**Jack Selzer** is a professor of English at Penn State, where he has taught courses in argument and in the rhetoric of science and technology since 1978. A native of Cincinnati and a graduate of Xavier University (B.A.) and Miami University (M.A. and Ph.D.), he has written and edited over a dozen books, including *Good Reasons: Designing and Writing Effective Arguments* (with Lester Faigley); *Conversations: Readings for Writing*; *Rhetorical Bodies* (with Sharon Crowley); *Understanding Scientific Prose*; and *Kenneth Burke in Greenwich Village: Conversing with the Moderns, 1915–1931*. He is currently completing another book on Kenneth Burke, beginning one on the rhetoric of the civil rights movement, and keeping up with his enduring loves: baseball and his family.

# Argument in America

## Essential Issues, Essential Texts

**Jack Selzer**
*The Pennsylvania State University*

PENGUIN ACADEMICS

PEARSON
Longman

New York   Boston   San Francisco
London   Toronto   Sydney   Tokyo   Singapore   Madrid
Mexico City   Munich   Paris   Cape Town   Hong Kong   Montreal

Senior Vice President and Publisher: Joseph Opiela
Vice President and Publisher: Eben W. Ludlow
Senior Supplements Editor: Donna Campion
Marketing Manager: Deborah Murphy
Production Manager: Charles Annis
Project Coordination, Text Design, and Electronic Page Makeup:
   PrePress Company, Inc.
Cover Designer/Manager: Wendy Fredericks
Cover Photo: © AP Wide World Photo
Manufacturing Buyer: Al Dorsey
Printer and Binder: Courier Corporation
Cover Printer: Coral Graphic Services

For permission to use copyrighted material, grateful acknowledgment is
made to the copyright holders on pp. 525–529, which are hereby made part
of this copyright page.

Library of Congress Cataloging-in-Publication Data

Argument in America : essential issues, essential texts / [compiled by] Jack
Selzer.
      p. cm.
Includes bibliographical references and index.
   ISBN 0-321-17278-7
   1. Persuasion (Rhetoric)--Problems, exercises, etc.  2. English language--
Rhetoric--Problems, exercises, etc.  3. Report writing--Problems, exercises,
etc.  4. College readers.  5. American essays.  I. Selzer, Jack.
   PE1431.A74 2004
   808'.0427--dc22
                                                              2003065709

Please visit our website at http://www.ablongman.com

ISBN 0-321-17278-7

1 2 3 4 5 6 7 8 9 10—CRW—06 05 04 03

# Contents

## Part Three Censorship 173

## Part Four Struggles for Liberation: Slavery, Women's Rights, Civil Rights 217

## Appendix  Some Arguments about Argument  481

# Contents by Argumentative Type

## Arguments Using Causal Analysis

## Arguments Using Comparison

## Proposal Arguments

# Preface

In the past decade the number of college courses on argument has increased exponentially: Some composition programs have changed their first-year course to feature argument; others have added or changed a required second composition course in order to accommodate argument; and still others have developed popular elective courses on argument. This move to feature argument follows from both social and intellectual forces. The general public has become increasingly interested in the tactics of argument, especially since argument has been featured so prominently in television and radio talk shows and in political campaigns. And scholars in composition studies have come to understand better the broadly argumentative nature of most discourse. In response to these developments, a number of people have been developing textbooks on argument as well as collections of sample arguments that can be used as classroom models and examples.

This particular collection of arguments has three key features not present in other books. First, *Argument in America: Essential Issues, Essential Texts* does what the title promises: It is organized around six essential argumentative issues that have dominated the national discourse in the United States for two centuries. Indeed, it could be said that the United States is defined as a unique community by its sustained and recurring discourses: about the environment, about the nature of the education that should be offered to U.S. citizens, about the propriety and reach of First-Amendment freedoms, about the challenge of extending civil liberties to broader constituencies, about the responsibilities of each individual citizen within our collective civic life (especially through the issue of civil disobedience), and about challenges to American identity posed by the processes of immigration and assimilation.

It is not that every argument in America comes down to one of these issues of course; people argue about everything from the merits of the designated hitter to the safety of cell phones. But it is nevertheless true that people in the United States have debated these six issues persistently since the nation's founding and that some of the most important, stirring, and seminal arguments in our history have centered on those topics: John Muir's pleas on behalf of environmental protection and Rachel Carson's *Silent Spring*; Ralph Waldo Emerson's "American Scholar" and W. E. B. DuBois's "The Talented Tenth"; Thomas Jefferson's Declaration of Independence, Frederick Douglass's "What, to the Slave, Is the Fourth of July?", and Elizabeth Cady Stanton's "The Seneca Falls Declaration"; Henry David Thoreau's "Civil Disobedience" and Martin Luther King, Jr.'s "Letter from Birmingham Jail"; James Baldwin's "Stranger in the Village" and Richard Rodriguez's "Aria: Memoir of a Bilingual Childhood." The issues that structure *Argument in America*, fundamental to American public life and civic identity, have prompted eloquent arguments that make this book a repository of respected and various voices.

Second, unlike many argument readers, which tend to present arguments in relative isolation, *Argument in America* is distinguished by an approach to argument that puts texts in implicit or explicit conversation with each other. Teachers will find that the book honors the principle that arguments are not one-sided or two-sided but multi-sided. Instead of featuring isolated pieces by Famous Authors or two or three selections on a great many issues, this book features sustained attention to specific themes that have generated an American dialogue. The writers included in the book often show a conscious awareness of people who have written before them—and who are themselves included in the book. Thus Jefferson's Declaration is responded to in pieces by Benjamin Banneker, Frederick Douglass, Elizabeth Cady Stanton, and Susan B. Anthony. John Muir's pleas on behalf of the Hetch Hetchy Valley are echoed by William Cronon, Aldo Leopold, and a series of visual arguments on a contemporary Web site. King's "Letter" recalls Thoreau and Gandhi—and is answered by Malcolm X's "Message to the Grassroots." Emma Lazarus's poem welcoming immigration (and inscribed on the Statue of Liberty) is answered by Thomas Bailey Aldrich's poem questioning the wisdom of a liberal immigration policy. And so on. Arguments, students will see, grow out of other arguments, not out of a vacuum; to write successfully on any topic, a student needs to learn how to situate himself or herself in what Kenneth Burke called "the unending conversation" on contemporary issues.

That brings me to the third unique feature of this reader. Its Appendix includes three important "arguments about argument" that might supplement (or even replace) a course textbook on argument. Kenneth Burke's "Rhetoric—Old and New" recommends that students base their arguments not on agonistic and antagonistic charges but on the principles of cooperation and identification. Deborah Tannen's "The Argument Culture" provides an eloquent plea to contemporary Americans to moderate the ways that they conduct public debate. And Anne Frances Wysocki offers a means for "Understanding the Visual in Textual Arguments."

Wysocki's discussion of how to understand visual arguments is especially appropriate in *Argument in America* because this book features all kinds of discourse—narrative arguments and argumentative essays, to be sure, but also fiction, poetry, cartoons, works of art, and photographs. The book also includes personal letters, speeches, satires, arguments on the World Wide Web, songs, and a play. In short, it features not just the arguments themselves but also the various argumentative forms (and argumentative styles) that students see in our culture today.

*Argument in America* is therefore flexible enough for teachers to adapt to their own course syllabi. To make the book easy for teachers to use, I have included an alternative table of contents that classifies the various selections, short introductions to each of the six major segments, a short headnote to each selection, and key questions that will give students a place to begin their own critical analyses. An Instructor's Manual, available separately, provides additional background information on each selection as well as suggestions for sustaining productive class discussions.

For their assistance in preparing this book, I must thank a great many people. If argument is a social activity, so is creating an argument reader. In addition to preparing the fine Instructor's Manual, Robert Davis suggested several of the selections that I ultimately included. Dominic Delli Carpini and Alysse Portnoy provided other helpful suggestions. Andrew Alexander assisted me in choosing selections, preparing headnotes, and developing the manuscript: his expertise is reflected everywhere in the book. Marika Siegel prepared the index, and Natalie Giboney obtained permissions. Katy Faria and Elsa van Bergen of Pre-Press Company, Inc. were patient and professional on the production end: they helped me out of any number of scrapes, including many that I'm sure I don't even know about. Eben Ludlow conceived of the project and encouraged me to bring it to completion. Deborah Anderson provided me great assistance in selecting photographs. I especially have appreciated the intellectual assistance of my colleagues at Penn State and at other universities who have shaped so profoundly my understanding of argument. Special mention in this regard goes to Marie Secor, Jeff Walker, and Lester Faigley, but I am profoundly aware of how many people—scholars and teachers of argument, textbook editors and writers, undergraduate and graduate students—have made this book what it is. I dedicate this book to all of them: colleagues in conversation.

Jack Selzer
*The Pennsylvania State University*

# Argument
# in America

# Introduction

What comes to mind when you think of "argument in America"? Yelling and screaming? People pointing fingers at each other, making accusations, ignoring the views of others, and interrupting each other? A verbal hand-to-hand combat in which someone wins and someone loses? Such a portrait of argument has indeed emerged from contemporary media, which has shaped profoundly the ways we think about argument in the United States. In television, radio, and films, arguments are very common these days—and are very commonly highly contentious and personalized affairs, verbal fisticuffs in which participants struggle to dominate their opponents and emerge victorious at all costs. Every four years presidential candidates, for example, engage in highly publicized debates, and candidates for state and local office also regularly engage in loud public exchanges: The implication is that every debate has a winner, and that whoever "wins" deserves to be elected. Or consider radio and TV talk shows: Often a moderator sponsors an argument on one topic or another by participants who battle for a verbal edge by talking loud, interrupting each other, and silencing or ridiculing their opponents. The guests on *Crossfire* or Bill O'Reilly's *No Spin Zone* often yell and scream at one another to get their points across because they understand argument as a contest that is all about winning. Testosterone seems to flow.

Or think of the courtroom dramas that animate so many TV shows and movies: *Law and Order* or *Erin Brockovitch* or *Chicago* or the many other courtroom shows that you can name pit larger-than-life lawyers against one another in win-or-lose contests in front of a jury. The stakes are conviction or acquittal, victory or defeat; the tactics are logical sleight of hand and verbal trickery. Unlike in real life, when most legal work involves patient, behind-the-scenes negotiations and compromises and when careful written briefs and counter-briefs are written and pondered in relative private, courtroom dramas show winners-taking-all through very public and very animated verbal and physical confrontation. What matters is the rhetorical virtuosity of the lawyer-heroes, whose cunning eloquence sways the jury, no matter the evidence, in one direction or the other.

This book occasionally reproduces arguments that work in that highly polarized way too. There is no denying that. Thomas Jefferson and his fellow composers of the Declaration of Independence pile up accusations against the British Crown in a way that is meant to inflame American opinion in favor of revolution, and Elizabeth Cady Stanton draws on the Declaration in order to dramatize the justice of the case for women's suffrage. Malcolm X ridicules the tactics of Martin Luther King, Jr., in order to further his own agenda, and Rachel Carson paints a portrait of a frightening Apocalypse that seems inevitable if Americans continue to use DDT and other devastating pesticides. There are heroes and villains in these arguments, the "right" way or the highway. When the stakes are high and the alternatives are limited, when there is little room for compromise or for sharing common ground, tempers can flare, arguers can grow self-righteous and uncompromising, and arguments can become highly emotional and combative. Sometimes those kinds of arguments are brilliant and memorable.

But far more frequently effective arguments actually involve a very reasonable process of negotiation through language about matters of public policy. Less heat, more light. Arguers and their audiences often act more as partners than adversaries; they put forth their views in an inevitably partisan way (for all arguers believe strongly in their causes!); but they nevertheless retain respect for their audiences and implicit goodwill toward those who disagree. People can disagree, in other words, without being disagreeable. Argument is usually less confrontational than it is invitational: rather than bludgeoning opponents into silent compliance, rather than seeking victory over a losing adversary, arguers invite people to reconsider their beliefs, values, and attitudes. They operate in a spirit in which everyone can win. Many times, indeed, arguments are presented in a tentative, experimental tone: An arguer puts forth a point of view in the expectation that he or she will be corrected in a respectful way (or ignored) if someone has a better idea to offer. That does not mean that arguers lack passion; far from it. Argument that is carried out in a spirit of cooperation is often highly emotional. And yet the arguer assumes the best in an audience, appeals to shared values and mutual benefit, and puts forth ideas that are designed to be a service for all. Everyone wins.

That, you will see, is the sense of argument that dominates *Argument in America*. According to this view (a view that is supported by the selections by Kenneth Burke and Deborah Tannen that are included in the Appendix), argument is a fundamental activity of a healthy democracy: People take turns giving their views and counter-views in open, public forums—pulpits, op-ed pages, magazine articles, televised speeches, government reports and hearings—and depend on informed readers and listeners to be persuaded by the best presentations of the evidence. If *Law and Order* and *The O'Reilly Factor* and presidential debates reflect a contentious view of argument, the second, more cooperative approach is dramatized in Michael Shaara's Civil War novel *The Killer Angels* and in the movie that developed out of that book, *Gettysburg*. In the book and the movie, the Northern hero is Colonel Joshua Chamberlain of Maine, who just happens to be a college teacher of rhetoric when he is not fighting the Civil War. And Chamberlain's expertise in argument shows: He saves the day for the Union cause at Gettysburg not just by heroic action (though he performs that too; there is tremendous battle valor on both sides)—but by means of argument. In two crucial scenes, Chamberlain invites a group of Northern deserters to rejoin the ranks by explaining the Union cause to them (and to those of us reading and watching) in a way that stirs their valor, not their animosity. Later, at Little Round Top, those would-be deserters, now loyally committed to the cause they are defending so courageously, play a crucial role in the Union victory. Chamberlain's counterpart on the Southern side is General James Longstreet, whose inability to argue effectively dooms the Southern cause. Longstreet is wise enough to know that the fight at Gettysburg will be a disaster for the South because the Northern troops control the high ground, and he knows Pickett's Charge is doomed to fail in particular. But in his arguments with General Lee he cannot deploy arguments effectively enough to make Lee change his mind about confronting the North at Gettysburg.

The movie *Gettysburg*, in other words, presents a central event in American history as a matter of argument. The other arguments collected in this book do much the same thing: *Argument in America* presents the most important arguments in American culture as models of effective argument. Could it not be said that the United States is defined as a unique community by its sustained and recurring discourses about the environment, about the nature of the education that should be offered to U.S. citizens, about the propriety and reach of First-Amendment freedoms, about the challenge of extending civil liberties to broader constituencies, about the responsibilities of each individual citizen within our collective civic life (especially through the issue of civil disobedience), and about challenges to American identity posed by the processes of immigration and assimilation? The issues that structure *Argument in America*, fundamental to American public life and civic identity, have prompted eloquent arguments that make this book a repository of respected and various voices. Martin Luther King, Jr.'s "Letter from Birmingham Jail" and "I Have a Dream" speech; Ralph Waldo Emerson's "The American Scholar"; Henry David Thoreau's "Civil Disobedience"; Thomas Cole's Hudson River School painting *Schroon Lake*, Carleton Watkins's pictures of Yosemite, and photographs of Rosa Parks and other civil rights workers that shaped American attitudes about their causes; works by Thomas Jefferson, W. E. B. DuBois, E. B. White, John Adams, Frederick Douglass, Harvey Milk, Betty Friedan, Malcolm X, Susan B. Anthony, Jesse Jackson, Cesar Chavez, Amy Tan, James Baldwin: All are here along with many other names and arguments that you will recognize because they have been especially admired and influential. You will find lots of essays, of course, for essays (in the form of editorials, op-ed contributions, sermons, and letters) remain a staple form for the presentation of essential arguments in America. But you will also find arguments in other forms as well—fiction, poetry, a play, songs. And you will find visual arguments also: cartoons and photographs that are part of the most central debates in American life. The forms of argument are various, and so are the styles and methods used to persuade.

The idea is that by reading *Argument in America* carefully, you will observe a range of effective tactics and learn to employ them yourself. The arguments in the book are generally effective because they employ key argumentative tactics. They offer clear central claims, and they support their points of view with compelling lines of argument—a series of "good reasons" that support their theses—and with solid evidence. Implicitly or explicitly, they are attentive to the viewpoints of others. (Indeed, this book often represents the argumentative "conversation" that has developed around topics such as education, censorship, and civil disobedience.) Often the arguments have an emotional impact because the points presented speak to their audience's deepest held attitudes and values. And the "voices" of the arguments—the character of the apparent "speaker" or "persona" who delivers the argument—are reliable, trustworthy, and fair. In short, the arguments presented here are models of their kind. The hope is that reading them will be both pleasant and instructive.

# PART ONE
# THE
# ENVIRONMENT

"We are the most dangerous species of life on the planet, and every other species, even the earth itself, has cause to fear our power to exterminate. But we are also the only species which, when it chooses to do so, will go to great effort to save what it might destroy." These words by Wallace Stegner express an urgent tension that has been fundamental to Americans since 1962, when Rachel Carson's *Silent Spring* stimulated the environmental movement in the United States. Carson's book explicitly indicted pesticides commonly used in the agriculture industry (particularly DDT), but implicitly she was arguing for something broader—for a new sense of our relation to the environment, for the conviction that Americans should be living in balance with nature, not in domination over it. Thus, Carson's book ultimately influenced not just agricultural practice but also efforts to protect endangered species, to regulate population growth, and to clean our air and water resources. When President Richard Nixon created the Environmental Protection Agency in 1973, environmental concern became institutionalized in the United States; most states created their own departments of natural resources or environmental protection soon after.

Then again, that environmental tension—the contradictory drive to exploit nature and to sustain it—had been an issue in the United States long before Carson wrote. For environmentalism is ingrained within the American character. It derives from a respect for the land—the sacred

American Eden—that is evident in the legend of Rip Van Winkle, in the work of Hudson River painters such as Thomas Cole (one of whose works is reproduced in this section), in the landscape architecture of Frederick Law Olmsted, in Henry David Thoreau's *Walden* and in Ralph Waldo Emerson's transcendentalist writings in the 1850s, in John Muir's and Carleton Watkins's testimonials about Yosemite (also reproduced here), and in Theodore Roosevelt's campaign to begin a system of national parks. Then again, the exploitation of the American green world for profit is also ingrained in our national character: Even as some Americans were reverencing the land as a special landscape that sustained them physically and spiritually, pioneers moving westward were subduing it for their own purposes, in the process spoiling rivers and air and virgin forests—and native peoples—in the name of development. That spoilage was perhaps first lamented in the argument included here by James Fenimore Cooper, "The Slaughter of the Pigeons."

In any event, the tension between the uses of nature and its protection is persistent, so arguments about environmental issues are prevalent in American public discourse. Are science and technology friends or foes of the environment? What is the proper relationship between people and the natural environment? What is a suitable balance between resource development and resource protection—resources including everything from timber and coal to streams and animals. How serious a problem is global warming, and what should be done about it? To what extent should Americans invest in the protection of little-known species or lands whose benefit to people has not been demonstrated? How can poorer nations develop economically without global environmental repercussions? Is it too late? Such questions are debated

each day in every kind of media, especially since organized environmental groups are legion, ranging from the activist Earth First!
(whose 10,000 members sometimes advocate direct action in support
of environmental aims) to more mainstream groups such as the Sierra
Club or the Nature Conservancy, which has created a membership of
nearly a million as an explicit effort to create partnerships between
scientists and businesspersons in the interests of environmental reform. On the other hand, conservatives such as Rush Limbaugh have
often ridiculed the efforts of environmentalists in the interest of a relatively unbridled developmentalism that is in the heady and optimistic
tradition of nineteenth-century free enterprise.

Debates about environmental issues, in other words, are part and
parcel of American culture. What follows is a sampling of several ar-
guments on which so much depends—Cole, Cooper, Watkins, and
Carson; but also Aldo Leopold's searching essay "The Land Ethic,"
William Cronon's reflective "The Trouble with Wilderness," Alice
Walker's haunting question, "Am I Blue?," and Scott Momaday's
Native American plea, "The Way to Rainy Mountain."

*James Fenimore Cooper is best remembered for inventing the fictional hero Natty Bumppo, "Leather-stocking," a prototype of the American western hero. Cooper would include him in several other novels, including* The Deerslayer *(1841),* The Last of the Mohicans *(1826), and* The Pioneers *(1823). "The Slaughter of the Pigeons" is a chapter in* The Pioneers. *In it, Natty Bumppo is in his early seventies; clad in a fox-skin hat and carrying a long rifle, his demeanor is one that captured and captivated the American imagination. The action is set in the spring of 1794, at Otsego Lake in central New York, about 50 miles west of Albany. The passenger pigeons described in the passage were one of the most commonly seen birds in North America—it was not considered unusual to see flocks that were miles wide and long, blocking out the daytime sky. The last passenger pigeon (named Martha) died in captivity in the Cincinnati Zoo on September 1, 1914.*

*James Fenimore Cooper*

# The Slaughter of the Pigeons

From this time to the close of April, the weather continued to be a succession of great and rapid changes. One day, the soft airs of spring would seem to be stealing along the valley, and, in unison with an invigorating sun, attempting, covertly, to rouse the dormant powers of the vegetable world; while on the next, the surly blasts from the north would sweep across the lake, and erase every impression left by their gentle adversaries. The snow, however, finally disappeared, and the green wheat fields were seen in every direction, spotted with the dark and charred stumps that had, the preceding season, supported some of the proudest trees of the forest.[1] Ploughs were in motion, wherever those useful implements could be used, and the smokes of the sugar-camps[2] were no longer seen issuing from the summits of the woods of maple. The lake had lost all the characteristic beauty of a field of ice, but still, a dark and gloomy covering concealed its waters, for the absence of currents left them yet hid under a porous crust, which, satu-

---

[1] A common practice was to raise timber in the spring, let it dry all summer, then burn the cleared area.

[2] Where sugar was made from maple sap.

rated with the fluid, barely retained enough of its strength to preserve the contiguity of its parts. Large flocks of wild geese were seen passing over the country, which would hover, for a time, around the hidden sheet of water, apparently searching for an opening, where they might obtain a resting-place; and then, on finding themselves excluded by the chill covering, would soar away to the north, filling the air with their discordant screams, as if venting their complaints at the tardy operations of nature.

For a week, the dark covering of the Otsego was left to the undisturbed possession of two eagles, who alighted on the centre of its field, and sat proudly eyeing the extent of their undisputed territory. During the presence of these monarchs of the air, the flocks of migrating birds avoided crossing the plain of ice, by turning into the hills, and apparently seeking the protection of the forests, while the white and bald heads of the tenants of the lake were turned upward, with a look of majestic contempt, as if penetrating to the very heavens, with the acuteness of their vision. But the time had come, when even these kings of birds were to be dispossessed. An opening had been gradually increasing, at the lower extremity of the lake, and around the dark spot where the current of the river had prevented the formation of ice, during even the coldest weather; and the fresh southerly winds, that now breathed freely up the valley, obtained an impression on the waters. Mimic waves began to curl over the margin of the frozen field, which exhibited an outline of crystallizations, that slowly receded towards the north. At each step the power of the winds and the waves increased, until, after a struggle of a few hours, the turbulent little billows succeeded in setting the whole field in an undulating motion, when it was driven beyond the reach of the eye, with a rapidity, that was as magical as the change produced in the scene by this expulsion of the lingering remnant of winter. Just as the last sheet of agitated ice was disappearing in the distance, the eagles rose over the border of crystals, and soared with a wide sweep far above the clouds, while the waves tossed their little caps of snow into the air, as if rioting in their release from a thraldom of five months duration.

The following morning Elizabeth[3] was awakened by the exhilarating sounds of the martins, who were quarrelling and chattering around the little boxes which were suspended above her windows, and the cries of Richard,[4] who was calling, in tones as animating as the signs of the season itself—

---

[3] Elizabeth Temple, a leading figure in *The Pioneers*, is the daughter of Judge Marmaduke Temple, the founder of the town of Templeton and its chief landowner.

[4] Richard Jones, the sheriff, is a cousin of Judge Temple and his close associate.

"Awake! awake! my lady fair! the gulls are hovering over the lake already, and the heavens are alive with the pigeons. You may look an hour before you can find a hole, through which, to get a peep at the sun. Awake! awake! lazy ones! Benjamin[5] is overhauling the ammunition, and we only wait for our breakfasts, and away for the mountains and pigeon-shooting."

5    There was no resisting this animated appeal, and in a few minutes Miss Temple and her friend[6] descended to the parlor. The doors of the hall were thrown open, and the mild, balmy air of a clear spring morning was ventilating the apartment, where the vigilance of the ex-steward had been so long maintaining an artificial heat, with such unremitted diligence. All of the gentlemen . . . were impatiently waiting their morning's repast, each being equipt in the garb of a sportsman. Mr. Jones made many visits to the southern door, and would cry—

"See, cousin Bess! see, 'duke![7] the pigeon-roosts of the south have broken up! They are growing more thick every instant. Here is a flock that the eye cannot see the end of. There is food enough in it to keep the army of Xerxes for a month, and feathers enough to make beds for the whole county. Xerxes, Mr. Edwards,[8] was a Grecian king, who— no, he was a Turk, or a Persian, who wanted to conquer Greece, just the same as these rascals will overrun our wheat-fields, when they come back in the fall.—Away! away! Bess; I long to pepper them from the mountain."

In this wish both Marmaduke and young Edwards seemed equally to participate, for really the sight was most exhilarating to a sportsman; and the ladies soon dismissed the party, after a hasty breakfast.

If the heavens were alive with pigeons, the whole village seemed equally in motion, with men, women, and children. Every species of fire-arms, from the French ducking-gun, with its barrel of near six feet in length, to the common horseman's pistol, was to be seen in the hands of the men and boys; while bows and arrows, some made of the simple stick of a walnut sapling, and others in a rude imitation of the ancient cross-bows, were carried by many of the latter.

The houses, and the signs of life apparent in the village, drove the alarmed birds from the direct line of their flight, towards the moun-

---

[5] Benjamin Penguillan (called Ben Pump). In the next paragraph Pump is referred to as "the ex-steward" because he had been a steward to the captain in his seagoing years. One of his duties at the Templeton house is to keep the stove in the parlor hot.
[6] Louisa Grant, daughter of the minister.
[7] The name "'duke" is a nickname for "Marmaduke," the judge.
[8] Oliver Edwards is a young stranger.

tains, along the sides and near the bases of which they were glancing in dense masses, that were equally wonderful by the rapidity of their motion, as by their incredible numbers.

10    We have already said, that across the inclined plane which fell from the steep ascent of the mountain to the banks of the Susquehanna, ran the highway, on either side of which a clearing of many acres had been made, at a very early day. Over those clearings, and up the eastern mountain, and along the dangerous path that was cut into its side, the different individuals posted themselves, as suited their inclinations; and in a few moments the attack commenced.

Amongst the sportsmen was to be seen the tall, gaunt form of Leather-stocking, who was walking over the field, with his rifle hanging on his arm, his dogs following close at his heels, now scenting the dead or wounded birds, that were beginning to tumble from the flocks, and then crouching under the legs of their master, as if they participated in his feelings, at this wasteful and unsportsmanlike execution.

The reports of the fire-arms became rapid, whole volleys rising from the plain, as flocks of more than ordinary numbers darted over the opening, covering the field with darkness, like an interposing cloud; and then the light smoke of a single piece would issue from among the leafless bushes on the mountain, as death was hurled on the retreat of the affrighted birds, who would rise from a volley, for many feet into the air, in a vain effort to escape the attacks of man. Arrows, and missiles of every kind, were seen in the midst of the flocks; and so numerous were the birds, and so low did they take their flight, that even long poles, in the hands of those on the sides of the mountain, were used to strike them to the earth.

During all this time, Mr. Jones, who disdained the humble and ordinary means of destruction used by his companions, was busily occupied, aided by Benjamin, in making arrangements for an assault of a more than ordinarily fatal character. Among the relics of the old military excursions, that occasionally are discovered throughout the different districts of the western part of New-York, there had been found in Templeton, at its settlement, a small swivel,[9] which would carry a ball of a pound weight. It was thought to have been deserted by a war-party of the whites, in one of their inroads into the Indian settlements, when, perhaps, their convenience or their necessities induced them to leave such an encumbrance to the rapidity of their march, behind them in the woods. This miniature cannon had been released from the rust, and mounted on little wheels, in a state for actual service. For

---

[9] A swivel, or small cannon, is capable of being swung higher or lower.

several years, it was the sole organ for extraordinary rejoicings that was used in those mountains. On the mornings of the Fourth of July, it would be heard, with its echoes ringing among the hills, and telling forth its sounds, for thirteen times, with all the dignity of a two-and-thirty pounder. . . . It was somewhat the worse for the service it had performed, it is true, there being but a trifling difference in size between the touch-hole and the muzzle. Still, the grand conceptions of Richard had suggested the importance of such an instrument, in hurling death at his nimble enemies. The swivel was dragged by a horse into a part of the open space, that the sheriff thought most eligible for planting a battery of the kind, and Mr. Pump proceeded to load it. Several handfuls of duck-shot were placed on top of the powder, and the Major-domo soon announced that his piece was ready for service.

The sight of such an implement collected all the idle spectators to the spot, who, being mostly boys, filled the air with their cries of exultation and delight. The gun was pointed on high, and Richard, holding a coal of fire in a pair of tongs, patiently took his seat on a stump, awaiting the appearance of a flock that was worthy of his notice.

15    So prodigious was the number of the birds, that the scattering fire of the guns, with the hurling of missiles, and the cries of the boys, had no other effect than to break off small flocks from the immense masses that continued to dart along the valley, as if the whole creation of the feathered tribe were pouring through that one pass. None pretended to collect the game, which lay scattered over the fields in such profusion, as to cover the very ground with the fluttering victims.

Leather-stocking was a silent, but uneasy spectator of all these proceedings, but was able to keep his sentiments to himself until he saw the introduction of the swivel into the sports.

"This comes of settling a country!" he said—"here have I known the pigeons to fly for forty long years, and, till you made your clearings, there was nobody to scare or to hurt them. I loved to see them come into the woods, for they were company to a body; hurting nothing; being, as it was, as harmless as a garter-snake. But now it gives me sore thoughts when I hear the frighty things whizzing through the air, for I know it's only a motion to bring out all the brats in the village at them. Well! the Lord won't see the waste of his creaters for nothing, and right will be done to the pigeons, as well as others, by-and-by.— There's Mr. Oliver, as bad as the rest of them, firing into the flocks as if he was shooting down nothing but the Mingo[10] warriors."

---

[10] In the *Leather-Stocking* novels, the Mingos (Iroquois) are depicted as the "bad Indians" while the Delawares are depicted as "good Indians."

Among the sportsmen was Billy Kirby,[11] who, armed with an old musket, was loading, and, without even looking into the air, was firing, and shouting as his victims fell even on his own person. He heard the speech of Natty, and took upon himself to reply—

"What's that, old Leather-stocking!" he cried; "grumbling at the loss of a few pigeons! If you had to sow your wheat twice, and three times, as I have done, you wouldn't be so massyfully[12] feeling'd to'ards the divils.—Hurrah, boys! scatter the feathers. This is better than shooting at a turkey's head and neck, old fellow."

20 "It's better for you, maybe, Billy Kirby," returned the indignant old hunter, "and all them as don't know how to put a ball down a rifle-barrel, or how to bring it up ag'in with a true aim; but it's wicked to be shooting into flocks in this wastey manner; and none do it, who know how to knock over a single bird. If a body has a craving for pigeon's flesh, why! it's made the same as all other creaters, for man's eating, but not to kill twenty and eat one. When I want such a thing, I go into the woods till I find one to my liking, and then I shoot him off the branches without touching a feather of another, though there might be a hundred on the same tree. But you couldn't do such a thing, Billy Kirby—you couldn't do it if you tried."

"What's that you say, you old, dried cornstalk! you sapless stub!" cried the wood-chopper. "You've grown mighty boasting, since you killed the turkey; but if you're for a single shot, here goes at that bird which comes on by himself."

The fire from the distant part of the field had driven a single pigeon below the flock to which it had belonged, and, frightened with the constant reports of the muskets, it was approaching the spot where the disputants stood, darting first from one side, and then to the other, cutting the air with the swiftness of lightning, and making a noise with its wings, not unlike the rushing of a bullet. Unfortunately for the wood-chopper, notwithstanding his vaunt, he did not see his bird until it was too late for him to fire as it approached, and he pulled his trigger at the unlucky moment when it was darting immediately over his head. The bird continued its course with incredible velocity.

Natty had dropped his piece from his arm, when the challenge was made, and, waiting a moment, until the terrified victim had got in a line with his eyes, and had dropped near the bank of the lake, he raised his rifle with uncommon rapidity, and fired. It might have been chance, or it might have been skill, that produced the result; it was

---

[11] Billy Kirby is a local woodchopper.
[12] Mercifully.

probably a union of both; but the pigeon whirled over in the air, and fell into the lake, with a broken wing. At the sound of his rifle, both his dogs started from his feet, and in a few minutes the "slut"[13] brought out the bird, still alive.

The wonderful exploit of Leather-stocking was noised through the field with great rapidity, and the sportsmen gathered in to learn the truth of the report.

25     "What," said young Edwards, "have you really killed a pigeon on the wing, Natty, with a single ball?"

"Haven't I killed loons before now, lad, that dive at the flash?" returned the hunter. "It's much better to kill only such as you want, without wasting your powder and lead, than to be firing into God's creaters in such a wicked manner. But I come out for a bird, and you know the reason why I like small game, Mr. Oliver, and now I have got one I will go home, for I don't like to see these wasty ways that you are all practysing, as if the least thing was not made for use, and not to destroy."

"Thou sayest well, Leather-stocking," cried Marmaduke, "and I begin to think it time to put an end to this work of destruction."

"Put an ind, Judge, to your clearings. An't the woods his work as well as the pigeons? Use, but don't waste. Wasn't the woods made for the beasts and birds to harbour in? and when man wanted their flesh, their skins, or their feathers, there's the place to seek them. But I'll go to the hut with my own game, for I wouldn't touch one of the harmless things that kiver the ground here, looking up with their eyes at me, as if they only wanted tongues to say their thoughts."

With this sentiment in his mouth, Leather-stocking threw his rifle over his arm, and, followed by his dogs, stepped across the clearing with great caution, taking care not to tread on one, of the hundreds of the wounded birds that lay in his path. He soon entered the bushes on the margin of the lake, and was hid from view.

## Questions for Discussion

How do the descriptive passages contribute to the argument that is being made?

What kind of impact on the reader is the narrator aiming for?

Which speak louder in this passage, words or actions?

[13] Female dog.

***Thomas Cole** (1801–1848), an immigrant from England who arrived in Ohio in the early nineteenth century, lived during a period of national expansion and gathering industrialism, when the issue of slavery was dividing the nation. But Cole's paintings seem removed from these events and concerns, for Cole was the most prominent member of the Hudson River School of painters. These artists took as their subject frontier and wilderness scenes associated with James Fenimore Cooper's fiction (see previous selection) and with American romanticism more generally. Schroon Lake 1846 is a typical product of the Hudson River School: Can you see within it an argument about the sacred character of the natural world?*

# Thomas Cole

## Schroon Lake 1846

Source: Thomas Cole, Schroon Lake, ca. 1846. Courtesy of The Adirondack Museum.

*The spectacular photographs of* **Carleton Watkins** *(1829–1916) documented the physical resources of America's western regions, especially in the
years 1860–1890. While he also photographed San Francisco; Mt. Shasta;
portions of Nevada, Arizona, and Oregon; and many other sites, he is especially remembered for the large images of Yosemite that he produced beginning in 1861. When Watkins entered the Yosemite Valley, the medium of photography was barely two decades old and Yosemite was barely known. By
1864, his photos had persuaded the public and Congress to declare Yosemite
"inviolate," a recognition that led to the eventual establishment of the
national park system. They also inspired the work of later photographers,
such as Ansel Adams, and of landscape painters, such as Albert Bierstadt.
As scholars Anne Demo and Kevine DeLuca have indicated, Watkins's photos
of Yosemite promote a vision of the environment that persists to this day.*

## *Carleton  Watkins*

# Photographs of Yosemite

(See pages 17 and 18.)

Yosemite Falls, ca. 1861

B 18 Glacier Point, 3200 Feet, Yo Semite.

Glacier Point 3200 feet, Yosemite

*The famous nineteenth-century naturalist **John Muir** (1838–1914) was born in Dunbar, Scotland, and emigrated to the United States with his family in 1849. The founder of the Sierra Club, Muir wrote many articles and books on the importance of preserving nature, including a series of articles published in* Century *magazine that played an instrumental role in the creation of Yosemite National Park in 1890 (many of Muir's writings are archived at www.sierraclub.org). Muir spent much of his life hiking the American West and recording what he saw in a way that persuaded people to value outstanding wilderness areas. Two of his best known books are* The Mountains of California *(1894) and* Our National Parks *(1901). The following appeal comes from Muir's* The Yosemite *(1912), although he wrote about the Hetch Hetchy Valley on numerous other occasions, as well. It was an effort—an unsuccessful effort, as it turned out—to block the construction of a dam in the Yosemite National Park area that was designed to provide water to the San Francisco area. Muir's was a prominent voice in the debate over the dam, which William Cronon (whose work is included later in this section) has called "the single most famous episode in American conservationist history."*

## John Muir

# Save the Hetch Hetchy Valley!

Yosemite is so wonderful that we are apt to regard it as an exceptional creation, the only valley of its kind in the world; but Nature is not so poor as to have only one of anything. Several other Yosemites have been discovered in the Sierra that occupy the same relative positions on the Range and were formed by the same forces in the same kind of granite. One of these, the Hetch Hetchy Valley, is in the Yosemite National Park about twenty miles from Yosemite and is easily accessible to all sorts of travelers by a road and trail that leaves the Big Oak Flat road at Bronson Meadows a few miles below Crane Flat, and to mountaineers by way of Yosemite Creek basin and the head of the middle fork of the Tuolumne.

It is said to have been discovered by Joseph Screech, a hunter, in 1850, a year before the discovery of the great Yosemite. After my first visit to it in the autumn of 1871, I have always called it the

"Tuolumne Yosemite," for it is a wonderfully exact counterpart of the Merced Yosemite, not only in its sublime rocks and waterfalls but in the gardens, groves and meadows of its flowery park-like floor. The floor of Yosemite is about 4000 feet above the sea; the Hetch Hetchy floor about 3700 feet. And as the Merced River flows through Yosemite, so does the Tuolumne through Hetch Hetchy. The walls of both are of gray granite, rise abruptly from the floor, are sculptured in the same style and in both every rock is a glacier monument.

Standing boldly out from the south wall is a strikingly picturesque rock called by the Indians, Kolana, the outermost of a group 2300 feet high, corresponding with the Cathedral Rocks of Yosemite both in relative position and form. On the opposite side of the Valley, facing Kolana, there is a counterpart of the El Capitan that rises sheer and plain to a height of 1800 feet, and over its massive brow flows a stream which makes the most graceful fall I have ever seen. From the edge of the cliff to the top of an earthquake talus it is perfectly free in the air for a thousand feet before it is broken into cascades among talus boulders. It is in all its glory in June, when the snow is melting fast, but fades and vanishes toward the end of summer. The only fall I know with which it may fairly be compared is the Yosemite Bridal Veil; but it excels even that favorite fall both in height and airy-fairy beauty and behavior. Lowlanders are apt to suppose that mountain streams in their wild career over cliffs lose control of themselves and tumble in a noisy chaos of mist and spray. On the contrary, on no part of their travels are they more harmonious and self-controlled. Imagine yourself in Hetch Hetchy on a sunny day in June, standing waist-deep in grass and flowers (as I have often stood), while the great pines sway dreamily with scarcely perceptible motion. Looking northward across the Valley you see a plain, gray granite cliff rising abruptly out of the gardens and groves to a height of 1800 feet, and in front of it Tueeulala's silvery scarf burning with irised sun-fire. In the first white outburst at the head there is abundance of visible energy, but it is speedily hushed and concealed in divine repose, and its tranquil progress to the base of the cliff is like that of a downy feather in a still room. Now observe the fineness and marvelous distinctness of the various sun-illumined fabrics into which the water is woven; they sift and float from form to form down the face of that grand gray rock in so leisurely and unconfused a manner that you can examine their texture, and patterns and tones of color as you would a piece of embroidery held in the hand. Toward the top of the fall you see groups of booming, comet-like masses, their solid, white heads separate, their tails like combed silk interlacing among delicate gray and purple shadows, ever forming and dissolving, worn out by friction in their rush through the air. Most of these vanish a few hundred feet below the summit, changing to varied forms of cloud-like drapery. Near the bottom the width of the fall has increased from about twenty-five feet to a hundred feet. Here it is composed of yet finer tissues, and is still without a trace of disorder—air, water and sunlight woven into stuff that spirits might wear.

So fine a fall might well seem sufficient to glorify any valley; but here, as in Yosemite, Nature seems in nowise moderate, for a short distance to the eastward of Tueeulala booms and thunders the great Hetch Hetchy Fall, Wapama, so near that you have both of them in full view from the same standpoint. It is the counterpart of the Yosemite Fall, but has a much greater volume of water, is about 1700 feet in height, and appears to be nearly vertical, though considerably inclined, and is dashed into huge outbounding bosses of foam on projecting shelves and knobs. No two falls could be more unlike—Tueeulala out in the open sunshine descending like thistledown; Wapama in a jagged, shadowy gorge roaring and thundering, pounding its way like an earthquake avalanche.

5    Besides this glorious pair there is a broad, massive fall on the main river a short distance above the head of the Valley. Its position is something like that of the Vernal in Yosemite, and its roar as it plunges into a surging trout-pool may be heard a long way, though it is only about twenty feet high. On Rancheria Creek, a large stream, corresponding in position with the Yosemite Tenaya Creek, there is a chain of cascades joined here and there with swift flashing plumes like the one between the Vernal and Nevada Falls, making magnificent shows as they go their glacier-sculptured way, sliding, leaping, hurrahing, covered with crisp clashing spray made glorious with sifting sunshine. And besides all these a few small streams come over the walls at wide intervals, leaping from ledge to ledge with bird-like song and watering many a hidden cliff-garden and fernery, but they are too unshowy to be noticed in so grand a place.

The correspondence between the Hetch Hetchy walls in their trends, sculpture, physical structure, and general arrangement of the main rock-masses and those of the Yosemite Valley has excited the wondering admiration of every observer. We have seen that the El Capitan and Cathedral rocks occupy the same relative positions in both valleys; so also do their Yosemite points and North Domes. Again, that part of the Yosemite north wall immediately to the east of the

Yosemite Fall has two horizontal benches, about 500 and 1500 feet above the floor; timbered with golden-cup oak. Two benches similarly situated and timbered occur on the same relative portion of the Hetch Hetchy north wall, to the east of Wapama Fall, and on no other. The Yosemite is bounded at the head by the great Half Dome. Hetch Hetchy is bounded in the same way, though its head rock is incomparably less wonderful and sublime in form.

The floor of the Valley is about three and a half miles long, and from a fourth to half a mile wide. The lower portion is mostly a level meadow about a mile long, with the trees restricted to the sides and the river banks, and partially separated from the main, upper, forested portion by a low bar of glacier-polished granite across which the river breaks in rapids.

The principal trees are the yellow and sugar pines, digger pine, incense cedar, Douglas spruce, silver fir, the California and golden-cup oaks, balsam cottonwood, Nuttall's flowering dogwood, alder, maple, laurel, tumion, etc. The most abundant and influential are the great yellow or silver pines like those of Yosemite, the tallest over two hundred feet in height, and the oaks assembled in magnificent groves with massive rugged trunks four to six feet in diameter, and broad, shady, wide-spreading heads. The shrubs forming conspicuous flowery clumps and tangles are manzanita, azalea, spiræa, brier-rose, several species of ceanothus, calycanthus, philadelphus, wild cherry, etc.; with abundance of showy and fragrant herbaceous plants growing about them or out in the open in beds by themselves—lilies, Mariposa tulips, brodiaeas, orchids, iris, spraguea, draperia, collomia, collinsia, castilleja, nemophila, larkspur, columbine, goldenrods, sunflowers, mints of many species, honeysuckle, etc. Many fine ferns dwell here also, especially the beautiful and interesting rock-ferns—pellaea, and cheilanthes of several species—fringing and rosetting dry rock-piles and ledges; woodwardia and asplenium on damp spots with fronds six or seven feet high; the delicate maidenhair in mossy nooks by the falls, and the sturdy, broad-shouldered pteris covering nearly all the dry ground beneath the oaks and pines.

It appears, therefore, that Hetch Hetchy Valley, far from being a plain, common, rock-bound meadow, as many who have not seen it seem to suppose, is a grand landscape garden, one of Nature's rarest and most precious mountain temples. As in Yosemite, the sublime rocks of its walls seem to glow with life, whether leaning back in repose or standing erect in thoughtful attitudes, giving welcome to storms and calms alike, their brows in the sky, their feet set in the

groves and gay flowery meadows, while birds, bees, and butterflies
help the river and waterfalls to stir all the air into music—things frail
and fleeting and types of permanence meeting here and blending, just
as they do in Yosemite, to draw her lovers into close and confiding
communion with her.

10   Sad to say, this most precious and sublime feature of the Yosemite
National Park, one of the greatest of all our natural resources for the
uplifting joy and peace and health of the people, is in danger of being
dammed and made into a reservoir to help supply San Francisco with
water and light, thus flooding it from wall to wall and burying its gardens and groves one or two hundred feet deep. This grossly destructive
commercial scheme has long been planned and urged (though water as
pure and abundant can be got from outside of the people's park, in a
dozen different places), because of the comparative cheapness of the
dam and of the territory which it is sought to divert from the great
uses to which it was dedicated in the Act of 1890 establishing the
Yosemite National Park.

The making of gardens and parks goes on with civilization all over
the world, and they increase both in size and number as their value is
recognized. Everybody needs beauty as well as bread, places to play in
and pray in, where Nature may heal and cheer and give strength to
body and soul alike. This natural beauty-hunger is made manifest in
the little window-sill gardens of the poor; though perhaps only a gera-
nium slip in a broken cup, as well as in the carefully tended rose and
lily gardens of the rich, the thousands of spacious city parks and
botanical gardens, and in our magnificent National Parks—the Yellowstone, Yosemite, Sequoia, etc.—Nature's sublime wonderlands, the admiration and joy of the world. Nevertheless, like anything else worth
while, from the very beginning, however well guarded, they have always been subject to attack by despoiling gainseekers and mischief-
makers of every degree from Satan to Senators, eagerly trying to make
everything immediately and selfishly commercial, with schemes disguised in smug-smiling philanthropy, industriously, sham-piously crying, "Conservation, conservation, panutilization," that man and beast
may be fed and the dear Nation made great. Thus long ago a few enterprising merchants utilized the Jerusalem temple as a place of business instead of a place of prayer; changing money, buying and selling
cattle and sheep and doves; and earlier still, the first forest reservation,
including only one tree, was likewise despoiled. Ever since the establishment of the Yosemite National Park, strife has been going on
around its borders and I suppose this will go on as part of the universal

battle between right and wrong, however much its boundaries may be shorn, or its wild beauty destroyed.

The first application to the Government by the San Francisco Supervisors for the commercial use of Lake Eleanor and the Hetch Hetchy Valley was made in 1903, and on December 22nd of that year it was denied by the Secretary of the Interior, Mr. Hitchcock, who truthfully said:

> Presumably the Yosemite National Park was created such by law because of the natural objects of varying degrees of scenic importance located within its boundaries, inclusive alike of its beautiful small lakes, like Eleanor, and its majestic wonders, like Hetch Hetchy and Yosemite Valley. It is the aggregation of such natural scenic features that makes the Yosemite Park a wonderland which the Congress of the United States sought by law to reserve for all coming time as nearly as practicable in the condition fashioned by the hand of the Creator—a worthy object of national pride and a source of healthful pleasure and rest for the thousands of people who may annually sojourn there during the heated months.

In 1907 when Mr. Garfield became Secretary of the Interior the application was renewed and granted; but under his successor, Mr. Fisher, the matter has been referred to a Commission, which as this volume goes to press still has it under consideration.

The most delightful and wonderful camp-grounds in the Park are its three great valleys—Yosemite, Hetch Hetchy, and Upper Tuolumne; and they are also the most important places with reference to their positions relative to the other great features—the Merced and Tuolumne Cañons, and the High Sierra peaks and glaciers, etc., at the head of the rivers. The main part of the Tuolumne Valley is a spacious flowery lawn four or five miles long, surrounded by magnificent snowy mountains, slightly separated from other beautiful meadows, which together make a series about twelve miles in length, the highest reaching to the feet of Mount Dana, Mount Gibbs, Mount Lyell and Mount McClure. It is about 8500 feet above the sea, and forms the grand central High Sierra camp-ground from which excursions are made to the noble mountains, domes, glaciers, etc.; across the Range to the Mono Lake and volcanoes and down the Tuolumne Cañon to Hetch Hetchy. Should Hetch Hetchy be submerged for a reservoir, as proposed, not only would it be utterly destroyed, but the sublime cañon way to the heart of the High Sierra would be hopelessly blocked and the great camping-ground, as the watershed of a city drinking system, virtually would be closed to the public. So far as I have learned, few of all the thousands who have seen the Park and seek rest and peace in it are in favor of this outrageous scheme.

15      One of my later visits to the Valley was made in the autumn of 1907 with the late William Keith, the artist. The leaf-colors were then ripe, and the great god-like rocks in repose seemed to glow with life. The artist, under their spell, wandered day after day along the river and through the groves and gardens, studying the wonderful scenery; and, after making about forty sketches, declared with enthusiasm that although its walls were less sublime in height, in picturesque beauty and charm Hetch Hetchy surpassed even Yosemite.

That any one would try to destroy such a place seems incredible; but sad experience shows that there are people good enough and bad enough for anything. The proponents of the dam scheme bring forward a lot of bad arguments to prove that the only righteous thing to do with the people's parks is to destroy them bit by bit as they are able. Their arguments are curiously like those of the devil, devised for the destruction of the first garden—so much of the very best Eden fruit going to waste; so much of the best Tuolumne water and Tuolumne scenery going to waste. Few of their statements are even partly true, and all are misleading.

Thus, Hetch Hetchy, they say, is a "low-lying meadow." On the contrary, it is a high-lying natural landscape garden, as the photographic illustrations show.

"It is a common minor feature, like thousands of others." On the contrary it is a very uncommon feature; after Yosemite, the rarest and in many ways the most important in the National Park.

"Damming and submerging it 175 feet deep would enhance its beauty by forming a crystal-clear lake." Landscape gardens, places of recreation and worship, are never made beautiful by destroying and burying them. The beautiful sham lake, forsooth, would be only an eyesore, a dismal blot on the landscape, like many others to be seen in the Sierra. For, instead of keeping it at the same level all the year, allowing Nature centuries of time to make new shores, it would, of course, be full only a month or two in the spring, when the snow is melting fast; then it would be gradually drained, exposing the slimy sides of the basin and shallower parts of the bottom, with the gathered drift and waste, death and decay of the upper basins, caught here instead of being swept on to decent natural burial along the banks of the river or in the sea. Thus the Hetch Hetchy dam-lake would be only a rough imitation of a natural lake for a few of the spring months, an open sepulcher for the others.

20      "Hetch Hetchy water is the purest of all to be found in the Sierra, unpolluted, and forever unpollutable." On the contrary, excepting that of the Merced below Yosemite, it is less pure than that of most of the other Sierra streams, because of the sewerage of camp-grounds draining into it, especially of the Big Tuolumne Meadows camp-ground, occupied by hundreds of tourists and mountaineers, with their animals, for months every summer, soon to be followed by thousands from all the world.

These temple destroyers, devotees of ravaging commercialism, seem to have a perfect contempt for Nature, and, instead of lifting their eyes to the God of the mountains, lift them to the Almighty Dollar.

Dam Hetch Hetchy! As well dam for water-tanks the people's cathedrals and churches, for no holier temple has ever been consecrated by the heart of man.

## Questions for Discussion

What image of himself does Muir convey?

Why does Muir go to such lengths to compare features of Hetch Hetchy to those of Yosemite?

Why did Muir choose to organize the piece in this particular way?

*Despite the efforts of John Muir and many others, the Hetch Hetchy Valley in the Sierra Nevadas of California was changed forever when O'Shaughnessy Dam was erected between 1922 and 1937 in order to create a water supply for the San Francisco Bay area. Many people feel that in a sense Hetch Hetchy was ruined by the existence of Yosemite, since the grandeur of Yosemite made nearby Hetch Hetchy expendable by comparison. In any event, environmentalists continue to call attention to their cause by appealing to the example of Hetch Hetchy. For example, before-and-after photos similar to the ones shown here and on the next page are on the Web site of the Sierra Nevada Gallery; the photos are intended to serve as a lament and a warning "that the beauty of their valley was expendable for a mere reservoir." See www.sierranevadaphotos.com/ gallery/hetch_hetchy.html.*

# Photos of Hetch Hetchy

Hetch Hetchy Valley, ca. 1911

Hetch Hetchy as it appears today

*Aldo Leopold (1887–1948), widely considered the "father of modern ecology," earned a Master of Forestry degree from Yale in 1909. He then worked in the U.S. Forest Service for nineteen years before beginning a long and productive teaching career at the University of Wisconsin, where he eventually chaired the newly created Department of Game Management. One of the most influential nature writers of the twentieth century, Leopold revised the following essay (first published in 1933) shortly before he died while fighting a brushfire in a neighbor's field; it appeared in his posthumously published* Sand County Almanac *(1949). Like much of Leopold's work—an effort to create what he called a new "ecological conscience"—"The Land Ethic" calls for a new way of understanding our relationship with the environment, a conception that has powerfully influenced environmental policy debates in the United States.*

# Aldo Leopold
# The Land Ethic

When god-like Odysseus returned from the wars in Troy, he hanged all on one rope a dozen slave-girls of his house-hold whom he suspected of misbehavior during his absence.

This hanging involved no question of propriety. The girls were property. The disposal of property was then, as now, a matter of expediency, not of right and wrong.

Concepts of right and wrong were not lacking from Odysseus' Greece: witness the fidelity of his wife through the long years before at last his black-prowed galleys clove the wine-dark seas for home. The ethical structure of that day covered wives, but had not yet been extended to human chattels. During the three thousand years which have since elapsed, ethical criteria have been extended to many fields of conduct, with corresponding shrinkages in those judged by expediency only.

## The Ethical Sequence

This extension of ethics, so far studied only by philosophers, is actually a process in ecological evolution. Its sequences may be described in ecological as well as in philosophical terms. An ethic, ecologically, is a limitation on freedom of action in the struggle for existence. An ethic, philosophically, is a differentiation of social from anti-social conduct. These are two definitions of one thing. The thing has its origin in the tendency of interdependent individuals or groups to evolve modes of co-operation. The ecologist calls these symbioses. Politics and economics are advanced symbioses in which the original free-for-all competition has been replaced, in part, by co-operative mechanisms with an ethical content.

5    The complexity of co-operative mechanisms has increased with population density, and with the efficiency of tools. It was simpler, for example, to define the anti-social uses of sticks and stones in the days of the mastodons than of bullets and billboards in the age of motors.

The first ethics dealt with the relation between individuals; the Mosaic Decalogue is an example. Later accretions dealt with the relation between the individual and society. The Golden Rule tries to integrate the individual to society; democracy to integrate social organization to the individual.

There is as yet no ethic dealing with man's relation to land and to the animals and plants which grow upon it. Land, like Odysseus' slave-girls, is still property. The land-relation is still strictly economic, entailing privileges but not obligations.

The extension of ethics to this third element in human environment is, if I read the evidence correctly, an evolutionary possibility and an ecological necessity. It is the third step in a sequence. The first two have already been taken. Individual thinkers since the days of Ezekiel and Isaiah have asserted that the despoliation of land is not only inexpedient but wrong. Society, however, has not yet affirmed their belief. I regard the present conservation movement as the embryo of such an affirmation.

An ethic may be regarded as a mode of guidance for meeting ecological situations so new or intricate, or involving such deferred reactions, that the path of social expediency is not discernible to the average individual. Animal instincts are modes of guidance for the individual in meeting such situations. Ethics are possibly a kind of community instinct in-the-making.

## The Community Concept

10  All ethics so far evolved rest upon a single premise: that the individual is a member of a community of interdependent parts. His instincts prompt him to compete for his place in that community, but his ethics prompt him also to co-operate (perhaps in order that there may be a place to compete for).

The land ethic simply enlarges the boundaries of the community to include soils, waters, plants, and animals, or collectively: the land. This sounds simple: do we not already sing our love for and obligation to the land of the free and the home of the brave? Yes, but just what and whom do we love? Certainly not the soil, which we are sending helter-skelter downriver. Certainly not the waters, which we assume have no function except to turn turbines, float barges, and carry off sewage. Certainly not the plants, of which we exterminate whole communities without batting an eye. Certainly not the animals, of which we have already extirpated many of the largest and most beautiful species. A land ethic of course cannot prevent the alteration, management, and use of these "resources," but it does affirm their right to continued existence, and, at least in spots, their continued existence in a natural state.

In short, a land ethic changes the role of *Homo sapiens* from conqueror of the land-community to plain member and citizen of it. It implies respect for his fellow-members, and also respect for the community as such.

In human history, we have learned (I hope) that the conqueror role is eventually self-defeating. Why? Because it is implicit in such a role that the conqueror knows, *ex cathedra*, just what makes the community clock tick, and just what and who is valuable, and what and who is worthless, in community life. It always turns out that he knows neither, and this is why his conquests eventually defeat themselves.

15    In the biotic community, a parallel situation exists. Abraham knew exactly what the land was for: it was to drip milk and honey into Abraham's mouth. At the present moment, the assurance with which we regard this assumption is inverse to the degree of our education.

The ordinary citizen today assumes that science knows what makes the community clock tick; the scientist is equally sure that he does not. He knows that the biotic mechanism is so complex that its workings may never be fully understood.

That man is, in fact, only a member of a biotic team is shown by an ecological interpretation of history. Many historical events, hitherto explained solely in terms of human enterprise, were actually biotic interactions between people and land. The characteristics of the land determined the facts quite as potently as the characteristics of the men who lived on it.

Consider, for example, the settlement of the Mississippi valley. In the years following the Revolution, three groups were contending for its control: the native Indian, the French and English traders, and the

American settlers. Historians wonder what would have happened if the English at Detroit had thrown a little more weight into the Indian side of those tipsy scales which decided the outcome of the colonial migration into the cane-lands of Kentucky. It is time now to ponder the fact that the cane-lands, when subjected to the particular mixture of forces represented by the cow, plow, fire, and axe of the pioneer, became bluegrass. What if the plant succession inherent in this dark and bloody ground had, under the impact of these forces, given us some worthless sedge, shrub, or weed? Would Boone and Kenton have held out? Would there have been any overflow into Ohio, Indiana, Illinois, and Missouri? Any Louisiana Purchase? Any transcontinental union of new states? Any Civil War?

Kentucky was one sentence in the drama of history. We are commonly told what the human actors in this drama tried to do, but we are seldom told that their success, or the lack of it, hung in large degree on the reaction of particular soils to the impact of the particular forces exerted by their occupancy. In the case of Kentucky, we do not even know where the bluegrass came from—whether it is a native species, or a stowaway from Europe.

20      Contrast the cane-lands with what hindsight tells us about the Southwest, where the pioneers were equally brave, resourceful, and persevering. The impact of occupancy here brought no bluegrass, or other plant fitted to withstand the bumps and buffetings of hard use. This region, when grazed by livestock, reverted through a series of more and more worthless grasses, shrubs, and weeds to a condition of unstable equilibrium. Each recession of plant types bred erosion; each increment to erosion bred a further recession of plants. The result today is a progressive and mutual deterioration, not only of plants and soils, but of the animal community subsisting thereon. The early settlers did not expect this: on the ciénegas of New Mexico some even cut ditches to hasten it. So subtle has been its progress that few residents of the region are aware of it. It is quite invisible to the tourist who finds this wrecked landscape colorful and charming (as indeed it is, but it bears scant resemblance to what it was in 1848).

This same landscape was "developed" once before, but with quite different results. The Pueblo Indians settled the Southwest in pre-Columbian times, but they happened *not* to be equipped with range livestock. Their civilization expired, but not because their land expired.

In India, regions devoid of any sod-forming grass have been settled, apparently without wrecking the land, by the simple expedient of carrying the grass to the cow, rather than vice versa. (Was this the result of some deep wisdom, or was it just good luck? I do not know.)

In short, the plant succession steered the course of history; the pioneer simply demonstrated, for good or ill, what successions inhered in the land. Is history taught in this spirit? It will be, once the concept of land as a community really penetrates our intellectual life.

## The Ecological Conscience

Conservation is a state of harmony between humans and land. Despite nearly a century of propaganda, conservation still proceeds at a snail's pace; progress still consists largely of letterhead pieties and convention oratory. On the back forty we still slip two steps backward for each forward stride.

25       The usual answer to this dilemma is "more conservation education." No one will debate this, but is it certain that only the *volume* of education needs stepping up? Is something lacking in the *content* as well?

It is difficult to give a fair summary of its content in brief form, but, as I understand it, the content is substantially this: obey the law, vote right, join some organizations, and practice what conservation is profitable on your own land; the government will do the rest.

Is not this formula too easy to accomplish anything worthwhile? It defines no right or wrong, assigns no obligation, calls for no sacrifice, implies no change in the current philosophy of values. In respect of land-use, it urges only enlightened self-interest. Just how far will such education take us? An example will perhaps yield a partial answer.

By 1930 it had become clear to all except the ecologically blind that south-western Wisconsin's topsoil was slipping seaward. In 1933 the farmers were told that if they would adopt certain remedial practices for five years, the public would donate CCC labor to install them, plus the necessary machinery and materials. The offer was widely accepted, but the practices were widely forgotten when the five-year contract period was up. The farmers continued only those practices that yielded an immediate and visible economic gain for themselves.

This led to the idea that maybe farmers would learn more quickly if they themselves wrote the rules. Accordingly the Wisconsin Legislature in 1937 passed the Soil Conservation District Law. This said to farmers, in effect: *We, the public, will furnish you free technical service and loan you specialized machinery, if you will write your own rules for land-use. Each county may write its own rules and these will have the force of law.* Nearly all the counties promptly organized to accept the proffered help, but after a decade of operation, *no county has yet written a single rule.* There has been visible progress in such practices as strip-cropping, pasture renovation, and soil liming, but none in fencing woodlots against grazing, and none in excluding plow and cow from steep slopes. The farmers, in short, have selected those remedial practices which were profitable anyhow, and ignored those which were profitable to the community, but not clearly profitable to themselves.

30    When one asks why no rules have been written, one is told that the community is not yet ready to support them; education must precede rules. But the education actually in progress makes no mention of obligations to land over and above those dictated by self-interest. The net result is that we have more education but less soil, fewer healthy woods, and as many floods as in 1937.

The puzzling aspect of such situations is that the existence of obligations over and above self-interest is taken for granted in such rural community enterprises as the betterment of roads, schools, churches, and baseball teams. Their existence is not taken for granted, nor as yet seriously discussed, in bettering the behavior of the water that falls on the land, or in the preserving of the beauty or diversity of the farm landscape. Land-use ethics are still governed wholly by economic self-interest, just as social ethics were a century ago.

To sum up: we asked the farmer to do what he conveniently could to save his soil, and he has done just that, and only that. The farmer who clears the woods off a 75 per cent slope, turns his cows into the clearing, and dumps its rainfall, rocks, and soil into the community creek, is still (if otherwise decent) a respected member of society. If he puts lime on his fields and plants his crops on contour he is still entitled to all the privileges and emoluments of his Soil Conservation District. The District is a beautiful piece of social machinery, but it is coughing along on two cylinders because we have been too timid, and too anxious for quick success, to tell the farmer the true magnitude of his obligations. Obligations have no meaning without conscience, and the problem we face is the extension of the social conscience from people to land.

No important change in ethics was ever accomplished without an internal change in our intellectual emphasis, loyalties, affections, and convictions. The proof that conservation has not yet touched these foundations of conduct lies in the fact that philosophy and religion have not yet heard of it. In our attempt to make conservation easy, we have made it trivial.

## Substitutes for a Land Ethic

When the logic of history hungers for bread and we hand out a stone, we are at pains to explain how much the stone resembles bread. I now describe some of the stones which serve in lieu of a land ethic.

35      One basic weakness in a conservation system based wholly on economic motives is that most members of the land community have no economic value. Wildflowers and songbirds are examples. Of the 22,000 higher plants and animals native to Wisconsin, it is doubtful whether more than 5 per cent can be sold, fed, eaten, or otherwise put to economic use. Yet these creatures are members of the biotic community, and if (as I believe) its stability depends on its integrity, they are entitled to continuance.

When one of these non-economic categories is threatened, and if we happen to love it, we invent subterfuges to give it economic importance. At the beginning of the century songbirds were supposed to be disappearing. Ornithologists jumped to the rescue with some distinctly shaky evidence to the effect that insects would eat us up if birds failed to control them. The evidence had to be economic in order to be valid.

It is painful to read these circumlocutions today. We have no land ethic yet, but we have at least drawn nearer the point of admitting that birds should continue as a matter of biotic right, regardless of the presence or absence of economic advantage to us.

A parallel situation exists in respect of predatory mammals, raptorial birds, and fish-eating birds. Time was when biologists somewhat overworked the evidence that these creatures preserve the health of game by killing weaklings, or that they control rodents for the farmer, or that they prey only on "worthless" species. Here again, the evidence had to be economic in order to be valid. It is only in recent years that we hear the more honest argument that predators are members of the community, and that no special interest has the right to exterminate them for the sake of a benefit, real or fancied, to itself. Unfortunately this enlightened view still in the talk stage. In the field the extermination of predators goes merrily on: witness the impending erasure of the timber wolf by fiat of Congress, the Conservation Bureaus, and many state legislatures.

Some species of trees have been "read out of the party" by economics-minded foresters because they grow too slowly, or have too low a sale value to pay as timber crops: white cedar, tamarack, cypress, beech, and hemlock are examples. In Europe, where forestry is ecologically more advanced, the non-commercial tree species are recognized as members of the native forest community, to be preserved as such, within reason. Moreover some (like beech) have been found to have a valuable function in building up soil fertility. The interdependence of the forest and its constituent tree species, ground flora, and fauna is taken for granted.

Lack of economic value is sometimes a character not only of species or groups, but of entire biotic communities: marshes, bogs, dunes, and "deserts" are examples. Our formula in such cases is to relegate their conservation to government as refuges, monuments, or parks. The difficulty is that these communities are usually interspersed with more valuable private lands; the government cannot possibly own or control such scattered parcels. The net effect is that we have relegated some of them to ultimate extinction over large areas. If the private owner were ecologically minded, he would be proud to be the custodian of a reasonable proportion of such areas, which add diversity and beauty to his farm and to his community.

40 In some instances, the assumed lack of profit in these "waste" areas has proved to be wrong, but only after most of them had been done away with. The present scramble to reflood muskrat marshes is a case in point.

There is a clear tendency in American conservation to relegate to government all necessary jobs that private landowners fail to perform. Government ownership, operation, subsidy, or regulation is now widely prevalent in forestry, range management, soil and watershed management, park and wilderness conservation, fisheries management, and migratory bird management, with more to come. Most of this growth in governmental conservation is proper and logical, some of it is inevitable. That I imply no disapproval of it is implicit in the fact that I have spent most of my life working for it. Nevertheless the question arises: What is the ultimate magnitude of the enterprise? Will the tax base carry its eventual ramifications? At what point will governmental conservation, like the mastodon, become handicapped by its own dimensions? The answer, if there is any, seems to be in a land ethic, or some other force which assigns more obligation to the private landowner.

Industrial landowners and users, especially lumbermen and stockmen, are inclined to wail long and loudly about the extension of government ownership and regulation to land, but (with notable exceptions) they show little disposition to develop the only visible alternative: the voluntary practice of conservation on their own lands.

When the private landowner is asked to perform some unprofitable act for the good of the community, he today assents only with outstretched palm. If the act costs him cash this is fair and proper, but when it costs only forethought, open-mindedness, or time, the issue is at least debatable. The overwhelming growth of land-use subsidies in recent years must be ascribed, in large part, to the government's own agencies for conservation education: the land bureaus, the agricultural colleges, and the extension services. As far as I can detect, no ethical obligation toward land is taught in these institutions.

To sum up: a system of conservation based solely on economic self-interest is hopelessly lopsided. It tends to ignore, and thus eventually to eliminate, many elements in the land community that lack commercial value, but that are (as far as we know) essential to its healthy functioning. It assumes, falsely, I think, that the economic parts of the biotic clock will function without the uneconomic parts. It tends to relegate to government many functions eventually too large, too complex, or too widely dispersed to be performed by government. 45 An ethical obligation on the part of the private owner is the only visible remedy for these situations.

## The Land Pyramid

An ethic to supplement and guide the economic relation to land presupposes the existence of some mental image of land as a biotic mechanism. We can be ethical only in relation to something we can see, feel, understand, love, or otherwise have faith in.

The image commonly employed in conservation education is "the balance of nature." For reasons too lengthy to detail here, this figure of speech fails to describe accurately what little we know about the land mechanism. A much truer image is the one employed in ecology: the biotic pyramid. I shall first sketch the pyramid as a symbol of land, and later develop some of its implications in terms of land-use.

Plants absorb energy from the sun. This energy flows through a circuit called the biota, which may be represented by a pyramid consisting of layers. The bottom layer is the soil. A plant layer rests on the soil, an insect layer on the plants, a bird and rodent layer on the insects, and so on up through various animal groups to the apex layer, which consists of the larger carnivores.

The species of a layer are alike not in where they came from, or in what they look like, but rather in what they eat. Each successive layer depends on those below it for food and often for other services, and each in turn furnishes food and services to those above. Proceeding upward, each successive layer decreases in numerical abundance. Thus, for every carnivore there are hundreds of his prey, thousands of their prey, millions of insects, uncountable plants. The pyramidal form of the system reflects this numerical progression from apex to base. Man shares an intermediate layer with the bears, raccoons, and squirrels which eat both meat and vegetables.

50 The lines of dependency for food and other services are called food chains. Thus soil-oak-deer-Indian is a chain that has now been largely converted to soil-corn-cow-farmer. Each species, including ourselves, is a link in many chains. The deer eats a hundred plants other than oak, and the cow a hundred plants other than corn. Both, then, are links in a hundred chains. The pyramid is a tangle of chains so complex as to seem disorderly, yet the stability of the system proves it to be a highly organized structure. Its functioning depends on the cooperation and competition of its diverse parts.

In the beginning, the pyramid of life was low and squat; the food chains short and simple. Evolution has added layer after layer, link after link. Man is one of thousands of accretions to the height and complexity of the pyramid. Science has given us many doubts, but it has given us at least one certainty: the trend of evolution is to elaborate and diversify the biota.

Land, then, is not merely soil; it is a fountain of energy flowing through a circuit of soils, plants, and animals. Food chains are the living channels which conduct energy upward; death and decay return it to the soil. The circuit is not closed; some energy is dissipated in decay, some is added by absorption from the air, some is stored in soils, peats, and long-lived forests; but it is a sustained circuit, like a slowly augmented revolving fund of life. There is always a net loss by downhill wash, but this is normally small and offset by the decay of rocks. It is deposited in the ocean and, in the course of geological time, raised to form new lands and new pyramids.

The velocity and character of the upward flow of energy depend on the complex structure of the plant and animal community, much as the upward flow of sap in a tree depends on its complex cellular organization. Without this complexity, normal circulation would presumably not occur. Structure means the characteristic numbers, as well as the characteristic kinds and functions, of the component species. This interdependence between the complex structure of the land and its smooth functioning as an energy unit is one of its basic attributes.

When a change occurs in one part of the circuit, many other parts must adjust themselves to it. Change does not necessarily obstruct or divert the flow of energy; evolution is a long series of self-induced changes, the net result of which has been to elaborate the flow mechanism and to lengthen the circuit. Evolutionary changes, however, are usually slow and local. Man's invention of tools has enabled him to make changes of unprecedented violence, rapidity, and scope.

55      One change is in the composition of floras and faunas. The larger predators are lopped off the apex of the pyramid; food chains, for the first time in history, become shorter rather than longer. Domesticated species from other lands are substituted for wild ones, and wild ones are moved to new habitats. In this world-wide pooling of faunas and floras, some species get out of bounds as pests and diseases, others are extinguished. Such effects are seldom intended or foreseen; they represent unpredicted and often untraceable readjustments in the structure. Agricultural science is largely a race between the emergence of new pests and the emergence of new techniques for their control.

Another change touches the flow of energy through plants and animals and its return to the soil. Fertility is the ability of soil to receive, store, and release energy. Agriculture, by overdrafts on the soil, or by too radical a substitution of domestic for native species in the superstructure, may derange the channels of flow or deplete storage. Soils depleted of their storage, or of the organic matter which anchors it, wash away faster than they form. This is erosion.

Waters, like soil, are part of the energy circuit. Industry, by polluting waters or obstructing them with dams, may exclude the plants and animals necessary to keep energy in circulation.

Transportation brings about another basic change; the plants or animals grown in one region are now consumed and returned to the soil in another. Transportation taps the energy stored in rocks, and in the air, and uses it elsewhere; thus we fertilize the garden with nitrogen gleaned by the guano birds from the fishes of seas on the other side of the equator. Thus the formerly localized and self-contained circuits are pooled on a world-wide scale.

The process of altering the pyramid for human occupation releases stored energy, and this often gives rise, during the pioneering period, to a deceptive exuberance of plant and animal life, both wild and tame. These releases of biotic capital tend to becloud or postpone the penalties of violence.

60      This thumbnail sketch of land as an energy circuit conveys three basic ideas:

1. That land is not merely soil.
2. That the native plants and animals kept the energy circuit open; others may or may not.

3. That man-made changes are of a different order than evolutionary changes, and have effects more comprehensive than is
intended or foreseen.

These ideas, collectively, raise two basic issues: Can the land adjust itself to the new order? Can the desired alterations be accomplished with less violence?

Biotas seem to differ in their capacity to sustain violent conversion. Western Europe, for example, carries a far different pyramid
than Caesar found there. Some large animals are lost; swampy forests
have become meadows or plowland; many new plants and animals are
introduced, some of which escape as pests; the remaining natives are
greatly changed in distribution and abundance. Yet the soil is still
there and, with the help of imported nutrients, still fertile; the waters
flow normally; the new structure seems to function and to persist.
There is no visible stoppage or derangement of the circuit.

Western Europe, then, has a resistant biota. Its inner processes
are tough, elastic, resistant to strain. No matter how violent the alterations, the pyramid, so far, has developed some new *modus
vivendi* which preserves its habitability for man, and for most of the
other natives.

Japan seems to present another instance of radical conversion
without disorganization.

65    Most other civilized regions, and some as yet barely touched by
civilization, display various stages of disorganization, varying from
initial symptoms to advanced wastage. In Asia Minor and North Africa
diagnosis is confused by climatic changes, which may have been either
the cause or the effect of advanced wastage. In the United States the
degree of disorganization varies locally; it is worst in the Southwest,
the Ozarks, and parts of the South, and least in New England and the
Northwest. Better land-uses may still arrest it in the less advanced regions. In parts of Mexico, South America, South Africa, and Australia
a violent and accelerating wastage is in progress, but I cannot assess
the prospects.

This almost world-wide display of disorganization in the land
seems to be similar to disease in an animal, except that it never culmi-
nates in complete disorganization or death. The land recovers, but at
some reduced level of complexity, and with a reduced carrying capacity for people, plants, and animals. Many biotas currently regarded as
"lands of opportunity" are in fact already subsisting on exploitative
agriculture, i.e., they have already exceeded their sustained carrying
capacity. Most of South America is overpopulated in this sense.

In arid regions we attempt to offset the process of wastage by reclamation, but it is only too evident that the prospective longevity of reclamation project is often short. In our own West, the best of them may not last a century.

The combined evidence of history and ecology seems to support one general deduction: the less violent the man-made changes, the greater the probability of successful readjustment in the pyramid. Violence, in turn, varies with human population density; a dense population requires a more violent conversion. In this respect, North America has a better chance for permanence than Europe, if she can contrive to limit her density.

This deduction runs counter to our current philosophy, which assumes that because a small increase in density enriched human life, that an indefinite increase will enrich it indefinitely. Ecology knows of no density relationship that holds for indefinitely wide limits. All gains from density are subject to a law of diminishing returns.

70    Whatever may be the equation for humans and land, it is improbable that we as yet know all its terms. Recent discoveries in mineral and vitamin nutrition reveal unsuspected dependencies in the up-circuit: incredibly minute quantities of certain substances determine the value of soils to plants, of plants to animals. What of the down-circuit? What of the vanishing species, the preservation of which we now regard as an esthetic luxury? They helped build the soil; in what unsuspected ways may they be essential to its maintenance? Professor Weaver proposes that we use prairie flowers to reflocculate the wasting soils of the dust bowl; who knows for what purpose cranes and condors, otters and grizzlies may some day be used?

## Land Health and the A-B Cleavage

A land ethic, then, reflects the existence of an ecological conscience, and this in turn reflects a conviction of individual responsibility for the health of the land. Health is the capacity of the land for self-renewal. Conservation is our effort to understand and preserve this capacity.

Conservationists are notorious for their dissensions. Superficially these seem to add up to mere confusion, but a more careful scrutiny reveals a single plane of cleavage common to many specialized fields. In each field one group (A) regards the land as soil, and its function as commodity-production; another group (B) regards the land as a biota, and its function as something broader. How much broader is admittedly in a state of doubt and confusion.

In my own field, forestry, group A is quite content to grow trees like cabbages, with cellulose as the basic forest commodity. It feels no inhibition against violence; its ideology is agronomic. Group B, on the other hand, sees forestry as fundamentally different from agronomy because it employs natural species, and manages a natural environment rather than creating an artificial one. Group B prefers natural reproduction on principle. It worries on biotic as well as economic grounds about the loss of species like chestnut, and the threatened loss of the white pines. It worries about a whole series of secondary forest functions: wildlife, recreation, watersheds, wilderness areas. To my mind, Group B feels the stirrings of an ecological conscience.

In the wildlife field, a parallel cleavage exists. For Group A the basic commodities are sport and meat; the yardsticks of production are ciphers of take in pheasants and trout. Artificial propagation is acceptable as a permanent as well as a temporary recourse—if its unit costs permit. Group B, on the other hand, worries about a whole series of biotic side-issues. What is the cost in predators of producing a game crop? Should we have further recourse to exotics? How can management restore the shrinking species, like prairie grouse, already hopeless as shootable game? How can management restore the threatened rarities, like trumpeter swan and whooping crane? Can management principles be extended to wildflowers? Here again it is clear to me that we have the same A-B cleavage as in forestry.

75     In the larger field of agriculture I am less competent to speak, but there seem to be somewhat parallel cleavages. Scientific agriculture was actively developing before ecology was born, hence a slower penetration of ecological concepts might be expected. Moreover the farmer, by the very nature of his techniques, must modify the biota more radically than the forester or the wildlife manager. Nevertheless, there are many discontents in agriculture which seem to add up to a new vision of "biotic farming."

Perhaps the most important of these is the new evidence that poundage or tonnage is no measure of the food-value of farm crops; the products of fertile soil may be qualitatively as well as quantitatively superior. We can bolster poundage from depleted soils by pouring on imported fertility, but we are not necessarily bolstering food-value. The possible ultimate ramifications of this idea are so immense that I must leave their exposition to abler pens.

The discontent that labels itself "organic farming," while bearing some of the earmarks of a cult, is nevertheless biotic in its direction, particularly in its insistence on the importance of soil flora and fauna.

The ecological fundamentals of agriculture are just as poorly known to the public as in other fields of land-use. For example, few educated people realize that the marvelous advances in technique made during recent decades are improvements in the pump, rather than the well. Acre for acre, they have barely sufficed to offset the sinking level of fertility.

In all of these cleavages, we see repeated the same basic paradoxes: man the conqueror *versus* man the biotic citizen; science the sharpener of his sword *versus* science the searchlight on his universe; land the slave and servant *versus* land the collective organism. Robinson's injunction to Tristram may well be applied, at this juncture, to *Homo sapiens* as a species in geological time:

> *Whether you will or not*
> *You are a King, Tristram, for you are one*
> *Of the time-tested few that leave the world,*
> *When they are gone, not the same place it was.*
> *Mark what you leave.*

## The Outlook

80 It is inconceivable to me that an ethical relation to land can exist without love, respect, and admiration for land, and a high regard for its value. By value, I of course mean something far broader than mere economic value; I mean value in the philosophical sense.

Perhaps the most serious obstacle impeding the evolution of a land ethic is the fact that our educational and economic system is headed away from, rather than toward, an intense consciousness of land. Your true modern is separated from the land by many middlemen, and by innumerable physical gadgets. He has no vital relation to it; to him it is the space between cities on which crops grow. Turn him loose for a day on the land, and if the spot does not happen to be a golf links or a "scenic" area, he is bored stiff. If crops could be raised by hydroponics instead of farming, it would suit him very well. Synthetic substitutes for wood, leather, wool, and other natural land products suit him better than the originals. In short, land is something he has "outgrown."

Almost equally serious as an obstacle to a land ethic is the attitude of the farmer for whom the land is still an adversary, or a taskmaster that keeps him in slavery. Theoretically, the mechanization of farming ought to cut the farmer's chains, but whether it really does is debatable.

One of the requisites for an ecological comprehension of land is an understanding of ecology, and this is by no means co-extensive with "education"; in fact, much higher education seems deliberately to avoid ecological concepts. An understanding of ecology does not necessarily originate in courses bearing ecological labels; it is quite as likely to be labeled geography, botany, agronomy, history, or economics. This is as it should be, but whatever the label, ecological training is scarce.

The case for a land ethic would appear hopeless but for the minority which is in obvious revolt against these "modern" trends.

85    The "key-log" which must be moved to release the evolutionary process for an ethic is simply this: quit thinking about decent land-use as solely an economical problem. Examine each question in terms of what is ethically and esthetically right, as well as what is economically expedient. A thing is right when it tends to preserve the integrity, stability, and beauty of the biotic community. It is wrong when it tends otherwise.

It of course goes without saying that economic feasibility limits the tether of what can or cannot be done for land. It always has and it always will. The fallacy the economic determinists have tied around our collective neck, and which we now need to cast off, is the belief that economics determines *all* land-use. This is simply not true. An innumerable host of actions and attitudes, comprising perhaps the bulk of all land relations, is determined by the land-user's tastes and predilections, rather than by his purse. The bulk of all land relations hinges on investments of time, forethought, skill, and faith rather than on investments of cash. As a land-user thinketh, so is he.

I have purposely presented the land ethic as a product of social evolution because nothing so important as an ethic is ever "written." Only the most superficial student of history supposes that Moses "wrote" the Decalogue; it evolved in the minds of a thinking community, and Moses wrote a tentative summary of it for a "seminar." I say tentative because evolution never stops.

The evolution of a land ethic is an intellectual as well as emotional process. Conservation is paved with good intentions which prove to be futile, or even dangerous, because they are devoid of critical understanding either of the land, or of economic land-use. I think it is a truism that as the ethical frontier advances from the individual to the community, its intellectual content increases.

The mechanism of operation is the same for any ethic: social approbation for right actions: social disapproval for wrong actions.

90     By and large, our present problem is one of attitudes and implements. We are remodeling the Alhambra with a steamshovel, and we
are proud of our yardage. We shall hardly relinquish the shovel, which
after all has many good points, but we are in need of gentler and more
objective criteria for its successful use.

## Questions for Discussion

How does Leopold use the languages of economics and ecology? Is it contradictory of Leopold to use the language of economics to help him support his case for a new ecology?

Has the idea of a "land ethic" been realized in contemporary society? Do
you think this essay is as compelling to a reader now as it was in the middle of the twentieth century?

**William Cronon** *(born in 1954) is the Frederick Jackson Turner Professor of History, Geography, and Environmental Studies at the University of Wisconsin–Madison. Cronon's research and writing frequently explore the interrelations between human culture and the natural environment, particularly the ways that human activities oftentimes provoke unpredictable reactions from the land, reactions which then create new conditions to which people must adapt. He is the author of many books, including* Changes in the Land: Indians, Colonists, and the Ecology of New England *(1983) and the prize-winning* Nature's Metropolis: Chicago and the Great West *(1991). The following essay is an excerpt from a piece that appeared in his* Uncommon Ground: Toward Reinventing Nature *(1995). Published in the inaugural issue of* Environmental History, *a magazine designed for academics, in January 1996, the essay elicited many heated responses.*

## William Cronon
# The Trouble with Wilderness

## The Time Has Come to Rethink Wilderness

This will seem a heretical claim to many environmentalists, since the idea of wilderness has for decades been a fundamental tenet—indeed, a passion—of the environmental movement, especially in the United States. For many Americans wilderness stands as the last remaining place where civilization, that all too human disease, has not fully infected the earth. It is an island in the polluted sea of urban-industrial modernity, the one place we can turn for escape from our own too-muchness. Seen in this way, wilderness presents itself as the best antidote to our human selves, a refuge we must somehow recover if we hope to save the planet. As Henry David Thoreau once famously declared, "In Wildness is the preservation of the World."[1]

But is it? The more one knows of its peculiar history, the more one realizes that wilderness is not quite what it seems. Far from being the one place on earth that stands apart from humanity, it is quite profoundly a human creation—indeed, the creation of very particular human cultures at very particular moments in human history. It is not a pristine sanctuary where the last remnant of an untouched, endangered, but still transcendent nature can for at least a little while longer be encountered without the contaminating taint of civilization. Instead, it is a product of that civilization, and could hardly be contaminated by the very stuff of which it is made. Wilderness hides its unnaturalness behind a mask that is all the more beguiling because it seems so natural. As we gaze into the mirror it holds up for us, we too easily imagine that what we behold is Nature when in fact we see the reflection of our own unexamined longings and desires. For this reason, we mistake ourselves when we suppose that wilderness can be the solution to our culture's problematic relationships with the nonhuman world, for wilderness is itself no small part of the problem.

To assert the unnaturalness of so natural a place will no doubt seem absurd or even perverse to many readers, so let me hasten to add that the nonhuman world we encounter in wilderness is far from being merely our own invention. I celebrate with others who love wilderness the beauty and power of the things it contains. Each of us who has spent time there can conjure images and sensations that seem all the more hauntingly real for having engraved themselves so indelibly on our memories. Such memories may be uniquely our own, but they are also familiar enough be to be instantly recognizable to others. Remember this? The torrents of mist shoot out from the base of a great waterfall in the depths of a Sierra canyon, the tiny droplets cooling your face as you listen to the roar of the water and gaze up toward the sky through a rainbow that hovers just out of reach. Remember this too: looking out across a desert canyon in the evening air, the only sound a lone raven calling in the distance, the rock walls dropping away into a chasm so deep that its bottom all but vanishes as you squint into the amber light of the setting sun. And this: the moment beside the trail as you sit on a sandstone ledge, your boots damp with the morning dew while you take in the rich smell of the pines, and the small red fox—or maybe for you it was a raccoon or a coyote or a deer—that suddenly ambles across your path, stopping for a long moment to gaze in your direction with cautious indifference before continuing on its way. Remember the feelings of such moments, and you will know as well as I do that you were in the presence of something irreducibly nonhuman, something profoundly Other than yourself. Wilderness is made of that too.

And yet: what brought each of us to the places where such memories became possible is entirely a cultural invention. Go back 250 years in American and European history, and you do not find nearly so many people wandering around remote corners of the planet looking for what today we would call "the wilderness experience." As late as the eighteenth century, the most common usage of the word "wilderness" in the English language referred to landscapes that generally carried adjectives far different from the ones they attract today. To be a wilderness then was to be "deserted," "savage," "desolate," "barren"—in short, a "waste," the word's nearest synonym. Its connotations were anything but positive, and the emotion one was most likely to feel in its presence was "bewilderment" or terror.[2]

5      Many of the word's strongest associations then were biblical, for it is used over and over again in the King James Version to refer to places on the margins of civilization where it is all too easy to lose oneself in moral confusion and despair. The wilderness was where Moses had wandered with his people for forty years, and where they had nearly abandoned their God to worship a golden idol.[3] "For Pharaoh will say of the Children of Israel," we read in Exodus, "They are entangled in the land, the wilderness hath shut them in."[4] The wilderness was where Christ had struggled with the devil and endured his temptations: "And immediately the Spirit driveth him into the wilderness. And he was there in the wilderness for forty days tempted of Satan; and was with the wild beasts; and the angels ministered unto him."[5] The "delicious Paradise" of John Milton's Eden was surrounded by "a steep wilderness, whose hairy sides / Access denied" to all who sought entry.[6] When Adam and Eve were driven from that garden, the world they entered was a wilderness that only their labor and pain could redeem. Wilderness, in short, was a place to which one came only against one's will, and always in fear and trembling. Whatever value it might have arose solely from the possibility that it might be "reclaimed" and turned toward human ends—planted as a garden, say, or a city upon a hill.[7] In its raw state, it had little or nothing to offer civilized men and women.

But by the end of the nineteenth century, all this had changed. The wastelands that had once seemed worthless had for some people come to seem almost beyond price. That Thoreau in 1862 could declare wildness to be the preservation of the world suggests the sea change that was going on. Wilderness had once been the antithesis of all that was orderly and good—it had been the darkness, one might say, on the far side of the garden wall—and yet now it was frequently likened to Eden itself. When John Muir arrived in the Sierra Nevada in

1869, he would declare, "No description of Heaven that I have ever heard or read of seems half so fine."[8] He was hardly alone in expressing such emotions. One by one, various corners of the American map came to be designated as sites whose wild beauty was so spectacular that a growing number of citizens had to visit and see them for themselves. Niagara Falls was the first to undergo this transformation, but it was soon followed by the Catskills, the Adirondacks, Yosemite, Yellowstone, and others. Yosemite was deeded by the U.S. government to the state of California in 1864 as the nation's first wildland park, and Yellowstone became the first true national park in 1872.[9]

By the first decade of the twentieth century, in the single most famous episode in American conservation history, a national debate had exploded over whether the city of San Francisco should be permitted to augment its water supply by damming the Tuolumne River in Hetch Hetchy valley, well within the boundaries of Yosemite National Park. The dam was eventually built, but what today seems no less significant is that so many people fought to prevent its completion. Even as the fight was being lost, Hetch Hetchy became the battle cry of an emerging movement to preserve wilderness. Fifty years earlier, such opposition would have been unthinkable. Few would have questioned the merits of "reclaiming" a wasteland like this in order to put it to human use. Now the defenders of Hetch Hetchy attracted widespread national attention by portraying such an act not as improvement or progress but as desecration and vandalism. Lest one doubt that the old biblical metaphors had been turned completely on their heads, listen to John Muir attack the dam's defenders. "Their arguments," he wrote, "are curiously like those of the devil, devised for the destruction of the first garden—so much of the very best Eden fruit going to waste; so much of the best Tuolumne water and Tuolumne scenery going to waste."[10] For Muir and the growing number of Americans who shared his views, Satan's home had become God's own temple.

The sources of this rather astonishing transformation were many, but for the purposes of this essay they can be gathered under two broad headings: the sublime and the frontier. Of the two, the sublime is the older and more pervasive cultural construct, being one of the most important expressions of that broad transatlantic movement we today label as romanticism; the frontier is more peculiarly American, though it too had its European antecedents and parallels. The two converged to remake wilderness in their own image, freighting it with moral values and cultural symbols that it carries to this day. Indeed, it is not too much to say that the modern environmental movement is itself a grandchild of romanticism and post-frontier ideology, which is why it is no accident that so much environmentalist discourse takes its bearings from the wilderness these intellectual movements helped create. Although wilderness may today seem to be just one environmental concern among many, it in fact serves as the foundation for a long list of other such concerns that on their face seem quite remote from it. That is why its influence is so pervasive and, potentially, so insidious.

To gain such remarkable influence, the concept of wilderness had to become loaded with some of the deepest core values of the culture that created and idealized it: it had to become sacred. This possibility had been present in wilderness even in the days when it had been a place of spiritual danger and moral temptation. If Satan was there, then so was Christ, who had found angels as well as wild beasts during His sojourn in the desert. In the wilderness the boundaries between human and nonhuman, between natural and supernatural, had always seemed less certain than elsewhere. This was why the early Christian saints and mystics had often emulated Christ's desert retreat as they sought to experience for themselves the visions and spiritual testing He had endured. One might meet devils and run the risk of losing one's soul in such a place, but one might also meet God. For some that possibility was worth almost any price.

10     By the eighteenth century this sense of the wilderness as a landscape where the supernatural lay just beneath the surface was expressed in the doctrine of the *sublime*, a word whose modern usage has been so watered down by commercial hype and tourist advertising that it retains only a dim echo of its former power.[11] In the theories of Edmund Burke, Immanuel Kant, William Gilpin, and others, sublime landscapes were those rare places on earth where one had more chance than elsewhere to glimpse the face of God.[12] Romantics had a clear notion of where one could be most sure of having this experience. Although God might, of course, choose to show Himself anywhere, He would most often be found in those vast, powerful landscapes where one could not help feeling insignificant and being reminded of one's own mortality. Where were these sublime places? The eighteenth century catalog of their locations feels very familiar, for we still see and value landscapes as it taught us to do. God was on the mountaintop, in the chasm, in the waterfall, in the thunder-cloud, in the rainbow, in the sunset. One has only to think of the sites that Americans chose for

their first national parks—Yellowstone, Yosemite, Grand Canyon, Rainier, Zion—to realize that virtually all of them fit one or more of these categories. Less sublime landscapes simply did not appear worthy of such protection; not until the 1940s, for instance, would the first swamp be honored, in Everglades National Park, and to this day there is no national park in the grasslands.[13]

Among the best proofs that one had entered a sublime landscape was the emotion it evoked. For the early romantic writers and artists who first began to celebrate it, the sublime was far from being a pleasurable experience. The classic description is that of William Wordsworth as he recounted climbing the Alps and crossing the Simplon Pass in his autobiographical poem *The Prelude*. There, surrounded by crags and waterfalls, the poet felt himself literally to be in the presence of the divine—and experienced an emotion remarkably close to terror:

The immeasurable height
Of woods decaying, never to be decayed,
The stationary blasts of waterfalls,
And in the narrow rent at every turn
Winds thwarting winds, bewildered and forlorn,
The torrents shooting from the clear blue sky,
The rocks that muttered close upon our ears,
Black drizzling crags that spake by the way-side
As if a voice were in them, the sick sight
And giddy prospect of the raving stream,
The unfettered clouds and region of the Heavens,
Tumult and peace, the darkness and the light—
Were all like workings of one mind, the features
Of the same face, blossoms upon one tree;
Characters of the great Apocalypse,
The types and symbols of Eternity,
Of first, and last, and midst, and without end.[14]

This was no casual stroll in the mountains, no simple sojourn in the gentle lap of nonhuman nature. What Wordsworth described was nothing less than a religious experience, akin to that of the Old Testament prophets as they conversed with their wrathful God. The symbols he detected in this wilderness landscape were more supernatural than natural, and they inspired more awe and dismay than joy or pleasure. No mere mortal was meant to linger long in such a place, so it was with considerable relief that Wordsworth and his companion made their way back down from the peaks to the sheltering valleys.

Lest you suspect that this view of the sublime was limited to timid Europeans who lacked the American know-how for feeling at home in the wilderness, remember Henry David Thoreau's 1846 climb of Mount Katahdin, in Maine. Although Thoreau is regarded by many today as one of the great American celebrators of wilderness, his emotions about Katahdin were no less ambivalent than Wordsworth's about the Alps.

> It was vast, Titanic; and such as man never inhabits. Some part of the beholder, even some vital part, seems to escape through the loose grating of his ribs as he ascends. He is more lone than you can imagine. . . . Vast, Titanic, inhuman Nature has got him at disadvantage, caught him alone, and pilfers him of some of his divine faculty. She does not smile on him as in the plains. She seems to say sternly, why came ye here before your time? This ground is not prepared for you. Is it not enough that I smile in the valleys? I have never made this soil for thy feet, this air for thy breathing, these rocks for thy neighbors. I cannot pity nor fondle thee here, but forever relentlessly drive thee hence to where I *am* kind. Why seek me where I have not called thee, and then complain because you find me but a stepmother?[15]

This is surely not the way a modern backpacker or nature lover would describe Maine's most famous mountain, but that is because Thoreau's description owes as much to Wordsworth and other romantic contemporaries as to the rocks and clouds of Katahdin itself. His words took the physical mountain on which he stood and transmuted it into an icon of the sublime: a symbol of God's presence on earth. The power and the glory of that icon were such that only a prophet might gaze on it for long. In effect, romantics like Thoreau joined Moses and the children of Israel in Exodus when "they looked toward the wilderness, and behold, the glory of the Lord appeared in the cloud."[16]

But even as it came to embody the awesome power of the sublime, wilderness was also being tamed—not just by those who were building settlements in its midst but also by those who most celebrated its inhuman beauty. By the second half of the nineteenth century, the terrible awe that Wordsworth and Thoreau regarded as the appropriately pious stance to adopt in the presence of their mountaintop God was giving way to a much more comfortable, almost sentimental demeanor. As more and more tourists sought out the wilderness as a spectacle to be looked at and enjoyed for its great beauty, the sublime in effect became domesticated. The wilderness was still sacred, but the religious sentiments it evoked were more those of a pleasant parish church than those of a grand cathedral or a harsh desert retreat. The writer who best captures this late romantic sense of a domesticated sublime is undoubtedly John Muir, whose descriptions of Yosemite and the Sierra Nevada reflect none of the anxiety or terror one finds in earlier writers. Here he is, for instance, sketching on North Dome in Yosemite Valley:

> No pain here, no dull empty hours, no fear of the past, no fear of the future. These blessed mountains are so compactly filled with God's beauty, no petty personal hope or experience has room to be. Drinking this champagne water is pure pleasure, so is breathing the living air, and every movement of limbs is pleasure, while the body seems to feel beauty when exposed to it as it feels the campfire or sunshine, entering not by the eyes alone, but equally through all one's flesh like radiant heat, making a passionate ecstatic pleasure glow not explainable.

The emotions Muir describes in Yosemite could hardly be more different from Thoreau's on Katahdin or Wordsworth's on the Simplon Pass. Yet all three men are participating in the same cultural tradition and contributing to the same myth: the mountain as cathedral. The three may differ in the way they choose to express their piety— Wordsworth favoring an awefilled bewilderment, Thoreau a stern loneliness, Muir a welcome ecstasy—but they agree completely about the church in which they prefer to worship. Muir's closing words on North Dome diverge from his older contemporaries only in mood, not in their ultimate content:

> Perched like a fly on this Yosemite dome, I gaze and sketch and bask, oftentimes settling down into dumb administration without definite hope of ever learning much, yet with the longing, unresting effort that lies at the door of hope, humbly prostrate before the vast display of God's power, and eager to offer self-denial and renunciation with eternal toil to learn any lesson in the divine manuscript.[17]

Muir's "divine manuscript" and Wordsworth's "Characters of the great Apocalypse" were in fact pages from the same holy book. The sublime wilderness had ceased to be a place of satanic temptation and become instead a sacred temple, much as it continues to be for those who love it today.

15  But the romantic sublime was not the only cultural movement that helped transform wilderness into a sacred American icon during the nineteenth century. No less important was the powerful romantic attraction of primitivism, dating back at least to Rousseau—the belief that the best antidote to the ills of an overly refined and civilized modern world

was a return to simpler, more primitive living. In the United States, this was embodied most strikingly in the national myth of the frontier. The historian Frederick Jackson Turner wrote in 1893 the classic academic statement of this myth, but it had been part of American cultural traditions for well over a century. As Turner described the process, easterners and European immigrants, in moving to the wild unsettled lands of the frontier, shed the trappings of civilization, rediscovered their primitive racial energies, reinvented direct democratic institutions, and thereby reinfused themselves with a vigor, an independence, and a creativity that were the source of American democracy and national character. Seen in this way, wild country became a place not just of religious redemption but of national renewal, the quintessential location for experiencing what it meant to be an American.

One of Turner's most provocative claims was that by the 1890s the frontier was passing away. Never again would "such gifts of free land offer themselves" to the American people. "The frontier has gone," he declared, "and with its going has closed the first period of American history."[18] Built into the frontier myth from its very beginning was the notion that this crucible of American identity was temporary and would pass away. Those who have celebrated the frontier have almost always looked backward as they did so, mourning an older, simpler, truer world that is about to disappear forever: That world and all of its attractions, Turner said, depended on free land—on wilderness. Thus, in the myth of the vanishing frontier lay the seeds of wilderness preservation in the United States, for if wild land had been so crucial in the making of the nation, then surely one must save its last remnants as monuments to the American past—and as an insurance policy to protect its future. It is no accident that the movement to set aside national parks and wilderness areas began to gain real momentum at precisely the time that laments about the passing frontier reached their peak. To protect wilderness was in a very real sense to protect the nation's most sacred myth of origin.

Among the core elements of the frontier myth was the powerful sense among certain groups of Americans that wilderness was the last bastion of rugged individualism. Turner tended to stress communitarian themes when writing frontier history, asserting that Americans in primitive conditions had been forced to band together with their neighbors to form communities and democratic institutions. For other writers, however, frontier democracy for communities was less compelling than frontier freedom for individuals.[19] By fleeing to the outer margins of settled land and society—so the story ran—an individual could escape the confining strictures of civilized life. The mood among writers who celebrated frontier individualism was almost always nostalgic; they lamented not just a lost way of life but the passing of the heroic men who had embodied that life. Thus Owen Wister in the introduction to his classic 1902 novel *The Virginian* could write of "a vanished world" in which "the horseman, the cow-puncher, the last romantic figure upon our soil" rode only "in his historic yesterday" and would "never come again." For Wister, the cowboy was a man who gave his word and kept it ("Wall Street would have found him behind the times"), who did not talk lewdly to women ("Newport would have thought him old-fashioned"), who worked and played hard, and whose "ungoverned hours did not unman him."[20] Theodore Roosevelt wrote with much the same nostalgic fervor about the "fine, manly qualities" of the "wild rough-rider of the plains." No one could be more heroically masculine, thought Roosevelt, or more at home in the western wilderness:

> There he passes his days, there he does his life-work, there, when he meets death, he faces it as he has faced many other evils, with quiet, uncomplaining fortitude. Brave, hospitable, hardy, and adventurous, he is the grim pioneer of our race; he prepares the way for the civilization from before whose face he must himself disappear. Hard and dangerous though his existence is, it has yet a wild attraction that strongly draws to it his bold, free spirit.[21]

This nostalgia for a passing frontier way of life inevitably implied ambivalence, if not downright hostility, toward modernity and all that it represented. If one saw the wild lands of the frontier as freer, truer, and more natural than other, more modern places, then one was also inclined to see the cities and factories of urban-industrial civilization as confining, false, and artificial. Owen Wister looked at the postfrontier "transition" that had followed "the horseman of the plains," and did not like what he saw: "a shapeless state, a condition of men and manners as unlovely as is that moment in the year when winter is gone and spring not come, and the face of Nature is ugly."[22] In the eyes of writers who shared Wister's distaste for modernity, civilization contaminated its inhabitants and absorbed them into the faceless, collective, contemptible life of the crowd. For all of its troubles and dangers, and despite the fact that it must pass away, the frontier had been a better place. If civilization was to be redeemed, it would be by men like the Virginian who could retain their frontier virtues even as they made the transition to post-frontier life.

The mythic frontier individualist was almost always masculine in gender: here, in the wilderness, a man could be a real man, the rugged individual he was meant to be before civilization sapped his energy and threatened his masculinity. Wister's contemptuous remarks about Wall Street and Newport suggest what he and many others of his generation believed—that the comforts and seductions of civilized life were especially insidious for men, who all too easily became emasculated by the femininizing tendencies of civilization. More often than not, men who felt this way came, like Wister and Roosevelt, from elite class backgrounds. The curious result was that frontier nostalgia became an important vehicle for expressing a peculiarly bourgeois form of antimodernism. The very men who most benefited from urban-industrial capitalism were among those who believed they must escape its debilitating effects. If the frontier was passing, then men who had the means to do so should preserve for themselves some remnant of its wild landscape so that they might enjoy the regeneration and renewal that came from sleeping under the stars, participating in blood sports, and living off the land. The frontier might be gone, but the frontier experience could still be had if only wilderness were preserved.

20     Thus the decades following the Civil War saw more and more of the nation's wealthiest citizens seeking out wilderness for themselves. The elite passion for wild land took many forms: enormous estates in the Adirondacks and elsewhere (disingenuously called "camps" despite their many servants and amenities), cattle ranches for would-be rough riders on the Great Plains, guided big-game hunting trips in the Rockies, and luxurious resort hotels wherever railroads pushed their way into sublime landscapes. Wilderness suddenly emerged as the landscape of choice for elite tourists, who brought with them strikingly urban ideas of the countryside through which they traveled. For them, wild land was not a site for productive labor and not a permanent home; rather, it was a place of recreation. One went to the wilderness not as a producer but as a consumer, hiring guides and other back-country residents who could serve as romantic surrogates for the rough riders and hunters of the frontier if one was willing to overlook their new status as employees and servants of the rich.

In just this way, wilderness came to embody the national frontier myth, standing for the wild freedom of America's past and seeming to represent a highly attractive natural alternative to the ugly artificiality of modern civilization. The irony, of course, was that in the process wilderness came to reflect the very civilization its devotees sought to escape. Ever since the nineteenth century, celebrating wilderness has been an activity mainly for well-to-do city folks. Country people generally know far too much about working the land to regard *un*worked land as their ideal. In contrast, elite urban tourists and wealthy sportsmen projected their leisure-time frontier fantasies onto the American landscape and so created wilderness in their own image.

There were other ironies as well. The movement to set aside national parks and wilderness areas followed hard on the heels of the final Indian wars, in which the prior human inhabitants of these areas were rounded up and moved onto reservations. The myth of the wilderness as "virgin," uninhabited land had always been especially cruel when seen from the perspective of the Indians who had once called that land home. Now they were forced to move elsewhere, with the result that tourists could safely enjoy the illusion that they were seeing their nation in its pristine, original state, in the new morning of God's own creation.[23] Among the things that most marked the new national parks as reflecting a post-frontier consciousness was the relative absence of human violence within their boundaries. The actual frontier had often been a place of conflict, in which invaders and invaded fought for control of land and resources. Once set aside within the fixed and carefully policed boundaries of the modern bureaucratic state, the wilderness lost its savage image and became safe: a place more of reverie than of revulsion or fear. Meanwhile, its original inhabitants were kept out by dint of force, their earlier uses of the land redefined as inappropriate or even illegal. To this day, for instance, the Blackfeet continue to be accused of "poaching" on the lands of Glacier National Park that originally belonged to them and that were ceded by treaty only with the proviso that they be permitted to hunt there.[24]

The removal of Indians to create an "uninhabited wilderness"— uninhabited as never before in the human history of the place— reminds us just how invented, just how constructed, the American wilderness really is. To return to my opening argument: there is nothing natural about the concept of wilderness. It is entirely a creation of the culture that holds it dear, a product of the very history it seeks to deny. Indeed, one of the most striking proofs of the cultural invention of wilderness is its thoroughgoing erasure of the history from which it sprang. In virtually all of its manifestations, wilderness represents a flight from history. Seen as the original garden, it is a place outside of time, from which human beings had to be ejected before the fallen world history could properly begin. Seen as the frontier, it is a savage world at the dawn of civilization, whose transformation represents the very beginning of the national historical epic. Seen as the bold landscape of frontier heroism, it is the place of youth and childhood, into which men escape by abandoning their pasts and entering a world of freedom where the constraints of civilization fade into memory. Seen as the sacred sublime, it is the home of a God who transcends history by standing as the One who remains untouched and unchanged by time's arrow. No matter what the angle from which we regard it, wilderness offers us the illusion that we can escape the cares and troubles of the world in which our past has ensnared us.[25]

This escape from history is one reason why the language we use to talk about wilderness is often permeated with spiritual and religious values that reflect human ideals far more than the material world of physical nature. Wilderness fulfills the old romantic project of secularizing Judeo-Christian values so as to make a new cathedral not in some pretty human building but in God's own creation, Nature itself. Many environmentalists who reject traditional notions of the Godhead and who regard themselves as agnostics or even atheists nonetheless express feelings tantamount to religious awe when in the presence of wilderness—a fact that testifies to the success of the romantic project. Those who have no difficulty seeing God as the expression of our human dreams and desires nonetheless have trouble recognizing that in a secular age Nature can offer precisely the same sort of mirror.

25      Thus it is that wilderness serves as the unexamined foundation on which so many of the quasi-religious values of modern environmentalism rest. The critique of modernity that is one of environmentalism's most important contributions to the moral and political discourse of our time more often than not appeals, explicitly or implicitly, to wilderness as the standard against which to measure the failings of our human world. Wilderness is the natural, unfallen antithesis of an unnatural civilization that has lost its soul. It is a place of freedom in which we can recover the true selves we have lost to the corrupting influences of our artificial lives. Most of all, it is the ultimate landscape of authenticity. Combining the sacred grandeur of the sublime with the primitive simplicity of the frontier, it is the place where we can see the world as it really is, and so know ourselves as we really are—or ought to be.

But the trouble with wilderness is that it quietly expresses and reproduces the very values its devotees seek to reject. The flight from history that is very nearly the core of wilderness represents the false hope of an escape from responsibility, the illusion that we can somehow wipe clean the slate of our past and return to the tabula rasa that supposedly existed before we began to leave our marks on the world. The dream of an unworked natural landscape is very much the fantasy of people who have never themselves had to work the land to make a living—urban folk for whom food comes from a supermarket or a restaurant instead of a field, and for whom the wooden houses in which they live and work apparently have no meaningful connection to the forests in which trees grow and die. Only people whose relation to the land was already alienated could hold up wilderness as a model for human life in nature, for the romantic ideology of wilderness leaves precisely nowhere for human beings actually to make their living from the land.

This, then, is the central paradox: wilderness embodies a dualistic vision in which the human is entirely outside the natural. If we allow ourselves to believe that nature, to be true, must also be wild, then our very presence in nature represents its fall. The place where we are is the place where nature is not. If this is so—if by definition wilderness leaves no place for human beings, save perhaps as contemplative so-journers enjoying their leisurely reverie in God's natural cathedral—then also by definition it can offer no solution to the environmental and other problems that confront us. To the extent that we celebrate wilderness as the measure with which we judge civilization, we repro-duce the dualism that sets humanity and nature at opposite poles. We thereby leave ourselves little hope of discovering what an ethical, sus-tainable, *honorable* human place in nature might actually look like.

Worse: to the extent that we live in an urban-industrial civilization but at the same time pretend to ourselves that our *real* home is in the wilderness, to just that extent we give ourselves permission to evade responsibility for the lives we actually lead. We inhabit civilization while holding some part of ourselves—what we imagine to be the most precious part—aloof from its entanglements. We work our nine-to-five jobs in its institutions, we eat its food, we drive its cars (not least to reach the wilderness), we benefit from the intricate and all too invisi-ble networks with which it shelters us, all the while pretending that these things are not an essential part of who we are. By imagining that our true home is in the wilderness, we forgive ourselves the homes we actually inhabit. In its flight from history, in its siren song of escape, in its reproduction of the dangerous dualism that sets human beings out-side of nature—in all of these ways, wilderness poses a serious threat to responsible environmentalism at the end of the twentieth century.

By now I hope it is clear that my criticism in this essay is not directed at wild nature per se, or even at efforts to set aside large tracts of wild land, but rather at the specific habits of thinking that flow from this com-plex cultural construction called wilderness. It is not the things we label as wilderness that are the problem—for nonhuman nature and large tracts of the natural world *do* deserve protection—but rather what we ourselves mean when we use the label. Lest one doubt how pervasive these habits of thought actually are in contemporary environmentalism, let me list some of the places where wilderness serves as the ideological underpinning for environmental concerns that might otherwise seem quite remote from it. Defenders of biological diversity, for instance, although sometimes appealing to more utilitarian concerns, often point to "untouched" ecosystems as the best and richest repositories of the undiscovered species we must certainly try to protect. Although at first blush an apparently more "scientific" concept than wilderness, biological diversity in fact invokes many of the same sacred values, which is why organizations like the Nature Conservancy have been so quick to employ it as an alternative to the seemingly fuzzier and more problematic concept of wilderness. There is a paradox here, of course. To the extent that biological diversity (indeed, even wilderness itself) is likely to survive in the future only by the most vigilant and self-conscious management of the ecosystems that sustain it, the ideology of wilderness is potentially in direct conflict with the very thing it encourages us to protect.[26]

30    The most striking instances of this have revolved around "endangered species," which serve as vulnerable symbols of biological diversity while at the same time standing as surrogates for wilderness itself. The terms of the Endangered Species Act in the United States have often meant that those hoping to defend pristine wilderness have had to rely on a single endangered species like the spotted owl to gain legal standing for their case—thereby making the full power of the sacred land inhere in a single numinous organism whose habitat then becomes the object of intense debate about appropriate management and use.[27] The ease with which anti-environmental forces like the wise-use movement have attacked such single-species preservation efforts suggests the vulnerability of strategies like these.

Perhaps partly because our own conflicts over such places and organisms have become so messy, the convergence of wilderness values with concerns about biological diversity and endangered species has helped produce a deep fascination for remote ecosystems, where it is easier to imagine that nature might somehow be "left alone" to flourish by its own pristine devices. The classic example is the tropical rain forest, which since the 1970s has become the most powerful modern icon of unfallen, sacred land—a veritable Garden of Eden—for many Americans and Europeans. And yet protecting the rain forest in the eyes of First World environmentalists all too often means protecting it from the people who live there. Those who seek to preserve such "wilderness" from the activities of native peoples run the risk of reproducing the same tragedy—being forceably removed from an ancient home—that befell American Indians. Third World countries face massive environmental problems and deep social conflicts, but these are not likely to be solved by a cultural myth that encourages us to "preserve" peopleless landscapes that have not existed in such places for millennia. At its worst, as environmentalists are beginning to realize, exporting American notions of wilderness in this way can become an unthinking and self-defeating form of cultural imperialism.[28]

Perhaps the most suggestive example of the way that wilderness thinking can underpin other environmental concerns has emerged in the recent debate about "global change." In 1989 the journalist Bill McKibben published a book entitled *The End of Nature*, in which he argued that the prospect of global climate change as a result of unintentional human manipulation of the atmosphere means that nature as we once knew it no longer exists.[29] Whereas earlier generations inhabited a natural world that remained more or less unaffected by their actions, our own generation is uniquely different. We and our children will henceforth live in a biosphere completely altered by our own activity, a planet in which the human and the natural can no longer be distinguished, because the one has overwhelmed the other. In McKibben's view, nature has died, and we are responsible for killing it. "The planet," he declares, "is utterly different now."[30]

But such a perspective is possible only if we accept the wilderness premise that nature, to be natural, must also be pristine—remote from humanity and untouched by our common past. In fact, everything we know about environmental history suggests that people have been manipulating the natural world on various scales for as long as we have a record of their passing. Moreover, we have unassailable evidence that many of the environmental changes we now face also occurred quite apart from human intervention at one time or another in the earth's past.[31] The point is not that our current problems are trivial, or that our devastating effects on the earth's ecosystems should be accepted as inevitable or "natural." It is rather that we seem unlikely to make much progress in solving these problems if we hold up to ourselves as the mirror of nature a wilderness we ourselves cannot inhabit.

To do so is merely to take to a logical extreme the paradox that was built into wilderness from the beginning: if nature dies because we enter it, then the only way to save nature is to kill ourselves. The absurdity of this proposition flows from the underlying dualism it expresses. Not only does it ascribe greater power to humanity than we in fact possess—physical and biological nature will surely survive in some form or another long after we ourselves have gone the way of all flesh—but in the end it offers us little more than a self-defeating counsel of despair. The tautology gives us no way out: if wild nature is the only thing worth saving, and if our mere presence destroys it, then the sole solution to our own unnaturalness, the only way to protect sacred wilderness from profane humanity, would seem to be suicide. It is not a proposition that seems likely to produce very positive or practical results.

35        And yet radical environmentalists and deep ecologists all too frequently come close to accepting this premise as a first principle. When they express, for instance, the popular notion that our environmental problems began with the invention of agriculture, they push the human fall from natural grace so far back into the past that all of civilized history becomes a tale of ecological declension. Earth First! founder Dave Foreman captures the familiar parable succinctly when he writes,

> Before agriculture was midwifed in the Middle East, humans were in the wilderness. We had no concept of "wilderness" because everything was wilderness and *we were a part of it*. But with irrigation ditches, crop surpluses, and permanent villages, we became *apart from* the natural world. . . . Between the wilderness that created us and the civilization created by us grew an ever-widening rift.[32]

In this view the farm becomes the first and most important battlefield in the long war against wild nature, and all else follows in its wake. From such a starting place, it is hard not to reach the conclusion that the only way human beings can hope to live naturally on earth is to follow the hunter-gatherers back into a wilderness Eden and abandon virtually everything that civilization has given us. It may indeed turn out that civilization will end in ecological collapse or nuclear disaster, whereupon one might expect to find any human survivors returning to a way of life closer to that celebrated by Foreman and his followers. For most of us, though, such a debacle would be cause for regret, a sign that humanity had failed to fulfill its own promise and failed to honor its own highest values—including those of the deep ecologists.

In offering wilderness as the ultimate hunter-gatherer alternative to civilization, Foreman reproduces an extreme but still easily recognizable version of the myth of frontier primitivism. When he writes of his fellow Earth Firsters that "we believe we must return to being animal, to glorying in our sweat, hormones, tears, and blood" and that "we struggle against the modern compulsion to become dull, passionless androids," he is following in the footsteps of Owen Wister.[33]

Although his arguments give primacy to defending biodiversity and the autonomy of wild nature, his prose becomes most passionate when he speaks of preserving "the wilderness experience." His own ideal "Big Outside" bears an uncanny resemblance to that of the frontier myth: wide open spaces and virgin land with no trails, no signs, no facilities, no maps, no guides, no rescues, no modern equipment. Tellingly, it is a land where hardy travelers can support themselves by hunting with "primitive weapons (bow and arrow, atlatl, knife, sharp rock)."[34] Foreman claims that "the primary value of wilderness is not as a proving ground for young Huck Finns and Annie Oakleys," but his heart is with Huck and Annie all the same. He admits that "preserving a quality wilderness experience for the human visitor, letting her or him flex Paleolithic muscles or seek visions, remains a tremendously important secondary purpose."[35] Just so does Teddy Roosevelt's rough rider live on in the greener garb of a new age.

However much one may be attracted to such a vision, it entails problematic consequences. For one, it makes wilderness the locus for an epic struggle between malign civilization and benign nature, compared with which all other social, political, and moral concerns seem trivial. Foreman writes, "The preservation of wildness and native diversity is *the* most important issue. Issues directly affecting only humans pale in comparison."[36] Presumably so do any environmental problems whose victims are mainly people, for such problems usually surface in landscapes that have already "fallen" and are no longer wild. This would seem to exclude from the radical environmentalist agenda problems of occupational health and safety in industrial settings, problems of toxic waste exposure on "unnatural" urban and agricultural sites, problems of poor children poisoned by lead exposure in the inner city, problems of famine and poverty and human suffering in the "overpopulated" places of the earth—problems, in short, of environmental justice. If we set too high a stock on wilderness, too many other corners of the earth become less than natural and too many other people become less than human, thereby giving us permission not to care much about their suffering or their fate.

It is no accident that these supposedly inconsequential environmental problems affect mainly poor people, for the long affiliation between wilderness and wealth means that the only poor people who count when wilderness is *the* issue are hunter-gatherers, who presumably do not consider themselves to be poor in the first place. The dualism at the heart of wilderness encourages its advocates to conceive of its protection as a crude conflict between the "human" and the "nonhuman"—or, more often, between those who value the nonhuman and those who do not. This in turn tempts one to ignore crucial differences *among* humans and the complex cultural and historical reasons why different peoples may feel very differently about the meaning of wilderness.

Why, for instance, is the "wilderness experience" so often conceived as a form of recreation best enjoyed by those whose class privileges give them the time and resources to leave their jobs behind and "get away from it all"? Why does the protection of wilderness so often seem to pit urban recreationists against rural people who actually earn their living from the land (excepting those who sell goods and services to the tourists themselves)? Why in the debates about pristine natural areas are "primitive" peoples idealized, even sentimentalized, until the moment they do something unprimitive, modern, and unnatural, and thereby fall from environmental grace? What are the consequences of a wilderness ideology that devalues productive labor and the very concrete knowledge that comes from working the land with one's own hands?[37] All of these questions imply conflicts among different groups of people, conflicts that are obscured behind the deceptive clarity of "human" vs. "nonhuman." If in answering these knotty questions we resort to so simplistic an opposition, we are almost certain to ignore the very subtleties and complexities we need to understand.

40    But the most troubling cultural baggage that accompanies the celebration of wilderness has less to do with remote rain forests and peoples than with the ways we think about ourselves—we American environmentalists who quite rightly worry about the future of the earth and the threats we pose to the natural world. Idealizing a distant wilderness too often means not idealizing the environment in which we actually live, the landscape that for better or worse we call home. Most of our most serious environmental problems start right here, at home, and if we are to solve those problems, we need an environmental ethic that will tell us as much about *using* nature as about *not* using it. The wilderness dualism tends to cast any use as *ab*-use, and thereby denies us a middle ground in which responsible use and non-use might attain some kind of balanced, sustainable relationship. My own belief is that only by exploring this middle ground will we learn ways of imagining a better world for all of us: humans and nonhumans, rich people and poor, women and men, First Worlders *and* Third Worlders, white folks and people of color, consumers and producers—a world better for humanity in all of its diversity and for all the rest of nature too. The middle ground is where we actually live. It is where we—all of us, in our different places and ways—make our homes.

That is why, when I think of the times I myself have come closest to experiencing what I might call the sacred in nature, I often find myself remembering wild places much closer to home. I think, for instance, of a small pond near my house where water bubbles up from limestone springs to feed a series of pools that rarely freeze in winter and so play home to waterfowl that stay here for the protective warmth even on the coldest of winter days, gliding silently through streaming mists as the snow falls from gray February skies. I think of a November evening long ago when I found myself on a Wisconsin hilltop in rain and dense fog, only to have the setting sun break through the clouds to cast an otherworldly golden light on the misty farms and woodlands below, a scene so unexpected and joyous that I lingered past dusk so as not to miss any part of the gift that had come my way. And I think perhaps most especially of the blown-out, bankrupt farm in the sand country of central Wisconsin where Aldo Leopold and his family tried one of the first American experiments in ecological restoration, turning ravaged and infertile soil into carefully tended ground where the human and the nonhuman could exist side by side in relative harmony. What I celebrate about such places is not *just* their wildness, though that certainly is among their most important qualities; what I celebrate even more is that they remind us of the wildness in our own backyards, of the nature that is all around us if only we have eyes to see it.

Indeed, my principal objection to wilderness is that it may teach us to be dismissive or even contemptuous of such humble places and experiences. Without our quite realizing it, wilderness tends to privilege some parts of nature at the expense of others. Most of us, I suspect, still follow the conventions of the romantic sublime in finding the mountaintop more glorious than the plains, the ancient forest nobler than the grasslands, the mighty canyon more inspiring than the humble marsh. Even John Muir, in arguing against those who sought to dam his beloved Hetch Hetchy valley in the Sierra Nevada, argued for alternative dam sites in the gentler valleys of the foothills—a preference that had nothing to do with nature and everything with the cultural traditions of the sublime.[38] Just as problematically, our frontier traditions have encouraged Americans to define "true" wilderness as requiring very large tracts of roadless land—what Dave Foreman calls "The Big Outside." Leaving aside the legitimate empirical question in conservation biology of how large a tract of land must be before a given species can reproduce on it, the emphasis on big wilderness reflects a romantic frontier belief that one hasn't really gotten away from civilization unless one can go for days at a time without encountering another human being. By teaching us to fetishize sublime places and wide open country, these peculiarly American ways of thinking about wilderness encourage us to adopt too high a standard for what counts as "natural." If it isn't hundreds of square miles big, if it doesn't give us God's-eye views or grand vistas, if it doesn't permit us the illusion that we are alone on the planet, then it really isn't natural. It's too small, too plain, or too crowded to be *authentically* wild.

In critiquing wilderness as I have done in this essay, I'm forced to confront my own deep ambivalence about its meaning for modern environmentalism. On the one hand, one of my own most important environmental ethics is that people should always be conscious that they are part of the natural world, inextricably tied to the ecological systems that sustain their lives. Any way of looking at nature that encourages us to believe we are separate from nature—as wilderness tends to do—is likely to reinforce environmentally irresponsible behavior. On the other hand, I also think it no less crucial for us to recognize and honor nonhuman nature as a world we did not create, a world with its own independent, nonhuman reasons for being as it is. The autonomy of nonhuman nature seems to me an indispensable corrective to human arrogance. Any way of looking at nature that helps us remember—as wilderness also tends to do—that the interests of people are not necessarily identical to those of every other creature or of the earth itself is likely to foster *responsible* behavior. To the extent that wilderness has served as an important vehicle for articulating deep moral values regarding our obligations and responsibilities to the nonhuman world, I would not want to jettison the contributions it has made to our culture's ways of thinking about nature.

If the core problem of wilderness is that it distances us too much from the very things it teaches us to value, then the question we must ask is what it can tell us about *home*, the place where we actually live. How can we take the positive values we associate with wilderness and bring them closer to home? I think the answer to this question will come by broadening our sense of the otherness that wilderness seeks to define and protect. In reminding us of the world we did not make, wilderness can teach profound feelings of humility and respect as we confront our fellow beings and the earth itself. Feelings like these argue for the importance of self-awareness and self-criticism as we exercise our own ability to transform the world around us, helping us set responsible limits to human mastery—which without such limits too easily becomes human hubris. Wilderness is the place where, symbolically at least, we try to withhold our power to dominate.

45    Wallace Stegner once wrote of

the special human mark, the special record of human passage, that distinguishes man from all other species. It is rare enough among men, impossible to any other form of life. *It is simply the deliberate and chosen refusal to make any marks at all*. . . . We are the most dangerous species of life on the planet, and every other species, even the earth itself, has cause to fear our power to exterminate. But we are also the only species which, when it chooses to do so, will go to great effort to save what it might destroy.[39]

The myth of wilderness, which Stegner knowingly reproduces in these remarks, is that we can somehow leave nature untouched by our passage. By now it should be clear that this for the most part is an illusion. But Stegner's deeper message then becomes all the more compelling. If living in history means that we cannot help leaving marks on a fallen world, then the dilemma we face is to decide what kinds of marks we wish to leave. It is just here that our cultural traditions of wilderness remain so important. In the broadest sense, wilderness teaches us to ask whether the Other must always bend to our will, and, if not, under what circumstances it should be allowed to flourish without our intervention. This is surely a question worth asking about everything we do, and not just about the natural world.

When we visit a wilderness area, we find ourselves surrounded by plants and animals and physical landscapes whose otherness compels our attention. In forcing us to acknowledge that they are not of our making, that they have little or no need of our continued existence, they recall for us a creation far greater than our own. In the wilderness, we need no reminder that a tree has its own reasons for being, quite apart from us. The same is less true in the gardens we plant and tend ourselves: there it is far easier to forget the otherness of the tree.[40] Indeed, one could almost measure wilderness by the extent to which our recognition of its otherness requires a conscious, willed act on our part. The romantic legacy means that wilderness is more a state of mind than a fact of nature, and the state of mind that today most defines wilderness is *wonder*. The striking power of the wild is that wonder in the face of it requires no act of will, but forces itself upon us—as an expression of the nonhuman world experienced through the lens of our cultural history—as proof that ours is not the only presence in the universe.

Wilderness gets us into trouble only if we imagine that this experience of wonder and otherness is limited to the remote corners of the planet, or that it somehow depends on pristine landscapes we ourselves do not inhabit. Nothing could be more misleading. The tree in the garden is in reality no less other, no less worthy of our wonder and respect, than the tree in an ancient forest that has never known an ax or a saw—even though the tree in the forest reflects a more intricate web of ecological relationships. The tree in the garden could easily have sprung from the same seed as the tree in the forest, and we can claim only its location and perhaps its form as our own. Both trees stand apart from us; both share our common world. The special power of the tree in the wilderness is to remind us of this fact. It can teach us to recognize the wildness we did not see in the tree we planted in our own backyard. By seeing the otherness in that which is most unfamiliar, we can learn to see it too in that which at first seemed merely ordinary. If wilderness can do this—if it can help us perceive and respect a nature we had forgotten to recognize as natural—then it will become part of the solution to our environmental dilemmas rather than part of the problem.

This will only happen, however, if we abandon the dualism that sees the tree in the garden as artificial—completely fallen and unnatural—and the tree in the wilderness as natural—completely pristine and wild. Both trees in some ultimate sense are wild; both in a practical sense now depend on our management and care. We are responsible for both, even though we can claim credit for neither. Our challenge is to stop thinking of such things according to a set of bipolar moral scales in which the human and the nonhuman, the unnatural and the natural, the fallen and the unfallen, serve as our conceptual map for understanding and valuing the world. Instead, we need to embrace the full continuum of a natural landscape that is also cultural, in which the city, the suburb, the pastoral, and the wild each has its proper place, which we permit ourselves to celebrate without needlessly denigrating the others. We need to honor the Other within and the Other next door as much as we do the exotic Other that lives far away—a lesson that applies as much to people as it does to (other) natural things. In particular, we need to discover a common middle ground in which all of these things, from the city to the wilderness, can somehow be encompassed in the word "home." Home, after all, is the place where finally we make our living. It is the place for which we take responsibility, the place we try to sustain so we can pass on what is best in it (and in ourselves) to our children.[41]

The task of making a home in nature is what Wendell Berry has called "the forever unfinished lifework of our species." "The only thing we have to preserve nature with," he writes, "is culture; the only thing we have to preserve wildness with is domesticity."[42] Calling a place home inevitably means that we will *use* the nature we find in it, for there can be no escape from manipulating and working and even killing some parts of nature to make our home. But if we acknowledge the autonomy and otherness of the things and creatures around us—an autonomy our culture has taught us to label with the word "wild"—then we will at least think carefully about the uses to which we put them, and even ask if we should use them at all. Just so can we still join Thoreau in declaring that "in Wildness is the preservation of the World," for *wildness* (as opposed to wilderness) can be found anywhere: in the seemingly tame fields and woodlots of Massachusetts, in the cracks of a Manhattan sidewalk, even in the cells of our own bodies. As Gary Snyder has wisely said, "A person with a clear heart and open mind can experience the wilderness anywhere on earth. It is a quality of one's own consciousness. The planet is a wild place and always will be."[43] To think ourselves capable of causing "the end of nature" is an act of great hubris, for it means forgetting the wildness that dwells everywhere within and around us.

50    Learning to honor the wild—learning to remember and acknowledge the autonomy of the other—means striving for critical self-consciousness in all of our actions. It means that deep reflection and respect must accompany each act of use, and means too that we must always consider the possibility of nonuse. It means looking at the part of nature we intend to turn toward our own ends and asking whether we can use it again and again and again—sustainably—without its being diminished in the process. In means never imagining that we can flee into a mythical wilderness to escape history and the obligation to take responsibility for our own actions that history inescapably entails. Most of all, it means practicing remembrance and gratitude, for thanksgiving is the simplest and most basic of ways for us to recollect the nature, the culture, and the history that have come together to make the world as we know it. If wildness can stop being (just) out there and start being (also) in here, if it can start being as humane as it is natural, then perhaps we can get on with the unending task of struggling to live rightly in the world—not just in the garden, not just in the wilderness, but in the home that encompasses them both.

# Notes

1. Henry David Thoreau, "Walking," *The Works of Thoreau*, ed. Henry S. Canby (Boston, Massachusetts: Houghton Mifflin, 1937), p. 672.

2. *Oxford English Dictionary*, s.v. "wilderness"; see also Roderick Nash, *Wilderness and the American Mind*, 3rd ed. (New Haven, Connecticut: Yale Univ. Press, 1982), pp. 1–22; and Max Oelschlaeger, *The Idea of Wilderness: From Prehistory to the Age of Ecology* (New Haven, Connecticut: Yale Univ. Press, 1991).

3. Exodus 32:1–35, KJV.

4. Exodus 14:3, KJV.

5. Mark 1:12–13, KJV; see also Matthew 4:1–11; Luke 4:1–13.

6. John Milton, "Paradise Lost," *John Milton: Complete Poems and Major Prose*, ed. Merritt Y. Hughes (New York: Odyssey Press, 1957), pp. 280–81, lines 131–42.

7. I have discussed this theme at length in "Landscapes of Abundance and Scarcity," in Clyde Milner et al., eds., *Oxford History of the American West* (New York: Oxford Univ. Press, 1994), pp. 603–37. The classic work on the Puritan "city on a hill" in colonial New England is Perry Miller, *Errand into the Wilderness* (Cambridge, Massachusetts: Harvard Univ. Press, 1956).

8. John Muir, *My First Summer in the Sierra* (1911), reprinted in *John Muir: Eight Wilderness Discovery Books* (London, England: Diadem; Seattle, Washington: Mountaineers, 1992), p. 211.

9. Alfred Runte, *National Parks: The American Experience*, 2nd ed. (Lincoln: Univ. of Nebraska Press, 1987).

10. John Muir, *The Yosemite* (1912), reprinted in *John Muir: Eight Wilderness Discovery Books*, p. 715.

11. Scholarly work on the sublime is extensive. Among the most important studies are Samuel Monk, *The Sublime: A Study of Critical Theories in XVII-Century England* (New York: Modern Language Association, 1935); Basil Willey, *The Eighteenth-Century Background: Studies on the Idea of Nature in the Thought of the Period* (London, England: Chattus and Windus, 1949); Marjorie Hope Nicolson, *Mountain Gloom and Mountain Glory: The Development of the Aesthetics of the Infinite* (Ithaca, New York: Cornell Univ. Press, 1959); Thomas Weiskel, *The Romantic Sublime: Studies in the Structure and Psychology of Transcendence* (Baltimore, Maryland: Johns Hopkins Univ. Press, 1976); Barbara Novak, *Nature and Culture: American Landscape Painting, 1825–1875* (New York: Oxford Univ. Press, 1980).

12. The classic works are Immanuel Kant, *Observations on the Feeling of the Beautiful and Sublime* (1764), trans. John T. Goldthwait (Berkeley: Univ. of California Press, 1960); Edmund Burke, *A Philosophical Enquiry into the Origin of Our Ideas of the Sublime and Beautiful*, ed. James T. Boulton (1958; Notre Dame, Indiana: Univ. of Notre Dame Press, 1968); William Gilpin, *Three Essays: On Picturesque Beauty; on Picturesque Travel; and on Sketching Landscape* (London, England, 1803).

13. See Ann Vileisis, "From Wastelands to Wetlands" (unpublished senior essay, Yale Univ., 1989); Runte, *National Parks*.

14. William Wordsworth, "The Prelude," bk. 6, in Thomas Hutchinson, ed., *The Poetical Works of Wordsworth* (London, England: Oxford Univ. Press, 1936), p. 536.

15.  Henry David Thoreau, *The Maine Woods* (1864), in *Henry David Thoreau* (New York: Library of America, 1985), pp. 640–41.

16.  Exodus 16:10, KJV.

17.  John Muir, *My First Summer in the Sierra*, p. 238. Part of the difference between these descriptions may reflect the landscapes the three authors were describing. In his essay, "Reinventing Common Nature: Yosemite and Mount Rushmore—A Meandering Tale of a Double Nature," Kenneth Olwig notes that early American travelers experienced Yosemite as much through the aesthetic tropes of the pastoral as through those of the sublime. The ease with which Muir celebrated the gentle divinity of the Sierra Nevada had much to do with the pastoral qualities of the landscape he described. See Olwig, "Reinventing Common Nature: Yosemite and Mount Rushmore—A Meandering Tale of a Double Nature," *Uncommon Ground: Toward Reinventing Nature*, ed. William Cronon (New York: W. W. Norton & Co., 1995), pp. 379–408.

18.  Frederick Jackson Turner, *The Frontier in American History* (New York: Henry Holt, 1920), pp. 37–38.

19.  Richard Slotkin has made this observation the linchpin of his comparison between Turner and Theodore Roosevelt. See Slotkin, *Gunfighter Nation: The Myth of the Frontier in Twentieth-Century America* (New York: Atheneum, 1992), pp. 29–62.

20.  Owen Wister, *The Virginian: A Horseman of the Plains* (New York: Macmillan, 1902), pp. viii–ix.

21.  Theodore Roosevelt, *Ranch Life and the Hunting Trail* (1888; New York: Century, 1899), p. 100.

22.  Wister, *Virginian*, p. x.

23.  On the many problems with this view, see William M. Denevan, "The Pristine Myth: The Landscape of the Americans in 1492," *Annals of the Association of American Geographers* 82 (1992): 369–85.

24.  Louis Warren, "The Hunter's Game: Poachers, Conservationists, and Twentieth-Century America" (Ph.D. diss., Yale University, 1994).

25.  Wilderness also lies at the foundation of the Clementsian ecological concept of the climax. See Michael Barbour, "Ecological Fragmentation in the Fifties" in Cronon, *Uncommon Ground*, pp. 233–55, and William Cronon, "Introduction: In Search of Nature," in Cronon, *Uncommon Ground*, pp. 23–56.

26.  On the many paradoxes of having to manage wilderness in order to maintain the appearance of an unmanaged landscape, see John C. Hendee et al., *Wilderness Management*, USDA Forest Service Miscellaneous Publication No. 1365 (Washington, D.C.: Government Printing Office, 1978).

27.  See James Proctor, "Whose Nature?: The Contested Moral Terrain of Ancient Forests," in Cronon, *Uncommon Ground*, pp. 269–97.

28.  See Candace Slater, "Amazonia as Edenic Narrative," in Cronon, *Uncommon Ground*, pp. 114–31. This argument has been powerfully made by Ramachandra Guha, "Radical American Environmentalism: A Third World Critique," *Environmental Ethics* 11 (1989): 71–83.

29.  Bill McKibben, *The End of Nature* (New York: Random House, 1989).

30.  McKibben, *The End of Nature*, p. 49.

31.  Even comparable extinction rates have occurred before, though we surely would not want to emulate the Cretaceous-Tertiary boundary extinctions as a model for responsible manipulation of the biosphere!

32.  Dave Foreman, *Confessions of an Eco-Warrior* (New York: Harmony Books, 1991), p. 69 (italics in original). For a sampling of other writings by followers of deep ecology and/or Earth First!, see Michael Tobias, ed., *Deep Ecology* (San Diego, California: Avant Books, 1984); Bill Devall and George Sessions, *Deep Ecology: Living as if Nature Mattered* (Salt Lake City, Utah: Gibbs Smith, 1985); Michael Tobias, *After Eden: History, Ecology, and Conscience* (San Diego, California: Avant Books, 1985); Dave Foreman and Bill Haywood, eds., *Ecodefense: A Field Guide to Monkey Wrenching*, 2nd ed. (Tucson, Arizona: Ned Ludd Books, 1987); Bill Devall, *Simple in Means, Rich in Ends: Practicing Deep Ecology* (Salt Lake City, Utah: Gibbs Smith, 1988); Steve Chase, ed., *Defending the Earth: A Dialogue between Murray Bookchin & Dave Foreman* (Boston, Massachusetts: South End Press, 1991); John Davis, ed., *The Earth First! Reader: Ten Years of Radical Environmentalism* (Salt Lake City, Utah: Gibbs Smith, 1991); Bill Devall, *Living Richly in an Age of Limits: Using Deep Ecology for an Abundant Life* (Salt Lake City, Utah: Gibbs Smith, 1993); Michael E. Zimmerman et al., eds., *Environmental Philosophy: From Animal Rights to Radical Ecology* (Englewood Cliffs, New Jersey: Prentice-Hall, 1993). A useful survey of the different factions of radical environmentalism can be found in Carolyn Merchant, *Radical Ecology: The Search for a Livable World* (New York: Routledge, 1992). For a very interesting critique of this literature (first published in the anarchist newspaper *Fifth Estate*), see George Bradford, *How Deep is Deep Ecology?* (Ojai, California: Times Change Press, 1989).

33.  Foreman, *Confessions of an Eco-Warrior*, p. 34.

34.  Foreman, *Confessions of an Eco-Warrior*, p. 65. See also Dave Foreman and Howie Wolke, *The Big Outside: A Descriptive Inventory of the Big Wilderness Areas of the U.S.* (Tucson, Arizona: Ned Ludd Books, 1989).

35.  Foreman, *Confessions of an Eco-Warrior*, p. 63.

36.  Foreman, *Confessions of an Eco-Warrior*, p. 27.

37.  See Richard White, "'Are You an Environmentalist or Do You Work for a Living?': Work and Nature," in Cronon, *Uncommon Ground*, pp. 171–85. Compare its analysis of environmental knowledge through work with Jennifer Price's analysis of environmental knowledge through consumption. It is not much of an exaggeration to say that the wilderness experience is essentially consumerist in its impulses.

38.  Compare with Muir, *Yosemite*, in *John Muir: Eight Wilderness Discovery Books*, p. 714.

39.  Wallace Stegner, ed. *This Is Dinosaur: Echo Park Country and Its Magic Rivers* (New York: Knopf, 1955), p. 17 (italics in original).

40.  Katherine Hayles helped me see the importance of this argument.

41.  Analogous arguments can be found in John Brinckerhoff Jackson, "Beyond Wilderness," *A Sense of Place, a Sense of Time* (New Haven, Connecticut: Yale Univ. Press, 1994), pp. 71–91, and in the wonderful collection of essays by Michael Pollan, *Second Nature: A Gardener's Education* (New York: Atlantic Monthly Press, 1991).

42.  Wendell Berry, *Home Economics* (San Francisco, California: North Point, 1987), pp. 138, 143.

43.  Gary Snyder, quoted in *New York Times*, "Week in Review," 18 September 1994, p. 6.

## Questions for Discussion

How has Cronon redefined "wilderness"?

What are some of the likely responses to an argument like this?

What kinds of roles does Cronon believe language can play in debates about the environment?

*Rachel Carson (1907–1964) has been called the most important writer of the twentieth century because, almost singlehandedly, she exposed the dangerous intersections of scientific progress and social and environmental degradation. Carson began her career as a marine biologist, earning a master's degree in marine biology from Johns Hopkins University in 1932. She worked for the U.S. Fish and Wildlife Service, taught university courses and conducted research in her field, and over the course of the next three decades*

*published many popular books and articles on the natural world, many of which established her reputation as a trained scientist who could communicate passionately and eloquently with nonspecialists about difficult and "academic" topics. In 1962, Carson published* Silent Spring, *her controversial and widely read exploration of the negative effects of pesticides. Her claims were sometimes met with great hostility by leaders in agriculture, many of whom continue to work to disprove her hypotheses. Ironically, Carson was battling breast cancer immediately after the publication of* Silent Spring, *a battle she lost in 1964. The following are the first two chapters of* Silent Spring.

# Rachel Carson
# Silent Spring

## I.

There was once a town in the heart of America where all life seemed to live in harmony with its surroundings. The town lay in the midst of a checkerboard of prosperous farms, with fields of grain and hillsides of orchards where, in spring, white clouds of bloom drifted above the green fields. In autumn, oak and maple and birch set up a blaze of color that flamed and flickered across a backdrop of pines. Then foxes barked in the hills and deer silently crossed the fields, half hidden in the mists of the fall mornings.

Along the roads, laurel, viburnum and alder, great ferns and wildflowers delighted the traveler's eye through much of the year. Even in winter the roadsides were places of beauty, where countless birds came to feed on the berries and on the seed heads of the dried weeds rising above the snow. The countryside was, in fact, famous for the abundance and variety of its bird life, and when the flood of migrants was pouring through in spring and fall people traveled from great distances to observe them. Others came to fish the streams, which flowed clear and cold out of the hills and contained shady pools where trout lay. So it had been from the days many years ago when the first settlers raised their houses, sank their wells, and built their barns.

Then a strange blight crept over the area and everything began to change. Some evil spell had settled on the community: mysterious maladies swept the flocks of chickens; the cattle and sheep sickened and died. Everywhere was a shadow of death. The farmers spoke of much illness among their families. In the town the doctors had become more and more puzzled by new kinds of sickness appearing among their patients. There had been several sudden and unexplained deaths, not only among adults but even among children, who would be stricken suddenly while at play and die within a few hours.

There was a strange stillness. The birds, for example—where had they gone? Many people spoke of them, puzzled and disturbed. The feeding stations in the backyards were deserted. The few birds seen anywhere were moribund; they trembled violently and could not fly. It was a spring without voices. On the mornings that had once throbbed with the dawn chorus of robins, catbirds, doves, jays, wrens, and scores of other bird voices there was now no sound; only silence lay over the fields and woods and marsh.

5    On the farms the hens brooded, but no chicks hatched. The farmers complained that they were unable to raise any pigs—the litters were small and the young survived only a few days. The apple trees were coming into bloom but no bees droned among the blossoms, so there was no pollination and there would be no fruit.

The roadsides, once so attractive, were now lined with browned and withered vegetation as though swept by fire. These, too, were silent, deserted by all living things. Even the streams were now lifeless. Anglers no longer visited them, for all the fish had died.

In the gutters under the eaves and between the shingles of the roofs, a white granular powder still showed a few patches: some weeks before it had fallen like snow upon the roofs and the lawns, the fields and streams.

No witchcraft, no enemy action had silenced the rebirth of new life in this stricken world. The people had done it themselves.

This town does not actually exist, but it might easily have a thousand counterparts in America or elsewhere in the world. I know of no community that has experienced all the misfortunes I describe. Yet every one of these disasters has actually happened somewhere, and many real communities have already suffered a substantial number of them. A grim specter has crept upon us almost unnoticed, and this imagined tragedy may easily become a stark reality we all shall know.

## II.

10  The history of life on earth has been a history of interaction between living things and their surroundings. To a large extent, the physical form and the habits of the earth's vegetation and its animal life have been molded by the environment. Considering the whole span of earthly time, the opposite effect, in which life actually modifies its surroundings, has been relatively slight. Only within the moment of time represented by the present century has one species—man—acquired significant power to alter the nature of his world.

During the past quarter century this power has not only increased to one of disturbing magnitude but it has changed in character. The most alarming of all man's assaults upon the environment is the contamination of air, earth, rivers, and sea with dangerous and even lethal materials. This pollution is for the most part irrecoverable; the chain of evil it initiates not only in the world that must support life but in living tissues is for the most part irreversible. In this now universal contamination of the environment, chemicals are the sinister and little-recognized partners of radiation in changing the very nature of the world—the very nature of its life. Strontium 90, released through nuclear explosions into the air, comes to earth in rain or drifts down as fallout, lodges in soil, enters into the grass or corn or wheat grown there, and in time takes up its abode in the bones of a human being, there to remain until his death. Similarly, chemicals sprayed on croplands or forests or gardens lie long in soil, entering into living organisms, passing from one to another in a chain of poisoning and death. Or they pass mysteriously by underground streams until they emerge and, through the alchemy of air and sunlight, combine into new forms that kill vegetation, sicken cattle, and work unknown harm on those who drink from once pure wells. As Albert Schweitzer has said, "Man can hardly even recognize the devils of his own creation."

It took hundreds of millions of years to produce the life that now inhabits the earth—eons of time in which that developing and evolving and diversifying life reached a state of adjustment and balance with its surroundings. The environment, rigorously shaping and directing the life it supported, contained elements that were hostile as well as supporting. Certain rocks gave out dangerous radiation; even within the light of the sun, from which all life draws its energy, there were short-wave radiations with power to injure. Given time—time not in years but in millennia—life adjusts, and a balance has been reached. For time is the essential ingredient; but in the modern world there is no time.

The rapidity of change and the speed with which new situations are created follow the impetuous and heedless pace of man rather than the deliberate pace of nature. Radiation is no longer merely the background radiation of rocks, the bombardment of cosmic rays, the ultraviolet of the sun that have existed before there was any life on earth; radiation is now the unnatural creation of man's tampering with the atom. The chemicals to which life is asked to make its adjustment are no longer merely the calcium and silica and copper and all the rest of the minerals washed out of the rocks and carried in rivers to the sea; they are the synthetic creations of man's inventive mind, brewed in his laboratories, and having no counterparts in nature.

To adjust to these chemicals would require time on the scale that is nature's; it would require not merely the years of a man's life but the life of generations. And even this, were it by some miracle possible, would be futile, for the new chemicals come from our laboratories in an endless stream; almost five hundred annually find their way into actual use in the United States alone. The figure is staggering and its implications are not easily grasped—500 new chemicals to which the bodies of men and animals are required somehow to adapt each year, chemicals totally outside the limits of biologic experience.

15    Among them are many that are used in man's war against nature. Since the mid-1940's over 200 basic chemicals have been created for use in killing insects, weeds, rodents, and other organisms described in the modern vernacular as "pests"; and they are sold under several thousand different brand names.

These sprays, dusts, and aerosols are now applied almost universally to farms, gardens, forests, and homes—nonselective chemicals that have the power to kill every insect, the "good" and the "bad," to still the song of birds and the leaping of fish in the streams, to coat the leaves with a deadly film, and to linger on in soil—all this though the intended target may be only a few weeds or insects. Can anyone believe it is possible to lay down such a barrage of poisons on the surface of the earth without making it unfit for all life? They should not be called "insecticides," but "biocides."

The whole process of spraying seems caught up in an endless spiral. Since DDT was released for civilian use, a process of escalation has been going on in which ever more toxic materials must be found. This has happened because insects, in a triumphant vindication of Darwin's principle of the survival of the fittest, have evolved super races immune to the particular insecticide used, hence a deadlier one has always to be developed—and then a deadlier one than that. It has happened also because, for reasons to be described later, destructive insects often undergo a "flareback," or resurgence, after spraying, in numbers greater than before. Thus the chemical war is never won, and all life is caught in its violent crossfire.

Along with the possibility of the extinction of mankind by nuclear war, the central problem of our age has therefore become the contamination of man's total environment with such substances of incredible potential for harm—substances that accumulate in the tissues of plants and animals and even penetrate the germ cells to shatter or alter the very material of heredity upon which the shape of the future depends.

Some would-be architects of our future look toward a time when it will be possible to alter the human germ plasm by design. But we may easily be doing so now by inadvertence, for many chemicals, like radiation, bring about gene mutations. It is ironic to think that man might determine his own future by something so seemingly trivial as the choice of an insect spray.

20 All this has been risked—for what? Future historians may well be amazed by our distorted sense of proportion. How could intelligent beings seek to control a few unwanted species by a method that contaminated the entire environment and brought the threat of disease and death even to their own kind? Yet this is precisely what we have done. We have done it, moreover, for reasons that collapse the moment we examine them. We are told that the enormous and expanding use of pesticides is necessary to maintain farm production. Yet is our real problem not one of *overproduction?* Our farms, despite measures to remove acreages from production and to pay farmers *not* to produce, have yielded such a staggering excess of crops that the American

taxpayer in 1962 is paying out more than one billion dollars a year as the total carrying cost of the surplus-food storage program. And is the situation helped when one branch of the Agriculture Department tries to reduce production while another states, as it did in 1958, "It is believed generally that reduction of crop acreages under provisions of the Soil Bank will stimulate interest in use of chemicals to obtain maximum production on the land retained in crops."

All this is not to say there is no insect problem and no need of control. I am saying, rather, that control must be geared to realities, not to mythical situations, and that the methods employed must be such that they do not destroy us along with the insects.

The problem whose attempted solution has brought such a train of disaster in its wake is an accompaniment of our modern way of life. Long before the age of man, insects inhabited the earth—a group of extraordinarily varied and adaptable beings. Over the course of time since man's advent, a small percentage of the more than half a million species of insects have come into conflict with human welfare in two principal ways: as competitors for the food supply and as carriers of human disease.

Disease-carrying insects become important where human beings are crowded together, especially under conditions where sanitation is poor, as in time of natural disaster or war or in situations of extreme poverty and deprivation. Then control of some sort becomes necessary. It is a sobering fact, however, as we shall presently see, that the method of massive chemical control has had only limited success, and also threatens to worsen the very conditions it is intended to curb.

Under primitive agricultural conditions the farmer had few insect problems. These arose with the intensification of agriculture—the devotion of immense acreages to a single crop. Such a system set the stage for explosive increases in specific insect populations. Single-crop farming does not take advantage of the principles by which nature works; it is agriculture as an engineer might conceive it to be. Nature has introduced great variety into the landscape, but man has displayed a passion for simplifying it. Thus he undoes the built-in checks and balances by which nature holds the species within bounds. One important natural check is a limit on the amount of suitable habitat for each species. Obviously then, an insect that lives on wheat can build up its population to much higher levels on a farm devoted to wheat than on one in which wheat is intermingled with other crops to which the insect is not adapted.

25    The same thing happens in other situations. A generation or more
ago, the towns of large areas of the United States lined their streets
with the noble elm tree. Now the beauty they hopefully created is
threatened with complete destruction as disease sweeps through the
elms, carried by a beetle that would have only limited chance to build
up large populations and to spread from tree to tree if the elms were
only occasional trees in a richly diversified planting.

Another factor in the modern insect problem is one that must be
viewed against a background of geologic and human history: the
spreading of thousands of different kinds of organisms from their native homes to invade new territories. This worldwide migration has
been studied and graphically described by the British ecologist Charles
Elton in his recent book *The Ecology of Invasions*. During the
Cretaceous Period, some hundred million years ago, flooding seas cut
many land bridges between continents and living things found themselves confined in what Elton calls "colossal separate nature reserves."
There, isolated from others of their kind, they developed many new
species. When some of the land masses were joined again, about 15
million years ago, these species began to move out into new territories—a movement that is not only still in progress but is now receiving
considerable assistance from man.

The importation of plants is the primary agent in the modern
spread of species, for animals have almost invariably gone along
with the plants, quarantine being a comparatively recent and not completely effective innovation. The United States Office of Plant
Introduction alone has introduced almost 200,000 species and vari-
eties of plants from all over the world. Nearly half of the 180 or so major insect enemies of plants in the United States are accidental imports
from abroad, and most of them have come as hitchhikers on plants.

In new territory, out of reach of the restraining hand of the natural
enemies that kept down its numbers in its native land, an invading
plant or animal is able to become enormously abundant. Thus it is no
accident that our most troublesome insects are introduced species.

These invasions, both the naturally occurring and those dependent
on human assistance, are likely to continue indefinitely. Quarantine
and massive chemical campaigns are only extremely expensive ways of
buying time. We are faced, according to Dr. Elton, "with a life-and-
death need not just to find new technological means of suppressing this
plant or that animal"; instead we need the basic knowledge of animal
populations and their relations to their surroundings that will "promote

an even balance and damp down the explosive power of outbreaks and new invasions."

30    Much of the necessary knowledge is now available but we do not use it. We train ecologists in our universities and even employ them in our governmental agencies but we seldom take their advice. We allow the chemical death rain to fall as though there were no alternative, whereas in fact there are many, and our ingenuity could soon discover many more if given opportunity.

Have we fallen into a mesmerized state that makes us accept as inevitable that which is inferior or detrimental, as though having lost the will or the vision to demand that which is good? Such thinking, in the words of the ecologist Paul Shepard, "idealizes life with only its head out of water, inches above the limits of toleration of the corruption of its own environment . . . Why should we tolerate a diet of weak poisons, a home in insipid surroundings, a circle of acquaintances who are not quite our enemies, the noise of motors with just enough relief to prevent insanity? Who would want to live in a world which is just not quite fatal?"

Yet such a world is pressed upon us. The crusade to create a chemically sterile, insect-free world seems to have engendered a fanatic zeal on the part of many specialists and most of the so-called control agencies. On every hand there is evidence that those engaged in spraying operations exercise a ruthless power. "The regulatory entomologists . . . function as prosecutor, judge and jury, tax assessor and collector and sheriff to enforce their own orders," said Connecticut entomologist Neely Turner. The most flagrant abuses go unchecked in both state and federal agencies.

It is not my contention that chemical insecticides must never be used. I do contend that we have put poisonous and biologically potent chemicals indiscriminately into the hands of persons largely or wholly ignorant of their potentials for harm. We have subjected enormous numbers of people to contact with these poisons, without their consent and often without their knowledge. If the Bill of Rights contains no guarantee that a citizen shall be secure against lethal poisons distributed either by private individuals or by public officials, it is surely only because our forefathers, despite their considerable wisdom and foresight, could conceive of no such problem.

I contend, furthermore, that we have allowed these chemicals to be used with little or no advance investigation of their effect on soil, water, wildlife, and man himself. Future generations are unlikely to condone our lack of prudent concern for the integrity of the natural world that supports all life.

35    There is still very limited awareness of the nature of the threat. This is an era of specialists, each of whom sees his own problem and is unaware of or intolerant of the larger frame into which it fits. It is also an era dominated by industry, in which the right to make a dollar at whatever cost is seldom challenged. When the public protests, confronted with some obvious evidence of damaging results of pesticide applications, it is fed little tranquilizing pills of half truth. We urgently need an end to these false assurances, to the sugar coating of unpalatable facts. It is the public that is being asked to assume the risks that the insect controllers calculate. The public must decide whether it wishes to continue on the present road, and it can do so only when in full possession of the facts. In the words of Jean Rostand, "The obligation to endure gives us the right to know."

## Questions for Discussion

Is Carson's use of "exaggeration" in her fable "fair" in this instance?

According to Carson, what kind of a relationship exists between the human and natural worlds? What is the proper balance between human and scientific interests?

*Silent Spring* was written during the Cold War, when the United States and the former Soviet Union were engaged in a nuclear arms race. How is that historical context evident in her work?

*The eighth child of sharecropper parents in Eatonton, Georgia, **Alice Walker** (born 1944) is best known for her Pulitzer Prize–winning 1982 novel* The Color Purple, *which was adapted into a film produced by Quincy Jones and directed by Steven Spielberg. But Walker has also written a great deal of other*  *material—poems, essays, short stories, other novels—over the past three decades, material that is a reflection of her upbringing in rural Georgia and a product of her commitments to social justice and women's issues. She was active in the civil rights movement in the 1960s and has become a powerful voice in many contemporary causes. Walker included "Am I Blue?" in her 1988 collection of essays called* Living by the Word, *which meditates on the insidious effects of power in our relationships with animals.*

## Alice Walker

# Am I Blue?

For about three years my companion and I rented a small house in the country that stood on the edge of a large meadow that appeared to run from the end of our deck straight into the mountains. The mountains, however, were quite far away, and between us and them there was, in fact, a town. It was one of the many pleasant aspects of the house that you never really were aware of this.

It was a house of many windows, low, wide, nearly floor to ceiling in the living room, which faced the meadow, and it was from one of these that I first saw our closest neighbor, a large white horse, cropping grass, flipping its mane, and ambling about—not over the entire meadow, which stretched well out of sight of the house, but over the five or so fenced-in acres that were next to the twenty-odd that we had rented. I soon learned that the horse, whose name was Blue, belonged to a man who lived in another town, but was boarded by our neighbors next door. Occasionally, one of the children, usually a stocky teenager, but sometimes a much younger girl or boy, could be seen riding Blue. They would appear in the meadow, climb up on his back, ride furiously for ten or fifteen minutes, then get off, slap Blue on the flanks, and not be seen again for a month or more.

There were many apple trees in our yard, and one by the fence that Blue could almost reach. We were soon in the habit of feeding him apples, which he relished, especially because by the middle of summer the meadow grasses—so green and succulent since January—had dried out from lack of rain, and Blue stumbled about munching the dried stalks half-heartedly. Sometimes he would stand very still just by the apple tree, and when one of us came out he would whinny, snort loudly, or stamp the ground. This meant, of course: I want an apple.

It was quite wonderful to pick a few apples, or collect those that had fallen to the ground overnight, and patiently hold them, one by one, up to his large, toothy mouth. I remained as thrilled as a child by his flexible dark lips, huge, cubelike teeth that crunched the apples, core and all, with such finality, and his high, broad-breasted *enormity*; beside which, I felt small indeed. When I was a child, I used to ride horses, and was especially friendly with one named Nan until the day I was riding and my brother deliberately spooked her and I was thrown, head first, against the trunk of a tree. When I came to, I was in bed and my mother was bending worriedly over me; we silently agreed that perhaps horseback riding was not the safest sport for me. Since then I have walked, and prefer walking, to horseback riding—but I had forgotten the depth of feeling one could see in horses' eyes.

5    I was therefore unprepared for the expression in Blue's. Blue was lonely. Blue was horribly lonely and bored. I was not shocked that this should be the case; five acres to tramp by yourself, endlessly, even in the most beautiful of meadows—and his was—cannot provide many interesting events, and once rainy season turned to dry that was about it. No, I was shocked that I had forgotten that human animals and nonhuman animals can communicate quite well; if we are brought up around animals as children we take this for granted. By the time we are adults we no longer remember. However, the animals have not changed. They are in fact *completed* creations (at least they seem to be, so much more than we) who are not likely *to* change; it is their nature to express themselves. What else are they going to express? And they do. And, generally speaking, they are ignored.

After giving Blue the apples, I would wander back to the house, aware that he was observing me. Were more apples not forthcoming then? Was that to be his sole entertainment for the day? My partner's small son had decided he wanted to learn how to piece a quilt; we worked in silence on our respective squares as I thought. . . .

Well, about slavery: about white children, who were raised by black people, who knew their first all-accepting love from black women, and then, when they were twelve or so, were told they must "forget" the deep levels of communication between themselves and "mammy" that they knew. Later they would be able to relate quite calmly, "My old mammy was sold to another good family." "My old mammy was __ __." Fill in the blank. Many more years later a white woman would say: "I can't understand these Negroes, these blacks. What do they want? They're so different from us."

And about the Indians, considered to be "like animals" by the "settlers" (a very benign euphemism for what they actually were), who did not understand their description as a compliment.

And about the thousands of American men who marry Japanese, Korean, Filipina, and other non-English-speaking women and of how happy they report they are, "*blissfully*," until their brides learn to speak English, at which point the marriages tend to fall apart. What then did the men see, when they looked into the eyes of the women they married, before they could speak English? Apparently only their own reflections.

10     I thought of society's impatience with the young. "Why are they playing the music so loud?" Perhaps the children have listened to much of the music of oppressed people their parents danced to before they were born, with its passionate but soft cries for acceptance and love, and they have wondered why their parents failed to hear.

I do not know how long Blue had inhabited his five beautiful, boring acres before we moved into our house; a year after we had arrived—and had also traveled to other valleys, other cities, other worlds—he was still there.

But then, in our second year at the house, something happened in Blue's life. One morning, looking out the window at the fog that lay like a ribbon over the meadow, I saw another horse, a brown one, at the other end of Blue's field. Blue appeared to be afraid of it, and for several days made no attempt to go near. We went away for a week. When we returned, Blue had decided to make friends and the two horses ambled or galloped along together, and Blue did not come nearly as often to the fence underneath the apple tree.

When he did, bringing his new friend with him, there was a different look in his eyes. A look of independence, of self-possession, of inalienable *horse*ness. His friend eventually became pregnant. For months and months there was, it seemed to me, a mutual feeling between me and the horses of justice, of peace. I fed apples to them both. The look in Blue's eyes was one of unabashed "this is *it*ness."

It did not, however, last forever. One day, after a visit to the city, I went out to give Blue some apples. He stood waiting, or so I thought, though not beneath the tree. When I shook the tree and jumped back from the shower of apples, he made no move. I carried some over to him. He managed to half-crunch one. The rest he let fall to the ground. I dreaded looking into his eyes—because I had of course noticed that Brown, his partner, had gone—but I did look. If I had been born into slavery, and my partner had been sold or killed, my eyes would have looked like that. The children next door explained that Blue's partner had been "put with him" (the same expression that old people used, I had noticed, when speaking of an ancestor during slavery who had been impregnated by her owner) so that they could mate and she conceive. Since that was accomplished, she had been taken back by her owner, who lived somewhere else.

15    Will she be back? I asked.

They didn't know.

Blue was like a crazed person. Blue *was*, to me, a crazed person. He galloped furiously, as if he were being ridden, around and around his five beautiful acres. He whinnied until he couldn't. He tore at the ground with his hooves. He butted himself against his single shade tree. He looked always and always toward the road down which his partner had gone. And then, occasionally, when he came up for apples, or I took apples to him, he looked at me. It was a look so piercing, so full of grief, a look so *human*, I almost laughed (I felt too sad to cry) to think there are people who do not know that animals suffer. People like me who have forgotten, and daily forget, all that animals try to tell us. "Everything you do to us will happen to you; we are your teachers, as you are ours. We are one lesson" is essentially it, I think. There are those who never once have even considered animals' rights: those who have been taught that animals actually want to be used and abused by us, as small children "love" to be frightened, or women "love" to be mutilated and raped. . . . They are the great-grandchildren of those who honestly thought, because someone taught them this: "Women can't think," and "niggers can't faint." But most disturbing of all, in Blue's large brown eyes was a new look, more painful than the look of despair: the look of disgust with human beings, with life; the look of hatred. And it was odd what the look of hatred did. It gave him, for the first time, the look of a beast. And what that meant was that he had put up a barrier within to protect himself from further violence; all the apples in the world wouldn't change that fact.

And so Blue remained, a beautiful part of our landscape, very peaceful to look at from the window, white against the grass. Once a friend came to visit and said, looking out on the soothing view: "And it *would* have to be a *white* horse; the very image of freedom." And I thought, yes, the animals are forced to become for us merely "images" of what they once so beautifully expressed. And we are used to drinking milk from containers showing "contented" cows, whose real lives we want to hear nothing about, eating eggs and drumsticks from "happy" hens, and munching hamburgers advertised by bulls of integrity who seem to command their fate.

As we talked of freedom and justice one day for all, we sat down to steaks. I am eating misery, I thought, as I took the first bite. And spit it out.

## Questions for Discussion

What is the significance of the title, "Am I Blue?" What does it reveal about Walker's objectives?

How does Walker go about establishing the kinship between humans and animals? How would you characterize this kinship?

**Navarre Scott Momaday** *(born 1934), raised on an Indian reservation in the American Southwest, won the Pulitzer Prize for fiction in 1969 for his first novel* House Made of Dawn. *He tells us something about himself in the following introductory chapter from his 1969 book* The Way to Rainy Mountain, *an account of his homeland in the Wichita Mountains of Oklahoma. Momaday's father was Kiowa and his mother was of white and Cherokee descent—so a concern with the complex relations between American subcultures has always permeated his work. In addition to essays, fiction, and poetry, Momaday has created paintings, prints, memoirs, and plays. He is now Regents Professor of English at the University of Arizona.*

# N. Scott Momaday
## The Way to Rainy Mountain

A single knoll rises out of the plain in Oklahoma, north and west of the Wichita Range. For many people, the Kiowas, it is an old landmark, and they gave it the name Rainy Mountain. The hardest weather in the world is there. Winter brings blizzards, hot tornadic winds arise in the spring, and in summer the prairie is an anvil's edge. The grass turns brittle and brown, and it cracks beneath your feet. There are green belts along the rivers and creeks, linear groves of hickory and pecan, willow and witch hazel. At a distance in July or August the steaming foliage seems almost to writhe in fire. Great green and yellow grasshoppers are everywhere in the tall grass, popping up like corn to sting the flesh, and tortoises crawl about on the red earth, going nowhere in the plenty of time. Loneliness is an aspect of the land. All things in the plain are isolate; there is no confusion of objects in the eye, but *one* hill or *one* tree or *one* man. To look upon that landscape in the early morning, with the sun at your back, is to lose the sense of proportion. Your imagination comes to life, and this, you think, is where Creation was begun.

I returned to Rainy Mountain in July. My grandmother had died in the spring, and I wanted to be at her grave. She had lived to be very old and at last infirm. Her only living daughter was with her when she died, and I was told that in death her face was that of a child.

I like to think of her as a child. When she was born, the Kiowas were living that last great moment of their history. For more than a hundred years they had controlled the open range from the Smoky Hill River to the Red, from the headwaters of the Canadian to the fork of the Arkansas and Cimarron. In alliance with the Comanches, they had ruled the whole of the southern plains. War was their sacred business, and they were among the finest horsemen the world has ever known. But warfare for the Kiowas was preeminently a matter of disposition rather than of survival, and they never understood the grim, unrelenting advance of the U.S. Cavalry. When at last, divided and ill-provisioned, they were driven onto the Staked Plains in the cold rains of autumn, they fell into panic. In Palo Duro Canyon they abandoned their crucial stores to pillage and had nothing then but their lives. In order to save themselves, they surrendered to the soldiers at Fort Sill and were imprisoned in the old stone corral that now stands as a military museum. My grandmother was spared the humiliation of those high gray walls by eight or ten years, but she must have known from birth the affliction of defeat, the dark brooding of old warriors.

Her name was Aho, and she belonged to the last culture to evolve in North America. Her forebears came down from the high country in western Montana nearly three centuries ago. They were a mountain people, a mysterious tribe of hunters whose language has never been positively classified in any major group. In the late seventeenth century they began a long migration to the south and east. It was a journey toward the dawn, and it led to a golden age. Along the way the Kiowas were befriended by the Crows, who gave them the culture and religion of the Plains. They acquired horses, and their ancient nomadic spirit was suddenly free of the ground. They acquired Tai-me, the sacred Sun Dance doll, from that moment the object and symbol of their worship, and so shared in the divinity of the sun. Not least, they acquired the sense of destiny, therefore courage and pride. When they entered upon the southern Plains they had been transformed. No longer were they slaves to the simple necessity of survival; they were a lordly and dangerous society of fighters and thieves, hunters and priests of the sun. According to their origin myth, they entered the world through a hollow log. From one point of view, their migration was the fruit of an old prophecy, for indeed they emerged from a sunless world.

5     Although my grandmother lived out her long life in the shadow of Rainy Mountain, the immense landscape of the continental interior lay like memory in her blood. She could tell of the Crows, whom she had

never seen, and of the Black Hills, where she had never been. I wanted to see in reality what she had seen more perfectly in the mind's eye, and traveled fifteen hundred miles to begin my pilgrimage.

Yellowstone, it seemed to me, was the top of the world, a region of deep lakes and dark timber, canyons and waterfalls. But, beautiful as it is, one might have the sense of confinement there. The skyline in all directions is close at hand, the high wall of the woods and deep cleavages of shade. There is a perfect freedom in the mountains, but it belongs to the eagle and the elk, the badger and the bear. The Kiowas reckoned their stature by the distance they could see, and they were bent and blind in the wilderness.

Descending eastward, the highland meadows are a stairway to the plain. In July the inland slope of the Rockies is luxuriant with flax and buckwheat, stonecrop and larkspur. The earth unfolds and the limit of the land recedes. Clusters of trees, and animals grazing far in the distance, cause the vision to reach away and wonder to build upon the mind. The sun follows a longer course in the day, and the sky is immense beyond all comparison. The great billowing clouds that sail upon it are shadows that move upon the grain like water, dividing light. Farther down, in the land of the Crows and Blackfeet, the plain is yellow. Sweet clover takes hold of the hills and bends upon itself to cover and seat the soil. There the Kiowas paused on their way; they had come to the place where they must change their lives. The sun is at home on the plains. Precisely there does it have the certain character of a god. When the Kiowas came to the land of the Crows, they could see the dark lees of the hills at dawn across the Bighorn River, the profusion of light on the grain shelves, the oldest deity ranging after the solstices. Not yet would they veer southward to the caldron of the land that lay below; they must wean their blood from the northern winter and hold the mountains a while longer in their view. They bore Tai-me in procession to the east.

A dark mist lay over the Black Hills, and the land was like iron. At the top of a ridge I caught sight of Devil's Tower upthrust against the gray sky as if in the birth of time the core of the earth had broken through its crust and the motion of the world was begun. There are things in nature that engender an awful quiet in the heart of man; Devil's Tower is one of them. Two centuries ago, because they could not do otherwise, the Kiowas made a legend at the base of the rock. My grandmother said:

> Eight children were there at play, seven sisters and their brother. Suddenly the boy was struck dumb; he trembled and began to run

upon his hands and feet. His fingers became claws, and his body was covered with fur. Directly there was a bear where the boy had been. The sisters were terrified; they ran, and the bear after them. They came to the stump of a great tree, and the tree spoke to them. It bade them climb upon it, and as they did so it began to rise into the air. The bear came to kill them, but they were just beyond its reach. It reared against the tree and scored the bark all around with its claws. The seven sisters were borne into the sky, and they became the stars of the Big Dipper.

From that moment, and so long as the legend lives, the Kiowas have kinsmen in the night sky. Whatever they were in the mountains, they could be no more. However tenuous their well-being, however much they had suffered and would suffer again, they had found a way out of the wilderness.

My grandmother had a reverence for the sun, a holy regard that now is all but gone out of mankind. There was a wariness in her, and an ancient awe. She was a Christian in her later years, but she had come a long way about, and she never forgot her birthright. As a child she had been to the Sun Dances; she had taken part in those annual rites, and by them she had learned the restoration of her people in the presence of Tai-me. She was about seven when the last Kiowa Sun Dance was held in 1887 on the Washita River above Rainy Mountain Creek. The buffalo were gone. In order to consummate the ancient sacrifice—to impale the head of a buffalo bull upon the medicine tree—a delegation of old men journeyed into Texas, there to beg and barter for an animal from the Goodnight herd. She was ten when the Kiowas came together for the last time as a living Sun Dance culture. They could find no buffalo; they had to hang an old hide from the sacred tree. Before the dance could begin, a company of soldiers rode out from Fort Sill under orders to disperse the tribe. Forbidden without cause the essential act of their faith, having seen the wild herds slaughtered and left to rot upon the ground, the Kiowas backed away forever from the medicine tree. That was July 20, 1890, at the great bend of the Washita. My grandmother was there. Without bitterness, and for as long as she lived, she bore a vision of deicide.

10    Now that I can have her only in memory, I see my grandmother in the several postures that were peculiar to her: standing at the wood stove on a winter morning and turning meat in a great iron skillet; sitting at the south window, bent above her beadwork, and afterwards, when her vision failed, looking down for a long time into the fold of her hands; going out upon a cane, very slowly as she did when the

weight of age came upon her; praying. I remember her most often at prayer. She made long, rambling prayers out of suffering and hope, having seen many things. I was never sure that I had the right to hear, so exclusive were they of all mere custom and company. The last time I saw her she prayed standing by the side of her bed at night, naked to the waist, the light of a kerosene lamp moving upon her dark skin. Her long, black hair, always drawn and braided in the day, lay upon her shoulders and against her breasts like a shawl. I do not speak Kiowa, and I never understood her prayers, but there was something inherently sad in the sound, some merest hesitation upon the syllables of sorrow. She began in a high and descending pitch, exhausting her breath to silence; then again and again—and always the same intensity of effort, of something that is, and is not, like urgency in the human voice. Transported so in the dancing light among the shadows of her room, she seemed beyond the reach of time. But that was illusion; I think I knew then that I should not see her again.

Houses are like sentinels in the plain, old keepers of the weather watch. There, in a very little while, wood takes on the appearance of great age. All colors wear soon away in the wind and rain, and then the wood is burned gray and the grain appears and the nails turn red with rust. The windowpanes are black and opaque; you imagine there is nothing within, and indeed there are many ghosts, bones given up to the land. They stand here and there against the sky, and you approach them for a longer time than you expect. They belong in the distance; it is their domain.

Once there was a lot of sound in my grandmother's house, a lot of coming and going, feasting and talk. The summers there were full of excitement and reunion. The Kiowas are a summer people; they abide the cold and keep to themselves, but when the season turns and the land becomes warm and vital they cannot hold still; an old love of going returns upon them. The aged visitors who came to my grandmother's house when I was a child were made of lean and leather, and they bore themselves upright. They wore great black hats and bright ample shirts that shook in the wind. They rubbed fat upon their hair and wound their braids with strips of colored cloth. Some of them painted their faces and carried the scars of old and cherished enmities. They were an old council of warlords, come to remind and be reminded of who they were. Their wives and daughters served them well. The women might indulge themselves; gossip was at once the mark and compensation of their servitude. They made loud and elaborate talk among themselves, full of jest and gesture, fright and false alarm. They went abroad in fringed and flowered shawls, bright bead-work and German silver. They were at home in the kitchen, and they prepared meals that were banquets.

There were frequent prayer meetings, and great nocturnal feasts. When I was a child I played with my cousins outside, where the lamp-light fell upon the ground and the singing of the old people rose up around us and carried away into the darkness. There were a lot of good things to eat, a lot of laughter and surprise. And afterwards, when the quiet returned, I lay down with my grandmother and could hear the frogs away by the river and feel the motion of the air.

Now there is a funeral silence in the rooms, the endless wake of some final word. The walls have closed in upon my grandmother's house. When I returned to it in mourning, I saw for the first time in my life how small it was. It was late at night, and there was a white moon, nearly full. I sat for a long time on the stone steps by the kitchen door. From there I could see out across the land; I could see the long row of trees by the creek, the low light upon the rolling plains, and the stars of the Big Dipper. Once I looked at the moon and caught sight of a strange thing. A cricket had perched upon the handrail, only a few inches away from me. My line of vision was such that the creature filled the moon like a fossil. It had gone there, I thought, to live and die, for there, of all places, was its small definition made whole and eternal. A warm wind rose up and purled like the longing within me.

15    The next morning I awoke at dawn and went out on the dirt road to Rainy Mountain. It was already hot, and the grasshoppers began to fill the air. Still, it was early in the morning, and the birds sang out of the shadows. The long yellow grass on the mountain shone in the bright light, and a scissortail hied above the land. There, where it ought to be, at the end of a long and legendary way, was my grand-mother's grave. Here and there on the dark stones were ancestral names. Looking back once, I saw the mountain and came away.

## Questions for Discussion

Why does Momaday begin the piece with a relatively straightforward de-scription of Rainy Mountain?

How is the piece organized? Is there an underlying pattern to the piece as a whole?

What part does the legend Momaday recounts in paragraph 8 play in his argument?

# PART TWO

# EDUCATION

Why have Americans always been so passionate about issues related to education? For one thing, education issues affect every American in a personal way because no other people strive for universal education with the zeal that Americans do. True, there is a strong anti-intellectual strain in American life, and true, not everyone appreciates the mandate for universal education; but it is also true that Americans do pursue with a passion the ideal of "education for all" both as a means of self-improvement and as the source of the enlightened citizenry required by democratic institutions. For another thing, education issues in America are decided locally and immediately. The relatively decentralized nature of our educational "system" (not that American education is as monolithic as the term "system" implies) encourages continuing and passionate public discussion among citizens interested in shaping the policies and practices of local schools.

What principles should guide educational policy in the United States? That fundamental question, which lies behind most of the debates about education, has been restated in a compelling way by the American philosopher and educational reformer John Dewey: *Should society be a function of education, or should education be a function of society?* In other words, should educational institutions be developed to perpetuate American institutions and values and to develop a skilled workforce for the American economy ("education as a function of society")? Or should educational institutions be developed chiefly in order to critique and reform American institutions in the interest of creating a more just and equitable society ("society as a function of education")? To put it yet another way: Should

Eva Rodriguez-Chavez teaches a language skills lesson to first
graders in Los Angeles

schools emphasize mastery of bodies of knowledge, "what every educated citizen needs to know"? Or instead should it emphasize practical
learning skills—problem-solving ability, flexibility, independent thinking, and resourcefulness? Most people would answer, "Both":
Education should equip people both with practical, vocational abilities
and with the critical and communication skills necessary to make for a
vibrant, resourceful, just society. Yet that answer only complicates the
issue, for in what proportion should schools develop creative criticizers
and questioners versus efficient and adjusted workers?

The highly influential arguments included in this part of
*Argument in America* bear directly on the issue of "education as a
function of society" versus "society as a function of education." Ralph
Waldo Emerson's famous "The American Scholar" offers a definition
of what a college student should be and do and how a college student
should learn—one that continues to shape institutions and individuals. Charles William Eliot's argument, another from the nineteenth
century, proposes the elective-based style of education, which still
dominates much of American higher education. W. E. B. DuBois next
offers (in "The Talented Tenth") an argument about the nature of
higher education for African Americans that counters the more
strictly vocational goals that were emphasized by Booker T.
Washington. Later a cartoon strip by Garry B. Trudeau and Adrienne

Rich's "Taking Women Students Seriously" both challenge Americans to make higher education a means of enhancing critical thinking and intellectual development.

Another group of arguments addresses the function of primary and secondary education. E. B. White in "Education" wonders whether schools should be large, efficient, and comprehensive—or whether schools would be better if they were smaller and more personal. Jerome Stern and Matt Groening complain that schools have become regimented, confining, and constricting places, places that value order and conformity over independence and freedom of inquiry. Finally, Jonathan Kozol and Benjamin R. Barber challenge Americans to improve funding for primary and secondary schools.

Arguments related to education are developed further in this book—in the section on censorship, for example, and in Richard Rodriguez's essay "Aria: A Memoir of a Bilingual Childhood." But in this part of *Argument in America*, the emphasis is on education in particular. The readings you encounter should give you a better understanding of the issues that you and your classmates are grappling with right now. As you read, remember that the perennial nature of debates about education can be frustrating, especially to educational leaders. But the very relentlessness of the debates probably brings out the best feature of a democratic society: the freedom of citizens to shape policy through open and public exchange.

*Ralph Waldo Emerson (1803–1882) originally trained to become a
Unitarian minister but instead left that profession to take up what would
be a long and celebrated career in writing and public speaking. Emerson
was a prolific and original thinker, with many of his ideas forming the
basis of the American transcendentalist movement, which valued spiritu-
ality, the natural world, human optimism, and a healthy skepticism toward reason and logic. Many of America's most important writers and
thinkers credit Emerson with beginning to define an "American" voice and
literary tradition responsive to the ideas, values, and problems of the new
country. In "The American Scholar," originally delivered before the Phi
Beta Kappa Society in 1837 and later collected in* Essays *(1841),
Emerson argues for a new and distinctly "American" brand of educational philosophy.*

# Ralph Waldo Emerson
## The American Scholar

Mr. President and Gentlemen,

I greet you on the re-commencement of our literary year. Our anniversary is one of hope, and, perhaps, not enough of labor. We do not meet
for games of strength or skill, for the recitation of histories, tragedies,
and odes, like the ancient Greeks; for parliaments of love and poesy,
like the Troubadours; nor for the advancement of science, like our
cotemporaries in the British and European capitals. Thus far, our holiday has been simply a friendly sign of the survival of the love of letters amongst a people too busy to give to letters any more. As such, it
is precious as the sign of an indestructible instinct. Perhaps the time is
already come, when it ought to be, and will be, something else; when
the sluggard intellect of this continent will look from under its iron
lids, and fill the postponed expectation of the world with something
better than the exertions of mechanical skill. Our day of dependence,
our long apprenticeship to the learning of other lands, draws to a
close. The millions, that around us are rushing into life, cannot always
be fed on the sere remains of foreign harvests. Events, actions arise,
that must be sung, that will sing themselves. Who can doubt, that poetry will revive and lead in a new age, as the star in the constellation
Harp, which now flames in our zenith, astronomers announce, shall
one day be the pole-star for a thousand years?

In this hope, I accept the topic which not only usage, but the nature of our association, seem to prescribe to this day,—the AMERICAN SCHOLAR. Year by year, we come up hither to read one more chapter of his biography. Let us inquire what light new days and events have thrown on his character, and his hopes.

It is one of those fables, which, out of an unknown antiquity, convey an unlooked-for wisdom, that the gods, in the beginning, divided Man into men, that he might be more helpful to himself; just as the hand was divided into fingers, the better to answer its end.

The old fable covers a doctrine ever new and sublime; that there is One Man,—present to all particular men only partially, or through one faculty; and that you must take the whole society to find the whole man. Man is not a farmer, or a professor, or an engineer, but he is all. Man is priest, and scholar, and statesman, and producer, and soldier. In the *divided* or social state, these functions are parcelled out to individuals, each of whom aims to do his stint of the joint work, whilst each other performs his. The fable implies, that the individual, to possess himself, must sometimes return from his own labor to embrace all the other laborers. But unfortunately, this original unit, this fountain of power, has been so distributed to multitudes, has been so minutely subdivided and peddled out, that it is spilled into drops, and cannot be gathered. The state of society is one in which the members have suffered amputation from the trunk, and strut about so many walking monsters,—a good finger, a neck, a stomach, an elbow, but never a man.

5    Man is thus metamorphosed into a thing, into many things. The planter, who is Man sent out into the field to gather food, is seldom cheered by any idea of the true dignity of his ministry. He sees his bushel and his cart, and nothing beyond, and sinks into the farmer, instead of Man on the farm. The tradesman scarcely ever gives an ideal worth to his work, but is ridden by the routine of his craft, and the soul is subject to dollars. The priest becomes a form; the attorney, a statute-book; the mechanic, a machine; the sailor, a rope of a ship.

In this distribution of functions, the scholar is the delegated intellect. In the right state, he is, *Man Thinking*. In the degenerate state, when the victim of society, he tends to become a mere thinker, or, still worse, the parrot of other men's thinking.

In this view of him, as Man Thinking, the theory of his office is contained. Him nature solicits with all her placid, all her monitory pictures; him the past instructs; him the future invites. Is not, indeed, every man a student, and do not all things exist for the student's behoof? And, finally, is not the true scholar the only true master? But the old oracle said, 'All things have two handles: beware of the wrong one.' In life, too often, the scholar errs with mankind and forfeits his privilege. Let us see him in his school, and consider him in reference to the main influences he receives.

I. The first in time and the first in importance of the influences upon the mind is that of nature. Every day, the sun; and, after sunset, night and her stars. Ever the winds blow; ever the grass grows. Every day, men and women, conversing, beholding and beholden. The scholar is he of all men whom this spectacle most engages. He must settle its value in his mind. What is nature to him? There is never a beginning, there is never an end, to the inexplicable continuity of this web of God, but always circular power returning into itself. Therein it resembles his own spirit, whose beginning, whose ending, he never can find,—so entire, so boundless. Far, too, as her splendors shine, system on system shooting like rays, upward, downward, without centre, without circumference,—in the mass and in the par-ticle, nature hastens to render account of herself to the mind. Classification begins. To the young mind, every thing is individual, stands by itself. By and by, it finds how to join two things, and see in them one nature; then three, then three thousand; and so, tyrannized over by its own unifying instinct, it goes on tying things together, di-minishing anomalies, discovering roots running under ground, whereby contrary and remote things cohere, and flower out from one stem. It presently learns, that, since the dawn of history, there has been a constant accumulation and classifying of facts. But what is classification but the perceiving that these objects are not chaotic, and are not foreign, but have a law which is also a law of the human mind? The astronomer discovers that geometry, a pure abstraction of the human mind, is the measure of planetary motion. The chemist finds proportions and intelligible method throughout matter; and science is nothing but the finding of analogy, identity, in the most re-mote parts. The ambitious soul sits down before each refractory fact; one after another, reduces all strange constitutions, all new powers, to their class and their law, and goes on for ever to animate the last fibre of organization, the outskirts of nature, by insight.

Thus to him, to this school-boy under the bending dome of day, is suggested, that he and it proceed from one root; one is leaf and one is flower; relation, sympathy, stirring in every vein. And what is that Root? Is not that the soul of his soul?—A thought too bold,—a dream too wild. Yet when this spiritual light shall have revealed the law of more earthly natures,—when he has learned to worship the soul, and to see that the natural philosophy that now is, is only the first gropings of its gigantic hand, he shall look forward to an ever expanding knowledge as to a becoming creator. He shall see, that nature is the opposite of the soul, answering to it part for part. One is seal, and one is print. Its beauty is the beauty of his own mind. Its laws are the laws of his own mind. Nature then becomes to him the measure of his attainments. So much of nature as he is ignorant of, so much of his own mind does he not yet possess. And, in fine, the ancient precept, "Know thyself," and the modern precept, "Study nature," become at last one maxim.

10  II. The next great influence into the spirit of the scholar, is, the mind of the Past,—in whatever form, whether of literature, of art, of institutions, that mind is inscribed. Books are the best type of the influence of the past, and perhaps we shall get at the truth,—learn the amount of this influence more conveniently,—by considering their value alone.

The theory of books is noble. The scholar of the first age received into him the world around; brooded thereon; gave it the new arrangement of his own mind, and uttered it again. It came into him, life; it went out from him, truth. It came to him, short-lived actions; it went out from him, immortal thoughts. It came to him, business; it went from him, poetry. It was dead fact; now, it is quick thought. It can stand, and it can go. It now endures, it now flies, it now inspires. Precisely in proportion to the depth of mind from which it issued, so high does it soar, so long does it sing.

Or, I might say, it depends on how far the process had gone, of transmuting life into truth. In proportion to the completeness of the distillation, so will the purity and imperishableness of the product be. But none is quite perfect. As no air-pump can by any means make a perfect vacuum, so neither can any artist entirely exclude the conventional, the local, the perishable from his book, or write a book of pure thought, that shall be as efficient, in all respects, to a remote posterity, as to contemporaries, or rather to the second age. Each age, it is found, must write its own books; or rather, each generation for the next succeeding. The books of an older period will not fit this.

Yet hence arises a grave mischief. The sacredness which attaches to the act of creation,—the act of thought,—is transferred to the record. The poet chanting, was felt to be a divine man: henceforth the chant is divine also. The writer was a just and wise spirit: henceforward it is settled, the book is perfect; as love of the hero corrupts into worship of his statue. Instantly, the book becomes noxious: the guide is a tyrant. The sluggish and perverted mind of the multitude, slow to open to the incursions of Reason, having once so opened, having once received this book, stands upon it, and makes an outcry, if it is disparaged. Colleges are built on it. Books are written on it by thinkers, not by Man Thinking; by men of talent, that is, who start wrong, who set out from accepted dogmas, not from their own sight of principles. Meek young men grow up in libraries, believing it their duty to accept the views, which Cicero, which Locke, which Bacon, have given, forgetful that Cicero, Locke, and Bacon were only young men in libraries, when they wrote these books.

Hence, instead of Man Thinking, we have the bookworm. Hence, the book-learned class, who value books, as such; not as related to nature and the human constitution, but as making a sort of Third Estate with the world and the soul. Hence, the restorers of readings, the emendators, the bibliomaniacs of all degrees.

15     Books are the best of things, well used; abused, among the worst. What is the right use? What is the one end, which all means go to effect? They are for nothing but to inspire. I had better never see a book, than to be warped by its attraction clean out of my own orbit, and made a satellite instead of a system. The one thing in the world, of value, is the active soul. This every man is entitled to; this every man contains within him, although, in almost all men, obstructed, and as yet unborn. The soul active sees absolute truth; and utters truth, or creates. In this action, it is genius; not the privilege of here and there a favorite, but the sound estate of every man. In its essence, it is progressive. The book, the college, the school of art, the institution of any kind, stop with some past utterance of genius. This is good, say they,— let us hold by this. They pin me down. They look backward and not forward. But genius looks forward: the eyes of man are set in his forehead, not in his hindhead: man hopes: genius creates. Whatever talents may be, if the man create not, the pure efflux of the Deity is not his;—cinders and smoke there may be, but not yet flame. There are creative manners, there are creative actions, and creative words; manners, actions, words, that is, indicative of no custom or authority, but springing spontaneous from the mind's own sense of good and fair.

On the other part, instead of being its own seer, let it receive from another mind its truth, though it were in torrents of light, without periods of solitude, inquest, and self-recovery, and a fatal disservice is done. Genius is always sufficiently the enemy of genius by over influence. The literature of every nation bear me witness. The English dramatic poets have Shakespearized now for two hundred years.

Undoubtedly there is a right way of reading, so it be sternly subordinated. Man Thinking must not be subdued by his instruments. Books are for the scholar's idle times. When he can read God directly, the hour is too precious to be wasted in other men's transcripts of their readings. But when the intervals of darkness come, as come they must,—when the sun is hid, and the stars withdraw their shining,— we repair to the lamps which were kindled by their ray, to guide our steps to the East again, where the dawn is. We hear, that we may speak. The Arabian proverb says, "A fig tree, looking on a fig tree, becometh fruitful."

It is remarkable, the character of the pleasure we derive from the best books. They impress us with the conviction, that one nature wrote and the same reads. We read the verses of one of the great English poets, of Chaucer, of Marvell, of Dryden, with the most modern joy,— with a pleasure, I mean, which is in great part caused by the abstraction of all *time* from their verses. There is some awe mixed with the joy of our surprise, when this poet, who lived in some past world, two or three hundred years ago, says that which lies close to my own soul, that which I also had wellnigh thought and said. But for the evidence thence afforded to the philosophical doctrine of the identity of all minds, we should suppose some preestablished harmony, some foresight of souls that were to be, and some preparation of stores for their future wants, like the fact observed in insects, who lay up food before death for the young grub they shall never see.

I would not be hurried by any love of system, by any exaggeration of instincts, to underrate the Book. We all know, that, as the human body can be nourished on any food, though it were boiled grass and the broth of shoes, so the human mind can be fed by any knowledge. And great and heroic men have existed, who had almost no other information than by the printed page. I only would say, that it needs a strong head to bear that diet. One must be an inventor to read well. As the proverb says, "He that would bring home the wealth of the Indies, must carry out the wealth of the Indies." There is then creative reading as well as creative writing. When the mind is braced by labor and invention, the page of whatever book we read becomes luminous with manifold allusion. Every sentence is doubly significant, and the sense of our author is as broad as the world. We then see, what is always true, that, as the seer's hour of vision is short and rare among heavy days and months, so is its record, perchance, the least part of his volume. The discerning will read, in his Plato or Shakespeare, only that least part,—only the authentic utterances of the oracle;—all the rest he rejects, were it never so many times Plato's and Shakespeare's.

20     Of course, there is a portion of reading quite indispensable to a wise man. History and exact science he must learn by laborious reading. Colleges, in like manner, have their indispensable office,— to teach elements. But they can only highly serve us, when they aim not to drill, but to create; when they gather from far every ray of various genius to their hospitable halls, and, by the concentrated fires, set the hearts of their youth on flame. Thought and knowledge are natures in which apparatus and pretension avail nothing. Gowns, and pecuniary foundations, though of towns of gold, can never countervail the least sentence or syllable of wit. Forget this, and our American colleges will recede in their public importance, whilst they grow richer every year.

III. There goes in the world a notion, that the scholar should be a recluse, a valetudinarian,—as unfit for any handiwork or public labor, as a penknife for an axe. The so-called 'practical men' sneer at speculative men, as if, because they speculate or *see*, they could do nothing. I have heard it said that the clergy,—who are always, more universally than any other class, the scholars of their day,—are addressed as women; that the rough, spontaneous conversation of men they do not hear, but only a mincing and diluted speech. They are often virtually disfranchised; and, indeed, there are advocates for their celibacy. As far as this is true of the studious classes, it is not just and wise. Action is with the scholar subordinate, but it is essential. Without it, he is not yet man. Without it, thought can never ripen into truth. Whilst the world hangs before the eye as a cloud of beauty, we cannot even see its beauty. Inaction is cowardice, but there can be no scholar without the heroic mind. The preamble of thought, the transition through which it passes from the unconscious to the conscious, is action. Only so much do I know, as I have lived. Instantly we know whose words are loaded with life, and whose not.

     The world,—this shadow of the soul, or *other me*, lies wide around. Its attractions are the keys which unlock my thoughts and make me acquainted with myself. I run eagerly into this resounding tumult. I grasp the hands of those next me, and take my place in the ring to suffer and to work, taught by an instinct, that so shall the dumb abyss be vocal with speech. I pierce its order; I dissipate its fear; I dispose of it within the circuit of my expanding life. So much only of life as I know by experience, so much of the wilderness have I van-

quished and planted, or so far have I extended my being, my dominion. I do not see how any man can afford, for the sake of his nerves
and his nap, to spare any action in which he can partake. It is pearls
and rubies to his discourse. Drudgery, calamity, exasperation, want,
are instructers in eloquence and wisdom. The true scholar grudges
every opportunity of action past by, as a loss of power.

It is the raw material out of which the intellect moulds her splendid products. A strange process too, this, by which experience is converted into thought, as a mulberry leaf is converted into satin. The
manufacture goes forward at all hours.

The actions and events of our childhood and youth, are now matters of calmest observation. They lie like fair pictures in the air. Not so
with our recent actions,—with the business which we now have in
hand. On this we are quite unable to speculate. Our affections as yet
circulate through it. We no more feel or know it, than we feel the feet,
or the hand, or the brain of our body. The new deed is yet a part of
life,—remains for a time immersed in our unconscious life. In some
contemplative hour, it detaches itself from the life like a ripe fruit, to
become a thought of the mind. Instantly, it is raised, transfigured; the
corruptible has put on incorruption. Henceforth it is an object of
beauty, however base its origin and neighborhood. Observe, too, the
impossibility of antedating this act. In its grub state, it cannot fly, it
cannot shine, it is a dull grub. But suddenly, without observation, the
selfsame thing unfurls beautiful wings, and is an angel of wisdom. So
is there no fact, no event, in our private history, which shall not,
sooner or later, lose its adhesive, inert form, and astonish us by soaring
from our body into the empyrean. Cradle and infancy, school and
playground, the fear of boys, and dogs, and ferules, the love of little
maids and berries, and many another fact that once filled the whole
sky, are gone already; friend and relative, profession and party, town
and country, nation and world, must also soar and sing.

25      Of course, he who has put forth his total strength in fit actions,
has the richest return of wisdom. I will not shut myself out of this
globe of action, and transplant an oak into a flower-pot, there to
hunger and pine; nor trust the revenue of some single faculty, and ex-
haust one vein of thought, much like those Savoyards, who, getting
their livelihood by carving shepherds, shepherdesses, and smoking
Dutchmen, for all Europe, went out one day to the mountain to find
stock, and discovered that they had whittled up the last of their pine-
trees. Authors we have, in numbers, who have written out their vein,
and who, moved by a commendable prudence, sail for Greece or

Palestine, follow the trapper into the prairie, or ramble round Algiers, to replenish their merchantable stock.

If it were only for a vocabulary, the scholar would be covetous of action. Life is our dictionary. Years are well spent in country labors; in town,—in the insight into trades and manufactures; in frank intercourse with many men and women; in science; in art; to the one end of mastering in all their facts a language by which to illustrate and embody our perceptions. I learn immediately from any speaker how much he has already lived, through the poverty or the splendor of his speech. Life lies behind us as the quarry from whence we get tiles and copestones for the masonry of today. This is the way to learn grammar. Colleges and books only copy the language which the field and the work-yard made.

But the final value of action, like that of books, and better than books, is, that it is a resource. That great principle of Undulation in nature, that shows itself in the inspiring and expiring of the breath; in desire and satiety; in the ebb and flow of the sea; in day and night; in heat and cold; and as yet more deeply ingrained in every atom and every fluid, is known to us under the name of Polarity,—these "fits of easy transmission and reflection," as Newton called them, are the law of nature because they are the law of spirit.

The mind now thinks; now acts; and each fit reproduces the other. When the artist has exhausted his materials, when the fancy no longer paints, when thoughts are no longer apprehended, and books are a weariness,—he has always the resource *to live.* Character is higher than intellect. Thinking is the function. Living is the functionary. The stream retreats to its source. A great soul will be strong to live, as well as strong to think. Does he lack organ or medium to impart his truths? He can still fall back on this elemental force of living them. This is a total act. Thinking is a partial act. Let the grandeur of justice shine in his affairs. Let the beauty of affection cheer his lowly roof. Those 'far from fame,' who dwell and act with him, will feel the force of his constitution in the doings and passages of the day better than it can be measured by any public and designed display. Time shall teach him, that the scholar loses no hour which the man lives. Herein he unfolds the sacred germ of his instinct, screened from influence. What is lost in seemliness is gained in strength. Not out of those, on whom systems of education have exhausted their culture, comes the helpful giant to destroy the old or to build the new, but out of unhandselled savage nature, out of terrible Druids and Berserkirs, come at last Alfred and Shakespeare.

I hear therefore with joy whatever is beginning to be said of the dignity and necessity of labor to every citizen. There is virtue yet in the hoe and the spade, for learned as well as for unlearned hands. And labor is everywhere welcome; always we are invited to work; only be this limitation observed, that a man shall not for the sake of wider activity sacrifice any opinion to the popular judgments and modes of action.

30    I have now spoken of the education of the scholar by nature, by books, and by action. It remains to say somewhat of his duties.

They are such as become Man Thinking. They may all be comprised in self-trust. The office of the scholar is to cheer, to raise, and to guide men by showing them facts amidst appearances. He plies the slow, unhonored, and unpaid task of observation. Flamsteed and Herschel, in their glazed observatories, may catalogue the stars with the praise of all men, and, the results being splendid and useful, honor is sure. But he, in his private observatory, cataloguing obscure and nebulous stars of the human mind, which as yet no man has thought of as such,—watching days and months, sometimes, for a few facts; correcting still his old records;—must relinquish display and immediate fame. In the long period of his preparation, he must betray often an ignorance and shiftlessness in popular arts, incurring the disdain of the able who shoulder him aside. Long he must stammer in his speech; often forego the living for the dead. Worse yet, he must accept,—how often! poverty and solitude. For the ease and pleasure of treading the old road, accepting the fashions, the education, the religion of society, he takes the cross of making his own, and, of course, the self-accusation, the faint heart, the frequent uncertainty and loss of time, which are the nettles and tangling vines in the way of the self-relying and self-directed; and the state of virtual hostility in which he seems to stand to society, and especially to educated society. For all this loss and scorn, what offset? He is to find consolation in exercising the highest functions of human nature. He is one, who raises himself from private considerations, and breathes and lives on public and illustrious thoughts. He is the world's eye. He is the world's heart. He is to resist the vulgar prosperity that retrogrades ever to barbarism, by preserving and communicating heroic sentiments, noble biographies, melodious verse, and the conclusions of history. Whatsoever oracles the human heart, in all emergencies, in all solemn hours, has uttered as its commentary on the world of actions,—these he shall receive and impart. And whatsoever new verdict Reason from her inviolable seat pronounces on the passing men and events of today,—this he shall hear and promulgate.

These being his functions, it becomes him to feel all confidence in himself, and to defer never to the popular cry. He and he only knows the world. The world of any moment is the merest appearance. Some great decorum, some fetish of a government, some ephemeral trade, or war, or man, is cried up by half mankind and cried down by the other half, as if all depended on this particular up or down. The odds are that the whole question is not worth the poorest thought which the scholar has lost in listening to the controversy. Let him not quit his belief that a popgun is a popgun, though the ancient and honorable of the earth affirm it to be the crack of doom. In silence, in steadiness, in severe abstraction, let him hold by himself; add observation to observation, patient of neglect, patient of reproach; and bide his own time,—happy enough, if he can satisfy himself alone, that this day he has seen something truly. Success treads on every right step. For the instinct is sure, that prompts him to tell his brother what he thinks. He then learns, that in going down into the secrets of his own mind, he has descended into the secrets of all minds. He learns that he who has mastered any law in his private thoughts, is master to that extent of all men whose language he speaks, and of all into whose language his own can be translated. The poet, in utter solitude remembering his spontaneous thoughts and recording them, is found to have recorded that, which men in crowded cities find true for them also. The orator distrusts at first the fitness of his frank confessions,—his want of knowledge of the persons he addresses,—until he finds that he is the complement of his hearers;—that they drink his words because he fulfils for them their own nature; the deeper he dives into his privatest, secretest presentiment, to his wonder he finds, this is the most acceptable, most public, and universally true. The people delight in it; the better part of every man feels, This is my music; this is myself.

In self-trust, all the virtues are comprehended. Free should the scholar be,—free and brave. Free even to the definition of freedom, "without any hindrance that does not arise out of his own constitution." Brave; for fear is a thing, which a scholar by his very function puts behind him. Fear always springs from ignorance. It is a shame to him if his tranquility, amid dangerous times, arise from the presumption, that, like children and women, his is a protected class; or if he seek a temporary peace by the diversion of his thoughts from politics or vexed questions, hiding his head like an ostrich in the flowering bushes, peeping into microscopes, and turning rhymes, as a boy whistles to keep his courage up. So is the danger a danger still; so is the fear worse. Manlike let him turn and face it. Let him look into its eye and search its nature, inspect its origin,—see the whelping of this lion,—which lies no great way back; he will then find in himself a perfect comprehension of its nature and extent; he will have made his hands meet on the other side, and can henceforth defy it, and pass on superior. The world is his, who can see through its pretension. What deafness, what stone-blind custom, what overgrown error you behold, is there only by sufferance,—by your sufferance. See it to be a lie, and you have already dealt it its mortal blow.

Yes, we are the cowed,—we the trustless. It is a mischievous notion that we are come late into nature; that the world was finished a long time ago. As the world was plastic and fluid in the hands of God, so it is ever to so much of his attributes as we bring to it. To ignorance and sin, it is flint. They adapt themselves to it as they may; but in proportion as a man has any thing in him divine, the firmament flows before him and takes his signet and form. Not he is great who can alter matter, but he who can alter my state of mind. They are the kings of the world who give the color of their present thought to all nature and all art, and persuade men by the cheerful serenity of their carrying the matter, that this thing which they do, is the apple which the ages have desired to pluck, now at last ripe, and inviting nations to the harvest. The great man makes the great thing. Wherever Macdonald sits, there is the head of the table. Linnaeus makes botany the most alluring of studies, and wins it from the farmer and the herb-woman; Davy, chemistry; and Cuvier, fossils. The day is always his, who works in it with serenity and great aims. The unstable estimates of men crowd to him whose mind is filled with a truth, as the heaped waves of the Atlantic follow the moon.

35      For this self-trust, the reason is deeper than can be fathomed,— darker than can be enlightened. I might not carry with me the feeling of my audience in stating my own belief. But I have already shown the ground of my hope, in adverting to the doctrine that man is one. I believe man has been wronged; he has wronged himself. He has almost lost the light, that can lead him back to his prerogatives. Men are become of no account. Men in history, men in the world of today are bugs, are spawn, and are called 'the mass' and 'the herd.' In a century, in a millennium, one or two men; that is to say,—one or two approximations to the right state of every man. All the rest behold in the hero or the poet their own green and crude being,—ripened; yes, and are content to be less, so *that* may attain to its full stature. What a testimony,—full of grandeur, full of pity, is borne to the demands of his own nature, by the poor clansman, the poor partisan, who rejoices in

the glory of his chief. The poor and the low find some amends to their immense moral capacity, for their acquiescence in a political and social inferiority. They are content to be brushed like flies from the path of a great person, so that justice shall be done by him to that common nature which it is the dearest desire of all to see enlarged and glorified. They sun themselves in the great man's light, and feel it to be their own element. They cast the dignity of man from their downtrod selves upon the shoulders of a hero, and will perish to add one drop of blood to make that great heart beat, those giant sinews combat and conquer. He lives for us, and we live in him.

Men such as they are, very naturally seek money or power; and power because it is as good as money,—the "spoils," so called, "of office." And why not? for they aspire to the highest, and this, in their sleep-walking, they dream is highest. Wake them, and they shall quit the false good, and leap to the true, and leave governments to clerks and desks. This revolution is to be wrought by the gradual domestication of the idea of Culture. The main enterprise of the world for splendor, for extent, is the upbuilding of a man. Here are the materials strown along the ground. The private life of one man shall be a more illustrious monarchy,—more formidable to its enemy, more sweet and serene in its influence to its friend, than any kingdom in history. For a man, rightly viewed, comprehendeth the particular natures of all men. Each philosopher, each bard, each actor, has only done for me, as by a delegate, what one day I can do for myself. The books which once we valued more than the apple of the eye, we have quite exhausted. What is that but saying, that we have come up with the point of view which the universal mind took through the eyes of one scribe; we have been that man, and have passed on. First, one; then, another; we drain all cisterns, and, waxing greater by all these supplies, we crave a better and more abundant food. The man has never lived that can feed us ever. The human mind cannot be enshrined in a person, who shall set a barrier on any one side to this unbounded, unboundable empire. It is one central fire, which, flaming now out of the lips of Etna, lightens the capes of Sicily; and, now out of the throat of Vesuvius, illuminates the towers and vineyards of Naples. It is one light which beams out of a thousand stars. It is one soul which animates all men.

But I have dwelt perhaps tediously upon this abstraction of the Scholar. I ought not to delay longer to add what I have to say, of nearer reference to the time and to this country.

Historically, there is thought to be a difference in the ideas which predominate over successive epochs, and there are data for marking the genius of the Classic, of the Romantic, and now of the Reflective or

Philosophical age. With the views I have intimated of the oneness or the identity of the mind through all individuals, I do not much dwell on these differences. In fact, I believe each individual passes through all three. The boy is a Greek; the youth, romantic; the adult, reflective. I deny not, however, that a revolution in the leading idea may be distinctly enough traced.

Our age is bewailed as the age of Introversion. Must that needs be evil? We, it seems, are critical; we are embarrassed with second thoughts; we cannot enjoy any thing for hankering to know whereof the pleasure consists; we are lined with eyes; we see with our feet; the time is infected with Hamlet's unhappiness,—

"Sicklied o'er with the pale cast of thought."

Is it so bad then? Sight is the last thing to be pitied. Would we be blind? Do we fear lest we should outsee nature and God, and drink truth dry? I look upon the discontent of the literary class, as a mere announcement of the fact, that they find themselves not in the state of mind of their fathers, and regret the coming state as untried; as a boy dreads the water before he has learned that he can swim. If there is any period one would desire to be born in,—is it not the age of Revolution; when the old and the new stand side by side, and admit of being compared; when the energies of all men are searched by fear and by hope; when the historic glories of the old, can be compensated by the rich possibilities of the new era? This time, like all times, is a very good one, if we but know what to do with it.

40      I read with joy some of the auspicious signs of the coming days, as they glimmer already through poetry and art, through philosophy and science, through church and state.

One of these signs is the fact, that the same movement which effected the elevation of what was called the lowest class in the state, assumed in literature a very marked and as benign an aspect. Instead of the sublime and beautiful; the near, the low, the common, was explored and poetized. That, which had been negligently trodden under foot by those who were harnessing and provisioning themselves for long journeys into far countries, is suddenly found to be richer than all foreign parts. The literature of the poor, the feelings of the child, the philosophy of the street, the meaning of household life, are the topics of the time. It is a great stride. It is a sign,—is it not? of new vigor, when the extremities are made active, when currents of warm life run into the hands and the feet. I ask not for the great, the remote, the romantic; what is doing in Italy or Arabia; what is Greek art, or Provencal minstrelsy; I embrace the common, I explore and sit at the feet of the familiar, the low. Give me insight into today, and you may have the antique and future worlds. What would we really know the meaning of? The meal in the firkin; the milk in the pan; the ballad in the street; the news of the boat; the glance of the eye; the form and the gait of the body;—show me the ultimate reason of these matters; show me the sublime presence of the highest spiritual cause lurking, as always it does lurk, in these suburbs and extremities of nature; let me see every trifle bristling with the polarity that ranges it instantly on an eternal law; and the shop, the plough, and the leger, referred to the like cause by which light undulates and poets sing;—and the world lies no longer a dull miscellany and lumber-room, but has form and order; there is no trifle; there is no puzzle; but one design unites and animates the farthest pinnacle and the lowest trench.

This idea has inspired the genius of Goldsmith, Burns, Cowper, and, in a newer time, of Goethe, Wordsworth, and Carlyle. This idea they have differently followed and with various success. In contrast with their writing, the style of Pope, of Johnson, of Gibbon, looks cold and pedantic. This writing is blood-warm. Man is surprised to find that things near are not less beautiful and wondrous than things remote. The near explains the far. The drop is a small ocean. A man is related to all nature. This perception of the worth of the vulgar is fruitful in discoveries. Goethe, in this very thing the most modern of the moderns, has shown us, as none ever did, the genius of the ancients.

There is one man of genius, who has done much for this philosophy of life, whose literary value has never yet been rightly estimated;—I mean Emanuel Swedenborg. The most imaginative of men, yet writing with the precision of a mathematician, he endeavored to engraft a purely philosophical Ethics on the popular Christianity of his time. Such an attempt, of course, must have difficulty, which no genius could surmount. But he saw and showed the connection between nature and the affections of the soul. He pierced the emblematic or spiritual character of the visible, audible, tangible world. Especially did his shade-loving muse hover over and interpret the lower parts of nature; he showed the mysterious bond that allies moral evil to the foul material forms, and has given in epical parables a theory of insanity, of beasts, of unclean and fearful things.

Another sign of our times, also marked by an analogous political movement, is, the new importance given to the single person. Every thing that tends to insulate the individual,—to surround him with barriers of natural respect, so that each man shall feel the world is his, and man shall treat with man as a sovereign state with a sovereign state;—tends to true union as well as greatness. "I learned," said the melancholy Pestalozzi, "that no man in God's wide earth is either willing or able to help any other man." Help must come from the bosom alone. The scholar is that man who must take up into himself all the ability of the time, all the contributions of the past, all the hopes of the future. He must be an university of knowledges. If there be one lesson more than another, which should pierce his ear, it is, The world is nothing, the man is all; in yourself is the law of all nature, and you know not yet how a globule of sap ascends; in yourself slumbers the whole of Reason; it is for you to know all, it is for you to dare all. Mr. President and Gentlemen, this confidence in the unsearched might of man belongs, by all motives, by all prophecy, by all preparation, to the American Scholar. We have listened too long to the courtly muses of Europe. The spirit of the American freeman is already suspected to be timid, imitative, tame. Public and private avarice make the air we breathe thick and fat. The scholar is decent, indolent, complaisant. See already the tragic consequence. The mind of this country, taught to aim at low objects, eats upon itself. There is no work for any but the decorous and the complaisant. Young men of the fairest promise, who begin life upon our shores, inflated by the mountain winds, shined upon by all the stars of God, find the earth below not in unison with these,—but are hindered from action by the disgust which the principles on which business is managed inspire, and turn drudges, or die of disgust,—some of them suicides. What is the remedy? They did not yet see, and thousands of young men as hopeful now crowding to the barriers for the career, do not yet see, that, if the single man plant himself indomitably on his instincts, and there abide, the huge world will come round to him. Patience,—patience;—with the shades of all the good and great for company; and for solace, the perspective of your own infinite life; and for work, the study and the communication of principles, the making those instincts prevalent, the conversion of the world. Is it not the chief disgrace in the world, not to be an unit;—not to be reckoned one character;—not to yield that peculiar fruit which each man was created to bear, but to be reckoned in the gross, in the hundred, or the thousand, of the party, the section, to which we belong; and our opinion predicted geographically, as the north, or the south? Not so, brothers and friends,—please God, ours shall not be so. We will walk on our own feet; we will work with our own hands; we will speak our own minds. The study of letters shall be no longer a name for pity, for doubt, and for sensual indulgence. The dread of man and the love of man shall be a wall of defence and a wreath of joy around all. A nation of men will for the first time exist, because each believes himself inspired by the Divine Soul which also inspires all men.

## Questions for Discussion

What idea of the "scholar" is Emerson trying to redefine?

Do you think any of Emerson's ideas are visible in the current American educational system? Should they be?

What is the effect of the figurative language that Emerson uses in this essay?

*Charles William Eliot (1834–1926) was president of Harvard University
for 40 years (1869–1909), transforming what had been a small college
into a respected university. Eliot's appointment as president was unusual
for the time, as his professional training was primarily in the sciences (he
was professor of mathematics and chemistry), not the ministry. His progressive and influential ideas about education, including his argument
here in favor of the relatively new idea of elective studies, responded to
the rapidly changing social, cultural, and economic landscape of his day
and helped transform twentieth-century higher education in America in
ways that are still visible. The following argument, excerpted from a
speech delivered in 1885, was later published in Eliot's* Educational
Reform: Essays and Adresses *(1898).*

# *Charles William Eliot*

# Liberty in Education

How to transform a college with one uniform curriculum into a university without any prescribed course of study at all is a problem
which more and more claims the attention of all thoughtful friends of
American learning and education. To-night I hope to convince you
that a university of liberal arts and sciences must give its students
Freedom in choice of studies.

Let me first present what I may call a mechanical argument on
this subject. . . . Now there are eighty teachers employed this year in
Harvard College, exclusive of laboratory assistants; and these eighty
teachers give about four hundred and twenty-five hours of public instruction a week without any repetitions, not counting the very important instruction which many of them give in laboratories. It is impossible for any undergraduate in his four years to take more than a tenth
part of the instruction given by the College; and since four fifths of this
instruction is of a higher grade than any which can be given in a college with a prescribed curriculum, a diligent student would need about
forty years to cover the present field; and during those years the field
would enlarge quite beyond his powers of occupation. Since the student cannot take the whole of the instruction offered, it seems to be
necessary to allow him to take a part. A college must either limit
closely its teaching, or provide some mode of selecting studies for the

individual student. The limitation of teaching is an intolerable alternative for any institution which aspires to become a university; for a university must try to teach every subject, above the grade of its admission requirements, for which there is any demand; and to teach it thoroughly enough to carry the advanced student to the confines of present knowledge, and make him capable of original research. These are the only limits which a university can properly set to its instruction—except indeed those rigorous limits which poverty imposes. The other alternative is selection or election of studies.

The elective system at Harvard has been sixty years in developing, and during fourteen of these years—from 1846 to 1860—the presidents and the majority of the faculty were not in favor of it; but they could find no way of escape from the dilemma which I have set before you. They could not deliberately reduce the amount of instruction offered, and election of studies in some degree was the inevitable alternative.

The practical question then is, At what age, and at what stage of his educational progress, can an American boy be offered free choice of studies? or, in other words, At what age can an American boy best go to a free university? Before answering this question I will ask your attention to four preliminary observations.

5    1. The European boy goes to free universities at various ages from seventeen to twenty; and the American boy is decidedly more mature and more capable of taking care of himself than the European boy of like age.

2. The change from school to university ought to be made as soon as it would be better for the youth to associate with older students under a discipline suited to their age, than with younger pupils under a discipline suited to theirs—as soon, in short, as it would be better for the youth to be the youngest student in a university than the oldest boy in a school. The school might still do much for the youth; the university may as yet be somewhat too free for him: there must be a balancing of advantages against disadvantages; but the wise decision is to withdraw him betimes from a discipline which he is outgrowing, and put him under a discipline which he is to grow up to. . . .

3. A young man is much affected by the expectations which his elders entertain of him. If they expect him to behave like a child, his lingering childishness will oftener rule his actions; if they expect him to behave like a man, his incipient manhood will oftener assert itself. The pretended parental or sham monastic régime of the common American college seems to me to bring out the childishness rather

than the manliness of the average student; as is evidenced by the pranks he plays, the secret societies in which he rejoices, and the barbarous or silly customs which he accepts and transmits. The conservative argument is: a college must deal with the student as he is; he will be what he has been, namely, a thoughtless, aimless, lazy, and possibly vicious boy; therefore a policy which gives him liberty is impracticable. The progressive argument is: adapt college policy to the best students, and not to the worst; improve the policy, and in time the evil fruits of a mistaken policy will disappear. I would only urge at this point that a far-seeing educational policy must be based upon potentialities as well as actualities, upon things which may be reasonably hoped for, planned, and aimed at, as well as upon things which are.

4. The condition of secondary education is an important factor in our problem. It is desirable that the young men who are to enjoy university freedom should have already received at school a substantial training, in which the four great subdivisions of elementary knowledge—languages, history, mathematics, and natural science—were all adequately represented; but it must be admitted that this desirable training is now given in very few schools, and that in many parts of the country there are not secondary schools enough of even tolerable quality. For this condition of secondary education the colleges are in part responsible; for they have produced few good teachers, except for the ancient languages; and they have required for admission to college hardly anything but the elements of Greek, Latin, and mathematics. But how should this condition of things affect the policy of an institution which sees its way to obtain a reasonable number of tolerably prepared students? Shall we stop trying to create a university because the condition of secondary education in the country at large is unsatisfactory? The difficulty with that policy of inaction is that the reform and development of secondary education depend upon the right organization and conduct of universities. It is the old problem: Which was first created, an egg or a hen? In considering the relation of college life to school life, many people are confused by a misleading metaphor—that of building. They say to themselves: on weak foundations no strong superstructure can be built; schools lay the foundations on which the university must build; therefore, if preparatory schools fail to do good work, no proper university work can subsequently be done. The analogy seems perfect, but has this fatal defect: education is a vital process, not a mechanical one. Let us, therefore, use an illustration drawn from a vital function, that of nutrition. A child has had poor

milk as an infant, and is not well developed; therefore, when its teeth are cut, and it is ready for bread, meat, and oatmeal, you are to hold back this substantial diet, and give it the sweetened milk and water, and Mellin's Food, which would have suited it when a baby. The mental food of a boy has not been as nourishing and abundant as it should have been at school; therefore when he goes to college or university his diet must be that which he should have had at school, but missed. Education involves growth or development from within in every part; and metaphors drawn from the process of laying one stone upon another are not useful in educational discussions. Harvard College now finds itself able to get nearly three hundred tolerably prepared students every year from one hundred or more schools and private tutors scattered over the country; and she is only just beginning to reap the fruit of the changes in her own policy and discipline which the past eighteen years have wrought. Schools follow universities, and will be what universities make them.

With these preliminary suggestions I proceed to answer the question, At what age can an American boy best go to a university where choice of studies is free? and to defend my answer. I believe the normal age under reasonably favorable conditions to be eighteen. In the first place, I hold that the temperament, physical constitution, mental aptitudes, and moral quality of a boy are all well determined by the time he is eighteen years old. The potential man is already revealed. His capacities and incapacities will be perfectly visible to his teacher, or to any observant and intimate friend, provided that his studies at school have been fairly representative. . . . The boy's future will depend greatly upon the influences, happy or unhappy, to which he is subjected; but given all favorable influences, his possibilities are essentially determined. The most fortunate intellectual influences will be within his reach, if he has liberty to choose the mental food which he can best assimilate. Secondly, at eighteen the American boy has passed the age when a compulsory external discipline is useful. Motives and inducements may be set vividly before him; he may be told that he must do so and so in order to win something which he desires or values; prizes and rewards near or remote may be held out to him; but he cannot be driven to any useful exercise of his mind. *Thirdly*, a well-instructed youth of eighteen can select for himself—not for any other boy, or for the fictitious universal boy, but for himself alone—a better course of study than any college faculty, or any wise man who does not know him and his ancestors and his previous life, can possibly select for him. In choosing his course he will naturally seek aid from teachers and friends who have intimate knowledge of him, and he will act under the dominion of that intense conservatism which fortunately actuates civilized man in the whole matter of education, and under various other safeguards which nature and not arbitrary regulation provides. When a young man whom I never saw before asks me what studies he had better take in college, I am quite helpless, until he tells me what he likes and what he dislikes to study, what kinds of exertion are pleasurable to him, what sports he cares for, what reading interests him, what his parents and grandparents were in the world, and what he means to be. In short, I can only show him how to think out the problem for himself with such lights as he has and nobody else can have. The proposition that a boy of eighteen can choose his own studies, with the natural helps, more satisfactorily than anybody else can choose them for him, seems at first sight absurd; but I believe it to be founded upon the nature of things, and it is also for me a clear result of observation. I will state first the argument from the nature of things, and then describe my own observations.

10    Every youth of eighteen is an infinitely complex organization, the duplicate of which neither does nor ever will exist. His inherited traits are different from those of every other human being; his environment has been different from that of every other child; his passions, emotions, hopes, and desires were never before associated in any other creature just as they are in him; and his will-force is aroused, stimulated, exerted, and exhausted in ways wholly his own. The infinite variety of form and feature, which we know human bodies to be capable of, presents but a faint image of the vastly deeper diversities of the minds and characters which are lodged in these unlike shells. To discern and take due account of these diversities no human insight or wisdom is sufficient, unless the spontaneous inclinations, natural preferences, and easiest habitual activities of each individual are given play. It is for the happiness of the individual and the benefit of society alike that these mental diversities should be cultivated, not suppressed. The individual enjoys most that intellectual labor for which he is most fit; and society is best served when every man's peculiar skill, faculty, or aptitude is developed and utilized to the highest possible degree. The presumption is, therefore, against uniformity in education, and in favor of diversity at the earliest possible moment.

What determines that moment? To my thinking, the limit of compulsory uniform instruction should be determined by the elementary quality and recognized universal utility of the subjects of such instruction. For instance, it is unquestionable that every child needs to know how to read, write, and, to a moderate extent, cipher. Therefore primary schools may have a uniform programme. One might naturally suppose that careful study of the mother-tongue and its literature would be considered a uniform need for all youth; but as a matter of fact there is no agreement to this effect. The English language and literature have hardly yet won a place for themselves in American schools. Only the elements of two foreign languages and the elements of algebra and geometry can be said to be generally recognized as indispensable to the proper training of all young people who are privileged to study beyond their seventeenth year. There is no consent as to the uniform desirableness of the elements of natural science, and there is much difference of opinion about the selection of the two foreign languages, the majority of educated people supposing two dead languages to be preferable, a minority thinking that living languages are permissible. The limit of that elementary knowledge, of which by common consent all persons who are to be highly educated stand in need, is therefore a narrow one, easily to be reached and passed, under respectable instruction, by any youth of fair ability before he is eighteen years old. There, at least, ceases justifiable uniformity in education. There, at least, election of studies should begin; and the safest guides to a wise choice will be the taste, inclination, and special capacity of each individual. When it comes to the choice of a profession, everybody knows that the only wisdom is to follow inclination. In my view, the only wisdom in determining those liberal studies which may be most profitably pursued after eighteen is to follow inclination. Hence it is only the individual youth who can select that course of study which will most profit him, because it will most interest him. The very fact of choice goes far to secure the cooperation of his will.

I give, in the next place, some results of my own observation upon the working of an elective system; and that you may have my credentials before you I will describe briefly my opportunities of observation. I had experience as an undergraduate of a college course almost wholly required; for I happened upon nearly the lowest stage to which the elective system in Harvard College ever fell, after its initiation in 1825. During the nine years from 1854 to 1863 I became intimately acquainted with the working of this mainly prescribed curriculum from the point of view of a tutor and assistant professor who had a liking for administrative details. After a separation from the University of six years, two of which were spent in Europe as a student and four at the Massachusetts Institute of Technology as a professor, I went back as president in 1869, to find a tolerably broad elective system already under way. The wishes of the governing boards and external circumstances all favoring it, the system was rapidly developed. . . . I have therefore had ample opportunity to observe at Harvard the working of almost complete prescription, of almost complete freedom, and of all intermediate methods. In Europe I studied the free university method; and at the Institute of Technology I saw the system—excellent for technical schools—of several well-defined courses branching from a common stock of uniformly prescribed studies.

The briefest form in which I can express the general result of my observation is this: I have never known a student of any capacity to select for himself a set of studies covering four years which did not apparently possess more theoretical and practical merit for his case than the required curriculum of my college days. Every prescribed curriculum is necessarily elementary from beginning to end, and very heterogeneous. Such is the press of subjects that no one subject can possibly be carried beyond its elements; no teacher, however learned and enthusiastic, can have any advanced pupils; and no scholar, however competent and eager, can make serious attainments in any single subject. Under an elective system the great majority of students use their liberty to pursue some subject or subjects with a reasonable degree of thoroughness. This concentration upon single lines develops advanced teaching, and results in a general raising of the level of instruction. . . .

Two common objections to an elective system shall next have our attention. The first is often put in the form of a query. Election of studies may be all very well for conscientious or ambitious students, or for those who have a strong taste for certain studies; but what becomes, under such a system, of the careless, indifferent, lazy boys who have no bent or intellectual ambition of any sort? I answer with a similar query: What became of such boys under the uniform compulsory system? Did they get any profit to speak of under that régime? Not within my observation. It really does not make much difference what these unawakened minds dawdle with. There is, however, much more chance that such young men will get roused from their lethargy under an elective system than under a required. When they follow such faint promptings of desire as they feel, they at least escape the sense of grievance and repugnance which an arbitrary assignment to certain teachers and certain studies often creates. An elective system does not mean liberty to do nothing.

15      Having said thus much about the effects of free choice of studies upon the unpromising student, I must add that the policy of an institution of education, of whatever grade, ought never to be determined by

the needs of the least capable students; and that a university should aim at meeting the wants of the best students at any rate, and the wants of inferior students only so far as it can meet them without impairing the privileges of the best. A uniform curriculum, by enacting superficiality and prohibiting thoroughness, distinctly sacrifices the best scholars to the average. Free choice of studies gives the young genius the fullest scope without impairing the chances of the drone and the dullard.

The second objection with which I wish to deal is this: free choice implies that there are no studies which are recognized as of supreme merit, so that every young man unquestionably ought to pursue them. Can this be? Is it possible that the accumulated wisdom of the race cannot prescribe with certainty the studies which will best develop the human mind in general between the ages of eighteen and twenty-two? At first it certainly seems strange that we have to answer no; but when we reflect how very brief the acquaintance of the race has been with the great majority of the subjects which are now taught in a university the negative answer seems less surprising. Out of the two hundred courses of instruction which stand on the list of Harvard University this year it would be difficult to select twenty which could have been given at the beginning of this century with the illustrations, materials, and methods now considered essential to the educational quality of the courses. One realizes more easily this absence of accumulated experience on considering that all the natural sciences, with comparative philology, political economy, and history, are practically new subjects, that all mathematics is new except the elements of arithmetic, algebra, and geometry, that the recent additions to ethics and metaphysics are of vast extent, and that the literatures of the eighteenth and nineteenth centuries have great importance in several European languages. The materials and methods of university education always have been, and always will be, changing from generation to generation. We think, perhaps with truth, that the nineteenth century has been a period of unprecedented growth and progress; but every century has probably witnessed an unprecedented advance in civilization, simply because the process is cumulative, if no catastrophes arrest it. It is one of the most important functions of universities to store up the accumulated knowledge of the race, and so to use these stores that each successive generation of youth shall start with all the advantages which their predecessors have won. Therefore a university, while not neglecting the ancient treasures of learning, has to keep a watchful eye upon the new fields of discovery, and has to invite its students to walk in new-made as well as in long-trodden paths. . . .

Before I leave the subject of election of studies, let me point out that there is not a university of competent resources upon the continent of Europe in which complete freedom of studies has not long prevailed; and that Oxford and Cambridge have recently provided an almost complete liberty for their students. In our own country respectable colleges now offer a considerable proportion of elective studies, and as a rule the greater their resources in teachers, collections, and money, the more liberal their application of the elective principle. Many colleges, however, still seem to have but a halting faith in the efficacy of the principle, and our educated public has but just begun to appreciate its importance. So fast as American institutions acquire the resources and powers of European universities, they will adopt the methods proper to universities wherever situate. At present our best colleges fall very far short of European standards in respect to number of teachers, and consequently in respect to amplitude of teaching.

As yet we have no university in America—only aspirants to that eminence. All the more important is it that we should understand the conditions under which a university can be developed—the most indispensable of which is freedom in choice of studies.

## Questions for Discussion

From our contemporary perspective, in what ways can Eliot's views be seen as antiquated? progressive?

Would you say that Eliot's ideas about education deny or build upon Emerson's?

*William Edward Burghardt DuBois (1868–1963) was determined to expedite the emancipation of African Americans throughout the first half of the twentieth century. Having received his education from Fisk (1885–1888) and from Harvard (where he received his Ph.D. in 1895), he launched a distinguished career as a social scientist, social critic, social reformer, and civil rights leader. He wrote many books, played a prominent role in the founding of the NAACP (in 1909), and for many years edited its magazine,* Crisis. *An advocate for black cultural nationalism, he ultimately renounced his American citizenship and moved to Ghana where he died August 27, 1963, within hours of the famous March on Washington.*

    *DuBois's theories brought him into conflict with the most influential African American working at the turn of the century, Booker T. Washington. Washington preached a policy of accommodation: He felt that African Americans could best achieve social and legal progress by gradually winning the respect of whites through hard work and personal virtue, and he founded Tuskegee Institute as a means of improving and extending vocational education. DuBois, by contrast, in his famous 1903 book* The Souls of Black Folk, *charged that Washington's approach would only perpetuate injustice. Later that year, in "The Talented Tenth," DuBois elaborated his position on higher education for African Americans. DuBois revisited the subject of "The Talented Tenth" throughout his career.*

## W. E. B. DuBois

# The Talented Tenth

The Negro race, like all races, is going to be saved by its exceptional men. The problem of education, then, among Negroes must first of all deal with the Talented Tenth: it is the problem of developing the Best of this race that they may guide the Mass away from the contamination and death of the Worst, in their own and other races. Now the training of men is a difficult and intricate task. Its technique is a matter for educational experts, but its object is for the vision of seers. If we make money the object of man-training, we shall develop money-makers but not necessarily men; if we make technical skill the object of education, we may possess artisans but not, in nature, men. Men we shall have only as we make manhood the object of the work of the schools—intelligence, broad sympathy, knowledge of the world that was and is, and of the relation of men to it—this is the curriculum of that Higher Education which must underlie true life. On this foundation we may build bread winning, skill of hand and quickness of brain, with never a fear lest the child and man mistake the means of living for the object of life.

If this be true—and who can deny it—three tasks lay before me: first to show from the past that the Talented Tenth as they have risen among American Negroes have been worthy of leadership; secondly to show how these men may be educated and developed; and thirdly to show their relation to the Negro problem.

You misjudge us because you do not know us. From the very first it has been the educated and intelligent of the Negro people that have led and elevated the mass, and the sole obstacles that nullified and retarded their efforts were slavery and race prejudice: for what is slavery but the legalized survival of the unfit and the nullification of the work of natural internal leadership? Negro leadership therefore sought from the first to rid the race of this awful incubus that it might make way for natural selection and the survival of the fittest. In colonial days came Phillis Wheatley and Paul Cuffe striving against the bars of prejudice; and Benjamin Banneker, the almanac maker, voiced their longings when he said to Thomas Jefferson, "I freely and cheerfully acknowledge that I am of the African race and in colour which is natural to them, of the deepest dye; and it is under a sense of the most profound gratitude to the Supreme Ruler of the Universe, that I now confess to you that I am not under that state of tyrannical thraldom and inhuman captivity to which too many of my brethren are doomed, but that I have abundantly tasted of the fruition of those blessings which proceed from that free and unequalled liberty with which you are favored."

Then came Dr. James Derham, who could tell even the learned Dr. Rush something of medicine, and Lemuel Haynes, to whom Middlebury College gave an honorary A. M. in 1804. These and others we may call the Revolutionary group of distinguished Negroes—they were persons of marked ability, leaders of a Talented Tenth, standing conspicuously among the best of their time. They strove by word and deed to save the color line from becoming the line between the bond and free, but all they could do was nullified by Eli Whitney and the Curse of Gold. So they passed into forgetfulness.

5      But their spirit did not wholly die; here and there in the early part of the century came other exceptional men. Some were natural sons of unnatural fathers and were given often a liberal training and thus a race of educated mulattoes sprang up to plead for black men's rights. There was Ira Aldridge, whom all Europe loved to honor; there was that Voice crying in the Wilderness, David Walker.

In 1831 there met that first Negro convention in Philadelphia, at which the world gaped curiously but which bravely attacked the problems of race and slavery, crying out against persecution and declaring that "Laws as cruel in themselves as they were unconstitutional and unjust, have in many places been enacted against our poor, unfriended and unoffending brethren (without a shadow of provocation on our part), at whose bare recital the very savage draws himself up for fear of contagion—looks noble and prides himself because he bears not the name of Christian." Side by side this free Negro movement, and the movement for abolition, strove until they merged in to one strong stream. Too little notice has been taken of the work which the Talented Tenth among Negroes took in the great abolition crusade. From the very day that a Philadelphia colored man became the first subscriber to Garrison's "Liberator," to the day when Negro soldiers made the Emancipation Proclamation possible, black leaders worked shoulder to shoulder with white men in a movement, the success of which would have been impossible without them. There was Purvis and Remond, Pennington and Highland Garnett, Sojourner Truth and Alexander Crummel, and above all, Frederick Douglass— what would the abolition movement have been without them? They stood as living examples of the possibilities of the Negro race, their own hard experiences and well wrought culture said silently more than all the drawn periods of orators—they were the men who made American slavery impossible.

And so we come to the present—a day of cowardice and vacillation, of strident wide-voiced wrong and faint hearted compromise; of double-faced dallying with Truth and Right. Who are today guiding the work of the Negro people? The "exceptions" of course. And yet so sure as this Talented Tenth is pointed out, the blind worshippers of the Average cry out in alarm: "These are exceptions, look here at death, disease and crime—these are the happy rule." Of course they are the rule, because a silly nation made them the rule: Because for three long centuries this people lynched Negroes who dared to be brave, raped black women who dared to be virtuous, crushed dark-hued youth who dared to be ambitious, and encouraged and made to flourish servility and lewdness and apathy. But not even this was able to crush all manhood and chastity and aspiration from black folk. A saving remnant continually survives and persists, continually aspires, continually shows itself in thrift and ability and character. Exceptional it is to be sure, but this is its chiefest promise; it shows the capability of Negro blood, the promise of black men. Do Americans ever stop to reflect that there are in this land a million men of Negro blood, well-educated, owners of homes, against the honor of whose womanhood no breath was ever raised, whose men occupy positions of trust and usefulness, and who, judged by any standard, have reached the full measure of the best type of modern European culture? Is it fair, is it decent, is it Christian to ignore these facts of the Negro problem, to belittle such aspiration, to nullify such leadership and seek to crush these people back into the mass out of which by toil and travail, they and their fathers have raised themselves?

Can the masses of the Negro people be in any possible way more quickly raised than by the effort and example of this aristocracy of talent and character? Was there ever a nation on God's fair earth civilized from the bottom upward? Never; it is, ever was and ever will be from the top downward that culture filters. The Talented Tenth rises and pulls all that are worth the saving up to their vantage ground. This is the history of human progress; and the two historic mistakes which have hindered that progress were the thinking first that no more could ever rise save the few already risen: or second, that it would better the unrisen to pull the risen down.

How then shall the leaders of a struggling people be trained and the hands of the risen few strengthened? There can be but one answer: The best and most capable of their youth must be schooled in the colleges and universities of the land. We will not quarrel as to just what the university of the Negro should teach or how it should teach it—I willingly admit that each soul and each race-soul needs its own peculiar curriculum. But this is true: A university is a human invention for the transmission of knowledge and culture from generation to generation, through the training of quick minds and pure hearts, and for this work no other human invention will suffice, not even trade and industrial schools.

10    All men cannot go to college but some men must; every isolated group or nation must have its yeast, must have for the talented few centers of training where men are not so mystified and befuddled by the hard and necessary toil of earning a living, as to have no aims higher than their bellies, and no God greater than Gold. This is true training, and thus in the beginning were the favored sons of the freedmen trained. Out of the colleges of the North came, after the blood of war, Ware, Cravath, Chase, Andrews, Bumstead and Spence to build the foundations of knowledge and civilization in the black South. Where ought they to have begun to build? At the bottom, of course, quibbles the mole with his eyes in the earth. Aye! truly at the bottom, at the very bottom; at the bottom of knowledge, down in the very depths of knowledge there where the roots of justice strike into the lowest soil of Truth. And so they did begin; they founded colleges, and up from the colleges shot normal schools, and out from the normal schools went teachers, and around the normal teachers clustered other teachers to teach the public schools; the college trained in Greek and Latin and mathematics, 2,000 men; and these men trained full 50,000 others in morals and manners, and they in turn taught thrift and the alphabet to nine millions of men, who today hold $300,000,000 of property. It was a miracle—the most wonderful peace-battle of the 19th century, and yet today men smile at it, and in fine superiority tell us that it was all a strange mistake; that a proper way to found a system of education is first to gather the children and buy them spelling books and hoes; afterward men may look about for teachers, if haply they may find them; or again they would teach men Work, but as for Life—why, what has Work to do with Life, they ask vacantly.

Was the work of these college founders successful; did it stand the test of time? Did the college graduates, with all their fine theories of life, really live? Are they useful men helping to civilize and elevate their less fortunate fellows? Let us see. Omitting all institutions which have not actually graduated students from a college course, there are today in the United States thirty-four institutions giving something above high school training to Negroes and designed especially for this race.

Three of these were established in border States before the War; thirteen were planted by the Freedmen's Bureau in the years 1864–1869; nine were established between 1870 and 1880 by various church bodies: five were established after 1881 by Negro churches; and four are state institutions supported by United States' agricultural funds. In most cases the college departments are small adjuncts to high and common schoolwork. As a matter of fact six institutions— Atlanta, Fisk, Howard, Shaw, Wilberforce and Leland—are the important Negro colleges so far as actual work and number of students are concerned. In all these institutions, seven hundred and fifty Negro college students are enrolled. In grade the best of these colleges are about a year behind the smaller New England colleges and a typical curriculum is that of Atlanta University. Here students from the grammar grades, after a three years' high school course, take a college course of 136 weeks. One-fourth of this time is given to Latin and Greek; one-fifth, to English and modern languages; one-sixth, to history and social science; one-seventh, to natural science; one-eighth to mathematics; and one-eighth to philosophy and pedagogy.

In addition to these students in the South, Negroes have attended Northern colleges for many years. As early as 1826 one was graduated from Bowdoin College, and from that time till today nearly every year has seen elsewhere, other such graduates. They have, of course, met much color prejudice. Fifty years ago very few colleges would admit them at all. Even today no Negro has ever been admitted to Princeton, and at some other leading institutions they are rather endured than encouraged. Oberlin was the great pioneer in the work of blotting out the color line in colleges, and has more Negro graduates by far than any other Northern college.

The total number of Negro college graduates up to 1899 (several of the graduates of that year not being reported), was as follows:

|  | Negro Colleges | White Colleges |
|---|---|---|
| Before '76 | 137 | 75 |
| '75–80 | 143 | 22 |
| '80–85 | 250 | 31 |
| '85–90 | 413 | 43 |
| '90–95 | 465 | 66 |
| '95–99 | 475 | 88 |
| Class Unknown | 57 | 64 |
| *Total* | 1,914 | 390 |

15   Of these graduates 2,079 were men and 252 were women; 50 per cent of Northern-born college men come South to work among the

masses of their people, at a sacrifice which few people realize; nearly 90 per cent of the Southern-born graduates instead of seeking that personal freedom and broader intellectual atmosphere which their training has led them, in some degree, to conceive, stay and labor and wait in the midst of their black neighbors and relatives.

The most interesting question, and in many respects the crucial question, to be asked concerning college-bred Negroes, is: Do they earn a living? It has been intimated more than once that the higher training of Negroes has resulted in sending into the world of work, men who could find nothing to do suitable to their talents. Now and then there comes a rumor of a colored college man working at menial service, etc. Fortunately, returns as to occupations of college-bred Negroes, gathered by the Atlanta conference, are quite full—nearly sixty per cent of the total number of graduates.

This enables us to reach fairly certain conclusions as to the occupations of all college-bred Negroes. Of 1,312 persons reported, there were:

701 Teachers:
    Presidents and Deans, 19
    Teacher of Music, 7
    Professors, Principals and Teachers, 675
221 Clergymen:
    Bishop, 1
    Chaplains U.S. Army, 2
    Missionaries, 9
    Presiding Elders, 12
    Preachers, 197
83 Physicians:
    Doctors of Medicine, 76
    Druggists, 4
    Dentists, 3
74 Students
62 Lawyers
53 in Civil Service:
    U.S. Minister Plenipotentiary, 1
    U.S. Consul, 1
    U.S. Deputy Collector, 1
    U.S. Gauger, 1
    U.S. Postmasters, 2

U.S. Clerks, 44
State Civil Service, 2
City Civil Service, 1
47 Business Men:
   Merchants, etc., 30
   Managers, 13
   Real Estate Dealers, 4
26 Farmers
22 Clerks and Secretaries:
   Secretary of National Societies, 7
   Clerks, etc., 15
9 Artisans
9 Editors
5 Miscellaneous

These figures illustrate vividly the function of the college-bred Negro. He is, as he ought to be, the group leader, the man who sets the ideals of the community where he lives, directs its thoughts and heads its social movements. It need hardly be argued that the Negro people need social leadership more than most groups; that they have no traditions to fall back upon, no long established customs, no strong family ties, no well defined social classes. All these things must be slowly and painfully evolved. The preacher was, even before the war, the group leader of the Negroes, and the church their greatest social institution. Naturally this preacher was ignorant and often immoral, and the problem of replacing the older type by better educated men has been a difficult one. Both by direct work and by direct influence on other preachers, and on congregations, the college-bred preacher has an opportunity for reformatory work and moral inspiration, the value of which cannot be overestimated.

It has, however, been in the furnishing of teachers that the Negro college has found its peculiar function. Few persons realize how vast a work, how mighty a revolution has been thus accomplished. To furnish five millions and more of ignorant people with teachers of their own race and blood, in one generation, was not only a very difficult undertaking, but a very important one, in that it placed before the eyes of almost every Negro child an attainable ideal. It brought the masses of the blacks in contact with modern civilization, made black men the leaders of their communities and trainers of the new generation. In this work college-bred Negroes were first teachers, and then teachers of teachers. And here it is that the broad culture of college work has been of peculiar value. Knowledge of life and its wider meaning, has been the point of the Negro's deepest ignorance, and the sending out of teachers whose training has not been simply for bread winning, but also for human culture, has been of inestimable value in the training of these men.

20      In earlier years the two occupations of preacher and teacher were practically the only ones open to the black college graduate. Of later years a larger diversity of life among his people, has opened new avenues of employment. Nor have these college men been paupers and spendthrifts: 557 college-bred Negroes owned in 1899, $1,342,862.50 worth of real estate (assessed value), or $2,411 per family. The real value of the total accumulations of the whole group is perhaps about $10,000,000, or $5,000 a piece. Pitiful is it not beside the fortunes of oil kings and steel trusts, but after all is the fortune of the millionaire the only stamp of true and successful living? Alas! it is, with many and there's the rub.

     The problem of training the Negro is today immensely complicated by the fact that the whole question of the efficiency and appropriateness of our present systems of education, for any kind of child, is a matter of active debate, in which final settlement seems still afar off. Consequently it often happens that persons arguing for or against certain systems of education for Negroes, have these controversies in mind and miss the real question at issue. The main question, so far as the Southern Negro is concerned, is: What under the present circumstance, must a system of education do in order to raise the Negro as quickly as possible in the scale of civilization? The answer to this question seems to me clear: It must strengthen the Negro's character, increase his knowledge and teach him to earn a living. Now it goes without saying that it is hard to do all these things simultaneously or suddenly and that at the same time it will not do to give all the attention to one and neglect the others: we could give black boys trades, but that alone will not civilize a race of ex-slaves; we might simply increase their knowledge of the world, but this would not necessarily make them wish to use this knowledge honestly; we might seek to strengthen character and purpose, but to what end if this people have nothing to eat or to wear? A system of education is not one thing, nor does it have a single definite object, nor is it a mere matter of schools. Education is that whole system of human training within and without the school house walls, which molds and develops men. If then we start out to train an ignorant and unskilled people with a heritage of bad habits, our system of training must set before itself two great aims—the one dealing with knowledge and character, the other part seeking to give the child the technical knowledge necessary for him to earn a living under the present circumstances. These objects are accomplished in part by the opening of the common schools on the one hand, and of the industrial schools on the other. But only in part, for there must also be trained those who are to teach these schools—men and women of knowledge and culture and technical skill who understand modern civilization, and have the training and aptitude to impart it to the children under them. There must be teachers, and teachers of teachers, and to attempt to establish any sort of a system of common and industrial school training, without *first* (and I say *first* advisedly) without *first* providing for the higher training of the very best teachers, is simply throwing your money to the winds. School houses do not teach themselves—piles of brick and mortar and machinery do not send out *men*. It is the trained, living human soul, cultivated and strengthened by long study and thought, that breathes the real breath of life into boys and girls and makes them human, whether they be black or white, Greek, Russian or American. Nothing, in these latter days, has so dampened the faith of thinking Negroes in recent educational movements, as the fact that such movements have been accompanied by ridicule and denouncement and decrying of those very institutions of higher training which made the Negro public school possible, and make Negro industrial schools thinkable. It was Fisk, Atlanta, Howard and Straight, those colleges born of the faith and sacrifice of the abolitionist, that placed in the black schools of the South the 30,000 teachers and more, which some, who depreciate the work of these higher schools, are using to teach their own new experiments. If Hampton, Tuskegee and the hundred other industrial schools prove in the future to be as successful as they deserve to be, then their success in training black artisans for the South will be due primarily to the white colleges of the North and the black colleges of the South, which trained the teachers who today conduct these institutions. There was a time when the American people believed pretty devoutly that a log of wood with a boy at one end and Mark Hopkins at the other represented the highest ideal of human training. But in these eager days it would seem that we have changed all that and think it necessary to add a couple of saw-mills and a hammer to this outfit, and, at a pinch, to dispense with the services of Mark Hopkins.

I would not deny, or for a moment seem to deny, the paramount necessity of teaching the Negro to work, and to work steadily and skillfully; or seem to depreciate in the slightest degree the important part industrial schools must play in the accomplishment of these ends, but I *do* say, and insist upon it, that it is industrialism drunk with its vision of success, to imagine that its own work can be accomplished without providing for the training of broadly cultured men and women to teach its own teachers, and to teach the teachers of the public schools.

But I have already said that human education is not simply a matter of schools; it is much more a matter of family and group life—the training of one's home, of one's daily companions, of one's social class. Now the black boy of the South moves in a black world—a world with its own leaders, its own thoughts, its own ideals. In this world he gets by far the larger part of his life training, and through the eyes of this dark world he peers into the veiled world beyond. Who guides and determines the education which he receives in his world? His teachers here are the group-leaders of the Negro people—the physicians and clergymen, the trained fathers and mothers, the influential and forceful men about him of all kinds; here it is, if at all, that the culture of the surrounding world trickles through and is handed on by the graduates of the higher schools. Can such culture training of group leaders be neglected? Can we afford to ignore it? Do you think that if the leaders of thought among Negroes are not trained and educated thinkers, that they will have no leaders? On the contrary a hundred half-trained demagogues will still hold the places they so largely occupy now, and hundreds of vociferous busy-bodies will multiply. You have no choice; either you must help furnish this race from within its own ranks with thoughtful men of trained leadership, or you must suffer the evil consequences of a headless misguided rabble.

I am an earnest advocate of manual training and trade teaching for black boys, and for white boys, too. I believe that next to the founding of Negro colleges the most valuable addition to Negro education since the war, has been industrial training for black boys. Nevertheless, I insist that the object of all true education is not to make men carpenters, it is to make carpenters men; there are two means of making the carpenter a man, each equally important: the first is to give the group and community in which he works, liberally trained teachers and leaders to teach him and his family what life means; the second is to give him sufficient intelligence and technical skill to make him an efficient workman. The first object demands the Negro college and college-bred men—not a quantity of such colleges, but a few of excellent quality; not too many college-bred men, but enough to leaven the lump, to inspire the masses, to raise the

Talented Tenth to leadership. The second object demands a good system of common schools, well-taught, conveniently located and properly equipped.

25    What is the chief need for the building up of the Negro public school in the South? The Negro race in the South needs teachers to-day above all else. This is the concurrent testimony of all who know the situation. For the supply of this great demand two things are needed—institutions of higher education and money for school houses and salaries. It is usually assumed that a hundred or more institutions for Negro training are today turning out so many teachers and college-bred men that the race is threatened with an over-supply. This is sheer nonsense. There are today less than 3,000 living Negro college graduates in the United States, and less than 1,000 Negroes in college. Moreover, in the 164 schools for Negroes, 95 per cent of their students are doing elementary and secondary work, work which should be done in the public schools. Over half the remaining 2,157 students are taking high school studies. The mass of so-called "normal" schools for the Negro are simply doing elementary common school work, or, at most, high school work, with a little instruction in methods. The Negro colleges and the post-graduate courses at other institutions are the only agencies for the broader and more careful training of teachers. The work of these institutions is hampered for lack of funds. It is getting increasingly difficult to get funds for training teachers in the best modern methods, and yet all over the South, from State Superintendents, county officials, city boards and school principals comes the wail, "We need TEACHERS!" and teachers must be trained. As the fairest minded of all white Southerners, Atticus G. Haygood, once said: "The defects of colored teachers are so great as to create an urgent necessity for training better ones. Their excellencies and their successes are sufficient to justify the best hopes of success in the effort, and to vindicate the judgment of those who make large investments of money and service to give to colored students opportunity for thoroughly preparing themselves for the work of teaching children of their people."

The truth of this has been strikingly shown in the marked improvement of white teachers in the South. Twenty years ago the rank and file of white public school teachers were not as good as the Negro teachers. But they, by scholarships and good salaries, have been encouraged to thorough normal and collegiate preparation, while the Negro teachers have been discouraged by starvation wages and the idea that any training will do for a black teacher. If carpenters are needed it is well and good to train men as carpenters. But to train men as carpenters, and then set them to teaching is wasteful and criminal; and to train men as teachers and then refuse them living wages, unless they become carpenters, is rank nonsense.

The United States Commissioner of Education says in his report for 1900: "For comparison between the white and colored enrollment in secondary and higher education, I have added together the enrollment in high schools and secondary schools, with the attendance on colleges and universities, not being sure of the actual grade of work done in the colleges and universities. The work done in the secondary schools is reported in such detail in this office, that there can be no doubt of its grade."

He then makes the following comparisons of persons in every million enrolled in secondary and higher education:

|  | **Whole Country** | **Negroes** |
|---|---|---|
| 1880 | 4,362 | 1,289 |
| 1900 | 10,743 | 2,061 |

And he concludes: "While the number in colored high schools and colleges had increased somewhat faster than the population, it had not kept pace with the average of the whole country, for it had fallen from 30 per cent to 24 per cent of the average quota. Of all colored pupils, one (1) in one hundred was engaged in secondary and higher work, and that ratio has continued substantially for the past twenty years. If the ratio of colored population in secondary and higher education is to be equal to the average for the whole country, it must be increased to five times its present average." And if this be true of the secondary and higher education, it is safe to say that the Negro has not one-tenth his quota in college studies. How baseless, therefore, is the charge of too much training! We need Negro teachers for the Negro common schools, and we need first-class normal schools and colleges to train them. This is the work of higher Negro education and it must be done.

Further than this, after being provided with group leaders of civilization, and a foundation of intelligence in the public schools, the carpenter, in order to be a man, needs technical skill. This calls for trade schools. Now trade schools are not nearly such simple things as people once thought. The original idea was that the "Industrial" school was to furnish education, practically free, to those willing to work for it: it was to "do" things—i.e.: become a center of productive industry, it was to be partially, if not wholly, self-supporting, and it was to teach trades. Admirable as were some of the ideas underlying this scheme, the whole thing simply would not work in practice; it was found that if you were to use time and material to teach trades thoroughly, you could not at the same time keep the industries on a commercial basis and make them pay. Many schools started out to do this on a large scale and went into virtual bankruptcy. Moreover, it was found also that it was possible to teach a boy a trade mechanically, without giving him the full educative benefit of the process, and, vice versa, that there was a distinctive educative value in teaching a boy to use his hands and eyes in carrying out certain physical processes, even though he did not actually learn a trade. It has happened, therefore, in the last decade, that a noticeable change has come over the industrial schools. In the first place the idea of commercially remunerative industry in a school is being pushed rapidly to the background. There are still schools with shops and farms that bring an income, and schools that use student labor partially for the erection of their buildings and the furnishing of equipment. It is coming to be seen, however, in the education of the Negro, as clearly as it has been seen in the education of the youths the world over, that it is the *boy* and not the material product, that is the true object of education. Consequently the object of the industrial school came to be the thorough training of boys regardless of the cost of the training, so long as it was thoroughly well done.

30    Even at this point, however, the difficulties were not surmounted. In the first place modern industry has taken great strides since the war, and the teaching of trades is no longer a simple matter. Machinery and long processes of work have greatly changed the work of the carpenter, the ironworker and the shoemaker. A really efficient workman must be today an intelligent man who has had good technical training in addition to thorough common school, and perhaps even higher training. To meet this situation the industrial schools began a further development; they established distinct Trade Schools for the thorough training of better class artisans, and at the same time they sought to preserve for the purposes of general education, such of the simpler processes of elementary trade learning as were best suited therefor. In this differentiation of the Trade School and manual training, the best of the industrial schools simply followed the plain trend of the present educational epoch. A prominent educator tells us that, in Sweden, "In the beginning the economic conception was generally adopted, and everywhere manual training was looked upon as a means of preparing the children of the common people to earn their living. But gradually it came to be recognized that manual training has a more elevated purpose, and one, indeed, more useful in the deeper meaning of the term. It came to be considered as an educative process

for the complete moral, physical and intellectual development of the child."

Thus, again, in the manning of trade schools and manual training schools we are thrown back upon the higher training as its source and chief support. There was a time when any aged and wornout carpenter could teach in a trade school. But not so today. Indeed the demand for college-bred men by a school like Tuskegee, ought to make Mr. Booker T. Washington the firmest friend of higher training. Here he has as helpers the son of a Negro senator, trained in Greek and the humanities and graduated at Harvard; the son of a Negro congressman and lawyer, trained in Latin and mathematics, and graduated at Oberlin; he has as his wife, a woman who read Virgil and Homer in the same class room with me; he has as college chaplain, a classical graduate of Atlanta University; as teacher of science, a graduate of Fisk; as teacher of history, a graduate of Smith,—indeed some thirty of his chief teachers are college graduates, and instead of studying French grammars in the midst of weeds, or buying pianos for dirty cabins, they are at Mr. Washington's right hand helping him in a noble work. And yet one of the effects of Mr. Washington's propaganda has been to throw doubt upon the expediency of such training for Negroes, as these persons have had.

Men of America, the problem is plain before you. Here is a race transplanted through the criminal foolishness of your fathers. Whether you like it or not the millions are here, and here they will remain. If you do not lift them up, they will pull you down. Education and work are the levers to uplift a people. Work alone will not do it unless inspired by the right ideals and guided by intelligence. Education must not simply teach work—it must teach Life. The Talented Tenth of the Negro race must be made leaders of thought and missionaries of culture among their people. No others can do this work and Negro colleges must train men for it. The Negro race, like all other races, is going to be saved by its exceptional men.

## Questions for Discussion

Why does DuBois focus on technical skills and on money making as problems? Do you agree with him?

Is the concept of "the talented tenth" an elitist concept or not?

*Elwyn Brooks White (1899–1985), who contributed regularly to* The
New Yorker *and whose work has been collected into several books, was
perhaps America's most popular essayist. Widely regarded as a master
stylist, White won many awards for his lifetime of writing, which included
numerous books, volumes of poetry, and published criticism on social and
political issues. Younger readers may be most familiar with his classic
children's books* Stuart Little *(1945) and* Charlotte's Web *(1952). First
published in* Harper's *in 1939 and collected later in White's* One Man's
Meat, *the following comparison of two educational philosophies remains
relevant over half a century later.*

# E. B. White

## Education

I have an increasing admiration for the teacher in the country school
where we have a third-grade scholar in attendance. She not only un-
dertakes to instruct her charges in all the subjects of the first three
grades, but she manages to function quietly and effectively as a
guardian of their health, their clothes, their habits, their mothers, and
their snowball engagements. She has been doing this sort of Augean
task for twenty years, and is both kind and wise. She cooks for the
children on the stove that heats the room, and she can cool their passions or warm their soup with equal competence. She conceives their
costumes, cleans up their messes, and shares their confidences. My boy
already regards his teacher as his great friend, and I think tells her a
great deal more than he tells us.

The shift from city school to country school was something we
worried about quietly all last summer. I have always rather favored
public school over private school, if only because in public school you
meet a greater variety of children. This bias of mine, I suspect, is
partly an attempt to justify my own past (I never knew anything but
public schools) and partly an involuntary defense against getting
kicked in the shins by a young ceramist on his way to the kiln. My wife
was unacquainted with public schools, never having been exposed (in
her early life) to anything more public than the washroom of Miss
Winsor's. Regardless of our backgrounds, we both knew that the
change in schools was something that concerned not us but the scholar
himself. We hoped it would work out all right. In New York our son
went to a medium-priced private institution with semi-progressive

ideas of education, and modern plumbing. He learned fast, kept well, and we were satisfied. It was an electric, colorful, regimented existence with moments of pleasurable pause and giddy incident. The day the Christmas angel fainted and had to be carried out by one of the Wise Men was educational in the highest sense of the term. Our scholar gave imitations of it around the house for weeks afterward, and I doubt if it ever goes completely out of his mind.

His days were rich in formal experience. Wearing overalls and an old sweater (the accepted uniform of the private seminary), he sallied forth at morn accompanied by a nurse or a parent and walked (or was pulled) two blocks to a corner where the school bus made a flag stop. This flashy vehicle was as punctual as death: seeing us waiting at the cold curb, it would sweep to a halt, open its mouth, suck the boy in, and spring away with an angry growl. It was a good deal like a train picking up a bag of mail. At school the scholar was worked on for six or seven hours by half a dozen teachers and a nurse, and was revived on orange juice in mid-morning. In a cinder court he played games supervised by an athletic instructor, and in a cafeteria he ate lunch worked out by a dietitian. He soon learned to read with gratifying facility and discernment and to make Indian weapons of a semi-deadly nature. Whenever one of his classmates fell low of a fever the news was put on the wires and there were breathless phone calls to physicians, discussing periods of incubation and allied magic.

In the country all one can say is that the situation is different, and somehow more casual. Dressed in corduroys, sweatshirt, and short rubber boots, and carrying a tin dinner pail, our scholar departs at the crack of dawn for the village school, two and a half miles down the road, next to the cemetery. When the road is open and the car will start, he makes the journey by motor, courtesy of his old man. When the snow is deep or the motor is dead or both, he makes it on the hoof. In the afternoons he walks or hitches all or part of the way home in fair weather, gets transported in foul. The schoolhouse is a two-room frame building, bungalow type, shingles stained a burnt brown with weather-resistant stain. It has a chemical toilet in the basement and two teachers above the stairs. One takes the first three grades, the other the fourth, fifth, and sixth. They have little or no time for individual instruction, and no time at all for the esoteric. They teach what they know themselves, just as fast and as hard as they can manage. The pupils sit still at their desks in class, and do their milling around outdoors during recess.

5     There is no supervised play. They play cops and robbers (only they call it "Jail") and throw things at one another—snowballs in winter, rose hips in fall. It seems to satisfy them. They also construct darts, pinwheels, and "pick-up-sticks" (jackstraws), and the school itself does a brisk trade in penny candy, which is for sale right in the classroom and which contains "surprises." The most highly prized surprise is a fake cigarette, made of cardboard, fiendishly lifelike.

The memory of how apprehensive we were at the beginning is still strong. The boy was nervous about the change too. The tension, on that first fair morning in September when we drove him to school, almost blew the windows out of the sedan. And when later we picked him up on the road, wandering along with his little blue lunch-pail, and got his laconic report "All right" in answer to our inquiry about how the day had gone, our relief was vast. Now, after almost a year of it, the only difference we can discover in the two school experiences is that in the country he sleeps better at night—and *that* probably is more the air than the education. When grilled on the subject of school-in-country vs. school-in-city, he replied that the chief difference is that the day seems to go so much quicker in the country. "Just like lightning," he reported.

## Questions for Discussion

Does White simply compare the two kinds of schools, or does the comparison argue in favor of one of them?

What form of evidence does White favor in this piece? How effective is it?

*The following essay was published in the* Los Angeles Times *in October
1991; it amounts to an excerpt from Kozol's polemical book* Savage
Inequalities: Children in America's Schools, *published in the same year.
An activist, educational reformer, and social critic, Jonathan Kozol lost
his first teaching job when he read a Langston Hughes poem to his class
in 1967.* Death at an Early Age, *an account of his first year teaching that
won the National Book Award in 1968, dramatically described the terrible conditions that he found in schools in poor neighborhoods.* Savage
Inequalities *emerged from his visits twenty-five years later to similar
schools in places like Camden, New Jersey; Bronx, New York; East St.
Louis, Illinois; and Washington, D.C.—and from his conviction that the
gap between schools for the rich and those for the poor in the United
States has only been widening, not narrowing.*

## *Jonathan Kozol*

# A Tale of Two Schools: How Poor Children Are Lost to the World

New Trier's physical setting might well make the students of Du Sable
High School envious. The Chicago suburb school is, says a student, "a
maple land of beauty and civility." While Du Sable is sited on one
crowded Chicago city block, New Trier students have the use of 27
acres. While Du Sable's science students have to settle for makeshift
equipment, New Trier's students have superior labs and up-to-date
technology. One wing of the school, a physical-education center that
includes three separate gyms, also contains a fencing room, a wrestling
room and studios for dance instruction. In all, the school has seven
gyms as well as an Olympic pool.

"This is a school with a lot of choices," says one student at New
Trier; and this hardly seems an overstatement if one studies the curriculum. Courses in music, art and drama are so varied and abundant
that students can virtually major in these subjects in addition to their
academic programs. The modern and classical language department
offers Latin and six other foreign languages. In a senior literature class,
students are reading Nietzsche, Darwin, Plato, Freud and Goethe.

Average class size is 24 children; classes for slower learners hold 15.

The wealth of New Trier's geographical district provides $340,000 worth of taxable property for each child; Chicago's property wealth affords only one-fifth this much. Nonetheless, *Town and Country*, which profiled the school, gives New Trier's parents credit for a "willingness to pay enough . . . in taxes" to make this one of the state's best-funded schools. New Trier, according to the magazine, is "a striking example of what is possible when citizens want to achieve the best for their children." Families move here "seeking the best," and their children "make good use" of what they're given. Both statements may be true, but *Town and Country* flatters the privileged for having privilege but terms it aspiration.

5      "Competition is the lifeblood of New Trier," *Town and Country* writes. But there is one kind of competition that these children will not need to face. They will not compete against the children who attended Du Sable.

Conditions at Du Sable High School, which I visited in 1990, seem in certain ways to be improved. Improvement, however, is a relative term. Du Sable is better than it was three or four years ago. It is still a school that would be shunned—or, probably, shut down—if it were serving a white middle-class community. The building, a three-story Tudor structure, is in fairly good repair and, in this respect, contrasts with its immediate surroundings, which are almost indescribably despairing. The school, whose student population is 100% black, has no campus and no schoolyard, but there is at least a full-sized playing field and track. Overcrowding is not a problem. Much to the reverse, it is uncomfortably empty. Built in 1935 and holding some 4,500 students in past years, its student population is now fewer than 1,600. Of these students, according to data provided by the school, 646 are "chronic truants."

The graduation rate is 25%. Of those who get to senior year, only 17% are in a college-preparation program. Twenty percent are in the general curriculum, a stunning 63% in vocational classes.

A vivid sense of loss is felt by standing in the cafeteria in early spring, when students file in to choose their courses for the following year. "These are the ninth graders," says a supervising teacher; but, of the official freshman class of some 600 children, only 350 fill the room. An hour later the 11th graders come to choose their classes: I count at most 170 students.

The faculty includes some excellent teachers, but there are others, says the principal, who don't belong in education. "I can't do anything with them but I'm not allowed to fire them," he says.

10   In a 12th-grade English class, the students are learning to pronounce a list of words. The words are not derived from any context; they are simply written on a list. A tall boy struggles to read "fastidious," "gregarious," "auspicious," "fatuous." When he struggles to pronounce "egregious," I ask him if he knows its meaning. It turns out that he has no idea. The teacher never asks the children to write the words or use them in a sentence. The lesson baffles me. It may be that these are words that will appear on a required test that states impose now in the name of "raising standards," but it all seems dreamlike and surreal.

After lunch, I talk with a group of students who are hoping to go on to college but do not seem sure of what they'll need to do to make this possible. Only one out of five seniors in the group has filed an application, and it is already April. Pamela, the one who did apply, however, tells me she neglected to submit her grades and college-entrance test results and therefore has to start again. The courses she is taking seem to rule out application to a four-year college. She tells me she is taking Spanish, literature, physical education, Afro-American history and a class she terms "job strategy." When I ask her what this is, she says, "It teaches how to dress and be on time and figure your deductions." She's a bright, articulate student, and it seems quite sad that she has not had any of the richness of curriculum that would have been given to her at a high school like New Trier.

The children in the group seem not just lacking in important, useful information that would help them to achieve their dreams, but, in a far more drastic sense, cut off and disconnected from the outside world. In talking of some recent news events, they speak of Moscow and Berlin, but all but Pamela are unaware that Moscow is the capital of the Soviet Union or that Berlin is in Germany. Several believe that Jesse Jackson is the mayor of New York City. Listening to their guesses and observing their confusion, I am thinking of the students at New Trier High. These children live in truly separate worlds. What do they have in common? Yet the kids before me seem so innocent and spiritually clean and also—most of all—so vulnerable. It's as if they have been stripped of all the armament—the reference points, the facts, the reasoning, the elemental weapons—that suburban children take for granted.

"It took an extraordinary combination of greed, racism, political cowardice and public apathy," writes James D. Squires, the former editor of the *Chicago Tribune*, "to let the public schools in Chicago get so bad." He speaks of the schools as a costly result of "the political orphaning of the urban poor . . . daytime warehouses for inferior students . . . a bottomless pit."

The results of these conditions are observed in thousands of low-income children in Chicago, who are virtually disjoined from the worldview, even from the basic reference points, of the American experience. A 16-year-old girl who has dropped out discusses her economic prospects with a TV interviewer.

15      "How much money would you like to make in a year?" asks the reporter.

"About $2,000," she replies.

The reporter looks bewildered by this answer. This teenage girl, he says, "has no clue that $2,000 a year isn't enough to survive anywhere in America, not even in her world."

## Questions for Discussion

Does Kozol's argument make use of primarily logical or emotional evidence?

How important a role does Kozol's description of the students play in the argument?

*Benjamin R. Barber is the Gershon and Carrol Kekst Professor of Civil
Society at the University of Maryland. He has written numerous scholarly and popular books which consistently explore the issues of politics,
education, democracy, community, and citizenship. He regularly contributes to the* Atlantic Monthly, *the* New York Times, *and* Harper's,
*where the following argument appeared in 1993. An educational and
political progressive, in the traditional sense of the term, Barber's main
concern is with sustaining a healthy democracy. His best known book is*
An Aristocracy of Everyone, *in which he argues for fundamental changes
in the ways Americans view the role of education in sustaining political
and social life.*

# Benjamin R. Barber

# America Skips School

On September 8, the day most of the nation's children were scheduled
to return to school, the Department of Education Statistics issued a report, commissioned by Congress, on adult literacy and numeracy in
the United States. The results? More than 90 million adult Americans
lacked simple literacy. Fewer than 20 percent of those surveyed could
compare two metaphors in a poem; not 4 percent could calculate the
cost of carpeting at a given price for a room of a given size, using a cal-
culator. As the DOE report was being issued, as if to echo its findings,
two of the nation's largest school systems had delayed their openings:
in New York, to remove asbestos from aging buildings; in Chicago, because of a battle over the budget.

Inspired by the report and the delays, pundits once again began
chanting the familiar litany of the education crisis. We've heard it all
many times before: 130,000 children bring guns along with their pen-
cils and books to school each morning; juvenile arrests for murder increased by 85 percent from 1987 to 1991; more than 3,000 youngsters
will drop out today and every day for the rest of the school year, until
about 600,000 are lost by June—in many urban schools, perhaps half
the enrollment. A lot of the dropouts will end up in prison, which is a
surer bet for young black males than college: one in four will pass
through the correctional system, and at least two out of three of those
will be dropouts.

In quiet counterpoint to those staggering facts is another set of statistics: teachers make less than accountants, architects, doctors, lawyers, engineers, judges, health professionals, auditors, and surveyors. They can earn higher salaries teaching in Berlin, Tokyo, Ottawa, or Amsterdam than in New York or Chicago. American children are in school only about 180 days a year, as against 240 days or more for children in Europe or Japan. The richest school districts (school financing is local, not federal) spend twice as much per student as poorer ones do. The poorer ones seem almost beyond help: children with venereal disease or AIDS (2.5 million adolescents annually contract a sexually transmitted disease), gangs in the schoolyard, drugs in the classroom, children doing babies instead of homework, playground firefights featuring Uzis and Glocks.

Clearly, the social contract that obliges adults to pay taxes so that children can be educated is in imminent danger of collapse. Yet for all the astonishing statistics, more astonishing still is that no one seems to be listening. The education crisis is kind of like violence on television: the worse it gets the more inert we become, and the more of it we require to rekindle our attention. We've had a "crisis" every dozen years or so at least since the launch of *Sputnik*, in 1957, when American schools were accused of falling behind the world standard in science education. Just ten years ago, the National Commission on Excellence in Education warned that America's pedagogical inattention was putting America "at risk." What the commission called "a rising tide of mediocrity" was imperiling "our very future as a Nation and a people." What was happening to education was an "act of war."

5      Since then, countless reports have been issued decrying the condition of our educational system, the DOE report being only the most recent. They have come from every side, Republican as well as Democrat, from the private sector as well as the public. Yet for all the talk, little happens. At times, the schools look more like they are being dismantled than rebuilt. How can this be? If Americans over a broad political spectrum regard education as vital, why has nothing been done?

I have spent thirty years as a scholar examining the nature of democracy, and even more as a citizen optimistically celebrating its possibilities, but today I am increasingly persuaded that the reason for the country's inaction is that Americans do not really care about education—the country has grown comfortable with the game of "let's pretend we care."

As America's educational system crumbles, the pundits, instead of looking for solutions, search busily for scapegoats. Some assail the teachers—those "Profscam" pedagogues trained in the licentious Sixties who, as aging hippies, are supposedly still subverting the schools—for producing a dire illiteracy. Others turn on the kids themselves, so that at the same moment as we are transferring our responsibilities to the shoulders of the next generation, we are blaming them for our generation's most conspicuous failures. Allan Bloom was typical of the many recent critics who have condemned the young as vapid, lazy, selfish, complacent, self-seeking, materialistic, small-minded, apathetic, greedy, and, of course, illiterate. E. D. Hirsch in his *Cultural Literacy* and Diane Ravitch and Chester E. Finn Jr. in their *What Do Our Seventeen-Year-Olds Know?* have lambasted the schools, the teachers, and the children for betraying the adult generation from which they were to inherit, the critics seemed confident, a precious cultural legacy.

How this captious literature reeks of hypocrisy! How sanctimonious all the hand-wringing over still another "education crisis" seems. Are we ourselves really so literate? Are our kids stupid or smart for ignoring what we preach and copying what we practice? The young, with their keen noses for hypocrisy, are in fact adept readers—but not of books. They are society-smart rather than school-smart, and what they read so acutely are the social signals emanating from the world in which they will have to make a living. Their teachers in that world, the nation's true pedagogues, are television, advertising, movies, politics, and the celebrity domains they define. We prattle about deficient schools and the gullible youngsters they turn out, so vulnerable to the siren song of drugs, but think nothing of letting the advertisers into the classroom to fashion what an *Advertising Age* essay calls "brand and product loyalties through classroom-centered, peer-powered lifestyle patterning."

Our kids spend 900 hours a year in school (the ones who go to school) and from 1,200 to 1,800 hours a year in front of the television set. From which are they likely to learn more? Critics such as Hirsch and Ravitch want to find out what our seventeen-year-olds know, but it's really pretty simple: they know exactly what our forty-seven-year-olds know and teach them by example—on television, in the boardroom, around Washington, on Madison Avenue, in Hollywood. The very first lesson smart kids learn is that it is much more important to heed what society teaches implicitly by its deeds and reward structures than what school teaches explicitly in its lesson plans and civic sermons. Here is a test for adults that may help reveal what the kids see when they look at our world.

## Real-World Cultural Literacy

1. According to television, having fun in America means
   a. going blond
   b. drinking Pepsi
   c. playing Nintendo
   d. wearing Air Jordans
   e. reading Mark Twain
2. A good way to prepare for a high-income career and to acquire status in our society is to
   a. win a slam-dunk contest
   b. take over a company and sell off its assets
   c. start a successful rock band
   d. earn a professional degree
   e. become a kindergarten teacher
3. Book publishers are financially rewarded today for publishing
   a. mega-cookbooks
   b. mega-cat books
   c. megabooks by Michael Crichton
   d. megabooks by John Grisham
   e. mini-books by Voltaire
4. A major California bank that advertised "no previous credit history required" in inviting Berkeley students to apply for Visa cards nonetheless turned down one group of applicants because
   a. their parents had poor credit histories
   b. they had never held jobs
   c. they had outstanding student loans
   d. they were "humanities majors"
5. Colleges and universities are financially rewarded today for
   a. supporting bowl-quality football games
   b. forging research relationships with large corporations
   c. sustaining professional programs in law and business
   d. stroking wealthy alumni
   e. fostering outstanding philosophy departments
6. Familiarity with *Henry; IV Part II* is likely to be of vital importance in
   a. planning a corporate takeover
   b. evaluating budget cuts in the Department of Education
   c. initiating a medical-malpractice lawsuit

      d.  writing an impressive job résumé

      e.  taking a test on what our seventeen-year-olds know

7.  To help the young learn that "history is a living thing," Scholastic, Inc., a publisher of magazines and paper-backs, recently distributed to 40,000 junior and senior high school classrooms

      a.  a complimentary video of the award-winning series *The Civil War*

      b.  free copies of Plato's *Dialogues*

      c.  an abridgment of Alexis Tocqueville's *Democracy in America*

      d.  a wall-size Periodic Table of the Elements

      e.  gratis copies of Billy Joel's hit single "We Didn't Start the Fire" (which recounts history via a vaguely chronological list of warbled celebrity names)

10    My sample of forty-seven-year-olds scored very well on the test. Not surprisingly, so did their seventeen-year-old children. (For each question, either the last entry is correct or all responses are correct except the last one.) The results of the test reveal again the deep hypocrisy that runs through our lamentations about education. The illiteracy of the young turns out to be our own reflected back to us with embarrassing force. We honor ambition, we reward greed, we celebrate materialism, we worship acquisitiveness, we cherish success, and we commercialize the classroom—and then we bark at the young about the gentle arts of the spirit. We recommend history to the kids but rarely consult it ourselves. We make a fuss about ethics but are satisfied to see it taught as an "add-on," as in "ethics in medicine" or "ethics in business"—as if Sunday morning in church could compensate for uninterrupted sinning from Monday to Saturday.

    The children are onto this game. They know that if we really valued schooling, we'd pay teachers what we pay stockbrokers; if we valued books, we'd spend a little something on the libraries so that adults could read, too; if we valued citizenship, we'd give national service and civic education more than pilot status; if we valued children, we wouldn't let them be abused, manipulated, impoverished, and killed in their beds by gang-war cross fire and stray bullets. Schools can and should lead, but when they confront a society that in every instance tells a story exactly opposite to the one they are supposed to be teaching, their job becomes impossible. When the society undoes each workday what the school tries to do each day, schooling can't make much of a difference.

Inner-city children are not the only ones who are learning the wrong lessons. TV sends the same messages to everyone, and the success of Donald Trump, Pete Rose, Henry Kravis, or George Steinbrenner makes them potent role models, whatever their values. Teen dropouts are not blind; teen drug sellers are not deaf; teen college students who avoid the humanities in favor of pre-business or pre-law are not stupid. Being apt pupils of reality, they learn their lessons well. If they see a man with a rubber arm and an empty head who can throw a ball at 95 miles per hour pulling down millions of dollars a year while a dedicated primary-school teacher is getting crumbs, they will avoid careers in teaching even if they can't make the major leagues. If they observe their government spending up to $35,000 a year to keep a young black behind bars but a fraction of that to keep him in school, they will write off school (and probably write off blacks as well).

Our children's illiteracy is merely our own, which they assume with commendable prowess. They know what we have taught them all too well: there is nothing in Homer or Virginia Woolf, in Shakespeare or Toni Morrison, that will advantage them in climbing to the top of the American heap. Academic credentials may still count, but schooling in and of itself is for losers. Bookworms. Nerds. Inner-city rappers and fraternity-house wise guys are in full agreement about that. The point is to start pulling down the big bucks. Some kids just go into business earlier than others. Dropping out is the national pastime, if by dropping out we mean giving up the precious things of the mind and the spirit in which America shows so little interest and for which it offers so little payback. While the professors argue about whether to teach the ancient history of a putatively white Athens or the ancient history of a putatively black Egypt, the kids are watching televised political campaigns driven by mindless image-mongering and inflammatory polemics that ignore history altogether. Why, then, are we so surprised when our students dismiss the debate over the origins of civilization, whether Eurocentric or Afrocentric, and concentrate on cash-and-carry careers? Isn't the choice a tribute not to their ignorance but to their adaptive intelligence? Although we can hardly be proud of ourselves for what we are teaching them, we should at least be proud of them for how well they've learned our lessons.

Not all Americans have stopped caring about the schools, however. In the final irony of the educational endgame, cynical entrepreneurs like Chris Whittle are insinuating television into the classroom itself, bribing impoverished school boards by offering free TV sets on which they can show advertising for children—sold to sponsors at premium rates. Whittle, the mergers and acquisitions mogul of education, is trying to get rich off the poverty of public schools and the fears of parents. Can he really believe advertising in the schools enhances education? Or is he helping to corrupt public schools in ways that will make parents even more anxious to use vouchers for private schools—which might one day be run by Whittle's latest entrepreneurial venture, the Edison Project.

15    According to Lifetime Learning Systems, an educational software company, "kids spend 40 percent of each day . . . where traditional advertising can't reach them." Not to worry, says Lifetime Learning in an *Advertising Age* promo: "Now, you can enter the classroom through custom-made learning materials created with your specific marketing objectives in mind. Communicate with young spenders directly and, through them, their teachers and families as well." If we redefine young learners as "young spenders," are the young really to be blamed for acting like mindless consumers? Can they become young spenders and still become young critical thinkers, let alone informed citizens? If we are willing to give TV cartoons the government's imprimatur as "educational television" (as we did a few years ago, until the FCC changed its mind), can we blame kids for educating themselves on television trash?

Everyone can agree that we should educate our children to be something more than young spenders molded by "lifestyle patterning." But what should the goals of the classroom be? In recent years it has been fashionable to define the educational crisis in terms of global competition and minimal competence, as if schools were no more than vocational institutions. Although it has talked sensibly about education, the Clinton Administration has leaned toward this approach, under the tutelage of Secretary of Labor Robert Reich.

The classroom, however, should not be merely a trade school. The fundamental task of education in a democracy is what Tocqueville once called the apprenticeship of liberty: learning to be free. I wonder whether Americans still believe liberty has to be learned and that its skills are worth learning. Or have they been deluded by two centuries of rhetoric into thinking that freedom is "natural" and can be taken for granted?

The claim that all men are born free, upon which America was founded, is at best a promising fiction. In real life, as every parent knows, children are born fragile, born needy, born ignorant, born unformed, born weak, born foolish, born dependent—born in chains. We acquire our freedom over time, if at all. Embedded in families, clans, communities, and nations, we must learn to be free. We may be natural consumers and born narcissists, but citizens have to be made. Liberal-arts education actually means education in the arts of liberty; the "servile arts" were the trades learned by unfree men in the Middle Ages, the vocational education of their day. Perhaps this is why Thomas Jefferson preferred to memorialize his founding of the University of Virginia on his tombstone rather than his two terms as president; it is certainly why he viewed his Bill for the More General Diffusion of Knowledge in Virginia as a centerpiece of his career (although it failed passage as legislation—times were perhaps not so different). John Adams, too, boasted regularly about Massachusetts's high literacy rates and publicly funded education.

Jefferson and Adams both understood that the Bill of Rights offered little protection in a nation without informed citizens. Once educated, however, a people was safe from even the subtlest tyrannies. Jefferson's democratic proclivities rested on his conviction that education could turn a people into a safe refuge—indeed "the only safe depository" for the ultimate powers of society. "Cherish therefore the spirit of our people," he wrote to Edward Carrington in 1787, "and keep alive their attention. Do not be severe upon their errors, but reclaim them by enlightening them. If once they become inattentive to public affairs, you and I and Congress and Assemblies, judges and governors, shall all become wolves."

20    The logic of democracy begins with public education, proceeds to informed citizenship, and comes to fruition in the securing of rights and liberties. We have been nominally democratic for so long that we presume it is our natural condition rather than the product of persistent effort and tenacious responsibility. We have decoupled rights from civic responsibilities and severed citizenship from education on the false assumption that citizens just happen. We have forgotten that the "public" in public schools means not just paid for by the public but procreative of the very idea of a public. Public schools are how a public—a citizenry—is forged and how young, selfish individuals turn into conscientious, community-minded citizens.

Among the several literacies that have attracted the anxious attention of commentators, civic literacy has been the least visible. Yet this is the fundamental literacy by which we live in a civil society. It encompasses the competence to participate in democratic communities, the ability to think critically and act with deliberation in a pluralistic world, and the empathy to identify sufficiently with others to live with them despite conflicts of interest and differences in character. At the most elementary level, what our children suffer from most, whether they're hurling racial epithets from fraternity porches or shooting one another down in schoolyards, is the absence of civility. Security guards and metal detectors are poor surrogates for civility, and they make our schools look increasingly like prisons (though they may be less safe than prisons). Jefferson thought schools would produce free men: we prove him right by putting dropouts in jail.

Civility is a work of the imagination, for it is through the imagination that we render others sufficiently like ourselves for them to become subjects of tolerance and respect, if not always affection. Democracy is anything but a "natural" form of association. It is an extraordinary and rare contrivance of cultivated imagination. Give the uneducated the right to participate in making collective decisions, and what results is not democracy but, as best, mob rule: the government of private prejudice once known as the tyranny of opinion. For Jefferson, the difference between the democratic temperance he admired in agrarian America and the rule of the rabble he condemned when viewing the social unrest of Europe's teeming cities was quite simply education. Madison had hoped to "filter" out popular passion through the device of representation. Jeferson saw in education a filter that could be installed within each individual, giving to each the capacity to rule prudently. Education creates a ruling aristocracy constrained by temperance and wisdom; when that education is public and universal, it is an aristocracy to which all can belong. At its best, the American dream of a free and equal society governed by judicious citizens has been this dream of an aristocracy of everyone.

To dream this dream of freedom is easy, but to secure it is difficult as well as expensive. Notwithstanding their lamentations, Americans do not appear ready to pay the price. There is no magic bullet for education. But I no longer can accept that the problem lies in the lack of consensus about remedies—in a dearth of solutions. There is no shortage of debate over how to repair our educational infrastructure. National standards or more local control? Vouchers or better public schools? More parental involvement or more teacher autonomy? A greater federal presence (only 5 or 6 percent of the nation's education budget is federally funded) or fairer local school taxes? More multicultural diversity or more emphasis on what Americans share in common? These are honest disputes. But I am convinced that the problem is simpler and more fundamental. Twenty years ago, writer and activist Frances Moore Lappé captured the essence of the world food crisis when she argued that starvation was caused not by a scarcity of food but by a global scarcity in democracy. The education crisis has the same genealogy. It stems from a dearth of democracy: an absence of democratic will and a consequent refusal to take our children, our schools, and our future seriously.

Most educators, even while they quarrel among themselves, will agree that a genuine commitment to any one of a number of different solutions could help enormously. Most agree that although money can't by itself solve problems, without money few problems can be solved. Money also can't win wars or put men in space, but it is the crucial facilitator. It is also how America has traditionally announced, We are serious about this!

25      If we were serious, we would raise teachers' salaries to levels that would attract the best young professionals in our society: starting lawyers get from $70,000 to $80,000—why don't starting kindergarten teachers get the same? Is their role in vouchsafing our future less significant? And although there is evidence suggesting that an increase in general educational expenditures doesn't translate automatically into better schools, there is also evidence that an increase aimed specifically at instructional service does. Can we really take in earnest the chattering devotion to excellence of a country so wedded in practice to mediocrity, a nation so ready to relegate teachers—conservators of our common future—to the professional backwaters?

If we were serious, we would upgrade physical facilities so that every school met the minimum standards of our better suburban institutions. Good buildings do not equal good education, but can any education at all take place in leaky, broken-down habitats of the kind described by Jonathan Kozol in his *Savage Inequalities?* If money is not a critical factor, why are our most successful suburban school districts funded at nearly twice the level of our inner-city schools? Being even at the starting line cannot guarantee that the runners will win or even finish the race, but not being even pretty much assures failure. We would rectify the balance not by penalizing wealthier communities but by bringing poorer communities up to standard, perhaps by finding other sources of funding for our schools besides property taxes.

If we were serious, we'd extend the school year by a month or two so that learning could take place throughout the year. We'd reduce class size (which means more teachers) and nurture more cooperative learning so that kids could become actively responsible for their own education and that of their classmates. Perhaps most important, we'd raise standards and make teachers and students responsible for them. There are two ways to breed success: to lower standards so that everybody "passes" in a way that loses all meaning in the real world; and to raise standards and then meet them, so that school success translates into success beyond the classroom. From Confucian China to Imperial England, great nations have built their success in the world upon an education of excellence. The challenge in a democracy is to find a way to maintain excellence while extending educational opportunity to everyone.

Finally, if we were serious, parents, teachers, and students would be the real players while administrators, politicians, and experts would be secondary, at best advisers whose chief skill ought to be knowing when and how to facilitate the work of teachers and then get out of the way. If the Democrats can clean up federal government bureaucracy (the Gore plan), perhaps we can do the same for educational bureaucracy. In New York up to half of the city's teachers occupy jobs outside the classroom. No other enterprise is run that way: Half the soldiers at company headquarters? Half the cops at stationhouse desks? Half the working force in the assistant manager's office? Once the teachers are back in the classroom, they will need to be given more autonomy, more professional responsibility for the success or failure of their students. And parents will have to be drawn in not just because they have rights or because they are politically potent but because they have responsibilities and their children are unlikely to learn without parental engagement. How to define the parental role in the classroom would become serious business for educators.

Some Americans will say this is unrealistic. Times are tough, money's short, and the public is fed up with almost all of its public institutions: the schools are just one more frustrating disappointment. With all the goodwill in the world, it is still hard to know how schools can cure the ills that stem from the failure of so many other institutions. Saying we want education to come first won't put it first.

30     America, however, has historically been able to accomplish what it sets its mind to. When we wish it and will it, what we wish and will has happened. Our successes are willed; our failures seem to happen when will is absent. There are, of course, those who benefit from the bankruptcy of public education and the failure of democracy. But their blame is no greater than our own: in a world where doing nothing has such dire consequences, complacency has become a greater sin than malevolence.

In wartime, whenever we have known why we were fighting and believed in the cause, we have prevailed. Because we believe in profits, we are consummate salespersons and efficacious entrepreneurs.

Because we love sports, ours are the dream teams. Why can't a Chicago junior high school be as good as the Chicago Bulls? Because we cherish individuality and mobility, we have created a magnificent (if costly) car culture and the world's largest automotive consumer market. Even as our lower schools are among the worst in the Western world, our graduate institutions are among the very best because professional training in medicine, law, and technology is vital to our ambitions and because corporate America backs up state and federal priorities in this crucial domain. Look at the things we do well and observe how very well we do them: those are the things that as a nation we have willed.

Then observe what we do badly and ask yourself, Is it because the challenge is too great? Or is it because, finally, we aren't really serious? Would we will an end to the carnage and do whatever it took—more cops, state militias, federal marshals, the Marines?—if the dying children were white and middle class? Or is it a disdain for the young—white, brown, and black—that inures us to the pain? Why are we so sensitive to the retirees whose future (however foreshortened) we are quick to guarantee—don't worry, no reduced cost-of-living allowances, no taxes on social security except for the well-off—and so callous to the young? Have you noticed how health care is on every politician's agenda and education on no one's?

To me, the conclusion is inescapable: we are not serious. We have given up on the public schools because we have given up on the kids; and we have given up on the kids because we have given up on the future—perhaps because it looks too multicolored or too dim or too hard. "Liberty," said Jean-Jacques Rousseau, "is a food easy to eat but hard to digest." America is suffering from a bad case of indigestion. Finally, in giving up on the future, we have given up on democracy. Certainly there will be no liberty, no equality, no social justice without democracy, and there will be no democracy without citizens and the schools that forge civic identity and democratic responsibility. If I am wrong (I'd like to be), my error will be easy to discern, for before the year is out we will put education first on the nation's agenda. We will put it ahead of the deficit, for if the future is finished before it starts, the deficit doesn't matter. Ahead of defense, for without democracy, what liberties will be left to defend? Ahead of all the other public issues and public goods, for without public education there can be no public and hence no truly public issues or public goods to advance. When the polemics are spent and we are through hyperventilating about the crisis in education, there is only one question worth asking:

are we serious? If we are, we can begin by honoring that old folk homily and put our money where for much too long our common American mouth has been. Our kids, for once, might be grateful.

## Questions for Discussion

What does Barber's title, "America Skips School," mean, in light of his argument?

How would you describe the debate that Barber is a part of? What are the other positions in the debate?

*Jerome Stern taught English and Creative Writing at Florida State University for many years until his death in 1996. He wrote about the craft of fiction writing (*Making Shapely Fiction*) and edited collections of short stories (*Micro Fiction: An Anthology of Really Short Stories*). He was also a frequent contributor of commentary to National Public Radio; many of those pieces were collected in* Radios: Short Takes on Life and Culture *(1997). The following "monologue" aired March 17, 1989, on National Public Radio's* All Things Considered. *It was later reprinted in* Harper's *magazine.*

# *Jerome Stern*

# What They Learn in School

In the schools now, they want them to know all about marijuana, crack, heroin, and amphetamines,

Because then they won't be interested in marijuana, crack, heroin, and amphetamines,

But they don't want to tell them anything about sex because if the schools tell them about sex, then they will be interested in sex,

But if the schools don't tell them anything about sex,

5    Then they will have high morals and no one will get pregnant, and everything will be all right,

And they do want them to know a lot about computers so they will outcompete the Japanese,

But they don't want them to know anything about real science because then they will lose their faith and become secular humanists,

And they do want them to know all about this great land of ours so they will be patriotic,

But they don't want them to learn about the tragedy and pain in its real history because then they will be critical about this great land of ours and we will be passively taken over by a foreign power,

10   And they want them to learn how to think for themselves so they can get good jobs and be successful,

But they don't want them to have books that confront them with real ideas because that will confuse their values,

And they'd like them to be good parents,

But they can't teach them about families because that takes them back to how you get to be a family,

And they want to warn them about how not to get AIDS
15 But that would mean telling them how not to get AIDS,

And they'd like them to know the Constitution,

But they don't like some of those amendments except when they are invoked by the people they agree with,

And they'd like them to vote,

But they don't want them to discuss current events because it might be controversial and upset them and make them want to take drugs, which they already have told them all about,
20 And they want to teach them the importance of morality,

But they also want them to learn that Winning is not everything— it is the Only Thing,

And they want them to be well-read,

But they don't want them to read Chaucer or Shakespeare or Aristophanes or Mark Twain or Ernest Hemingway or John Steinbeck, because that will corrupt them,

And they don't want them to know anything about art because that will make them weird,
25 But they do want them to know about music so they can march in the band,

And they mainly want to teach them not to question, not to challenge, not to imagine, but to be obedient and behave well so that they can hold them forever as children to their bosoms as the second millennium lurches toward its panicky close.

## Questions for Discussion

How does the form of the piece contribute to its effectiveness?

Are the contradictions Stern explores in this piece accurate? How fair is Stern to debates surrounding secondary education?

*Gwendolyn Brooks (1917–2000), who lived in and frequently wrote about Chicago, was one of the most important American poets of the past century. In many of her books of poetry she often concentrated on the struggle of the individual against difficult circumstances, especially an urban landscape which provided as many struggles as it did opportunities. Brooks received numerous awards throughout her long and distinguished career, including a Pulitzer Prize in 1950 and the National Endowment for the Arts Lifetime Achievement Award. The following poem, "We Real Cool," first appeared in* The Bean Eaters *(1960). Can you tell why it is one of the most anthologized poems on race and education?*

## Gwendolyn Brooks

# We Real Cool

We real cool. We
Left school. We

Lurk late. We
Strike straight. We

5  Sing sin. We
Thin gin. We

Jazz June. We
Die soon.

## Questions for Discussion

Why is rhyme so important to this poem?

What is Brooks's argument in this poem?

What is significant about the progression of statements in this poem?

What does repetition add to the impact of the poem's point?

*A selection from his popular collection* School Is Hell *(1987), this cartoon by* **Matt Groening** *(born 1954) captures some of the feelings students associate with high school. Groening's sensitivity to and sense of humor about popular culture, including every level of school, is also captured in the highly popular and critically successful television show* The Simpsons. *Groening's success with* The Simpsons *came after* School Is Hell, *but it is already possible to see the seeds of the later work. What exactly is the argument Groening makes here? How does he support it?*

*Garry B. Trudeau* (born 1948) is one of America's most influential (and controversial) political and social commentators. His vehicle is the comic strip "Doonesbury," which appears in more than 850 newspapers and whose audience may top 100 million readers. What exactly does this cartoon argue about the nature of current higher education?

# Garry B. Trudeau

## Teaching Is Dead

***Adrienne Rich*** *(born 1929) is a noted writer who won the National Book Award for poetry in 1974 for her book* Diving into the Wreck. *Rich taught at many prestigious private universities, including Swarthmore, Columbia, and Stanford, as well as at public institutions such as City College of New York and Douglass College of Rutgers University. Her experiences at Douglass contributed to the insight she brings to the unequal treatment of women in schooling. She has long been active with movements for social justice, including the movement for women's liberation and lesbian/gay liberation. Do you agree with Rich that girls and women are at a disadvantage in American institutions of learning today?*

## *Adrienne Rich*

# Taking Women Students Seriously

I see my function here today as one of trying to create a context, delineate a background, against which we might talk about women as students and students as women. I would like to speak for awhile about this background, and then I hope that we can have, not so much a question period, as a raising of concerns, a sharing of questions for which we as yet may have no answers, an opening of conversations which will go on and on.

When I went to teach at Douglass, a women's college, it was with a particular background which I would like briefly to describe to you. I had graduated from an all-girls' school in the 1940s, where the head and the majority of the faculty were independent, unmarried women. One or two held doctorates, but had been forced by the Depression (and by the fact that they were women) to take secondary school teaching jobs. These women cared a great deal about the life of the mind, and they gave a great deal of time and energy—beyond any limit of teaching hours—to those of us who showed special intellectual interest or ability. We were taken to libraries, art museums, lectures at neighboring colleges, set to work on extra research projects, given extra French or Latin reading. Although we sometimes felt "pushed" by them, we held those women in a kind of respect which even then we dimly perceived was not generally accorded to women in the world at large. They were vital individuals, defined not by their relationships but by their personalities; and although under the pressure of the culture we were all certain we wanted to get married, their lives did not appear empty or dreary to us. In a kind of cognitive dissonance, we knew they were "old maids" and therefore supposed to be bitter and lonely; yet we saw them vigorously involved with life. But despite their existence as alternate models of women, the *content* of the education they gave us in no way prepared us to survive as women in a world organized by and for men.

From that school, I went on to Radcliffe, congratulating myself that now I would have great men as my teachers. From 1947 to 1951, when I graduated, I never saw a single woman on a lecture platform, or in front of a class, except when a woman graduate student gave a paper on a special topic. The "great men" talked of other "great men," of the nature of Man, the history of Mankind, the future of Man; and never again was I to experience, from a teacher, the kind of prodding, the insistence that my best could be even better, that I had known in high school. Women students were simply not taken very seriously. Harvard's message to women was an elite mystification: we were, of course, part of Mankind; we were special, achieving women, or we would not have been there; but of course our real goal was to marry—if possible, a Harvard graduate.

In the late sixties, I began teaching at the City College of New York—a crowded, public, urban, multiracial institution as far removed from Harvard as possible. I went there to teach writing in the SEEK Program, which predated Open Admissions and which was then a kind of model for programs designed to open up higher education to poor, black, and Third World students. Although during the next few years we were to see the original concept of SEEK diluted, then violently attacked and betrayed, it was for a short time an extraordinary and intense teaching and learning environment. The characteristics of this environment were a deep commitment on the part of teachers to the minds of their students; a constant, active effort to create or discover the conditions for learning, and to educate ourselves to meet the needs of the new college population; a philosophical attitude based on open discussion of racism, oppression, and the politics of literature and language; and a belief that learning in the classroom could not be isolated from the student's experience as a member of an urban minority group in white America. Here are some of the kinds of questions we, as teachers of writing, found ourselves asking:

1. What has been the student's experience of education in the inadequate, often abusively racist public school system, which rewards passivity and treats a questioning attitude or independent mind as a behavior problem? What has been her or his experience in a society that consistently undermines the selfhood of the poor and the nonwhite? How can such a student gain that sense of self which is necessary for active participation in education? What does all this mean for us as teachers?

2. How do we go about teaching a canon of literature which has consistently excluded or depreciated nonwhite experience?

3. How can we connect the process of learning to write well with the student's own reality, and not simply teach her/him how to write acceptable lies in standard English?

5    When I went to teach at Douglass College in 1976, and in teaching women's writing workshops elsewhere, I came to perceive stunning parallels to the questions I had first encountered in teaching the so-called disadvantaged students at City. But in this instance, and against the specific background of the women's movement, the questions framed themselves like this:

1. What has been the student's experience of education in schools which reward female passivity, indoctrinate girls and boys in stereotypic sex roles, and do not take the female mind seriously? How does a woman gain a sense of her *self* in a system—in this case, patriarchal capitalism—which devalues work done by women, denies the importance and uniqueness of female experience, and is physically violent toward women? What does this mean for a woman teacher?

2. How do we, as women, teach women students a canon of literature which has consistently excluded or depreciated female experience, and which often expresses hostility to women and validates violence against us?

3. How can we teach women to move beyond the desire for male approval and getting "good grades" and seek and write their own truths that the culture has distorted or made taboo? (For women, of course, language itself is exclusive: I want to say more about this further on.)

In teaching women, we have two choices: to lend our weight to the forces that indoctrinate women to passivity, self-depreciation, and a sense of powerlessness, in which case the issue of "taking women students seriously" is a moot one; or to consider what we have to work against, as well as with, in ourselves, in our students, in the content of the curriculum, in the structure of the institution, in the society at large. And this means, first of all, taking ourselves seriously: Recognizing that central responsibility of a woman to herself, without which we remain always the Other, the defined, the object, the victim; believing that there is a unique quality of validation, affirmation, challenge, support, that one woman can offer another. Believing in the value and significance of women's experience, traditions, perceptions. Thinking of ourselves seriously, not as one of the boys, not as neuters, or androgynes, but *as women.*

Suppose we were to ask ourselves, simply: What does a woman need to know? Does she not, as a self-conscious, self-defining human being, need a knowledge of her own history, her much-politicized biology, an awareness of the creative work of women of the past, the skills and crafts and techniques and powers exercised by women in different times and cultures, a knowledge of women's rebellions and organized movements against our oppression and how they have been routed or diminished? Without such knowledge women live and have lived without context, vulnerable to the projections of male fantasy, male prescriptions for us, estranged from our own experience because our education has not reflected or echoed it. I would suggest that not biology, but ignorance of our selves, has been the key to our powerlessness.

But the university curriculum, the high-school curriculum, do not provide this kind of knowledge for women, the knowledge of Womankind, whose experience has been so profoundly different from that of Mankind. Only in the precariously budgeted, much-condescended-to area of women's studies is such knowledge available to women students. Only there can they learn about the lives and work of women other than the few select women who are included in the "mainstream" texts, usually misrepresented even when they do appear. Some students, at some institutions, manage to take a majority of courses in women's studies, but the message from on high is that this is self-indulgence, soft-core education: the "real" learning is the study of Mankind.

If there is any misleading concept, it is that of "coeducation": that because women and men are sitting in the same classrooms, hearing the same lectures, reading the same books, performing the same laboratory experiments, they are receiving an equal education. They are not, first because the content of education itself validates men even as it invalidates women. Its very message is that men have been the shapers and thinkers of the world, and that this is only natural. The bias of higher education, including the so-called sciences, is white and male, racist and sexist; and this bias is expressed in both subtle and blatant ways. I have mentioned already the exclusiveness of grammar itself: "The student should test himself on the above questions"; "The poet is representative. He stands among partial men for the complete man." Despite a few half-hearted departures from custom, what the linguist Wendy Martyna has named "He-Man" grammar prevails throughout the culture. The efforts of feminists to reveal the profound ontological implications of sexist grammar are routinely ridiculed by academicians and journalists, including the professedly liberal *Times* columnist, Tom Wicker, and the professed humanist, Jacques Barzun. Sexist grammar burns into the brains of little girls and young women a message that the male is the norm, the standard, the central figure beside which we are the deviants, the marginal, the dependent variables. It lays the foundation for androcentric thinking, and leaves men safe in their solipsistic tunnel-vision.

10     Women and men do not receive an equal education because outside the classroom women are perceived not as sovereign beings but as prey. The growing incidence of rape on and off the campus may or may not be fed by the proliferations of pornographic magazines and X-rated films available to young males in fraternities and student unions; but it is certainly occurring in a context of widespread images of sexual violence against women, on billboards and in so-called high art. More subtle, more daily than rape is the verbal abuse experienced by the woman student on many campuses—Rutgers for example— where, traversing a street lined with fraternity houses, she must run a gauntlet of male commentary and verbal assault. The undermining of self, of a woman's sense of her right to occupy space and walk freely in the world, is deeply relevant to education. The capacity to think independently, to take intellectual risks, to assert ourselves mentally, is inseparable from our physical way of being in the world, our feelings of personal integrity. If it is dangerous for me to walk home late of an evening from the library, *because I am a woman and can be raped*, how self-possessed, how exuberant can I feel as I sit working in that library? how much of my working energy is drained by the subliminal knowledge that, as a woman, I test my physical right to exist each time I go out alone? Of this knowledge, Susan Griffin has written:

> . . . more than rape itself, the fear of rape permeates our lives. And what does one do from day to day, with *this* experience, which says, without words and directly to the heart, *your existence, your experience, may*

*end at any moment.* Your experience may end, and the best defense against this is not to be, to deny being in the body, as a self, to . . . avert your gaze, make yourself, as a presence in the world, less felt.[1]

Finally, rape of the mind. Women students are more and more often now reporting sexual overtures by male professors—one part of our overall growing consciousness of sexual harassment in the workplace. At Yale a legal suit has been brought against the university by a group of women demanding an explicit policy against sexual advances toward female students by male professors. Most young women experience a profound mixture of humiliation and intellectual self-doubt over seductive gestures by men who have the power to award grades, open doors to grants and graduate school, or extend special knowledge and training. Even if turned aside, such gestures constitute mental rape, destructive to a woman's ego. They are acts of domination, as despicable as the molestation of the daughter by the father.

But long before entering college the woman student has experienced her alien identity in a world which misnames her, turns her to its own uses, denying her the resources she needs to become self-affirming, self-defined. The nuclear family teaches her that relationships are more important than selfhood or work; that "whether the phone rings for you, and how often," having the right clothes, doing the dishes, take precedence over study or solitude; that too much intelligence or intensity may make her unmarriageable; that marriage and children—service to others—are, finally, the points on which her life will be judged a success or a failure. In high school, the polarization between feminine attractiveness and independent intelligence comes to an absolute. Meanwhile, the culture resounds with messages. During Solar Energy Week in New York I saw young women wearing "ecology" T-shirts with the legend: CLEAN, CHEAP AND AVAILABLE; a reminder of the 1960s antiwar button which read: CHICKS SAY YES TO MEN WHO SAY NO. Department store windows feature female mannequins in chains, pinned to the wall with legs spread, smiling in positions of torture. Feminists are depicted in the media as "shrill," "strident," "puritanical," or "humorless," and the lesbian choice—the choice of the woman-identified woman—as pathological or sinister. The young woman sitting in the philosophy classroom, the political science lecture, is already gripped by tensions between her nascent sense of self-worth, and the battering force of messages like these.

[1] *Rape: The Power of Consciousness* (New York, 1979).

Look at a classroom: look at the many kinds of women's faces, postures, expressions. Listen to the women's voices. Listen to the silences, the unasked questions, the blanks. Listen to the small, soft voices, often courageously trying to speak up, voices of women taught early that tones of confidence, challenge, anger, or assertiveness, are strident and unfeminine. Listen to the voices of the women and the voices of the men; observe the space men allow themselves, physically and verbally, the male assumption that people will listen, even when the majority of the group is female. Look at the faces of the silent, and of those who speak. Listen to a woman groping for language in which to express what is on her mind, sensing that the terms of academic discourse are not her language, trying to cut down her thought to the dimensions of a discourse not intended for her (*for it is not fitting that a woman speak in public*); or reading her paper aloud at breakneck speed, throwing her words away, deprecating her own work by a reflex prejudgment: *I do not deserve to take up time and space.*

As women teachers, we can either deny the importance of this context in which women students think, write, read, study, project their own futures; or try to work with it. We can either teach passively, accepting these conditions, or actively, helping our students identify and resist them.

15      One important thing we can do is *discuss* the context. And this need not happen only in a women's studies course; it can happen anywhere. We can refuse to accept passive, obedient learning and insist upon critical thinking. We can become harder on our women students, giving them the kinds of "cultural prodding" that men receive, but on different terms and in a different style. Most young women need to have their intellectual lives, their work, legitimized against the claims of family, relationships, the old message that a woman is always available for service to others. We need to keep our standards very high, not to accept a woman's preconceived sense of her limitations; we need to be hard to please, while supportive of risk-taking, because self-respect often comes only when exacting standards have been met. At a time when adult literacy is generally low, we need to demand more, not less, of women, both for the sake of their futures as thinking beings, and because historically women have always had to be better than men to do half as well. A romantic sloppiness, an inspired lack of rigor, a self-indulgent incoherence, are symptoms of female self-depreciation. We should help our women students to look very critically at such symptoms, and to understand where they are rooted.

Nor does this mean we should be training women students to "think like men." Men in general think badly: in disjuncture from their personal lives, claiming objectivity where the most irrational passions seethe, losing, as Virginia Woolf observed, their senses in the pursuit of professionalism. It is not easy to think like a woman in a man's world, in the world of the professions; yet the capacity to do that is a strength which we can try to help our students develop. To think like a woman in a man's world means thinking critically, refusing to accept the givens, making connections between facts and ideas which men have left unconnected. It means remembering that every mind resides in a body; remaining accountable to the female bodies in which we live; constantly retesting given hypotheses against lived experience. It means a constant critique of language, for as Wittgenstein (no feminist) observed, "The limits of my language are the limits of my world." And it means that most difficult thing of all: listening and watching in art and literature, in the social sciences, in all the descriptions we are given of the world, for the silences, the absences, the nameless, the unspoken, the encoded—for there we will find the true knowledge of women. And in breaking those silences, naming our selves, uncovering the hidden, making ourselves present, we begin to define a reality which resonates to *us*, which affirms *our* being, which allows the woman teacher and the woman student alike to take ourselves, and each other, seriously: meaning, to begin taking charge of our lives.

## Questions for Discussion

In what ways does a culture "argue" for certain (different) roles for men and women?

What does Rich mean when she refers to the need "to think like a woman in a man's world" in the last paragraph of the essay?

# PART THREE

# CENSORSHIP

"Congress shall make no law . . . abridging the freedom of
speech, or of the press," stoutly declares the First Amendment to the United States Constitution. Ever since the
Constitution was ratified, First Amendment absolutists
have made that declaration one of the most familiar sentences in American public life. After all, as Benjamin
Franklin has implied in his plea for freedom of the press
reprinted in this section, free speech is simply essential to
public debate and democratic exchange.

And yet legitimate abridgements of free speech have
been a part of American life since the beginning as well.
Chief Justice Oliver Wendell Holmes in 1919 articulated a
commonsense principle that has guided much American
practice: "The most stringent protection of free speech would
not protect a man in falsely shouting 'Fire!' in a crowded
theater and causing a panic. The question in every case is
whether the words used are used in such circumstances and
are of such a nature as to create a clear and present danger
that they will bring about substantive evils that Congress has
a right to prevent." Consequently, Americans have attempted to control any number of types of "free speech"
when such speech appears to be harmful or dangerous.
Cigarette advertising has been banned from television, for
example, on the grounds that such ads promote a dangerous
habit. Some citizens have attempted to suppress violence in
the media in the wake of stubborn and sensational real-life
violence that seems endemic to American life. Still others
have moved to restrict certain books and other materials
from being used in the schools. And in recent years concern
has shifted to the Internet. To protect intellectual property,
Congress has supported restrictions on Napster and similar

Demonstrators outside the Contemporary Arts Center in Cincinnati rally in support of freedom of expression—in this case, a controversial exhibit by photographer Robert Mapplethorpe.

software that would permit people to download music, photography, and other copyrighted materials without paying a fee. (Paul Winston and Ruben Bolling in this section debate the merits of such restrictions.)

Moreover, shocked by the prevalence of pornography on the Internet (sometimes including the dissemination of sexually explicit photographs without the permission of the person photographed), by Web sites created by extremist militia groups and hate groups, or by individuals who offer guns—or advice on bomb construction—on the Internet, many have called for schools and libraries to install censorware on computers. In 1996 Congress passed a Communications Decency Act in an effort to regulate pornography online; when it was declared unconstitutional, Congress then responded in 1998 with the Child Online Protection Act, which prohibits the publication of materials online that could be harmful to children. (After all, do we really want children—or anyone, for that matter—exploring sites that feature beastiality, child pornography, or necrophilia? Estimates are that more than half of all current requests on search engines are for sexually explicit sites and that over 25 percent of teens have visited X-rated sites.) Such efforts to restrict Internet access are supported in this section by an argument by Cathleen Cleaver and a cartoon by Walt Handelsman—and are refuted by William Bennett Turner.

Proposals to ban or restrict pornography are not limited to the Internet, of course (and indeed the Supreme Court has ruled that pornography itself is not "protected speech"). Lately the war of words on pornography has continued, with reasonable arguments on both sides—as well as extreme censors attempting to restrict the kind of art supported by the National Endowment for the Arts, and extreme free speech advocates uneasily defending Larry Flint and his misogynist magazines. Here are included several cogent arguments in the debate about pornography: Susan Brownmiller's "Let's Put Pornography Back in the Closet"; Nadine Strossen's "The Perils of Pornophobia"; and Irving Kristol's "Pornography, Obscenity, and the Case for Censorship."

Do laws designed to restrict speech and writing and images violate the Constitution? Does violence on television and in movies teach violence to children, and should it therefore be restricted in some way? Is it a good idea to regulate so-called hate speech on campuses? Or to keep people from placing pornography, or hate speech, or other destructive messages on the Internet? Such issues will continue to be argued in America, you can be sure.

*Benjamin Franklin (1706–1790) was a remarkable polymath: business-
man, inventor, publisher, scientist, civic leader, public servant, educator.
He contributed to the Declaration of Independence as a member of the
Second Continental Congress. Born in Boston, Franklin arrived penniless
in Philadelphia in 1723 and eventually acquired his own printing business. In 1733, he began producing* Poor Richard's Almanack, *a compila-
tion of weather forecasts, planetary descriptions, and witty maxims and
humor, which quickly became popular. Always with wit and civic consciousness, Franklin often wrote on controversial matters for contemporary newspapers, sometimes under his own name and sometimes anony-
mously. He published the following piece in 1731 in response to public
outcry against an advertisement that ran in his* Pennsylvania Gazette
*newspaper.*

## Benjamin Franklin

# Apology for Printers

Being frequently censur'd and condemn'd by different Persons for
printing Things which they say ought not to be printed, I have sometimes thought it might be necessary to make a standing Apology for
my self, and publish it once a Year, to be read upon all Occasions of
that Nature. Much Business has hitherto hindered the execution of this
Design; but having very lately given extraordinary Offence by printing
an Advertisement with a certain *N.B.* at the End of it, I find an
Apology more particularly requisite at this Juncture, tho' it happens
when I have not yet Leisure to write such a thing in the proper Form,
and can only in a loose manner throw those Considerations together
which should have been the Substance of it.

I request all who are angry with me on the Account of printing
things they don't like, calmly to consider these following Particulars:

1. That the Opinions of Men are almost as various as their Faces;
   an Observation general enough to become a common Proverb,
   *So many Men so many Minds.*
2. That the Business of Printing has chiefly to do with Men's
   Opinions; most things that are printed tending to promote
   some, or oppose others.
3. That hence arises the peculiar Unhappiness of that Business,
   which other Callings are no way liable to; they who follow

Printing being scarce able to do any thing in their way of getting a Living, which shall not probably give Offence to some, and perhaps to many; whereas the Smith, the Shoemaker, the Carpenter, or the Man of any other Trade, may work indifferently for People of all Persuasions, without offending any of them: and the Merchant may buy and sell with Jews, Turks, Hereticks, and Infidels of all sorts, and get Money by every one of them, without giving Offence to the most orthodox, of any sort; or suffering the least Censure or ill-will on the Account from any Man whatever.

4. That it is as unreasonable in any one Man or Set of Men to expect to be pleas'd with every thing that is printed, as to think that nobody ought to be pleas'd but themselves.

5. Printers are educated in the Belief, that when Men differ in Opinion, both Sides ought equally to have the Advantage of being heard by the Publick; and that when Truth and Error have fair Play, the former is always an overmatch for the latter: Hence they cheerfully serve all contending Writers that pay them well, without regarding on which side they are of the Question in Dispute.

6. Being thus continually employ'd in serving all Parties, Printers naturally acquire a vast Unconcernedness as to the right or wrong Opinions contain'd in what they print; regarding it only as the Matter of their daily labour: They print things full of Spleen and Animosity, with the utmost Calmness and Indifference, and without the least Ill-will to the Persons reflected on; who nevertheless unjustly think the Printer as much their Enemy as the Author, and join both together in their Resentment.

7. That it is unreasonable to imagine Printers approve of every thing they print, and to censure them on any particular thing accordingly; since in the way of their Business they print such great variety of things opposite and contradictory. It is likewise as unreasonable what some assert, *That Printers ought not to print any Thing but what they approve;* since if all of that Business should make such a Resolution, and abide by it, an End would thereby be put to Free Writing, and the World would afterwards have nothing to read but what happen'd to be the Opinions of Printers.

8. That if all Printers were determin'd not to print any thing till they were sure it would offend no body, there would be very little printed.

9. That if they sometimes print vicious or silly things not worth reading, it may not be because they approve such things themselves, but because the People are so viciously and corruptly educated that good things are not encouraged. I have known a very numerous Impression of *Robin Hood's Songs* go off in this Province at 2s. [two shillings] per Book, in less than a Twelvemonth; when a small Quantity of *David's Psalms* (an excellent Version) have lain upon my Hands above twice the Time.

10. That notwithstanding what might be urg'd in behalf of a Man's being allow'd to do in the Way of his Business whatever he is paid for, yet Printers do continually discourage the Printing of great Numbers of bad things, and stifle them in the Birth. I my self have constantly refused to print any thing that might countenance Vice, or promote Immorality; tho' by complying in such Cases with the corrupt Taste of the Majority, I might have got much Money. I have also always refus'd to print such things as might do real Injury to any Person, how much soever I have been solicited, and tempted with Offers of great Pay; and how much soever I have by refusing got the Ill-will of those who would have employ'd me. I have heretofore fallen under the Resentment of large Bodies of Men, for refusing absolutely to print any of their Party or Personal Reflections. In this Manner I have made my self many Enemies, and the constant Fatigue of denying is almost insupportable. But the Publick being unacquainted with all this, whenever the poor Printer happens either through Ignorance or much Persuasion, to do any thing that is generally thought worthy of Blame, he meets with no more Friendship or Favour on the above Account, than if there were no Merit in't at all. Thus, as Waller says,

> *Poets loose half the Praise they would have got*
> *Were it but known what they discreetly blot;*

Yet are censur'd for every bad Line found in their Works with the utmost Severity.

I come now to the particular Case of the *N.B.* above-mention'd, about which there has been more Clamour against me, than ever before on any other Account. In the Hurry of other Business an Advertisement was brought to me to be printed; it signified that such a Ship lying at such a Wharff, would sail for Barbadoes in such a Time, and that Freighters and Passengers might agree with the Captain at such a Place; so far is what's common: But at the Bottom this odd Thing was added, N.B. *No Sea Hens nor Black Gowns will be admitted on any Terms.* I printed it, and receiv'd my Money; and the Advertisement was stuck up round the Town as usual. I had not so much Curiosity at that time as to enquire the Meaning of it, nor did I in the least imagine it would give so much Offence. Several good Men are very angry with me on this Occasion; they are pleas'd to say I have too much Sense to do such things ignorantly; that if they were Printers they would not have done such a thing on any Consideration; that it could proceed from nothing but my abundant Malice against Religion and the Clergy: They therefore declare they will not take any more of my Papers, nor have any farther Dealings with me; but will hinder me of all the Custom they can. All this is very hard!

I believe it had been better if I had refused to print the said Advertisement. However, 'tis done and cannot be revok'd. I have only the following few Particulars to offer, some of them in my Behalf, by way of Mitigation, and some not much to the Purpose; but I desire none of them may be read when the Reader is not in a very good Humour.

1. That I really did it without the least Malice, and imagin'd the *N.B.* was plac'd there only to make the Advertisement star'd at, and more generally read.

2. That I never saw the Word *Sea-Hens* before in my Life; nor have I yet ask'd the meaning of it; and tho' I had certainly known that *Black Gowns* in that Place signified the Clergy of the Church of England, yet I have that confidence in the generous good Temper of such of them as I know, as to be well satisfied such a trifling mention of their Habit gives them no Disturbance.

3. That most of the Clergy in this and the neighbouring Provinces, are my Customers, and some of them my very good Friends; and I must be very malicious indeed, or very stupid, to print this thing for a small Profit, if I had thought it would have given them just Cause of Offence.

4. That if I have much Malice against the Clergy, and withal much Sense; 'tis strange I never write or talk against the Clergy my self. Some have observed that 'tis a fruitful Topic, and the easiest to be witty upon of all others. I can print any thing I write at less Charge than others; yet I appeal to the Publick that I am never guilty this way, and to all my Acquaintance as to my Conversation.

5. That if a Man of Sense had Malice enough to desire to injure the Clergy, this is the foolishest Thing he could possibly contrive for that Purpose.

6. That I got Five Shillings by it.

7. That none who are angry with me would have given me so much to let it alone.

8. That if all the People of different Opinions in this Province would engage to give me as much for not printing things they don't like, as I can get by printing them, I should probably live a very easy Life; and if all Printers were every where so dealt by, there would be very little printed.

9. That I am oblig'd to all who take my Paper, and am willing to think they do it out of mere Friendship. I only desire they would think the same when I deal with them. I thank those who leave off, that they have taken it so long. But I beg they would not endeavour to disuade others, for that will look like Malice.

10. That 'tis impossible any Man should know what he would do if he was a Printer.

11. That notwithstanding the Rashness and Inexperience of Youth, which is most likely to be prevail'd with to do things that ought not to be done; yet I have avoided printing such Things as usually give Offence either to Church or State, more than any Printer that has followed the Business in this Province before.

12. And lastly, That I have printed above a Thousand Advertisements which made not the least mention of *Sea-Hens* or *Black Gowns;* and this being the first Offence, I have the more Reason to expect Forgiveness.

5    I take leave to conclude with an old Fable, which some of my Readers have heard before, and some have not.

"A certain well-meaning Man and his Son, were travelling towards a Market Town, with an Ass which they had to sell. The Road was bad; and the old Man therefore rid, but the Son went a-foot. The first Passenger they met, asked the Father if he was not ashamed to ride by himself, and suffer the poor Lad to wade along thro' the Mire; this induced him to take up his Son behind him: He had not travelled far, when he met others, who said, they were two unmerciful Lubbers to get both on the Back of that poor Ass, in such a deep Road. Upon this the old Man gets off, and lets his Son ride alone. The next they met called the Lad a graceless, rascally young Jackanapes, to ride in that Manner thro' the Dirt, while his aged Father trudged along on Foot; and they said the old Man was a Fool, for suffering it. He then bid his

Son come down, and walk with him, and they travell'd on leading the Ass by the Halter; 'till they met another Company, who called them a Couple of sensless Blockheads, for going both on Foot in such a dirty Way, when they had an empty Ass with them, which they might ride upon. The old Man could bear no longer; My Son, said he, it grieves me much that we cannot please all these People: Let us throw the Ass over the next Bridge, and be no farther troubled with him."

Had the old Man been seen acting this last Resolution, he would probably have been call'd a Fool for troubling himself about the different Opinions of all that were pleas'd to find Fault with him: Therefore, tho' I have a Temper almost as complying as his, I intend not to imitate him in this last Particular. I consider the Variety of Humours among Men, and despair of pleasing every Body: yet I shall not therefore leave off Printing. I shall continue my Business. I shall not burn my Press and melt my Letters.

## Questions for Discussion

How serious is Franklin about his "apology"?

What kind of tone does Franklin take in this piece? How does it help him achieve his objectives?

To what degree is Franklin's "Apology" applicable to contemporary discussions about the media?

*Susan Brownmiller is a journalist, novelist, activist, and a founder of Women against Pornography. Her book,* Against Our Will: Men, Women, and Rape *(1975), articulated a strong position on pornography that has been developed recently by feminists such as Andrea Dworkin and Catherine McKinnon. The following essay, in which Brownmiller attempts to clarify her position on the issues of pornography and censorship, originally appeared in* Newsday, *a Long Island newspaper, in 1979. A year later it was included in* Take Back the Night, *a collection of essays about violence against women.*

## Susan Brownmiller

# Let's Put Pornography Back in the Closet

Free speech is one of the great foundations on which our democracy rests. I am old enough to remember the Hollywood Ten, the screenwriters who went to jail in the late 1940s because they refused to testify before a congressional committee about their political affiliations. They tried to use the First Amendment as a defense, but they went to jail because in those days there were few civil liberties lawyers around who cared to champion the First Amendment right to free speech, when the speech concerned the Communist Party.

The Hollywood Ten were correct in claiming the First Amendment. Its high purpose is the protection of unpopular ideas and political dissent. In the dark, cold days of the 1950s, few civil libertarians were willing to declare themselves First Amendment absolutists. But in the brighter, though frantic, days of the 1960s, the principle of protecting unpopular political speech was gradually strengthened.

It is fair to say now that the battle has largely been won. Even the American Nazi Party has found itself the beneficiary of the dedicated, tireless work of the American Civil Liberties Union. But—and please notice the quotation marks coming up—"To equate the free and robust exchange of ideas and political debate with commercial exploitation of obscene material demeans the grand conception of the First Amendment and its high purposes in the historic struggle for freedom. It is a misuse of the great guarantees of free speech and free press."

I didn't say that, although I wish I had, for I think the words are thrilling. Chief Justice Warren Burger said it in 1973, in the United

States Supreme Court's majority opinion in *Miller* v. *California*. During the same decades that the right to political free speech was being strengthened in the courts, the nation's obscenity laws also were undergoing extensive revision.

5      It's amazing to recall that in 1934 the question of whether James Joyce's *Ulysses* should be banned as pornographic actually went before the Court. The battle to protect *Ulysses* as a work of literature with redeeming social value was won. In later decades, Henry Miller's *Tropic* books, *Lady Chatterley's Lover* and the *Memoirs of Fanny Hill* also were adjudged not obscene. These decisions have been important to me. As the author of *Against Our Will*, a study of the history of rape that does contain explicit sexual material, I shudder to think how my book would have fared if James Joyce, D. H. Lawrence and Henry Miller hadn't gone before me.

I am not a fan of *Chatterley* or the *Tropic* books, I should quickly mention. They are not to my literary taste, nor do I think they represent female sexuality with any degree of accuracy. But I would hardly suggest that we ban them. Such a suggestion wouldn't get very far anyway. The battle to protect these books is ancient history. Time does march on, quite methodically. What, then, is unlawfully obscene, and what does the First Amendment have to do with it?

In the Miller case of 1973 (not Henry Miller, by the way, but a porn distributor who sent unsolicited stuff through the mails), the Court came up with new guidelines that it hoped would strengthen obscenity laws by giving more power to the states. What it did in actuality was throw everything into confusion. It set up a three-part test by which materials can be adjudged obscene. The materials are obscene if they depict patently offensive, hard-core sexual conduct; lack serious scientific, literary, artistic or political value; and appeal to the prurient interest of an average person—as measured by contemporary community standards.

"Patently offensive," "prurient interest" and "hard-core" are indeed words to conjure with. "Contemporary community standards" are what we're trying to redefine. The feminist objection to pornography is not based on prurience, which the dictionary defines as lustful, itching desire. We are not opposed to sex and desire, with or without the itch, and we certainly believe that explicit sexual material has its place in literature, art, science and education. Here we part company rather swiftly with old-line conservatives who don't want sex education in the high schools, for example.

No, the feminist objection to pornography is based on our belief that pornography represents hatred of women, that pornography's intent is to humiliate, degrade and dehumanize the female body for the purpose of erotic stimulation and pleasure. We are unalterably opposed to the presentation of the female body being stripped, bound, raped, tortured, mutilated and murdered in the name of commercial entertainment and free speech.

10    These images, which are standard pornographic fare, have nothing to do with the hallowed right of political dissent. They have everything to do with the creation of a cultural climate in which a rapist feels he is merely giving in to a normal urge and a woman is encouraged to believe that sexual masochism is healthy, liberated fun. Justice Potter Stewart once said about hard-core pornography, "You know it when you see it," and that certainly used to be true. In the good old days, pornography looked awful. It was cheap and sleazy, and there was no mistaking it for art.

Nowadays, since the porn industry has become a multimillion dollar business, visual technology has been employed in its service. Pornographic movies are skillfully filmed and edited, pornographic still shots using the newest tenets of good design artfully grace the covers of *Hustler*, *Penthouse* and *Playboy*; and the public—and the courts—are sadly confused.

The Supreme Court neglected to define "hard-core" in the Miller decision. This was a mistake. If "hard-core" refers only to explicit sexual intercourse, then that isn't good enough. When women or children or men—no matter how artfully—are shown tortured or terrorized in the service of sex, that's obscene. And "patently offensive," I would hope, to our "contemporary community standards."

Justice William O. Douglas wrote in his dissent to the Miller case that no one is "compelled to look." This is hardly true. To buy a paper at the corner newsstand is to subject oneself to a forcible immersion in pornography, to be demeaned by an array of dehumanized, chopped-up parts of the female anatomy, packaged like cuts of meat at the supermarket. I happen to like my body and I work hard at the gym to keep it in good shape, but I am embarrassed for my body and for the bodies of all women when I see the fragmented parts of us so frivolously, and so flagrantly, displayed.

Some constitutional theorists (Justice Douglas was one) have maintained that any obscenity law is a serious abridgement of free speech. Others (and Justice Earl Warren was one) have maintained that the First Amendment was never intended to protect obscenity. We live quite compatibly with a host of free-speech abridgements. There are restraints against false and misleading advertising or statements—

shouting "fire" without cause in a crowded movie theater, etc.—that do not threaten, but strengthen, our societal values. Restrictions on the public display of pornography belong in this category.

15    The distinction between permission to publish and permission to display publicly is an essential one and one which I think consonant with First Amendment principles. Justice Burger's words which I quoted above support this without question. We are not saying "Smash the presses" or "Ban the bad ones," but simply "Get the stuff out of our sight." Let the legislatures decide—using realistic and humane contemporary community standards—what can be displayed and what cannot. The courts, after all, will be the final arbiters.

## Questions for Discussion

How does Brownmiller portray herself in her text? How does this construction of ethos—of credibility and authority—contribute to her point?

What kind of audience is Brownmiller appealing to? What assumptions does she make about the audience's preexisting views?

*Nadine Strossen, Professor of Law at New York Law School, is president of the American Civil Liberties Union, an organization famous for defending the rights of U.S. citizens. She was the youngest person to hold that office, as well as the first woman. Strossen frequently publishes and delivers speeches on the topics of civil liberties and human rights; in addition, she regularly contributes columns and opinion pieces to Web-zines and appears on national political talk shows. She has earned numerous awards for her writing and her work on civil rights and social equality. The following essay on feminist responses to the regulation of pornography appeared in* The Humanist *in the spring of 1995. Her essay was adapted from her book* Defending Pornography: Free Speech, Sex, and the Fight for Women's Rights *(1995).*

## *Nadine Strossen*

# The Perils of Pornophobia

In 1992, in response to a complaint, officials at Pennsylvania State University unceremoniously removed Francisco de Goya's masterpiece, *The Nude Maja*, from a classroom wall. The complaint had not been lodged by Jesse Helms or some irate member of the Christian Coalition. Instead, the complainant was a feminist English professor who protested that the eighteenth-century painting of a recumbent nude woman made her and her female students "uncomfortable."

This was not an isolated incident. At the University of Arizona at Tucson, feminist students physically attacked a graduate student's exhibit of photographic self-portraits. Why? The artist had photographed *herself* in her *underwear*. And at the University of Michigan Law School feminist students who had organized a conference on "Prostitution: From Academia to Activism" removed a feminist-curated art exhibition held in conjunction with the conference. Their reason? Conference speakers had complained that a composite video-tape containing interviews of working prostitutes was "pornographic" and therefore unacceptable.

What is wrong with this picture? Where have they come from—these feminists who behave like religious conservatives, who censor works of art because they deal with sexual themes? Have not feminists long known that censorship is a dangerous weapon which, if permitted, would inevitably be turned against them? Certainly that was the irrefutable lesson of the early women's rights movement, when

Margaret Sanger, Mary Ware Dennett, and other activists were arrested, charged with "obscenity" and prosecuted for distributing educational pamphlets about sex and birth control. Theirs was a struggle for freedom of sexual expression and full gender equality, which they understood to be mutually reinforcing.

Theirs was also a lesson well understood by the second wave of feminism in the 1970s, when writers such as Germaine Greer, Betty Friedan, and Betty Dodson boldly asserted that women had the right to be free from discrimination not only in the workplace and in the classroom but in the bedroom as well. Freedom from limiting, conventional stereotypes concerning female sexuality was an essential aspect of what we then called "women's liberation." Women should not be seen as victims in their sexual relations with men but as equally assertive partners, just as capable of experiencing sexual pleasure.

5      But it is a lesson that, alas, many feminists have now forgotten. Today, an increasingly influential feminist pro-censorship movement threatens to impair the very women's rights movement it professes to serve. Led by law professor Catharine MacKinnon and writer Andrea Dworkin, this faction of the feminist movement maintains that sexually oriented *expression*—not sex-segregated labor markets, sexist concepts of marriage and family, or pent-up rage—is the preeminent cause of discrimination and violence against women. Their solution is seemingly simple: suppress all "pornography."

Censorship, however, is never a simple matter. First, the offense must be described. And how does one define something so infinitely variable, so deeply personal, so uniquely individualized as the image, the word, and the fantasy that cause sexual arousal? For decades, the U.S. Supreme Court has engaged in a Sisyphean struggle to craft a definition of *obscenity* that the lower courts can apply with some fairness and consistency. Their dilemma was best summed up in former Justice Potter Stewart's now famous statement: "I shall not today attempt further to define [obscenity]; and perhaps I could never succeed in intelligibly doing so. But I know it when I see it."

The censorious feminists are not so modest as Justice Stewart. They have fashioned an elaborate definition of *pornography* that encompasses vastly more material than does the currently recognized law of *obscenity*. As set out in their model law (which has been considered in more than a dozen jurisdictions in the United States and overseas, and which has been substantially adopted in Canada), pornography is "the sexually explicit subordination of women through pictures and/or words." The model law lists eight different criteria that attempt to illustrate their concept of "subordination," such as depictions in which "women are presented in postures or positions of sexual submission, servility, or display" or "women are presented in scenarios of degradation, humiliation, injury, torture . . . in a context that makes these conditions sexual." This linguistic driftnet can ensnare anything from religious imagery and documentary footage about the mass rapes in the Balkans to self-help books about women's health. Indeed, the Boston Women's Health Book Collective, publisher of the now-classic book on women's health and sexuality, *Our Bodies, Ourselves*, actively campaigned against the MacKinnon-Dworkin model law when it was proposed in Cambridge, Massachusetts, in 1985, recognizing that the book's explicit text and pictures could be targeted as pornographic under the law.

Although the "MacDworkinite" approach to pornography has an intuitive appeal to many feminists, it is *itself* based on subordinating and demeaning stereotypes about women. Central to the pornophobic feminists—and to many traditional conservatives and right-wing fundamentalists, as well—is the notion that *sex* is inherently degrading to women (although not to men). Not just sexual expression but sex itself—even consensual, nonviolent sex—is an evil from which women, like children, must be protected.

MacKinnon puts it this way: "Compare victims' reports of rape with women's reports of sex. They look a lot alike. . . . The major distinction between intercourse (normal) and rape (abnormal) is that the normal happens so often that one cannot get anyone to see anything wrong with it." And from Dworkin: "Intercourse remains a means or the means of physiologically making a woman inferior." Given society's pervasive sexism, she believes, women cannot freely consent to sexual relations with men; those who do consent are, in Dworkin's words, "collaborators . . . experiencing pleasure in their own inferiority."

10    These ideas are hardly radical. Rather, they are a reincarnation of disempowering puritanical, Victorian notions that feminists have long tried to consign to the dustbin of history: woman as sexual victim; man as voracious satyr. The MacDworkinite approach to sexual expression is a throwback to the archaic stereotypes that formed the basis for nineteenth-century laws which prohibited "vulgar" or sexually suggestive language from being used in the presence of women and girls.

In those days, women were barred from practicing law and serving as jurors lest they be exposed to such language. Such "protective" laws have historically functioned to bar women from full legal equality. Paternalism always leads to exclusion, discrimination, and the loss of freedom and autonomy. And in its most extreme form, it leads to purdah, in which women are completely shrouded from public view.

The pro-censorship feminists are not fighting alone. Although they try to distance themselves from such traditional "family-values" conservatives as Jesse Helms, Phyllis Schlafly, and Donald Wildmon, who are less interested in protecting women than in preserving male dominance, a common hatred of sexual expression and fondness for censorship unite the two camps. For example, the Indianapolis City Council adopted the MacKinnon-Dworkin model law in 1984 thanks to the hard work of former council member Beulah Coughenour, a leader of the Indiana Stop ERA movement. (Federal courts later declared the law unconstitutional.) And when Phyllis Schlafly's Eagle Forum and Beverly LaHaye's Concerned Women for America launched their "Enough Is Enough" anti-pornography campaign, they trumpeted the words of Andrea Dworkin in promotional materials.

This mutually reinforcing relationship does a serious disservice to the fight for women's equality. It lends credibility to and strengthens the right wing and its anti-feminist, anti-choice, homophobic agenda. This is particularly damaging in light of the growing influence of the religious right in the Republican Party and the recent Republican sweep of both Congress and many state governments. If anyone doubts that the newly empowered GOP intends to forge ahead with anti-woman agendas, they need only read the party's "Contract with America" which, among other things, reintroduces the recently repealed "gag rule" forbidding government-funded family-planning clinics from even discussing abortion with their patients.

The pro-censorship feminists base their efforts on the largely unexamined assumption that ridding society of pornography would reduce sexism and violence against women. If there were any evidence that this were true, anti-censorship feminists—myself included—would be compelled at least to reexamine our opposition to censorship. But there is no such evidence to be found.

15      A causal connection between exposure to pornography and the commission of sexual violence has never been established. The National Research Council's Panel on Understanding and Preventing Violence concluded in a 1993 survey of laboratory studies that "demonstrated empirical links between pornography and sex crimes in general are weak or absent." Even according to another research literature survey that former U.S. Surgeon General C. Everett Koop conducted at the behest of the staunchly anti-pornography Meese

Commission, only two reliable generalizations could be made about the impact of "degrading" sexual material on its viewers: it caused them to think that a variety of sexual practices was more common than they had previously believed, and to more accurately estimate the prevalence of varied sexual practices.

15    Correlational studies are similarly unsupportive of the pro-censorship cause. There are no consistent correlations between the availability of pornography in various communities, states, and countries and their rates of sexual offenses. If anything, studies suggest an inverse relationship: a greater availability of sexually explicit material seems to correlate not with higher rates of sexual violence but, rather, with higher indices of gender equality. For example, Singapore, with its tight restrictions on pornography, has experienced a much greater increase in rape rates than has Sweden, with its liberalized obscenity laws.

There *is* mounting evidence, however, that MacDworkinite-type laws will be used against the very people they are supposed to protect—namely, women. In 1992, for example, the Canadian Supreme Court incorporated the MacKinnon-Dworkin concept of pornography into Canadian obscenity law. Since that ruling, in *Butler* v. *The Queen*—which MacKinnon enthusiastically hailed as "a stunning victory for women"—well over half of all feminist bookstores in Canada have had materials confiscated or detained by customs. According to the *Feminist Bookstore News*, a Canadian publication, "The *Butler* decision has been used . . . only to seize lesbian, gay, and feminist material."

Ironically but predictably, one of the victims of Canada's new law is Andrea Dworkin herself. Two of her books, *Pornography: Men Possessing Women* and *Women Hating*, were seized, customs officials said, because they "illegally eroticized pain and bondage." Like the MacKinnon-Dworkin model law, the *Butler* decision makes no exceptions for material that is part of a feminist critique of pornography or other feminist presentation. And this inevitably overbroad sweep is precisely why censorship is antithetical to the fight for women's rights.

The pornophobia that grips MacKinnon, Dworkin, and their followers has had further counterproductive impacts on the fight for women's rights. Censorship factionalism within the feminist movement has led to an enormously wasteful diversion of energy from the real cause of and solutions to the ongoing problems of discrimination and violence against women. Moreover, the "porn-made-me-do-it" defense, whereby convicted rapists cite MacKinnon and Dworkin in seeking to reduce their sentences, actually impedes the aggressive enforcement of criminal laws against sexual violence.

A return to the basic principles of women's liberation would put the feminist movement back on course. We women are entitled to freedom of expression—to read, think, speak, sing, write, paint, dance, dream, photograph, film, and fantasize as we wish. We are also entitled to our dignity, autonomy, and equality. Fortunately, we can—and will—have both.

## Questions for Discussion

What are the "perils of pornophobia" Strossen refers to in her title?

What is Strossen's view of feminism? What is the "right" form? What should its tenets be?

How does Strossen characterize her feminist counterparts? Does she treat them "fairly"?

---

*Irving Kristol (1920–1999) wrote the following essay for the* New York
Times Magazine *in 1971, just after the National Commission on Pornography had issued its minority and majority reports. He later included it
in his 1983 book* Reflections of a Neoconservative. *The father of William
Kristol, a leading conservative Republican theorist, Irving Kristol began
his writing career in New York as a fervent leftist in the 1930s, but he
grew increasingly disaffected with communism after World War II and
wrote as a conservative New York intellectual for the next five decades.*

# *Irving Kristol*
# Pornography, Obscenity, and the Case for Censorship

Being frustrated is disagreeable, but the real disasters in life begin
when you get what you want. For almost a century now, a great many
intelligent, well-meaning and articulate people have argued eloquently
against any kind of censorship of art and entertainment. Within the
past ten years, courts and legislatures have found these arguments so
persuasive that censorship is now a relative rarity in most states.

Is there triumphant exhilaration in the land? Hardly. Somehow,
things have not worked out as they were supposed to, and many civil-
libertarians have said this was not what they meant. They wanted a
world in which Eugene O'Neill's *Desire under the Elms* could be produced, or James Joyce's *Ulysses* published, without interference. They
got that, of course; but they also got a world in which homosexual rape
is simulated on the stage, in which the public flocks to witness professional fornication, in which New York's Times Square has become a
hideous marketplace for printed filth. But does this really matter?
Might not our disquiet be merely a cultural hangover? Was anyone
ever corrupted by a book?

This last question, oddly enough, is asked by the same people
who seem convinced that advertisements in magazines or displays of
violence on television do have the power to corrupt. It is also asked,
incredibly enough and in all sincerity, by university professors and
teachers whose very lives provide the answer. After all, if you believe
that no one was ever corrupted by a book, you have also to believe

that no one was ever improved by a book. You have to believe, in other words, that art is morally trivial and that education is morally irrelevant.

To be sure, it is extremely difficult to trace the effects of any single book (or play or movie) on any reader. But we all know that the ways in which we use our minds and imaginations do shape our characters and help define us as persons. That those who certainly know this are moved to deny it merely indicates how a dogmatic resistance to the idea of censorship can result in a mindless insistence on the absurd.

5    For the plain fact is that we all believe that there is a point at which the public authorities ought to step in to limit the "self-expression" of an individual or a group. A theatrical director might find someone willing to commit suicide on the stage. We would not allow that. And I know of no one who argues that we ought to permit public gladiatorial contests, even between consenting adults.

No society can be utterly indifferent to the ways its citizens publicly entertain themselves. Bearbaiting and cockfighting are prohibited only in part out of compassion for the animals; the main reason is that such spectacles were felt to debase and brutalize the citizenry who flocked to witness them. The question with regard to pornography and obscenity is whether they will brutalize and debase our citizenry. We are, after all, not dealing with one book or one movie. We are dealing with a general tendency that is suffusing our entire culture.

Pornography's whole purpose, it seems to me, is to treat human beings obscenely, to deprive them of their specifically human dimension. Imagine a well-known man in a hospital ward, dying an agonizing death. His bladder and bowels empty themselves of their own accord. His consciousness is overwhelmed by pain, so that he cannot communicate with us, nor we with him. Now, it would be technically easy to put a television camera in his room and let the whole world witness this spectacle. We don't do it—at least not yet—because we regard this as an obscene invasion of privacy. And what would make the spectacle obscene is that we would be witnessing the extinguishing of humanity in a human animal.

Sex—like death—is an activity that is both animal and human. There are human sentiments and human ideals involved in this animal activity. But when sex is public, I do not believe the viewer can see the sentiments and the ideals, but sees only the animal coupling. And that is why when most men and women make love, they prefer to be alone—because it is only when you are alone that you can make love, as distinct from merely copulating. When sex is a public spectacle, a human relationship has been debased into a mere animal connection.

But even if all this is granted, it doubtless will be said that we ought not to be unduly concerned. Free competition in the cultural marketplace, it is argued by those who have never otherwise had a kind word to say for laissez-faire, will dispose of the problem: in the course of time, people will get bored with pornography and obscenity.

10    I would like to be able to go along with this reasoning, but I think it is false, and for two reasons. The first reason is psychological, the second, political.

In my opinion, pornography and obscenity appeal to and provoke a kind of sexual regression. The pleasure one gets from pornography and obscenity is infantile and autoerotic; put bluntly, it is a masturbatory exercise of the imagination. Now, people who masturbate do not get bored with masturbation, just as sadists don't get bored with sadism, and voyeurs don't get bored with voyeurism. In other words, like all infantile sexuality, it can quite easily become a permanent self-reinforcing neurosis. And such a neurosis, on a mass scale, is a threat to our civilization and humanity, nothing less.

I am already touching upon a political aspect of pornography when I suggest that it is inherently subversive of civilization. But there is another political aspect, which has to do with the relationship of pornography and obscenity to democracy, and especially to the quality of public life on which democratic government ultimately rests.

Today a "managerial" conception of democracy prevails, wherein democracy is seen as a set of rules and procedures, and nothing but a set of rules and procedures, by which majority rule and minority rights are reconciled into a state of equilibrium. Thus, the political system can be fully reduced to its mechanical arrangements.

There is, however, an older idea of democracy—fairly common until about the beginning of this century—for which the conception of the quality of public life is absolutely crucial. This idea starts from the proposition that democracy is a form of self-government, and that you are entitled to it only if that "self" is worthy of governing. Because the desirability of self-government depends on the character of the people who govern, the older idea of democracy was very solicitous of the condition of this character. This older democracy had no problem in principle with pornography and obscenity; it censored them; it was not about to permit people to corrupt themselves. But can a liberal— today—be for censorship? Yes, but he ought to favor a liberal form of censorship.

15    I don't think this is a contradiction.

I therefore see no reason why we should not be able to distinguish repressive censorship from liberal censorship of the written and spoken word. In Britain, until a few years ago, you could perform almost any play you wished, but certain plays, judged to be obscene, had to be performed in private theatrical clubs. In the United States, all of us who grew up using public libraries are familiar with the circumstances under which certain books could be circulated only to adults, while still other books had to be read in the library. In both cases, a small minority that was willing to make a serious effort to see an obscene play or book could do so. But the impact of obscenity was circumscribed, and the quality of public life was only marginally affected.

It is a distressing fact that any system of censorship is bound, upon occasion, to treat unjustly a particular work of art—to find pornography where there is only gentle eroticism, to find obscenity where none really exists, or to find both where the work's existence ought to be tolerated because it serves a larger moral purpose. That is the price one has to be prepared to pay for censorship, even liberal censorship.

But if you look at the history of American or English literature, there is precious little damage you can point to as a consequence of the censorship that prevailed throughout most of that history. I doubt that many works of real literary merit ever were suppressed. Nor did I notice that hitherto suppressed masterpieces flooded the market when censorship was eased. I should say, to the contrary, that literature has lost quite a bit now that so much is permitted. It seems to me that the cultural market in the United States today is awash in dirty books, dirty movies, dirty theater. Our cultural condition has not improved as a result of the new freedom.

I'll put it bluntly: if you care for the quality of life in our American democracy, then you have to be for censorship.

## Questions for Discussion

Are the analogies Kristol draws between pornography and staged suicide or gladiator battles fair and persuasive?

What is the "specifically human dimension" Kristol refers to in paragraph 7? How does Kristol develop this concept?

*Currently the editorial cartoonist for the New Orleans* Times-Picayune *newspaper,* **Walt Handelsman** *won a Pulitzer Prize for his work in 1997.*

# Walt Handelsman

## Traffic on the Information Superhighway

*Cathleen Cleaver was working in Washington, D.C., at the Family Research Council (a research and advocacy organization) as director of legal policy when, in October 1997, she was invited to deliver the following speech as part of Boston University's Great Debate series. Cleaver was invited to take the affirmative position on the question of whether the Internet ought to be regulated, and her argument was later posted on the Web. Since then, she has appeared frequently on television in support of her contention that children's exposure to adult materials on the Internet poses a social menace. She also contributes op-ed articles on subjects related to the protection of children and families, as well as on the free exercise of religion. She now works as counsel to the U.S. House of Representatives Subcommittee on the Constitution.*

## Cathleen Cleaver

# The Internet: A Clear and Present Danger?

- Someone breaks through your firewall and steals proprietary information from your computer systems. You find out and contract a lawyer who says, "Man, you shouldn't have had your stuff online." The thief becomes a millionaire using your ideas, and you go broke, if laws against copyright violation don't protect material on the Internet.

- You visit the Antiques Anonymous Web site and decide to pay their hefty subscription fee for a year's worth of exclusive estate sale previews in their private online monthly magazine. They never deliver, and, in fact, never intended to—they don't even have a magazine. You have no recourse, if laws against fraud don't apply to online transactions.

- Bob Guccione decides to branch out into the lucrative child porn market, and creates a Teen Hustler Web site featuring nude adolescents and preteens. You find out and complain, but nothing can be done, if child pornography distribution laws don't apply to computer transmissions.

- A major computer software vendor who dominates the market develops his popular office software so that it works only with his browser. You're a small browser manufacturer who is completely squeezed out of the market, but you have to find a new line of work, if antitrust laws don't apply online.

- Finally, a pedophile e-mails your son, misrepresenting himself as a 12-year-old named Jenny. They develop an online relationship and one day arrange to meet after school, where he intends to rape your son. Thankfully, you learn in advance about the meeting and go there yourself, where you find a 40-year-old man instead of Jenny. You flee to the police, who'll tell you there's nothing they can do, if child-stalking laws don't apply to the Internet.

## The Issue

The awesome advances in interactive telecommunication that we've witnessed in just the last few years have changed the way in which many Americans communicate and interact. No one can doubt that the Internet is a technological revolution of enormous proportion, with outstanding possibilities for human advancement.

As lead speaker for the affirmative, I'm asked to argue that the Internet poses a "clear and present danger," but the Internet, as a whole, isn't dangerous. In fact, it continues to be a positive and highly beneficial tool, which will undoubtedly improve education, information exchange, and commerce in years to come. In other words, the Internet will enrich many aspects of our daily life. Thus, instead of defending this rather apocalyptic view of the Internet, I'll attempt to explain why some industry and government regulation of certain aspects of the Internet is necessary—or, stated another way, why people who use the Internet should not be exempt from many of the laws and regulations that govern their conduct elsewhere. My opening illustrations were meant to give examples of some illegal conduct which should not become legal simply because someone uses the Internet. In looking at whether Internet regulation is a good idea, I believe we should consider whether regulation is in the public interest. In order to do that, we have to ask the question: Who is the public? More specifically, does the "public" whose interests we care about tonight include children?

## Children and the Internet

Dave Barry describes the Internet as a "worldwide network of university, government, business, and private computer systems, run by a thirteen-year-old named Jason." This description draws a smile precisely because we acknowledge the highly advanced computer literacy of our children. Most children demonstrate computer proficiency that far surpasses that of their parents, and many parents know only what their children have taught them about the Internet, which gives new relevance to Wordsworth's insight: "The child is father of the man." In fact, one could go so far as to say that the Internet is as accessible to many children as it is inaccessible to many adults. This technological evolution is new in many ways, not the least of which is its accessibility to children, wholly independent of their parents.

When considering what's in the public interest, we must consider the whole public, including children, as individual participants in this new medium.

## Pornography and the Internet

5   This new medium is unique in another way. It provides, through a single avenue, the full spectrum of pornographic depictions, from the more familiar convenience store fare to pornography of such violence and depravity that it surpasses the worst excesses of the normal human imagination. Sites displaying this material are easily accessible, making pornography far more freely available via the Internet than from any other communications medium in the United States. Pornography is the third largest sector of sales on the Internet, generating $1 billion annually. There are an estimated seventy-two thousand pornographic sites on the World Wide Web alone, with approximately thirty-nine new explicit sex sites every day. Indeed, the *Washington Post* has called the Internet the largest pornography store in the history of mankind.

There is little restriction of pornography-related activity in cyberspace. While there are some porn-related laws, the specter of those laws does not loom large in cyberspace. There's an implicit license there that exists nowhere else with regard to pornography—an environment where people are free to exploit others for profit and be virtually untroubled by legal deterrent. Indeed, if we consider cyberspace to be a little world of its own, it's the type of world for which groups like the ACLU have long fought, but, so far, fought in vain.

I believe it will not remain this way, but until it changes, we should take the opportunity to see what this world looks like, if for no other reason than to reassure ourselves that our decades-old decisions to control pornography were good ones.

With a few clicks of the mouse, anyone, any child, can get graphic and often violent sexual images—the kind of stuff it used to be difficult to find without exceptional effort and some significant personal risk. Anyone with a computer and a modem can set up public sites featuring the perversion of their choice, whether it's mutilation of female genitals, eroticized urination and defecation, bestiality, or sites featuring depictions of incest. These pictures can be sold for profit, they can be sent to harass others, or posted to shock people. Anyone can describe the fantasy rape and murder of a specific person and display it for all to read. Anyone can meet children in chat rooms or via e-mail and send them pornography and find out where they live. An adult who signs onto an AOL chat room as a thirteen-year-old girl is hit on thirty times within the first half hour.

All this can be done from the seclusion of the home, with the feeling of near anonymity and with the comfort of knowing that there's little risk of legal sanction.

10      The phenomenon of this kind of pornography finding such a welcome home in this new medium presents abundant opportunities for social commentary. What does Internet pornography tell us about human sexuality? Photographs, videos, and virtual games that depict rape and the dehumanization of women in sexual scenes send powerful messages about human dignity and equality. Much of the pornography freely available without restriction on the Internet celebrates unhealthy and antisocial kinds of sexual activity, such as sadomasochism, abuse, and degradation. Of course, by its very nature, pornography encourages voyeurism.

Beyond the troubling social aspects of unrestricted porn, we face the reality that children are accessing it and that predators are accessing children. We have got to start considering what kind of society we'll have when the next generation learns about human sexuality from what the Internet teaches. What does unrestricted Internet pornography teach children about relationships, about the equality of women? What does it teach little girls about themselves and their worth?

Opponents of restrictions are fond of saying that it's up to the parents to deal with the issue of children's exposure. Well, of course it is, but placing the burden solely on parents is illogical and ineffective. It's far easier for a distributor of pornography to control his material than it is for parents, who must, with the help of software, search for and find the pornographic sites, which change daily, and then attempt to block them. Any pornographer who wants to can easily subvert these efforts, and a recent Internet posting from a teenager wanting to know how to disable the filtering software on his computer received several effective answers. Moreover, it goes without saying that the most sophisticated software can only be effective where it's installed, and children will have access to many computers that don't have filtering software, such as those in libraries, schools, and at neighbors' houses.

## Internet Transactions Should Not Be Exempt

Opponents of legal restrictions often argue simply that the laws just cannot apply in this new medium, but the argument that old laws can't apply to changing technology just doesn't hold. We saw this argument last in the early '80s with the advent of the videotape. Then, certain groups tried to argue that, since you can't view videotapes without a VCR, you can't make the sale of child porn videos illegal, because, after all, they're just plastic boxes with magnetic tape inside. Technological change mandates legal change only insofar as it affects the justification for a law. It just doesn't make sense that the government may take steps to restrict illegal material in *every* medium— video, television, radio, the private telephone, *and* print—but that it may do *nothing* where people distribute the material by the Internet. While old laws might need redefinition, the old principles generally stand firm.

The question of enforcement usually is raised here, and it often comes in the form of: "How are you going to stop people from doing it?" Well, no law stops people from doing things—a red light at an intersection doesn't force you to stop but tells you that you should stop and that there could be legal consequences if you don't. Not everyone who runs a red light is caught, but that doesn't mean the law is futile. The same concept holds true for Internet laws. Government efforts to temper harmful conduct online will never be perfect, but that doesn't mean they shouldn't undertake the effort at all.

15      There's clearly a role for industry to play here. Search engines don't have to run ads for porn sites or prioritize search results to highlight porn. One new search engine even has *sex* as the default search term. Internet service providers can do something about unsolicited e-mail with hotlinks to porn, and they can and should carefully monitor any chat rooms designed for kids.

Some charge that industry standards or regulations that restrict explicit pornography will hinder the development of Internet technology. But that is to say that its advancement *depends upon* unrestricted exhibition of this material, and this cannot be true. The Internet does not belong to pornographers, and it's clearly in the public interest to see that they don't usurp this great new technology. We don't live in a perfect society, and the Internet is merely a reflection of the larger social community. Without some mitigating influences, the strong will exploit the weak, whether a Bill Gates or a child predator.

## Conclusion: Technology Must Serve Man

To argue that the strength of the Internet is chaos or that our liberty depends upon chaos is to misunderstand not only the Internet but also the fundamental nature of our liberty. It's an illusion to claim social or moral neutrality in the application of technology, even if its development may be neutral. It can be a valuable resource only when placed at the service of humanity and when it promotes our integral development for the benefit of all.

Guiding principles simply cannot be inferred from mere technical efficiency or from the usefulness accruing to some at the expense of others. Technology by its very nature requires unconditional respect for the fundamental interests of society.

Internet technology must be at the service of humanity and of our inalienable rights. It must respect the prerogatives of a civil society, among which is the protection of children.

## Questions for Discussion

What does Cleaver accomplish through the use of the bulleted list at the start of her argument?

Cleaver argues that "placing the burden solely on parents is illogical and ineffective." How and how well does she support that claim?

What counterpoints might someone who disagreed with Cleaver ("opponents of legal restrictions") make to the arguments she presents here? How does she handle the ideas and arguments of her opposition?

*William Bennett Turner practices law in San Francisco, specializing in First Amendment issues. Turner also teaches a course called The First Amendment and the Press at the University of California, Berkeley. He has worked as a legal affairs correspondent for television and with the NAACP's Legal Defense Fund and argued First Amendment cases in front of the Supreme Court. The following essay first appeared in* Wired, *a magazine devoted to innovations and controversies associated with the advent of the Information Age.*

# William Bennett Turner

# What Part of "No Law" Don't You Understand?

It's hard to imagine that our antique First Amendment, written in 1789, is up to the task of dealing with 21st-century digital communication. James Madison would have had a hard time getting his mind around instant worldwide electronic communication. The Supreme Court has said, ominously, that "differences in the characteristics of new media justify differences in the First Amendment standards applied to them." In light of this, some thoughtful observers of new technology have proposed constitutional amendments to ensure that government does not censor, manage, or restrict electronic communications.

The truth, however, is that we don't need a new First Amendment for digital communication. All we need is adherence to the bedrock principles of First Amendment interpretation that have grown up with us over the first two centuries of the republic. Madison's 18th-century framework is flexible enough to protect our freedoms in any century.

## Reality Check: Free Speech Is Not Absolute

The First Amendment speaks in seemingly absolute terms: "Congress shall make no law . . . abridging the freedom of speech or of the press." This has never meant, however, that people can say *whatever* they want *whenever* they want. Freedom of speech does not mean speech totally uninhibited by any legal restraint. It has always been true that some forms of speech can be outlawed or penalized—and many have been. Common examples include fraudulent advertising, child pornography, obscenity, "fighting words," help-wanted ads that discriminate on the basis of race, words used in a criminal transaction ("I'll kill your husband for US$10,000"), unkept promises, unlicensed broadcasts, libel, speech that infringes a copyright, and unauthorized disclosure of data used to make atomic weapons.

Correctly interpreted, the First Amendment does not prohibit all restrictions on speech. It doesn't prohibit private restrictions at all. Our constitution is a series of constraints on government, not on individuals or even powerful corporations. It is not a violation of the First Amendment for the Microsoft Network, if it so desired, to forbid postings that criticize Bill Gates. Microsoft is not the government, at least not yet. Similarly, CompuServe's censorship of sex newsgroups may offend freedom lovers but does not violate the First
5 Amendment.

The amendment prohibits government restrictions on "the freedom of speech," not on all speech, and it's a mistake to argue that no speech can be restricted. In every case, the question is whether the particular "speech" is within the "freedom" comprehended by the amendment.

## No Fine Print

The First Amendment means what the courts say it means. Since the amendment's words themselves don't tell us what falls within its "freedom," it is up to the courts, faced with the necessity of deciding particular cases, to spell out the rules for deciding exactly what speech is free, in the sense that it cannot legally be prohibited or penalized. While the courts sometimes go astray, it remains true that Americans have freer speech than any other people because our freedoms have been forthrightly defined and enforced by the courts.

In every case in which government tries to restrict speech, some highminded—or at least plausible—reason is offered. When the Nixon Administration tried to suppress publication of the Pentagon Papers, it was argued that their publication would undermine national security. When Congress acted to prohibit phone sex, it said that such action was necessary to protect children from exposure to indecent material. When state governments forbid publication of the names of rape victims, they say it is necessary to protect privacy and encourage the reporting of sex crimes. And so on. In each new case, a court has to decide whether the government's justification prevails over the interest in free speech.

## Fundamental Free Speech Principles

In deciding free speech cases, the courts have elaborated some bedrock principles that inform First Amendment decision-making. What the First Amendment "freedom" means, in fact, is basically this set of principles. We should remind ourselves of them and ask whether they need adjustment for the 21st century. Here are some of them:

- Government may not restrict or penalize speech because of its content or its viewpoint. It must remain neutral in the marketplace of ideas.
- There is no such thing as a "false idea." This principle rests on the belief that bad ideas will be driven out not by censorship but by good ideas, that the remedy for offensive speech is not suppression, but more speech.
- Restrictions on speech must not be vague or uncertain but sufficiently precise so that everyone understands exactly what is unlawful. No overly broad meat-axe regulation is allowed—any restriction must be a sensitive tool that cuts no more than is necessary to serve the precise government interest involved.
- "Journalism" is not a licensed, credentialed profession. Under our legal system, the "lonely pamphleteer" has the same First Amendment rights as the publisher of the *New York Times*.
- The press cannot be ordered to print statements it does not wish to print.
- "Prior restraints" on speech—government orders that certain information not be published—are prohibited.
- Penalties (like damages in libel suits) may not be imposed for innocent mistakes that happen to defame someone.
- Advocacy—including advocacy of the overthrow of the government—cannot be outlawed, so long as it does not amount to inciting people to imminent lawless action. Speech short of incitement cannot be banned because of the anticipated adverse reaction of the audience.
- Punishment for "seditious libel"—scathing criticism of government—is not tolerated under the First Amendment.
- No one can own or control facts or ideas (though a person can copyright the unique way he or she expresses those facts or ideas).

These are all great protections that allow us to call ourselves free people. And these principles apply regardless of the means of communication: via big newspapers, small magazines, telephones, television, radio, or the street-corner orator. There is no reason to fear that these principles will not apply with full force to all forms of digital communication.

10    On the other hand, one must recognize that some of these principles—like the First Amendment itself—are not absolute. There can be exceptions. For example, government can restrict certain speech because of its content, if it proves that there's a "compelling" government interest (like protecting national security or shielding children from sexual exploitation) and there's no less onerous means of protecting the government interest. Even a "prior restraint" on certain speech may be warranted if the government proves, say, that disclosure of the locations of strategic missiles in wartime world sabotage the war effort or endanger troops.

The question, then, is whether anything about the nature of digital communication would justify exceptions to the basic principles of our longstanding First Amendment freedom.

## New Media, New Rules?

The Supreme Court spoke too loosely when it said that differences in new media justify different First Amendment standards. The notion first surfaced in a 1949 case (*Kovacs* v. *Cooper*) involving restrictions on the use of sound trucks in congested cities. The court not surprisingly ruled that cities could keep the "new medium" from disrupting sleep and drowning out all conversation by blaring slogans at all hours and decibel levels. Such a regulation is a reasonable "time, place, and manner" restriction that does not forbid any speech based on its content. Government can more easily justify regulating the way the message is delivered rather than the message itself.

Unfortunately, the Supreme Court retrieved the thought about new media years later, reformulated it, and unthinkingly applied it to a case in which the issue was government regulation of content. In 1969, the court handed down *Red Lion*, the most important decision ever on broadcasting.

The Court upheld the FCC's "Fairness Doctrine," which required licensed broadcasters to cover important public issues and to give voice to contrasting views on the issues. In other words, broadcasters were required to air information they would otherwise have chosen not to air, including views with which they vehemently disagreed. For example, a broadcaster strongly in favor of constructing a nuclear power plant would have to air the anti-nuke point of view as well as his or her own.

15    The Court's rationale in *Red Lion* was that the airwaves were a public resource, and those licensed to monopolize one of the scarce frequencies could be required to use this government-bestowed benefit in the public interest. Scarcity of frequencies justified both government allocation of frequencies and regulation of content. The court said that requiring broadcasters to air diverse views enhanced rather than hobbled our First Amendment marketplace of ideas.

Just five years later, people concerned about the increasing concentration of media power in large corporations owning newspapers tried to get a similar concept applied to the world of print. They asked the Supreme Court to uphold a Florida law giving political candidates a "right of reply" to newspaper attacks against them during campaigns. The law was a lot like the FCC's "personal attack" rule (part of the Fairness Doctrine), one that the court had enforced against broadcasters in *Red Lion*. But in the *Miami Herald* case, the Court rejected the argument as completely inconsistent with the First Amendment right of newspapers to exercise editorial discretion in deciding what to publish and what not to publish. The result left one rule for print and another for broadcast—the most prominent illustration to date of the different-media, different-standards rule.

Now that print is becoming electronic, will it lose its preferred status? Certainly not. There is far less need for a government-enforced right of reply regarding digital communication than there is for print. There is no "scarcity" problem. You can reply instantly without permission, and you don't have to worry about economic or license barriers to entry. Your ability to respond, virtually free of charge, makes it silly to think that government should strive for some kind of "fairness" or balance in digital communication.

Whatever the merits of the Fairness Doctrine (it was abandoned by the FCC in 1987, though the *Red Lion* precedent stands), the Supreme Court should not extend the broad statement that new media justify different First Amendment rules. Former Justice Robert Jackson's original statement in the sound-truck case was that "the moving picture screen, the radio, the newspaper, the handbill, the sound truck, and the street-corner orator have differing natures, values, abuses, and dangers. Each, in my view, is a law unto itself." In *Red Lion*, the Court gave too much emphasis to the "law unto itself" part. If all the Court meant to say is that the law must reflect the "differing natures, values, abuses, and dangers" of each medium, that's fine—the unique characteristics of computer-mediated communication favor greater freedom.

## Not Broadcast, Not Print

Computer-mediated communication should have much greater freedom than, for example, broadcast. Instead of being one-way—from a broadcaster with a government license to a captive audience—it's interactive and from many to many. Its decentralization and user control are vastly different from the monopolistic control of scarce frequencies by powerful broadcasters.

20      Nor is the medium "intrusive" in the sense that our kids might be surprised and "assaulted" by hearing dirty words, such as when they scan radio stations. (This is what led the Court, in the 1978 *Pacifica* decision, to uphold the FCC prohibition of "indecency" on the radio.) User control means you need to work at it in a fairly sophisticated way to participate, and you have an incredible range of choice about exposing yourself to communication. Parental control should not be a thing of the past.

Of course, the fact that digital communication is cheap means anybody can become a publisher. There's no built-in preference for speech by the rich and powerful—those who own printing presses, tons of newsprint, or broadcast licenses—or for speech whose main appeal is to generate paid advertisements. It's far more democratic even than print.

Unfortunately, the Supreme Court has repeated the new-media new-rules statement in recent cases. In 1994, for example, the Court quoted the line from the *Red Lion* decision in deciding a case (*Turner Broadcasting* v. *FCC*) on whether cable television operators could be required to carry local broadcast and public television channels. I hope the Court, when it gets its first digital communication case, does not woodenly recite the same slogan.

The idea that there should be special First Amendment rules for new media makes little sense. The basic principles of First Amendment jurisprudence apply to all media. And, to the extent that digital communication is different—because it is fast, cheap, interactive, and controlled by decentralized users—the differences call for less regulation than traditional media, not more. The application of the basic principles should reflect these characteristics of the new technology.

## New Wine into Old Vessels

So how would First Amendment principles established for older media apply to digital communication? Check out the bedrock principles already listed. They ought to resolve just about any restriction on digital communication that you can imagine.

25     Yes, the new technology will present different kinds of issues. It has occurred to many people that libel or "indecency" on the Internet presents novel problems, and that hate speech and the invasion of privacy will have to be dealt with. Cases involving the liability of access providers and bulletin board operators already have appeared in the lower courts. And issues about anonymous speech and encryption have been hotly debated, though not decided by the courts.

In my view, none of these problems requires alteration of any of the fundamental First Amendment principles. Deciding cases involving these new issues should be done the old-fashioned way: by looking to precedent, reasoning by analogy, and considering the policy implications of ruling one way or another.

The most immediate example is the impending telecommunications law prohibiting "obscene" or "indecent" speech on the Internet. Like it or not, this is a no-brainer. Material that is so gross as to fall within the Supreme Court's strict definition of obscenity, which is really hardcore material that has no artistic, political, or social value, is unprotected by the First Amendment regardless of the medium in which it appears. So, for better or for worse, we have to accept that Congress can make a law outlawing obscene speech on the Internet. To be sure, there are knotty issues involving whose "community standards" are being used to judge obscenity when an alleged dirty picture is uploaded in libertine San Francisco and downloaded in Logan, Utah, by a recipient with no geographic address.

This is a rule that could profit by reexamination in light of the new manner of communication. And maybe there should be a new, nongeographic definition of "community" that prevents federal prosecution of, for example, those who wish to discuss safe-sex options for preventing AIDS. But there's no basis for arguing either that obscene speech is now legal because it's communicated by computer or that obscenity must now be judged by the standards of the most prudish community a prosecutor can find.

Indecent material—dirty words or pictures that the government can't prohibit adults from seeing but can keep from children—is treated differently from obscene material. The ban on "indecent" communications on the Internet is plainly invalid under the recognized principles that forbid vague, overly broad, content-based restrictions promoting interests that can be served by less restrictive means. The Supreme Court threw out, on those grounds, the comparable prohibition of "indecent" speech on the telephone in the Sable Communications case in 1989—it must do the same with the new law. The availability of less restrictive means, like filtering technology, will allow parents to control their children's access instead of reducing all communication to the level of what is fit for children.

30    Consider also what adjustments need to be made in the law of libel. More people will be "publishing" all over the country and presumably saying false and defamatory things about more people, and it won't be long before defamation cases work their way up the court system. Since *New York Times* v. *Sullivan* in 1964, all libel cases are governed, at least in part, by First Amendment rules. A public figure can't sue for an innocent mistake but basically has to prove that the publisher deliberately lied. Whether you are a public figure depends on whether you have ready access to the media to combat an untruth published about you, and whether you inject yourself into a particular controversy.

Well, if you are actively participating in a chat room or posting material on a bulletin board, you probably ought to be considered a "limited purpose" public figure and you will have to shrug off false—but not deliberately false—statements made about you in that forum. And because it's within your power to respond to statements instantaneously and to the very same audience that saw the falsehoods, any damages should be limited. Digital libel ought to be harder, not easier, to prove.

But what about the system operator, the one who allows "indecent" or libelous speech to be published on his or her system? The rule ought to be that the operator is not liable as a "publisher" unless the operator actually knows that the system is being used for plainly unlawful speech. The operator cannot be a guarantor of the accuracy of all posted information. He or she cannot reasonably be expected to monitor all postings, to screen for possible torts or even dirty words. The analogy is to a bookstore owner, not a magazine publisher.

Hate speech and harassment can be found on the Internet, just as they can be found on college dormitory bulletin boards or over the telephone. They may wreck one's enjoyment of the digital conversation but they don't present any unique First Amendment problems that can't be dealt with by the established principles. Again, we have to remember that private regulation is not unconstitutional and there is no First Amendment prohibition against expelling those whose speech is abusive or unwelcome from your digital circle. If you want government to do it for you, you're asking that First Amendment principles be diluted. Remember, we don't protect speech because it can cause no harm but because we don't trust government to decide what expression is acceptable in our discourse.

## Questions for Discussion

What kind of reader is Turner targetting? What attitude does Turner's typical reader bring to this argument?

What is the rationale for the "progression" of Turner's argument (its organization)? How does each section set up or grow out of its neighbors?

---

**Paul Winston** *writes frequently for a variety of Internet publications. The following argument appeared in September 2000 in a magazine called* Business Insurance *(available at* www.businessinsurance.com*), to which Winston contributes a regular column exploring the intersection of current cultural phenomena and their potential impact on the business community.*

## Paul Winston
# Copying This Article Is Strictly Forbidden

There is a legal battle being waged whose outcome could dramatically affect how business is done in the new millennium.

You may have heard of this dispute, involving a software program called Napster, and figured it had little to do with you because: a) You don't listen to Metallica, and b) You couldn't download a music file from the Internet even if you wanted to. I believe, however, that the Napster dispute has the potential to destroy current copyright protections for any material—including this column—and wreak havoc on free market economies.

Napster is a program that enables computer users to copy and exchange digital music files, resulting in a vast, automated exchange where files are freely traded. Essentially, Napster allows your computer to search the files on other computers using its software and download copies of whatever you like. If you want to find a particular song by Metallica, for example, you put your query online, and the software matches you with people who have these selections, just as people are perusing your hard drive and wondering whether to download your Toto music library. It's an automated process, so you can enter your search parameters, go away, and come back to find the job has been completed.

I mention Metallica because that band has taken the lead in trying to shut down Napster, charging that this free exchange of its music is copyright infringement and theft. Contrary to the warm fuzzy feelings that Metallica invokes, the band does what it does for the money, and it has no interest in giving its work away for free. While many other artists share Metallica's view, some do not; they see the free exchange of their music as an excellent way to gain recognition and interest. Often, though, these Napster supporters are bands that are not now making any money on their music anyway, and as soon as people start paying for their CDs, they'll likely change their minds and start to vote Republican.

5 The issue, as I see it, boils down to one of choice: Whether an original literary or artistic work is freely copied and shared should be up to the person or entity that created it in the first place.

If Metallica says no, that should be its right, and violators should be prosecuted. If Ned's Garage Band from Pocatello, Idaho, wants its musical message to spread as widely as possible, it should be free to use Napster, MP3 or whatever other technology exists to share its songs of potato love.

Current U.S. copyright statutes clearly protect the ability of the originator of material to control the copying, publishing and sale of that work. So it is amazing to me that the courts hearing the Napster dispute are even contemplating any argument that would contravene that right, which long existed under common law before it was the subject of legislation. While a trial court moved recently to block Napster Inc., creator of the software, a federal appeals court that will hear arguments next month has stayed that move.

If courts ultimately rule that copyrights do not block the exchange and copying of music or published material, not only will a lot of musicians find their revenue streams dry up but so too will any business that relies on intellectual property as an asset or source of income.

Book publishers, broadcasters, newspapers and software developers are among those that would be especially hard hit. If people were free to copy, print and exchange books, instead of buying them, pretty soon authors and publishers would have to find other lines of work to feed themselves. Where would Harry Potter be in this brave new world? And what about Amazon.com, let alone the corner bookstore?

10 Technology is the source of this new battle over ownership of the right to distribute information. Technology has enabled images, sounds and words to be broken down into a digital code. With the spread of personal computers and the growth of the Internet, it has become quite easy to share these perfect copies with millions of others.

Not only does Web technology make this possible but it also has conditioned us to expect to receive free information. As early companies sought to stake out a place on the Internet and lure visitors to their sites, they often offered free information. Book publishers offered free excerpts. Music companies offered free electronic singles. News organizations put all their information online for free.

I believe that the resulting mindset—that we are entitled to whatever we find on the Web—is at least partly responsible for the belief by some individuals that copyrights aren't worth the pixels used to display them.

If this view that all information should be free prevails, eventually there will be nothing worthwhile for those pixels to display. The vast majority of companies and individuals will likely conclude, despite lip service to such noble concepts as art for art's sake and media's duty to serve the masses, that if no one is willing to pay for their efforts, then why should they bother?

## Questions for Discussion

Compare Winston's argument to Turner's. Whose case is stronger? Who uses better "evidence" Why?

How does humor help Winston's argument?

*"Tom the Dancing Bug"* cartoons by **Ruben Bolling** are distributed to many publications by the Universal Press Syndicate; this one appeared in 2000. How effectively does it support its argument in favor of permitting people to download copyrighted materials from the Internet?

# Ruben Bolling

# Library System Terrorizes Publishing Industry!

# PART FOUR

# STRUGGLES

# FOR

# LIBERATION:
## SLAVERY,
## WOMEN'S RIGHTS,
## CIVIL RIGHTS

No words in American life are more respected, even reverenced, than these words expressed by Thomas Jefferson in the Declaration of Independence, July 4, 1776:

> We hold these Truths to be self-evident, that all Men are created equal, that they are endowed by their Creator with certain unalienable Rights, that among these are Life, Liberty and the Pursuit of Happiness.—That to secure these rights, Governments are instituted among Men . . .

The readings in this part of *Argument in America* test out some of the implications of those words.

The first such test was presented by those who wished to end the practice of slavery. If the Declaration of Independence could assert that "all men are created equal"

Suffragettes marching c. 1910

and "are endowed by their Creator with certain unalienable Rights," including "liberty," then how could slavery be permitted in the United States? That question was raised immediately after provisions to perpetuate slavery were written into the original United States Constitution. Here in this section of *Argument in America* are reprinted (in addition to Jefferson's Declaration and in addition to several Negro spirituals which articulated the dream of freedom within the African American community) Benjamin Banneker's letter to Jefferson challenging the constitutional provision for slavery, composed as the Constitution was being ratified in 1791; and Frederick Douglass's "What, to the Slave, Is the Fourth of July?" Douglass, a key figure in the emancipation movement, eloquently laid out the arguments against slavery and pointed to the contradiction between the Declaration and the Constitution. His argument articulated the reasons for the Civil War, for Lincoln's 1863 Emancipation Proclamation and his Gettysburg Address, and for the Thirteenth Amendment to the Constitution, which outlawed slavery once and for all when it was ratified in 1865.

But abolitionists have not been the only people to use the words of the Declaration to support arguments for one or another form of liberation. While Jefferson had said that "all *men* are created equal," women nonetheless have used the Declaration as justification for their own campaigns for political and social liberation. John Adams and his wife Abigail were quite aware of the implications that the Declaration held, as their letters reprinted here indicate. Elizabeth Cady Stanton, in "The Seneca Falls Declaration" (1848), explicitly echoed the Declaration in order to make her revolutionary case for women's rights. In addition to Stanton, reprinted here are other memorable nineteenth-century arguments in support of women's liberation: Sarah Grimké's "Letters on Women's Rights," Sojourner Truth's thrilling speech in support of the same end, and Susan B. Anthony's stirring defense "On Women's Right to Suffrage." Also included here are several photographs of suffragettes, twentieth-century women who employed the new technology of photography to reinforce their argumentative claims. (Photographs were employed to resist women's suffrage too, of course!) Women were finally granted the right to vote in 1920, with the ratification of the Nineteenth Amendment to the Constitution.

The struggle for equality in the United States did not end with the Thirteenth and Nineteenth Amendments. Later waves of political and argumentative action in the twentieth and twenty-first centuries have continued to challenge Americans to make good the words of the Declaration of Independence. Arguments in favor of women's social and economic equality are represented here in several different forms: Susan Glaspell's one-act play *Trifles* (1916), Betty Friedan's "An Open Letter to *True* Men" (1974), Cindy Lauper's anthem "Girls Just Wanna Have Fun" (1983), and Paula Gunn Allen's essay "Where I Come From Is Like This" (1986). In addition, you will encounter several vital statements that have furthered the cause of civil rights for African Americans: Claude McKay's poem "If We Must Die" and the solidarity anthem "We Shall Overcome," Martin Luther King, Jr.'s "I Have a Dream" speech (delivered on the steps of the Lincoln Memorial as part of an observance of the one hundredth anniversary of the Emancipation Proclamation), Jesse Jackson's speech at the 1984 Democratic National Convention, and several visual arguments in support of civil rights. (You might also examine King's "Letter from Birmingham Jail," reprinted in Part Five, and arguments by James Baldwin and Richard Rodriguez in Part Six on "Becoming America(n).") This section also includes Harvey Milk's "The Hope Speech," an early argument in support of gay rights that has inspired later liberation efforts.

*Thomas Jefferson (1743–1826), the third president of the United States, was a lawyer, legislator, statesman, educator, inventor, architect, author, scientist, and philosopher. Overall, Jefferson spent nearly forty years in public service, including his two terms as president; during that time he developed and shaped many of the political ideas and practices we now take for granted. Considered by many to be the quintessential American representative of the Enlightenment, Jefferson studied many of the ideas of famous European theorists like John Locke, adapting them to the unique circumstances of the developing and highly volatile situation in America. Jefferson drafted the Declaration of Independence for the Continental Congress in June of 1776 as a means of generating public support, both at home and abroad, for the colonists' grievances against King George III. It was submitted on July 1 and adopted by the Congress (with some revision) on July 4, 1776.*

## Thomas Jefferson

# The Declaration of Independence

WHEN in the Course of human Events, it becomes necessary for one People to dissolve the Political Bands which have connected them with another, and to assume among the Powers of the Earth, the separate and equal Station to which the Laws of Nature and of Nature's God entitle them, a decent Respect to the Opinions of Mankind requires that they should declare the causes which impel them to the Separation.

WE hold these Truths to be self-evident, that all Men are created equal, that they are endowed by their Creator with certain unalienable Rights, that among these are Life, Liberty and the Pursuit of Happiness—That to secure these Rights, Governments are instituted among Men, deriving their just Powers from the Consent of the Governed, that whenever any Form of Government becomes destructive of these Ends, it is the Right of the People to alter or to abolish it, and to institute new Government, laying its Foundation on such Principles, and organizing its Powers in such Form, as to them shall seem most likely to effect their Safety and Happiness. Prudence, indeed, will dictate that Governments long established should not be changed for light and transient Causes; and accordingly all Experience hath shewn, that Mankind are more disposed to suffer, while Evils are sufferable, than to right themselves by abolishing the Forms to which they are accustomed. But when a long Train of Abuses and Usurpations, pursuing invariably the same Object, evinces a Design to reduce them under absolute Despotism, it is their Right, it is their Duty, to throw off such Government, and to provide new Guards for their future Security. Such has been the patient Sufferance of these Colonies; and such is now the Necessity which constrains them to alter their former Systems of Government. The History of the present King of Great-Britain is a History of repeated Injuries and Usurpations, all having in direct Object the Establishment of an absolute Tyranny over these States. To prove this, let Facts be submitted to a candid World.

He has refused his Assent to Laws, the most wholesome and necessary for the public Good.

HE has forbidden his Governors to pass Laws of immediate and pressing Importance, unless suspended in their Operation till his Assent should be obtained; and when so suspended, he has utterly neglected to attend to them.

5 HE has refused to pass other Laws for the Accommodation of large Districts of People, unless those People would relinquish the Right of Representation in the Legislature, a Right inestimable to them, and formidable to Tyrants only.

HE has called together Legislative Bodies at Places unusual, uncomfortable, and distant from the Depository of their public Records, for the sole Purpose of fatiguing them into Compliance with his Measures.

HE has dissolved Representative Houses repeatedly, for opposing with manly Firmness his Invasions on the Rights of the People.

HE has refused for a long Time, after such Dissolutions, to cause others to be elected; whereby the Legislative Powers, incapable of the Annihilation, have returned to the People at large for their exercise; the State remaining in the mean time exposed to all the Dangers of Invasion from without, and the Convulsions within.

HE has endeavoured to prevent the Population of these States; for that Purpose obstructing the Laws for Naturalization of Foreigners; refusing to pass others to encourage their Migrations hither, and raising the Conditions of new Appropriations of Lands.

10 HE has obstructed the Administration of Justice, by refusing his Assent to Laws for establishing Judiciary Powers.

HE has made Judges dependent on his Will alone, for the Tenure of their Offices, and the Amount and Payment of their Salaries.

HE has erected a Multitude of new Offices, and sent hither Swarms of Officers to harrass our People, and eat out their Substance.

HE has kept among us, in Times of Peace, Standing Armies, without the consent of our Legislatures.

HE has affected to render the Military independent of and superior to the Civil Power.

15 HE has combined with others to subject us to a Jurisdiction foreign to our Constitution, and unacknowledged by our Laws; giving his Assent to their Acts of pretended Legislation:

FOR quartering large Bodies of Armed Troops among us;

FOR protecting them, by a mock Trial, from Punishment for any Murders which they should commit on the Inhabitants of these States:

FOR cutting off our Trade with all Parts of the World:

FOR imposing Taxes on us without our Consent:

20 FOR depriving us, in many Cases, of the Benefits of Trial by Jury:

FOR transporting us beyond Seas to be tried for pretended Offences:

FOR abolishing the free System of English Laws in a neighbouring Province, establishing therein an arbitrary Government, and enlarging its Boundaries, so as to render it at once an Example and fit Instrument for introducing the same absolute Rules into these Colonies:

FOR taking away our Charters, abolishing our most valuable Laws, and altering fundamentally the Forms of our Governments:

FOR suspending our own Legislatures, and declaring themselves invested with Power to legislate for us in all Cases whatsoever.

25 HE has abdicated Government here, by declaring us out of his Protection and waging War against us.

HE has plundered our Seas, ravaged our Coasts, burnt our Towns, and destroyed the Lives of our People.

HE is, at this Time, transporting large Armies of foreign Mercenaries to compleat the Works of Death, Desolation, and Tyranny, already begun with circumstances of Cruelty and Perfidy, scarcely paralleled in the most barbarous Ages, and totally unworthy the Head of a civilized Nation.

HE has constrained our fellow Citizens taken Captive on the high Seas to bear Arms against their Country, to become the Executioners of their Friends and Brethren, or to fall themselves by their Hands.

HE has excited domestic Insurrections amongst us, and has endeavoured to bring on the Inhabitants of our Frontiers, the merciless Indian Savages, whose known Rule of Warfare, is an undistinguished Destruction, of all Ages, Sexes and Conditions.

30 IN every stage of these Oppressions we have Petitioned for Redress in the most humble Terms: Our repeated Petitions have been answered only by repeated Injury. A Prince, whose Character is thus marked by every act which may define a Tyrant, is unfit to be the Ruler of a free People.

NOR have we been wanting in Attentions to our British Brethren. We have warned them from Time to Time of Attempts by their Legislature to extend an unwarrantable Jurisdiction over us. We have reminded them of the Circumstances of our Emigration and Settlement here. We have appealed to their native Justice and Magnanimity, and we have conjured them by the Ties of our common Kindred to disavow these Usurpations, which, would inevitably interrupt our Connections and Correspondence. They too have been deaf to the Voice of Justice and of Consanguinity. We must, therefore, acquiesce in the Necessity, which denounces our Separation, and hold them, as we hold the rest of Mankind, Enemies in War, in Peace, Friends.

WE, therefore, the Representatives of the UNITED STATES OF AMERICA, in GENERAL CONGRESS, Assembled, appealing to the Supreme Judge of the World for the Rectitude of our Intentions, do, in the Name, and by Authority of the good People of these Colonies, solemnly Publish and Declare, That these United Colonies are, and of Right ought to be, FREE AND INDEPENDENT STATES; that they are absolved from all Allegiance to the British Crown, and that all political Connection between them and the State of Great-Britain, is and

ought to be totally dissolved; and that as FREE AND INDEPENDENT
STATES, they have full Power to levy War, conclude Peace, contract
Alliances, establish Commerce, and to do all other Acts and Things
which INDEPENDENT STATES may of right do. And for the support
of this Declaration, with a firm Reliance on the Protection of divine
Providence, we mutually pledge to each other our Lives, our Fortunes,
and our sacred Honor.

## Questions for Discussion

How well do the first few paragraphs set the stage for the list of "offenses"
Jefferson supplies? How effective is this way of arranging things, given the
document's primary objectives?

Is the Declaration of Independence an argument—an effort to change
minds—or is it simply a "declaration" of principles shared by those who
signed it?

*Benjamin Banneker (1731–1806) was a free and educated (although by no means wealthy) African American during a period in American history when that was unusual. He was interested in almost everything mechanical (in his early twenties, he carved a large-scale clock based on detailed drawings and measurements he took of a neighbor's pocket watch); but he specialized in mathematics and astronomy, two disciplines he drew on to compile reliable and highly popular almanacs. As a surveyor, he also played a crucial role in the original planning of the District of Columbia. In 1791, Banneker sent the following letter, and an almanac he had compiled, to then Secretary of State Thomas Jefferson in response to Jefferson's implications in* Notes on the State of Virginia *that African Americans were inferior. Banneker was also probably aware that Jefferson's initial drafts of the Declaration of Independence had contained passages concerning the need to limit the spread of slavery in the new nation, passages that were eventually excised from the final edition.*

# Benjamin Banneker
## Letter to Thomas Jefferson

Sir, I am fully sensible of the greatness of that freedom which I take with you on the present occasion; a liberty which seemed to me scarcely allowable, when I reflected on that distinguished and dignified station in which you stand; and the almost general prejudice and prepossession which is so prevalent in the world against those of my complexion.

I suppose it is a truth too well attested to you to need of proof here, that we are a race of beings who have long labored under the abuse and censure of the world, that we have long been looked upon with an eye of contempt, and that we have long been considered rather as brutish than human, and scarcely capable of mental endowments.

Sir, I hope I may safely admit, in consequence of that report which hath reached me, that you are a man far less inflexible in sentiments of this nature than many others, that you are measurably friendly and well disposed towards us, and that you are willing and ready to lend your aid and assistance to our relief from those many distresses and numerous calamities to which we are reduced.

Now, sir, if this is founded in truth, I apprehend you will readily embrace every opportunity to eradicate that train of absurd and false ideas and opinions which so generally prevail with respect to us, and that your sentiments are concurrent with mine, which are that one universal father hath given being to us all, and that he hath not only made us all of one flesh, but that he hath also without partiality afforded us all the same sensations, and endued us all with the same faculties, and that however variable we may be in society or religion, however diversified in situation or color, we are all of the same family, and stand in the same relation to him.

Sir, if these are sentiments of which you are fully persuaded, I hope you cannot but acknowledge that it is the indispensable duty of those who maintain for themselves the rights of human nature, and who profess the obligations of Christianity, to extend their power and influence to the relief of every part of the human race from whatever burthen or oppression they may unjustly labor under; and this I apprehend a full conviction of the truth and obligation of these principles should lead all to.

Sir, I have long been convinced that if your love for your selves and for those inesteemable laws which preserve to you the rights of human nature was founded on sincerity, you could not but be solicitous that every individual, of whatsoever rank or distinction, might with you equally enjoy the blessings thereof; neither could you rest satisfied, short of the most active diffusion of your exertions, in order to their promotion from any state of degradation to which the unjustifiable cruelty and barbarism of men may have reduced them.

Sir, I freely and cheerfully acknowledge that I am of the African race, and in that color which is natural to them of the deepest dye, and it is under a sense of the most profound gratitude to the Supreme Ruler of the universe that I now confess to you, that I am not under that state of tyrannical thraldom, and inhuman captivity, to which too many of my brethren are doomed; but that I have abundantly tasted of the fruition of those blessings which proceed from that free and unequaled liberty with which you are favored and which I hope you will willingly allow you have received from the immediate hand of that being from whom proceedeth every good and perfect gift.

Sir, suffer me to recall to your mind that time in which the arms and tyranny of the British Crown were exerted with every powerful effort in order to reduce you to a state of servitude; look back, I intreat you, on the variety of dangers to which you were exposed, reflect on that time in which every human aid appeared unavailable, and in which even hope and fortitude wore the aspect of inability to the conflict, and you cannot but be led to a serious and grateful sense of your miraculous and providential preservation; you cannot but acknowledge that the present freedom and tranquility which you enjoy you have mercifully received, and that it is the peculiar blessing of heaven.

This, sir, was a time in which you clearly saw into the injustice of a state of slavery, and in which you had just apprehensions of the horrors of its condition; it was now, Sir, that your abhorrence thereof was so excited, that you publicly held forth this true and invaluable doctrine which is worthy to be recorded and remembered in all succeeding ages. "We hold these truths to be self evident, that all men are created equal, and that they are endowed by their creator with certain unalienable rights, that amongst these are life, liberty, and the pursuit of happiness."

Here, sir, was a time in which your tender feelings for yourselves engaged you thus to declare, you were then impressed with proper ideas of the great valuation of liberty, and the free possession of those blessings to which you were entitled by nature; but, Sir, how pitiable is it to reflect, that although you were so fully convinced of the benevolence of the father of mankind, and of his equal and impartial distribution of those rights and privileges which he had conferred upon them, that you should at the same time counteract his mercies, in detaining by fraud and violence so numerous a part of my brethren under groaning captivity and cruel oppression, that you should at the same time be found guilty of that most criminal act, which you professedly detested in others, with respect to yourselves.

Sir, I suppose that your knowledge of the situation of my brethren is too extensive to need a recital here; neither shall I presume to prescribe methods by which they may be relieved; otherwise than by recommending to you, and all others, to wean yourselves from those narrow prejudices which you have imbibed with respect to them, and as Job proposed to his friends, "Put your souls in their souls stead," thus shall your hearts be enlarged with kindness and benevolence towards them, and thus shall you need neither the direction of myself or others in what manner to proceed herein.

And now, Sir, although my sympathy and affection for my brethren hath caused my enlargement thus far, I ardently hope that your candour and generosity will plead with you in my behalf, when I make known to you, that it was not originally my design; but that having taken up my pen in order to direct to you as a present, a copy of an almanac which I have calculated for the succeeding year, I was unexpectedly and unavoidably led thereto.

This calculation, sir, is the production of my arduous study, in this my advanced stage of life; for having long had unbounded desires to become acquainted with the secrets of nature, I have had to gratify my curiosity herein through my own assiduous application to astronomical study, in which I need not to recount to you the many difficulties and disadvantages which I have had to encounter.

And although I had almost declined to make my calculation for the ensuing year, in consequence of that time which I had allotted therefore being taking up at the federal territory by the request of Mr. Andrew Ellicott, yet finding myself under several engagements to printers of this state to whom I had communicated my design, on my return to my place of residence, I industriously applied myself thereto, which I hope I have accomplished with correctness and accuracy, a copy of which I have taken the liberty to direct to you, and which I humbly request you will favorably receive, and although you may have the opportunity of perusing it after its publication, yet I chose to send it to you in manuscript previous thereto, that thereby you might not only have an earlier inspection, but that you might also view it in my own hand-writing.

And now, Sir, I shall conclude and subscribe myself with the most profound respect, your most obedient humble servant,

*Benjamin Banneker*

## Questions for Discussion

How does Banneker handle the differences in "station" between himself and Thomas Jefferson?

What role does the almanac play in Banneker's argument? How effective is it for Banneker to offer up his own work as a form of evidence against slavery?

*Frederick Douglass's rise from obscurity to prominence was even more astounding than the rise of Benjamin Franklin. Born a slave in Maryland in 1818 under the name Frederick Bailey—he never knew his father and seldom saw his mother after he was taken from her as a child—Douglass escaped to the North in 1839 and assumed a new identity. He quickly became active in abolitionist circles and, after a decade of flight, was able, with assistance, to purchase his freedom for $700. Later, he began his own weekly newspaper,* The North Star, *in Rochester, New York, as a vehicle for his beliefs and causes. A prominent orator and essayist, during the Civil War he urged President Lincoln to enlist African Americans in the army, and after the war he continued to campaign for freedom, not only by advocating antilynching laws and better conditions for tenant farmers but also by supporting women's suffrage.*

*Douglass is best known for his* Narrative of the Life of Frederick Douglass, an American Slave *(1845), the most famous of the many "slave narratives" (i.e., firsthand accounts of slave life) that were published in the years before the Civil War. Publication of the* Narrative *established him as a major voice in the antislavery movement and he was highly sought as an orator for the rest of his life (he died in 1895). The following speech, slightly edited here for length, was delivered at a meeting of an antislavery society in Rochester on July 5, 1852.*

# Frederick Douglass

# What, to the Slave, Is the Fourth of July?

Friends and Fellow Citizens: He who could address this audience without a quailing sensation has stronger nerves than I have. I do not remember ever to have appeared as a speaker before any assembly more shrinkingly, nor with greater distrust of my ability, than I do this day. A feeling has crept over me, quite unfavorable to the exercise of my limited powers of speech. The task before me is one which requires much previous thought and study for its proper performance. I know that apologies of this sort are generally considered flat and unmeaning. I trust, however, that mine will not be so considered. Should I seem at ease, my appearance would much misrepresent me. The little experience I have had in addressing public meetings, in country school houses, avails me nothing on the present occasion.

The papers and placards say that I am to deliver a Fourth [of] July oration. This certainly sounds large, and out of the common way, for me. It is true that I have often had the privilege to speak in this beautiful Hall, and to address many who now honor me with their presence. But neither their familiar faces, nor the perfect gage I think I have of Corinthian Hall, seems to free me from embarrassment.

The fact is, ladies and gentlemen, the distance between this platform and the slave plantation, from which I escaped, is considerable—and the difficulties to be overcome in getting from the latter to the former, are by no means slight. That I am here today is, to me, a matter of astonishment as well as of gratitude. You will not, therefore, be surprised, if in what I have to say, I evince no elaborate preparation, nor grace my speech with any high sounding exordium. With little experience and with less learning, I have been able to throw my thoughts hastily and imperfectly together; and trusting to your patient and generous indulgence, I will proceed to lay them before you.

This, for the purpose of this celebration, is the Fourth of July. It is the birthday of your National Independence, and of your political freedom. This, to you, is what the Passover was to the emancipated people of God. It carries your minds back to the day, and to the act of your great deliverance; and to the signs, and to the wonders, associated with that act, and that day. This celebration also marks the beginning of another year of your national life; and reminds you that the Republic of America is now seventy-six years old. I am glad, fellow-citizens, that your nation is so young. Seventy-six years, though a good old age for a man, is but a mere speck in the life of a nation. Three score years and ten is the allotted time for individual men; but nations number their years by thousands. According to this fact, you are, even now, only in the beginning of your national career, still lingering in the period of childhood. I repeat, I am glad this is so. There is hope in the thought, and hope is much needed, under the dark clouds which lower above the horizon. The eye of the reformer is met with angry flashes, portending disastrous times; but his heart may well beat lighter at the thought that America is young, and that she is still in the impressible stage of her existence. May he not hope that high lessons of wisdom, of justice and of truth, will yet give direction to her destiny? Were the nation older, the patriot's heart might be sadder, and the reformer's brow heavier. Its future might be shrouded in gloom, and the hope of its prophets go out in sorrow. There is consolation in the thought that America is young. Great streams are not easily turned from channels, worn deep in the course of ages. They may sometimes rise in quiet and stately majesty, and inundate the land, refreshing and fertilizing the earth with their mysterious properties. They may also rise in wrath and fury, and bear away, on their angry waves, the accumulated wealth of years of toil and hardship. They, however, gradually flow back to the same old channel, and flow on as serenely as ever. But, while the river may not be turned aside, it may dry up, and leave nothing behind but the withered branch, and the unsightly rock, to howl in the abyss-sweeping wind, the sad tale of departed glory. As with rivers so with nations.

5  Fellow-citizens, I shall not presume to dwell at length on the associations that cluster about this day. The simple story of it is that, seventy-six years ago, the people of this country were British subjects. The style and title of your "sovereign people" (in which you now glory) was not then born. You were under the British Crown. Your fathers esteemed the English Government as the home government; and England as the fatherland. This home government, you know, although a considerable distance from your home, did, in the exercise of its parental prerogatives, impose upon its colonial children, such restraints, burdens and limitations, as, in its mature judgment, it deemed wise, right and proper.

But, your fathers, who had not adopted the fashionable idea of this day, of the infallibility of government, and the absolute character of its acts, presumed to differ from the home government in respect to the wisdom and the justice of some of those burdens and restraints. They went so far in their excitement as to pronounce the measures of government unjust, unreasonable, and oppressive, and altogether such as ought not to be quietly submitted to. I scarcely need say, fellow-citizens, that my opinion of those measures fully accords with that of your fathers. Such a declaration of agreement on my part would not be worth much to anybody. It would, certainly, prove nothing, as to what part I might have taken, had I lived during the great controversy of 1776. To say *now* that America was right, and England wrong, is exceedingly easy. Everybody can say it; the dastard, not less than the noble brave, can flippantly discant on the tyranny of England towards the American Colonies. It is fashionable to do so; but there was a time when to pronounce against England, and in favor of the cause of the colonies, tried men's souls.[1] They who did so were accounted in their day, plotters of mischief, agitators and rebels, dangerous men. To side with the right, against the wrong, with the weak against the strong, and with the oppressed against the oppressor! *Here* lies the merit, and the one which, of all others, seems unfashionable in our day. The cause of liberty may be stabbed by the men who glory in the deeds of your fathers. But, to proceed.

Feeling themselves harshly and unjustly treated by the home government, your fathers, like men of honesty, and men of spirit, earnestly sought redress. They petitioned and remonstrated; they did so in a decorous, respectful, and loyal manner. Their conduct was wholly unexceptionable. This, however, did not answer the purpose. They saw themselves treated with sovereign indifference, coldness and scorn. Yet they persevered. They were not the men to look back.

As the sheet anchor takes a firmer hold, when the ship is tossed by the storm, so did the cause of your fathers grow stronger, as it breasted the chilling blasts of kingly displeasure. The greatest and best of British statesmen admitted its justice, and the loftiest eloquence of the British Senate came to its support. But, with that blindness which seems to be the unvarying characteristic of tyrants, since Pharaoh and his hosts were drowned in the Red Sea, the British Government persisted in the exactions complained of.

The madness of this course, we believe, is admitted now, even by England; but we fear the lesson is wholly lost on our present rulers.

10    Oppression makes a wise man mad. Your fathers were wise men, and if they did not go mad, they became restive under this treatment. They felt themselves the victims of grievous wrongs, wholly incurable in their colonial capacity. With brave men there is always a remedy for oppression. Just here, the idea of a total separation of the colonies from the crown was born! It was a startling idea, much more so, than we, at this distance of time, regard it. The timid and the prudent (as has been intimated) of that day, were, of course, shocked and alarmed by it.

Such people lived then, had lived before, and will, probably, ever have a place on this planet; and their course, in respect to any great

---

[1] This note and some others on this selection draw on the edition of Douglass's speeches prepared by John W. Blassingame et al. (Yale University Press, 1982). An allusion to the opening line of a Revolutionary-era pamphlet by agitator Thomas Paine: "These are the times that try men's souls."

change (no matter how great the good to be attained, or the wrong to be redressed by it), may be calculated with as much precision as can be the course of the stars. They hate all changes, but silver, gold and copper change! Of this sort of change they are always strongly in favor.

These people were called Tories in the days of your fathers; and the appellation, probably, conveyed the same idea that is meant by a more modern, though a somewhat less euphonious term, which we often find in our papers, applied to some of our old politicians.

Their opposition to the then dangerous thought was earnest and powerful; but, amid all their terror and affrighted vociferations against it, the alarming and revolutionary idea moved on, and the country with it.

On the second of July, 1776, the old Continental Congress, to the dismay of the lovers of ease, and the worshippers of property, clothed that dreadful idea with all the authority of national sanction. They did so in the form of a resolution; and as we seldom hit upon resolutions, drawn up in our day, whose transparency is at all equal to this, it may refresh your minds and help my story if I read it:

> Resolved, That these united colonies *are*, and of right, ought to be free and Independent States; that they are absolved from all allegiance to the British Crown; and that all political connection between them and the State of Great Britain *is*, and ought to be, dissolved.

15

Citizens, your fathers made good that resolution. They succeeded; and today you reap the fruits of their success. The freedom gained is yours; and you, therefore, may properly celebrate this anniversary. The Fourth of July is the first great fact in your nation's history—the very ring-bolt in the chain of your yet undeveloped destiny.

Pride and patriotism, not less than gratitude, prompt you to celebrate and to hold it in perpetual remembrance. I have said that the Declaration of Independence is the RING-BOLT to the chain of your nation's destiny; so, indeed, I regard it. The principles contained in that instrument are saving principles. Stand by those principles, be true to them on all occasions, in all places, against all foes, and at whatever cost.

From the round top of your ship of state, dark and threatening clouds may be seen. Heavy billows, like mountains in the distance, disclose to the leeward huge forms of flinty rocks! That *bolt* drawn, that *chain* broken, and all is lost. *Cling to this day—cling to it*, and to its principles, with the grasp of a storm-tossed mariner to a spar at midnight.

The coming into being of a nation, in any circumstances, is an interesting event. But, besides general considerations, there were peculiar circumstances which make the advent of this republic an event of special attractiveness.

The whole scene, as I look back to it, was simple, dignified and sublime.

20　　The population of the country, at the time, stood at the insignificant number of three millions. The country was poor in the munitions of war. The population was weak and scattered, and the country a wilderness unsubdued. There were then no means of concert and combination, such as exist now. Neither steam nor lightning had then been reduced to order and discipline. From the Potomac to the Delaware was a journey of many days. Under these, and innumerable other disadvantages, your fathers declared for liberty and independence and triumphed.

Fellow Citizens, I am not wanting in respect for the fathers of this republic. The signers of the Declaration of Independence were brave men. They were great men too—great enough to give fame to a great age. It does not often happen to a nation to raise, at one time, such a number of truly great men. The point from which I am compelled to view them is not, certainly, the most favorable; and yet I cannot contemplate their great deeds with less than admiration. They were statesmen, patriots and heroes, and for the good they did, and the principles they contended for, I will unite with you to honor their memory.

They loved their country better than their own private interests; and, though this is not the highest form of human excellence, all will concede that it is a rare virtue, and that when it is exhibited, it ought to command respect. He who will, intelligently, lay down his life for his country, is a man whom it is not in human nature to despise. Your fathers staked their lives, their fortunes, and their sacred honor, on the cause of their country. In their admiration of liberty, they lost sight of all other interests.

They were peace men; but they preferred revolution to peaceful submission to bondage. They were quiet men; but they did not shrink from agitating against oppression. They showed forbearance; but that they knew its limits. They believed in order; but not in the order of tyranny. With them, nothing was *"settled"* that was not right. With them, justice, liberty and humanity were *"final"*; not slavery and oppression. You may well cherish the memory of such men. They were great in their day and generation. Their solid manhood stands out the more as we contrast it with these degenerate times.

How circumspect, exact and proportionate were all their movements! How unlike the politicians of an hour! Their statesmanship looked beyond the passing moment, and stretched away in strength into the distant future. They seized upon eternal principles, and set a glorious example in their defence. Mark them!

25　　Fully appreciating the hardship to be encountered, firmly believing in the right of their cause, honorably inviting the scrutiny of an onlooking world, reverently appealing to heaven to attest their sincerity, soundly comprehending the solemn responsibility they were about to assume, wisely measuring the terrible odds against them, your fathers, the fathers of this republic, did, most deliberately, under the inspiration of a glorious patriotism, and with a sublime faith in the great principles of justice and freedom, lay deep the corner-stone of the national superstructure, which has risen and still rises in grandeur around you.

Of this fundamental work, this day is the anniversary. Our eyes are met with demonstrations of joyous enthusiasm. Banners and pennants wave exultingly on the breeze. The din of business, too, is hushed. Even Mammon seems to have quitted his grasp on this day.[2] The ear-piercing fife and the stirring drum unite their accents with the ascending peal of a thousand church bells. Prayers are made, hymns are sung, and sermons are preached in honor of this day; while the quick martial tramp of a great and multitudinous nation, echoed back by all the hills, valleys and mountains of a vast continent, bespeak the occasion one of thrilling and universal interest—a nation's jubilee. . . .

## The Present

Fellow-citizens, pardon me, allow me to ask, why am I called upon to speak here today? What have I, or those I represent, to do with your national independence? Are the great principles of political freedom and of natural justice, embodied in that Declaration of Independence, extended to us? and am I, therefore, called upon to bring our humble offering to the national altar, and to confess the benefits and express devout gratitude for the blessings resulting from your independence to us?

---

[2] In Matthew 6:24, Jesus personifies Mammon as a god of material and earthly interests, whom people are tempted to worship in place of the true God.

Would to God, both for your sakes and ours, that an affirmative answer could be truthfully returned to these questions! Then would my task be light, and my burden easy and delightful. For *who* is there so cold, that a nation's sympathy could not warm him? Who so obdurate and dead to the claims of gratitude, that would not thankfully acknowledge such priceless benefits? Who so stolid and selfish, that would not give his voice to swell the hallelujahs of a nation's jubilee, when the chains of servitude had been torn from his limbs? I am not that man. In a case like that, the dumb might eloquently speak, and the "lame man leap as an hart."

But, such is not the state of the case. I say it with a sad sense of the disparity between us. I am not included within the pale of this glorious anniversary! Your high independence only reveals the immeasurable distance between us. The blessings in which you, this day, rejoice, are not enjoyed in common. The rich inheritance of justice, liberty, prosperity and independence, bequeathed by your fathers, is shared by you, not by me. The sunlight that brought life and healing to you, has brought stripes and death to me. This Fourth [of] July is *yours*, not *mine*. *You* may rejoice, *I* must mourn. To drag a man in fetters into the grand illuminated temple of liberty, and call upon him to join you in joyous anthems, were inhuman mockery and sacrilegious irony. Do you mean, citizens, to mock me, by asking me to speak today? If so, there is a parallel to your conduct. And let me warn you that it is dangerous to copy the example of a nation whose crimes, towering up to heaven, were thrown down by the breath of the Almighty, burying that nation in irrecoverable ruin! I can today take up the plaintive lament of a peeled and woe-smitten people!

30   "By the rivers of Babylon, there we sat down. Yea! we wept when we remembered Zion. We hanged our harps upon the willows in the midst thereof. For there, they that carried us away captive, required of us a song; and they who wasted us required of us mirth, saying, Sing us one of the songs of Zion. How can we sing the Lord's song in a strange land? If I forget thee, O Jerusalem, let my right hand forget her cunning. If I do not remember thee, let my tongue cleave to the roof of my mouth.[3]

Fellow-citizens; above your national, tumultuous joy, I hear the mournful wall of millions! whose chains, heavy and grievous yesterday, are, today, rendered more intolerable by the jubilee shouts that

---

[3] Psalms 137:1–6 describes the sorrow of the Jewish captives who were taken away to Babylon after the fall of Jerusalem.

reach them. If I do forget, if I do not faithfully remember those bleeding children of sorrow this day, "may my right hand forget her cunning, and may my tongue cleave to the roof of my mouth!" To forget them, to pass lightly over their wrongs, and to chime in with the popular theme, would be treason most scandalous and shocking, and would make me a reproach before God and the world. My subject, then fellow-citizens, is AMERICAN SLAVERY. I shall see, this day, and its popular characteristics, from the slave's point of view. Standing, there, identified with the American bondman, making his wrongs mine, I do not hesitate to declare, with all my soul, that the character and conduct of this nation never looked blacker to me than on this Fourth of July! Whether we turn to the declarations of the past, or to the professions of the present, the conduct of the nation seems equally hideous and revolting. America is false to the past, false to the present, and solemnly binds herself to be false to the future. Standing with God and the crushed and bleeding slave on this occasion, I will, in the name of humanity which is outraged, in the name of liberty which is fettered, in the name of the constitution and the Bible, which are disregarded and trampled upon, dare to call in question and to denounce, with all the emphasis I can command, everything that serves to perpetuate slavery—the great sin and shame of America! "I will not equivocate; I will not excuse";[4] I will use the severest language I can command; and yet not one word shall escape me that any man, whose judgment is not blinded by prejudice, or who is not at heart a slaveholder, shall not confess to be right and just.

But I fancy I hear some one of my audience say, it is just in this circumstance that you and your brother abolitionists fail to make a favorable impression on the public mind. Would you argue more, and denounce less, would you persuade more, and rebuke less, your cause would be much more likely to succeed. But, I submit, where all is plain there is nothing to be argued. What point in the antislavery creed would you have me argue? On what branch of the subject do the people of this country need light? Must I undertake to prove that the slave is a man? That point is conceded already. Nobody doubts it. The slaveholders themselves acknowledge it in the enactment of laws for their government. They acknowledge it when they punish disobedience on the part of the slave. There are seventy-two crimes in the State

---

[4] Douglass alludes to the first issue of *The Liberator* (1831): there William Lloyd Garrison promised, "I am in earnest—I will not equivocate—I will not excuse—I will not retreat a single inch—and *I will be heard.*"

of Virginia, which, if committed by a black man (no matter how ignorant he be), subject him to the punishment of death; while only two of the same crimes will subject a white man to the like punishment. What is this but the acknowledgement that the slave is a moral, intellectual and responsible being? The manhood of the slave is conceded. It is admitted in the fact that Southern statute books are covered with enactments forbidding, under severe fines and penalties, the teaching of the slave to read or to write. When you can point to any such laws, in reference to the beasts of the field, then I may consent to argue the manhood of the slave. When the dogs in your streets, when the fowls of the air, when the cattle on your hills, when the fish of the sea, and the reptiles that crawl, shall be unable to distinguish the slave from a brute, *then* will I argue with you that the slave is a man!

For the present, it is enough to affirm the equal manhood of the negro race. Is it not astonishing that, while we are ploughing, planting and reaping, using all kinds of mechanical tools, erecting houses, constructing bridges, building ships, working in metals of brass, iron, copper, silver and gold; that, while we are reading, writing and cyphering, acting as clerks, merchants and secretaries, having among us lawyers, doctors, ministers, poets, authors, editors, orators and teachers; that, while we are engaged in all manner of enterprises common to other men, digging gold in California, capturing the whale in the Pacific, feeding sheep and cattle on the hillside, living, moving, acting, thinking, planning, living in families as husbands, wives and children, and, above all, confessing and worshipping the Christian's God, and looking hopefully for life and immortality beyond the grave, we are called upon to prove that we are men!

Would you have me argue that man is entitled to liberty? that he is the rightful owner of his own body? You have already declared it. Must I argue the wrongfulness of slavery? . . . Is it to be settled by the rules of logic and argumentation, as a matter beset with great difficulty, involving a doubtful application of the principle of justice, hard to be understood? How should I look today, in the presence of Americans, dividing, and subdividing a discourse, to show that men have a natural right to freedom? speaking of it relatively, and positively, negatively, and affirmatively. To do so, would be to make myself ridiculous, and to offer an insult to your understanding. There is not a man beneath the canopy of heaven, that does not know that slavery is wrong *for him.*

35     What, am I to argue that it is wrong to make men brutes, to rob them of their liberty, to work them without wages, to keep them ignorant of their relations to their fellow men, to beat them with sticks, to

flay their flesh with the lash, to load their limbs with irons, to hunt them with dogs, to sell them at auction, to sunder their families, to knock out their teeth, to burn their flesh, to starve them into obedience and submission to their masters? Must I argue that a system thus marked with blood, and stained with pollution, is *wrong?* No! I will not. I have better employments for my time and strength, than such arguments would imply.

What, then, remains to be argued? Is it that slavery is not divine; that God did not establish it; that our doctors of divinity are mistaken? There is blasphemy in the thought. That which is inhuman, cannot be divine! *Who* can reason on such a proposition? They that can, may; I cannot. The time for such argument is past.

At a time like this, scorching irony, not convincing argument, is needed. O! had I the ability, and could I reach the nation's ear, I would today, pour out a fiery stream of biting ridicule, blasting reproach, withering sarcasm, and stern rebuke. For it is not light that is needed, but fire; it is not the gentle shower, but thunder. We need the storm, the whirlwind and the earthquake. The feeling of the nation must be quickened; the conscience of the nation must be roused; the propriety of the nation must be startled; the hypocrisy of the nation must be exposed; and its crime against God and man must be proclaimed and denounced.

What, to the American slave, is your Fourth of July? I answer: a day that reveals to him, more than all other days in the year, the gross injustice and cruelty to which he is the constant victim. To him, your celebration is a sham; your boasted liberty, an unholy license; your national greatness, swelling vanity; your sounds of rejoicing are empty and heartless; your denunciations of tyrants, brass fronted impudence; your shouts of liberty and equality, hollow mockery; your prayers and hymns, your sermons and thanksgivings, with all your religious parade, and solemnity, are, to him, mere bombast, fraud, deception, impiety, and hypocrisy—a thin veil to cover up crimes which would disgrace a nation of savages. There is not a nation on the earth guilty of practices, more shocking and bloody, than are the people of these United States, at this very hour.

Go where you may, search where you will, roam through all the monarchies and despotisms of the old world, travel through South America, search out every abuse, and when you have found the last, lay your facts by the side of the everyday practices of this nation, and you will say with me, that, for revolting barbarity and shameless hypocrisy, America reigns without a rival.

## The Internal Slave Trade

40 Take the American slave-trade, which, we are told by the papers, is especially prosperous just now. Ex-Senator Benton[5] tells us that the price of men was never higher than now. He mentions the fact to show that slavery is in no danger. This trade is one of the peculiarities of American institutions. It is carried on in all the large towns and cities in one-half of this confederacy; and millions are pocketed every year, by dealers in this horrid traffic. In several states, this trade is a chief source of wealth. It is called (in contradistinction to the foreign slave-trade) *"the internal slave-trade."* It is probably, called so, too, in order to divert from it the horror with which the foreign slave-trade is contemplated. That trade has long since been denounced by this government, as piracy. It has been denounced with burning words, from the high places of the nation, as an execrable traffic. To attest it, to put an end to it, this nation keeps a squadron, at immense cost, on the coast of Africa. Everywhere, in this country, it is safe to speak of this foreign slave-trade, as a most inhuman traffic, opposed alike to the laws of God and of man. The duty to extirpate and destroy it, is admitted even by our DOCTORS OF DIVINITY. In order to put an end to it, some of these last have consented that their colored brethren (nominally free) should leave this country, and establish themselves on the western coast of Africa! It is, never, a notable fact that, while so much execration is poured out by Americans upon those engaged in the foreign slave-trade, the men engaged in the slave-trade between the states pass without condemnation, and their business is deemed honorable.

Behold the practical operation of this internal slave-trade, the American slave-trade, sustained by American politics and American religion. Here you will see men and women reared like swine for the market. You know what is a swine-drover? I will show you a man-drover. They inhabit all our Southern States. They perambulate the country, and crowd the highways of the nation, with droves of human stock. You will see one of these human flesh-jobbers, armed with pistol, whip and bowie-knife, driving a company of a hundred men, women, and children, from the Potomac to the slave market at New Orleans. These wretched people are to be sold singly, or in lots, to suit purchasers. They are food for the cotton-field, and the deadly sugar-mill. Mark the sad procession, as it moves wearily along, and the inhu-

---

[5] Thomas Hart Benton served as U.S. senator from Missouri from 1821 to 1851.

man wretch who drives them. Hear his savage yells and his blood-chilling oaths, as he hurries on his affrighted captives! There, see the old man, with locks thinned and gray. Cast one glance, if you please, upon that young mother, whose shoulders are bare to the scorching sun, her briny tears falling on the brow of the babe in her arms. See, too, that girl of thirteen, weeping, *yes!* weeping, as she thinks of the mother from whom she has been torn! The drove moves tardily. Heat and sorrow have nearly consumed their strength; suddenly you hear a quick snap, like the discharge of a rifle; the fetters clank, and the chain rattles simultaneously; your ears are saluted with a scream, that seems to have torn its way to the centre of your soul! The crack you heard, was the sound of the slave-whip; the scream you heard, was from the woman you saw with the babe. Her speed had faltered under the weight of her child and her chains! that gash on her shoulder tells her to move on. Follow this drove to New Orleans. Attend the auction; see men examined like horses; see the forms of women rudely and bru-tally exposed to the shocking gaze of American slave-buyers. See this drove sold and separated forever; and never forget the deep, sad sobs that arose from that scattered multitude. Tell me citizens, WHERE, un-der the sun, you can witness a spectacle more fiendish and shocking. Yet this is but a glance at the American slave-trade, as it exists, at this moment, in the ruling part of the United States.

I was born amid such sights and scenes. To me the American slave-trade is a terrible reality. When a child, my soul was often pierced with a sense of its horrors. I lived on Philpot Street, Fell's Point, Baltimore, and have watched from the wharves, the slave ships in the Basin, anchored from the shore, with their cargoes of human flesh, waiting for favorable winds to waft them down the Chesapeake. There was, at that time, a grand slave mart kept at the head of Pratt Street, by Austin Woldfolk. His agents were sent into every town and county in Maryland, announcing their arrival, through the papers, and on flaming *"hand-bills,"* headed CASH FOR NEGROES. These men were generally well dressed men, and very captivating in their manners. Ever ready to drink, to treat, and to gamble. The fate of many a slave has depended upon the turn of a single card; and many a child has been snatched from the arms of its mother by bargains arranged in a state of brutal drunkenness.

The flesh-mongers gather up their victims by dozens, and drive them chained, to the general depot at Baltimore. When a sufficient number have been collected here, a ship is chartered, for the purpose of conveying the forlorn crew to Mobile, or to New Orleans. From the slave prison to the ship, they are usually driven in the darkness of night; for since the antislavery agitation, a certain caution is observed.

In the deep still darkness of midnight, I have been often aroused by the dead heavy footsteps, and the piteous cries of the chained gangs that passed our door. The anguish of my boyish heart was intense; and I was often consoled, when speaking to my mistress in the morning, to hear her say that the custom was very wicked; that she hated to hear the rattle of the chains, and the heart-rending cries. I was glad to find one who sympathised with me in my horror.

45 Fellow-citizens, this murderous traffic is, today, in active operation in this boasted republic. In the solitude of my spirit, I see clouds of dust raised on the highways of the South; I see the bleeding footsteps; I hear the doleful wail of fettered humanity, on the way to the slave-markets, where the victims are to be sold like *horses*, *sheep*, and *swine*, knocked off to the highest bidder. There I see the tenderest ties ruthlessly broken, to gratify the lust, caprice and rapacity of the buyers and sellers of men. My soul sickens at the sight.

> *Is this the land your Fathers loved,*
> *The freedom which they toiled to win?*
>
> *Is this the earth whereon they moved?*
> *Are these the graves they slumber in?*[6]

## The Fugitive Slave Law

But a still more inhuman, disgraceful, and scandalous state of things remains to be presented.

By an act of the American Congress, not yet two years old, slavery has been nationalized in its most horrible and revolting form. By that act, Mason & Dixon's line has been obliterated; New York has become as Virginia; and the power to hold, hunt, and sell men, women, and children as slaves remains no longer a mere state institution, but is now an institution of the whole United States. The power is co-extensive with the star spangled banner and American Christianity. Where these go, may also go the merciless slave-hunter. Where these are, man is not sacred. He is a bird for the sportsman's gun. By that most foul and fiendish of all human decrees, the liberty and person of every man are put in peril. Your broad republican domain is hunting ground for *men*.

[6] From John Greenleaf Whittier's "Stanzas for the Times."

*Not* for thieves and robbers, enemies of society, merely, but for men guilty of no crime. Your law-makers have commanded all good citizens to engage in this hellish sport. Your President, your Secretary of State, your *lords*, *nobles*, and ecclesiastics, enforce, as a duty you owe to your free and glorious country, and to your God, that you do this accursed thing. Not fewer than forty Americans have, within the past two years, been hunted down and, without a moment's warning, hurried away in chains, and consigned to slavery and excruciating torture. Some of these have had wives and children, dependent on them for bread; but of this, no account was made. The right of the hunter to his prey stands superior to the right of marriage, and to *all* rights in this republic, the rights of God included! For black men there are neither law, justice, humanity, nor religion. The Fugitive Slave *Law* makes MERCY TO THEM, A CRIME; and bribes the judge who tries them. An American JUDGE GETS TEN DOLLARS FOR EVERY VICTIM HE CONSIGNS to slavery, and five, when he fails to do so. The oath of any two villains is sufficient, under this hell-black enactment, to send the most pious and exemplary black man into the remorseless jaws of slavery! His own testimony is nothing. He can bring no witnesses for himself. The minister of American justice is bound by the law to hear but *one* side; and *that* side, is the side of the oppressor. Let this damning fact be perpetually told. Let it be thundered around the world, that, in tyrant-killing, king-hating, people-loving, democratic, Christian America, the seats of justice are filled with judges, who hold their offices under an open and palpable *bribe*, and are bound, in deciding in the case of a man's liberty, *to hear only his accusers!*

In glaring violation of justice, in shameless disregard of the forms of administering law, in cunning arrangement to entrap the defenseless, and in diabolical intent, this Fugitive Slave Law stands alone in the annals of tyrannical legislation. I doubt if there be another nation on the globe, having the brass and the baseness to put such a law on the statute-book. If any man in this assembly thinks differently from me in this matter, and feels able to disprove my statements, I will gladly confront him at any suitable time and place he may select. I take this law to be one of the grossest infringements of Christian Liberty, and, if the churches and ministers of our country were not stupidly blind or most wickedly indifferent, they, too, would so regard it.

At the very moment that they are thanking God for the enjoyment of civil and religious liberty, and for the right to worship God according to the dictates of their own consciences, they are utterly silent in respect to a law which robs religion of its chief significance, and makes it utterly worthless to a world lying in wickedness. Did this law concern the *"mint, anise* and *cummin"*[7]—abridge the right to sing psalms, to partake of the sacrament, or to engage in any of the ceremonies of religion, it would be smitten by the thunder of a thousand pulpits. A general shout would go up from the church, demanding *repeal, repeal, instant repeal!* And it would go hard with that politician who presumed to solicit the votes of the people without inscribing this motto on his banner. Further, if this demand were not complied with, another Scotland would be added to the history of religious liberty, and the stern old Covenanters would be thrown into the shade. A John Knox would be seen at every church door, and heard from every pulpit, and Fillmore would have no more quarter than was shown by Knox, to the beautiful, but treacherous Queen Mary of Scotland.[8] The fact that the church of our country (with fractional exceptions) does not esteem "the Fugitive Slave Law" as a declaration of war against religious liberty implies that that church regards religion simply as a form of worship, an empty ceremony, and *not* a vital principle, requiring active benevolence, justice, love and good will towards man. It esteems sacrifice above mercy; psalm-singing above right doing; solemn meetings above practical righteousness. A worship that can be conducted by persons who refuse to give shelter to the houseless, to give bread to the hungry, clothing to the naked, and who enjoin obedience to a law forbidding these acts of mercy, is a curse, not a blessing to mankind. The Bible addresses all such persons as "scribes, pharisees, hypocrites, who pay tithe of *mint, anise,* and *cummin,* and have omitted the weightier matters of the law, judgment, mercy and faith." . . .

## Religion in England and Religion in America

50  One is struck with the difference between the attitude of the American church towards the antislavery movement, and that occupied by the churches in England towards a similar movement in that country. There, the church, true to its mission of ameliorating, elevating, and

---

[7] Matt. 23:23: "Woe unto you, scribes and Pharisees, hypocrites! For ye pay tithe of mint, anise and cummin, and have omitted the weightier *matters* of the law, judgment, mercy and faith."

[8] Knox, a sixteenth-century leader of Calvinist Protestantism in Scotland, and his followers forced Roman Catholic Mary Stuart, queen of Scotland, to abdicate when she tried to suppress their form of religion. She was later executed. Millard Fillmore (1800–1874) was president in 1852.

improving the condition of mankind, came forward promptly, bound up the wounds of the West Indian slave, and restored him to his liberty. There, the question of emancipation was a high[ly] religious question. It was demanded, in the name of humanity, and according to the law of the living God. The Sharps, the Clarksons, the Wilberforces, the Buxtons, and Burchells and the Knibbs, were alike famous for their piety, and for their philanthropy. The antislavery movement *there* was not an anti-church movement, for the reason that the church took its full share in prosecuting that movement: and the antislavery movement in this country will cease to be an anti-church movement, when the church of this country shall assume a favorable, instead of a hostile position towards that movement.

Americans! your republican politics, not less than your republican religion, are flagrantly inconsistent. You boast of your love of liberty, your superior civilization, and your pure Christianity, while the whole political power of the nation (as embodied in the two great political parties), is solemnly pledged to support and perpetuate the enslavement of three millions of your countrymen. You hurl your anathemas at the crowned headed tyrants of Russia and Austria, and pride yourselves on your Democratic institutions, while you yourselves consent to be the mere *tools* and *body-guards* of the tyrants of Virginia and Carolina. You invite to your shores fugitives of oppression from abroad, honor them with banquets, greet them with ovations, cheer them, toast them, salute them, protect them, and pour out your money to them like water; but the fugitives from your own land you advertise, hunt, arrest, shoot and kill. You glory in your refinement and your universal education; yet you maintain a system as barbarous and dreadful as ever stained the character of a nation—a system begun in avarice, supported in pride, and perpetuated in cruelty. You shed tears over fallen Hungary, and make the sad story of her wrongs the theme of your poets, statesmen and orators, till your gallant sons are ready to fly to arms to vindicate her cause against her oppressors;[9] but, in regard to the ten thousand wrongs of the American slave, you would enforce the strictest silence, and would hail him as an enemy of the nation who dares to make those wrongs the subject of public discourse! You are all on fire at the mention of liberty for France or for Ireland; but are as cold as an iceberg at the thought of liberty for the enslaved of America. You discourse eloquently on the dignity of labor; yet, you

---

[9] In 1848 Hungarian patriot Louis Kossuth led an unsuccessful attempt to establish an independent Hungarian government.

sustain a system which, in its very essence, casts a stigma upon labor. You can bare your bosom to the storm of British artillery to throw off a threepenny tax on tea; and yet wring the last hard-earned farthing from the grasp of the black laborers of your country. You profess to believe "that, of one blood, God made all nations of men to dwell on the face of all the earth,"[10] and hath commanded all men, everywhere to love one another; yet you notoriously hate, (and glory in your hatred), all men whose skins are not colored like your own. You declare, before the world, and are understood by the world to declare, that you *"hold these truths to be self evident, that all men are created equal; and are endowed by their Creator with certain inalienable rights; and that, among these are, life, liberty, and the pursuit of happiness;"* and yet, you hold securely . . . *a seventh part* of the inhabitants of your country.

Fellow-citizens! I will not enlarge further on your national inconsistencies. The existence of slavery in this country brands your republicanism as a sham, your humanity as a base pretence, and your Christianity as a lie. It destroys your moral power abroad; it corrupts your politicians at home. It saps the foundation of religion; it makes your name a hissing, and a by-word to a mocking earth. It is the antagonistic force in your government, the only thing that seriously disturbs and endangers your *Union*. It fetters your progress; it is the enemy of improvement, the deadly foe of education; it fosters pride; it breeds insolence; it promotes vice; it shelters crime; it is a curse to the earth that supports it; and yet, you cling to it, as if it were the sheet anchor of all your hopes. Oh! be warned! be warned! a horrible reptile is coiled up in your nation's bosom; the venomous creature is nursing at the tender breast of your youthful republic; *for the love of God, tear away*, and fling from you the hideous monster, and *let the weight of twenty millions crush and destroy it forever!* . . .

I have detained my audience entirely too long already. At some future period I will gladly avail myself of an opportunity to give this subject a full and fair discussion.

Allow me to say, in conclusion, notwithstanding the dark picture I have this day presented of the state of the nation, I do not despair of this country. There are forces in operation, which must inevitably work the downfall of slavery. *"The arm of the Lord is not shortened,"*[11] and the doom of slavery is certain. I, therefore, leave off where I be-

---

[10] A paraphrase of Acts 17–26.

[11] Isaiah 59:1: "Behold, the Lord's hand is not shortened, that it cannot save, neither His ear heavy, that it cannot hear."

gan, with *hope*. While drawing encouragement from the Declaration of Independence, the great principles it contains, and the genius of American Institutions, my spirit is also cheered by the obvious tendencies of the age. Nations do not now stand in the same relation to each other that they did ages ago. No nation can now shut itself up from the surrounding world, and trot round in the same old path of its fathers without interference. The time *was* when such could be done. Long established customs of hurtful character could formerly fence themselves in, and do their evil work with social impunity. Knowledge was then confined and enjoyed by the privileged few, and the multitude walked on in mental darkness. But a change has now come over the affairs of mankind. Walled cities and empires have become unfashionable. The arm of commerce has borne away the gates of the strong city. Intelligence is penetrating the darkest corners of the globe. It makes its pathway over and under the sea, as well as on the earth. Wind, steam, and lightning are its chartered agents. Oceans no longer divide, but link nations together. From Boston to London is now a holiday excursion. Space is comparatively annihilated. Thoughts expressed on one side of the Atlantic are distinctly heard on the other.

55      The far off and almost fabulous Pacific rolls in grandeur at our feet. The Celestial Empire, the mystery of ages, is being solved.[12] The fiat of the Almighty, *"Let there be Light,"* has not yet spent its force. No abuse, no outrage whether in taste, sport or avarice, can now hide itself from the all-pervading light. . . . *Africa must rise and put on her yet unwoven garment. "Ethiopia shall stretch out her hand unto God."*[13] In the fervent aspirations of William Lloyd Garrison, I say, and let every heart join in saying it:

> *God speed the year of jubilee*
>     *the wide world o'er!*
> *When from their galling chains set free,*
> *Th' oppress'd shall vilely bend the knee,*
> *And wear the yoke of tyranny*
>     *Like brutes no more.*
> *that year will come, and freedom's reign,*
> *To man his plundered rights again*
>     *Restore. . . .*

                    . . .

---

[12] The "Celestial Empire" is China.
[13] Psalms 68:31: "Princes shall come out of Egypt; Ethiopia shall soon stretch out her hands unto God."

## Questions for Discussion

The Fourth of July commemorates the signing of the Declaration of Independence. How does Douglass capitalize on that in his speech?

Is Douglass "preaching to the converted," or does it appear that he sees himself as doing more than reinforcing the values and opinions his audience already holds?

What does the arrangement of Douglass's argument add to the force of his speech? Does the order of the sections of his speech suggest an overall design to the speech?

*Before the Civil War and emancipation (and after), spiritual songs played a variety of crucial roles in the African-American slave culture. According to Bernard Bell, these "singing telegraphs" were more than simple expressions of Christian piety; in fact, they often helped slaves subvert the brutal practices supported by the dominant religious and legal institutions of the day, especially since slave owners and politicians frequently cited the Bible to justify slavery. That motive is apparent in "We Raise de Wheat" and "You Got a Right." Many spirituals also played critical communication roles in support of the Underground Railroad, which used lyrics as code to convey specific messages to fugitive slaves and the communities that could help them escape. Thus, "Follow the Drinkin' Gourd" famously implored slaves escaping to follow the North Star. Finally, for those who were left behind in slavery, these songs served as sources of protection and consolation; "Go Down, Moses" is one illustration. During a time when slaves, by law, were forcibly prevented from learning to read and write, these songs were complex forms of communication that, as their communal authorship suggests, served as a way to uphold and protect the values and lives of an enslaved community. In what ways can they be understood as arguments?*

# Three Spirituals

## We Raise de Wheat

We raise de wheat,
Dey gib us de corn;
We bake de bread,
Dey gib us de cruss;
5 We sif de meal,
Dey gib us de huss;
We peal de meat,
Dey gib us de skin
And dat's de way
10 Dey takes us in.

**You Got a Right**

*Chorus*:
You got a right, I got a right,
We all got a right to de tree of life.
Yes, tree of life.

De every time I thought I was los'
5 De dungeon shuck an' de chain fell off.
You may hinder me here
But you cannot dere,
'Cause God in de heav'n gwinter answer prayer.

(*Chorus*)

O bretheren, O sisteren, You got a right,
10 You got a right, I got a right,
We all got a right to de tree of life.
Yes, tree of life.

**Go Down, Moses**

When Israel was in Egypt's Land,
Let my people go,
Oppressed so hard they could not stand,
Let my people go.

*Chorus*:
5 *Go down, Moses,*
*Way down in Egypt's Land.*
*Tell ol' Pharaoh,*
*Let my people go.*

Thus saith the Lord, bold Moses said,
10 Let my people go,
If not, I'll smite your first-born dead,
Let my people go.

(*Chorus*)

No more shall they in bondage toil,
Let my people go,
15 Let them come out with Egypt's spoil,
Let my people go.

(*Chorus*)

The Lord told Moses what to do,
Let my people go,
To lead the Hebrew children through,
20 Let my people go.

(*Chorus*)

O come along Moses, you'll not get lost,
Let my people go,
Stretch out your rod and come across,
Let my people go.

(*Chorus*)

25 As Israel stood by the waterside,
Let my people go,
At God's command it did divide,
Let my people go.

(*Chorus*)

When they reached the other shore,
30 Let my people go,
They sang a song of triumph o'er,
Let my people go.

(*Chorus*)

Pharaoh said he'd go across,
Let my people go,
35 But Pharaoh and his host were lost,
Let my people go.

(*Chorus*)

Jordan shall stand up like a wall,
Let my people go,
And the walls of Jericho shall fall,
40 Let my people go.

(*Chorus*)

Your foes shall not before you stand,
Let my people go,
And you'll possess fair Canaan's land,
Let my people go.

(*Chorus*)

45 O let us all from bondage flee,
Let my people go,
And let us all in Christ be free,
Let my people go.

(*Chorus*)

We need not always weep and mourn,
50 Let my people go,
And wear these slavery chains forlorn,
Let my people go.

(*Chorus*)

*Here are two letters and part of a third written by* **John Adams** *of Massachusetts, one of the founders and later the second president of the United States, and his wife* **Abigail Adams** *(a formidable person as well) in the spring of 1776—while the nation was considering declaring its freedom from British rule. Abigail sent the first letter to John while he was in Philadelphia debating with his colleagues the merits of a declaration of independence: Note how Abigail uses the occasion to press her husband to "remember the ladies" in his discussions about freedom from tyranny. She was probably thinking not of suffrage—too radical an idea—but of fairer laws regarding inheritance, wife beating, and so forth. John's response to that letter follows. The third letter, from John Adams to* **James Sullivan** *(who had proposed that one's power at the ballot box should be proportional to one's financial worth), indicates that John Adams understood all too well the probable long-term implications of what was being written in the Declaration.*

# John Adams and Abigail Adams
# Letters

## Letter from Abigail Adams to John Adams, March 31, 1776

I long to hear that you have declared an independancy—and by the way in the new Code of Laws which I suppose it will be necessary for you to make I desire you would Remember the Ladies, and be more generous and favourable to them than your ancestors. Do not put such unlimited power into the hands of the Husbands. Remember all Men would be tyrants if they could. If perticuliar care and attention is not paid to the Laidies we are determined to foment a Rebelion, and will not hold ourselves bound by any Laws in which we have no voice, or Representation.

That your Sex are Naturally Tyrannical is a Truth so thoroughly established as to admit of no dispute, but such of you as wish to be happy willingly give up the harsh title of Master for the more tender and endearing one of Friend. Why then, not put it out of the power of the vicious and the Lawless to use us with cruelty and indignity with impunity. Men of Sense in all Ages abhor those customs which treat us only as the vassals of your Sex. Regard us then as Beings placed by providence under your protection and in immitation of the Supreem Being make use of that power only for our happiness.

## Letter from John Adams to Abigail Adams, April 14, 1776

As to Declarations of Independency, be patient. Read our Privateering Laws, and our Commercial Laws. What signifies a Word.

As to your extraordinary Code of Laws, I cannot but laugh. We have been told that our Struggle has loosened the bands of Government every where. That Children and Apprentices were disobedient—that schools and Colledges were grown turbulent—that Indians slighted their Guardians and Negroes grew insolent to their Masters. But your Letter was the first Intimation that another Tribe more numerous and powerfull, than all the rest were grown discontented.—This is rather too coarse a Compliment but you are so saucy, I wont blot it out.

Depend upon it, We know better than to repeal our Masculine systems. Altho they are in full Force, you know they are little more than Theory. We dare not exert our Power in its full Latitude. We are obliged to go fair, and softly, and in Practice you know We are the subjects. We have only the Name of Masters, and rather than give up this, which would compleatly subject Us to the Despotism of the Peticoat, I hope General Washington, and all our brave Heroes would fight. I am sure every good Politician would plot, as long as he would against Despotism, Empire, Monarchy, Aristocracy, Oligarchy or Ochlocracy.—A fine Story indeed. I begin to think the Ministry as deep as they are wicked. After stirring up Tories Landjobbers, Trimmers, Bigots, Canadians, Indians, Negroes, Hanoverians, Hessians, Russians, Irish Roman Catholicks, Scotch Renegadoes, at last they have stimulated the[m] to demand new Priviledges and threaten to rebell.

## Letter from John Adams to James Sullivan, May 26, 1776

. . . The same reasoning which will induce you to admit all men who have no property, to vote, with those who have, for those laws which affect the person, will prove that you ought to admit women and children; for, generally speaking, women and children have as good judgments, and as independent minds, as those men who are wholly destitute of property; these last being to all intents and purposes as much dependent upon others, who will please to feed, clothe, and employ them, as women are upon their husbands, or children on their parents.

As to your idea of proportioning the votes of men, in money matters, to the property they hold, it is utterly impracticable. There is no possible way of ascertaining, at any one time, how much every man in a community is worth; and if there was, so fluctuating is trade and property, that this state of it would change in half an hour. . . .

Depend upon it, Sir, it is dangerous to open so fruitful a source of controversy and altercation as would be opened by attempting to alter the qualifications of voters; there will be no end of it. New claims will arise; women will demand a vote; lads from twelve to twenty-one will think their rights not enough attended to; and every man who has not a farthing, will demand an equal voice with any other, in all acts of state. It tends to confound all distinctions, and prostrate all ranks to one common level.

## Questions for Discussion

How does her "intimate" knowledge of her audience affect Abigail Adams's reasoning and strategies?

To what extent does John Adams actually respond to his wife's reasons? Does he fully understand her? Does he ignore some of her appeals for strategic reasons?

*Sarah Grimké (1792–1873) was born into a wealthy and respected family in South Carolina. Her father, a judge, owned slaves, and it was this firsthand experience that galvanized her hatred of slavery and her desire to speak out against the restrictions on women's rights. Both Sarah and her sister Angelina became popular and controversial public speakers on abolitionist and women's rights issues; in fact, their groundbreaking speeches (it was generally considered inappropriate for women to speak in public, let alone on political topics) were so incendiary that they once narrowly escaped a mob that burned down the arena they were speaking in.*

*Sarah Grimké is regarded as a central figure in the "first generation" of the women's movement in America. Grimké is also heralded today as one of the first activists to reach out to working-class and African-American women in the fight for women's rights. Grimké drew heavily on biblical principles and teachings that held that both men and women had been created in their maker's image. The following letter, which responds to common criticisms made against the women's movement and its tactics (including a "Pastoral Letter" written by Congregational clergy), was originally addressed to Mary Parker, president of the Boston Female Anti-Slavery Society; it (along with several others) was subsequently published in the abolitionist newspaper,* The Liberator, *in 1837, and in Grimké's book* Letters on the Equality of the Sexes and the Condition of Woman, *which came out the following year.*

## Sarah Grimké
# Letter on Women's Rights

## The Pastoral Letter of the General Association of Congregationalist Ministers of Massachusetts

Haverill, 7th Mo. 1837

Dear Friend,

When I last addressed thee, I had not seen the Pastoral Letter of the General Association. It has since fallen into my hands, and I must digress from my intention of exhibiting the condition of women in different parts of the world, in order to make some remarks on this extraordinary document. I am persuaded that when the minds of men and women become emancipated from the thraldom of superstition and "traditions of men," the sentiments contained in the Pastoral

Letter will be recurred to with as much astonishment as the opinions of Cotton Mather and other distinguished men of his day, on the subject of witchcraft; nor will it be deemed less wonderful, that a body of divines should gravely assemble and endeavor to prove that woman has no right to "open her mouth for the dumb," than it now is that judges should have sat on the trials of witches, and solemnly condemned nineteen persons and one dog to death for witchcraft.

But to the letter. It says, "We invite your attention to the dangers which at present seem to threaten the FEMALE CHARACTER with widespread and permanent injury." I rejoice that they have called the attention of my sex to this subject, because I believe if woman investigates it, she will soon discover that danger is impending, though from a totally different source from that which the Association apprehends,—danger from those who, having long held the reins of *usurped* authority, are unwilling to permit us to fill that sphere which God created us to move in, and who have entered into league to crush the immortal mind of woman. I rejoice, because I am persuaded that the rights of woman, like the rights of slaves, need only be examined to be understood and asserted, even by some of those, who are now endeavoring to smother the irrepressible desire for mental and spiritual freedom which glows in the breast of many, who hardly dare to speak their sentiments.

"The appropriate duties and influence of women are clearly stated in the New Testament. Those duties are unobtrusive and private, but the sources of *mighty power*. When the mild, *dependent*, softening influence of woman upon the sternness of man's opinions is fully exercised, society feels the effects of it in a thousand ways." No one can desire more earnestly than I do, that woman may move exactly in the sphere which her Creator has assigned her; and I believe her having been displaced from that sphere has introduced confusion into the world. It is, therefore, of vast importance to herself and to all the rational creation, that she should ascertain what are her duties and her privileges as a responsible and immortal being. The New Testament has been referred to, and I am willing to abide by its decisions, but must enter my protest against the false translation of some passages by the MEN who did that work, and against the perverted interpretation by the MEN who undertook to write commentaries thereon. I am inclined to think, when we are admitted to the honor of studying Greek and Hebrew, we shall produce some various readings of the Bible a little different from those we now have.

The Lord Jesus defines the duties of his followers in his Sermon on the Mount. He lays down grand principles by which they should be

governed, without any reference to sex or condition.—"Ye are the light
of the world. A city that is set on a hill cannot be hid. Neither do men
light a candle and put it under a bushel, but on a candlestick, and it
giveth light unto all that are in the house. Let your light so shine before men, that they may see your good works, and glorify your Father
which is in Heaven" [Matt. 5:14–16]. I follow him through all his pre-
cepts, and find him giving the same directions to women as to men,
never even referring to the distinction now so strenuously insisted
upon between masculine and feminine virtues: this is one of the anti-
Christian "traditions of men" which are taught instead of the "com-
mandments of God." Men and women were CREATED EQUAL; they are
both moral and accountable beings, and whatever is *right* for man to
do, is *right* for woman.

5      But the influence of woman, says the Association, is to be private
and unobtrusive; her light is not to shine before man like that of her
brethren; but she is passively to let the lords of the creation, as they
call themselves, put the bushel over it, lest peradventure it might appear that the world has been benefitted by the rays of *her* candle. So
that her quenched light, according to their judgment, will be of more
use than if it were set on the candlestick. "Her influence is the source
of mighty power." This has ever been the flattering language of man
since he laid aside the whip as a means to keep woman in subjection.
He spares her body; but the war he has waged against her mind, her
heart, and her soul, has been no less destructive to her as a moral being. How monstrous, how anti-Christian, is the doctrine that woman is
to be dependent on man! Where, in all the sacred Scriptures, is this
taught? Alas! she has too well learned the lesson, which MAN has labored to teach her. She has surrendered her dearest RIGHTS, and been
satisfied with the privileges which man has assumed to grant her; she
has been amused with the show of power, whilst man has absorbed all
the reality into himself. He has adorned the creature whom God gave
him as a companion, with baubles and gewgaws, turned her attention
to personal attractions, offered incense to her vanity, and made her the
instrument of his selfish gratification, a plaything to please his eye and
amuse his hours of leisure. "Rule by obedience and by submission
sway," or in other words, study to be a hypocrite, pretend to submit,
but gain your point, has been the code of household morality which
woman has been taught. The poet has sung, in sickly strains, the love-
liness of woman's dependence upon man, and now we find it reechoed
by those who profess to teach the religion of the Bible. God says,
"Cease ye from man whose breath is in his nostrils, for wherein is he to

be accounted of?" Man says, depend upon me. God says, "HE will teach us of his ways." Man says, believe it not, I am to be your teacher. This doctrine of dependence upon man is utterly at variance with the doctrine of the Bible. In that book I find nothing like the softness of woman, nor the sternness of man: both are equally commanded to bring forth the fruits of the Spirit, love, meekness, gentleness, &c.

But we are told, "the power of woman is in her dependence, flowing from a consciousness of that weakness which God has given her for her protection." If physical weakness is alluded to, I cheerfully concede the superiority; if brute force is what my brethren are claiming, I am willing to let them have all the honor they desire; but if they mean to intimate, that mental or moral weakness belongs to woman, more than to man, I utterly disclaim the charge. Our powers of mind have been crushed, as far as man could do it, our sense of morality has been impaired by his interpretation of our duties; but no where does God say that he made any distinction between us, as moral and intelligent beings.

"We appreciate," say the Association, "the *unostentatious* prayers and efforts of woman in advancing the cause of religion at home and abroad, in leading religious inquirers TO THE PASTOR for instruction." Several points here demand attention. If public prayers and public efforts are necessarily ostentatious, then "Anna the prophetess, (or preacher,) who departed not from the temple, but served God with fastings and prayers night and day," "and spake of Christ to all them that looked for redemption in Israel," was ostentatious in her efforts [Luke 2:36–38]. Then, the apostle Paul encourages women to be ostentatious in their efforts to spread the gospel, when he gives them directions how they should appear, when engaged in praying, or preaching in the public assemblies. Then, the whole association of Congregational ministers are ostentatious, in the efforts they are making in preaching and praying to convert souls.

But woman may be permitted to lead religious inquirers to the PASTORS for instruction. Now this is assuming that all pastors are better qualified to give instruction than woman. This I utterly deny. I have suffered too keenly from the teaching of man, to lead any one to him for instruction. The Lord Jesus says,—"Come unto me and learn of me" [Matt. 11:29]. He points his followers to no man; and when woman is made the favored instrument of rousing a sinner to his lost and helpless condition, she has no right to substitute any teacher for Christ; all she has to do is, to turn the contrite inquirer to the "Lamb of God which taketh away the sins of the world" [John 1:29]. More souls have probably been lost by going down to Egypt for help, and by trusting in man in the early stages of religious experience, than by any other error. Instead of the petition being offered to God,—"Lead me in thy truth, and TEACH me, for thou art the God of my salvation" [Ps. 25:5],—instead of relying on the precious promises—"What man is he that feareth the Lord? him shall HE TEACH in the way that he shall choose" [Ps. 25:12]—"I will instruct thee and TEACH thee in the way which thou shalt go—I will guide thee with mine eye" [Ps. 27:11]—the young convert is directed to go to man, as if he were in the place of God, and his instructions essential to an advancement in the path of righteousness. That woman can have but a poor conception of the privilege of being taught of God, what he alone can teach, who would turn the "religious inquirer aside" from the fountain of living waters, where he might slake his thirst for spiritual instruction, to those broken cisterns which can hold no water, and therefore cannot satisfy the panting spirit. The business of men and women, who are ORDAINED OF GOD to preach the unsearchable riches of Christ to a lost and perishing world, is to lead souls to Christ, and not to Pastors for instruction.

The General Association say; that "when woman assumes the place and tone of man as a public reformer, our care and protection of her seem unnecessary; we put ourselves in self-defence against her, and her character becomes unnatural." Here again the unscriptural notion is held up, that there is a distinction between the duties of men and women as moral beings; that what is virtue in man, is vice in woman; and women who dare to obey the command of Jehovah, "Cry aloud, spare not, lift up thy voice like a trumpet, and show my people their transgression" [Isa. 58:1], are threatened with having the protection of the brethren withdrawn. If this is all they do, we shall not even know the time when our chastisement is inflicted; our trust is in the Lord Jehovah, and in him is everlasting strength. The motto of woman, when she is engaged in the great work of public reformation should be,—"The Lord is my light and my salvation; whom shall I fear? The Lord is the strength of my life; of whom shall I be afraid?" [Ps. 27:1]. She must feel, if she feels rightly, that she is fulfilling one of the important duties laid upon her as an accountable being, and that her character, instead of being "unnatural," is in exact accordance with the will of Him to whom, and to no other, she is responsible for the talents and the gifts confided to her. As to the pretty simile, introduced into the "Pastoral Letter," "If the vine whose strength and beauty is to lean upon the trellis work, and half conceal its clusters, thinks to assume the independence and the overshadowing nature of the elm," &c. I shall only remark that it might well suit the poet's fancy, who sings of sparkling eyes and coral lips, and knights in armor clad; but it seems to me utterly inconsistent with the dignity of a Christian body, to endeavor to draw such an antiscriptural distinction between men and women. Ah! how many of my sex feel in the dominion, thus unrighteously exercised over them, under the gentle appellation of *protection*, that what they have leaned upon has proved a broken reed at best, and oft a spear.

10       Thine in the bonds of womanhood,

*Sarah M. Grimké*

## Questions for Discussion

While Grimké addresses her argument to her "friend," she is clearly imagining that it might come to the attention of a wider audience. Nevertheless, how does her "dear friend" format function in the letter?

How do Grimké's readings of biblical teachings differ from those of her opponents? How does she use this difference to her advantage?

*Elizabeth Cady Stanton (1815–1902) is widely recognized as a central figure in the "first generation" of the women's movement, despite the fact that she had seven children to raise while the movement was getting started in the 1840s. Stanton, along with Lucretia Mott (a Quaker activist from Philadelphia), began planning the 1848 Seneca Falls Convention after they were denied entry to the World Anti-Slavery Convention in London in 1840. The Seneca Falls Women's Rights Convention was a watershed moment in the*  *history of the women's movement, for the meeting and the ideas that emerged from it were widely reported (and widely criticized). Like Thomas Jefferson before her, Stanton drafted an original version of the Declaration that was ratified with minor changes by conference delegates. Stanton remained active in the fight for extension of rights to women throughout the remainder of her life, although oftentimes she needed to veil her identity by writing speeches for others, including for Susan B. Anthony, with whom she worked (sometimes more cordially than other times) up until her death in 1902. Stanton also coedited a women's rights newspaper, The Revolution (1868–1870), and served as president of the National Woman Suffrage Association from 1869 to 1892. Many subsequent women's activists consider Elizabeth Cady Stanton to be the first and perhaps most influential theorist of women's legal, social, economic, and religious rights in the history of women's rights in America.*

# *Elizabeth Cady Stanton*

# The Seneca Falls Declaration

## 1. Declaration of Sentiments

When, in the course of human events, it becomes necessary for one portion of the family of man to assume among the people of the earth a position different from that which they have hitherto occupied, but one to which the laws of nature and of nature's God entitle them, a decent respect to the opinions of mankind requires that they should declare the causes that impel them to such a course.

We hold these truths to be self-evident: that all men and women are created equal; that they are endowed by their Creator with certain inalienable rights; that among these are life, liberty, and the pursuit of happiness; that to secure these rights governments are instituted, deriving their just powers from the consent of the governed. Whenever any form of government becomes destructive of these ends, it is the right of those who suffer from it to refuse allegiance to it, and to insist upon the institution of a new government, laying its foundation on such principles, and organizing its powers in such form, as to them shall seem most likely to effect their safety and happiness. Prudence, indeed, will dictate that governments long established should not be changed for light and transient causes; and accordingly all experience hath shown that mankind are more disposed to suffer, while evils are sufferable, than to right themselves by abolishing the forms to which they are accustomed. But when a long train of abuses and usurpations, pursuing invariably the same object, evinces a design to reduce them under absolute despotism, it is their duty to throw off such government, and to provide new guards for their future security. Such has been the patient sufferance of the women under this government, and such is now the necessity which constrains them to demand the equal station to which they are entitled. The history of mankind is a history of repeated injuries and usurpations on the part of man toward woman, having in direct object the establishment of an absolute tyranny over her. To prove this, let facts be submitted to a candid world.

He has never permitted her to exercise her inalienable right to the elective franchise.

He has compelled her to submit to laws, in the formation of which she had no voice.

5 He has withheld from her rights which are given to the most ignorant and degraded men, both natives and foreigners.

Having deprived her of this first right of a citizen, the elective franchise, thereby leaving her without representation in the halls of legislation, he has oppressed her on all sides.

He has made her, if married, in the eye of the law, civilly dead.

He has taken from her all right in property, even to the wages she earns.

He has made her, morally, an irresponsible being, as she can commit many crimes with impunity, provided they be done in the presence of her husband.

10 In the covenant of marriage, she is compelled to promise obedience to her husband, he becoming, to all intents and purposes, her master, the law giving him power to deprive her of her liberty and to administer chastisement.

He has so framed the laws of divorce, as to what shall be the proper causes, and in case of separation, to whom the guardianship of the children shall be given, as to be wholly regardless of the happiness of women—the law, in all cases, going upon a false supposition of the supremacy of man, and giving all power into his hands.

After depriving her of all rights as a married woman, if single, and the owner of property, he has taxed her to support a government which recognizes her only when her property can be made profitable to it.

He has monopolized nearly all the profitable employments, and from those she is permitted to follow, she receives but a scanty remuneration. He closes against her all the avenues to wealth and distinction which he considers most honorable to himself. As a teacher of theology, medicine, or law, she is not known.

He has denied her the facilities for obtaining a thorough education, all colleges being closed against her.

15 He allows her in Church, as well as State, but a subordinate position, claiming Apostolic authority for her exclusion from the ministry, and, with some exceptions, from any public participation in the affairs of the Church.

He has created a false public sentiment by giving to the world a different code of morals for men and women, by which moral delinquencies which exclude women from society, are not only tolerated, but deemed of little account in man.

He has usurped the prerogative of Jehovah himself, claiming it as his right to assign for her a sphere of action, when that belongs to her conscience and to her God.

He has endeavored, in every way that he could, to destroy her confidence in her own powers, to lessen her self-respect and to make her willing to lead a dependent and abject life.

Now, in view of this entire disfranchisement of one-half the people of this country, their social and religious degradation [and] in view of the unjust laws above mentioned, and because women do feel themselves aggrieved, oppressed, and fraudulently deprived of their most sacred rights, we insist that they have immediate admission to all the rights and privileges which belong to them as citizens of the United States.

20 In entering upon the great work before us, we anticipate no small amount of misconception, misrepresentation, and ridicule; but we shall use every instrumentality within our power to effect our object. We shall employ agents, circulate tracts, petition the State and National legislatures, and endeavor to enlist the pulpit and the press in our behalf. We hope this Convention will be followed by a series of Conventions embracing every part of the country.

## 2. Resolutions

WHEREAS, The great precept of nature is conceded to be, that "man shall pursue his own true and substantial happiness." Blackstone in his Commentaries remarks, that this law of Nature being coeval with mankind, and dictated by God himself, is of course superior in obligation to any other. It is binding over all the globe, in all countries and at all times; no human laws are of any validity if contrary to this, and such of them as are valid, derive all their force, and all their validity, and all their authority, mediately and immediately, from this original; therefore,

Resolved, That such laws as conflict, in any way with the true and substantial happiness of woman, are contrary to the great precept of nature and of no validity, for this is "superior in obligation to any other."

Resolved, That all laws which prevent woman from occupying such a station in society as her conscience shall dictate, or which place her in a position inferior to that of man, are contrary to the great precept of nature, and therefore of no force or authority.

Resolved, That woman is man's equal, was intended to be so by the Creator, and the highest good of the race demands that she should be recognized as such.

25 Resolved, That the women of this country ought to be enlightened in regard to the laws under which they live, that they may no longer publish their degradation by declaring themselves satisfied with their present position, nor their ignorance, by asserting that they have all the rights they want.

Resolved, That inasmuch as man, while claiming for himself intellectual superiority, does accord to woman moral superiority, it is preeminently his duty to encourage her to speak and teach, as she has an opportunity, in all religious assemblies.

Resolved, That the same amount of virtue, delicacy, and refinement of behavior that is required of woman in the social state, should also be required of man, and the same transgressions should be visited with equal severity on both man and woman.

Resolved, That the objection of indelicacy and impropriety, which is so often brought against woman when she addresses a public audience, comes with a very ill-grace from those who encourage, by their attendance, her appearance on the stage, in the concert, or in feats of the circus.

Resolved, That woman has too long rested satisfied in the circumscribed limits which corrupt customs and a perverted application of the Scriptures have marked out for her, and that it is time she should move in the enlarged sphere which her great Creator has assigned her.

30 Resolved, That it is the duty of the women of this country to secure to themselves their sacred right to the elective franchise.

Resolved, That the equality of human rights results necessarily from the fact of the identity of the race in capabilities and responsibilities.

Resolved, therefore, That, being invested by the Creator with the same capabilities, and the same consciousness of responsibility for their exercise, it is demonstrably the right and duty of woman, equally with man, to promote every righteous cause by every righteous means; and especially in regard to the great subjects of morals and religion, it is self-evidently her right to participate with her brother in teaching them, both in private and in public, by writing and by speaking, by any instrumentalities proper to be used, and in any assemblies proper to be held; and this being a self-evident truth growing out of the divinely implanted principles of human nature, any custom or authority adverse to it, whether modern or wearing the hoary sanction of antiquity, is to be regarded as a self-evident falsehood, and at war with mankind.

Resolved, That the speedy success of our cause depends upon the zealous and untiring efforts of both men and women, for the overthrow of the monopoly of the pulpit, and for the securing to women an equal participation with men in the various trades, professions, and commerce.

## Questions for Discussion

How does imitating the Declaration of Independence help Cady's argument?

What grievances articulated in the Declaration are still at issue today?

*Sojourner Truth's story is fascinating and moving. Born into slavery in Ulster County, New York, around 1797, and given the name Isabella, she was sold three times before she turned twelve. Perhaps sexually abused by one of her owners, she fled to freedom in 1827, a year before slavery was outlawed in New York. In New York City, she worked as a domestic and fell in with an evangelical preacher who encouraged her efforts to convert prostitutes. Though illiterate, she managed to prevent the sale of her son Peter by her former "owner." In 1843, inspired by mystical visions, she took the name Sojourner Truth and set off alone and undeterred by her illiteracy to preach and sing about religion and the abolition of slavery. By 1850, huge crowds were coming to witness the oratory of the ex-slave with the resounding voice and message. During the Civil War she was presented to President Lincoln at the White House. After the war she spoke out for women's suffrage, but she never gave up her spiritual and racial themes—or her humor and exuberance. She continued to lecture until her death in Battle Creek, Michigan, in 1883.*

*Sojourner Truth accepted neither the physical inferiority of women nor the idea that they should be placed on pedestals; nor did she subordinate women's rights to the pursuit of racial equality. At a women's rights convention in May 1851, Sojourner Truth rose extemporaneously to rebut speakers who had impugned the rights and capabilities of women. According to an eyewitness who recorded the scene in his diary, this is an approximation of what she said:*

## *Sojourner Truth*

# Ain't I a Woman?

Well, children, where there is so much racket there must be something out of kilter. I think that 'twixt the negroes of the South and the women at the North, all talking about rights, the white men will be in a fix pretty soon. But what's all this here talking about?

That man over there says that women need to be helped into carriages, and lifted over ditches, and to have the best place everywhere. Nobody ever helps me into carriages, or over mud-puddles, or gives me any best place! And ain't I a woman? Look at me! Look at my arm! I have ploughed and planted, and gathered into barns, and no man could head me! And ain't I a woman? I could work as much and eat as much as a man—when I could get it—and bear the lash as well! And ain't I a woman? I have borne thirteen children, and seen them most all sold off to slavery, and when I cried out with my mother's grief, none but Jesus heard me! And ain't I a woman?

Then they talk about this thing in the head; what's this they call it? [Intellect, someone whispers.] That's it, honey. What's that got to do with women's rights or negro's rights? If my cup won't hold but a pint, and yours holds a quart, wouldn't you be mean not to let me have my little half-measure full?

Then that little man in black there, he says women can't have as much rights as men, 'cause Christ wasn't a woman! Where did your Christ come from? Where did your Christ come from? From God and a woman! Man had nothing to do with Him.

If the first woman God ever made was strong enough to turn the world upside down all alone, these women together ought to be able to turn it back, and get it right side up again! And now they is asking to do it, the men better let them.

Obliged to you for hearing on me, and now old Sojourner ain't got nothing more to say.

## Questions for Discussion

Why does Truth repeat the question, "Ain't I a woman?"

What kind of supporting evidence does Truth rely on to make her point?

*Like Elizabeth Cady Stanton, who wrote a number of Anthony's speeches,*
**Susan B. Anthony** *(1820–1896) was one of the most prominent figures in
the fight for women's rights in the nineteenth century. Her career closely
parallels Stanton's, and the two coedited* The Revolution *(a women's
rights newspaper) although Anthony was a far more public and controversial figure. Although her main cause was suffrage (she served with
Stanton on the National Woman Suffrage Association and headed up that
organization between 1892 and 1900), she also spoke and worked on behalf of temperance, abolitionism, educational reform, and workplace reform (including the right of women to form unions). Anthony delivered the
following speech (shortened here for reasons of space) a number of times
after she was arrested in New York State and fined $100 for illegally vot-
ing in the 1872 presidential election. In it, she addresses her fellow citizens as if they were jurors.*

# Susan B. Anthony

# On Women's Right to Suffrage

Friends and Fellow-citizens: I stand before you tonight, under indict-
ment for the alleged crime of having voted at the last Presidential election, without having a lawful right to vote. It shall be my work this
evening to prove to you that in thus voting, I not only committed no
crime, but, instead, simply exercised my *citizen's right,* guaranteed to
me and all United States citizens by the National Constitution, beyond
the power of any State to deny.

Our democratic-republican government is based on the idea of the
natural right of every individual member thereof to a voice and a vote
in making and executing the laws. We assert the province of government to be to secure the people in the enjoyment of their unalienable
rights. We throw to the winds the old dogma that governments can
give rights. Before governments were organized, no one denies that
each individual possessed the right to protect his own life, liberty and
property. And when 100 or 1,000,000 people enter into a free government, they do not barter away their natural rights; they simply pledge
themselves to protect each other in the enjoyment of them, through
prescribed judicial and legislative tribunals. They agree to abandon

the methods of brute force in the adjustment of their differences, and adopt those of civilization.

Nor can you find a word in any of the grand documents left us by the fathers that assumes for government the power to create or to confer rights. The Declaration of Independence, the United States Constitution, the constitutions of the several States and the organic laws of the territories, all alike propose to protect the people in the exercise of their God-given rights. Not one of them pretends to bestow rights.

> All men are created equal, and endowed by their Creator with certain unalienable rights. Among these are life, liberty and the pursuit of happiness. That to secure these, governments are instituted among men, deriving their just powers from the consent of the governed.

Here is no shadow of government authority over rights, nor exclusion of any class from their full and equal enjoyment. Here is pronounced the right of all men, and "consequently," as the Quaker preacher said, "of all women," to a voice in the government.

5       Surely, the right of the whole people to vote is here clearly implied. For however destructive to their happiness this government might become, a disfranchised class could neither alter nor abolish it, nor institute a new one, except by the old brute force method of insurrection and rebellion. One-half of the people of this nation today are utterly powerless to blot from the statute books an unjust law, or to write there a new and a just one. The women, dissatisfied as they are with this form of government, that enforces taxation without representation,—that compels them to obey laws to which they have never given their consent,—that imprisons and hangs them without a trial by a jury of their peers, that robs them, in marriage, of the custody of their own persons, wages and children,—are this half of the people left wholly at the mercy of the other half, in direct violation of the spirit and letter of the declarations of the framers of this government, every one of which was based on the immutable principle of equal rights to all.

The preamble of the Federal Constitution says:

> We, the people of the United States, in order to form a more perfect union, establish justice, insure *domestic* tranquility, provide for the common defence, promote the general welfare and secure the blessings of liberty to ourselves and our posterity, do ordain and establish this constitution for the United States of America.

It was we, the people, not we, the white male citizens, nor yet we, the male citizens; but we, the whole people, who formed this Union. And we formed it, not to give the blessings of liberty, but to secure them; not to the half of ourselves and the half of our posterity, but to the whole people—women as well as men. And it is downright mockery to talk to women of their enjoyment of the blessings of liberty while they are denied the use of the only means of securing them provided by this democratic-republican government—the ballot. . . .

For any State to make sex a qualification that must ever result in the disfranchisement of one entire half of the people, is to pass a bill of attainder, or an *ex post facto* law, and is therefore a violation of the supreme law of the land. By it, the blessings of liberty are forever withheld from women and their female posterity. To them, this government has no just powers derived from the consent of the governed. To them this government is not a democracy. It is not a republic. It is an odious aristocracy; a hateful oligarchy of sex. The most hateful aristocracy ever established on the face of the globe. An oligarchy of wealth, where the rich govern the poor; an oligarchy of learning, where the educated govern the ignorant; or even an oligarchy of race, where the Saxon rules the African, might be endured; but this oligarchy of sex, which makes father, brothers, husband, sons, the oligarchs over the mother and sisters, the wife and daughters of every household; which ordains all men sovereigns, all women subjects, carries dissension, discord and rebellion into every home of the nation. And this most odious aristocracy exists, too, in the face of Section 4, of Article 4, which says: "The United States shall guarantee to every State in the Union a Republican form of government."

What, I ask you, is the distinctive difference between the inhabitants of a monarchical and those of a republican form of government, save that in the monarchical the people are subjects, helpless, powerless, bound to obey laws made by superiors—while in the republican, the people are citizens, individual sovereigns, all clothed with equal power, to make and unmake both their laws and law makers, and the moment you deprive a person of his right to voice in the government, you degrade him from the status of a citizen of the republic, to that of a subject, and it matters very little to him whether his monarch be an individual tyrant, as is the Czar of Russia, or a 15,000,000 headed monster, as here in the United States; he is a powerless subject, serf or slave; not a free and independent citizen in any sense.

10    But, it is urged, the use of the masculine pronouns *he*, *his*, and *him*, in all the constitutions and laws, is proof that only men were

meant to be included in their provisions. If you insist on this version of the letter of the law, we shall insist that you be consistent, and accept the other horn of the dilemma, which would compel you to exempt women from taxation for the support of the government, and from penalties for the violation of laws.

In all the penalties and burdens of the government, (except the military,) women are reckoned as citizens, equally with men. Also, in all the privileges and immunities, save those of the jury box and ballot box, the two fundamental privileges on which rest all the others. The United States government not only taxes, fines, imprisons and hangs women, but it allows them to pre-empt lands, register ships, and take out passport and naturalization papers. . . .

But, whatever room there was for a doubt, under the old regime, the adoption of the fourteenth amendment settled that question forever, in its first sentence: "All persons born or naturalized in the United States and subject to the jurisdiction thereof, are citizens of the United States and of the State wherein they reside."

And the second settles the equal status of all persons—all citizens: "No State shall make or enforce any law which shall abridge the privileges or immunities of citizens; nor shall any State deprive any person of life, liberty or property, without due process of law, nor deny to any person within its jurisdiction the equal protection of the laws."

The only question left to be settled, now, is: Are women persons? And I hardly believe any of our opponents will have the hardihood to say they are not. Being persons, then, women are citizens, and no State has a right to make any new law, or to enforce any old law, that shall abridge their privileges or immunities. Hence, every discrimination against women in the constitutions and laws of the several States, is to-day null and void, precisely as is every one against negroes.

15     Is the right to vote one of the privileges or immunities of citizens? I think the disfranchised ex-rebels, and the ex-state prisoners will all agree with me, that it is not only one of them, but the one without which all the others are nothing. Seek first the kingdom of the ballot, and all things else shall be given thee, is the political injunction. . . .

And it is upon this just interpretation of the United States Constitution that our National Woman Suffrage Association, which celebrates the twenty-fifth anniversary of the woman's rights movement in New York on the 6th of May next, has based all its arguments and action the past five years.

We no longer petition Legislature or Congress to give us the right to vote. We appeal to the women everywhere to exercise their too long neglected "citizen's right to vote." We appeal to the inspectors of election everywhere to receive the votes of all United States citizens as it is their duty to do. We appeal to United States commissioners and marshals to arrest the inspectors who reject the names and votes of United States citizens, as it is their duty to do, and leave those alone who, like our eighth ward inspectors, perform their duties faithfully and well.

We ask the juries to fail to return verdicts of "guilty" against honest, law-abiding, tax-paying United States citizens for offering their votes at our elections. Or against intelligent, worthy young men, inspectors of elections, for receiving and counting such citizens' votes.

We ask the judges to render true and unprejudiced opinions of the law, and wherever there is room for a doubt to give its benefit on the side of liberty and equal rights to women, remembering that "the true rule of interpretation under our national Constitution, especially since its amendments, is that anything for human rights is constitutional, everything against human rights is unconstitutional."

20     And it is on this line that we propose to fight our battle for the ballot—all peaceably, but nevertheless persistently through to complete triumph, when all United States citizens shall be recognized as equals before the law.

## Questions for Discussion

How would you characterize Anthony's tactics? What forms of evidence does she favor? Why are these forms best suited to her likely audience?

What kind of response is Anthony trying to elicit from her audience?

The suffrage movement for women developed alongside improvements in literacy and a consequent expansion in the number of newspapers and magazines. Hence the movement was a frequent subject for both satire and support not only by writers but by illustrators, photographers, and cartoonists. Posters and political cartoons at the end of the nineteenth century and the beginning of the twentieth represented specific events and argued about the issue. In the process, cartoonists and engravers offered images of men and women in contemporary dress in the midst of daily activities: Images of hen-pecked men and domineering women reflected male fears about the loss of power—and established stereotypes about women's liberation that persist in visual rhetoric today.

# Visual Arguments: The Suffrage Movement

This lithograph by the famous and prolific Currier and Ives depicts a crowd of women joining the National Woman Suffrage Association. The women are shown voting for Susan Sharp Tongue (Susan B. Anthony) at a table supervised by Elizabeth Cady Stanton.

This 1909 illustration by E. W. Gurtin presented an argument embedded, in part, in the costumes of the people depicted.

**Susan Glaspell** *(1882–1948), an Iowan by birth and education,
moved east in 1911. A Pulitzer Prize–winning dramatist and a
prolific fiction writer, she cofounded the Provincetown Playhouse
on Cape Cod in 1915, which became a center for experimental
and innovative drama. In 1916, she wrote* Trifles, *the one-act
play reprinted here; then she adapted it a few months later into
the story,* "A Jury of Her Peers."

# Susan Glaspell

# Trifles

*Characters*
GEORGE HENDERSON, *County Attorney*
HENRY PETERS, *Sheriff*
LEWIS HALE, *A Neighboring Farmer*
MRS. PETERS
MRS. HALE

SCENE
*The kitchen in the now abandoned farmhouse of* JOHN WRIGHT,
*a gloomy kitchen, and left without having been put in order—
unwashed pans under the sink, a loaf of bread outside the
breadbox, a dish towel on the table—other signs of incom-
pleted work. At the rear the outer door opens and the* SHERIFF
*comes in followed by the* COUNTY ATTORNEY *and* HALE. *The*
SHERIFF *and* HALE *are men in middle life, the* COUNTY ATTORNEY
*is a young man; all are much bundled up and go at once to the
stove. They are followed by two women—the* SHERIFF'S *wife
first; she is a slight wiry woman, a thin nervous face.* MRS. HALE
*is larger and would ordinarily be called more comfortable look-
ing, but she is disturbed now and looks fearfully about as she
enters. The women have come in slowly, and stand close together near the door.*

County Attorney: [*Rubbing his hands.*] This feels good.
Come up to the fire, ladies.

*Mrs. Peters:* [*After taking a step forward.*] I'm not—cold.

*Sheriff:* [*Unbuttoning his overcoat and stepping away from the stove as if to mark the beginning of official business.*] Now, Mr. Hale, before we move things about, you explain to Mr. Henderson just what you saw when you came here yesterday morning.

*County Attorney:* By the way, has anything been moved? Are things just as you left them yesterday?

5  *Sheriff:* [*Looking about.*] It's just the same. When it dropped below zero last night I thought I'd better send Frank out this morning to make a fire for us—no use getting pneumonia with a big case on, but I told him not to touch anything except the stove—and you know Frank.

*County Attorney:* Somebody should have been left here yesterday.

*Sheriff:* Oh—yesterday. When I had to send Frank to Morris Center for that man who went crazy—I want you to know I had my hands full yesterday. I knew you could get back from Omaha by today and as long as I went over everything here myself—

*County Attorney:* Well, Mr. Hale, tell just what happened when you came here yesterday morning.

*Hale:* Harry and I had started to town with a load of potatoes. We came along the road from my place and as I got here I said, "I'm going to see if I can't get John Wright to go in with me on a party telephone." I spoke to Wright about it once before and he put me off, saying folks talked too much anyway, and all he asked was peace and quiet—I guess you know about how much he talked himself; but I thought maybe if I went to the house and talked about it before his wife, though I said to Harry that I didn't know as what his wife wanted made much difference to John—

10  *County Attorney:* Let's talk about that later, Mr. Hale. I do want to talk about that, but tell now just what happened when you got to the house.

*Hale:* I didn't hear or see anything; I knocked at the door, and still it was all quiet inside. I knew they must be up, it was past eight o'clock. So I knocked again, and I thought I heard somebody say, "Come in." I wasn't sure, I'm not sure yet, but I opened the door—this door [*Indicating the door by which the two women are still standing]* and there in that rocker—*[Pointing to it.]* sat Mrs. Wright. *[They all look at the rocker.]*

*County Attorney:* What—was she doing?

*Hale:* She was rockin' back and forth. She had her apron in her hand and was kind of—pleating it.

*County Attorney:* And how did she—look?

15   *Hale:* Well, she looked queer.

*County Attorney:* How do you mean—queer?

*Hale:* Well, as if she didn't know what she was going to do next. And kind of done up.

*County Attorney:* How did she seem to feel about your coming?

*Hale:* Why, I don't think she minded—one way or other. She didn't pay much attention. I said, "How do, Mrs. Wright, it's cold, ain't it?" And she said, "Is it?"—and went on kind of pleating at her apron. Well, I was surprised; she didn't ask me to come up to the stove, or to set down, but just sat there, not even looking at me, so I said, "I want to see John." And then she—laughed. I guess you would call it a laugh. I thought of Harry and the team outside, so I said a little sharp: "Can't I see John?" "No," she says, kind o' dull like. "Ain't he home?" says I. "Yes," says she, "he's home." "Then why can't I see him?" I asked her, out of patience. "Cause he's dead," says she. "*Dead?*" says I. She just nodded her head, not getting a bit excited, but rockin' back and forth. "Why—where is he?" says I, not knowing what to say. She just pointed upstairs—like that *[Himself pointing to the room above.]* I got up, with the idea of going up there. I walked from there to here—then I says, "Why, what did he die of?" "He died of a rope round his neck," says she, and just went on pleatin' at her apron. Well, I went out and called Harry. I thought I might—need help. We went upstairs and there he was lyin'—

20   *County Attorney:* I think I'd rather have you go into that upstairs, where you can point it all out. Just go on now with the rest of the story.

*Hale:* Well, my first thought was to get that rope off. It looked . . . *[Stops, his face twitches.]* . . . but Harry, he went up to him, and he said, "No, he's dead all right, and we'd better not touch anything." So we went back down stairs. She was still sitting that same way. "Has anybody been notified?" I asked. "No," says she, unconcerned. "Who did this, Mrs. Wright?" said Harry. He said it businesslike—and she stopped pleatin' of her apron. "I don't know," she says. "You don't *know?*" says Harry. "No," says she. "Weren't you sleepin' in bed with him?" says Harry. "Yes," says she, "but I was on the inside." "Somebody slipped a rope round his neck and strangled him and you didn't wake up?" says Harry. "I didn't wake up," she said after him. We must 'a looked as if we didn't see how that could be, for after a minute she said, "I sleep sound." Harry was going to ask her more questions but I said maybe we ought to let her tell her story first to the coroner, or the sheriff, so Harry went fast as he could to Rivers' place, where there's a telephone.

*County Attorney:* And what did Mrs. Wright do when she knew that you had gone for the coroner?

*Hale:* She moved from that chair to this one over here [*Pointing to a small chair in the corner.*] and just sat there with her hands held together and looking down. I got a feeling that I ought to make some conversation, so I said I had come in to see if John wanted to put in a telephone, and at that she started to laugh, and then she stopped and looked at me—scared. [*The* COUNTY ATTORNEY, *who has had his notebook out, makes a note.*] I dunno, maybe it wasn't scared. I wouldn't like to say it was. Soon Harry got back, and then Dr. Lloyd came, and you, Mr. Peters, and so I guess that's all I know that you don't.

*County Attorney:* [*Looking around.*]I guess we'll go upstairs first—and then out to the barn and around there. [*To the* SHERIFF] You're convinced that there was nothing important here—nothing that would point to any motive.

25    *Sheriff:* Nothing here but kitchen things. [*The* COUNTY ATTORNEY, *after again looking around the kitchen, opens the door of a cupboard closet. He gets up on a chair and looks on a shelf. Pulls his hand away, sticky.*]

*County Attorney:* Here's a nice mess.

[*The women draw nearer.*]

*Mrs. Peters:* [*To the other woman.*]Oh, her fruit; it did freeze. [*To the* COUNTY ATTORNEY:] She worried about that when it

turned so cold. She said the fire'd go out and her jars
would break.

*Sheriff:* Well, can you beat the women! Held for murder and
worryin' about her preserves.

*County Attorney:* I guess before we're through she may have
something more serious than preserves to worry about.

30 *Hale:* Well, women are used to worrying over trifles. [*The
two women move a little closer together.*]

*County Attorney:* [*With the gallantry of a young politician.*]
And yet, for all their worries, what would we do without
the ladies? [*The women do not unbend. He goes to the
sink, takes a dipperful of water from the pail and pouring
it into a basin, washes his hands. Starts to wipe them on
the roller towel, turns it for a cleaner place.*] Dirty towels!
[*Kicks his foot against the pans under the sink.*] Not
much of a housekeeper, would you say, ladies?

*Mrs. Hale:* [*Stiffly.*] There's a great deal of work to be done
on a farm.

*County Attorney:* To be sure. And yet [*With a little bow to
her.*] I know there are some Dickson county farmhouses
which do not have such roller towels.

[*He gives it a pull to expose its full length again.*]

*Mrs. Hale:* Those towels get dirty awful quick. Men's hands
aren't always as clean as they might be.

35 *County Attorney:* Ah, loyal to your sex, I see. But you and
Mrs. Wright were neighbors. I suppose you were friends,
too.

*Mrs. Hale:* [*Shaking her head.*]I've not seen much of her of
late years. I've not been in this house—it's more than a
year.

*County Attorney:* And why was that? You didn't like her?

*Mrs. Hale:* I liked her all well enough. Farmers' wives have
their hands full, Mr. Henderson. And then—

*County Attorney:* Yes—?

40 *Mrs. Hale:* [*Looking about.*]It never seemed a very cheerful
place.

*County Attorney:* No—it's not cheerful. I shouldn't say she
had the homemaking instinct.

*Mrs. Hale:* Well, I don't know as Wright had, either.

*County Attorney:* You mean that they didn't get on very
well?

*Mrs. Hale:* No, I don't mean anything. But I don't think a place'd be any cheerfuller for John Wright's being in it.

45 *County Attorney:* I'd like to talk more of that a little later. I want to get the lay of things upstairs now.

[*He goes to the left, where three steps lead to a stair door.*]

*Sheriff:* I suppose anything Mrs. Peters does'll be all right. She was to take in some clothes for her, you know, and a few little things. We left in such a hurry yesterday.

*County Attorney:* Yes, but I would like to see what you take, Mrs. Peters, and keep an eye out for anything that might be of use to us.

*Mrs. Peters:* Yes, Mr. Henderson.

[*The women listen to the men's steps on the stairs, then look about the kitchen.*]

*Mrs. Hale:* I'd hate to have men coming into my kitchen, snooping around and criticising.

[*She arranges the pans under sink which the* COUNTY AT-TORNEY *had shoved out of place.*]

50 *Mrs. Peters:* Of course it's no more than their duty.

*Mrs. Hale:* Duty's all right, but I guess that deputy sheriff that came out to make the fire might have got a little of this on.

[*Gives the roller towel a pull.*] Wish I'd thought of that sooner. Seems mean to talk about her for not having things slicked up when she had to come away in such a hurry.

*Mrs. Peters:* [*Who has gone to a small table in the left rear corner of the room, and lifted one end of a towel that covers a pan.*] She had bread set.

[*Stands still.*]

*Mrs. Hale:* [*Eyes fixed on a loaf of bread beside the bread-box, which is on a low shelf at the other side of the room. Moves slowly toward it.*] She was going to put this in there. [*Picks up loaf, then abruptly drops it. In a manner of returning to familiar things.*] It's a shame about her fruit. I wonder if it's all gone. [*Gets up on the chair and looks.*] I think there's some here that's all right, Mrs. Peters. Yes—here; [*Holding it toward the window.*] this is cherries too. [*Looking again.*] I declare I believe that's the only one. [*Gets down, bottle in her hand. Goes to the sink *and wipes it off on the outside.*] She'll feel awful bad after all her hard work in the hot weather. I remember the afternoon I put up my cherries last summer. [*She puts the bottle on the big kitchen table, center of the room. With a sigh, is about to sit down in the rocking-chair. Before she is seated realizes what chair it is; with a slow look at it, steps back. The chair which she has touched rocks back and forth.*]

Mrs. Peters: Well, I must get those things from the front room closet. [*She goes to the door at the right, but after looking into the other room, steps back.*] You coming with me, Mrs. Hale? You could help me carry them.

[*They go in the other room; reappear,* MRS. PETERS *carrying a dress and skirt,* MRS. HALE *following with a pair of shoes.*]

55 Mrs. Peters: My, it's cold in there.

[*She puts the clothes on the big table, and hurries to the stove.*]

Mrs. Hale: [*Examining her skirt.*] Wright was close. I think maybe that's why she kept so much to herself. She didn't even belong to the Ladies Aid. I suppose she felt she couldn't do her part, and then you don't enjoy things when you feel shabby. She used to wear pretty clothes and be lively, when she was Minnie Foster, one of the town girls singing in the choir. But that—oh, that was thirty years ago. This all you was to take in?

Mrs. Peters: She said she wanted an apron. Funny thing to want, for there isn't much to get you dirty in jail, goodness knows. But I suppose just to make her feel more natural. She said they was in the top drawer in this cupboard. Yes, here. And then her little shawl that always hung behind the door. [*Opens stair door and looks.*] Yes, here it is.

[*Quickly shuts door leading upstairs.*]

Mrs. Hale: [*Abruptly moving toward her.*] Mrs. Peters?

Mrs. Peters: Yes, Mrs. Hale?

60 Mrs. Hale: Do you think she did it?

Mrs. Peters: [*In a frightened voice.*] Oh, I don't know.

Mrs. Hale: Well, I don't think she did. Asking for an apron and her little shawl. Worrying about her fruit.

*Mrs. Peters:* [*Starts to speak, glances up, where footsteps are heard in the room above. In a low voice.*] Mr. Peters says it looks bad for her. Mr. Henderson is awful sarcastic in a speech and he'll make fun of her sayin' she didn't wake up.

*Mrs. Hale:* Well, I guess John Wright didn't wake when they was slipping that rope under his neck.

65  *Mrs. Peters:* No, it's strange. It must have been done awful crafty and still. They say it was such a—funny way to kill a man, rigging it all up like that.

*Mrs. Hale:* That's just what Mr. Hale said. There was a gun in the house. He says that's what he can't understand.

*Mrs. Peters:* Mr. Henderson said coming out that what was needed for the case was a motive; something to show anger, or—sudden feeling.

*Mrs. Hale:* [*Who is standing by the table.*] Well, I don't see any signs of anger around here. [*She puts her hand on the dish towel which lies on the table, stands looking down at table, one half of which is clean, the other half messy.*] It's wiped to here. [*Makes a move as if to finish work, then turns and looks at loaf of bread outside the breadbox. Drops towel. In that voice of coming back to familiar things.*] Wonder how they are finding things upstairs. I hope she had it a little more red-up up there. You know, it seems kind of *sneaking*. Locking her up in town and then coming out here and trying to get her own house to turn against her!

*Mrs. Peters:* But Mrs. Hale, the law is the law.

70  *Mrs. Hale:* I s'pose 'tis. [*Unbuttoning her coat.*] Better loosen up your things, Mrs. Peters. You won't feel them when you go out.

[MRS. PETERS *takes off her fur tippet, goes to hang it on hook at back of room, stands looking at the under part of the small corner table.*]

*Mrs. Peters:* She was piecing a quilt.

[*She brings the large sewing basket and they look at the bright pieces.*]

*Mrs. Hale:* It's log cabin pattern. Pretty, isn't it? I wonder if she was goin' to quilt it or just knot it?

[*Footsteps have been heard coming down the stairs. The* SHERIFF *enters followed by* HALE *and the* COUNTY ATTORNEY.]

*Sheriff:* They wonder if she was going to quilt it or just knot it!

[*The men laugh; the women look abashed.*]

*County Attorney:* [*Rubbing his hands over the stove.*] Frank's fire didn't do much up there, did it? Well, let's go out to the barn and get that cleared up.

[*The men go outside.*]

75 *Mrs. Hale:* [*Resentfully.*] I don't know as there's anything so strange, our takin' up our time with little things while we're waiting for them to get the evidence. [*She sits down at the big table smoothing out a block with decision.*] I don't see as it's anything to laugh about.

*Mrs. Peters:* [*Apologetically.*] Of course they've got awful important things on their minds.

[*Pulls up a chair and joins* MRS. HALE *at the table.*]

*Mrs. Hale:* [*Examining another block.*] Mrs. Peters, look at this one. Here, this is the one she was working on, and look at the sewing! All the rest of it has been so nice and even. And look at this! It's all over the place! Why, it looks as if she didn't know what she was about!

[*After she has said this they look at each other, then start to glance back at the door. After an instant* MRS. HALE *has pulled at a knot and ripped the sewing.*]

*Mrs. Peters:* Oh, what are you doing, Mrs. Hale?

*Mrs. Hale:* [*Mildly.*] Just pulling out a stitch or two that's not sewed very good. [*Threading a needle.*] Bad sewing always made me fidgety.

80 *Mrs. Peters:* [*Nervously.*] I don't think we ought to touch things.

*Mrs. Hale:* I'll just finish up this end. [*Suddenly stopping and leaning forward.*] Mrs. Peters?

*Mrs. Peters:* Yes, Mrs. Hale?

*Mrs. Hale:* What do you suppose she was so nervous about?

*Mrs. Peters:* Oh—I don't know. I don't know as she was nervous. I sometimes sew awful queer when I'm just tired. [MRS. HALE *starts to say something, looks at* MRS. PETERS, *then goes on sewing.*] Well, I must get these things wrapped up. They may be through sooner than we think. [*Putting apron and other things together.*] I wonder where I can find a piece of paper, and string.

85 *Mrs. Hale:* In that cupboard, maybe.

*Mrs. Peters:* [*Looking in cupboard.*] Why, here's a birdcage. [*Holds it up.*] Did she have a bird, Mrs. Hale?

*Mrs. Hale:* Why, I don't know whether she did or not—I've not been here for so long. There was a man around last year selling canaries cheap, but I don't know as she took one; maybe she did. She used to sing real pretty herself.

*Mrs. Peters:* [*Glancing around.*] Seems funny to think of a bird here. But she must have had one, or why would she have a cage? I wonder what happened to it.

*Mrs. Hale:* I s'pose maybe the cat got it.

90 *Mrs. Peters:* No, she didn't have a cat. She's got that feeling some people have about cats—being afraid of them. My cat got in her room and she was real upset and asked me to take it out.

*Mrs. Hale:* My sister Bessie was like that. Queer, ain't it?

*Mrs. Peters:* [*Examining the cage.*] Why, look at this door. It's broke. One hinge is pulled apart.

*Mrs. Hale:* [*Looking too.*] Looks as if someone must have been rough with it.

*Mrs. Peters:* Why, yes.

[*She brings the cage forward and puts it on the table.*]

95 *Mrs. Hale:* I wish if they're going to find any evidence they'd be about it. I don't like this place.

*Mrs. Peters:* But I'm awful glad you came with me, Mrs. Hale. It would be lonesome for me sitting here alone.

*Mrs. Hale:* It would, wouldn't it? [*Dropping her sewing.*] But I tell you what I do wish, Mrs. Peters. I wish I had come over sometimes when *she* was here. I—[*Looking around the room.*]—wish I had.

*Mrs. Peters:* But of course you were awful busy, Mrs. Hale—your house and your children.

*Mrs. Hale:* I could've come. I stayed away because it weren't cheerful—and that's why I ought to have come. I—I've never liked this place. Maybe because it's down in a hollow and you don't see the road. I dunno what it is but it's a lonesome place and always was. I wish I had come over to see Minnie Foster sometimes. I can see now—[*Shakes her head.*]

100 *Mrs. Peters:* Well, you mustn't reproach yourself, Mrs. Hale. Somehow we just don't see how it is with other folks until—something comes up.

*Mrs. Hale:* Not having children makes less work—but it makes a quiet house, and Wright out to work all day, and no company when he did come in. Did you know John Wright, Mrs. Peters?

*Mrs. Peters:* Not to know him; I've seen him in town. They say he was a good man.

*Mrs. Hale:* Yes—good; he didn't drink, and kept his word as well as most, I guess, and paid his debts. But he was a hard man, Mrs. Peters. Just to pass the time of day with him—[*Shivers.*] Like a raw wind that gets to the bone. [*Pauses, her eye falling on the cage.*] I should think she would'a wanted a bird. But what do you suppose went with it?

*Mrs. Peters:* I don't know, unless it got sick and died. [*She reaches over and swings the broken door, swings it again. Both women watch it.*]

105  *Mrs. Hale:* You weren't raised round here, were you? [MRS. PETERS *shakes her head.*] You didn't know—her?

*Mrs. Peters:* Not till they brought her yesterday.

*Mrs. Hale:* She—come to think of it, she was kind of like a bird herself—real sweet and pretty, but kind of timid and—fluttery. How—she—did—change. [*Silence; then as if struck by a happy thought and relieved to get back to every day things.*] Tell you what, Mrs. Peters, why don't you take the quilt in with you? It might take up her mind.

*Mrs. Peters:* Why, I think that's a real nice idea, Mrs. Hale. There couldn't possibly be any objection to it, could there? Now, just what would I take? I wonder if her patches are in here—and her things. [*They look in the sewing basket.*]

*Mrs. Hale:* Here's some red. I expect this has got sewing things in it. [*Brings out a fancy box.*] What a pretty box. Looks like something somebody would give you. Maybe her scissors are in here. [*Opens box. Suddenly puts her hand to her nose.*] Why—[MRS. PETERS *bends nearer, then turns her face away.*] There's something wrapped up in this piece of silk.

110  *Mrs. Peters:* Why, this isn't her scissors.

*Mrs. Hale:* [*Lifting the silk.*] Oh, Mrs. Peters—its—[MRS. PETERS *bends closer.*]

*Mrs. Peters:* It's the bird.

*Mrs. Hale:* [*Jumping up.*] But, Mrs. Peters—look at it! Its neck! Look at its neck! It's all—other side *to*.

*Mrs. Peters:* Somebody—wrung—its—neck.

[*Their eyes meet. A look of growing comprehension, of horror. Steps are heard outside.* MRS. HALE *slips box under quilt pieces, and sinks into her chair. Enter* SHERIFF *and* COUNTY ATTORNEY. MRS. PETERS *rises.*]

115 *County Attorney:* [*As one turning from serious things to little pleasantries.*] Well, ladies, have you decided whether she was going to quilt it or knot it?

*Mrs. Peters:* We think she was going to—knot it.

*County Attorney:* Well, that's interesting, I'm sure. [*Seeing the birdcage.*] Has the bird flown?

*Mrs. Hale:* [*Putting more quilt pieces over the box.*] We think the—cat got it.

*County Attorney:* [*Preoccupied.*] Is there a cat?

[MRS. HALE *glances in a quick covert way at* MRS. PETERS.]

120 *Mrs. Peters:* Well, not *now*. They're superstitious, you know. They leave.

*County Attorney:* [*To* SHERIFF PETERS, *continuing an interrupted conversation.*] No sign at all of anyone having come from the outside. Their own rope. Now let's go up again and go over it piece by piece. [*They start upstairs.*] It would have to have been someone who knew just the— [MRS. PETERS *sits down. The two women sit there not looking at one another, but as if peering into something and at the same time holding back. When they talk now it is in the manner of feeling their way over strange ground, as if afraid of what they are saying, but as if they can not help saying it.*]

*Mrs. Hale:* She liked the bird. She was going to bury it in that pretty box.

*Mrs. Peters:* [*In a whisper.*] When I was a girl—my kitten— there was a boy took a hatchet, and before my eyes—and before I could get there—[*Covers her face an instant.*] If they hadn't held me back I would have—[*Catches herself, looks upstairs where steps are heard, falters weakly.*]— hurt him.

*Mrs. Hale:* [*With a slow look around her.*] I wonder how it would seem never to have had any children around.

[*Pause.*] No, Wright wouldn't like the bird—a thing that sang. She used to sing. He killed that, too.

125 Mrs. Peters: [*Moving uneasily.*] We don't know who killed the bird.

Mrs. Hale: I knew John Wright.

Mrs. Peters: It was an awful thing was done in this house that night, Mrs. Hale. Killing a man while he slept, slipping a rope around his neck that choked the life out of him.

Mrs. Hale: His neck. Choked the life out of him. [*Her hand goes out and rests on the birdcage.*]

Mrs. Peters: [*With rising voice.*] We don't know who killed him. We don't know.

130 Mrs. Hale: [*Her own feeling not interrupted.*] If there'd been years and years of nothing, then a bird to sing to you, it would be awful—still, after the bird was still.

Mrs. Peters: [*Something within her speaking.*] I know what stillness is. When we homesteaded in Dakota, and my first baby died—after he was two years old, and me with no other then—

Mrs. Hale: [*Moving.*] How soon do you suppose they'll be through, looking for the evidence?

Mrs. Peters: I know what stillness is. [*Pulling herself back.*] The law has got to punish crime, Mrs. Hale.

Mrs. Hale: [*Not as if answering that.*] I wish you'd seen Minnie Foster when she wore a white dress with blue ribbons and stood up there in the choir and sang. [*A look around the room.*] Oh, I *wish* I'd come over here once in a while! That was a crime! That was a crime! Who's going to punish that?

135 Mrs. Peters: [*Looking upstairs.*] We mustn't—take on.

Mrs. Hale: I might have known she needed help! I know how things can be—for women. I tell you, it's queer, Mrs. Peters. We live close together and we live far apart. We all go through the same things—it's all just a different kind of the same thing. [*Brushes her eyes; noticing the bottle of fruit, reaches out for it.*] If I was you I wouldn't tell her her fruit was gone. Tell her it *ain't.* Tell her it's all right. Take this in to prove it to her. She—she may never know whether it was broke or not.

Mrs. Peters: [*Takes the bottle, looks about for something to wrap it in; takes petticoat from the clothes brought from the other room, very nervously begins winding this around the bottle. In a false voice.*] My, it's a good thing the men couldn't hear us. Wouldn't they just laugh! Getting all stirred up over a little thing like a—dead canary. As if that could have anything to do with—with—wouldn't they *laugh!*

[*The men are heard coming down stairs..*]

*Mrs. Hale:*  [*Under her breath.*] Maybe they would—maybe they wouldn't.

*County Attorney:*  No, Peters, it's all perfectly clear except a reason for doing it. But you know juries when it comes to women. If there was some definite thing. Something to show—something to make a story about—a thing that would connect up with this strange way of doing it—[*The women's eyes meet for an instant. Enter* HALE *from outer door.*]

140  *Hale:*  Well, I've got the team around. Pretty cold out there.

*County Attorney:*  I'm going to stay here a while by myself. [*To the* SHERIFF.] You can send Frank out for me, can't you? I want to go over everything. I'm not satisfied that we can't do better.

*Sheriff:*  Do you want to see what Mrs. Peters is going to take in? [*The* COUNTY ATTORNEY *goes to the table, picks up the apron, laughs.*]

*County Attorney:*  Oh, I guess they're not very dangerous things the ladies have picked out. [*Moves a few things about, disturbing the quilt pieces which cover the box. Steps back.*] No, Mrs. Peters doesn't need supervising. For that matter, a sheriff's wife is married to the law. Ever think of it that way, Mrs. Peters?

*Mrs. Peters:*  Not—just that way.

145  *Sheriff:*  [*Chuckling.*] Married to the law. [*Moves toward the other room.*] I just want you to come in here a minute, George. We ought to take a look at these windows.

*County Attorney:*  [*Scoffingly.*] Oh, windows!

*Sheriff:*  We'll be right out, Mr. Hale.

[HALE *goes outside. The* SHERIFF *follows the* COUNTY ATTORNEY *into the other room. Then* MRS. HALE *rises, hands tight together, looking intensely at* MRS. PETERS, *whose eyes make a slow turn, finally meeting* MRS. HALE'S. *A mo-*

*ment* MRS. HALE *holds her, then her own eyes point the way to where the box is concealed. Suddenly* MRS. PETERS *throws back quilt pieces and tries to put the box in the bag she is wearing. It is too big. She opens box, starts to take bird out, cannot touch it, goes to pieces, stands there helpless. Sound of a knob turning in the other room.* MRS. HALE *snatches the box and puts it in the pocket of her big coat. Enter* COUNTY ATTORNEY *and* SHERIFF.]

County Attorney: [*Facetiously.*] Well, Henry, at least we found out that she was not going to quilt it. She was going to—what is it you call it, ladies?

Mrs. Hale: [*Her hand against her pocket.*] We call it—knot it, Mr. Henderson.

CURTAIN

## Questions for Discussion

Should Glaspell's play be considered an "argument"? What is its thesis?

Are the two women right for withholding evidence?

How do men and women see things differently, noticing different things?

Does Glaspell's play represent an instance of male-bashing?

***Betty Friedan*** *(born 1921), author and co-founder of the National Organization of Women (NOW), wrote the groundbreaking study* The Feminine Mystique *(1963), which is widely regarded as the most important and influential critique of women's oppression in the twentieth-century United States. While raising three children and working part-time as a journalist, Friedan undertook the study of the way women are defined and positioned in Western culture as a result of her observation that many women, including herself, were profoundly dissatisfied with the opportunities and expectations that conventional culture held for them. Friedan's book became an immediate, although controversial, best-seller, and "the feminine mystique" became a widely used term for describing the suffering and alienation of women. After helping to found NOW and the National Women's Political Caucus (in 1971), she has continued to write and speak in support of a variety of social causes, including civil rights and the treatment of the elderly. In "An Open Letter to True Men," Friedan spells out the advantages that dismantling "the feminine mystique" would hold—for men. It first appeared in* True—*a men's magazine—in January 1974.*

# *Betty Friedan*

# An Open Letter to *True* Men

The word is that you feel threatened by the women's liberation movement. You thought it was a joke, at first, but it's begun to get to you—through your wife, girl friend, daughter, even your mother, to say nothing of the women in the office who say you shouldn't call them girls any more.

Well, it's not a joke, and I don't think you can turn it off, or even that you would really want to, if you understood how the women's movement is going to affect your own life—how it can liberate you to be more truly yourself as a man than ever before.

Before I go further, I want you to know that I am taking a risk, myself, in writing this letter to you. Because some of my sisters think you are the enemy, in which case it is a waste of time, or dangerous, or treason, to venture into enemy territory like this. And some of you are the enemy, or think you are. But I think you don't have to be the enemy of the women's movement. For if this were a class war of women against men, women could never win it, not just because men have too much power—which they do—but because most women wouldn't have the will to fight such a war. Most women wouldn't want to live without men, most want to be able to love men.

But what the women's movement actually implies, in change or risk or promise, for all our lives, both women's and men's, is serious enough, and maybe even slightly frightening, to us both. Before we lock ourselves into fixed positions we might never find our way out of, I'd like to know what honestly frightens you, or makes you mad, about women's liberation. And I'd like to tell you honestly what has been making women madder and madder. Because it seems to me we'll come to a dead end soon if we keep on talking just to ourselves—men to men, women to women. But if we can talk honestly to each other about what we fear, resent and want, those bitter battle lines of sex might look a little different to us both.

5    First, what you have heard about "women's lib" may bear only a slight relationship to what the women's movement really means, to me and to most women in America. A freaky bunch of bra-burners? Bitter losers who couldn't get a man and have it in now for all men—uncombed hippies who won't take the responsibility of home and kids? That's the image the media has been giving of "women's lib," though no woman in the movement, to my knowledge, ever burned a bra. (A number of researchers and reporters have been assigned the job of tracking down the original "bra-burning" by major news agencies and encyclopedias, and have never been able to find evidence it ever happened. The braless fashion was actually begun by a *male* fashion designer in the mid-sixties, about the same time as the women's movement began making headlines.) The people who started the women's movement were hardly hippies: they were women in their forties and fifties and thirties, housewives with children who'd gone back to school or work, or women who had worked for years. Most were or had been married; some were single, divorced, widows, even nuns. Most were white, middle class, and middle-aged, in the beginning— Middle American, really—though black women were among the

founders. (Most black women at that time were putting their energies into the black civil rights movement.) Then more and more younger women began to rebel at women's role in the student movement, even among the hippies—those "chicks" at the mimeograph machine.

The women's movement exploded in America in the mid-sixties not because I or any other witch of Salem seduced otherwise happy housewives who would still be putting on false eyelashes to wax the kitchen floor if we hadn't put other ideas in their heads. It happened because women couldn't live their whole lives through husband and children any more. With women's life span now stretching seventy-five years, most of those years will not be filled with kids at home to care for, and too many marriages end in divorce for a woman to count on a man to take care of her all her life. And with so much work that used to be done at home now being done in offices and specialized profes-sions—the teaching of kids, baking of bread, butchering, canning, doctoring, the making of clothing, all of it costing more and more money—a woman had to be able to move, work, earn, out in society where the action was, where the men and the children were most of the day now, whether or not she was married or had kids herself.

Women began to take themselves seriously as people, and to real-ize they weren't freaks when they resented being put down or ex-ploited, or taken advantage of in the office or at home. We began to organize, using the law and the tactics of demonstration and con-frontation that had worked for blacks and workers—and invented tac-tics of our own.

But "equality" for women—equal opportunity, human dignity, in-dividual identity, freedom of choice, which is what all the American revolutions have been about—really can't be seen in quite the same class-war terms as workers striking a boss for a pay raise, or blacks sitting down at a "whites only" lunch counter. Some of the man-hating image of the movement comes from this extremist ideology of sex-class warfare—and the temporary explosion of hostility which fuels it. But the media, in its hunger for sensationalism, plays up the extremists and their exhibitionist tactics far beyond their importance for the movement as a whole.

The movement has grown much too large in ten years to be con-tained in a single organization or single ideology. By now some 3,000,000 women have bought my book *The Feminine Mystique*, which many regard as having started it all in 1963; they consider themselves "liberated," have changed their lives and the way they think about themselves whether or not they belong to an organized group. Recent Gallup and Harris polls indicate that the *majority* of all American women now agree with the basic goals of the women's movement for equality—even those who say they don't like "women's lib."

10     The actions women have taken together to change their lives in recent years are the real women's movement, not the rhetoric or media image of "women's lib." The movement is women at the telephone company, who were never allowed to apply for jobs beyond operator, winning over $100,000,000 in back raises for the better jobs they now can get. It's airline stewardesses, no longer forced to resign at age thirty or thirty-five or because of marriage. There are over 1,000 lawsuits against universities and other institutions who will lose their government contracts if they continue to keep women out of the better jobs. Little girls in Midwest towns are getting the right to be in the Little League—or on high school track or tennis teams. It is now illegal in many states to discriminate against women in mortgages, credit loans, to set different quotas and standards for men and women for admission to college or law school, to ban women from restaurants where male-only business lunches take place. The movement is winning maternity leave, and even paternity leave, clauses in union contracts, and a demand for child-care centers in both national party platforms. It's demanding income tax deduction for expenses of working women, such as child care and housework, in the same way that men can deduct martini business lunches; attacking pension plans and Social Security laws that don't give men and women the right to retire at the same age with the same benefits, and that deny the husband of a deceased woman worker who has paid Social Security all her life the same benefits as the widow of the male worker.

And it's women from Texas and Georgia arguing and winning a historic case in the U.S. Supreme Court attesting as a constitutional right a woman's right to choose whether or not or when to have a baby, and therefore have medical access to abortion, according to the privacy of her own conscience. It's women calling themselves Ms., whether or not they are married, single or divorced, as all men are called Mr. It's objecting to Janey and Junior's readers and television programs which show women only with aprons on, cooking supper or bandaging children's knees; never as doctor, lawyer, or space explorer. It's women beginning to go to law school, and medical school, and business school, not yet in equal proportion to men but *many* times the one or two women in the classes before. It's many daughters of policemen, not just their sons, entering the police force in New York this year, women breaking through the barriers that have kept them out of major sports and varsity programs and physical training, from grade school on, and women getting ordained as ministers, priests, deacons, rabbis; twice as many delegates to both political conventions as ever before. Women are getting elected to state offices which women never ran for before, and are seriously running for President and Vice President—and are demanding, in all parties, the chance to "make policy, not coffee."

It's also the young couples beginning to really share the work and the fun of the home and children they make together. And girls in high school, or college, or working, not expecting the boys always to pay, when they go out . . .

All of this cannot be summed up as equal pay for equal work, or as women wanting to be just like men.

Where does this leave men? Does it really threaten your masculinity, your power, your sense of your own importance, all that's made life worth living for a man? It seems to me the real result will be to relieve you, as men, from some burdens that have become almost too difficult to bear, the way things are. I think you will live longer. And certain pressures that can make a man's life seem not worth living will no longer be, at home or in the office or at school. Maybe you won't have to be so touchy about your masculinity, because you will be able to feel more important for who you really are yourself.

15    Men have been dying ten years younger than their wives because of the heart attacks and ulcers brought on by the burdens a man is supposed to carry by himself, the rat race he has to keep running to win, the tears and fears he's not supposed to feel. You grew up knowing you were going to have to take complete care of yourself, your wife, whatever children you had, until death or until the kids went off on their own. It was unfair that a woman could grow up expecting to be taken care of all her life—and unfair to her if death, divorce or circumstance ended that dream, and she had never gotten the confidence or skills to take care of herself in the world. It's only when the subject of alimony comes up that you bewail the unfairness to you. But aren't there times, even in a good marriage, when you panic at the burden? Wouldn't it be a relief if your wife could get a job that paid well enough to ease that burden on you? Or that you could be free to take more time to do things you have always wanted to do?

As for your relationship with your wife—or any woman—has it ever seemed to you that whatever you do, it's wrong . . . that nothing ever satisfies her . . . that whatever you give her it's not enough? As if underneath she has some secret complaint or grievance against you?

Or do you feel lonesome sometimes, left out when at home with her and the kids, uncomfortable, as if you're an outsider, that they're ganging up against you, so it's a relief to get out with the boys? It might be a greater relief for you if your woman could just feel better about herself. When you feel as if you're nobody yourself, you can't feel good about other people. A recent study of Long Island housewives showed that they saw their husbands first of all as breadwinners, then as fathers, then as husbands, and last of all, as themselves. When women no longer have to depend on husbands first of all as breadwinners, and no longer feel so bad about themselves that they can't see any good in their husbands, they will be able to love you for yourselves. There would be less nagging, less guilt, fewer problems, more love from the woman with whom a man feels at home.

As for that masculinity supposedly being threatened, wouldn't it be a relief if it didn't get measured any more by the big-muscle bluster some aren't born with—and all can lose—or by winning the rat race that is always stacked against you? It's the sexual and economic *testing* that can make a man feel inadequate even before he begins. I think it might be just as much a relief for true men to break out of that iron mask which makes you so unnecessarily vulnerable—and other men your enemies—as it has been for women to break out of our false, simpering, ruffled masks which made us feel such contempt for ourselves and other women, and feel such rage and fear of men. Beneath the phony togetherness, wearing those masks, we are both alone.

You've heard, of course, that "women's lib" wants to destroy marriage, the family, motherhood, and take the pants off men . . . that it's turning women against their own husbands, children, homes, even sex. There is a lot of bitterness and rage exploding in women today, with good reason. It may turn, temporarily, against the very husband, children, marriage and home women were supposed to live for. Because she wants nothing to do with men, it may even temporarily turn a woman off of sex. The women's movement is not the cause of this exploding rage, but it may be the only hope for its cure. Because all this hostility is a symptom that something is terribly wrong with the way marriages, family and home are structured right now, built around those separate, obsolete and unequal roles women and men have been trying to play.

Medical and psychiatric experts have noted that marriage, the way it is structured now, works out much better for men than women, even though the men die younger. On scales of happiness and general well-being, married men and single women are much better off than married women. Police and missing persons bureaus report an enormous increase in runaway wives. In one instance, the husband was asked by the police to describe his wife. "Sort of average." "What color are her eyes?" "Blue, I guess, or is it brown?" He couldn't remember, it was so long since he had looked at her as a person, really seen her. But if a woman feels like nobody—"a service station," as one woman I interviewed put it—it's bound to rub off on her husband and children, even if she doesn't get desperate enough to run away. And it's bound to affect the way she feels, or doesn't feel, in bed with her husband at night. And not all the sex manuals, sexploitation films, pornographic titillators, vibrators, Playboy Bunnies, or Masters and Johnson techniques may cure what seems to be happening, or not happening, in the American bedroom at night. Can they change the conditions of women's lives, the routine all day, every day, at home, in the office, that have driven them to this desperation?

20      Only the extremists think women's liberation has to mean the end of marriage and the family, but it certainly will change marriage, the family, the way we raise the children, even the architecture of the home, when we liberate ourselves and each other from the old sex roles. I hope, and believe, women will *enjoy* being mothers when they stop living through and for their children, and feel better about themselves. (And it may be better for the kids to take the bus themselves and butter their own sandwiches and do their own homework instead of mother's chauffeuring them, doing it all for them.) I think marriages may last longer, and we may find in them the love, comfort, intimacy, peace, and support we still need and seek from each other, and so rarely find today.

Can you finally look at your woman in a way you've never looked at her before—not as the old lady who gets you breakfast, or as your kids' mother, or as a sex object—but as the person she really is herself? Are you afraid to do that, true man? Well, let me tell you she is even more afraid than you are. When all we were supposed to be were wives and mothers, we never had to face the world, to be tested as individuals. It's easier to blame things on you than to face that lonely test of who we are ourselves in this fast-changing human world. This test you can no longer take for us, true men, we have to do it ourselves. When we know who we truly are, as women, you'll be able to be truly yourselves, as men. When we break out of the roles that have kept us from being ourselves, and know each other for who we really are—woman and man—then, and only then, will come real sexual liberation, and the end of loneliness—and men and women will truly be able to make love, not war.

## Questions for Discussion

What kind of "true man" is Friedan targeting? How can you tell?

How well does Friedan understand her audience? What does she do to demonstrate this understanding?

Do the "advances" Friedan discusses seem as striking now as they seemed in 1974? How far has American culture come since this argument was made?

*Singer and songwriter **Cyndi Lauper** (born 1953) began her music career singing cover songs in the New York club scene. She briefly formed the band Blue Angel in the late 1970s before embarking on a successful solo career in 1983 with her debut album,* She's So Unusual, *on which the following song first appeared. The album sold millions of copies and contained many hit singles, including the controversial "She Bop" and the ballad "Time After Time," which was later covered by Miles Davis. Lauper's work is marked by a mixture of humor and seriousness, perhaps best exemplified by her association with professional wrestling while she was at the top of her career in the mid 1980s. Lauper won a Grammy for Best New Artist in 1984.*

# *Cyndi Lauper*
# Girls Just Wanna Have Fun

I come home in the morning light
My mother says when you're gonna live your life right
Oh mother dear we're not the fortunate ones
And girls they want to have fun
5 Oh girls just want to have fun

The phone rings in the middle of the night
My father yells what you're gonna do with your life
Oh daddy dear you know you're still number one
But girls they want to have fun
10 Oh girls just want to have . . .

That's all they really want—Some fun
When the working day is done
Girls . . . they want to have fun
Oh girls just want to have fun

15 Some boys take a beautiful girl
And hide her away from the rest of the world
I want to be the one to walk in the sun
Oh girls they want to have fun
Oh girls just want to have

20 That's all they really want—Some fun
When the working day is done
Oh girls . . . they want to have fun
Oooh girls just want to have fun,

They just want to . . .
25 They just want to . . .
They just want to have fun . . .

When the working day is done . . .
When the working day is done . . .
Ohh girls just want to . . .
30 Girls just want to have fun . . .

***Paula Gunn Allen** (born 1939), born into a family with a long and various heritage—Lebanese, Laguna-Sioux, Scottish—grew up in the New Mexican Pueblo culture. A professor of English with a doctorate in American Studies, Allen, until her retirement in 1999, studied and advocated successfully for including Native American literary and cultural studies alongside the study of Western literature and culture. She taught and developed Native American literatures and curricula with tremendous innovation: Witness her 1983 book* Studies in American Indian Literature: Critical Essays and Course Designs. *In addition to her academic career, Allen also has written poetry, novels, and essays, the latter for both academic and popular audiences. The following argument appears in her collection of essays* The Sacred Hoop *(1986), a meditation on women's issues in the Native American community.*

## Paula Gunn Allen

# Where I Come From Is Like This

## I

Modern American Indian women, like their non-Indian sisters, are deeply engaged in the struggle to redefine themselves. In their struggle they must reconcile traditional tribal definitions of women with industrial and postindustrial non-Indian definitions. Yet while these definitions seem to be more or less mutually exclusive, Indian women must somehow harmonize and integrate both in their own lives.

An American Indian woman is primarily defined by her tribal identity. In her eyes, her destiny is necessarily that of her people, and her sense of herself as a woman is first and foremost prescribed by her tribe. The definitions of woman's roles are as diverse as tribal cultures in the Americas. In some she is devalued; in others she wields considerable power. In some she is a familial/clan adjunct; in some she is as close to autonomous as her economic circumstances and psychological traits permit. But in no tribal definitions is she perceived in the same way as are women in western industrial and postindustrial cultures.

In the west, few images of women form part of the cultural mythos, and these are largely sexually charged. Among Christians, the madonna is the female prototype, and she is portrayed as essentially passive: her contribution is simply that of birthing. Little else is attributed to her and she certainly possesses few of the characteristics that are attributed to mythic figures among Indian tribes. This image is countered (rather than balanced) by the witch-goddess/whore characteristics designed to reinforce cultural beliefs about women, as well as western adversarial and dualistic perceptions of reality.

The tribes see women variously, but they do not question the power of femininity. Sometimes they see women as fearful, sometimes peaceful, sometimes omnipotent and omniscient, but they never portray women as mindless, helpless, simple, or oppressed. And while the women in a given tribe, clan, or band may be all these things, the individual woman is provided with a variety of images of women from the interconnected supernatural, natural, and social worlds she lives in.

5    As a half-breed American Indian woman, I cast about in my mind for negative images of Indian women, and I find none that are directed to Indian women alone. The negative images I do have are of Indians in general and in fact are more often of males than of females. All these images come to me from non-Indian sources, and they are always balanced by a positive image. My ideas of womanhood, passed on largely by my mother and grandmothers, Laguna Pueblo women, are about practicality, strength, reasonableness, intelligence, wit, and competence. I also remember vividly the women who came to my father's store, the women who held me and sang to me, the women at Feast Day, at Grab Days, the women in the kitchen of my Cubero home, the women I grew up with; none of them appeared weak or helpless, none of them presented herself tentatively. I remember a certain reserve on those lovely brown faces; I remember the direct gaze of eyes framed by bright-colored shawls draped over their heads and cascading down their backs. I remember the clean cotton dresses and carefully pressed hand-embroidered aprons they always wore; I remember laughter and good food, especially the sweet bread and the oven bread they gave us. Nowhere in my mind is there a foolish woman, a dumb woman, a vain woman, or a plastic woman, though the Indian women I have known have shown a wide range of personal style and demeanor.

My memory includes the Navajo woman who was badly beaten by her Sioux husband; but I also remember that my grandmother abandoned her Sioux husband long ago. I recall the stories about the Laguna woman beaten regularly by her husband in the presence of her children so that the children would not believe in the strength and power of femininity. And I remember the women who drank, who got into fights with other women and with the men, and who often won those battles. I have memories of tired women, partying women, stubborn women, sullen women, amicable women, selfish women, shy women, and aggressive women. Most of all I remember the women who laugh and scold and sit uncomplaining in the long sun on feast days and who cook wonderful food on wood stoves, in beehive mud ovens, and over open fires outdoors.

Among the images of women that come to me from various tribes as well as my own are White Buffalo Woman, who came to the Lakota long ago and brought them the religion of the Sacred Pipe, which they still practice; Tinotzin the goddess, who came to Juan Diego to remind him that she still walked the hills of her people and sent him with her message, her demand and her proof to the Catholic bishop in the city nearby. And from Laguna I take the images of Yellow Woman, Coyote Woman, Grandmother Spider (Spider Old Woman), who brought the light, who gave us weaving and medicine, who gave us life. Among the Keres she is known as Thought Woman, who created us all and who keeps us in creation even now. I remember Iyatiku, Earth Woman, Corn Woman, who guides and counsels the people to peace and who welcomes us home when we cast off this coil of flesh as huskers cast off the leaves that wrap the corn. I remember Iyatiku's sister, Sun Woman, who held metals and cattle, pigs and sheep, highways and engines and so many things in her bundle, who went away to the east saying that one day she would return.

## II

Since the coming of the Anglo-Europeans beginning in the fifteenth century, the fragile web of identity that long held tribal people secure has gradually been weakened and torn. But the oral tradition has prevented the complete destruction of the web, the ultimate disruption of tribal ways. The oral tradition is vital; it heals itself and the tribal web by adapting to the flow of the present while never relinquishing its connection to the past. Its adaptability has always been required, as many generations have experienced. Certainly the modern American Indian woman bears slight resemblance to her forebears—at least on superficial examination—but she is still a tribal woman in her deepest being. Her tribal sense of relationship to all that is continues to flourish. And though she is at times beset by her knowledge of the enormous gap between the life she lives and the life she was raised to live, and while she adapts her mind and being to the circumstances of her present life, she does so in tribal ways, mending the tears in the web of being from which she takes her existence as she goes.

My mother told me stories all the time, though I often did not recognize them as that. My mother told me stories about cooking and childbearing; she told me stories about menstruation and pregnancy; she told me stories about gods and heroes, about fairies and elves, about goddesses and spirits; she told me stories about the land and the sky, about cats and dogs, about snakes and spiders; she told me stories about climbing trees and exploring the mesas; she told me stories about going to dances and getting married; she told me stories about dressing and undressing, about sleeping and waking; she told me stories about herself, about her mother, about her grandmother. She told me stories about grieving and laughing, about thinking and doing; she told me stories about school and about people; about darning and mending; she told me stories about turquoise and about gold; she told me European stories and Laguna stories; she told me Catholic stories and Presbyterian stories; she told me city stories and country stories; she told me political stories and religious stories. She told me stories about living and stories about dying. And in all of those stories she told me who I was, who I was supposed to be, whom I came from, and who would follow me. In this way she taught me the meaning of the words she said, that all life is a circle and everything has a place within it. That's what she said and what she showed me in the things she did and the way she lives.

10    Of course, through my formal, white, Christian education, I discovered that other people had stories of their own—about women, about Indians, about fact, about reality—and I was amazed by a number of startling suppositions that others made about tribal customs and beliefs. According to the un-Indian, non-Indian view, for instance, Indians barred menstruating women from ceremonies and indeed segregated them from the rest of the people, consigning them to some space specially designed for them. This showed that Indians considered menstruating women unclean and not fit to enjoy the company of decent (nonmenstruating) people, that is, men. I was surprised and confused to hear this because my mother had taught me that white people had strange attitudes toward menstruation: they thought something was bad about it, that it meant you were sick, cursed, sinful, and weak and that you had to be very careful during that time. She taught me that menstruation was a normal occurrence, that I could go swimming or hiking or whatever else I wanted to do during my period. She actively scorned women who took to their beds, who were incapacitated by cramps, who "got the blues."

As I struggled to reconcile these very contradictory interpretations of American Indians' traditional beliefs concerning menstruation, I realized that the menstrual taboos were about power, not about sin or filth. My conclusion was later borne out by some tribes' own explanations, which, as you may well imagine, came as quite a relief to me.

The truth of the matter as many Indians see it is that women who are at the peak of their fecundity are believed to possess power that throws male power totally out of kilter. They emit such force that, in their presence, any male-owned or -dominated ritual or sacred object cannot do its usual task. For instance, the Lakota say that a menstruating woman anywhere near a yuwipi man, who is a special sort of psychic, spirit-empowered healer, for a day or so before he is to do his ceremony will effectively disempower him. Conversely, among many, if not most, tribes, important ceremonies cannot be held without the presence of women. Sometimes the ritual woman who empowers the ceremony must be unmarried and virginal so that the power she channels is unalloyed, unweakened by sexual arousal and penetration by a male. Other ceremonies require tumescent women, others the presence of mature women who have borne children, and still others depend for empowerment on postmenopausal women. Women may be segregated from the company of the whole band or village on certain occasions, but on certain occasions men are also segregated. In short, each ritual depends on a certain balance of power, and the positions of women within the phases of womanhood are used by tribal people to empower certain rites. This does not derive from a male-dominant view; it is not a ritual observance imposed on women by men. It derives from a tribal view of reality that distinguishes tribal people from feudal and industrial people.

Among the tribes, the occult power of women, inextricably bound to our hormonal life, is thought to be very great; many hold that we possess innately the blood-given power to kill—with a glance, with a step, or with a judicious mixing of menstrual blood into somebody's soup. Medicine women among the Pomo of California cannot practice until they are sufficiently mature; when they are immature, their power is diffuse and is likely to interfere with their practice until time and experience have it under control. So women of the tribes are not especially inclined to see themselves as poor helpless victims of male domination. Even in those tribes where something akin to male domination was present, women are perceived as powerful, socially, physically, and metaphysically. In times past, as in times present, women carried enormous burdens with aplomb. We were far indeed from the "weaker sex," the designation that white aristocratic sisters unhappily earned for us all.

I remember my mother moving furniture all over the house when she wanted it changed. She didn't wait for my father to come home and help—she just went ahead and moved the piano, a huge upright from the old days, the couch, the refrigerator. Nobody had told her she was too weak to do such things. In imitation of her, I would delight in loading trucks at my father's store with cases of pop or fifty-pound sacks of flour. Even when I was quite small I could do it, and it gave me a belief in my own physical strength that advancing middle age can't quite erase. My mother used to tell me about the Acoma Pueblo women she had seen as a child carrying huge ollas (water pots) on their heads as they wound their way up the tortuous stairwell carved into the face of the "Sky City" mesa, a feat I tried to imitate with books and tin buckets. ("Sky City" is the term used by the Chamber of Commerce for the mother village of Acoma, which is situated atop a high sandstone table mountain.) I was never very successful, but even the attempt reminded me that I was supposed to be strong and balanced to be a proper girl.

15 Of course, my mother's Laguna people are Keres Indian, reputed to be the last extreme mother-right people on earth. So it is no wonder that I got notably nonwhite notions about the natural strength and prowess of women. Indeed, it is only when I am trying to get non-Indian approval, recognition, or acknowledgment that my "weak sister" emotional and intellectual ploys get the better of my tribal woman's good sense. At such times I forget that I just moved the piano or just wrote a competent paper or just completed a financial transaction satisfactorily or have supported myself and my children for most of my adult life.

Nor is my contradictory behavior atypical. Most Indian women I know are in the same bicultural bind: we vacillate between being dependent and strong, self-reliant and powerless, strongly motivated and hopelessly insecure. We resolve the dilemma in various ways: some of us party all the time; some of us drink to excess; some of us travel and move around a lot; some of us land good jobs and then quit them; some of us engage in violent exchanges; some of us blow our brains out. We act in these destructive ways because we suffer from the societal conflicts caused by having to identify with two hopelessly opposed cultural definitions of women. Through this destructive dissonance we are unhappy prey to the self-disparagement common to, indeed demanded of, Indians living in the United States today. Our situation is caused by the exigencies of a history of invasion, conquest, and colonization whose searing marks are probably ineradicable. A popular bumper sticker on many Indian cars proclaims: "If You're Indian You're In," to which I always find myself adding under my breath, "Trouble."

# III

No Indian can grow to any age without being informed that her people were "savages" who interfered with the march of progress pursued by respectable, loving, civilized white people. We are the villains of the scenario when we are mentioned at all. We are absent from much of white history except when we are calmly, rationally, succinctly, and systematically dehumanized. On the few occasions we are noticed in any way other than as howling, bloodthirsty beings, we are acclaimed for our noble quaintness. In this definition, we are exotic curios. Our ancient arts and customs are used to draw tourist money to state coffers, into the pocketbooks and bank accounts of scholars, and into support of the American-in-Disneyland promoters' dream.

As a Roman Catholic child I was treated to bloody tales of how the savage Indians martyred the hapless priests and missionaries who went among them in an attempt to lead them to the one true path. By the time I was through high school I had the idea that Indians were people who had benefited mightily from the advanced knowledge and superior morality of the Anglo-Europeans. At least I had, perforce, that idea to lay beside the other one that derived from my daily experience of Indian life, an idea less dehumanizing and more accurate because it came from my mother and the other Indian people who raised me. That idea was that Indians are a people who don't tell lies, who care for their children and their old people. You never see an Indian orphan, they said. You always know when you're old that someone will take care of you—one of your children will. Then they'd list the old folks who were being taken care of by this child or that. No child is ever considered illegitimate among the Indians, they said. If a girl gets pregnant, the baby is still part of the family, and the mother is too. That's what they said, and they showed me real people who lived according to those principles.

Of course the ravages of colonization have taken their toll; there are orphans in Indian country now, and abandoned, brutalized old folks; there are even illegitimate children, though the very concept still strikes me as absurd. There are battered children and neglected children, and there are battered wives and women who have been raped by Indian men. Proximity to the "civilizing" effects of white Christians has not improved the moral quality of life in Indian country, though each group, Indian and white, explains the situation differently. Nor is there much yet in the oral tradition that can enable us to adapt to these inhuman changes. But a force is growing in that direction, and it is helping Indian women reclaim their lives. Their power, their sense of direction and of self will soon be visible. It is the force of the women who speak and work and write, and it is formidable.

20 Through all the centuries of war and death and cultural and psychic destruction have endured the women who raise the children and tend the fires, who pass along the tales and the traditions, who weep and bury the dead, who are the dead, and who never forget. There are always the women, who make pots and weave baskets, who fashion clothes and cheer their children on at powwow, who make fry bread and piki bread, and corn soup and chili stew, who dance and sing and remember and hold within their hearts the dream of their ancient peoples—that one day the woman who thinks will speak to us again, and everywhere there will be peace. Meanwhile we tell the stories and write the books and trade tales of anger and woe and stories of fun and scandal and laugh over all manner of things that happen every day. We watch and we wait.

My great-grandmother told my mother: Never forget you are Indian. And my mother told me the same thing. This, then, is how I have gone about remembering, so that my children will remember too.

## Questions for Discussion

What does Paula Gunn Allen mean by "definitions of women?"

What is the role of "stories" in her life? What roles do stories play in other cultures you are familiar with? How do they differ?

*Harvey Milk (1930–1978) is generally recognized as the first openly gay man elected to public office in the United States, serving as a member of the San Francisco Board of Supervisors in 1977. A charismatic speaker and savvy grassroots organizer, Milk energized the gay community and the gay liberation movement, in San Francisco and throughout the country, with his ideas about how gays should assert their identities, form political coalitions with other minority and special interest groups (including unions), and openly fight for their rights. Unfortunately, Milk and San Francisco Mayor George Moscone were assassinated only eleven months after Milk's election. Tens of thousands of mourners held a procession to City Hall the night of his death; and in fact, the march, known as the "Candlelight March," is still held every year. Milk often delivered one version or another of the following speech, commonly known as "The Hope Speech"; this version was given at the meeting of the gay caucus of the California Democratic Council (CDC) in 1978.*

## Harvey Milk
# The Hope Speech

My name is Harvey Milk and I'm here to recruit you.

I've been saving this one for years. It's a political joke. I can't help it—I've got to tell it. I've never been able to talk to this many political people before, so if I tell you nothing else you may be able to go home laughing a bit.

This ocean liner was going across the ocean and it sank. And there was one little piece of wood floating and three people swam to it and they realized only one person could hold on to it. So they had a little debate about which was the person. It so happened the three people were the Pope, the President, and Mayor Daley. The Pope said he was titular head of one of the great religions of the world and he was spiritual adviser to many, many millions and he went on and pontificated and they thought it was a good argument. Then the President said he was leader of the largest and most powerful nation of the world. What takes place in this country affects the whole world and they thought that was a good argument. And Mayor Daley said he was mayor of the backbone of the United States and what took place in Chicago affected the world, and what took place in the archdiocese of Chicago affected Catholicism. And they thought that was a good argument. So they did it the democratic way and voted. And Daley won, seven to two.

About six months ago, Anita Bryant in her speaking to God said that the drought in California was because of the gay people.[1] On November 9, the day after I got elected, it started to rain. On the day I got sworn in, we walked to City Hall and it was kinda nice, and as soon as I said the word "I do," it started to rain again. It's been raining since then and the people of San Francisco figure the only way to stop it is to do a recall petition. That's a local joke.

5      So much for that. Why are we here? Why are gay people here? And what's happening? What's happening to me is the antithesis of what you read about in the papers and what you hear about on the radio. You hear about and read about this movement to the right. That we must band together and fight back this movement to the right. And I'm here to go ahead and say that what you hear and read is what they want you to think because it's not happening. The major media in this country has talked about the movement to the right so much that they've got even us thinking that way. Because they want the legislators to think that there is indeed a movement to the right and that the Congress and the legislators and the city councils will start to move to the right the way the major media want them. So they keep on talking about this move to the right.

So let's look at 1977 and see if there was indeed a move to the right. In 1977, gay people had their rights taken away from them in Miami. But you must remember that in the week before Miami and the week after that, the word homosexual or gay appeared in every single newspaper in this nation in articles both pro and con. In every radio station, in every TV station and every household. For the first time in the history of the world, everybody was talking about it, good or bad. Unless you have dialogue, unless you open the walls of dialogue, you can never reach to change people's opinion. In those two weeks, more good and bad, but *more* about the word homosexual and gay was written than probably in the history of mankind. Once you have dialogue starting, you know you can break down the prejudice. In 1977 we saw a dialogue start. In 1977, we saw a gay person elected in San Francisco. In 1977 we saw the state of Mississippi decriminalize marijuana. In 1977, we saw the convention of conventions in Houston. And I want to know where the movement to the right is happening.

What that is is a record of what happened last year. What we must do is make sure that 1978 continues the movement that is really happening that the media don't want you to know about, that is the

---

[1] In 1977 Anita Bryant, former Miss America and spokesperson for the Florida orange juice industry, was blaming many of the nation's economic and social ills on gay citizens.

movement to the left. It's up to CDC to put the pressures on Sacramento—not to just bring flowers to Sacramento—but to break down the walls and the barriers so the movement to the left continues and progress continues in the nation. We have before us coming up several issues we must speak out on. Probably the most important issue outside the Briggs—which we will come to—but we do know what will take place this June. We know there's an issue on the ballot called Jarvis-Gann. We hear the taxpayers talk about it on both sides. But what you don't hear is that it's probably the most racist issue on the ballot in a long time. In the city and county of San Francisco, if it passes and we indeed have to lay off people, who will they be? The last in, not the first in, and who are the last in but the minorities? Jarvis-Gann is a racist issue. We must address that issue. We must not talk away from it. We must not allow them to talk about the money it's going to save, because look at who's going to save the money and who's going to get hurt.

We also have another issue that we've started in some of the north counties and I hope in some of the south counties it continues. In San Francisco elections we're asking—at least we hope to ask—that the U.S. government put pressure on the closing of the South African consulate. That must happen. There is a major difference between an embassy in Washington which is a diplomatic bureau, and a consulate in major cities. A consulate is there for one reason only—to promote business, economic gains, tourism, investment. And every time you have business going to South Africa, you're promoting a regime that's offensive.

In the city of San Francisco, if everyone of 51 percent of that city were to go to South Africa, they would be treated as second-class citizens. That is an offense to the people of San Francisco and I hope all my colleagues up there will take every step we can to close down that consulate and hope that people in other parts of the state follow us in that lead. The battles must be started some place and CDC is the greatest place to start the battles.

10      I know we are pressed for time so I'm going to cover just one more little point. That is to understand why it is important that gay people run for office and that gay people get elected. I know there are many people in this room who are running for central committee who are gay. I encourage you. There's a major reason why. If my non-gay friends and supporters in this room understand it, they'll probably understand why I've run so often before I finally made it. Y'see right now, there's a controversy going on in this convention about the governor. Is he speaking out enough? Is he strong enough for gay rights? And there

is a controversy and for us to say it is not would be foolish. Some people are satisfied and some people are not.

You see there is a major difference—and it remains a vital difference—between a friend and a gay person, a friend in office and a gay person in office. Gay people have been slandered nationwide. We've been tarred and we've been brushed with the picture of pornography. In Dade County, we were accused of child molestation. It's not enough anymore just to have friends represent us. No matter how good that friend may be.

The black community made up its mind to that a long time ago. That the myths against blacks can only be dispelled by electing black leaders, so the black community could be judged by the leaders and not by the myths or black criminals. The Spanish community must not be judged by Latin criminals or myths. The Asian community must not be judged by Asian criminals or myths. The Italian community should not be judged by the mafia, myths. And the time has come when the gay community must not be judged by our criminals and myths.

Like every other group, we must be judged by our leaders and by those who are themselves gay, those who are visible. For invisible, we remain in limbo—a myth, a person with no parents, no brothers, no sisters, no friends who are straight, no important positions in employment. A tenth of a nation supposedly composed of stereotypes and would-be seducers of children—and no offense meant to the stereotypes. But today, the black community is not judged by its friends, but by its black legislators and leaders. And we must give people the chance to judge us by our leaders and legislators. A gay person in office can set a tone, can command respect not only from the larger community, but from the young people in our own community who need both examples and hope.

The first gay people we elect must be strong. They must not be content to sit in the back of the bus. They must not be content to accept pablum. They must be above wheeling and dealing. They must be—for the good of all of us—independent, unbought. The anger and the frustrations that some of us feel is because we are misunderstood, and friends can't feel that anger and frustration. They can sense it in us, but they can't feel it. Because a friend has never gone through what is known as coming out. I will never forget what it was like coming out and having nobody to look up toward. I remember the lack of hope—and our friends can't fulfill that.

15    I can't forget the looks on faces of people who've lost hope. Be they gay, be they seniors, be they blacks looking for an almost impossible

job, be they Latins trying to explain their problems and aspirations in a tongue that's foreign to them. I personally will never forget that people are more important than buildings. I use the word "I" because I'm proud. I stand here tonight in front of my gay sisters, brothers and friends because I'm proud of you. I think it's time that we have many legislators who are gay and proud of that fact and do not have to remain in the closet. I think that a gay person, up-front, will not walk away from a responsibility and be afraid of being tossed out of office. After Dade County, I walked among the angry and the frustrated night after night and I looked at their faces. And in San Francisco, three days before Gay Pride Day, a person was killed just because he was gay. And that night, I walked among the sad and the frustrated at City Hall in San Francisco and later that night as they lit candles on Castro Street and stood in silence, reaching out for some symbolic thing that would give them hope. These were strong people, people whose faces I knew from the shop, the streets, meetings and people who I never saw before but I knew. They were strong, but even they needed hope.

And the young gay people in the Altoona, Pennsylvanias and the Richmond, Minnesotas who are coming out and hear Anita Bryant on television and her story. The only thing they have to look forward to is hope. And you have to give them hope. Hope for a better world, hope for a better tomorrow, hope for a better place to come to if the pressures at home are too great. Hope that all will be all right. Without hope, not only gays, but the blacks, the seniors, the handicapped, the us'es, the us'es will give up. And if you help elect to the central committee and other offices, more gay people, that gives a green light to all who feel disenfranchised, a green light to move forward. It means hope to a nation that has given up, because if a gay person makes it, the doors are open to everyone.

So if there is a message I have to give, it is that if I've found one overriding thing about my personal election, it's the fact that if a gay person can be elected, it's a green light. And you and you and you, you have to give people hope. Thank you very much.

## Questions for Discussion

Why does Milk choose to spend so much of his speech talking about other minorities' tactics and struggles?

What kind of ethos does Milk construct? How does that ethos contribute to the points he is making? Why does Milk start his speech with jokes?

*Claude McKay (1889–1948) was an influential and fascinating poet, novelist, and journalist during the Harlem Renaissance, that flowering of the arts and intellectual life that is associated with the Harlem area of New York City after 1920. Actually, McKay was from Jamaica, and throughout his life he travelled widely and spent significant parts of his professional and artistic life in Europe, Africa, and America. The influence of McKay's work extended well beyond the Harlem Renaissance period, for he was gifted at turning angry protest into magnificent verse: "If We Must Die," a sonnet which appeared in the radical magazine* The Liberator *in 1919, is a stirring example. Thus, many of McKay's words and themes later shaped the thinking behind the civil rights movement of the 1950s and 1960s.*

# Claude McKay

# If We Must Die

If we must die, let it not be like hogs
Hunted and penned in an inglorious spot,
While round us bark the mad and hungry dogs,
Making their mock at our accursed lot.
5 If we must die, O let us nobly die,
So that our precious blood may not be shed
In vain; then even the monsters we defy
Shall be constrained to honor us though dead!
O kinsmen! we must meet the common foe!
10 Though far outnumbered let us show us brave,
And for their thousand blows deal one deathblow!
What though before us lies the open grave?
Like men we'll face the murderous, cowardly pack,
Pressed to the wall, dying, but fighting back!

*The song "We Shall Overcome" has had a remarkable history in America. Its tune derives from a nineteenth-century, antebellum spiritual called "No More Auction Block for Me," and its lyrics were adapted from the gospel song "I'll Overcome Some Day," written around World War I. The song became the anthem of the civil rights movement in the 1960s after its lyrics and music were rediscovered and then adapted by folksingers Pete Seeger and Guy Carawan. (Carawan, according to Taylor Branch's Parting the Waters, was the "resident folksinger" at Highlander Folk School, an incubator for civil rights activists in the late 1950s and early 1960s.) The song spread quickly when it was appropriated by other folk entertainers like Peter, Paul, and Mary and Joan Baez. In all its forms, the song has expressed the feelings and plight of oppressed peoples and has unified the hopeful voices of those who share the common goal of striving to overturn injustice—not only African Americans, but also people engaged in human rights campaigns in other nations such as South Africa.*

# We Shall Overcome

We shall overcome,
We shall overcome.
We shall overcome some day,
Oh, deep in my heart I do believe
5   We shall overcome some day.

We'll walk hand in hand,
We'll walk hand in hand,
We'll walk hand in hand some day,
Oh, deep in my heart I do believe
10   We shall overcome some day.

We are not afraid,
We are not afraid,
We are not afraid today,
Oh, deep in my heart I do believe
15   We shall overcome some day.

We shall stand together,
We shall stand together,
We shall stand together—now,
Oh, deep in my heart I do believe
20   We shall overcome some day.

The truth will make us free,
The truth will make us free,
The truth will make us free some day,
Oh, deep in my heart I do believe
25    We shall overcome some day.

The Lord will see us through,
The Lord will see us through,
The Lord will see us through some day,
Oh, deep in my heart I do believe
30    We shall overcome some day.

We shall be like Him,
We shall be like Him,
We shall be like Him some day,
Oh, deep in my heart I do believe
35    We shall overcome some day.

We shall live in peace,
We shall live in peace,
We shall live in peace some day,
Oh, deep in my heart I do believe
40    We shall overcome some day.

The whole wide world around,
The whole wide world around,
The whole wide world around some day,
Oh, deep in my heart I do believe
45    We shall overcome some day.

We shall overcome,
We shall overcome,
We shall overcome some day,
Oh, deep in my heart I do believe
50    We shall overcome some day.

*On August 28, 1963,* **Martin Luther King, Jr.**, *standing in the shadow of the Lincoln Memorial, delivered the following speech, perhaps the most famous and oft-quoted of the civil rights era, to a crowd of over 200,000 people who had come together in support of civil rights for African Americans. The speech secured wider national acceptance of the need for civil rights from all segments of the American population, for it was immediately recognized for its thrilling eloquence. The following year, Congress ratified the Twenty-Fourth Amendment to the Constitution, which outlawed the poll tax, and passed the Civil Rights Act of 1964, which outlawed racial discrimination in education, employment, and public facilities. In the same year, King was awarded the Nobel Peace Prize, and when he was assassinated in 1968, the nation mourned. (For more on King, see pages 356–371.)*

## *Martin Luther King, Jr.*

# I Have a Dream

I am happy to join with you today in what will go down in history as the greatest demonstration for freedom in the history of our nation.

Five score years ago, a great American, in whose symbolic shadow we stand today, signed the Emancipation Proclamation. This momentous decree came as the great beacon light of hope for millions of Negro slaves who had been seared in the flames of withering injustice. It came as the joyous daybreak to end the long night of their captivity.

But one hundred years later the Negro still is not free. One hundred years later, the life of the Negro is still badly crippled by the manacles of segregation and the chains of discrimination. One hundred years later, the Negro lives on a lonely island of poverty in the midst of a vast ocean of material prosperity. One hundred years later, the Negro is still languished in the corners of American society and finds himself an exile in his own land. So we have come here today to dramatize the shameful condition.

In a sense we've come to our Nation's Capital to cash a check. When the architects of our republic wrote the magnificent words of the Constitution and the Declaration of Independence, they were signing a promissory note to which every American was to fall heir. This note was a promise that all men, yes, black men as well as white men, should be guaranteed the unalienable rights of life, liberty and the pursuit of happiness.

5    It is obvious today that America has defaulted on this promissory note insofar as her citizens of color are concerned. Instead of honoring this sacred obligation, America has given the Negro people a bad check, a check which has come back marked "Insufficient Funds." But we refuse to believe the bank of justice is bankrupt. We refuse to believe that there are insufficient funds in the great vaults of opportunity of this nation. So we have come to cash this check, a check that will give us upon demand, the riches of freedom and the security of justice. We have also come to this hallowed spot to remind America of the fierce urgency of now.

This is no time to engage in the luxury of cooling off or to take the tranquilizing drug of gradualism. Now is the time to make real the promises of democracy. Now is the time to rise from the dark, the desolate valley of segregation to the sunlit path of racial justice. Now is the time to lift our nation from the quicksands of racial injustice to the solid rock of brotherhood. Now is the time to make justice a reality for all of God's children.

It would be fatal for the nation to overlook the urgency of the moment. This sweltering summer of the Negro's legitimate discontent will not pass until there is an invigorating autumn of freedom and equality. Nineteen sixty-three is not an end but a beginning. Those who hoped that the Negro needed to blow off steam and will now be content will have a rude awakening if the nation returns to business as usual. There will be neither rest nor tranquility in America until the Negro is guaranteed his citizenship rights. The whirlwinds of revolt will continue to shake the foundations of our nation until the bright day of justice emerges.

But there is something I must say to my people who stand on the warm threshold which leads them to the palace of justice. In the process of gaining our rightful place we must not be guilty of wrongful deeds. Let us not seek to satisfy our thirst for freedom by drinking from the cup of bitterness and hatred. We must forever conduct our struggle on the high plane of dignity and discipline. We must not allow our creative protest to degenerate into physical violence. Again and again we must rise to the majestic heights of meeting physical force with soul force.

The marvelous new militancy which has engulfed the Negro community must not lead us to a distrust of all white people, for many of our white brothers, as evidenced by their presence here today, have come to realize that their destiny is tied up with our destiny. They have come to realize that their freedom is inextricably bound to our freedom. We cannot walk alone.

10      And as we walk we must make the pledge that we shall always march ahead. We cannot turn back. There are those who are asking the devotees of civil rights: "When will you be satisfied?" We can never be satisfied as long as our bodies, heavy with the fatigue of travel, cannot gain lodging in the motels of the highways and the hotels of the cities. We cannot be satisfied as long as the Negro's basic mobility is from a smaller ghetto to a larger one. We can never be satisfied as long as our children are stripped of their selfhood and robbed of their dignity by signs stating: "For Whites Only." We cannot be satisfied as long as the Negro in Mississippi cannot vote and the Negro in New York believes he has nothing for which to vote. No, no, we are not satisfied and we will not be satisfied until justice rolls down like the waters and righteousness like a mighty stream.

     I am not unmindful that some of you have come here out of great trials and tribulations, some of you have come fresh from narrow jail cells, some of you have come from areas where your quest for freedom left you battered by the storms of persecution and staggered by the winds of police brutality. You have been the veterans of creative suffering. Continue to work with the faith that unearned suffering is redemptive.

     Go back to Mississippi, go back to Alabama, go back to South Carolina, go back to Georgia, go back to Louisiana, go back to the slums and ghettos of our northern cities, knowing that somehow this situation can and will be changed. Let us not wallow in the valley of despair.

     I say to you today, my friends, even though we face the difficulties of today and tomorrow, I still have a dream. It is a dream deeply rooted in the American dream. I have a dream that one day this nation will rise up and live out the true meaning of its creed: "We hold these truths to be self-evident that all men are created equal."

     I have a dream that one day on the red hills of Georgia the sons of former slaves and the sons of former slave owners will be able to sit down together at the table of brotherhood.

15      I have a dream that one day even the State of Mississippi, a state sweltering with the heat of injustice, sweltering with the heat of oppression, will be transformed into an oasis of freedom and justice. I have a dream that my four little children will one day live in a nation where they will not be judged by the color of their skin but by the content of their character. I have a dream today.

     I have a dream that one day down in Alabama with its vicious racists, with its Governor having his lips dripping with the words of interposition and nullification—one day right there in Alabama, little black boys and black girls will be able to join hands with little white boys and white girls as sisters and brothers.

I have a dream today.

I have a dream that one day every valley shall be exalted, every hill and mountain shall be made low, the rough places will be made plain and the crooked places will be made straight, and the glory of the Lord shall be revealed, and all flesh shall see it together.

This is our hope. This is the faith that I go back to the South with. With this faith we will be able to hew out of the mountain of despair a stone of hope. With this faith we will be able to transform the jangling discords of our nation into a beautiful symphony of brotherhood. With this faith we will be able to work together, to pray together, to struggle together, to go to jail together, to stand up for freedom together, knowing that we will be free one day.

20    This will be the day when all of God's children will be able to sing with new meaning:

> *My country 'tis of thee,*
> *Sweet land of liberty,*
> *Of thee I sing:*
> *Land where my fathers died,*
> *Land of the pilgrims' pride.*
> *From every mountain-side*
> *Let Freedom ring.*

And if America is to be a great nation, this must become true. So, let freedom ring from the prodigious hill tops of New Hampshire. Let freedom ring from the mighty mountains of New York. Let freedom ring from the heightening Alleghenies of Pennsylvania. Let freedom ring from the snowcapped Rockies of Colorado. Let freedom ring from the curvaceous slopes of California. But not only that, let freedom ring from Stone Mountain of Georgia.

Let freedom ring from Lookout Mountain of Tennessee.

Let freedom ring from every hill and molehill of Mississippi. From every mountainside, let freedom ring. And when we allow freedom to ring, when we let it ring from every village, from every hamlet, from every state and every city, we will be able to speed up that day when all of God's children, black men and white men, Jews and Gentiles, Protestants and Catholics, will be able to join hands and sing in the words of the old Negro spiritual: "Free at last! free at last! thank God almighty, we are free at last!"

## Questions for Discussion

What figures of speech and thought does King rely on most in the speech?

How do those figures strengthen his effectiveness?

Why does King start with historical references? How does the conscious use of "history" work to his advantage?

What kinds of different audiences is King addressing? How does he accommodate them all?

*Jesse Jackson (born 1941) is perhaps America's most visible leader of the African-American community: minister, activist, statesman, humanitarian, world ambassador, and presidential candidate. After graduating from college, Jackson attended the Chicago Theological Seminary and was ordained as a Baptist minister in 1968. In 1965, Jackson joined the voter registration campaign led by Martin Luther King, Jr., and the Southern Christian Leadership Conference in Alabama, and he was standing near King when King was assassinated in 1968. In 1971 he started his own organization, People United to Save Humanity (PUSH), an effort to improve the material conditions facing African-American citizens and to inspire young people to improve their lives through their own efforts. He has remained active on behalf of various social causes—prevention of crime and drug abuse, health care and prevention of teen pregnancy, voting rights. He has traveled to Iraq, Cuba, Syria, South Africa, Yugoslavia, and elsewhere on missions to preserve peace and free political prisoners. Jackson ran as a Democrat for president in 1984 and 1988, with support from a Rainbow Coalition of his own inspiration, garnering almost 7 million votes and finishing a strong second in the primaries. The following speech was delivered at the Democratic National Convention in San Francisco in July of 1984.*

# Jesse Jackson

# Speech at the Democratic National Convention, 1984

Tonight we come together bound by our faith in a mighty God, with genuine respect and love for our country, and inheriting the legacy of a great party, the Democratic Party, which is the best hope for redirecting our nation on a more humane, just and peaceful course.

This is not a perfect party. We are not a perfect people. Yet, we are called to a perfect mission: our mission to feed the hungry; to clothe the naked; to house the homeless; to teach the illiterate; to provide jobs for the jobless; and to choose the human race over the nuclear race. We are gathered here this week to nominate a candidate and adopt a platform which will expand, unify, direct and inspire our Party and the Nation to fulfill this mission. . . .

Our flag is red, white and blue, but our Nation is a rainbow—Red, Yellow, Brown, Black and White—we're all precious in God's sight.

America is not like a blanket—one piece of unbroken cloth, the same color, the same texture, the same size. America is more like a quilt—many patches, many pieces, many colors, many sizes, all woven and held together by a common thread. The White, the Hispanic, the Black, the Arab, the Jew, the woman, the Native American, the small farmer, the businessperson, the environmentalist, the peace activist, the young, the old, the lesbian, the gay and the disabled make up the American quilt.

5      Even in our fractured state, all of us count and fit somewhere. We have proven that we can survive without each other. But we have not proven that we can win and make progress without each other. We must come together.

From Fannie Lou Hamer in Atlantic City in 1964 to the Rainbow Coalition in San Francisco today; from the Atlantic to the Pacific, we have experienced pain but progress as we ended America's apartheid laws, we got public accommodations, we secured voting rights, we obtained open housing, as young people got the right to vote. We lost Malcolm, Martin, Medgar, Bobby and John and Viola. The team that got us here must be expanded, not abandoned.[1]

Twenty years ago, tears welled up in our eyes as the bodies of Schwerner, Goodman, and Cheney were dredged from the depths of a river in Mississippi. Twenty years later, our communities, Black and Jewish, are in anguish, anger and in pain. Feelings have been hurt on both sides.

There is a crisis in communications. Confusion is in the air, but we cannot afford to lose our way. We may agree to agree or agree to disagree on issues; we must bring back civility to the tensions.

We are co-partners in a long and rich religious history—the Judeo-Christian traditions. Many Blacks and Jews have a shared passion for social justice at home and peace abroad. We must seek a revival of the spirit inspired by a new vision and new possibilities. We must return to higher ground.

---

[1] Fannie Lou Hamer was an important civil right activist who played a prominent role in the Democratic Convention in 1964. The others referred to in the paragraph are Malcolm X (assassinated in 1965), Martin Luther King, Jr. (assassinated in 1968), Medgar Evers (a civil rights activist assassinated in 1963), John and Robert Kennedy (both assassinated), and Viola Liuzzo (a civil right activist murdered in 1965). The next paragraph refers to the murders in 1964 of activists Michael Schwerner, Andrew Goodman, and James Cheney.

10      We are bound by Moses and Jesus, but also connected with Islam and Mohammed. These three great religions—Judaism, Christianity, and Islam—were all born in the revered and Holy City of Jerusalem. We are bound by Dr. Martin Luther King, Jr., and Rabbi Abraham Heschel, crying out from their graves for us to reach common ground. We are bound by shared blood and shared sacrifices. We are much too intelligent; much too bound by our Judeo-Christian heritage; much too victimized by racism, sexism, militarism, and anti-Semitism; much too threatened as historical scapegoats to go on divided one from another. We must turn from finger-pointing to clasped hands. We must share our burdens and our joys with each other once again. We must turn to each other and not on each other, and choose higher ground.

Twenty years later, we cannot be satisfied by just restoring the old coalition. Old wine skins must make room for new wine. We must heal and expand. The Rainbow Coalition is making room for Arab Americans. They, too, know the pain and hurt of racial and religious rejection. They must not continue to be made pariahs. The Rainbow Coalition is making room for Hispanic Americans who this very night are living under the threat of the Simpson-Mazzoli bill. And [for] farm workers from Ohio who are fighting the Campbell Soup Company with a boycott to achieve legitimate workers' rights.

The Rainbow is making room for the Native American, the most exploited people of all, a people with the greatest moral claim amongst us. We support them as they seek the restoration of land and water rights, as they seek to preserve their ancestral homelands and the beauty of a land that was once all theirs. They can never receive a fair share for all they have given us. They must finally have a fair chance to develop their great resources and to preserve their people and their culture.

The Rainbow Coalition includes Asian Americans, now being killed in our streets, scapegoats for the failures of corporate, industrial and economic policies. The Rainbow is making room for young Americans. . . . The Rainbow includes disabled veterans. The color scheme fits in the Rainbow. The disabled have their handicap revealed and their genius concealed; while the able-bodied have their genius revealed and their disability concealed. But ultimately, we must judge people by their values and their contribution. Don't leave anybody out. I would rather have Roosevelt in a wheelchair than Reagan on a horse. The Rainbow is making room for small farmers. . . . The Rainbow includes lesbians and gays. No American citizen ought to be denied equal protection under the law.

15     We must be unusually committed and caring as we expand our family to include new members. All of us must be tolerant and understanding as the fears and anxieties of the rejected . . . express themselves in many different ways. Too often, what we call hate, as if it were some deeply rooted philosophy or strategy, is simply ignorance, anxiety, paranoia, fear and insecurity. . . .

In 1984, my heart is made to feel glad, because I know there is a way out—justice. The requirement for rebuilding America is justice. The linchpin of progressive politics in our Nation will not come from the North. . . . [It] in fact will come from the South.

That is why I argue over and over again. We look from Virginia around to Texas. There is only one Black Congressperson out of 115. Nineteen years later, we are locked out of the Congress, the Senate, and the Governor's Mansion.

What does this large black vote mean? Why do I fight to win second primaries and fight gerrymandering and annexation and at-large elections? Why do we fight over that? Because I tell you, you cannot hold someone in the ditch unless you linger there with them. . . .

If you want a change in this Nation, you enforce that Voting Rights Act. We will get 12 to 20 Black, Hispanic, female and progressive congresspersons from the South. We can save the cotton, but we have got to fight the boll weevils. We have got to make a judgment. . . .

20     It is not enough to hope ERA[2] will pass. How can we pass ERA? If Blacks vote in great numbers, progressive Whites win. It is the only way progressive Whites win. If Blacks vote in great numbers, Hispanics win. When Blacks, Hispanics, and progressive Whites vote, women win. When women win, children win. When women and children win, workers win. We must all come together. We must come up together. . . .

I have a message for our youth. I challenge them to put hope in their brains and not dope in their veins. I told them that like Jesus, I, too, was born in the slum, and just because you are born in the slum does not mean the slum is born in you, and you can rise above it if your mind is made up. I told them in every slum there are two sides. When I see a broken window, that is the slummy side. Train some youth to become a glazier; that is the sunny side. When I see a missing brick, that is the slummy side. Let that child in the union and become a brick mason and build; that is the sunny side. When I see a missing door, that is the slummy side. Train some youth to become a carpen-

---

[2] The Equal Rights Amendment, proposed in the 1970s, was under consideration by state legislators in 1984.

ter; that is the sunny side. And when I see the vulgar words and hiero-
glyphics of destitution on the walls, that's the slummy side. Train some
youth to become a painter, an artist; that is the sunny side.

We leave this place looking for the sunny side because there is a
brighter side somewhere. I am more convinced than ever that we can
win. We will vault up the rough side of the mountain. We can win. I
just want young America to do me one favor: Exercise the right to
dream. You must face reality—that which is; but then dream of the reality that ought to be—that must be. Live beyond the pain of reality
with the dream of a bright tomorrow. Use hope and imagination as
weapons of survival and progress. Use love to motivate you and obli-
gate you to serve the human family.

Young America, dream. Choose the human race over the nuclear
race. Bury the weapons and don't burn the people. Dream—dream of
a new value system.

Teachers who teach for life and not just for a living, teach because
they can't help it. Dream of lawyers more concerned about justice than
a judgeship. Dream of doctors more concerned about public health
than personal wealth. Dream of preachers and priests who will proph-
esy and not just profiteer. Preach and dream! Our time has come. Our
time has come.

25    Suffering breeds character, character breeds faith, and faith will
not disappoint. Our time has come. Our faith, hopes and dreams will
prevail. Our time has come. Weeping has endured for night, but now
joy cometh in the morning.

Our time has come. No grave can hold our body down. Our time
has come. No lie can live forever. Our time has come. We must leave
the racial battleground and find the economic common ground and
moral higher ground. America, our time has come.

We come from disgrace to Amazing Grace. Our time has come.
Give me your tired, give me your poor, your huddled masses who
yearn to breathe free, and come November there will be a change because our time has come.

Thank you and God bless you.

## Questions for Discussion

What is Jackson's central point? What themes, metaphors, and forms of
evidence does he use to support that point?

How might hearing this speech be a different experience than simply reading it?

*The victories in the civil rights movement during the 1950s and 1960s, culminating in the Voting Rights Act and the Civil Rights Act of 1964, were achieved through the heroic efforts of a great many people, famous and not so famous. But also important to the success of the movement was the news media, especially photojournalism and the new medium of television.* Look *and* Life *magazines achieved wide circulation after World War II, and network news programs began appearing on television early in the 1960s, so visual arguments about the civil rights movement— including photos of atrocities committed by opponents, such as lynchings, church bombings, and other acts of intimidation that contrasted with the nonviolent methods of activists—circulated widely and influenced public opinion. Among the many famous images that dramatized the cause of civil rights were the four reproduced here on these pages; a fifth is reprinted on page 332.*

# Visual Arguments:
# The Civil Rights
# Movement

Segregated water fountains in North Carolina, 1960s.

Rosa Parks sits patiently and contemplatively on a bus seat in front of a white man in Montgomery, Alabama, 1955.

A teacher oversees her students' work in a segregated, one-room schoolhouse in Georgia.

Freedom Riders in May, 1961, rode Greyhound buses across the South in order to protest segregation. Beaten and harassed, they were also endangered when one of the buses, disabled by a flat tire, was firebombed near Anniston, Alabama.

# PART FIVE

# THE
# INDIVIDUAL
# AND THE
# COMMUNITY:
## CIVIL
# DISOBEDIENCE

The conflict between the individual and society has been persistent in the selections in this book: Environmental disputes poise the rights of individual developers and users against the rights of all to enjoy clean water, air, and unspoiled natural surroundings *in perpetuity*; discussions about public education place individual needs and desires against the public good, especially since public education serves the political imperatives of a democracy; arguments over censorship regularly pit private citizens and free speech advocates against guardians of social norms; arguments about civil rights for African Americans, women, and other groups consistently assert the rights of individuals as against traditional civic and cultural practices; and immigration customs force Americans to ask about the

Three students resisting Jim Crow at a Woolworth's lunch counter in Jackson, Mississippi, in 1963 are harassed by a crowd of whites.

rights of illegal aliens and student visitors, especially in the wake of September 11. The conflict between the individual and society is pervasive in American culture because Americans value both the dignity of the private individual and the importance of public institutions and practices sanctioned through the democratic process.

Faced with the dilemma of paying taxes to support a popular war, which he disagreed with, Henry David Thoreau proposed civil disobedience—a private act of personal conscience against "the tyranny of the majority." Later Mahatma Gandhi and Martin Luther King, Jr., refined civil disobedience into an effective tactic for achieving public justice and political equality, and ever since, civil disobedience has been a common tactic in campaigns to expand the civil rights of African Americans and women. Sit-ins, bus boycotts, freedom rides, marches: All can be forms of nonviolent resistance. Civil disobedience has also been employed at times by pro-life groups eager to see the practice of abortion restricted in the United States. What exactly is civil disobedience anyway? Is it a legitimate political tool or an invitation to anarchy that would destroy the principle of democratic rule? What should people do when "higher laws" put them in conflict with majority rule? What else can a democratic society do except be ruled by a majority? Can such a majority be a "tyranny," or is it the resistance to legitimate, democratic authority that is arrogant and tyrannical? Could civil disobedience even exist in a truly tyrannical society, one without a free press and trial by jury, one in which political minorities disappear in the middle of the night?

The selections in this section of *Argument in America* debate the legitimacy of civil disobedience and offer a critical context for understanding a central document of civil disobedience and the American civil rights movement: King's "Letter from Birmingham Jail." In addition to King's "Letter," Thoreau's "Civil Disobedience," and Gandhi's "Letter to Lord Irvin," you will find photographs of civil disobedience, some of them in support of Martin Luther King, Jr.'s Birmingham Campaign of 1963—as well as two criticisms of the tactics of civil disobedience: a philosophical and legal argument by Lewis Van Dusen that would eliminate civil disobedience in general and a more specific rebuttal of King's tactics of nonviolent resistance that was produced soon after "Letter from Birmingham Jail" by King's rival Malcolm X ("Message from the Grassroots"). The section concludes with Cesar Chavez's speech "Lessons from Martin Luther King," which applies the tactics of nonviolent resistance in support of the unionization of farm workers—and additional photographic arguments that support the same cause.

*Henry David Thoreau (1817–1862) is best known for his American
classic* Walden, *an autobiographical, satiric, spiritual, scientific, and
naturalistic "self-help book" based on his two years' stay at Walden
Pond, near Boston. A friend of Ralph Waldo Emerson and other trans-
cendentalists, Thoreau expressed his idealism in a number of concrete
ways, for example, in his opposition to slavery and the Mexican War. His
refusal to pay taxes to support the Mexican War inspired his essay "Civil
Disobedience" (1849). First delivered as a lecture in 1848, this seminal
essay (very slightly edited here for length) influenced the thinking of
Mahatma Gandhi and Martin Luther King, Jr., among others.*

# Henry David Thoreau
# Civil Disobedience

I heartily accept the motto,—"That government is best which governs
least"; and I should like to see it acted up to more rapidly and systematically. Carried out, it finally amounts to this, which also I believe,—
"That government is best which governs not at all": and when men are
prepared for it, that will be the kind of government which they will
have. Government is at best but an expedient; but most governments
are usually, and all governments are sometimes, inexpedient. The objections which have been brought against a standing army, and they
are many and weighty, and deserve to prevail, may also at last be
brought against a standing government. The standing army is only an
arm of the standing government. The government itself, which is only
the mode which the people have chosen to execute their will, is equally
liable to be abused and perverted before the people can act through it.
Witness the present Mexican war; the work of comparatively a few individuals using the standing government as their tool; for, in the out-
set, the people would not have consented to this measure.

This American government—what is it but a tradition, though a
recent one, endeavoring to transmit itself unimpaired to posterity, but
each instant losing some of its integrity? It has not the vitality and
force of a single living man; for a single man can bend it to his will. It
is a sort of wooden gun to the people themselves. But it is not the less
necessary for this; for the people must have some complicated machinery or other, and hear its din, to satisfy that idea of government which
they have. Governments show thus how successfully men can be imposed on, even impose on themselves, for their own advantage. It is ex-

cellent, we must all allow. Yet this government never of itself furthered any enterprise, but by the alacrity with which it got out of its way. *It does not keep the country free. It does not settle the West. It does not educate.* The character inherent in the American people has done all that has been accomplished; and it would have done somewhat more, if the government had not sometimes got in its way. For government is an expedient by which men would fain succeed in letting one another alone; and, as has been said, when it is most expedient, the governed are most let alone by it. Trade and commerce, if they were not made of India-rubber, would never manage to bounce over the obstacles which legislators are continually putting in their way; and, if one were to judge these men wholly by the effects of their actions and not partly by their intentions, they would deserve to be classed and punished with those mischievous persons who put obstructions on the railroads.

But, to speak practically and as a citizen, unlike those who call themselves no-government men, I ask for, not at once no government, but *at once* a better government. Let every man make known what kind of government would command his respect, and that will be one step toward obtaining it.

After all, the practical reason why, when the power is once in the hands of people, a majority are permitted, and for a long period continue, to rule is not because they are most likely to be in the right, nor because this seems fairest to the minority, but because they are physically the strongest. But a government in which the majority rule in all cases cannot be based on justice, even as far as men understand it. Can there not be a government in which majorities do not virtually decide right and wrong, but conscience?—in which majorities decide only those questions to which the rule of expediency is applicable? Must the citizen ever for a moment, or in the least degree, resign his conscience to the legislator? Why has every man a conscience, then? I think that we should be men first, and subjects afterward. It is not desirable to cultivate a respect for the law, so much as for the right. The only obligation which I have a right to assume is to do at any time what I think right. It is truly enough said, that a corporation has no conscience; but a corporation of conscientious men is a corporation *with* a conscience. Law never made men a whit more just; and, by means of their respect for it, even the well-disposed are daily made the agents of injustice. A common and natural result of an undue respect for law is, that you may see a file of soldiers, colonel, captain, corporal, privates, powder-monkeys, and all, marching in admirable order over hill and dale to the wars, against their will, ay, against their common sense and consciences, which makes it very steep marching indeed, and produces a palpitation of the heart. They have no doubt that it is a damnable business in which they are concerned; they are all peaceably inclined. Now, what are they? Men at all? or small movable forts and magazines, at the service of some unscrupulous man in power? Visit the Navy-Yard, and behold a marine, such a man as an American government can make, or such as it can make a man with its black arts,—a mere shadow and reminiscence of humanity, a man laid out alive and standing, and already, as one may say, buried under arms with funeral accompaniments, though it may be,—

> Not a drum was heard, not a funeral note,
> As his corse to the rampart we hurried;
> Not a soldier discharged his farewell shot
> O'er the grave where our hero we buried.[1]

5      The mass of men serve the state thus, not as men mainly, but as machines, with their bodies. They are the standing army, and the militia, jailers, constables, posse comitatus, etc. In most cases there is no free exercise whatever of the judgment or of the moral sense; but they put themselves on a level with wood and earth and stones; and wooden men can perhaps be manufactured that will serve the purpose as well. Such command no more respect than men of straw or a lump of dirt. They have the same sort of worth only as horses and dogs. Yet such as these even are commonly esteemed good citizens. Others—as most legislators, politicians, lawyers, ministers, and office-holders—serve the state chiefly with their heads; and, as they rarely make any moral distinctions, they are as likely to serve the Devil, without *intending* it, as God. A very few, as heroes, patriots, martyrs, reformers in the great sense, and *men*, serve the state with their consciences also, and so necessarily resist it for the most part; and they are commonly treated as enemies by it. A wise man will only be useful as a man, and will not submit to be "clay," and "stop a hole to keep the wind away," but leave that office to his dust at least:—

> I am too high-born to be propertied,
> To be a secondary at control,
> Or useful serving-man and instrument
> To any sovereign state throughout the world.[2]

---

[1] From "Burial of St. John Moore at Corunna" by Charles Wolfe (1817).
[2] The line before the quotation is from *Hamlet* V. i. 236–37; the quotation is from Shakespeare's *King John* V. ii 79–82.

He who gives himself entirely to his fellow-men appears to them useless and selfish; but he who gives himself partially to them is pronounced a benefactor and philanthropist.

How does it become a man to behave toward this American government today? I answer, that he cannot without disgrace be associated with it. I cannot for an instant recognize that political organization as *my* government which is the *slave's* government also.

All men recognize the right of revolution; that is, the right to refuse allegiance to, and to resist, the government, when its tyranny or its inefficiency are great and unendurable. But almost all say that such is not the case now. But such was the case, they think, in the Revolution of '75. If one were to tell me that this was a bad government because it taxed certain foreign commodities brought to its ports, it is most probable that I should not make and do about it, for I can do without them. All machines have their friction; and possibly this does enough good to counterbalance the evil. At any rate, it is a great evil to make a stir about it. But when the friction comes to have its machine, and oppression and robbery are organized, I say, let us not have such a machine any longer. In other words, when a sixth of the population of a nation which has undertaken to be the refuge of liberty are slaves, and a whole country is unjustly overrun and conquered by a foreign army, and subjected to military law, I think that it is not too soon for honest men to rebel and revolutionize. What makes this duty the more urgent is the fact that the country so overrun is not our own, but ours is the invading army.

Paley,[3] a common authority with many on moral questions, in his chapter on the "Duty of Submission to Civil Government," resolves all civil obligation into expediency; and he proceeds to say, "that so long as the interest of the whole society requires it, that is, so long as the established government cannot be resisted or changed without public inconveniency, it is the will of God that the established government be obeyed, and no longer. . . . This principle being admitted, the justice of every particular case of resistance is reduced to a computation of the quantity of the danger and grievance on the one side, and of the probability and expense of redressing it on the other." Of this, he says, every man shall judge for himself. But Paley appears never to have contemplated those cases to which the rule of expediency does not apply, in which a people, as

---

[3] William Paley (1743–1805), English theologian.

well as an individual, must do justice, cost what it may. If I have unjustly wrested a plank from a drowning man, I must restore it to
him though I drown myself. This, according to Paley, would be in-
convenient. But he that would save his life, in such a case, shall
lose it. This people must cease to hold slaves, and to make war on
Mexico, though it cost them their existence as a people.

10      In their practice, nations agree with Paley; but does any one think
that Massachusetts does exactly what is right at the present crisis?

> A drab of state, a cloth-o'-silver slut,
> To have her train borne up, and her soul trail in the dirt.

Practically speaking the opponents to a reform in Massachusetts are
not a hundred thousand politicians at the South, but a hundred thousand merchants and farmers here, who are more interested in commerce and agriculture than they are in humanity, and are not prepared
to do justice to the slave and to Mexico, *cost what it may*. I quarrel not
with far-off foes, but with those who, near at home, cooperate with,
and do the bidding of, those far away, and without whom the latter
would be harmless. We are accustomed to say, that the mass of men
are unprepared; but improvement is slow, because the few are not ma-
terially wiser or better than the many. It is not so important that many
should be as good as you, as that there be some absolute goodness
somewhere; for that will leaven the whole lump. There are thousands
who are *in opinion* opposed to slavery and to the war, who yet in effect
do nothing to put an end to them; who, esteeming themselves children
of Washington and Franklin, sit down with their hands in their pock-
ets, and say that they know not what to do, and do nothing; who even
postpone the question of freedom to the question of free-trade, and
quietly read the prices-current along with the latest advices from
Mexico, after dinner, and, it may be, fall asleep over them both. What
is the price-current of an honest man and patriot to-day? They hesitate, and they regret, and sometimes they petition; but they do nothing
in earnest and with effect. They will wait, well disposed, for others to
remedy the evil, that they may no longer have it to regret. At most,
they give only a cheap vote, and a feeble countenance and Godspeed,
to the right, as it goes by them. There are nine hundred and ninety-
nine patrons of virtue to one virtuous man. But it is easier to deal with
the real possessor of a thing than with the temporary guardian of it.
      All voting is a sort of gaming, like checkers or backgammon,
with a slight moral tinge to it, a playing with right and wrong, with

moral questions; and betting naturally accompanies it. The character of the voters is not staked. I cast my vote, perchance, as I think right; but I am not vitally concerned that that right should prevail. I am willing to leave it to the majority. Its obligation, therefore, never exceeds that of expediency. Even voting *for the right* is *doing* nothing for it. It is only expressing to men feebly your desire that it should prevail. A wise man will not leave the right to the mercy of chance, nor wish it to prevail through the power of the majority. There is but little virtue in the action of masses of men. When the majority shall at length vote for the abolition of slavery, it will be because they are indifferent to slavery, or because there is but little slavery left to be abolished by their vote. *They* will then be the only slaves. Only *his* vote can hasten the abolition of slavery who asserts his own freedom by his vote.

I hear of a convention to be held at Baltimore, or elsewhere, for the selection of a candidate for the Presidency, made up chiefly of editors, and men who are politicians by profession; but I think, what is it to any independent, intelligent, and respectable man what decision they may come to? Shall we not have the advantage of his wisdom and honesty, nevertheless? Can we not count upon some independent votes? Are there not many individuals in the country who do not attend conventions? But no: I find that the respectable man, so called, has immediately drifted from his position, and despairs of his country, when his country has more reason to despair of him. He forthwith adopts one of the candidates thus selected as the only *available* one, thus proving that he is himself *available* for any purposes of the demagogue. His vote is of no more worth than that of any unprincipled foreigner or hireling native, who may have been bought. O for a man who is a *man*, and, as my neighbor says, has a bone in his back which you cannot pass your hand through! Our statistics are at fault: the population has been returned too large. How many *men* are there to a square thousand miles in this country? Hardly one. Does not America offer any inducement for men to settle here? The American has dwindled into an Odd Fellow,—one who may be known by the development of his organ of gregariousness, and a manifest lack of intellect and cheerful self-reliance; whose first and chief concern, on coming into the world, is to see that the Almshouses are in good repair; and, before yet he has lawfully donned the virile garb, to collect a fund for the support of the widows and orphans that may be; who, in short, ventures to live only by the aid of the Mutual Insurance company, which has promised to bury him decently.

It is not a man's duty, as a matter of course, to devote himself to the eradication of any, even the most enormous wrong; he may still properly have other concerns to engage him; but it is his duty, at least, to wash his hands of it, and, if he gives it no thought longer, not to give it practically his support. If I devote myself to other pursuits and contemplations, I must first see, at least, that I do not pursue them sitting upon another man's shoulders. I must get off him first, that he may pursue his contemplations too. See what gross inconsistency is tolerated. I have heard some of my townsmen say, "I should like to have them order me out to help put down an insurrection of the slaves, or to march to Mexico;—see if I would go"; and yet these very men have each, directly by their allegiance, and so indirectly, at least, by their money, furnished a substitute. The soldier is applauded who refuses to serve in an unjust war by those who do not refuse to sustain the unjust government which makes the war; is applauded by those whose own act and authority he disregards and sets at naught; as if the state were penitent to that degree that it hired one to scourge it while it sinned, but not to that degree that it left off sinning for a moment. Thus, under the name of Order and Civil Government, we are all made at last to pay homage to and support our own meanness. After the first blush of sin comes its indifference; and from immoral it becomes, as it were, *un*moral, and not quite unnecessary to that life which we have made.

The broadest and most prevalent error requires the most disinterested virtue to sustain it. The slight reproach to which the virtue of patriotism is commonly liable, the noble are most likely to incur. Those who, while they disapprove of the character and measures of a government, yield to it their allegiance and support are undoubtedly its most conscientious supporters, and so frequently the most serious obstacles to reform. Some are petitioning the state to dissolve the Union, to disregard the requisitions of the President. Why do they not dissolve it themselves,—the union between themselves and the state,—and refuse to pay their quota into its treasury? Do not they stand in the same relation to the state that the state does to the Union? And have not the same reasons prevented the state from resisting the Union which have prevented them from resisting the state?

15     How can a man be satisfied to entertain an opinion merely, and enjoy *it?* Is there any enjoyment in it, if his opinion is that he is aggrieved? If you are cheated out of a single dollar by your neighbor, you do not rest satisfied with knowing that you are cheated, or with saying that you are cheated, or even with petitioning him to pay you your due; but you take effectual steps at once to obtain the full amount, and see that you are never cheated again. Action from principle, the per-

ception and the performance of right, changes things and relations; it is essentially revolutionary, and does not consist wholly with anything which was. It not only divides states and churches, it divides families; ay, it divides the *individual*, separating the diabolical in him from the divine.

Unjust laws exist: shall we be content to obey them, or shall we endeavor to amend them, and obey them until we have succeeded, or shall we transgress them at once? Men generally, under such a government as this, think that they ought to wait until they have persuaded the majority to alter them. They think that, if they should resist, the remedy would be worse than the evil. But it is the fault of the government itself that the remedy *is* worse than the evil. *It* makes it worse. Why is it not more apt to anticipate and provide for reform? Why does it not cherish its wise minority? Why does it cry and resist before it is hurt? Why does it not encourage its citizens to be on the alert to point out its faults, and *do* better than it would have them? Why does it always crucify Christ, and excommunicate Copernicus and Luther, and pronounce Washington and Franklin rebels?

One would think, that a deliberate and practical denial of its authority was the only offense never contemplated by government; else, why has it not assigned its definite, its suitable and proportionate penalty? If a man who has no property refuses but once to earn nine shillings for the state, he is put in prison for a period unlimited by any law that I know, and determined only by the discretion of those who place him there; but if he should steal ninety times nine shillings from the state, he is soon permitted to go at large again.

If the injustice is part of the necessary friction of the machine of government, let it go, let it go; perchance it will wear smooth,—certainly the machine will wear out. If the injustice has a spring, or a pulley, or a rope, or a crank, exclusively for itself, then perhaps you may consider whether the remedy will not be worse than the evil; but if it is of such a nature that it requires you to be the agent of injustice to another, then, I say, break the law. Let your life be a counter friction to stop the machine. What I have to do is to see, at any rate, that I do not lend myself to the wrong which I condemn.

As for adopting the ways which the state has provided for remedying the evil, I know not of such ways. They take too much time, and a man's life will be gone. I have other affairs to attend to. I came into this world, not chiefly to make this a good place to live in, but to live in it, be it good or bad. A man has not everything to do, but something; and because he cannot do *everything*, it is not necessary that he should do *something* wrong. It is not my business to be petitioning the

Governor or the Legislature any more than it is theirs to petition me; and if they should not hear my petition, what should I do then? But in this case the state has provided no way; its very Constitution is the evil. This may seem to be harsh and stubborn and unconciliatory; but it is to treat with the utmost kindness and consideration the only spirit that can appreciate or deserves it. So is all change for the better, like birth and death, which convulse the body.

20     I do not hesitate to say, that those who call themselves Abolitionists should at once effectually withdraw their support, both in person and property, from the government of Massachusetts, and not wait till they constitute a majority of one, before they suffer the right to prevail through them. I think that it is enough if they have God on their side, without waiting for that other one. Moreover, any man more right than his neighbors constitutes a majority of one already.

    I meet this American government, or its representative, the state government, directly, and face to face, once a year—no more—in the person of its tax-gatherer; this is the only mode in which a man situated as I am necessarily meets it; and it then says distinctly, Recognize me; and the simplest, the most effectual, and, in the present posture of affairs, the indispensablest mode of treating with it on this head, of expressing your little satisfaction with and love for it, is to deny it then. My civil neighbor, the tax-gatherer, is the very man I have to deal with,—for it is, after all, with men and not with parchment that I quarrel,—and he has voluntarily chosen to be an agent of the government. How shall he ever know well what he is and does as an officer of the government, or as a man, until he is obliged to consider whether he shall treat me, his neighbor, for whom he has respect, as a neighbor and well-disposed man, or as a maniac and disturber of the peace, and see if he can get over this obstruction to his neighborliness without a ruder and more impetuous thought or speech corresponding with his action. I know this well, that if one thousand, if one hundred, if ten men whom I could name,—if ten *honest* men only,—ay, if *one* HONEST man, in this State of Massachusetts, *ceasing to hold slaves*, were actually to withdraw from this copartnership, and be locked up in the county jail therefor, it would be the abolition of slavery in America. For it matters not how small the beginning may seem to be; what is once well done is done forever. But we love better to talk about it: that we say is our mission. Reform keeps many scores of newspapers in its service, but not one man. If my esteemed neighbor, the State's ambassador, who will devote his days to the settlement of the question of human rights in the Council Chamber, instead of being threatened with the prisons of Carolina, were to sit down the prisoner of Massachusetts, that State which is so anxious to foist the sin of slavery upon her sister,—though at present she can discover only an act of inhospitality to be the ground of a quarrel with her—the Legislature would not wholly waive the subject the following winter.

Under a government which imprisons any unjustly, the true place for a just man is also a prison. The proper place today, the only place which Massachusetts has provided for her freer and less desponding spirits, is in her prisons, to be put out and locked out of the State by her own act, as they have already put themselves out by their principles. It is there that the fugitive slave, and the Mexican prisoner on parole, and the Indian come to plead the wrongs of his race should find them; on that separate, but more free and honorable ground, where the State places those who are not *with* her, but *against* her,—the only house in a slave State in which a free man can abide with honor. If any think that their influence would be lost there, and their voices no longer afflict the ear of the State, that they would not be as an enemy within its walls, they do not know by how much truth is stronger than error, nor how much more eloquently and effectively he can combat injustice who has experienced a little in his own person. Cast your whole vote, not a strip of paper merely, but your whole influence. A minority is powerless while it conforms to the majority; it is not even a minority then; but it is irresistible when it clogs by its whole weight. If the alternative is to keep all just men in prison, or give up war and slavery, the State will not hesitate which to choose. If a thousand men were not to pay their tax-bills this year, that would not be a violent and bloody measure, as it would be to pay them, and enable the State to commit violence and shed innocent blood. This is, in fact, the definition of a peaceable revolution, if any such is possible. If the tax-gatherer, or any other public officer, asks me, as one has done, "But what shall I do?" my answer is, "If you really wish to do anything, resign your office." When the subject has refused allegiance, and the officer has resigned his office, then the revolution is accomplished. But even suppose blood should flow. Is there not a sort of blood shed when the conscience is wounded? Through this wound a man's real manhood and immortality flow out, and he bleeds to an everlasting death. I see this blood flowing now.

I have contemplated the imprisonment of the offender, rather than the seizure of his goods,—though both will serve the same purpose,—because they who assert the purest right, and consequently are most dangerous to a corrupt State, commonly have not spent much time in accumulating property. To such the State renders comparatively small service, and a slight tax is wont to appear exorbitant, particularly if they are obliged to earn it by special labor with their hands. If there were one who lived wholly without the use of money, the State itself would hesitate to demand it of him. But the rich man—not to make any invidious comparison—is always sold to the institution which makes him rich. Absolutely speaking, the more money, the less virtue; for money comes between a man and his objects, and obtains them for him; and it was certainly no great virtue to obtain it. It puts to rest many questions which he would otherwise be taxed to answer; while the only new question which it puts is the hard but superfluous one, how to spend it. Thus his moral ground is taken from under his feet. The opportunities of living are diminished in proportion as what are called the "means" are increased. The best thing a man can do for his culture when he is rich is to endeavor to carry out those schemes which he entertained when he was poor. Christ answered the Herodians according to their condition. "Show me the tribute-money," said he;—and one took a penny out of his pocket;—if you use money which has the image of Caesar on it, and which he has made current and valuable, that is, *if you are men of the State*, and gladly enjoy the advantages of Caesar's government, then pay him back some of his own when he demands it. "Render therefore to Caesar that which is Caesar's, and to God those things which are God's,"—leaving them no wiser than before as to which was which; for they did not wish to know.

When I converse with the freest of my neighbors, I perceive that, whatever they may say about the magnitude and seriousness of the question, and their regard for the public tranquillity, the long and the short of the matter is, that they cannot spare the protection of the existing government, and they dread the consequences to their property and families of disobedience to it. For my own part, I should not like to think that I ever rely on the protection of the State. But, if I deny the authority of the State when it presents its tax-bill, it will soon take and waste all my property, and so harass me and my children without end. This is hard. This makes it impossible for a man to live honestly, and at the same time comfortably, in outward respects. It will not be worth the while to accumulate property; that would be sure to go again. You must hire or squat somewhere, and raise but a small crop, and eat that soon. You must live within yourself, and depend upon yourself always tucked up and ready for a start, and not have many affairs. A man may grow rich in Turkey even, if he will be in all respects a good subject of the Turkish government. Confucius said: "If a state is governed by the principles of reason, poverty and misery are subjects of shame; if a state is not governed by the principles of reason, riches and honors are the subjects of shame." No: until I want the protection of Massachusetts to be extended to me in some distant Southern port, where my liberty is endangered, or until I am bent solely on building up an estate at home by peaceful enterprise, I can afford to refuse allegiance to Massachusetts, and her right to my property and life. It costs me less in every sense to incur the penalty of disobedience to the State than it would to obey. I should feel as if I were worth less in that case.

25    Some years ago, the State met me in behalf of the Church, and commanded me to pay a certain sum toward the support of a clergyman whose preaching my father attended, but never I myself. "Pay," it said, "or be locked up in the jail." I declined to pay. But, unfortunately, another man saw fit to pay it. I did not see why the schoolmaster should be taxed to support the priest, and not the priest the schoolmaster; for I was not the State's schoolmaster, but I supported myself by voluntary subscription. I did not see why the lyceum should not present its tax-bill, and have the State to back its demand, as well as the Church. However, at the request of the selectmen, I condescended to make some such statement as this in writing:—"Know all men by these presents, that I, Henry Thoreau, do not wish to be regarded as a member of any incorporated society which I have not joined." This I gave to the town clerk; and he has it. The State, having thus learned that I did not wish to be regarded as a member of that church, has never made a like demand on me since; though it said that it must adhere to its original presumption that time. If I had known how to name them, I should then have signed off in detail from all the societies which I never signed on to; but I did not know where to find a complete list.

I have paid no poll-tax[4] for six years. I was put into jail once on this account, for one night; and, as I stood considering the walls of solid stone, two or three feet thick, the door of wood and iron, a foot thick, and the iron grating which strained the light, I could not help being struck with the foolishness of that institution which treated me as if I were mere flesh and blood and bones, to be locked up. I wondered that it should have concluded at length that this was the best use

---

[4] Tax assessed against a person (not property); payment was frequently prerequisite for voting.

it could put me to, and had never thought to avail itself of my services in some way. I saw that, if there was a wall of stone between me and my townsmen, there was still a more difficult one to climb or break through before they could get to be as free as I was. I did not for a moment feel confined, and the walls seemed a great waste of stone and mortar. I felt as if I alone of all my townsmen had paid my tax. They plainly did not know how to treat me, but behaved like persons who are underbred. In every threat and in every compliment there was a blunder; for they thought that my chief desire was to stand the other side of that stone wall. I could not but smile to see how industriously they locked the door on my meditations, which followed them out again without let or hindrance, and *they* were really all that was dangerous. As they could not reach me, they had resolved to punish my body; just as boys, if they cannot come at some person against whom they have a spite, will abuse his dog. I saw that the State was half-witted, that it was timid as a lone woman with her silver spoons, and that it did not know its friends from its foes, and I lost all my remaining respect for it, and pitied it.

Thus the State never intentionally confronts a man's sense, intellectual or moral, but only his body, his senses. It is not armed with superior wit or honesty, but with superior physical strength. I was not born to be forced. I will breathe after my own fashion. Let us see who is the strongest. What force has a multitude? They only can force me who obey a higher law than I. They force me to become like themselves. I do not hear of *men* being *forced* to live this way or that by masses of men. What sort of life were that to live? When I meet a government which says to me, "Your money or your life," why should I be in haste to give it my money? It may be in a great strait, and not know what to do: I cannot help that. It must help itself; do as I do. It is not worth the while to snivel about it. I am not responsible for the successful working of the machinery of society. I am not the son of the engineer. I perceive that, when an acorn and a chestnut fall side by side, the one does not remain inert to make way for the other, but both obey their own laws, and spring and grow and flourish as best they can, till one, perchance, overshadows and destroys the other. If a plant cannot live according to its nature, it dies; and so a man.

The night in prison was novel and interesting enough. The prisoners in their shirt-sleeves were enjoying a chat and the evening air in the doorway, when I entered. But the jailer said, "Come, boys, it is time to lock up;" and so they dispersed, and I heard the sound of their steps returning into the hollow apartments. My room-mate was intro-

duced to me by the jailer as "a first-rate fellow and a clever man."
When the door was locked, he showed me where to hang my hat, and
how he managed matters there. The rooms were whitewashed once a
month; and this one, at least, was the whitest, most simply furnished,
and probably the neatest apartment in the town. He naturally wanted
to know where I came from, and what brought me there; and, when I
had told him, I asked him in my turn how he came there, presuming
him to be an honest man, of course; and, as the world goes, I believe
he was. "Why," said he, "they accuse me of burning a barn; but I
never did it." As near as I could discover, he had probably gone to bed
in a barn when drunk, and smoked his pipe there; and so a barn was
burnt. He had the reputation of being a clever man, had been there
some three months waiting for his trial to come on, and would have to
wait as much longer; but he was quite domesticated and contented,
since he got his board for nothing, and thought that he was well
treated.

He occupied one window, and I the other; and I saw that if one
stayed there long, his principal business would be to look out the window. I had soon read all the tracts that were left there, and examined
where former prisoners had broken out, and where a grate had been
sawed off, and heard the history of the various occupants of that room;
for I found that even here there was a history and a gossip which never
circulated beyond the walls of the jail. Probably this is the only house
in the town where verses are composed, which are afterward printed in
a circular form, but not published. I was shown quite a long list of
verses which were composed by some young men who had been detected in an attempt to escape, who avenged themselves by singing
them.

30    I pumped my fellow-prisoner as dry as I could, for fear I should
never see him again; but at length he showed me which was my bed,
and left me to blow out the lamp.

It was like traveling into a far country, such as I had never expected to behold, to lie there for one night. It seemed to me that I
never had heard the town-clock strike before, nor the evening sounds
of the village; for we slept with the windows open, which were inside
the grating. It was to see my native village in the light of the Middle
Ages, and our Concord was turned into a Rhine stream, and visions of
knights and castles passed before me. They were the voices of old
burghers that I heard in the streets. I was an involuntary spectator and
auditor of whatever was done and said in the kitchen of the adjacent
village-inn,—a wholly new and rare experience to me. It was a closer

view of my native town. I was fairly inside of it. I never had seen its institutions before. This is one of its peculiar institutions; for it is a shire town. I began to comprehend what its inhabitants were about.

In the morning, our breakfasts were put through the hole in the door, in small oblong-square tin pans, made to fit, and holding a pint of chocolate, with brown bread, and an iron spoon. When they called for the vessels again, I was green enough to return what bread I had left; but my comrade seized it, and said that I should lay that up for lunch or dinner. Soon after he was let out to work at having in a neighboring field, whither he went every day, and would not be back till noon; so he bade me good-day, saying that he doubted if he should see me again.

When I came out of prison—for some one interfered, and paid that tax,—I did not perceive that great changes had taken place on the common, such as he observed who went in a youth and emerged a tottering and gray-headed man; and yet a change had to my eyes come over the scene,—the town, and State, and country,—greater than any that mere time could effect. I saw yet more distinctly the State in which I lived. I saw to what extent the people among whom I lived could be trusted as good neighbors and friends; that their friendship was for summer weather only; that they did not greatly propose to do right; that they were a distinct race from me by their prejudices and superstitions, as the Chinamen and Malays are; that in their sacrifices to humanity they ran no risks, not even to their property; that after all they were not so noble but they treated the thief as he had treated them, and hoped, by a certain outward observance and a few prayers, and by walking in a particular straight though useless path from time to time, to save their souls. This may be to judge my neighbors harshly; for I believe that many of them are not aware that they have such an institution as the jail in their village.

It was formerly the custom in our village, when a poor debtor came out of jail, for his acquaintances to salute him, looking through their fingers, which were crossed to represent the grating of a jail window, "How do ye do?" My neighbors did not thus salute me, but first looked at me, and then at one another, as if I had returned from a long journey. I was put into jail as I was going to the shoemaker's to get a shoe which was mended. When I was let out the next morning, I proceeded to finish my errand, and, having put on my mended shoe, joined a huckleberry party, who were impatient to put themselves under my conduct; and in half an hour,—for the horse was soon tackled,—was in the midst of a huckleberry field, on one of our highest hills, two miles off, and then the State was nowhere to be seen.

This is the whole history of "My Prisons."

## Questions for Discussion

Does Thoreau himself seem reliable, trustworthy, admirable, and sympathetic in "Civil Disobedience?"

What role does humor play in Thoreau's argument?

What does Thoreau mean when he tells the reader "Let your life be a counter friction to stop the machine"?

*Mahatma Gandhi (Mahatma means "of great soul") was born in India in 1869, studied law in London, and in 1893 went to South Africa, where he opposed discriminatory legislation against Indians, was exposed to the writings of Henry David Thoreau, and carried on a famous correspondence with the Russian novelist Leo Tolstoy concerning civil disobedience. In 1914, he returned to India, and about 1920 began a lifetime of committed support for India's independence from England—notably through the practice and encouragement of nonviolent resistance (satyagraha). After a decade of sporadic civil disobedience and periodic imprisonments, Gandhi in 1930 prepared a Declaration of Independence for India and soon after led a remarkable (and famous) 200-mile march to the sea to collect salt in symbolic defiance of the English government's monopoly on that product; by the end of the year, more than 100,000 people were jailed in the campaign. India of course did finally achieve independence, in 1947. The following year, while trying to calm tensions between Hindus and Moslems, Gandhi was assassinated.*

*The following letter was sent by Gandhi to the British viceroy in India, Lord Irwin, in March 1930, just ten days before the salt march was to begin. It was sent from Satyagraha Ashram, a community established to practice Gandhi's method of nonviolent resistance. While not strictly an "American" argument, it deserves inclusion here for building on the insights of Henry David Thoreau and for inspiring the work of Martin Luther King, Jr.*

# *Mahatma Gandhi*
# Letter to Lord Irwin

Satyagraha Ashram, Sabarmati,
March 2, 1930

Dear Friend,

Before embarking on civil disobedience and taking the risk I have dreaded to take all these years, I would fain approach you and find a way out.

My personal faith is absolutely clear. I cannot intentionally hurt anything that lives, much less fellow human beings, even though they may do the greatest wrong to me and mine. Whilst, therefore, I hold the British rule to be a curse, I do not intend harm to a single Englishman or to any legitimate interest he may have in India.

I must not be misunderstood. Though I hold the British rule in India to be a curse, I do not, therefore, consider Englishmen in general to be worse than any other people on earth. I have the privilege of claiming many Englishmen as dearest friends. Indeed much that I have learnt of the evil of British rule is due to the writings of frank and courageous Englishmen who have not hesitated to tell the unpalatable truth about that rule.

And why do I regard the British rule as a curse?

5    It has impoverished the dumb millions by a system of progressive exploitation and by a ruinously expensive military and civil administration which the country can never afford.

It has reduced us politically to serfdom. It has sapped the foundations of our culture. And, by the policy of cruel disarmament, it has degraded us spiritually. Lacking the inward strength, we have been reduced, by all but universal disarmament, to a state bordering on cowardly helplessness.

In common with many of my countrymen, I had hugged the fond hope that the proposed Round Table Conference might furnish a solution. But, when you said plainly that you could not give any assurance that you or the British Cabinet would pledge yourselves to support a scheme of full Dominion Status, the Round Table Conference could not possibly furnish the solution for which vocal India is consciously, and the dumb millions are unconsciously, thirsting.

It seems as clear as daylight that responsible British statesmen do not contemplate any alteration in British policy that might adversely affect Britain's commerce with India or require an impartial and close scrutiny of Britain's transactions with India. If nothing is done to end the process of exploitation India must be bled with an ever increasing speed. The Finance Member regards as a settled fact the 1/6 ratio which by a stroke of the pen drains India of a few crores.[1] And when a serious attempt is being made through a civil form of direct action, to unsettle this fact, among many others, even you cannot help appealing to the wealthy landed classes to help you to crush that attempt in the name of an order that grinds India to atoms.

Unless those who work in the name of the nation understand and keep before all concerned the motive that lies behind the craving for independence, there is every danger of independence coming to us so changed as to be of no value to those toiling voiceless millions for whom it is sought and for whom it is worth taking. It is for that reason

[1] In Indian currency, a crore is equivalent to ten million rupees.

that I have been recently telling the public what independence should really mean.

10     Let me put before you some of the salient points.

The terrific pressure of land revenue, which furnishes a large part of the total, must undergo considerable modification in an independent India. Even the much vaunted permanent settlement benefits the few rich zamindars,[2] not the ryots.[3] The ryot has remained as helpless as ever. He is a mere tenant at will. Not only, then, has the land revenue to be considerably reduced, but the whole revenue system has to be so revised as to make the ryot's good its primary concern. But the British system seems to be designed to crush the very life out of him. Even the salt he must use to live is so taxed as to make the burden fall heaviest on him, if only because of the heartless impartiality of its incidence. The tax shows itself still more burdensome on the poor man when it is remembered that salt is the one thing he must eat more than the rich man both individually and collectively.

The iniquities sampled above are maintained in order to carry on a foreign administration, demonstrably the most expensive in the world. Take your own salary. It is over Rs. 21,000 per month, besides many other indirect additions. The British Prime Minister gets £5,000 per year, i.e., over Rs. 5,400 per month at the present rate of exchange. You are getting over Rs. 700 per day against India's average income of less than annas 2 per day. The Prime Minister gets Rs. 180 per day against Great Britain's average income of nearly Rs. 2 per day. Thus you are getting much over five thousand times India's average income. The British Prime Minister is getting only ninety times Britain's average income. On bended knees I ask you to ponder over this phenomenon. I have taken a personal illustration to drive home a painful truth. I have too great a regard for you as a man to wish to hurt your feelings. I know that you do not need the salary you get. Probably the whole of your salary goes for charity. But a system that provides for such an arrangement deserves to be summarily scrapped.

If India is to live as a nation, if the slow death by starvation of her people is to stop, some remedy must be found for immediate relief. The proposed Conference is certainly not the remedy. It is not a matter of carrying conviction by argument. The matter resolves itself into one of matching forces. Conviction or no conviction, Great Britain would defend her Indian commerce and interests by all the forces at her com-

---

[2] A zamindar is a landowner.
[3] A ryot is a tenant farmer.

mand. India must consequently evolve force enough to free herself from that embrace of death.

It is common cause that, however disorganized and, for the time being, insignificant it may be, the party of violence is gaining ground and making itself felt. Its end is the same as mine. But I am convinced that it cannot bring the desired relief to the dumb millions. And the conviction is growing deeper and deeper in me that nothing but unadulterated non-violence can check the organized violence of the British Government. Many think that non-violence is not an active force. My experience, limited though it undoubtedly is, shows that non-violence can be an intensely active force. It is my purpose to set in motion that force as well against the organized violent force of the British rule as [against] the unorganized violent force of the growing party of violence. To sit still would be to give rein to both the forces above mentioned. Having an unquestioning and immovable faith in the efficacy of non-violence as I know it, it would be sinful on my part to wait any longer.

15    This non-violence will be expressed through civil disobedience, for the moment confined to the inmates of the Satyagraha Ashram, but ultimately designed to cover all those who choose to join the movement with its obvious limitations.

I know that in embarking on non-violence I shall be running what might fairly be termed a mad risk. But the victories of truth have never been won without risks, often of the gravest character. Conversion of a nation that has consciously or unconsciously preyed upon another, far more numerous, far more ancient and no less cultured than itself, is worth any amount of risk.

I have deliberately used the word "conversion." For my ambition is no less than to convert the British people through non-violence, and thus make them see the wrong they have done to India. I do not seek to harm your people. I want to serve them even as I want to serve my own. I believe that I have always served them. I served them up to 1919 blindly. But when my eyes were opened and I conceived non-cooperation, the object still was to serve them. I employed the same weapon that I have in all humility successfully used against the dearest members of my family. If I have equal love for your people with mine it will not long remain hidden. It will be acknowledged by them even as the members of my family acknowledged it after they had tried me for several years. If the people join me as I expect they will, the sufferings they will undergo, unless the British nation sooner retraces its steps, will be enough to melt the stoniest hearts.

The plan through civil disobedience will be to combat such evils as I have sampled out. If we want to sever the British connection it is because of such evils. When they are removed the path becomes easy. Then the way to friendly negotiation will be open. If the British commerce with India is purified of greed, you will have no difficulty in recognizing our independence. I respectfully invite you then to pave the way for immediate removal of those evils, and thus open a way for a real conference between equals, interested only in promoting the common good of mankind through voluntary fellowship and in arranging terms of mutual help and commerce equally suited to both. You have unnecessarily laid stress upon the communal problems that unhappily affect this land. Important though they undoubtedly are for the consideration of any scheme of government, they have little bearing on the greater problems which are above communities and which affect them all equally. But if you cannot see your way to deal with these evils and my letter makes no appeal to your heart, on the 11th day of this month, I shall proceed with such co-workers of the Ashram as I can take, to disregard the provisions of the salt laws. I regard this tax to be the most iniquitous of all from the poor man's standpoint. As the independence movement is essentially for the poorest in the land the beginning will be made with this evil. The wonder is that we have submitted to the cruel monopoly for so long. It is, I know, open to you to frustrate my design by arresting me. I hope that there will be tens of thousands ready, in a disciplined manner, to take up the work after me, and, in the act of disobeying the Salt Act to lay themselves open to the penalties of a law that should never have disfigured the Statute-book.

I have no desire to cause you unnecessary embarrassment, or any at all, so far as I can help. If you think that there is any substance in my letter, and if you will care to discuss matters with me, and if to that end you would like me to postpone publication of this letter, I shall gladly refrain on receipt of a telegram to that effect soon after this reaches you. You will, however, do me the favour not to deflect me from my course unless you can see your way to conform to the substance of this letter.

20  This letter is not in any way intended as a threat but is a simple and sacred duty peremptory on a civil resister. Therefore I am having it specially delivered by a young English friend who believes in the Indian cause and is a full believer in non-violence and whom Providence seems to have sent to me, as it were, for the very purpose.

I remain,
Your sincere friend,
*M.K. Gandhi*

## Questions for Discussion

How does Gandhi treat his audience? What kind of impact is he after by treating him this way?

Gandhi says at one point that he is appealing to Lord Irwin's "heart"—is this argument primarily one about values and emotions?

*Born in Atlanta and educated at Morehouse College, Crozer Theological Seminary (near Philadelphia), and Boston University,* **Martin Luther King, Jr.** *(1929–1968) was the most visible leader of the civil rights movement of the 1960s. An ordained minister with a doctorate in theology from Boston University, he worked especially in the South and through nonviolent means to overturn segregation statutes, to increase the number of African-American voters, and to support other civil rights initiatives. Reverend King won the Nobel Peace Prize in 1964 after delivering his famous "I Have a Dream" speech (reprinted elsewhere in this book). He was assassinated in 1968.*

*On April 12, 1963, in order to have himself arrested on a symbolic day (Good Friday), Reverend King disobeyed a court injunction forbidding demonstrations in Birmingham, Alabama. That same day, eight leading white Birmingham clergymen (Christian and Jewish) published a letter in the* Birmingham News *calling for the end of protests and exhorting protesters to work through the courts for the redress of their grievances. On the morning after his arrest, while held in solitary confinement, King began his response to these clergymen—his famous "Letter from Birmingham Jail." Begun in the margins of newspapers and on scraps of paper and finished the following Tuesday, the letter was widely distributed and later became a central chapter in King's* Why We Can't Wait *(1964).*

# Martin Luther King, Jr.

# Letter from Birmingham Jail

April 16, 1963

My Dear Fellow Clergymen:

While confined here in the Birmingham city jail, I came across your recent statement calling my present activities "unwise and untimely." Seldom do I pause to answer criticism of my work and ideas. If I sought to answer all the criticisms that cross my desk, my secretaries would have little time for anything other than such correspondence in the course of the day, and I would have no time for constructive work. But since I feel that you are men of genuine good will and that your criticisms are sincerely set forth, I want to try to answer your statement in what I hope will be patient and reasonable terms.

I think I should indicate why I am here in Birmingham, since you have been influenced by the view which argues against "outsiders coming in." I have the honor of serving as president of the Southern Christian Leadership Conference, an organization operating in every southern state, with headquarters in Atlanta, Georgia. We have some eighty-five affiliated organizations across the South, and one of them is the Alabama Christian Movement for Human Rights. Frequently we share staff, educational and financial resources with our affiliates. Several months ago the affiliate here in Birmingham asked us to be on call to engage in a nonviolent direct-action program if such were deemed necessary. We readily consented, and when the hour came we lived up to our promise. So I, along with several members of my staff, am here because I was invited here. I am here because I have organizational ties here.

But more basically, I am in Birmingham because injustice is here. Just as the prophets of the eighth century B.C. left their villages and carried their "thus saith the Lord" far beyond the boundaries of their home towns, and just as the Apostle Paul left his village of Tarsus and carried the gospel of Jesus Christ to the far corners of the Greco-Roman world, so am I compelled to carry the gospel of freedom beyond my own home town. Like Paul, I must constantly respond to the Macedonian call for aid.

Moreover, I am cognizant of the interrelatedness of all communities and states. I cannot sit idly by in Atlanta and not be concerned about what happens in Birmingham. Injustice anywhere is a threat to justice everywhere. We are caught in an inescapable network of mutuality, tied in a single garment of destiny. Whatever affects one directly, affects all indirectly. Never again can we afford to live with the narrow, provincial "outside agitator" idea. Anyone who lives inside the United States can never be considered an outsider anywhere within its bounds.

5    You deplore the demonstrations taking place in Birmingham. But your statement, I am sorry to say, fails to express a similar concern for the conditions that brought about the demonstrations. I am sure that none of you would want to rest content with the superficial kind of social analysis that deals merely with effects and does not grapple with underlying causes. It is unfortunate that demonstrations are taking place in Birmingham, but it is even more unfortunate that the city's white power structure left the Negro community with no alternative.

In any nonviolent campaign there are four basic steps: collection of the facts to determine whether injustices exist; negotiation; self-purification; and direct action. We have gone through all these steps in

Birmingham. There can be no gain-saying the fact that racial injustice engulfs this community. Birmingham is probably the most thoroughly segregated city in the United States. Its ugly record of brutality is widely known. Negroes have experienced grossly unjust treatment in the courts. There have been more unsolved bombings of Negro homes and churches in Birmingham than in any other city in the nation. These are the hard, brutal facts of the case. On the basis of these conditions, Negro leaders sought to negotiate with the city fathers. But the latter consistently refused to engage in good-faith negotiation.

Then, last September, came the opportunity to talk with leaders of Birmingham's economic community. In the course of the negotiations, certain promises were made by the merchants—for example, to remove the stores' humiliating racial signs. On the basis of these promises, the Reverend Fred Shuttlesworth and the leaders of the Alabama Christian Movement for Human Rights agreed to a moratorium on all demonstrations. As the weeks and months went by, we realized that we were the victims of a broken promise. A few signs, briefly removed, returned; the others remained.

As in so many past experiences, our hopes had been blasted, and the shadow of deep disappointment settled upon us. We had no alternative except to prepare for direct action, whereby we would present our very bodies as a means of laying our case before the conscience of the local and the national community. Mindful of the difficulties involved, we decided to undertake a process of self-purification. We began a series of workshops on nonviolence, and we repeatedly asked ourselves: "Are you able to accept blows without retaliating?" "Are you able to endure the ordeal of jail?" We decided to schedule our direct-action program for the Easter season, realizing that except for Christmas, this is the main shopping period of the year. Knowing that a strong economic-withdrawal program would be the by-product of direct action, we felt that this would be the best time to bring pressure to bear on the merchants for the needed change.

Then it occurred to us that Birmingham's mayoral election was coming up in March, and we speedily decided to postpone action until after election day. When we discovered that the Commissioner of Public Safety, Eugene "Bull" Connor, had piled up enough votes to be in the run-off, we decided again to postpone action until the day after the run-off so that the demonstrations could not be used to cloud the issues. Like many others, we waited to see Mr. Connor defeated, and to this end we endured postponement after postponement. Having aided in this community need, we felt that our direct action program could be delayed no longer.

10    You may well ask: "Why direct action? Why sit-ins, marches and so forth? Isn't negotiation a better path?" You are quite right in calling for negotiation. Indeed, this is the very purpose of direct action. Nonviolent direct action seeks to create such a crisis and foster such a tension that a community which has constantly refused to negotiate is forced to confront the issue. It seeks so to dramatize the issue that it can no longer be ignored. My citing the creation of tension as part of the work of the nonviolent-resister may sound rather shocking. But I must confess that I am not afraid of the word "tension." I have earnestly opposed violent tension, but there is a type of constructive, nonviolent tension which is necessary for growth. Just as Socrates felt that it was necessary to create a tension in the mind so that individuals could rise from the bondage of myths and half-truths to the unfettered realm of creative analysis and objective appraisal, so must we see the need for nonviolent gadflies to create the kind of tension in society that will help men rise from the dark depths of prejudice and racism to the majestic heights of understanding and brotherhood.

The purpose of our direct-action program is to create a situation so crisis-packed that it will inevitably open the door to negotiation. I therefore concur with you in your call for negotiation. Too long has our beloved Southland been bogged down in a tragic effort to live in monologue rather than dialogue.

One of the basic points in your statement is that the action that I and my associates have taken in Birmingham is untimely. Some have asked: "Why didn't you give the new city administration time to act?" The only answer that I can give to this query is that the new Birmingham administration must be prodded about as much as the outgoing one, before it will act. We are sadly mistaken if we feel that the election of Albert Boutwell as mayor will bring the millennium to Birmingham. While Mr. Boutwell is a much more gentle person than Mr. Connor, they are both segregationists, dedicated to maintenance of the status quo. I have hope that Mr. Boutwell will be reasonable enough to see the futility of massive resistance to desegregation. But he will not see this without pressure from devotees of civil rights. My friends, I must say to you that we have not made a single gain in civil rights without determined legal and nonviolent pressure. Lamentably, it is an historical fact that privileged groups seldom give up their privileges voluntarily. Individuals may see the moral light and voluntarily give up their unjust posture; but, as Reinhold Niebuhr has reminded us, groups tend to be more immoral than individuals.

We know through painful experience that freedom is never voluntarily given by the oppressor; it must be demanded by the oppressed.

Frankly, I have yet to engage in a direct-action campaign that was "well timed" in the view of those who have not suffered unduly from the disease of segregation. For years now I have heard the word "Wait!" It rings in the ear of every Negro with piercing familiarity. This "Wait" has almost always meant "Never." We must come to see, with one of our distinguished jurists, that "justice too long delayed is justice denied."

We have waited for more than 340 years for our constitutional and God-given rights. The nations of Asia and Africa are moving with jetlike speed toward gaining political independence, but we still creep at horse-and-buggy pace toward gaining a cup of coffee at a lunch counter. Perhaps it is easy for those who have never felt the stinging darts of segregation to say, "Wait." But when you have seen vicious mobs lynch your mothers and fathers at will and drown your sisters and brothers at whim; when you have seen hate-filled policemen curse, kick and even kill your black brothers and sisters; when you see the vast majority of your twenty million Negro brothers smothering in an airtight cage of poverty in the midst of an affluent society; when you suddenly find your tongue twisted and your speech stammering as you seek to explain to your six-year-old daughter why she can't go to the public amusement park that has just been advertised on television, and see tears welling up in her eyes when she is told that Funtown is closed to colored children, and see ominous clouds of inferiority beginning to form in her little mental sky, and see her beginning to distort her personality by developing an unconscious bitterness toward white people; when you have to concoct an answer for a five-year-old son who is asking: "Daddy, why do white people treat colored people so mean?"; when you take a cross-country drive and find it necessary to sleep night after night in the uncomfortable corners of your automobile because no motel will accept you; when you are humiliated day in and day out by nagging signs reading "white" and "colored"; when your first name becomes "nigger," your middle name becomes "boy" (however old you are) and your last name becomes "John," and your wife and mother are never given the respected title "Mrs."; when you are harried by day and haunted by night by the fact that you are a Negro, living constantly at tiptoe stance, never quite knowing what to expect next, and are plagued with inner fears and outer resentments; when you are forever fighting a degenerating sense of "nobodiness"— then you will understand why we find it difficult to wait. There comes a time when the cup of endurance runs over, and men are no longer willing to be plunged into the abyss of despair. I hope, sirs, you can understand our legitimate and unavoidable impatience.

15    You express a great deal of anxiety over our willingness to break laws. This is certainly a legitimate concern. Since we so diligently urge people to obey the Supreme Court's decision of 1954 outlawing segregation in the public schools, at first glance it may seem rather paradoxical for us consciously to break laws. One may well ask: "How can you advocate breaking some laws and obeying others?" The answer lies in the fact that there are two types of laws: just and unjust. I would be the first to advocate obeying just laws. One has not only a legal but a moral responsibility to obey just laws. Conversely, one has a moral responsibility to disobey unjust laws. I would agree with St. Augustine that "an unjust law is no law at all."

Now, what is the difference between the two? How does one determine whether a law is just or unjust? A just law is a manmade code that squares with the moral law or the law of God. An unjust law is a code that is out of harmony with the moral law. To put it in the terms of St. Thomas Aquinas: An unjust law is a human law that is not rooted in eternal law and natural law. Any law that uplifts human personality is just. Any law that degrades human personality is unjust. All segregation statutes are unjust because segregation distorts the soul and damages the personality. It gives the segregator a false sense of superiority and the segregated a false sense of inferiority. Segregation, to use the terminology of the Jewish philosopher Martin Buber, substitutes an "I-it" relationship for an "I-thou" relationship and ends up relegating persons to the status of things. Hence segregation is not only politically, economically and sociologically unsound, it is morally wrong and sinful. Paul Tillich has said that sin is separation. Is not segregation an existential expression of man's tragic separation, his awful estrangement, his terrible sinfulness? Thus it is that I can urge men to obey the 1954 decision of the Supreme Court, for it is morally right; and I can urge them to disobey segregation ordinances, for they are morally wrong.

Let us consider a more concrete example of just and unjust laws. An unjust law is a code that a numerical or power majority group compels a minority group to obey but does not make binding on itself. This is *difference* made legal. By the same token, a just law is a code that a majority compels a minority to follow and that it is willing to follow itself. This is *sameness* made legal.

Let me give another explanation. A law is unjust if it is inflicted on a minority that, as a result of being denied the right to vote, had no part in enacting or devising the law. Who can say that the legislature of Alabama which set up that state's segregation laws was democratically elected? Throughout Alabama all sorts of devious methods are used to prevent Negroes from becoming registered voters, and there are some counties in which, even though Negroes constitute a majority of the population, not a single Negro is registered. Can any law enacted under such circumstances be considered democratically structured?"

Sometimes a law is just on its face and unjust in its application. For instance, I have been arrested on a charge of parading without a permit. Now, there is nothing wrong in having an ordinance which requires a permit for a parade. But such an ordinance becomes unjust when it is used to maintain segregation and to deny citizens the First-Amendment privilege of peaceful assembly and protest.

20          I hope you are able to see the distinction I am trying to point out. In no sense do I advocate evading or defying the law, as would the rabid segregationist. That would lead to anarchy. One who breaks an unjust law must do so openly, lovingly, and with a willingness to accept the penalty. I submit that an individual who breaks a law that conscience tells him is unjust, and who willingly accepts the penalty of imprisonment in order to arouse the conscience of the community over its injustice, is in reality expressing the highest respect for law.

Of course, there is nothing new about this kind of civil disobedience. It was evidenced sublimely in the refusal of Shadrach, Meshach and Abednego to obey the laws of Nebuchadnezzar, on the ground that a higher moral law was at stake. It was practiced superbly by the early Christians, who were willing to face hungry lions and the excruciating pain of chopping blocks rather than submit to certain unjust laws of the Roman Empire. To a degree, academic freedom is a reality today because Socrates practiced civil disobedience. In our own nation, the Boston Tea Party represented a massive act of civil disobedience.

We should never forget that everything Adolf Hitler did in Germany was "legal" and everything the Hungarian freedom fighters did in Hungary was "illegal." It was "illegal" to aid and comfort a Jew in Hitler's Germany. Even so, I am sure that, had I lived in Germany at the time, I would have aided and comforted my Jewish brothers. If today I lived in a Communist country where certain principles dear to the Christian faith are suppressed, I would openly advocate disobeying that country's antireligious laws.

I must make two honest confessions to you, my Christian and Jewish brothers. First, I must confess that over the past few years I have been gravely disappointed with the white moderate. I have almost reached the regrettable conclusion that the Negro's great stumbling block in his stride toward freedom is not the White Citizen's Counciler or the Ku Klux Klanner, but the white moderate, who is more devoted to "order" than to justice; who prefers a negative peace which is the absence of tension to a positive peace which is the presence of justice; who constantly says: "I agree with you in the goal you seek, but I cannot agree with your methods of direct action"; who paternalistically believes he can set the timetable for another man's freedom; who lives by a mythical concept of time and who constantly advises the Negro to wait for a "more convenient season." Shallow understanding from people of good will is more frustrating than absolute misunderstanding from people of ill will. Lukewarm acceptance is much more bewildering than outright rejection.

I had hoped that the white moderate would understand that law and order exist for the purpose of establishing justice and that when they fail in this purpose they become the dangerously structured dams that block the flow of social progress. I had hoped that the white moderate would understand that the present tension in the South is a necessary phase of the transition from an obnoxious negative peace, in which the Negro passively accepted his unjust plight, to a substantive and positive peace, in which all men will respect the dignity and worth of human personality. Actually, we who engage in nonviolent direct action are not the creators of tension. We merely bring to the surface the hidden tension that is already alive. We bring it out in the open, where it can be seen and dealt with. Like a boil that can never be cured so long as it is covered up but must be opened with all its ugliness to the natural medicines of air and light, injustice must be exposed, with all the tension its exposure creates, to the light of human conscience and the air of national opinion before it can be cured.

25    In your statement you assert that our actions, even though peaceful, must be condemned because they precipitate violence. But is this a logical assertion? Isn't this like condemning a robbed man because his possession of money precipitated the evil act of robbery? Isn't this like condemning Socrates because his unswerving commitment to truth and his philosophical inquiries precipitated the act by the misguided populace in which they made him drink hemlock? Isn't this like condemning Jesus because his unique God-consciousness and never-ceasing devotion to God's will precipitated the evil act of crucifixion? We must come to see that, as the federal courts have consistently affirmed, it is wrong to urge an individual to cease his efforts to gain his basic constitutional rights because the quest may precipitate violence. Society must protect the robbed and punish the robber.

I had also hoped that the white moderate would reject the myth concerning time in relation to the struggle for freedom. I have just received a letter from a white brother in Texas. He writes: "All

Christians know that the colored people will receive equal rights eventually, but it is possible that you are in too great a religious hurry. It has taken Christianity almost two thousand years to accomplish what it has. The teachings of Christ take time to come to earth." Such an attitude stems from a tragic misconception of time, from the strangely irrational notion that there is something in the very flow of time that will inevitably cure all ills. Actually, time itself is neutral; it can be used either destructively or constructively. More and more I feel that the people of ill will have used time much more effectively than have the people of good will. We will have to repent in this generation not merely for the hateful words and actions of the bad people but for the appalling silence of the good people. Human progress never rolls in on wheels of inevitability; it comes through the tireless efforts of men willing to be co-workers with God, and without this hard work, time itself becomes an ally of the forces of social stagnation. We must use time creatively, in the knowledge that time is always ripe to do right. Now is the time to make real the promise of democracy and transform our pending national elegy into a creative psalm of brotherhood. Now is the time to lift our national policy from the quicksand of racial injustice to the solid rock of human dignity.

You speak of our activity in Birmingham as extreme. At first I was rather disappointed that fellow clergymen would see my nonviolent efforts as those of an extremist. I began thinking about the fact that I stand in the middle of two opposing forces in the Negro community. One is a force of complacency, made up in part of Negroes who, as a result of long years of oppression, are so drained of self-respect and a sense of "somebodiness" that they have adjusted to segregation; and in part of a few middle-class Negroes who, because of a degree of academic and economic security and because in some ways they profit by segregation, have become insensitive to the problems of the masses. The other force is one of bitterness and hatred, and it comes perilously close to advocating violence. It is expressed in the various black nationalist groups that are springing up across the nation, the largest and best-known being Elijah Muhammad's Muslim movement. Nourished by the Negro's frustration over the continued existence of racial discrimination, this movement is made up of people who have lost faith in America, who have absolutely repudiated Christianity, and who have concluded that the white man is an incorrigible "devil."

I have tried to stand between these two forces, saying that we need emulate neither the "do-nothingism" of the complacent nor the hatred and despair of the black nationalist. For there is the more excellent way of love and nonviolent protest. I am grateful to God that, through the influence of the Negro church, the way of nonviolence became an integral part of our struggle.

If this philosophy had not emerged, by now many streets of the South would, I am convinced, be flowing with blood. And I am further convinced that if our white brothers dismiss as "rabble-rousers" and "outside agitators" those of us who employ nonviolent direct action, and if they refuse to support our nonviolent efforts, millions of Negroes will, out of frustration and despair, seek solace and security in black-nationalist ideologies—a development that would inevitably lead to a frightening racial nightmare.

30   Oppressed people cannot remain oppressed forever. The yearning for freedom eventually manifests itself, and that is what has happened to the American Negro. Something within has reminded him of his birthright of freedom, and something without has reminded him that it can be gained. Consciously or unconsciously, he has been caught up by the *Zeitgeist*, and with his black brothers of Africa and his brown and yellow brothers of Asia, South America and the Caribbean, the United States Negro is moving with a sense of great urgency toward the promised land of racial justice. If one recognizes this vital urge that has engulfed the Negro community, one should readily understand why public demonstrations are taking place. The Negro has many pent-up resentments and latent frustrations, and he must release them. So let him march; let him make prayer pilgrimages to the city hall; let him go on freedom rides—and try to understand why he must do so. If his repressed emotions are not released in nonviolent ways, they will seek expression through violence; this is not a threat but a fact of history. So I have not said to my people: "Get rid of your discontent." Rather, I have tried to say that this normal and healthy discontent can be channeled into the creative outlet of nonviolent direct action. And now this approach is being termed extremist.

But though I was initially disappointed at being categorized as an extremist, as I continued to think about the matter I gradually gained a measure of satisfaction from the label. Was not Jesus an extremist for love: "Love your enemies, bless them that curse you, do good to them that hate you, and pray for them which despitefully use you, and persecute you." Was not Amos an extremist for justice: "Let justice roll down like waters and righteousness like an ever-flowing stream." Was not Paul an extremist for the Christian gospel: "I bear in my body the marks of the Lord Jesus." Was not Martin Luther an extremist: "Here I stand; I cannot do otherwise, so help me God." And John Bunyan: "I will stay in jail to the end of my days before I make a butchery of my conscience." And Abraham Lincoln: "This nation cannot survive half slave and half free." And Thomas Jefferson: "We hold these truths to be self-evident, that all men are created equal . . ." So the question is not whether we will be extremists, but what kind of extremists we will be. Will we be extremists for hate or for love? Will we be extremists for the preservation of injustice or for the extension of justice? In that dramatic scene on Calvary's hill three men were crucified. We must never forget that all three were crucified for the same crime—the crime of extremism. Two were extremists for immorality, and thus fell below their environment. The other, Jesus Christ, was an extremist for love, truth and goodness, and thereby rose above his environment. Perhaps the South, the nation and the world are in dire need of creative extremists.

I had hoped that the white moderate would see this need. Perhaps I was too optimistic; perhaps I expected too much. I suppose I should have realized that few members of the oppressor race can understand the deep groans and passionate yearnings of the oppressed race, and still fewer have the vision to see that injustice must be rooted out by strong, persistent and determined action. I am thankful, however, that some of our white brothers in the South have grasped the meaning of this social revolution and committed themselves to it. They are still all too few in quantity, but they are big in quality. Some—such as Ralph McGill, Lillian Smith, Harry Golden, James McBride Dabbs, Ann Braden and Sarah Patton Boyle—have written about our struggle in eloquent and prophetic terms. Others have marched with us down nameless streets of the South. They have languished in filthy, roach-infested jails, suffering the abuse and brutality of policemen who view them as "dirty nigger-lovers." Unlike so many of their moderate brothers and sisters, they have recognized the urgency of the moment and sensed the need for powerful "action" antidotes to combat the disease of segregation.

Let me take note of my other major disappointment. I have been so greatly disappointed with the white church and its leadership. Of course, there are some notable exceptions. I am not unmindful of the fact that each of you has taken some significant stands on this issue. I commend you, Reverend Stallings, for your Christian stand on this past Sunday, in welcoming Negroes to your worship service on a non-segregated basis. I commend the Catholic leaders of this state for integrating Spring Hill College several years ago.

But despite these notable exceptions, I must honestly reiterate that I have been disappointed with the church. I do not say this as one of those negative critics who can always find something wrong with the church. I say this as a minister of the gospel, who loves the church; who was nurtured in its bosom; who has been sustained by its spiritual blessings and who will remain true to it as long as the cord of life shall lengthen.

35    When I was suddenly catapulted into the leadership of the bus protest in Montgomery, Alabama, a few years ago, I felt we would be supported by the white church. I felt that the white ministers, priests and rabbis of the South would be among our strongest allies. Instead, some have been outright opponents, refusing to understand the freedom movement and misrepresenting its leaders; all too many others have been more cautious than courageous and have remained silent behind the anesthetizing security of stained-glass windows.

In spite of my shattered dreams, I came to Birmingham with the hope that the white religious leadership of this community would see the justice of our cause and, with deep moral concern, would serve as the channel through which our just grievances could reach the power structure. I had hoped that each of you would understand. But again I have been disappointed.

I have heard numerous southern religious leaders admonish their worshipers to comply with a desegregation decision because it is the law, but I have longed to hear white ministers declare: "Follow this decree because integration is morally right and because the Negro is your brother." In the midst of blatant injustices inflicted upon the Negro, I have watched white churchmen stand on the sideline and mouth pious irrelevancies and sanctimonious trivialities. In the midst of a mighty struggle to rid our nation of racial and economic injustice, I have heard many ministers say: "Those are social issues, with which the gospel has no real concern." And I have watched many churches commit themselves to a completely otherworldly religion which makes a strange, un-Biblical distinction between body and soul, between the sacred and the secular.

I have traveled the length and breadth of Alabama, Mississippi and all the other southern states. On sweltering summer days and crisp autumn mornings I have looked at the South's beautiful churches with their lofty spires pointing heavenward. I have beheld the impressive outlines of her massive religious-education buildings. Over and over I have found myself asking: "What kind of people worship here? Who is their God? Where were their voices when the lips of Governor Barnett dripped with words of interposition and nullification? Where were they when Governor Wallace gave a clarion call for defiance and hatred? Where were their voices of support when bruised and weary

Negro men and women decided to rise from the dark dungeons of complacency to the bright hills of creative protest?"

Yes, these questions are still in my mind. In deep disappointment I have wept over the laxity of the church. But be assured that my tears have been tears of love. There can be no deep disappointment where there is not deep love. Yes, I love the church. How could I do otherwise? I am in the rather unique position of being the son, the grandson and the great-grandson of preachers. Yes, I see the church as the body of Christ. But, oh! How we have blemished and scarred that body through social neglect and through fear of being non-conformists.

40     There was a time when the church was very powerful—in the time when the early Christians rejoiced at being deemed worthy to suffer for what they believed. In those days the church was not merely a thermometer that recorded the ideas and principles of popular opinion; it was a thermostat that transformed the mores of society. Whenever the early Christians entered a town, the people in power became disturbed and immediately sought to convict the Christians for being "disturbers of the peace" and "outside agitators." But the Christians pressed on, in the conviction that they were "a colony of heaven," called to obey God rather than man. Small in number, they were big in commitment. They were too God-intoxicated to be "astronomically intimidated." By their effort and example they brought an end to such ancient evils as infanticide and gladiatorial contests.

Things are different now. So often the contemporary church is a weak, ineffectual voice with an uncertain sound. So often it is an arch-defender of the status quo. Far from being disturbed by the presence of the church, the power structure of the average community is consoled by the church's silent—and often even vocal—sanction of things as they are.

But the judgment of God is upon the church as never before. If today's church does not recapture the sacrificial spirit of the early church, it will lose its authenticity, forfeit the loyalty of millions, and be dismissed as an irrelevant social club with no meaning for the twentieth century. Every day I meet young people whose disappointment with the church has turned into outright disgust.

Perhaps I have once again been too optimistic. Is organized religion too inextricably bound to the status quo to save our nation and the world? Perhaps I must turn my faith to the inner spiritual church, the church within the church, as the true *ekklesia* and the hope of the world. But again I am thankful to God that some noble souls from the ranks of organized religion have broken loose from the paralyzing chains of conformity and joined us as active partners in the struggle for freedom. They have left their secure congregations and walked the streets of Albany, Georgia, with us. They have gone down the highways of the South on tortuous rides for freedom. Yes, they have gone to jail with us. Some have been dismissed from their churches, have lost the support of their bishops and fellow ministers. But they have acted in the faith that right defeated is stronger than evil triumphant. Their witness has been the spiritual salt that has preserved the true meaning of the gospel in these troubled times. They have carved a tunnel of hope through the dark mountain of disappointment.

I hope the church as a whole will meet the challenge of this decisive hour. But even if the church does not come to the aid of justice, I have no despair about the future. I have no fear about the outcome of our struggle in Birmingham, even if our motives are at present misunderstood. We will reach the goal of freedom in Birmingham and all over the nation, because the goal of America is freedom. Abused and scorned though we may be, our destiny is tied up with America's destiny. Before the pilgrims landed at Plymouth, we were here. Before the pen of Jefferson etched the majestic words of the Declaration of Independence across the pages of history, we were here. For more than two centuries our forebears labored in this country without wages; they made cotton king; they built the homes of their masters while suffering gross injustice and shameful humiliation—and yet out of a bottomless vitality they continued to thrive and develop. If the inexpressible cruelties of slavery could not stop us, the opposition we now face will surely fail. We will win our freedom because the sacred heritage of our nation and the eternal will of God are embodied in our echoing demands.

45    Before closing I feel impelled to mention one other point in your statement that has troubled me profoundly. You warmly commended the Birmingham police force for keeping "order" and "preventing violence." I doubt that you would have so warmly commended the police force if you had seen its dogs sinking their teeth into unarmed, nonviolent Negroes. I doubt that you would so quickly commend the policemen if you were to observe their ugly and inhumane treatment of Negroes here in the city jail; if you were to watch them push and curse old Negro women and young Negro girls; if you were to see them slap and kick old Negro men and young boys; if you were to observe them, as they did on two occasions, refuse to give us food because we wanted to sing our grace together. I cannot join you in your praise of the Birmingham Police Department.

It is true that the police have exercised a degree of discipline in handling the demonstrators. In this sense they have conducted themselves rather "nonviolently" in public. But for what purpose? To preserve the evil system of segregation. Over the past few years I have consistently preached that nonviolence demands that the means we use must be as pure as the ends we seek. I have tried to make clear that it is wrong to use immoral means to attain moral ends. But now I must affirm that it is just as wrong, or perhaps even more so, to use moral means to preserve immoral ends. Perhaps Mr. Connor and his policemen have been rather nonviolent in public, as was Chief Pritchett in Albany, Georgia, but they have used the moral means of nonviolence to maintain the immoral end of racial injustice. As T. S. Eliot has said: "The last temptation is the greatest treason: To do the right deed for the wrong reason."

I wish you had commended the Negro sit-inners and demonstrators of Birmingham for their sublime courage, their willingness to suffer and their amazing discipline in the midst of great provocation. One day the South will recognize its real heroes. They will be the James Merediths, with the noble sense of purpose that enables them to face jeering and hostile mobs, and with the agonizing loneliness that characterizes the life of the pioneer. They will be old, oppressed, battered Negro women, symbolized in a seventy-two-year-old woman in Montgomery, Alabama, who rose up with a sense of dignity and with her people decided not to ride segregated buses, and who responded with ungrammatical profundity to one who inquired about her weariness: "My feets is tired, but my soul is at rest." They will be the young high school and college students, the young ministers of the gospel and a host of their elders, courageously and nonviolently sitting in at lunch counters and willingly going to jail for conscience sake. One day the South will know that when these disinherited children of God sat down at lunch counters, they were in reality standing up for what is best in the American dream and for the most sacred values in our Judaeo-Christian heritage, thereby bringing our nation back to those great wells of democracy which were dug deep by the founding fathers in their formulation of the Constitution and the Declaration of Independence.

Never before have I written so long a letter. I'm afraid it is much too long to take your precious time. I can assure you that it would have been much shorter if I had been writing from a comfortable desk, but what else can one do when he is alone in a narrow jail cell, other than write long letters, think long thoughts and pray long prayers?

If I have said anything in this letter that overstates the truth and indicates an unreasonable impatience, I beg you to forgive me. If I have said anything that understates the truth and indicates my having a patience that allows me to settle for anything less than brotherhood, I beg God to forgive me.

50    I hope this letter finds you strong in the faith. I also hope that circumstances will soon make it possible for me to meet each of you, not as an integrationist or a civil-rights leader but as a fellow clergyman and a Christian brother. Let us all hope that the dark clouds of racial prejudice will soon pass away and the deep fog of misunderstanding will be lifted from our fear-drenched communities, and in some not too distant tomorrow the radiant stars of love and brotherhood will shine over our great nation with all their scintillating beauty.

Yours for the cause of Peace and Brotherhood,
*Martin Luther King Jr.*

## Questions for Discussion

What methods does King use to apply "pressure" to his audience? How does he create "tension"?

What assumptions does King make about his audience? How does he attempt to address these assumptions?

*The campaign for civil rights described by Martin Luther King's "Letter from Birmingham Jail" was ultimately successful, not least because the campaign was highly publicized in the news media. Newspapers and television news programs covered the event in great detail, and in the process they mounted a large number of "visual arguments" about the issue. On these two pages are reproduced three photographs from the Birmingham campaign.*

# Visual Arguments: The Birmingham Campaign

The Birmingham city police turned waterhoses, at a force of 100 pounds per square inch, on demonstrators who huddled where they could for shelter.

Members of the National States Rights Party resisted civil rights protesters in Birmingham, May 6, 1963. They lynched-in-effigy the leader of the demonstrations, Martin Luther King, Jr.

Dr. King took a controversial course of action by permitting children to participate in the dangerous protests. When masses of the children were arrested in spite of their model decorum, the nation was outraged.

*The remarkable life of **Malcolm X** is well known because of Alex Haley's*
The Autobiography of Malcolm X *and Spike Lee's adoring film* Malcolm X.
*Born in 1925 into challenging circumstances, the victim of a tortured*
*childhood that created a seething alienation, and drawn first to a life of*
*petty crime, Malcolm X was converted in prison to Islam and thereafter be-*
*came a leader in the Black Muslims and the black nationalist movement of*
*the early 1960s. A charismatic speaker who was assassinated in 1965*
*(only months after returning from a pilgrimage to Africa and the Near East*
*and renouncing his separatist agenda), Malcolm X was a foil to his contem-*
*porary, Martin Luther King, Jr. The following speech was delivered on*
*November 10, 1963 (six months after King wrote his "Letter from*
*Birmingham Jail," two weeks before President Kennedy was assassinated,*
*and fifteen months before Malcolm X's own death), to an all-black audi-*
*ence gathered in Detroit for a Northern Negro Leadership Conference; it*
*was also broadcast over the radio. The speech reveals the terms of Malcolm*
*X's differences with King; at the time the two disagreed about the wisdom*
*of segregation versus integration and about whether nonviolent resistance*
*or violent revenge is the better means of countering racism.*

## *Malcolm X*
# Message to the Grassroots

We want to have just an off-the-cuff chat between you and me, us. We
want to talk right down to earth in a language that everybody here can
easily understand. We all agree tonight, all of the speakers have
agreed, that America has a very serious problem. Not only does
America have a very serious problem, but our people have a very serious problem. America's problem is us. We're her problem. The only
reason she has a problem is she doesn't want us here. And every time
you look at yourself, be you black, brown, red or yellow, a so-called
Negro, you represent a person who poses such a serious problem for
America because you're not wanted. Once you face this as a fact, then
you can start plotting a course that will make you appear intelligent,
instead of unintelligent.

What you and I need to do is learn to forget our differences. When
we come together, we don't come together as Baptists or Methodists.
You don't catch hell because you're a Baptist, and you don't catch hell
because you're a Methodist. You don't catch hell because you're a
Methodist or Baptist, you don't catch hell because you're a Democrat

or a Republican, you don't catch hell because you're a Mason or an Elk, and you sure don't catch hell because you're an American; because if you were an American, you wouldn't catch hell. You catch hell because you're a black man. You catch hell, all of us catch hell, for the same reason.

So we're all black people, so-called Negroes, second-class citizens, ex-slaves. You're nothing but an ex-slave. You don't like to be told that. But what else are you? You are ex-slaves. You didn't come here on the "Mayflower." You came here on a slave ship. In chains, like a horse, or a cow, or a chicken. And you were brought here by the people who came here on the "Mayflower," you were brought here by the so-called Pilgrims, or Founding Fathers. They were the ones who brought you here.

We have a common enemy. We have this in common: We have a common oppressor, a common exploiter, and a common discriminator. But once we all realize that we have a common enemy, then we unite—on the basis of what we have in common. And what we have foremost in common is that enemy—the white man. He's an enemy to all of us. I know some of you all think that some of them aren't enemies. Time will tell.

5     In Bandung back in, I think, 1954, was the first unity meeting in centuries of black people. And once you study what happened at the Bandung conference, and the results of the Bandung conference, it actually serves as a model for the same procedure you and I can use to get our problems solved. At Bandung all the nations came together, the dark nations from Africa and Asia. Some of them were Buddhists, some of them were Muslims, some of them were Christians, some were Confucianists, some were atheists. Despite their religious differences, they came together. Some were communists, some were socialists, some were capitalists—despite their economic and political differences, they came together. All of them were black, brown, red or yellow.

The number-one thing that was not allowed to attend the Bandung conference was the white man. He couldn't come. Once they excluded the white man, they found that they could get together. Once they kept him out, everybody else fell right in and fell in line. This is the thing that you and I have to understand. And these people who came together didn't have nuclear weapons, they didn't have jet planes, they didn't have all of the heavy armaments that the white man has. But they had unity.

They were able to submerge their little petty differences and agree on one thing: That there one African came from Kenya and was being colonized by the Englishman, and another African came from the Congo and was being colonized by the Belgian, and another African came from Guinea and was being colonized by the French, and another came from Angola and was being colonized by the Portuguese. When they came to the Bandung conference, they looked at the Portuguese, and at the Frenchman, and at the Englishman, and at the Dutchman, and learned or realized the one thing that all of them had in common—they were all from Europe, they were all Europeans, blond, blue-eyed and white skins. They began to recognize who their enemy was. The same man that was colonizing our people in Kenya was colonizing our people in the Congo. The same one in the Congo was colonizing our people in South Africa, and in Southern Rhodesia, and in Burma, and in India, and in Afghanistan, and in Pakistan. They realized all over the world where the dark man was being oppressed, he was being oppressed by the white man; where the dark man was being exploited, he was being exploited by the white man. So they got together on this basis—that they had a common enemy.

And when you and I here in Detroit and in Michigan and in America who have been awakened today look around us, we too realize here in America we all have a common enemy, whether he's in Georgia or Michigan, whether he's in California or New York. He's the same man—blue eyes and blond hair and pale skin—the same man. So what we have to do is what they did. They agreed to stop quarreling among themselves. Any little spat that they had, they'd settle it among themselves, go into a huddle—don't let the enemy know that you've got a disagreement.

Instead of airing our differences in public, we have to realize we're all the same family. And when you have a family squabble, you don't get out on the sidewalk. If you do, everybody calls you uncouth, unrefined, uncivilized, savage. If you don't make it at home, you settle it at home; you get in the closet, argue it out behind closed doors, and then when you come out on the street, you pose a common front, a united front. And this is what we need to do in the community, and in the city, and in the state. We need to stop airing our differences in front of the white man, put the white man out of our meetings, and then sit down and talk shop with each other. That's what we've got to do.

10   I would like to make a few comments concerning the difference between the black revolution and the Negro revolution. Are they both the same? And if they're not, what is the difference? What is the difference between a black revolution and a Negro revolution? First, what is a revolution? Sometimes I'm inclined to believe that many of

our people are using this word "revolution" loosely, without taking careful consideration of what this word actually means, and what its historic characteristics are. When you study the historic nature of revolutions, the motive of a revolution, the objective of a revolution, the result of a revolution, and the methods used in a revolution, you may change words. You may devise another program, you may change your goal and you may change your mind.

Look at the American Revolution in 1776. That revolution was for what? For land. Why did they want land? Independence. How was it carried out? Bloodshed. Number one, it was based on land, the basis of independence. And the only way they could get it was bloodshed. The French Revolution—what was it based on? The landless against the landlord. What was it for? Land. How did they get it? Bloodshed. Was no love lost, was no compromise, was no negotiation. I'm telling you—you don't know what a revolution is. Because when you find out what it is, you'll get back in the alley, you'll get out of the way.

The Russian Revolution—what was it based on? Land; the landless against the landlord. How did they bring it about? Bloodshed. You haven't got a revolution that doesn't involve bloodshed. And you're afraid to bleed. I said, you're afraid to bleed.

As long as the white man sent you to Korea, you bled. He sent you to Germany, you bled. He sent you to the South Pacific to fight the Japanese, you bled. You bleed for white people, but when it comes to seeing your own churches being bombed and little black girls murdered, you haven't got any blood. You bleed when the white man says bleed; you bite when the white man says bite; and you bark when the white man says bark. I hate to say this about us, but it's true. How are you going to be nonviolent in Mississippi, as violent as you were in Korea? How can you justify being nonviolent in Mississippi and Alabama, when your churches are being bombed, and your little girls are being murdered, and at the same time you are going to get violent with Hitler, and Tojo, and somebody else you don't even know?

If violence is wrong in America, violence is wrong abroad. If it is wrong to be violent defending black women and black children and black babies and black men, then it is wrong for America to draft us and make us violent abroad in defense of her. And if it is right for America to draft us, and teach us how to be violent in defense of her, then it is right for you and me to do whatever is necessary to defend our own people right here in this country.

15     The Chinese Revolution—they wanted land. They threw the British out, along with the Uncle Tom Chinese. Yes, they did. They set a

good example. When I was in prison, I read an article—don't be shocked when I say that I was in prison. You're still in prison. That's what America means: prison. When I was in prison, I read an article in *Life* magazine showing a little Chinese girl, nine years old; her father was on his hands and knees and she was pulling the trigger because he was an Uncle Tom Chinaman. When they had the revolution over there, they took a whole generation of Uncle Toms and just wiped them out. And within ten years that little girl became a full-grown woman. No more Toms in China. And today it's one of the toughest, roughest, most feared countries on this earth—by the white man. Because there are no Uncle Toms over there.

Of all our studies, history is best qualified to reward our research. And when you see that you've got problems, all you have to do is examine the historic method used all over the world by others who have problems similar to yours. Once you see how they got theirs straight, then you know how you can get yours straight. There's been a revolution, a black revolution, going on in Africa. In Kenya, the Mau Mau were revolutionary; they were the ones who brought the word "Uhuru" to the fore. The Mau Mau, they were revolutionary, they believed in scorched earth, they knocked everything aside that got in their way, and their revolution also was based on land, a desire for land. In Algeria, the northern part of Africa, a revolution took place. The Algerians were revolutionists, they wanted land. France offered to let them be integrated into France. They told France, to hell with France, they wanted some land, not some France. And they engaged in a bloody battle.

So I cite these various revolutions, brothers and sisters, to show you that you don't have a peaceful revolution. You don't have a turn-the-other-cheek revolution. There's no such thing as a nonviolent revolution. The only kind of revolution that is nonviolent is the Negro revolution. The only revolution in which the goal is loving your enemy is the Negro revolution. It's the only revolution in which the goal is a desegregated lunch counter, a desegregated theater, a desegregated park, and a desegregated public toilet; you can sit down next to white folks—on the toilet. That's no revolution. Revolution is based on land. Land is the basis of all independence. Land is the basis of freedom, justice, and equality.

The white man knows what a revolution is. He knows that the black revolution is world-wide in scope and in nature. The black revolution is sweeping Asia, is sweeping Africa, is rearing its head in Latin America. The Cuban Revolution—that's a revolution. They overturned the system. Revolution is in Asia, revolution is in Africa, and the white man is screaming because he sees revolution in Latin America. How do you think he'll react to you when you learn what a real revolution is? You don't know what a revolution is. If you did, you wouldn't use that word.

Revolution is bloody, revolution is hostile, revolution knows no compromise, revolution overturns and destroys everything that gets in its way. And you, sitting around here like a knot on the wall, saying, "I'm going to love these folks no matter how much they hate me." No, you need a revolution. Whoever heard of a revolution where they lock arms, as Rev. Cleage was pointing out beautifully, singing "We Shall Overcome"? You don't do that in a revolution. You don't do any singing, you're too busy swinging. It's based on land. A revolutionary wants land so he can set up his own nation, an independent nation. These Negroes aren't asking for any nation—they're trying to crawl back on the plantation.

20      When you want a nation, that's called nationalism. When the white man became involved in a revolution in this country against England, what was it for? He wanted this land so he could set up another white nation. That's white nationalism. The American Revolution was white nationalism. The French Revolution was white nationalism. The Russian Revolution too—yes, it was—white nationalism. You don't think so? Why do you think Khrushchev and Mao can't get their heads together? White nationalism. All the revolutions that are going on in Asia and Africa today are based on what?—black nationalism. A revolutionary is a black nationalist. He wants a nation. I was reading some beautiful words by Rev. Cleage, pointing out why he couldn't get together with someone else in the city because all of them were afraid of being identified with black nationalism. If you're afraid of black nationalism, you're afraid of revolution. And if you love revolution, you love black nationalism.

To understand this, you have to go back to what the young brother here referred to as the house Negro and the field Negro back during slavery. There were two kinds of slaves, the house Negro and the field Negro. The house Negroes—they lived in the house with master, they dressed pretty good, they ate good because they ate his food—what he left. They lived in the attic or the basement, but still they lived near the master; and they loved the master more than the master loved himself. They would give their life to save the master's house—quicker than the master would. If the master said, "We got a good house here," the house Negro would say, "Yeah, we got a good house here." Whenever the master said "we," he said "we." That's how you can tell a house Negro.

If the master's house caught on fire, the house Negro would fight harder to put the blaze out than the master would. If the master got sick, the house Negro would say, "What's the matter, boss, *we* sick?" *We* sick! He identified himself with his master, more than his master identified with himself. And if you came to the house Negro and said, "Let's run away, let's escape, let's separate," the house Negro would look at you and say, "Man, you crazy. What you mean, separate? Where is there a better house than this? Where can I wear better clothes than this? Where can I eat better food than this?" That was that house Negro. In those days he was called a "house nigger." And that's what we call them today, because we've still got some house niggers running around here.

This modern house Negro loves his master. He wants to live near him. He'll pay three times as much as the house is worth just to live near his master, and then brag about "I'm the only Negro out here." "I'm the only one on my job." "I'm the only one in this school." You're nothing but a house Negro. And if someone comes to you right now and says, "Let's separate," you say the same thing that the house Negro said on the plantation. "What you mean, separate? From America, this good white man? Where you going to get a better job than you get here?" I mean, this is what you say "I ain't left nothing in Africa," that's what you say. Why, you left your mind in Africa.

On that same plantation, there was the field Negro. The field Negroes—those were the masses. There were always more Negroes in the field than there were Negroes in the house. The Negro in the field caught hell. He ate leftovers. In the house they ate high up on the hog. The Negro in the field didn't get anything but what was left of the insides of the hog. They call it "chitt'lings" nowadays. In those days they called them what they were—guts. That's what you were—gut-eaters. And some of you are still gut-eaters.

25    The field Negro was beaten from morning to night; he lived in a shack, in a hut; he wore old, castoff clothes. He hated his master. I say he hated his master. He was intelligent. That house Negro loved his master, but that field Negro—remember, they were in the majority, and they hated the master. When the house caught on fire, he didn't try to put it out; that field Negro prayed for a wind, for a breeze. When the master got sick, the field Negro prayed that he'd die. If someone came to the field Negro and said, "Let's separate, let's run," he didn't say "Where we going?" He'd say, "Any place is better than here." You've got field Negroes in America today. I'm a field Negro. The masses are the field Negroes. When they see this man's house on fire, you don't hear the little Negroes talking about "*our* government is in

trouble." They say, "*The* government is in trouble." Imagine a Negro: "*Our* government"! I even heard one say "*our* astronauts." They won't even let him near the plant—and "*our* astronauts"! "*Our* Navy"— that's a Negro that is out of his mind, a Negro that is out of his mind.

Just as the slavemaster of that day used Tom, the house Negro, to keep the field Negroes in check, the same old slavemaster today has Negroes who are nothing but modern Uncle Toms, twentieth-century Uncle Toms, to keep you and me in check, to keep us under control, keep us passive and peaceful and nonviolent. That's Tom making you nonviolent. It's like when you go to the dentist, and the man's going to take your tooth. You're going to fight him when he starts pulling. So he squirts some stuff in your jaw called novocaine, to make you think they're not doing anything to you. So you sit there and because you've got all of that novocaine in your jaw, you suffer—peacefully. Blood running all down your jaw, and you don't know what's happening. Because someone has taught you to suffer—peacefully.

The white man does the same thing to you in the street, when he wants to put knots on your head and take advantage of you and not have to be afraid of your fighting back. To keep you from fighting back, he gets these old religious Uncle Toms to teach you and me, just like novocaine, to suffer peacefully. Don't stop suffering—just suffer peacefully. As Rev. Cleage pointed out, they say you should let your blood flow in the streets. This is a shame. You know he's a Christian preacher. If it's a shame to him, you know what it is to me.

There is nothing in our book, the Koran, that teaches us to suffer peacefully. Our religion teaches us to be intelligent. Be peaceful, be courteous, obey the law, respect everyone; but if someone puts his hand on you, send him to the cemetery. That's a good religion. In fact, that's that old-time religion. That's the one that Ma and Pa used to talk about: an eye for an eye, and a tooth for a tooth, and a head for a head, and a life for a life. That's a good religion. And nobody resents that kind of religion being taught but a wolf, who intends to make you his meal.

This is the way it is with the white man in America. He's a wolf— and you're sheep. Any time a shepherd, a pastor, teaches you and me not to run from the white man and, at the same time, teaches us not to fight the white man, he's a traitor to you and me. Don't lay down a life all by itself. No, preserve your life, it's the best thing you've got. And if you've got to give it up, let it be even-steven.

30  The slavemaster took Tom and dressed him well, fed him well and even gave him a little education—a *little* education; gave him a long coat and a top hat and made all the other slaves look up to him. Then

he used Tom to control them. The same strategy that was used in those days is used today, by the same white man. He takes a Negro, a so-called Negro, and makes him prominent, builds him up, publicizes him, makes him a celebrity. And then he becomes a spokesman for Negroes—and a Negro leader.

I would like to mention just one other thing quickly, and that is the method that the white man uses, how the white man uses the "big guns," or Negro leaders, against the Negro revolution. They are not a part of the Negro revolution. They are used against the Negro revolution.

When Martin Luther King failed to desegregate Albany, Georgia, the civil-rights struggle in America reached its low point. King became bankrupt almost, as a leader. The Southern Christian Leadership Conference was in financial trouble; and it was in trouble, period, with the people when they failed to desegregate Albany, Georgia. Other Negro civil-rights leaders of so-called national stature became fallen idols. As they became fallen idols, began to lose their prestige and influence, local Negro leaders began to stir up the masses. In Cambridge, Maryland, Gloria Richardson; in Danville, Virginia, and other parts of the country, local leaders began to stir up our people at the grass-roots level. This was never done by these Negroes of national stature. They control you, but they have never incited you or excited you. They control you, they contain you, they have kept you on the plantation.

As soon as King failed in Birmingham, Negroes took to the streets. King went out to California to a big rally and raised I don't know how many thousands of dollars. He came to Detroit and had a march and raised some more thousands of dollars. And recall, right after that Roy Wilkins attacked King. He accused King and CORE [Congress Of Racial Equality] of starting trouble everywhere and then making the NAACP [National Association for the Advancement of Colored People] get them out of jail and spend a lot of money; they accused King and CORE of raising all the money and not paying it back. This happened; I've got it in documented evidence in the newspaper. Roy started attacking King, and King started attacking Roy, and Farmer started attacking both of them. And as these Negroes of national stature began to attack each other, they began to lose their control of the Negro masses.

The Negroes were out there in the streets. They were talking about how they were going to march on Washington. Right at that time Birmingham had exploded, and the Negroes in Birmingham—remember, they also exploded. They began to stab the crackers in the back and bust them up 'side their head—yes, they did. That's when Kennedy sent in the troops, down in Birmingham. After that, Kennedy got on the television and said "this is a moral issue." That's when he said he was going to put out a civil-rights bill. And when he mentioned civil-rights bill and the Southern crackers started talking about how they were going to boycott or filibuster it, then the Negroes started talking—about what? That they were going to march on Washington, march on the Senate, march on the White House, march on the Congress, and tie it up, bring it to a halt, not let the government proceed. They even said they were going out to the airport and lay down on the runway and not let any airplanes land. I'm telling you what they said. That was revolution. That was revolution. That was the black revolution.

35     It was the grass roots out there in the street. It scared the white man to death, scared the white power structure in Washington, D.C., to death; I was there. When they found out that this black steamroller was going to come down on the capital, they called in Wilkins, they called in Randolph, they called in these national Negro leaders that you respect and told them, "Call it off." Kennedy said, "Look, you all are letting this thing go too far." And Old Tom said, "Boss, I can't stop it, because I didn't start it." I'm telling you what they said. They said, "I'm not even in it, much less at the head of it." They said, "These Negroes are doing things on their own. They're running ahead of us." And that old shrewd fox, he said, "If you all aren't in it, I'll put you in it. I'll put you at the head of it. I'll endorse it. I'll welcome it. I'll help it. I'll join it."

A matter of hours went by. They had a meeting at the Carlyle Hotel in New York City. The Carlyle Hotel is owned by the Kennedy family; that's the hotel Kennedy spent the night at, two nights ago; it belongs to his family. A philanthropic society headed by a white man named Stephen Currier called all the top civil-rights leaders together at the Carlyle Hotel. And he told them, "By you all fighting each other, you are destroying the civil-rights movement. And since you're fighting over money from white liberals, let us set up what is known as the Council for United Civil Rights Leadership. Let's form this council, and all the civil-rights organizations will belong to it, and we'll use it for fund-raising purposes." Let me show you how tricky the white man is. As soon as they got it formed, they elected Whitney Young as its chairman, and who do you think became the co-chairman? Stephen Currier, the white man, a millionaire. Powell was talking about it down at Cobo Hall today. This is what he was talking about.

Powell knows it happened. Randolph knows it happened. Wilkins knows it happened. King knows it happened. Every one of that Big Six—they know it happened.

Once they formed it, with the white man over it, he promised them and gave them $800,000 to split up among the Big Six; and told them that after the march was over they'd give them $700,000 more. A million and a half dollars—split up between leaders that you have been following, going to jail for, crying crocodile tears for. And they're nothing but Frank James and Jesse James and the what-do-you-call-'em brothers.

As soon as they got the setup organized, the white man made available to them top public-relations experts; opened the news media across the country at their disposal, which then began to project these Big Six as the leaders of the march. Originally they weren't even in the march. You were talking this march talk on Hastings Street, you were talking march talk on Lenox Avenue, and on Fillmore Street, and on Central Avenue, and 32nd Street and 63rd Street. That's where the march talk was being talked. But the white man put the Big Six at the head of it; made them the march. They became the march. They took it over. And the first move they made after they took it over, they invited Walter Reuther, a white man; they invited a priest, a rabbi, and an old white preacher, yes, an old white preacher. The same white element that put Kennedy into power—labor, the Catholics, the Jews, and liberal Protestants; the same clique that put Kennedy in power, joined the march on Washington.

It's just like when you've got some coffee that's too black, which means it's too strong. What do you do? You integrate it with cream, you make it weak. But if you pour too much cream in it, you won't even know you ever had coffee. It used to be hot, it becomes cool. It used to be strong, it becomes weak. It used to wake you up, now it puts you to sleep. This is what they did with the march on Washington. They joined it. They didn't integrate it, they infiltrated it. They joined it, became a part of it, took it over. And as they took it over, it lost its militancy. It ceased to be angry, it ceased to be hot, it ceased to be uncompromising. Why, it even ceased to be a march. It became a picnic, a circus. Nothing but a circus, with clowns and all. You had one right here in Detroit—I saw it on television—with clowns leading it, white clowns and black clowns. I know you don't like what I'm saying, but I'm going to tell you anyway. Because I can prove what I'm saying. If you think I'm telling you wrong, you bring me Martin Luther King and A. Philip Randolph and James Farmer and those other three, and see if they'll deny it over a microphone.

40    No, it was a sellout. It was a takeover. When James Baldwin came in from Paris, they wouldn't let him talk, because they couldn't make him go by the script. Burt Lancaster read the speech that Baldwin was supposed to make; they wouldn't let Baldwin get up there, because they know Baldwin is liable to say anything. They controlled it so tight, they told those Negroes what time to hit town, how to come, where to stop, what signs to carry, what song to sing, what speech they could make, and what speech they couldn't make; and then told them to get out of town by sundown. And every one of those Toms was out of town by sundown. Now I know you don't like my saying this. But I can back it up. It was a circus, a performance that beat anything Hollywood could ever do, the performance of the year. Reuther and those other three devils should get an Academy Award for the best actors because they acted like they really loved Negroes and fooled a whole lot of Negroes. And the six Negro leaders should get an award too, for the best supporting cast.

## Questions for Discussion

To what extent would you say that Malcolm X's "message" is a direct response to King's "Letter from Birmingham Jail"?

Does Malcolm X's use of history and historical episodes help his case?

*Lewis H. Van Dusen, Jr. (1910–) has been practicing law in Phila-
delphia since 1935 and served as president of the Pennsylvania Bar
Association in 1974–1975. Decorated for valor during World War II, he
also served with the State Department during his distinguished career. He
has written many essays for professional journals; the following one
appeared in 1969 in the* American Bar Association Journal.

# Lewis H. Van Dusen, Jr.

# Civil Disobedience: Destroyer of Democracy

As Charles E. Wyzanski, Chief Judge of the United States District
Court in Boston, wrote in the February 1968, *Atlantic:* "Disobedience
is a long step from dissent. Civil disobedience involves a deliberate and
punishable breach of legal duty." Protesters might prefer a different
definition. They would rather say that civil disobedience is the peaceful resistance of conscience.

The philosophy of civil disobedience was not developed in our
American democracy, but in the very first democracy of Athens. It was
expressed by the poet Sophocles and the philosopher Socrates. In
Sophocles' tragedy, Antigone chose to obey her conscience and violate
the state edict against providing burial for her brother, who had been
decreed a traitor. When the dictator Creon found out that Antigone
had buried her fallen brother, he confronted her and reminded her
that there was a mandatory death penalty for this deliberate disobedience of the state law. Antigone nobly replied, "Nor did I think your orders were so strong that you, a mortal man, could overrun the gods'
unwritten and unfailing laws."

Conscience motivated Antigone. She was not testing the validity of
the law in the hope that eventually she would be sustained. Appealing
to the judgment of the community, she explained her action to the chorus. She was not secret and surreptitious—the interment of her brother
was open and public. She was not violent; she did not trespass on another citizen's rights. And finally, she accepted without resistance the
death sentence—the penalty for violation. By voluntarily accepting the
law's sanctions, she was not a revolutionary denying the authority of

the state. Antigone's behavior exemplifies the classic case of civil disobedience.

Socrates believed that reason could dictate a conscientious disobedience of state law, but he also believed that he had to accept the legal sanctions of the state. In Plato's *Crito*, Socrates from his hanging basket accepted the death penalty for his teaching of religion to youths contrary to state laws.

5    The sage of Walden, Henry David Thoreau, took this philosophy of nonviolence and developed it into a strategy for solving society's injustices. First enunciating it in protest against the Mexican War, he then turned it to use against slavery. For refusing to pay taxes that would help pay the enforcers of the fugitive slave law, he went to prison. In Thoreau's words, "If the alternative is to keep all just men in prison or to give up slavery, the state will not hesitate which to choose."

Sixty years later, Gandhi took Thoreau's civil disobedience as his strategy to wrest Indian independence from England. The famous salt march against a British imperial tax is his best-known example of protest.

But the conscientious law breaking of Socrates, Gandhi, and Thoreau is to be distinguished from the conscientious law testing of Martin Luther King, Jr., who was not a civil disobedient. The civil disobedient withholds taxes or violates state laws knowing he is legally wrong, but believing he is morally right. While he wrapped himself in the mantle of Gandhi and Thoreau, Dr. King led his followers in violation of state laws he believed were contrary to the Federal Constitution. But since Supreme Court decisions in the end generally upheld his many actions, he should not be considered a true civil disobedient.

The civil disobedience of Antigone is like that of the pacifist who withholds paying the percentage of his taxes that goes to the Defense Department, or the Quaker who travels against State Department regulations to Hanoi to distribute medical supplies, or the Vietnam war protester who tears up his draft card. This civil disobedient has been nonviolent in his defiance of the law; he has been unfurtive in his violation; he has been submissive to the penalties of the law. He has neither evaded the law nor interfered with another's rights. He has been neither a rioter nor a revolutionary. The thrust of his cause has not been the might of coercion but the martyrdom of conscience.

# Was the Boston Tea Party Civil Disobedience?

Those who justify violence and radical action as being in the tradition of our Revolution show a misunderstanding of the philosophy of democracy.

10     James Farmer, former head of the Congress of Racial Equality, in defense of the mass action confrontation method, has told of a famous organized demonstration that took place in opposition to political and economic discrimination. The protestors beat back and scattered the law enforcers and then proceeded to loot and destroy private property. Mr. Farmer then said he was talking about the Boston Tea Party and implied that violence as a method for redress of grievances was an American tradition and a legacy of our revolutionary heritage. While it is true that there is no more sacred document than our Declaration of Independence, Jefferson's "inherent right of rebellion" was predicated on the tyrannical denial of democratic means. If there is no popular assembly to provide an adjustment of ills, and if there is no court system to dispose of injustices, then there is, indeed, a right to rebel.

The seventeenth century's John Locke, the philosophical father of the Declaration of Independence, wrote in his *Second Treatise on Civil Government*: "Wherever law ends, tyranny begins . . . and the people are absolved from any further obedience. Governments are dissolved from within when the legislative [chamber] is altered. When the government [becomes] . . . arbitrary disposers of lives, liberties and fortunes of the people, such revolutions happen. . . ."

But there are some sophisticated proponents of the revolutionary redress of grievances who say that the test of the need for radical action is not the unavailability of democratic institutions but the ineffectuality of those institutions to remove blatant social inequalities. If social injustice exists, they say, concerted disobedience is required against the constituted government, whether it be totalitarian or democratic in structure.

Of course, only the most bigoted chauvinist would claim that America is without some glaring faults. But there has never been a utopian society on earth and there never will be unless human nature is remade. Since inequities will mar even the best-framed democracies, the injustice rationale would allow a free right of civil resistance to be available always as a shortcut alternative to the democratic way of petition, debate and assembly. The lesson of history is that civil insurgency spawns far more injustices than it removes. The Jeffersons, Washingtons, and Adamses resisted tyranny with the aim of promoting the procedures of democracy. They would never have resisted a democratic government with the risk of promoting the techniques of tyranny.

## Legitimate Pressures and Illegitimate Results

There are many civil rights leaders who show impatience with the process of democracy. They rely on the sit-ins, boycott or mass picketing to gain speedier solutions to the problems that face every citizen. But we must realize that the legitimate pressures that won concessions in the past can easily escalate into the illegitimate power plays that might extort demands in the future. The victories of these civil rights leaders must not shake our confidence in the democratic procedures, as the pressures of demonstration are desirable only if they take place within the limits allowed by law. Civil rights gains should continue to be won by the persuasion of Congress and other legislative bodies and by the decision of courts. Any illegal entreaty for the rights of some can be an injury to the rights of others, for mass demonstrations often trigger violence.

15     Those who advocate taking the law into their own hands should reflect that when they are disobeying what they consider to be an immoral law, they are deciding on a possibly immoral course. Their answer is that the process for democratic relief is too slow, that only mass confrontation can bring immediate action, and that any injuries are the inevitable cost of the pursuit of justice. Their answer is, simply put, that the end justifies the means. It is this justification of any form of demonstration as a form of dissent that threatens to destroy a society built on the rule of law.

Our Bill of Rights guarantees wide opportunities to use mass meetings, public parades, and organized demonstrations to stimulate sentiment, to dramatize issues, and to cause change. The Washington freedom march of 1963 was such a call for action. But the rights of free expression cannot be mere force cloaked in the garb of free speech. As the courts have decreed in labor cases, free assembly does not mean mass picketing or sit-down strikes. These rights are subject to limitations of time and place so as to secure the rights of others. When militant students storm a college president's office to achieve demands, when certain groups plan rush-hour car stalling to protest discrimination in employment, these are not dissent, but a denial of rights to others. Neither is it the lawful use of mass protest, but rather the unlawful use of mob power.

Justice Black, one of the foremost advocates and defenders of the right of protest and dissent, has said:

> . . . Experience demonstrates that it is not a far step from what to many seems to be the earnest, honest, patriotic, kind-spirited multitude of today, to the fanatical, threatening, lawless mob of tomorrow. And the crowds that press in the streets for noble goals today can be supplanted tomorrow by street mobs pressuring the courts for precisely opposite ends.[1]

Society must censure those demonstrators who would trespass on the public peace, as it must condemn those rioters whose pillage would destroy the public peace. But more ambivalent is society's posture toward the civil disobedient. Unlike the rioter, the true civil disobedient commits no violence. Unlike the mob demonstrator, he commits no trespass on others' rights. The civil disobedient, while deliberately violating a law, shows an oblique respect for the law by voluntarily submitting to its sanctions. He neither resists arrest nor evades punishment. Thus, he breaches the law but not the peace.

But civil disobedience, whatever the ethical rationalization, is still an assault on our democratic society, an affront to our legal order and an attack on our constitutional government. To indulge civil disobedience is to invite anarchy, and the permissive arbitrariness of anarchy is hardly less tolerable than the repressive arbitrariness of tyranny. Too often the license of liberty is followed by the loss of liberty, because into the desert of anarchy comes the man on horseback, a Mussolini or a Hitler.

## Violations of Law Subvert Democracy

20 Law violations, even for ends recognized as laudable, are not only assaults on the rule of law, but subversions of the democratic process. The disobedient act of conscience does not ennoble democracy; it erodes it.

First, it courts violence, and even the most careful and limited use of nonviolent acts of disobedience may help sow the dragon-teeth of civil riot. Civil disobedience is the progenitor of disorder, and disorder is the sire of violence.

Second, the concept of civil disobedience does not invite principles of general applicability. If the children of light are morally privileged to resist particular laws on grounds of conscience, so are the children

---

[1] In *Cox v. Louisiana*, 379 U.S. 536, 575, 584 (1965).

of darkness. Former Deputy Attorney General Burke Marshall said: "If the decision to break the law really turned on individual conscience, it is hard to see in law how [the civil rights leader] is better off than former Governor Ross Barnett of Mississippi who also believed deeply in his cause and was willing to go to jail."[2]

Third, even the most noble act of civil disobedience assaults the rule of law. Although limited as to method, motive and objective, it has the effect of inducing others to engage in different forms of law breaking characterized by methods unsanctioned and condemned by classic theories of law violation. Unfortunately, the most patent lesson of civil disobedience is not so much nonviolence of action as defiance of authority.

Finally, the greatest danger in condoning civil disobedience as a permissible strategy for hastening change is that it undermines our democratic processes. To adopt the techniques of civil disobedience is to assume that representative government does not work. To resist the decisions of courts and the laws of elected assemblies is to say that democracy has failed.

25     There is no man who is above the law, and there is no man who has a right to break the law. Civil disobedience is not above the law, but against the law. When the civil disobedient disobeys one law, he invariably subverts all law. When the civil disobedient says that he is above the law, he is saying that democracy is beneath him. His disobedience shows a distrust for the democratic system. He is merely saying that since democracy does not work, why should he help make it work. Thoreau expressed well the civil disobedient's disdain for democracy:

> As for adopting the ways which the state has provided for remedying the evil, I know not of such ways. They take too much time and a man's life will be gone. I have other affairs to attend to. I came into this world not chiefly to make this a good place to live in, but to live in it, be it good or bad.[3]

Thoreau's position is not only morally irresponsible but politically reprehensible. When citizens in a democracy are called on to make a profession of faith, the civil disobedients offer only a confession of failure. Tragically, when civil disobedients for lack of faith abstain from democratic involvement, they help attain their own gloomy prediction. They help create the social and political basis for their own despair. By foreseeing failure, they help forge it. If citizens rely on antidemocratic

---

[2] "The Protest movement and the Law," *Virginia Legal Review* 51 (1965), 785.
[3] Thoreau, "Civil Disobedience" (see page 334).

means of protest, they will help bring about the undemocratic result of an authoritarian or anarchic state.

How far demonstrations properly can be employed to produce political and social change is a pressing question, particularly in view of the provocations accompanying the National Democratic Convention in Chicago last August and the reaction of the police to them. A line must be drawn by the judiciary between the demands of those who seek absolute order, which can lead only to a dictatorship, and those who seek absolute freedom, which can lead only to anarchy. The line, wherever it is drawn by our courts, should be respected on the college campus, on the streets, and elsewhere.

Undue provocation will inevitably result in overreaction, human emotions being what they are. Violence will follow. This cycle undermines the very democracy it is designed to preserve. The lesson of the past is that democracies will fall if violence, including the intentional provocations that will lead to violence, replaces democratic procedures, as in Athens, Rome, and the Weimar Republic. This lesson must be constantly explained by the legal profession.

We should heed the words of William James:

> Democracy is still upon its trial. The civic genius of our people is its only bulwark and . . . neither battleships nor public libraries nor great newspapers nor booming stocks: neither mechanical invention nor political adroitness, nor churches nor universities nor civil service examinations can save us from degeneration if the inner mystery be lost.

30    That mystery, at once the secret and the glory of our English-speaking race, consists of nothing but two habits. . . . [O]ne of them is the habit of trained and disciplined good temper towards the opposite party when it fairly wins its innings. The other is that of fierce and merciless resentment toward every man or set of men who break the public peace.[4]

## Questions for Discussion

Examine the placement of Van Dusen's claims—is there anything significant about the arrangement of his argument?

How does Van Dusen treat his audience? Does he show understanding for other opinions? Are there any counterclaims that he hasn't considered?

---

[4] James, *Pragmatism* (1907), pp. 127–128.

*In order to help his family earn a living during the Great Depression,*
**Cesar Estrada Chavez** *(1927–1993) left school after the eighth grade
and began working throughout the Southwest as an itinerant fruit and
vegetable picker. He thus experienced firsthand the hardships of the
migrant farmworkers, whose livelihood depends on seasonal harvests
and who toil in difficult working conditions. After serving in the Navy in
World War II, Chavez returned to the migrant community and in 1948
began what would turn into a lifelong struggle for safe working conditions and livable wages for seasonal agriculture workers. In 1962, Chavez
formed the National Farm Workers Association, later renamed the United
Farm Workers. In the tradition of Martin Luther King, Jr., and Mahatma
Gandhi, Chavez led successful hunger strikes and product boycotts,
including a five-year boycott of table grapes, to raise public awareness.
In 1977, the UFW finally earned the right to represent migrant field
workers. Chavez's lifetime commitment to social and economic justice was
posthumously recognized in 1994, when President Clinton awarded him
the Presidential Medal of Freedom. Chavez delivered the following speech
on January 12, 1990, in observance of Martin Luther King, Jr.'s birthday.*

# Cesar Chavez

# Lessons of Dr. Martin Luther King, Jr.

My friends, today we honor a giant among men; today we honor the
reverend Martin Luther King, Jr. Dr. King was a powerful figure of
destiny, of courage, of sacrifice, and of vision. Few people in the long
history of this nation can rival his accomplishment, his reason, or his
selfless dedication to the cause of peace and social justice. Today we
honor a wise teacher, an inspiring leader, and a true visionary, but to
truly honor Dr. King we must do more than say words of praise. We
must learn his lessons and put his views into practice, so that we may
truly be free at last.

Who was Dr. King?

Many people will tell you of his wonderful qualities and his many
accomplishments, but what makes him special to me, the truth many
people don't want you to remember, is that Dr. King was a great activist, fighting for radical social change with radical methods. While

other people talked about change, Dr. King used direct action to challenge the system. He welcomed it, and used it wisely. In his famous "Letter from the Birmingham Jail," Dr. King wrote that "The purpose of direct action is to create a situation so crisis-packed that it will inevitably open the door to negotiation."

Dr. King was also radical in his beliefs about violence. He learned how to successfully fight hatred and violence with the unstoppable power of nonviolence. He once stopped an armed mob, saying: "We are not advocating violence. We want to love our enemies. I want you to love our enemies. Be good to them. This is what we live by. We must meet hate with love." Dr. King knew that he very probably wouldn't survive the struggle that he led so well. But he said "If I am stopped, the movement will not stop. If I am stopped, our work will not stop. For what we are doing is right. What we are doing is just, and God is with us."

5    My friends, as we enter a new decade, it should be clear to all of us that there is an unfinished agenda, that we have miles to go before we reach the promised land. The men who rule this country today never learned the lessons of Dr. King, they never learned that non-violence is the only way to peace and justice. Our nation continues to wage war upon its neighbors, and upon itself. The powers that be rule over a racist society, filled with hatred and ignorance. Our nation continues to be segregated along racial and economic lines. The powers that be make themselves richer by exploiting the poor. Our nation continues to allow children to go hungry, and will not even house its own people.

The time is now for people, of all races and backgrounds, to sound the trumpets of change. As Dr. King proclaimed "There comes a time when people get tired of being trampled over by the iron feet of oppression." My friends, the time for action is upon us. The enemies of justice want you to think of Dr. King as only a civil rights leader, but he had a much broader agenda. He was a tireless crusader for the rights of the poor, for an end to the war in Vietnam long before it was popular to take that stand, and for the rights of workers everywhere.

Many people find it convenient to forget that Martin was murdered while supporting a desperate strike on that tragic day in Memphis, Tennessee. He died while fighting for the rights of sanitation workers. Dr. King's dedication to the rights of the workers who are so often exploited by the forces of greed has profoundly touched my life and guided my struggle. During my first fast in 1968, Dr. King reminded me that our struggle was his struggle too. He sent me a telegram which said "Our separate struggles are really one. A struggle for freedom, for dignity, and for humanity." I was profoundly moved that someone facing such a tremendous struggle himself would take the time to worry about a struggle taking place on the other side of the continent.

Just as Dr. King was a disciple of Gandhi and Christ, we must now be Dr. King's disciples. Dr. King challenged us to work for a greater humanity. I only hope that we are worthy of his challenge. The United Farm Workers are dedicated to carrying on the dream of Reverend Martin Luther King, Jr. My friends, I would like to tell you about the struggle of the farmworkers who are waging a desperate struggle for our rights, for our children's rights and for our very lives.

Many decades ago the chemical industry promised the growers that pesticides would bring great wealth and bountiful harvests to the fields. Just recently, the experts are learning what farmworkers, and the truly organized farmers have known for years. The prestigious National Academy of Sciences recently concluded an exhaustive five-year study which determined that pesticides do not improve profits and do not produce more crops. What, then, is the effect of pesticides? Pesticides have created a legacy of pain, and misery, and death for farmworkers and consumers alike.

10    The crop which poses the greatest danger, and the focus of our struggle, is the table grape crop. These pesticides soak the fields. They drift with the wind, pollute the water, and are eaten by unwitting consumers. These poisons are designed to kill, and pose a very real threat to consumers and farmworkers alike. The fields are sprayed with pesticides like Captan, Parathion, Phosdrin, and Methyl Bromide. These poisons cause cancer, DNA mutation, and horrible birth defects.

The Central Valley of California is one of the wealthiest agricultural regions in the world. In its midst are clusters of children dying from cancer. The children live in communities surrounded by the grape fields that employ their parents. The children come into contact with the poisons when they play outside, when they drink the water, and when they hug their parents returning from the fields. And the children are dying.

They are dying slow, painful, cruel deaths in towns called cancer clusters, in cancer clusters like McFarland, where the children's cancer rate is 800 percent above normal. A few months ago, the parents of a brave little girl in the agricultural community of Earlimart came to the United Farm Workers to ask for help. The Ramirez family knew about our protests in nearby McFarland and thought there might be a similar problem in Earlimart. Our union members went door to door in Earlimart, and found that the Ramirez family's worst fears were true:

There are at least four other children suffering from cancer in the little town of Earlimart, a rate 1200 percent above normal. In Earlimart, little Jimmy Caudillo died recently from leukemia at the age of three. Three other young children in Earlimart, in addition to Jimmy and Natalie, are suffering from similar fatal diseases that the experts believe are caused by pesticides. These same pesticides can be found on the grapes you buy in the stores.

My friends, the suffering must end. So many children are dying, so many babies are born without limbs and vital organs, so many workers are dying in the fields. We have no choice, we must stop the plague of pesticides.

15   The growers responsible for this outrage are blinded by greed, by racism, and by power. The same inhumanity displayed at Selma, in Birmingham, in so many of Dr. King's battlegrounds, is displayed every day in the vineyards of California. The farm labor system in place today is a system of economic slavery.

My friends, even those farmworkers who do not have to bury their young children are suffering from abuse, neglect, and poverty. Our workers labor for many hours every day under the hot sun, often without safe drinking water or toilet facilities. Our workers are constantly subjected to incredible pressures and intimidation to meet excessive quotas. The women who work in the fields are routinely subjected to sexual harassment and sexual assaults by the growers' thugs. When our workers complain, or try to organize, they are fired, assaulted, and even murdered. Just as Bull Connor turned the dogs loose on nonviolent marchers in Alabama, the growers turn armed foremen on innocent farmworkers in California.

The stench of injustice in California should offend every American. Some people, especially those who just don't care, or don't understand, like to think that the government can take care of these problems. The government should, but won't. The growers used their wealth to buy good friends like Governor George Deukmajian, Ronald Reagan, and George Bush.

My friends, if we are going to end the suffering, we must use the same people power that vanquished injustice in Montgomery, Selma, and Birmingham. I have seen many boycotts succeed. Dr. King showed us the way with the bus boycott, and with our first boycott we were able to get DDT, Aldrin, and Dieldrin banned in our first contracts with grape growers. Now, even more urgently, we are trying to get deadly pesticides banned. The growers and their allies have tried to stop us for years with intimidation, with character assassination, with public relations campaigns, with outright lies, and with murder. But those same tactics did not stop Dr. King, and they will not stop us.

Once social change begins, it cannot be reversed. You cannot un-educate the person who has learned to read. You cannot humiliate the person who feels pride. And you cannot oppress the people who are not afraid anymore.

20    In our life and death struggle for justice we have turned to the court of last resort: the American people. And the people are ruling in our favor. As a result, grape sales keep falling. We have witnessed truckloads of grapes being dumped because no one would stop to buy them. As demand drops, so do prices and profits. The growers are un-der tremendous economic pressure.

We are winning, but there is still much hard work ahead of us. I hope that you will join our struggle. The simple act of refusing to buy table grapes laced with pesticides is a powerful statement that the growers understand. Economic pressure is the only language the grow-ers speak, and they are beginning to listen. Please, boycott table grapes. For your safety, for the workers, and for the children, we must act together.

My friends, Dr. King realized that the only real wealth comes from helping others. I challenge each and every one of you to be a true dis-ciple of Dr. King, to be truly wealthy. I challenge you to carry on his work by volunteering to work for a just cause you believe in. Consider joining our movement because the farmworkers, and so many other oppressed peoples, depend upon the unselfish dedication of its volun-teers, people just like you.

Thousands of people have worked for our cause and have gone on to achieve success in many different fields. Our non-violent cause will give you skills that will last a lifetime. When Dr. King sounded the call for justice, the freedom riders answered the call in droves. I am giving you the same opportunity to join the same cause, to free your fellow human beings from the yoke of oppression.

I have faith that in this audience there are men and women with the same courage and the same idealism that put young Martin Luther King, Jr. on the path to social change. I challenge you to join the strug-gle of the United Farm Workers. And if you don't join our cause, then seek out the many organizations seeking peaceful social change. Seek out the many outstanding leaders who will speak to you this week, and make a difference.

25     If we fail to learn that each and every person can make a difference, then we will have betrayed Dr. King's life's work. The Reverend Martin Luther King, Jr. had more than just a dream, he had the love and the faith to act.

God bless you.

## Questions for Discussion

What does Chavez's speech argue for? What is his primary focus? What are his secondary purposes?

In what ways does Chavez exploit Martin Luther King, Jr. and his ideas to his own end?

What kind of balance does Chavez strike between logical and emotional appeals in the speech? Do they complement each other?

*In order to dramatize the justice of labor reform for migrant farm work-
ers, Cesar Chavez and his followers in California copied the tactics of
nonviolent resistance employed in the civil rights movement. In 1968, for
example, when tensions between police and protesters were highly in-
flamed, Chavez went on a hunger strike to underscore the need for nonviolence and justice in the campaign against grape growers. The visual argument on this page comments powerfully on that strike; the one on the
next page indicates that the struggle was still continuing five years later.*

# Visual Arguments: Nonviolent Resistance in the Hispanic Community

Senator Robert Kennedy, running for President of the United
States, breaks bread during a Mass of Thanksgiving. The
ceremony marked the end of Chavez's 23-day hunger strike,
March 10, 1968.

A deputy sheriff restrains a terrified teenage picketer during a police attack on farmworkers near Edison, California, August 1, 1973. The protester is wearing a scarf designed to help ward off tear gas.

# PART SIX

# BECOMING AMERICA(N):
## IMMIGRATION AND ASSIMILATION

Just about everyone can quote parts of the famous inscription on the base of New York's Statue of Liberty—"Give me your tired, your poor, your huddled masses, yearning to be free. / The wretched refuse of your teeming shore, send these, the homeless, tempest-tost to me"—because the United States prides itself on being a nation of immigrants. And recently the nation has made good on the promise, it seems: More than 10 percent of our people, over 30 million in all (and up from 10 million in 1970), were born in other countries. Steady increases in immigration after World War II developed into a boom during the 1980s and 1990s in part because the 1965 Immigration Act (amended in 1990) looked favorably on the immigration of relatives of U.S. citizens, repealed quotas on immigrants from certain nations, and therefore encouraged immigrants from Asia, Latin America, and Africa. While immigrants in the late nineteenth and early twentieth century mostly came from southern and central Europe (a wave of such immigrants between 1890 and 1920 peaked at 1.3 million people in 1907), most of today's immigrants come from Mexico, the Caribbean islands, the former Soviet Union, and Asian

nations such as China, Vietnam, the Philippines, and India. While those earlier immigrants typically passed by the Statue of Liberty and were processed at Ellis Island (opened in 1892) before going on to northern cities, more than half of recent immigrants have been attracted to Florida, Texas, and California.

Nevertheless, there has also been a long history of resistance to immigration in the United States, dating at least to those who proudly enrolled in the "Know Nothing" political party of the 1840s and 1850s. Members of that political faction, as you may have seen in the 2002 film *The Gangs of New York*, resisted the immigrants arriving from famine-torn Ireland and politically unstable Germany, and they and their successors have tended to blame all the nation's ills on immigration—crime, economic problems, social stresses. The questions (and fears) raised by those early critics persist today, except that now they are raised in connection with Asians, Arabs, and Latin

Americans.

Just what are the social and economic effects of immigration? How quickly and how completely do immigrants become assimilated— learning the majority language, identifying themselves with American cultural values, participating in American political life? Do immigrants constitute a threat to the nation's economic well-being because they are commonly poor and less educated, because they take jobs away from native workers, and because they require expensive social services—welfare, education, health? Or do immigrants in fact increase the national wealth because they are highly motivated and because they supply labor to a perennially labor-hungry economy? Do immigrants endanger our national democracy because they cling to their original national identities, are slow to learn English, and participate only fitfully in political life—or do immigrants assimilate well, enriching the nation with their values and beliefs, ideas and ideals, hopes and hard work?

Here we reprint several arguments that address those questions. In praise of immigration are Emma Lazarus's nineteenth-century poem "The New Colossus" and James Fallows's recent essay "Immigration— How It's Affecting Us." Rebuttals are by Thomas Bailey Aldrich (in his nineteenth-century poem "The Unguarded Gates") and by Francis Walker, whose "Restriction of Immigration" was published in 1896, just as a wave of immigrants was passing through Ellis Island. Visual arguments on immigration—Ellis Island and after—are also included. As for the attractiveness of coming to America, St. Jean de Crèvecoeur, writing at the time of the nation's founding, provides a sunny advertisement for immigration—"What Is an American?"—that is contradicted by Leslie Marmon Silko's more recent, more biting appraisal. Finally, three writers provide very thoughtful and very different perspectives on the challenges associated with assimilation: James Baldwin (an African American), Richard Rodriguez (a Hispanic American), and Amy Tan (an Asian American).

*The title question of the following argument was timely indeed when it
was posed by its author in the early years of the new American nation.*
**St. Jean de Crèvecoeur** *was born in France in 1735, and educated there
and in England. In 1755 he came to the New World, traveled extensively
for a decade, and settled into a farmer's life in Orange County, New York.
His agricultural vocation was interrupted by the Revolutionary War (he
was sympathetic to the British), and he was forced to return to Europe
where in 1782 he published* Letters from an American Farmer, *a series of
twelve epistolary essays describing the new American nation: one of those
"letters" was "What Is an American?" De Crèvecoeur finished his career in
Europe as a successful diplomat working to improve relations between
England, France, and the new United States. He died in 1813.*

*What follows is actually an excerpt from Letter III (the paragraphs
that have been deleted deal with the religious communities in America,
the ways of life of the frontier settlers, and descriptions of how Americans
differ from Europeans). Do you agree with those who hold that this piece
amounts to an argument advertising the new nation to skeptical English
men and women?*

## St. Jean de Crèvecoeur

# What Is an American?

I wish I could be acquainted with the feelings and thoughts which
must agitate the heart and present themselves to the mind of an enlightened Englishman, when he first lands on this continent. He must
greatly rejoice that he lived at a time to see this fair country discovered
and settled. He must necessarily feel a share of national pride when he
views the chain of settlements which embellish these extended shores.
When he says to himself, this is the work of my countrymen, who,
when convulsed by factions, afflicted by a variety of miseries and
wants, restless and impatient, took refuge here. They brought along
with them their national genius, to which they principally owe what
liberty they enjoy and what substance they possess. Here he sees the
industry of his native country displayed in a new manner, and traces,
in their works, the embryos of all the arts, sciences, and ingenuity,
which flourish in Europe. Here he beholds fair cities, substantial villages, extensive fields, an immense country filled with decent houses,
good roads, orchards, meadows, and bridges, where, a hundred years
ago, all was wild, woody, and uncultivated! What a train of pleasing

ideas this fair spectacle must suggest! It is a prospect which must inspire a good citizen with the most heartfelt pleasure! The difficulty consists in the manner of viewing so extensive a scene. He is arrived on a new continent: a modern society offers itself to his contemplation, different from what he had hitherto seen. It is not composed, as in Europe, of great lords who possess every thing, and of a herd of people who have nothing. Here are no aristocratical families, no courts, no kings, no bishops, no ecclesiastical dominion, no invisible power giving to a few a very visible one, no great manufactures employing thousands, no great refinements of luxury. The rich and the poor are not so far removed from each other as they are in Europe. Some few towns excepted, we are all tillers of the earth, from Nova Scotia to West Florida. We are a people of cultivators, scattered over an immense territory, communicating with each other by means of good roads and navigable rivers, united by the silken bands of mild government, all respecting the laws, without dreading their power, because they are equitable. We are all animated with the spirit of an industry which is unfettered and unrestrained, because each person works for himself. If he travels through our rural districts, he views not the hostile castle and the haughty mansion contrasted with the clay-built hut and miserable cabin, where cattle and men help to keep each other warm, and dwell in meanness, smoke, and indigence. A pleasing uniformity of decent competence appears throughout our habitations. The meanest of our log-houses is a dry and comfortable habitation. Lawyer or merchant are the fairest titles our towns afford: that of a farmer is the only appellation of the rural inhabitants of our country. It must take some time ere he can reconcile himself to our dictionary, which is but short in words of dignity and names of honour. There, on a Sunday, he sees a congregation of respectable farmers and their wives, all clad in neat homespun, well mounted, or riding in their own humble waggons. There is not among them an esquire, saving the unlettered magistrate. There he sees a parson as simple as his flock, a farmer who does not riot on the labour of others. We have no princes, for whom we toil, starve, and bleed. We are the most perfect society now existing in the world. Here man is free as he ought to be; nor is this pleasing equality so transitory as many others are. Many ages will not see the shores of our great lakes replenished with inland nations, nor the unknown bounds of North America entirely peopled. Who can tell how far it extends? Who can tell the millions of men whom it will feed and contain? for no European foot has, as yet, travelled half the extent of this mighty continent.

The next wish of this traveller will be, to know whence came all these people? They are a mixture of English, Scotch, Irish, French, Dutch, Germans, and Swedes. From this promiscuous breed, that race, now called Americans, have arisen. The Eastern provinces must indeed be excepted, as being the unmixed descendents of Englishmen. I have heard many wish that they had been more intermixed also: for my part, I am no wisher, and think it much better as it has happened. They exhibit a most conspicuous figure in this great and variegated picture. They too enter for a great share in the pleasing perspective displayed in these thirteen provinces. I know it is fashionable to reflect on them, but I respect them for what they have done; for the accuracy and wisdom with which they have settled their territory; for the decency of their manners; for their early love of letters; their antient college, the first in this hemisphere; for their industry; which to me, who am but a farmer, is the criterion of every thing. There never was a people, situated as they are, who, with so ungrateful a soil, have done more in so short a time. Do you think that the monarchical ingredients, which are more prevalent in other governments, have purged them from all foul stains? Their histories assert the contrary.

In this great American asylum, the poor of Europe have by some means met together, and in consequence of various causes. To what purpose should they ask one another what countrymen they are? Alas, two thirds of them had no country. Can a wretch, who wanders about, who works and starves, whose life is a continual scene of sore affliction or pinching penury; can that man call England or any other kingdom his country? A country that had no bread for him; whose fields procured him no harvest; who met with nothing but the frowns of the rich, the severity of the laws, with jails and punishments; who owned not a single foot of the extensive surface of this planet. No! Urged by a variety of motives here they came. Every thing has tended to regenerate them. New laws, a new mode of living, a new social system. Here they are become men. In Europe they were as so many useless plants, wanting vegetative mould and refreshing showers. They withered; and were mowed down by want, hunger, and war; but now, by the power of transplantation, like all other plants, they have taken root and flourished! Formerly they were not numbered in any civil lists of their country, except in those of the poor: here they rank as citizens. By what invisible power hath this surprising metamorphosis been performed? By that of the laws and that of their industry. The laws, the indulgent laws, protect them as they arrive, stamping on them the symbol of adoption: they receive ample rewards for their labours:

these accumulated rewards procure them lands: those lands confer on them the title of freemen, and to that title every benefit is affixed which men can possibly require. This is the great operation daily performed by our laws. Whence proceed these laws? From our government. Whence that government? It is derived from the original genius and strong desire of the people ratified and confirmed by the crown. This is the great chain which links us all; this is the picture which every province exhibits, Nova Scotia excepted. There the crown has done all. Either there were no people who had genius, or it was not much attended to. The consequence is, that the province is very thinly inhabited indeed. The power of the crown, in conjunction with the musketoes, has prevented men from settling there. Yet some parts of it flourished once, and it contained a mild harmless set of people. But, for the fault of a few leaders, the whole was banished. The greatest political error, the crown ever committed in America, was, to cut off men from a country which wanted nothing but men.

What attachment can a poor European emigrant have for a country where he had nothing? The knowledge of the language, the love of a few kindred as poor as himself, were the only cords that tied him. His country is now that which gives him his land, bread, protection, and consequence. *Ubi panis ibi patria* is the motto of all emigrants. What then is the American, this new man? He is neither an European, nor the descendent of an European: hence that strange mixture of blood, which you will find in no other country. I could point out to you a family, whose grandfather was an Englishman, whose wife was Dutch, whose son married a French woman, and whose present four sons have now four wives of different nations. He is an American, who, leaving behind him all his antient prejudices and manners, receives new ones from the new mode of life he has embraced, the new government he obeys, and the new rank he holds. He becomes an American by being received in the broad lap of our great *alma mater*. Here individuals of all nations are melted into a new race of men, whose labours and posterity will one day cause great changes in the world. Americans are the western pilgrims, who are carrying along with them that great mass of arts, sciences, vigour, and industry, which began long since in the east. They will finish the great circle. The Americans were once scattered all over Europe. Here they are incorporated into one of the finest systems of population which has ever appeared, and which will hereafter become distinct by the power of the different climates they inhabit. The American ought therefore to love this country much better than that wherein either he or his forefathers were born. Here the rewards of his industry follow, with equal steps, the progress of his labour. His labour is founded on the basis of nature, *self-interest:* can it want a stronger allurement? Wives and children, who before in vain demanded of him a morsel of bread, now, fat and frolicksome, gladly help their father to clear those fields whence exuberant crops are to arise, to feed and to clothe them all, without any part being claimed, either by a despotic prince, a rich abbot, or a mighty lord. Here religion demands but little of him; a small voluntary salary to the minister, and gratitude to God: can he refuse these? The American is a new man, who acts upon new principles; he must therefore entertain new ideas and form new opinions. From involuntary idleness, servile dependence, penury, and useless labour, he has passed to toils of a very different nature, rewarded by ample subsistence.—This is an American.

## Questions for Discussion

What do de Crèvecoeur's descriptions of the New World imply about the Old World?

What distinctively American traits in common usage today do you see foreshadowed in de Crèvecoeur's definition?

What is de Crèvecoeur's attitude toward nonwhite peoples?

*Emma Lazarus (1849–1887) was born into a well-established Jewish family in New York City, was well educated, and became an influential figure in the rapidly changing New York artistic scene. She wrote poetry and essays on a wide variety of topics that were published in the best-known magazines of her time. She worked to improve the conditions of Jews both at home and abroad by establishing programs to educate new immigrants and by founding the Society for the Improvement and Colonization of Eastern European Jews. Her most famous sonnet, reprinted below, was written in 1883 to help raise money for the Statue of Liberty's pedestal, then being raised in New York Harbor in close proximity to Ellis Island. Although "The New Colossus" did not actually become a part of the monument until 1901, the poem's final lines have become a canonical statement of America's promise.*

# Emma Lazarus
## The New Colossus

Not like the brazen giant of Greek fame,
With conquering limbs astride from land to land;
Here at our sea-washed, sunset gates shall stand
A mighty woman with a torch, whose flame
5  Is the imprisoned lightning, and her name
Mother of Exiles. From her beacon-hand
Glows world-wide welcome; her mild eyes command
The air-bridged harbor that twin cities frame.
"Keep ancient lands, your storied pomp!" cries she
10  With silent lips. "Give me your tired, your poor,
Your huddled masses yearning to breathe free,
The wretched refuse of your teeming shore.
Send these, the homeless, tempest-tost to me,
I lift my lamp beside the golden door!"

## Questions for Discussion

Why is Lazarus's poem such an appropriate choice for the inscription at the base of the Statue of Liberty?

What "message" does the poem send to different audiences? Immigrants? Average Americans? Politicians? Children?

*Not everyone was as enthusiastic as Emma Lazarus about the prospect of welcoming to America large numbers of immigrants.* **Thomas Bailey Aldrich** *(1836–1907), a prominent and prolific New England writer whose 1870 novel* Story of a Bad Boy *served as one inspiration for* Tom Sawyer, *articulated the fears of many Americans in "The Unguarded Gates."*

# *Thomas Bailey Aldrich*

# The Unguarded Gates

Wide open and unguarded stand our gates.
And through them press a wild, a motley throng—
Men from the Volga and the Tartar steppes,
Featureless figures of the Hoang Ho,
5 Malayan, Scythian, Teuton, Kelt, and Slav,
Flying the Old World's poverty and scorn;
These bringing with them unknown gods and rites,
Those tiger passions, here to stretch their claws.
In street and alley what strange tongues are these,
10 Accents of menace alien to our air,
Voices that once the tower of Babel knew!
O, Liberty, white goddess, is it well
To leave the gate unguarded? On thy breast
Fold sorrow's children, soothe the hurts of fate,
15 Lift the downtrodden, but with the hand of steel
Stay those who to thy sacred portals come
To waste the fight of freedom. Have a care
Lest from thy brow the clustered stars be torn
And trampled in the dust. For so of old
20 The thronging Goth and Vandal trampled Rome,
And where the temples of the Caesars stood
The lean wolf unmolested made her lair.

## Questions for Discussion

Aldrich appeals to history to support his argument about the danger of immigration. What particular historical developments does he refer to?

How does "The Unguarded Gates" serve as a refutation of Emma Lazarus's "The New Colossus"?

What is the argument of Aldrich's poem? What is the thesis?

The political battle over immigration has always been fought with pictures as well as with words, particularly after the advent of photojournalism, which coincided with one of the great periods of immigration into
America, 1890–1920. Advocates for immigration seized on images of the
new Statue of Liberty, near the Ellis Island receiving facility in New York
harbor, to make arguments about the justice and decency of an open
immigration policy, while opponents seized on images of crime, disorder,
and exaggerated Old World ethnicity to raise questions about the consequences of immigration. Compare the four visual arguments about immigration policy that are reproduced on this page and the following spread,
two from the 1890s, two from a century later.

# Visual Arguments
# on Immigration:
# Ellis Island and After

In an 1887 engraving, immigrants arriving in New York
pass by the Statue of Liberty.

In 1891, Grant Hamilton used the Statue of Liberty as part of the setting for a cartoon blaming immigration for social ills such as crime, anarchy, socialism, and the Mafia.

New American citizens from several different nations swear allegiance to the United States at a naturalization ceremony, c. 1990.

California citizens protest American immigration policy at a demonstration near the Mexican border, c. 1990.

*In 1896, just as the "frontier" was closing to immigrants in search of free land to farm, **Francis Walker** warned readers of* The Atlantic Monthly *(then a leading national public affairs magazine with a progressive reputation based on its antislavery roots) that eastern and southern European immigrants, at the time regarded as separate "races," were threatening to overwhelm and degrade American cultural institutions.*

## Francis Walker

# Restriction of Immigration

When we speak of the restriction of immigration, at the present time, we have not in mind measures undertaken for the purpose of straining out from the vast throngs of foreigners arriving at our ports a few hundreds, or possibly thousands of persons, deaf, dumb, blind, idiotic, insane, pauper, or criminal, who might otherwise become a hopeless burden upon the country, perhaps even an active source of mischief. The propriety, and even the necessity of adopting such measures is now conceded by men of all shades of opinion concerning the larger subject. There is even noticeable a rather severe public feeling regarding the admission of persons of any of the classes named above; perhaps one might say, a certain resentment at the attempt of such persons to impose themselves upon us. We already have laws which cover a considerable part of this ground; and so far as further legislation is needed, it will only be necessary for the proper executive department of the government to call the attention of Congress to the subject. There is a serious effort on the part of our immigration officers to enforce the regulations prescribed, though when it is said that more than five thousand persons have passed through the gates at Ellis Island, in New York harbor, during the course of a single day, it will be seen that no very careful scrutiny is practicable.

It is true that in the past there has been gross and scandalous neglect of this matter on the part both of government and people, here in the United States. For nearly two generations, great numbers of persons utterly unable to earn their living, by reason of one or another form of physical or mental disability, and others who were, from widely different causes, unfit to be members of any decent community, were admitted to our ports without challenge or question. It is a matter of official record that in many cases these persons had been directly shipped to us by states or municipalities desiring to rid themselves of a burden and a nuisance; while it could reasonably be believed that the proportion of such instances was far greater than could be officially ascertained. But all this is past. The question of the restriction of immigration today does not deal with that phase of the subject. What is proposed is, not to keep out some hundreds, or possibly thousands of persons, against whom lie specific objections like those above indicated, but to exclude perhaps hundreds of thousands, the great majority of whom would be subject to no individual objections; who, on the contrary, might fairly be expected to earn their living here in this new country, at least up to the standard known to them at home, and probably much more. The question today is, not of preventing the wards of our almshouses, our insane asylums, and our jails from being stuffed to repletion by new arrivals from Europe; but of protecting the American rate of wages, the American standard of living, and the quality of American citizenship from degradation through the tumultuous access of vast throngs of ignorant and brutalized peasantry from the countries of eastern and southern Europe.

The first thing to be said respecting any serious proposition importantly to restrict immigration into the United States is, that such a proposition necessarily and properly encounters a high degree of incredulity, arising from the traditions of our country. From the beginning, it has been the policy of the United States, both officially and according to the prevailing sentiment of our people, to tolerate, to welcome, and to encourage immigration, without qualification and without discrimination. For generations, it was the settled opinion of our people, which found no challenge anywhere, that immigration was a source of both strength and wealth. Not only was it thought unnecessary carefully to scrutinize foreign arrivals at our ports, but the figures of any exceptionally large immigration were greeted with noisy gratulation. In those days the American people did not doubt that they derived a great advantage from this source. It is, therefore, natural to ask, Is it possible that our fathers and our grandfathers were so far wrong in this matter? Is it not, rather, probable that the present anxiety and apprehension on the subject are due to transient causes or to distinctly false opinions, prejudicing the public mind? The challenge which current proposals for the restriction of immigration thus encounter is a perfectly legitimate one, and creates a presumption which their advocates are bound to deal with. Is it, however, necessarily true that if our fathers and grandfathers were right in their view of immigration in their own time, those who advocate the restriction of immigration today must be in the wrong? Does it not sometimes happen, in the course of national development, that great and permanent changes in condition require corresponding changes of opinion and of policy?

We shall best answer this question by referring to an instance in an altogether different department of public interest and activity. For nearly a hundred years after the peace of 1783 opened to settlement the lands beyond the Alleghanies, the cutting away of the primeval forest was regarded by our people not only with toleration, but with the highest approval. No physical instrument could have been chosen which was so fairly entitled to be called the emblem of American civilization as the Axe of the Pioneer. As the forests of the Ohio Valley bowed themselves before the unstaying enterprise of the adventurous settlers of that region, all good citizens rejoiced. There are few chapters of human history which recount a grander story of human achievement. Yet today all intelligent men admit that the cutting down of our forests, the destruction of the tree-covering of our soil, has already gone too far; and both individual States and the nation have united in efforts to undo some of the mischief which has been wrought to our agriculture and to our climate from carrying too far the work of denudation. In precisely the same way, it may be true that our fathers were right in their view of immigration; while yet the patriotic American of today may properly shrink in terror from the contemplation of the vast hordes of ignorant and brutalized peasantry thronging to our shores.

5 Before inquiring as to general changes in our national condition which may justify a change of opinion and policy in this respect, let us deal briefly, as we must, with two opinions regarding the immigration of the past, which stand in the way of any fair consideration of the subject. These two opinions were, first, that immigration constituted a net reinforcement of our population; secondly, that, in addition to this, or irrespective of this, immigration was necessary, in order to supply the laborers who should do certain kinds of work, imperatively demanded for the building up of our industrial and social structure, which natives of the soil were unwilling to undertake.

The former of these opinions was, so far as I am aware, held with absolute unanimity by our people; yet no popular belief was ever more unfounded. Space would not serve for the full statistical demonstration of the proposition that immigration, during the period from 1830 to 1860, instead of constituting a net reinforcement to the population, simply resulted in a replacement of native by foreign elements; but I believe it would be practicable to prove this to the satisfaction of every fair-minded man. Let it suffice to state a few matters which are beyond controversy.

The population of 1790 was almost wholly a native and wholly an acclimated population, and for forty years afterwards immigration remained at so low a rate as to be practically of no account; yet the people of the United States increased in numbers more rapidly than has ever elsewhere been known, in regard to any considerable population, over any considerable area, through any considerable period of time. Between 1790 and 1830 the nation grew from less than four millions to nearly thirteen millions,—an increase, in fact, of two hundred and twenty-seven per cent, a rate unparalleled in history. That increase was wholly out of the loins of our own people. Each decade had seen a growth of between thirty-three and thirty-eight percent, a doubling once in twenty-two or twenty-three years. During the thirty years which followed 1830, the conditions of life and reproduction in the United States were not less, but more favorable than in the preceding period. Important changes relating to the practice of medicine, the food and clothing of people, the general habits of living, took place, which were of a nature to increase the vitality and reproductive capability of the American people. Throughout this period, the standard of height, of weight, and of chest measurement was steadily rising, with the result that, of the men of all nationalities in the giant army formed to suppress the slaveholders' rebellion, the native American bore off the palm in respect to physical stature. The decline of this rate of increase among Americans began at the very time when foreign immigration first assumed considerable proportions; it showed itself first and in the highest degree in those regions, in those States, and in the very counties into which the foreigners most largely entered. It proceeded for a long time in such a way as absolutely to offset the foreign arrivals, so that in 1850, in spite of the incoming of two and a half millions of foreigners during thirty years, our population differed by less than ten thousand from the population which would have existed, according to the previous rate of increase, without reinforcement from abroad. These three facts, which might be shown by tables and diagrams, constitute a statistical demonstration such as is rarely attained in regard to the operation of any social or economic force.

But it may be asked, Is the proposition that the arrival of foreigners brought a check to the native increase a reasonable one? Is the cause thus suggested one which has elsewhere appeared as competent to produce such an effect? I answer, Yes. All human history shows that the principle of population is intensely sensitive to social and economic changes. Let social and economic conditions remain as they were, and population will go on increasing from year to year, and from decade to decade, with a regularity little short of the marvelous. Let social and economic conditions change, and population instantly responds. The arrival in the United States, between 1830 and 1840, and thereafter increasingly, of large numbers of degraded peasantry created for the first time in this country distinct social classes, and produced an alteration of economic relations which could not fail powerfully to affect population. The appearance of vast numbers of men, foreign in birth and often in language, with a poorer standard of living, with habits repellent to our native people, of an industrial grade suited only to the lowest kind of manual labor, was exactly such a cause as by any student of population would be expected to affect profoundly the growth of the native population. Americans shrank alike from the social contact and the economic competition thus created. They became increasingly unwilling to bring forth sons and daughters who should be obliged to compete in the market for labor and in the walks of life with those whom they did not recognize as of their own grade and condition. It has been said by some that during this time habits of luxury were entering, to reduce both the disposition and the ability to increase among our own population. In some small degree, in some restricted localities, this undoubtedly was the case; but prior to 1860 there was no such general growth of luxury in the United States as is competent to account for the effect seen. Indeed, I believe this was almost wholly due to the cause which has been indicated,—a cause recognized by every student of statistics and economics.

The second opinion regarding the immigration of the past, with which it seems well to deal before proceeding to the positive argument of the case, is that, whether desirable on other accounts or not, foreign immigration prior to 1860 was necessary in order to supply the country with a laboring class which should be able and willing to perform the lowest kind of work required in the upbuilding of our industrial and social structure, especially the making of railroads and canals. The opinion which has been cited constitutes, perhaps, the best example known to me of that putting the cart before the horse which is so commonly seen in sociological inquiry. When was it that native Americans first refused to do the lowest kinds of manual labor? I answer, When the foreigner came. Did the foreigner come because the native American refused longer to perform any kind of manual labor? No; the American refused because the foreigner came. Through all our early history, Americans, from Governor Winthrop, through Jonathan

Edwards, to Ralph Waldo Emerson, had done every sort of work which was required for the comfort of their families and for the up-building of the state, and had not been ashamed. They called nothing common or unclean which needed to be done for their own good or for the good of all. But when the country was flooded with ignorant and unskilled foreigners, who could do nothing but the lowest kind of labor, Americans instinctively shrank from the contact and the competition thus offered to them. So long as manual labor, in whatever field, was to be done by all, each in his place, there was no revolt at it; but when working on railroads and canals became the sign of a want of education and of a low social condition, our own people gave it up, and left it to those who were able to do that, and nothing better.

10 We have of late had a very curious demonstration of the entire fallacy of the popular mode of reasoning on this subject, due to the arrival of a still lower laboring class. Within a few years *Harper's Weekly* had an article in which the editor, after admitting that the Italians who have recently come in such vast numbers to our shores do not constitute a desirable element of the population, either socially or politically, yet claimed that it was a highly providential arrangement, since the Irish, who formerly did all the work of the country in the way of ditching and trenching, were now standing aside. We have only to meet the argument thus in its second generation, so to speak, to see the complete fallacy of such reasoning. Does the Italian come because the Irishman refuses to work in ditches and trenches, in gangs; or has the Irishman taken this position because the Italian has come? The latter is undoubtedly the truth; and if the administrators of Baron Hirsch's estate send to us two millions of Russian Jews, we shall soon find the Italians standing on their dignity, and deeming themselves too good to work on streets and sewers and railroads. But meanwhile, what of the republic? what of the American standard of living? what of the American rate of wages?

All that sort of reasoning about the necessity of having a mean kind of man to do a mean kind of work is greatly to be suspected. It is not possible to have a man who is too good to do any kind of work which the welfare of his family and of the community requires to be done. So long as we were left to increase out of the loins of our people such a sentiment as that we are now commenting upon made no appearance in American life. It is much to be doubted whether any material growth which is to be secured only by the degradation of our citizenship is a national gain, even from the most materialistic point of view.

Let us now inquire what are the changes in our general conditions which seem to demand a revision of the opinion and policy heretofore held regarding immigration. Three of these are subjective, affecting our capability of easily and safely taking care of a large and tumultuous access of foreigners; the fourth is objective, and concerns the character of the immigration now directed upon our shores. Time will serve for only a rapid characterization.

First, we have the important fact of the complete exhaustion of the free public lands of the United States. Fifty years ago, thirty years ago, vast tracts of arable laud were open to every person arriving on our shores, under the Preemption Act, or later, the Homestead Act. A good farm of one hundred and sixty acres could be had at the minimum price of $1.25 an acre, or for merely the fees of registration. Under these circumstances it was a very simple matter to dispose of a large immigration. Today there is not a good farm within the limits of the United States which is to be had under either of these acts. The wild and tumultuous scenes which attended the opening to settlement of the Territory of Oklahoma, a few years ago, and, a little later, of the so-called Cherokee Strip, testify eloquently to the vast change in our national conditions in this respect. This is not to say that more people cannot and will not, sooner or later, with more or less of care and pains and effort, be placed upon the land of the United States; but it does of itself alone show how vastly the difficulty of providing for immigration has increased. The immigrant must now buy his farm from a second hand, and he must pay the price which the value of the land for agricultural purposes determines. In the case of ninety-five out of a hundred immigrants, this necessity puts an immediate occupation of the soil out of the question.

A second change in our national condition, which importantly affects our capability of taking care of large numbers of ignorant and unskilled foreigners, is the fall of agricultural prices which has gone on steadily since 1873. It is not of the slightest consequence to inquire into the causes of this fall, whether we refer it to the competition of Argentina and of India or the appreciation of gold. We are interested only in the fact. There has been a great reduction in the cost of producing crops in some favored regions where steam-ploughs and steam-reaping, steam-threshing, and steam-sacking machines can be employed; but there has been no reduction in the cost of producing crops upon the ordinary American farm at all corresponding to the reduction in the price of the produce. It is a necessary consequence of this that the ability to employ a large number of uneducated and unskilled hands in agriculture has greatly diminished.

15    Still a third cause which may be indicated, perhaps more important than either of those thus far mentioned, is found in the fact that we have now a labor problem. We in the United States have been wont

to pride ourselves greatly upon our so easily maintaining peace and keeping the social order unimpaired. We have, partly from a reasonable patriotic pride, partly also from something like Phariseeism, been much given to pointing at our European cousins, and boasting superiority over them in this respect. Our self-gratulation has been largely due to overlooking social differences between us and them. That boasted superiority has been owing mainly, not to our institutions, but to our more favorable conditions. There is no country of Europe which has not for a long time had a labor problem; that is, which has not so largely exploited its own natural resources, and which has not a labor supply so nearly meeting the demands of the market at their fullest, that hard times and periods of industrial depression have brought a serious strain through extensive non-employment of labor. From this evil condition we have, until recently, happily been free. During the last few years, however, we have ourselves come under the shadow of this evil, in spite of our magnificent natural resources. We know what it is to have even intelligent and skilled labor unemployed through considerable periods of time. This change of conditions is likely to bring some abatement to our national pride. No longer is it a matter of course that every industrious and temperate man can find work in the United States. And it is to be remembered that, of all nations, we are the one which is least qualified to deal with a labor problem. We have not the machinery, we have not the army, we have not the police, we have not the traditions and instincts, for dealing with such a matter, as the great railroad and other strikes of the last few years have shown.

I have spoken of three changes in the national condition, all subjective, which greatly affect our capability of dealing with a large and tumultuous immigration. There is a fourth, which is objective. It concerns the character of the foreigners now resorting to our shores. Fifty, even thirty years ago, there was a rightful presumption regarding the average immigrant that he was among the most enterprising, thrifty, alert, adventurous, and courageous of the community from which he came. It required no small energy, prudence, forethought, and pains to conduct the inquiries relating to his migration, to accumulate the necessary means, and to find his way across the Atlantic. Today the presumption is completely reversed. So thoroughly has the continent of Europe been crossed by railways, so effectively has the business of emigration there been exploited, so much have the rates of railroad fares and ocean passage been reduced, that it is now among the least thrifty and prosperous members of any European community that the emigration agent finds his best recruiting-ground. The care and pains required have been reduced to a minimum; while the agent of the Red Star Line or the White Star Line is everywhere at hand, to suggest migration to those who are not getting on well at home. The intending emigrants are looked after from the moment they are locked into the cars in their native villages until they stretch themselves upon the floors of the buildings on Ellis Island, in New York. Illustrations of the ease and facility with which this Pipe Line Immigration is now carried on might be given in profusion. So broad and smooth is the channel, there is no reason why every foul and stagnant pool of population in Europe, which no breath of intellectual or industrial life has stirred for ages, should not be decanted upon our soil. Hard times here may momentarily check the flow; but it will not be permanently stopped so long as any difference of economic level exists between our population and that of the most degraded communities abroad.

But it is not alone that the presumption regarding the immigrant of today is so widely different from that which existed regarding the immigrant of thirty or fifty years ago. The immigrant of the former time came almost exclusively from western and northern Europe. We have now tapped great reservoirs of population then almost unknown to the passenger lists of our arriving vessels. Only a short time ago, the immigrants from southern Italy, Hungary, Austria, and Russia together made up hardly more than one per cent of our immigration. Today the proportion has risen to something like forty per cent, and threatens soon to become fifty or sixty per cent, or even more. The entrance into our political, social, and industrial life of such vast masses of peasantry, degraded below our utmost conceptions, is a matter which no intelligent patriot can look upon without the gravest apprehension and alarm. These people have no history behind them which is of a nature to give encouragement. They have none of the inherited instincts and tendencies which made it comparatively easy to deal with the immigration of the olden time. They are beaten men from beaten races; representing the worst failures in the struggle for existence. Centuries are against them, as centuries were on the side of those who formerly came to us. They have none of the ideas and aptitudes which fit men to take up readily and easily the problem of self-care and self-government, such as belong to those who are descended from the tribes that met under the oak-trees of old Germany to make laws and choose chieftains.

Their habits of life, again, are of the most revolting kind. Read the description given by Mr. Riis of the police driving from the garbage dumps the miserable beings who try to burrow in those depths of unutterable filth and slime in order that they may eat and sleep there! Was it in cement like this that the foundations of our republic were laid? What effects must be produced upon our social standards, and upon the ambitions and aspirations of our people, by a contact so foul and loathsome? The influence upon the American rate of wages of a competition like this cannot fail to be injurious and even disastrous. Already it has been seriously felt in the tobacco manufacture, in the clothing trade, and in many forms of mining industry; and unless this access of vast numbers of unskilled workmen of the lowest type, in a market already fully supplied with labor, shall be checked, it cannot fail to go on from bad to worse, in breaking down the standard which has been maintained with so much care and at so much cost. The competition of paupers is far more telling and more killing than the competition of pauper-made goods. Degraded labor in the slums of foreign cities may be prejudicial to intelligent, ambitious, self-respecting labor here; but it does not threaten half so much evil as does degraded labor in the garrets of our native cities.

Finally, the present situation is most menacing to our peace and political, safety. In all the social and industrial disorders of this country since 1877, the foreign elements have proved themselves the ready tools of demagogues in defying the law, in destroying property, and in working violence. A learned clergyman who mingled with the socialistic mob which, two years ago, threatened the State House and the governor of Massachusetts, told me that during the entire disturbance he heard no word spoken in any language which he knew,—either in English, in German, or in French. There may be those who can contemplate the addition to our population of vast numbers of persons having no inherited instincts of self-government and respect for law; knowing no restraint upon their own passions but the club of the policeman or the bayonet of the soldier; forming communities, by the tens of thousands, in which only foreign tongues are spoken, and into which can steal no influence from our free institutions and from popular discussion. But I confess to being far less optimistic. I have conversed with one of the highest officers of the United States army and with one of the highest officers of the civil government regarding the state of affairs which existed during the summer of 1894; and the revelations they made of facts not generally known, going to show how the ship of state grazed along its whole side upon the rocks, were enough to appall the most sanguine American, the most hearty believer in free government. Have we the right to expose the republic to any increase of the dangers from this source which now so manifestly threaten our peace and safety?

20      For it is never to be forgotten that self-defense is the first law of nature and of nations. If that man who careth not for his own house-

hold is worse than an infidel, the nation which permits its institutions to be endangered by any cause which can fairly be removed is guilty not less in Christian than in natural law. Charity begins at home; and while the people of the United States have gladly offered an asylum to millions upon millions of the distressed and unfortunate of other lands and climes, they have no right to carry their hospitality one step beyond the line where American institutions, the American rate of wages, the American standard of living, are brought into serious peril. All the good the United States could do by offering indiscriminate hospitality to a few millions more of European peasants, whose places at home will, within another generation, be filled by others as miserable as themselves, would not compensate for any permanent injury done to our republic. Our highest duty to charity and to humanity is to make this great experiment, here, of free laws and educated labor, the most triumphant success that can possibly be attained. In this way we shall do far more for Europe than by allowing its city slums and its vast stagnant reservoirs of degraded peasantry to be drained off upon our soil. Within the decade between 1880 and 1890 five and a quarter millions of foreigners entered our ports! No nation in human history ever undertook to deal with such masses of alien population. That man must be a sentimentalist and an optimist beyond all bounds of reason who believes that we can take such a load upon the national stomach without a failure of assimilation, and without great danger to the health and life of the nation. For one, I believe it is time that we should take a rest, and give our social, political, and industrial system some chance to recuperate. The problems which so sternly confront us today are serious enough without being complicated and aggravated by the addition of some millions of Hungarians, Bohemians, Poles, south Italians, and Russian Jews.

## Questions for Discussion

Does Walker's argument remind you of arguments you have read concerning U.S. immigration policy? Which of Walker's points seem the most outdated? Which seem most current?

What prejudices are at play in Walker's argument?

*James Fallows (born 1948) has written hundreds of articles and several books on topics as varied as computer software, national defense, travel, and the Far East, where he lived for several years. He has been the editor of* U.S. News & World Report *and served as a speechwriter for President Jimmy Carter. In 1983, just as immigration from Mexico was increasing significantly in Texas and California, Fallows investigated its impact on the English language, on racial and ethnic relations, and on national order. His subsequent essay "Immigration: How It's Affecting Us" was published in* The Atlantic Monthly, *a prestigious magazine that takes pride in its discussions of cultural and political affairs. The following is an excerpt from Fallow's essay on the economic impact of immigration.*

## James Fallows

# Immigration: How It's Affecting Us

Economists who study the effects of immigration take two very different approaches. One school views immigrants primarily as additional people—new workers in the labor force, extra purchasers in the national market. From this perspective, immigration can sometimes be valuable, if the labor it provides alleviates a shortage. Thus Western Europe needed immigrant "guest workers" to ease its labor shortage in the 1960s. And thus, contends the economist Julian Simon, immigrants can help the United States. The value of immigrants Simon says, is that they "represent additional *people* as people . . . [and] lead to faster economic growth by increasing the size of the market, and hence boosting productivity and investment." In addition, since so many of the immigrants are young, they can help offset the aging of the American work force. Most of those who see immigration from the labor-market perspective conclude, unlike Simon, that immigrants hurt a mature economy like that of the United States. If the immigrants are uneducated and unskilled—farmers, peasant craftsmen— they will drag down the overall productivity rate. They will, in effect, more narrowly divide the economic pie.

The other economic approach pays little attention to how many immigrants arrive. It concentrates instead on the economic behavior of those who survive the process of migration. This view is propounded by economists who place great stress on "human capital," the mixture of talents and cultural incentives that makes Germany economically different from England and Hong Kong from Macao. From this perspective, the ingenuity and perseverance that immigrants possess can make an economy richer, because immigrants will adapt and innovate and sacrifice in ways that non-immigrants are too comfortable to try. They make the pie larger for everyone to share.

I came to find the second approach more realistic, for reasons I can best present through the story of the Nguyen family, formerly of Saigon, now of Los Angeles.

In 1975, the four brothers and six sisters of the immediate Nguyen family lived in Saigon with their parents plus the extended family of nephews and brothers-in-law. The father ran a small import-export business. The children held clerical or professional jobs. Two were in the Army of the Republic of Vietnam (ARVN); one of them had been a law student before he was drafted. One son was an architectural draftsman, and one was a lawyer. Two daughters worked as secretaries, one in a South Vietnamese government ministry, the other at the U.S. Embassy. Although the family was not part of Saigon's moneyed elite, it was respectably successful. Because of the daughter who worked for the Americans, the family was on a list of people the U.S. planned to evacuate if Saigon fell.

5    In the chaos that engulfed Saigon in April of 1975, the onetime law student, Mr. Nguyen, was the first of the family out of Saigon. (He has asked that his given name not be used.) How did he escape? "In panic," he says. He made his way to Tan Son Nhut airport, where the rescue helicopters were supposed to land. He was thirty years old and spoke no English.

Mr. Nguyen was taken to Clark Air Base in the Philippines, then to Guam, and eventually to a resettlement base at Camp Pendleton, California. There he spent the next six months. In camp, he volunteered to work for the U.S. Catholic Conference, which was (and remains) heavily involved in resettling refugees. In time he came to be paid $5 a day for helping to coordinate the many details in finding homes for the refugees. When the camp closed, at the end of October 1975, he was the last refugee released.

Across the vast expanse of the Los Angeles basin Mr. Nguyen traveled in search of work. His first break came in November. In El Segundo he found work as an assembler in a waterbed factory, for $2.10 an hour, then the minimum wage. After Mr. Nguyen had accepted the job, the foreman asked him for his address. "I told him I didn't know, because I didn't live any place yet. I was only going to rent a place after I got a job."

Mr. Nguyen had his first foothold, but not much more than that. He was taking home less than $400 per month, and was paying $120 for his room. On leaving the camp, Mr. Nguyen had been entitled to $300 for resettlement expenses, but he had refused the money. "I had pride. I wanted to feel that I had made it without any help," he says. "But I felt lonely and miserable. In those factories, you can't slow down." He was buoyed only by his glimpses of other Vietnamese adjusting to industrial life. "You see one person in the corner, he might have been a farmer in Vietnam. He survived, I can survive."

Three weeks later, he heard of another possibility, an opening with RCA. On his time off, he went to the RCA record factory and said that he'd had experience with studios and music back in Vietnam. The personnel man listened with feigned attentiveness and told him that he sounded like the man for the job. When Mr. Nguyen reported for work, he found that he would be putting labels on records for $3 an hour.

10      "I learned that money is really valuable in this country," he says. "You pay for it with blood and tears. I started thinking about that $300. Money is money. Why not collect it and put it in the bank and earn interest instead of just ignoring it?"

Having steeled himself to claim his resettlement bonus, Mr. Nguyen went into a religious-charities office to apply. While there he ran into the resettlement director, who knew of his work in the camp. The charities were looking for a man like him, she said. Mr. Nguyen started to tell her he couldn't speak English well enough, but she shushed him with the reassurance that he'd be put in a training program. The pay would be $660 a month. He accepted. By the end of 1975, Mr. Nguyen was a white-collar worker.

Meanwhile, the rest of the family was adapting to life in the newly christened Ho Chi Minh City. Nguyen Ninh, the brother who had been a draftsman, escaped purges directed at other technicians because, as he remembers now, "they needed our skills to make the machinery run." Yet he suspected that sooner or later his usefulness would end. One of his brothers, named Viet, had been a lieutenant in the South Vietnamese Army and was being held in a "re-education camp." When Viet escaped from the camp, after two years' detention, he joined Ninh in a plan to flee the country.

With friends, the brothers bought an old boat from country people and then covertly brought it to the city to fortify it for an ocean voyage. None of them had been on the water, but they tried to teach themselves seamanship. One night in 1977, they set out, seven people in a boat that Nguyen Ninh says was not more than twelve feet long.

They hoped to reach Malaysia, but the winds blew hard from that quarter. On the eighth day at sea, the boat's engine failed, and they drifted where the wind pushed them.

15 "After the broken engine, we figure 99 percent that we die in the ocean," Ninh said this spring. "Nearly everyone who goes in a boat dies." Commercial ships passed, but they kept on going, some even adjusting their course so as to avoid entanglement with the troublesome boat people. The boat began to leak, and then it sank. The men were in the water, swimming, reckoning their remaining time in hours.

In the distance, a large, dark shape loomed. It was a freighter from Kuwait. Its captain, looking through his binoculars, was startled by the sight of men swimming in the ocean. When rescued, they were 200 miles from Vietnam.

They had avoided death, but for the next year the two Nguyen brothers lived as stateless men. Immigration officials would not let them go ashore at the ship's next stop, Singapore. They lived aboard ship till it returned to Kuwait, and when it got there they were jailed. Its next voyage was to Vietnam, they were told, and it would take them back home. The brothers tried to reach embassies, the Red Cross, the UN, but they got nowhere until a sailor agreed to mail a letter to Mr. Nguyen in California.

With efforts under way in Los Angeles and Kuwait, the men were classified as refugees and, after three months in jail, were turned over to the UN. They spent eight more months in a UN refugee camp in Greece, where they worked as farm laborers. After Mr. Nguyen was certified as their sponsor in the U.S., they were accepted as refugees. On June 22, 1978, they arrived in America.

Like their brother, they spoke no English on arrival, but they began learning as they looked for work. Beyond supporting themselves, they hoped to send money to the family members still in Vietnam, to help them buy their way out. Viet, the former ARVN lieutenant, got a job at a valet-parking outfit at the Los Angeles International Airport, for the minimum wage. Ninh became a carpenter's helper. A few months later, he found a place as a trainee draftsman with a machine-tool company.

20 Four sisters and a nephew were the next Nguyens to come over. They went by boat to a refugee camp in Indonesia. In 1979, they joined their brothers in Los Angeles.

Then the other two sisters escaped. One, Hai, had been a student; the other, Mai, had worked at the U.S. Embassy. In 1980 they set out on foot. With two children, they traveled west to Cambodia and then walked for seven days through the jungles of Cambodia to the Thai border. In Thailand, they were admitted to a refugee camp. There they stayed for six months. In 1980, with Mr. Nguyen acting as their sponsor, they entered the United States. They were among the 808,000 admissions that alarmed many Americans that year.

The family with which they were reunited had changed dramatically in the previous five years. Mr. Nguyen had become a citizen and was married to another Vietnamese immigrant. He and the other brothers were established in a way that would have been hard to imagine when they first arrived, as dispossessed persons. They had assimilated so fully as to see that in Southern California in the late seventies the road to financial independence was real estate. After Ninh and Viet arrived, in 1978, the three brothers had pooled their money in hopes of buying a house. Each of them was eventually bringing home about $1,000 a month; by sharing living expenses, they saved about $2,000 a month. By 1979, they had accumulated enough for a down payment on a house in Downey, a respectable middle-class suburb. All three signed the mortgage.

Viet had saved enough money from his work at the parking lot to buy a small furniture store, too. As he was contemplating the investment, he told Mr. Nguyen that it would consume all his savings. Mr. Nguyen replied that if he lost the money, he could always earn it back, but if the gamble paid off, he'd be independent. Ninh was by then earning $10 an hour as a professional draftsman.

Mr. Nguyen, the Benjamin Franklin of the family, encouraged his sisters to train for better jobs. Hai took a course in accounting and wound up working for a Vietnamese dentist in Long Beach. Mai studied cosmetology. She did not like it, but her brother pushed her to see it through. She finished, and found a job in West Los Angeles. She made the sixty-mile commute daily, and by the end of 1980 she was earning $2,000 a month doing nails. By 1982, she had a chance to buy her own salon. The family pooled its assets and took out loans, and now she runs Mai's Beauty Salon, in Beverly Hills, hard by Rodeo Drive. The family's father finally arrived, having first escaped to Belgium and established himself as a baker.

25    All the while, Mr. Nguyen was improving his own position. He rented the house in Downey to other members of his family, eight siblings and in-laws. They pay $100 a month apiece, which covers the mortgage. Mr. Nguyen has moved with his wife to a second house. They have carefully worked out their financial timetable. In a few years, they will have retired the second mortgage on their home, and his wife can quit her job as a chief bank teller to have children.

When I went to visit the house in Downey, home to nearly a dozen people, counting the children, I was prepared for a sense of confinement, or of brave endurance amid squalor, or of practically anything except the serene order I found. It sits amid other unexceptional, modern California houses, with a vista of a distant freeway, on a street like a thousand others in the Los Angeles basin. Inside the house, the sisters and brothers, arriving late after long commutes from their farflung businesses, changed quickly into Vietnamese pajamas and kimonos and took their leisure in the living room. Delicately colored prints of Asian scenes hung on the walls. The dining table stood on a platform with a canopy overhead, giving the effect of an indoor gazebo. The only external indication of the struggle for advancement going on within was the seven cars that jammed the driveway and lined the curb.

The adults, thin and short, spoke in heavily accented English about their arrivals, which in some cases were only a year in the past. Two elementary school children, whose father was still in jail in Vietnam, appeared in American-style pajamas and shyly answered questions in American tones. The family is still saving money, in preparation for the mother and for the spouses and siblings yet to arrive.

Mr. Nguyen's job involves assisting many new arrivals from Indochina. He tells them that they must adjust to the "new life" in the United States, as his family has done. He warns them against welfare, although he says he cannot blame people for accepting the $600 a month, plus food stamps and medical benefits, that welfare provides. "I tell them, If you go on job training, you will learn the English faster. Welfare will make you lazy. You will hesitate to work and hesitate to speak English."

The Nguyen family is, of course, not typical of all immigrants. Its members, with their education and their white-collar backgrounds, started out several steps ahead of the peasants and farmers who fled at the same time. The refugee camps, however cheerless, and the resettlement bonuses, however small, were more help than many other immigrants receive. Most important, the Nguyens' status as legal, fully entitled participants in American society made it easier for them to establish credit, buy homes, start businesses, and move up the ladder rung by rung.

30    Still, there *is* something in their story that is typical of immigrants' histories. However hard it was to continue living in Ho Chi Minh City (or, in earlier eras, Pinsk or Palermo), it took a certain daring to set out in the boat or walk through the jungle. At worst, the emigrants

would die or be captured. At best, they would arrive as uprooted foreigners, ignorant of the language and the mores that compose their new culture.

Some theorists speculate that the act of emigration is a kind of natural selection: those who are passive or fatalistic—or comfortable—do not take the step. Others suggest that the rigors of the passage teach the immigrants the skills they need to survive. In any case, there is little dispute that an "immigrant personality" exists, and that its elements are the same ones that, in retrospect, are so apparent in the nation's previous immigrants.

Compared with people who have not been forced to land on their feet, immigrants are generally more resourceful and determined. (A twenty-three-year-old man from El Salvador, who had come to the U.S. illegally and was working in Houston, told me that he could not understand all the talk about unemployment. Why, he himself was holding three jobs.) The full story of the immigrant personality would also include the psychological burdens of dislocation. But looked at from the economic point of view, the immigrant's grit and courage, and even his anxieties, impart productive energy to the society he joins.

This is different from saying that immigrants are valuable primarily for their specific talents. Some are, of course; the harvest ranges from Albert Einstein to Rod Carew. But through American history, the great masses of immigrants have not brought with them special skills. Most have come from the lower, but not the bottom, ranks of their native societies. They are people without advantages of birth who are nonetheless on the way up.

"Those who do come to the United States are those who are advancing within their own societies," says Ray Marshall, now of the University of Texas; "those who have attained the necessary knowledge of America and how to get here, and who have accumulated or been able to borrow the funds they need to pay for their airline tickets or to pay their smugglers."

35    The single most important quality in immigrants is the willingness to adapt. The very traits that persuade someone to move from Guatemala to Los Angeles, or even from Detroit to Houston, often enable the immigrant to find and fill economic gaps, which is what the Nguyen family did, and what many other immigrants have done.

Not every immigrant becomes an entrepreneur; a man who pushed a hand plow in a Mexican village will probably pick vegetables or wash dishes if he comes to the United States. The more temporary the visit, the more likely the immigrant is merely to sell his unskilled labor, rather than look for a special niche. Economists distinguish such "sojourner" behavior from the attitude of the true immigrant. It typified many Italian sojourners in the United States eighty years ago and French-Canadians in New England until several decades ago, and probably typifies most illegal immigrants from Mexico in recent years.

Still, there is evidence beyond the anecdotal about the economic benefits immigration can bring to the new homeland. The Urban Institute, which has been conducting a study of the California economy in the 1970s, recently released its preliminary findings:

During the 1970s, when Southern California received more immigrants than any other part of the country, it also created jobs faster than any other, and its per capita income increased by 25 percent, also higher than the norm. Immigration was far from the only factor in these increases, the study reported; but, it said, the findings suggest, "at least at the aggregate level, that large-scale immigration did not depress, and perhaps increased, per capita income in the state"—that is, it did not divide the pie. On balance, the study said, the economic benefits to the region—results of the new human energy, the entrepreneurship, the adaptability—outweighed the costs, which primarily came from the immigrants' use of public services, such as hospitals and schools.

Although immigration is a divisive issue in Miami, almost no one disputes the economic bonus the Cuban community now represents. The first to flee Castro were mainly professionals and businessmen, who soon repeated their success here. The second and third waves were less select, more like America's other immigrants; the first-wave Cubans grumbled that those who had lived under communism had lost their drive. Still, they were absorbed into Little Havana, where they opened shops and restaurants and kept the town alive. Miami's Cuban population has helped make it the entrepot for Latin American trade, to the occasional sorrow of the Drug Enforcement Administration, but to the satisfaction of financiers.

40      Immigrants eagerly join the American race to get ahead. According to Barry Chiswick, of the University of Illinois, the sons and daughters of immigrants earn 5 to 10 percent more than others of the same age and educational level whose parents were native-born. The immigrants themselves, compared with native-born people of the same race and with the same amount of schooling, start out at a big earnings disadvantage. But, in a matter of years, even the first generation catches up with and then passes the native-born. This "earnings

crossover" occurs after fifteen years for Mexican immigrants and after eleven for black immigrants. According to Thomas Sowell, a conservative black scholar, second-generation black-skinned West Indians in the United States have a higher average income than native-born white Americans.

Those opposed to immigration respond to these tales of success with three objections.

The first is demographic. One by one, immigrants may add to the national wealth, but collectively they frustrate efforts to limit America's population. Arguments about the ultimate "carrying capacity" of America's farmland, water supply, and other natural resources have been muted in the past decade, as American fertility rates have fallen. But many who are concerned about population growth naturally believe that each new immigrant puts ecological equilibrium that much further out of reach.

Those who advance this case often claim that immigration now accounts for half the total increase in the U.S. population. That is almost certainly not true. During the 1970s, the American population grew by less than one percent a year. The roughly 4 million legal immigrants admitted during that decade accounted for 21 percent of the growth. In comparison, the population grew by 2 percent per year from 1900 to 1910, and immigrants accounted for 40 percent of the increase.

If legal and illegal immigration combined did, as many environmentalists assert, account for half the increase in the 1970s, then there must have been more illegal than legal immigrants during that period. No one familiar with the subject believes that so many came. Lawrence Fuchs is a professor at Brandeis University who was executive director of the staff of the Select Commission on Immigration and Refugee Policy, the government body that in 1981 recommended changes in immigration law. The Census Bureau has estimated, he says, that in 1978 between 3.5 million and 6 million illegal immigrants were present in the U.S. Fuchs says, "Since we know that some of those have been coming since long before 1970, and since we also know that a large proportion of them are persons who go back and forth and are definitely not permanent residents, it is clearly fallacious to assert a number such as 50 percent without carefully qualifying it."

45      The demographic argument cannot be dismissed. But if immigrants bring adaptability to an economy, they may thereby increase the chances of finding new ways to use and conserve resources. Environmental concern means that we must strike a balance between

two competing virtues: a sustainable population and the invigorating effects of immigration. Too many of the environmental activists sound as if immigration is an unrelieved evil.

The second objection concerns international equity, even morality. It starts with the premise that immigration is a naturally selective process. Precisely because immigrants are so industrious, it is argued, the United States should not be skimming them from the poor nations of the world. Roger Conner, the executive director of the Federation for American Immigration Reform (FAIR), told a congressional committee in 1981 that the 808,000 legal immigrants and refugees admitted the previous year represented one five-thousandth of the population of the world. "Out of 5,000 impoverished people, we took one, taking the brightest, most able, most energetic, the best organized," he said. "We are taking the cream of each social class by the standards of their society. . . . We are taking the most energetic and talented."

In a human family of great riches and greater deprivation, a country as comfortable as the United States has an obligation to help. But of the varied ways in which America might advance the interests of poor countries, closing the door on their people seems one of the least effective, direct, or fair.

"We never heard this argument from experts in economic development or from the developing countries themselves," says Lawrence Fuchs. "We only heard it from Americans who oppose immigration."

Third, many people object to immigration because of the Americans it hurts. Overall, the nation might gain from immigration, they concede. But the benefits go to the most comfortable Americans, and the costs are absorbed by the least powerful and privileged.

50    Roger Conner is one of the foremost apostles of this view.

Conner is a compact, sandy-haired lawyer, thirty-five years old, with a puckishly all-American look. Like many other lobbyists in Washington, he seems to be struggling to resist grabbing his listeners by the lapels so as to be sure they'll hear all he has to say. In the past, he channeled his enthusiasm into the environmental movement, but, he says, he came to feel that immigration was the biggest environmental question of all. For the past four years, as executive director of and chief spokesman for FAIR, he has been asking Americans to re-examine their assumptions about immigration.

Conner is exasperated by the notion that you can understand the effects of immigration by looking at the immigrants. "They are the last people you'd want to talk with," he said this spring. "Of course it's been good for them. Especially for the first ten years, they will work very hard. But what no one ever does, when they're out talking with the aliens and hearing their success stories, is talk to the people who are paying the price."

Conner admits that most people may profit from immigration. The immigrants themselves do, and so do those Americans who don't compete with immigrant labor and therefore are free to enjoy its blessings. The benefits include fresher food (picked by immigrant field hands, instead of by machine), more pliant domestic service (provided by Mexican maids), smaller bills in restaurants (with Salvadorans in the kitchen), and lower prices for new houses (because of lower pay for the construction crew).

Whom does that leave out? In Conner's view, those who pay the price are the black teenagers, the white working-class fathers, the ambitious children of maids and janitors, who are just as eager as any Vietnamese or Mexican to move up the ladder but who find that the rungs have been knocked out. This is a disaster for them but not, Conner says, for the classes that make the laws and run the businesses.

55      "If the illegal aliens were flooding into the legal, medical, educational, and business occupations of this country, this problem would have received national attention at the highest level and it would have been solved," the labor economist Vernon Briggs, of Cornell University, has written. Lawrence Fuchs says that according to public-opinion polls the college-educated are the only group in favor of more immigration.

The economic argument against immigration is particularly troublesome for liberals. It pits the rest of the world's poor against the two American groups thought to have the most to lose from increased immigration: unionized labor, which says its wage levels would be depressed, and young, unskilled blacks, who would be nudged out of place for entry-level jobs.

At this point, it is important to emphasize the distinction, not always clearly stated, between legal and illegal immigration. If one were searching for the pure immigrant spirit, the place to look would be among the illegals, for every one of them has overcome some obstacle in order to be here. But because they cannot compete fully in the aboveboard economy (they have no legal redress if underpaid or mistreated; they have difficulty getting loans or rising into the white-collar world), their climb up the occupational ladder ends early. More important, from Conner's perspective, they put unfair pressure on the American citizens competing for similar jobs. A man outside the law will accept working conditions a citizen would not—and should not.

Once the illegal immigrant has the job, the citizen must choose between accepting similar conditions or going without work.

What kind of work do the illegals perform? According to some academic theory, and to the folk wisdom of the Southwest, immigrants do the jobs that Americans "won't" do. Michael Piore, an economist from MIT, has developed a model of a "dual" labor market: some jobs are so dirty, so onerous, so poorly paid, that if immigrants were not there to take them, the jobs would not exist. Therefore, the immigrants who are filling them have not really displaced anyone else.

"People say, 'Why aren't blacks like the Haitians?'" says T. Willard Fair, the president of the Urban League of Greater Miami, where Haitians now hold many of the maid and bellman jobs in which blacks once got their start. "'Why don't they want to work?' The Haitians are behaving the way we did thirty years ago. We would work for anything, take any abuse in the workplace."

60    To most of those directly involved in the industries where illegal immigrants concentrate, it seems obvious that no one else is lining up for the jobs. Last December, Merle Linda Wolin, of *The Wall Street Journal*, went to see a number of businesses where illegal immigrants had been rounded up during the spring of 1982 in Project Jobs, a short-lived sweep against employed illegal immigrants.

At a furniture factory in Santa Ana, California, on a railroad-construction gang in Texas, in a food-processing plant in Chicago, and at other sites of hard work, Wolin found that American citizens had in fact turned up for the jobs when the immigrants were gone—but soon afterward, they had quit. The pay was too bad; unemployment compensation was, by comparison, an attractive deal. Former truck drivers and carpenters found it humiliating to sweep parking lots or to keep up with a racing assembly line. By the time the *Journal*'s reporter arrived, six months after Project Jobs, the plants were again full of illegal aliens. A team of researchers, headed by Wayne Cornelius, the director of the Center for U.S.-Mexican Studies at the University of California, San Diego, found a similar pattern in California. "The attitude of many young people is that this is the dirty work of society," Cornelius has said, "and that people born, brought up and educated in the U.S. shouldn't have to do it."

What I learned on my tours over the same territory supported Cornelius's point. At a packing house in San Antonio, for example, men grunted as they hauled sides of meat from trucks into refrigerators. They disappeared as I, an Anglo in a rented car, drove up; Project Jobs had struck here. The beefy, red-haired foreman said that he'd be "happy" to have citizens in his work force if he could get them. Of course, he had "no idea" whether there were any illegal immigrants there. "It's against the law to ask." This is the convenient fiction that permits many employers to hire an illegal work force and pretend they haven't.

The agricultural industry in California, Texas, and Florida depends more heavily on illegal labor than any other industry does, and the growers have a more fully developed self-justifying rationale. Many protect themselves by saying they don't know who works for them, since the hiring is done by crew chiefs, acting as "independent agents." In the Rio Grande Valley of Texas, "independent" contracting means that people cross the river between 4 and 6 A.M. and stand near the bridges in Brownsville and Progreso, waiting for crew chiefs to drive up and hire truckloads of workers for the day. In the inland reaches of Texas and other large agricultural states, commuter labor is not so feasible, and resident camps of illegal immigrants are an open secret. Growers say they have no alternative: they need Mexicans (or, in Florida, Haitians) to work the fields, because no one else would stick with the job. Americans can get food stamps and live like kings on welfare, I was told by orange growers in the Rio Grande Valley; but the Mexicans are grateful for the work. They are even grateful for the piece-rate wages—40 cents for a bushel of cucumbers, 35 cents for a sack of oranges—that usually work out to well under the minimum wage.

Even Alfred Giugni, whose job is preventing illegal-immigration, says the growers may have a point. Giugni, a gigantic, mirthful man of mixed Italian and Hawaiian parentage, is the district director of the Immigration and Naturalization Service office in El Paso. "In the 1950s, the people picking strawberries in Oregon were high school and college students," he says. "Now they're Vietnamese and illegal Hispanics. The employers like it, because they will work harder. Your high school student will work long enough to earn as much money as he wants, and then he'll quit."

65 In Houston, a city swollen with immigrants from the declining industrial cities of Michigan and Indiana and the turbulent societies of Central and South America, I spent several days talking with illegal immigrants from Mexico and El Salvador. All had been successful by their own standards, but all operated along the margin that separates jobs "with a future" from work Americans "won't" do.

One of the women was in her forties and was wearing a housekeeper's jacket from an office-maintenance firm. She had been raised in El Salvador, and for several years taught elementary school there.

She came to the United States in 1970, when she was in her late twenties, on a tourist visa. It expired after three months, but she decided to stay. She began to work as a live-in maid for three immigrant families who shared one house. Her pay was $40 a week plus room and board. By 1974, she was earning $75 a week for the same work.

"Next, I learn to drive, so I can make more money," she said. With more of the city to choose her employers from, she was able to raise her rate to $125 a week. "But I am so tired of living in. I look for other work." In 1977, she found a job as a nighttime janitor—"bathroom lady"—in an office building. After a month and a half there, "the company sees that I speak a little English," she said. "They have other Latin people working there. They put me in a supervisory position, give me $2.65 an hour. During the days, I still clean house for $30 a day. I take the bus, and from six to ten in the evening I clean the offices. I am working thirteen hours a day."

She maintained this pace until 1981. As she had moved toward bigger, more institutionalized employers, her treatment had improved, and she hoped to continue that trend. She went to the employment manager at one of Houston's best-known hotels and applied to be supervisor of the housekeeping staff. She was eventually hired, and after several months moved to a similar position at a new office center. She now earns and pays taxes on $18,000 a year. "Nobody ever asks me for my paper," she says. "Never. But my wages are too low. I take care of a big place; I would be making more than $18,000 if I had my papers."

I also met in Houston an eighteen-year-old with a tousle-haired country-boy look, who was dressed in shiny black polyester trousers and a matching vest, worn over a white-on-white shirt. He left his farming village in El Salvador late in 1980, because, he said, "it is dangerous to be on either side." He took buses through Guatemala and Mexico, offered *mordida*—bribes—of $10 and $20 a shot to Mexican officials along the way, and reached the frontier near Nuevo Laredo, Mexico, by the end of the year. He crossed the Rio Grande, which at most places means nothing more than a wade, and hitchhiked out of Laredo to Houston. He located friends from his village, lived with them, and found a job at $3.40 an hour washing dishes in a well-known hotel. This wage was typical: outside of agriculture and domestic service, I found almost no illegal immigrants working for less than the federal minimum wage of $3.35 an hour, but many working at the minimum or just above it.

70    After a few days in the kitchen, the young man had heard enough from his friends to believe that he could find a less grueling way to

earn his money. He found a job in a metal-pipe yard, which at least was outdoor work. He tried to improve his English, and, although it is still not good, he was able to apply for jobs in which he would deal with the public. He returned to the hotel, where he now works as a bartender, earning $4.25 an hour.

His companion, also from El Salvador, was a twenty-four-year-old with the intense, committed look of a radical intellectual. Of the several dozen Salvadorans I met in California and Texas, perhaps one quarter explained their immigration in terms of political oppression and human rights. The rest said they were hunting for work. This young man was one of the quarter. He said he had reluctantly left his wife and child behind, because he was "Looking for a country that would respect human rights." He took buses through Mexico until he neared the U.S. border, then waded the Rio Grande near Brownsville. He worked on farm-labor gangs on the vast, flat ranches of South Texas, hitched a ride to Houston, and started as a minimum-wage dishwasher in a hotel, the job he still holds. After he was established, he called for his wife to join him. She left their first child at home with her parents. Their second child was born in Houston late last year, a U.S. citizen.

These dishwashers and maids think they are doing jobs most Americans would refuse. But there is another view of illegal immigration: it holds that men and women like those I met in Houston are displacing Americans, directly or indirectly.

Donald Huddle, of Rice University, contends that citizens do want the jobs immigrants now hold. Huddle and other researchers surveyed the jobs that illegal immigrants were holding when they were caught and found that they paid from $4 to $9.50 an hour. He concluded, "These wages debunk the commonly held notion that illegal aliens are taking only those jobs that Americans don't want because they are so lowly paid." Vernon Briggs points out that in every broad category of work in which illegal immigrants are found, most of the workers are still American citizens. He says that therefore it is misleading to talk about "immigrant work."

A more fundamental objection raised to the "Americans won't do dirty work" argument is that it ignores the dynamic aspect of economics. Perhaps it proves nothing that citizens won't take the jobs now available in the packing house and the tomato field; perhaps those jobs are dirty and low-paid precisely because so much cheap labor is available to fill them. "If there were no illegals," says Ray Marshall, "the jobs would be different."

75    Businesses in the service sector, such as restaurants and hotels, would pass along the modest additional cost of hiring legal help. Who would notice the extra dollar on the dinner bill? Some farmers would be able to pass along the extra cost of picking grapes or oranges; others would use labor more efficiently or mechanize their fields.

Still other businesses would fold, but for them the restrictionists shed no tears. In part, they would be service "businesses," such as household help. What would happen if the border were closed tomorrow? I asked Alfred Giugni, in El Paso. "The only serious impact would be the maid situation," he said. "Everything else would work out. You get the impression that the only maids who are paid the minimum wage in El Paso are the ones who work for people in the INS [Immigration and Naturalization Service]."

The other likely casualties would be garment factories, leather works, and other low-wage, labor-intensive businesses. "The jobs in which illegal aliens are not displacing American workers are those jobs in which American industry is competing with workers in newly developed countries," Dan Stein, an official of FAIR, has written. America's future lies with a skillful work force and high tech. "The fewer unskilled laborers there are in this country, the better off we should be," Vernon Briggs says.

In any case, Conner, Briggs, and others argue, it is a strange and greedy kind of social arithmetic that tots up those who might hypothetically be hurt by restriction but ignores those who are now paying the costs of uncontrolled borders.

Briggs notes government estimates that 29 million people, or nearly 30 percent of the employed civilian labor force, work in what he calls "the kinds of low-skilled industrial, service, and agricultural jobs in which illegal aliens typically seek employment." He contends that "farm workers, dishwashers, laborers, garbage collectors, building cleaners, restaurant employees, gardeners, maintenance workers, to name a few occupations, perform useful and often indispensable work. Unfortunately, their remuneration is often poor, in part because there is a large pool of persons available for these jobs."

80    "The victims of immigration are the marginal workers, with low education, who may not be hot to work sixty hours a week," says Roger Conner. "My own life as an employer teaches me that if an employer is looking for a minimum of hassle, he will look past these people—unless he has a reason to have to make it work with them. There is just enough truth to the notion that aliens make better workers that it nourishes the stereotypes and creates a self-fulfilling prophecy. One

reason there are so few opportunities for young black people on construction sites is that the aliens on the scene always have somebody available to bring in with them."

When Conner was a boy, in Dallas, his mother took in ironing and later did domestic work. He cites today's counterparts of his younger self as among the Americans the immigrant hurts. "To the extent that the initial targets of immigrants tend to be unskilled jobs and low-skill entrepreneurial opportunities—say a small construction company—those are the ways out of poverty for the energetic American. The guy who wants to work his way up—to him the immigrant is an obstacle. I would concede a gain in efficiency from immigration, but the cost is what we lose in upward mobility from the lower classes."

Conner's "concession" distills the economic argument against immigration to its pure form: immigrants can make the economy more efficient, but they can hurt the American lower class. Is this grounds for closing the door? I believe not.

For one thing, the analysis may be totally incorrect. Sixty years ago, Progressives and conservatives joined to oppose the New Immigration. The Progressives based their argument on the damage done to America's poor. Robert Hunter's *Poverty*, an influential Progressive tract, concluded that the immigrant stood between the American workingman and a better life. The Dillingham Commission, a government panel whose forty-two-volume study laid the groundwork for the immigration laws of the 1920s, also said that immigrants displaced American workers. Even so, the commission concluded that displaced workers found better jobs in an expanding economy. Oscar Handlin has said of its findings, "To the extent that immigrants contributed to that expansion, they actually helped to lift the condition of the laborers they found already there."

Is it necessarily any different now? In Texas and California, Mexican-Americans have been displaced by Mexican immigrants. Ricardo Romo, who teaches history at the University of Texas, says that his parents were displaced from their migrant laborers' jobs in South Texas. But "no one should assume that those who leave are worse off than if they had stayed," he says. "In many cases, there is substantial improvement when people move on. The kids go to better schools than their parents, they get into skilled trades."

85    Through the past decade, unemployment has been low in the very places where immigration, legal and illegal, has been the greatest: California, Florida, Texas. True, this is partly tautology—why would immigrants go where there were no jobs? But it also suggests that a

growing economy, even though washed by waves of immigration, can create more opportunities for Americans than a stagnant one that freezes competitors out.

The Urban Institute's study of Southern California reported that the region's unemployment rates for all races and age groups were lower than the national average, and that the difference between rates for whites and for non-whites was less than elsewhere. This was true though Southern California is rivaled only by Miami in its concentration of immigrants and has a higher proportion of illegals. "One can conclude that the large undocumented population in Los Angeles did not increase unemployment among Hispanics or other groups in Los Angeles," the report said.

Even if the case against illegal immigrants is assumed to be true, is the solution to shield the entire economy from the bracing effects of immigration? Restrictionists often cite the case of Kemah, Texas, to suggest the tensions that even legal immigrants create. In Kemah, the commercial fishermen who had long worked the Gulf Coast found their waters dotted with Vietnamese in rival boats. The Vietnamese were here legally, admitted as refugees. They had scrimped, like the Nguyens, to lease or buy their fishing craft. The working-class whites of the region had initially tolerated them. When the Vietnamese "took low income jobs cleaning fish or working in restaurant kitchens, they were acceptable," Paul D. Starr, a sociologist from Auburn University, said recently in the *Texas Observer*. "But when they became fishermen—and competitors—attitudes toward them changed. . . . The unpleasant fact is that the Vietnamese work harder and longer and under more difficult conditions than do most Americans."

The Vietnamese won, and American citizens lost—but they lost in the kind of economic competition that is supposed to be the engine of capitalism. Should the fishermen have been protected against the Vietnamese's willingness to work longer hours? Are we ready to say that fair competition is too much for Americans to withstand? Unless we are, there is no economic case against legal immigration.

Unfair competition is something else. Illegal immigrants, however admirable as individuals, are unfair rivals. They are often exploited, but that is not the real inequity. After all, they are here by their own choice. They are most unfair to the struggling Americans who hold similar jobs. Appreciating the immigrants' adaptability, we should welcome their lawful presence. Can anyone contend that what the Nguyen family enjoys it has "taken" from someone else? But recognizing the barriers that the black teenager, the white laborer, and the

Mexican-American father confront, and the strains their frustration puts on the entire society, we should attempt to ensure that less of America's immigration takes place outside the law.

## Questions for Discussion

How objective is Fallows's exploration of the issue? What kinds of evidence does he use?

How compelling are Fallows's anecdotes of immigrant families and individuals? Why does he rely so heavily on telling immigrants' stories?

*An influential and admired essayist, novelist, poet and playwright,* **James Baldwin** *(1924–1987) grew up in Harlem, New York City. As a teenager, Baldwin preached in local churches until he gave up the ministry to pursue a writing career in Greenwich Village. The success of his first novel,* Go Tell It on the Mountain *(1953), permitted him to devote full time to his writing, and he moved to France to escape the stifling oppression he felt in the United States. Although he wrote about many topics, including homosexuality, Baldwin maintained a lifelong interest in exploring race relations and racial identity in America, themes central to his famous* The Fire Next Time *(1963) and to the following essay, "Stranger in the Village," from his* Notes of a Native Son *(1955).*

## *James Baldwin*

# Stranger in the Village

From all available evidence no black man had ever set foot in this tiny Swiss village before I came. I was told before arriving that I would probably be a "sight" for the village; I took this to mean that people of my complexion were rarely seen in Switzerland, and also that city people are always something of a "sight" outside of the city. It did not occur to me—possibly because I am an American—that there could be people anywhere who had never seen a Negro.

It is a fact that cannot be explained on the basis of the inaccessibility of the village. The village is very high, but it is only four hours from Milan and three hours from Lausanne. It is true that it is virtually unknown. Few people making plans for a holiday would elect to come here. On the other hand, the villagers are able, presumably, to come and go as they please—which they do: to another town at the foot of the mountain, with a population of approximately five thousand, the nearest place to see a movie or go to the bank. In the village there is no movie house, no bank, no library, no theater; very few radios, one jeep, one station wagon; and, at the moment, one typewriter, mine, an invention which the woman next door to me here had never seen. There are about six hundred people living here, all Catholic—I conclude this from the fact that the Catholic church is open all year round, whereas the Protestant chapel, set off on a hill a little removed from the village, is open only in the summertime when the tourists arrive. There are four or five hotels, all closed now, and four or five *bistros*, of which, however, only two do any business during the winter. These two do not do a great deal, for life in the village seems to end around nine or ten o'clock. There are a few stores, butcher, baker, *épicerie*, a hardware store, and a money-changer—who cannot change travelers' checks, but must send them down to the bank, an operation which takes two or three days. There is something called the *Ballet Haus*, closed in the winter and used for God knows what, certainly not ballet, during the summer. There seems to be only one schoolhouse in the village, and this for the quite young children; I suppose this to mean that their older brothers and sisters at some point descend from these mountains in order to complete their education—possibly, again, to the town just below. The landscape is absolutely forbidding, mountains towering on all four sides, ice and snow as far as the eye can reach. In this white wilderness, men and women and children move all day, carrying washing, wood, buckets of milk or water, sometimes skiing on Sunday afternoons. All week long boys and young men are to be seen shoveling snow off the rooftops, or dragging wood down from the forest in sleds.

The village's only real attraction, which explains the tourist season, is the hot spring water. A disquietingly high proportion of these tourists are cripples, or semi-cripples, who come year after year—from other parts of Switzerland, usually—to take the waters. This lends the village, at the height of the season, a rather terrifying air of sanctity, as though it were a lesser Lourdes. There is often something beautiful, there is always something awful, in the spectacle of a person who has lost one of his faculties, a faculty he never questioned until it was gone, and who struggles to recover it. Yet people remain people, on crutches or indeed on deathbeds; and wherever I passed, the first summer I was here, among the native villagers or among the lame, a wind passed with me—of astonishment, curiosity, amusement, and outrage. The first summer I stayed two weeks and never intended to return. But I did return in the winter, to work; the village offers, obviously, no distractions whatever and has the further advantage of being extremely cheap. Now it is winter again, a year later, and I am here again. Everyone in the village knows my name, though they scarcely ever use it, knows that I come from America—though this, apparently, they will never really believe: black men come from Africa—and everyone knows that I am the friend of the son of a woman who was born here, and that I am staying in their chalet. But I remain as much a stranger today as I was the first day I arrived, and the children shout *Neger! Neger!* as I walk along the streets.

It must be admitted that in the beginning I was far too shocked to have any real reaction. In so far as I reacted at all, I reacted by trying to be pleasant—it being a great part of the American Negro's education (long before he goes to school) that he must make people "like" him. This smile-and-the-world-smiles-with-you routine worked about as well in this situation as it had in the situation for which it was designed, which is to say that it did not work at all. No one, after all, can be liked whose human weight and complexity cannot be, or has not been, admitted. My smile was simply another unheard-of phenomenon which allowed them to see my teeth—they did not, really, see my smile and I began to think that, should I take to snarling, no one would notice any difference. All of the physical characteristics of the Negro which had caused me, in America, a very different and almost forgotten pain were nothing less than miraculous—or infernal—in the eyes of the village people. Some thought my hair was the color of tar, that it had the texture of wire, or the texture of cotton. It was jocularly suggested that I might let it all grow long and make myself a winter coat. If I sat in the sun for more than five minutes some daring creature was certain to come along and gingerly put his fingers on my hair, as though he were afraid of an electric shock, or put his hand on my hand, astonished that the color did not rub off. In all of this, in which it must be conceded there was the charm of genuine wonder and in which there was certainly no element of intentional unkindness, there was yet no suggestion that I was human: I was simply a living wonder.

5      I knew that they did not mean to be unkind, and I know it now; it is necessary, nevertheless, for me to repeat this to myself each time I walk out of the chalet. The children who shout *Neger!* have no way of knowing the echoes this sound raises in me. They are brimming with good humor and the more daring swell with pride when I stop to speak with them. Just the same, there are days when I cannot pause and smile, when I have no heart to play with them; when, indeed, I mutter sourly to myself, exactly as I muttered on the streets of a city these children have never seen, when I was no bigger than these children are now: *Your* mother *was a nigger.* Joyce is right about history being a nightmare—but it may be the nightmare from which no one *can* awaken. People are trapped in history and history is trapped in them.

There is a custom in the village—I am told it is repeated in many villages—of "buying" African natives for the purpose of converting them to Christianity. There stands in the church all year round a small box with a slot for money, decorated with a black figurine, and into this box the villagers drop their francs. During the *carnaval* which precedes Lent, two village children have their faces blackened—out of which bloodless darkness their blue eyes shine like ice—and fantastic horsehair wigs are placed on their blond heads; thus disguised, they solicit among the villagers for money for the missionaries in Africa. Between the box in the church and the blackened children, the village "bought" last year six or eight African natives. This was reported to me with pride by the wife of one of the *bistro* owners and I was careful to express astonishment and pleasure at the solicitude shown by the village for the souls of black folk. The *bistro* owner's wife beamed with a pleasure far more genuine than my own and seemed to feel that I might now breathe more easily concerning the souls of at least six of my kinsmen.

I tried not to think of these so lately baptized kinsmen, of the price paid for them, or the peculiar price they themselves would pay, and said nothing about my father, who having taken his own conversion too literally never, at bottom, forgave the white world (which he described as heathen) for having saddled him with a Christ in whom, to judge at least from their treatment of him, they themselves no longer believed. I thought of white men arriving for the first time in an African village, strangers there, as I am a stranger here, and tried to imagine the astounded populace touching their hair and marveling at the color of their skin. But there is a great difference between being the first white man to be seen by Africans and being the first black man to be seen by whites. The white man takes the astonishment as tribute, for he arrives to conquer and to convert the natives, whose inferiority in relation to himself is not even to be questioned; whereas I, without a thought of conquest, find myself among a people whose culture controls me, has even, in a sense, created me, people who have cost me more in anguish and rage than they will ever know, who yet do not even know of my existence. The astonishment with which I might have greeted them, should they have stumbled into my African village a few hundred years ago, might have rejoiced their hearts. But the astonishment with which they greet me today can only poison mine.

And this is so despite everything I may do to feel differently, despite my friendly conversations with the *bistro* owner's wife, despite their three-year-old son who has at last become my friend, despite the *saluts* and *bonsoirs* which I exchange with people as I walk, despite the fact that I know that no individual can be taken to task for what history is doing, or has done. I say that the culture of these people controls me—but they can scarcely be held responsible for European culture. America comes out of Europe, but these people have never seen America nor have most of them seen more of

Europe than the hamlet at the foot of their mountain. Yet they move with an authority which I shall never have; and they regard me, quite rightly, not only as a stranger in their village but as a suspect latecomer, bearing no credentials, to everything they have—however unconsciously—inherited.

For this village, even were it incomparably more remote and incredibly more primitive, is the West, the West onto which I have been so strangely grafted. These people cannot be, from the point of view of power, strangers anywhere in the world; they have made the modern world, in effect, even if they do not know it. The most illiterate among them is related, in a way that I am not, to Dante, Shakespeare, Michelangelo, Aeschylus, Da Vinci, Rembrandt, and Racine; the cathedral at Chartres says something to them which it cannot say to me, as indeed would New York's Empire State Building, should anyone here ever see it. Out of their hymns and dances come Beethoven and Bach. Go back a few centuries and they are in their full glory—but I am in Africa, watching the conquerors arrive.

10       The rage of the disesteemed is personally fruitless, but it is also absolutely inevitable; this rage, so generally discounted, so little understood even among the people whose daily bread it is, is one of the things that makes history. Rage can only with difficulty, and never entirely, be brought under the domination of the intelligence and is therefore not susceptible to any arguments whatever. This is a fact which ordinary representatives of the *Herrenvolk*, having never felt this rage and being unable to imagine it, quite fail to understand. Also, rage cannot be hidden, it can only be dissembled. This dissembling deludes the thoughtless, and strengthens rage and adds, to rage, contempt. There are, no doubt, as many ways of coping with the resulting complex of tensions as there are black men in the world, but no black man can hope ever to be entirely liberated from this internal warfare— rage, dissembling, and contempt having inevitably accompanied his first realization of the power of white men. What is crucial here is that, since white men represent in the black man's world so heavy a weight, white men have for black men a reality which is far from being reciprocal; and hence all black men have toward all white men an attitude which is designed, really, either to rob the white man of the jewel of his naïveté, or else to make it cost him dear.

The black man insists, by whatever means he finds at his disposal, that the white man cease to regard him as an exotic rarity and recognize him as a human being. This is a very charged and difficult moment, for there is a great deal of will power involved in the white man's naïveté. Most people are not naturally reflective any more than they are naturally malicious, and the white man prefers to keep the black man at a certain human remove because it is easier for him thus to preserve his simplicity and avoid being called to account for crimes committed by his forefathers, or his neighbors. He is inescapably aware, nevertheless, that he is in a better position in the world than black men are, nor can he quite put to death the suspicion that he is hated by black men therefore. He does not wish to be hated, neither does he wish to change places, and at this point in his uneasiness he can scarcely avoid having recourse to those legends which white men have created about black men, the most usual effect of which is that the white man finds himself enmeshed, so to speak, in his own language which describes hell, as well as the attributes which lead one to hell, as being as black as night.

Every legend, moreover, contains its residuum of truth, and the root function of language is to control the universe by describing it. It is of quite considerable significance that black men remain, in the imagination, and in overwhelming numbers in fact, beyond the disciplines of salvation; and this despite the fact the West has been "buying" African natives for centuries. There is, I should hazard, an instantaneous necessity to be divorced from this so visibly unsaved stranger, in whose heart, moreover, one cannot guess what dreams of vengeance are being nourished; and, at the same time, there are few things on earth more attractive than the idea of the unspeakable liberty which is allowed the unredeemed. When, beneath the black mask, a human being begins to make himself felt one cannot escape a certain awful wonder as to what kind of human being it is. What one's imagination makes of other people is dictated, of course, by the laws of one's own personality and it is one of the ironies of black-white relations that, by means of what the white man imagines the black man to be, the black man is enabled to know who the white man is.

I have said, for example, that I am as much a stranger in this village today as I was the first summer I arrived, but this is not quite true. The villagers wonder less about the texture of my hair than they did then, and wonder rather more about me. And the fact that their wonder now exists on another level is reflected in their attitudes and in their eyes. There are the children who make those delightful, hilarious, sometimes astonishingly grave overtures of friendship in the unpredictable fashion of children; other children, having been taught that the devil is a black man, scream in genuine anguish as I approach. Some of the older women never pass without a friendly greeting, never pass, indeed, if it seems that they will be able to engage me in conversation; other women look down or look away or rather contemptuously smirk. Some of the men drink with me and suggest that I learn how to ski—partly, I gather, because they cannot imagine what I would look like on skis—and want to know if I am married, and ask questions about my *métier*. But some of the men have accused *le sale négre*—behind my back—of stealing wood and there is already in the eyes of some of them that peculiar, intent, paranoiac malevolence which one sometimes surprises in the eyes of American white men when, out walking with their Sunday girl, they see a Negro male approach.

There is a dreadful abyss between the streets of this village and the streets of the city in which I was born, between the children who shout *Neger!* today and those who shouted *Nigger!* Yesterday—the abyss is experience, the American experience. The syllable hurled behind me today expresses, above all, wonder: I am a stranger here. But I am not a stranger in America and the same syllable riding on the American air expresses the war my presence has occasioned in the American soul.

15     For this village brings home to me this fact: that there was a day, and not really a very distant day, when Americans were scarcely Americans at all but discontented Europeans, facing a great unconquered continent and strolling, say, into a marketplace and seeing black men for the first time. The shock this spectacle afforded is suggested, surely, by the promptness with which they decided that these black men were not really men but cattle. It is true that the necessity on the part of the settlers of the New World of reconciling their moral assumptions with the fact—and the necessity—of slavery enhanced immensely the charm of this idea, and it is also true that this idea expresses, with a truly American bluntness, the attitude which to varying extents all masters have had toward all slaves.

But between all former slaves and slave owners and the drama which begins for Americans over three hundred years ago at Jamestown, there are at least two differences to be observed. The American Negro slave could not suppose, for one thing, as slaves in past epochs had supposed and often done, that he would ever be able to wrest the power from his master's hands. This was a supposition which the modern era, which was to bring about such vast changes in the aims and dimensions of power, put to death; it only begins, in unprecedented fashion, and with dreadful implications, to be resurrected today. But even had this supposition persisted with undiminished force, the American Negro slave could not have used it to lend his condition dignity, for the reason that this supposition rests on another: that the slave in exile yet remains related to his past, has some means—if only in memory—of revering and sustaining the forms of his former life, is able, in short, to maintain his identity.

This was not the case with the American Negro slave. He is unique among the black men of the world in that his past was taken from him, almost literally, at one blow. One wonders what on earth the first slave found to say to the first dark child he bore. I am told that there are Haitians able to trace their ancestry back to African kings, but any American Negro wishing to go back so far will find his journey through time abruptly arrested by the signature on the bill of sale which served as the entrance paper for his ancestor. At the time—to say nothing of the circumstances—of the enslavement of the captive black man who was to become the American Negro, there was not the remotest possibility that he would ever take power from his master's hands. There was no reason to suppose that his situation would ever change, nor was there, shortly, anything to indicate that his situation had ever been different. It was his necessity, in the words of E. Franklin Frazier, to find a "motive for living under American culture or die." The identity of the American Negro comes out of this extreme situation, and the evolution of this identify was a source of the most intolerable anxiety in the minds and the lives of his masters.

For the history of the American Negro is unique also in this: that the question of his humanity, and of his rights therefore as a human being, became a burning one for several generations of Americans, so burning a question that it ultimately became one of those used to divide the nation. It is out of this argument that the venom of the epithet *Nigger!* is derived. It is an argument which Europe has never had, and hence Europe quite sincerely fails to understand how or why the argument arose in the first place, why its effects are so frequently disastrous and always so unpredictable, why it refuses until today to be entirely settled. Europe's black possessions remained—and do remain—in Europe's colonies, at which remove they represented no threat whatever to European identity. If they posed any problem at all for the European conscience, it was a problem which remained comfortingly abstract: in effect, the black man, *as a man*, did not exist for Europe. But in America, even as a slave, he was an inescapable part of the general social fabric and no American could escape having an attitude toward him. Americans attempt until today to make an abstraction of the Negro, but the very nature of these abstractions reveals the tremendous effects the presence of the Negro has had on the American character.

When one considers the history of the Negro in America it is of the greatest importance to recognize that the moral beliefs of a person, or a people, are never really as tenuous as life—which is not moral—very often causes them to appear; these create for them a frame of reference and a necessary hope, the hope being that when life has done its worst they will be enabled to rise above themselves and to triumph over life. Life would scarcely be bearable if this hope did not exist. Again, even when the worst has been said, to betray a belief is not by any means to have put oneself beyond its power; the betrayal of a belief is not the same thing as ceasing to believe. If this were not so there would be no moral standards in the world at all. Yet one must also recognize that morality is based on ideas and that all ideas are dangerous—dangerous because ideas can only lead to action and where the action leads no man can say. And dangerous in this respect that confronted with the impossibility of becoming free of them, one can be driven to the most inhuman excesses. The ideas on which American beliefs are based are not, though Americans often seem to think so, ideas which originated in America. They came out of Europe. And the establishment of democracy on the American continent was scarcely as radical a break with the past as was the necessity, which Americans faced, of broadening this concept to include black men.

20      This was, literally, a hard necessity. It was impossible, for one thing, for Americans to abandon their beliefs, not only because these beliefs alone seemed able to justify the sacrifices they had endured and the blood that they had spilled, but also because these beliefs afforded them their only bulwark against a moral chaos as absolute as the physical chaos of the continent it was their destiny to conquer. But in the situation in which Americans found themselves, these beliefs threatened an idea which, whether or not one likes to think so, is the very warp and woof of the heritage of the West, the idea of white supremacy.

Americans have made themselves notorious by the shrillness and the brutality with which they have insisted on this idea, but they did not invent it; and it has escaped the world's notice that those very excesses of which Americans have been guilty imply a certain, unprecedented uneasiness over the idea's life and power, if not, indeed, the idea's validity. The idea of white supremacy rests simply on the fact that white men are the creators of civilization (the present civilization, which is the only one that matters; all previous civilizations are simply "contributions" to our own) and are therefore civilization's guardians and defenders. Thus it was impossible for Americans to accept the black man as one of themselves, for to do so was to jeopardize their status as white men. But not so to accept him was to deny his human reality, his human weight and complexity, and the strain of denying the overwhelmingly undeniable forced Americans into rationalizations so fantastic that they approached the pathological.

At the root of the American Negro problem is the necessity of the American white man to find a way of living with the Negro in order to be able to live with himself. And the history of this problem can be reduced to the means used by Americans—lynch law and law, segregation and legal acceptance, terrorization and concession—either to come to terms with this necessity, or to find a way around it, or (most usually) to find a way of doing both these things at once. The resulting spectacle, at once foolish and dreadful, led someone to make the quite accurate observation that "the Negro-in-America is a form of insanity which overtakes white men."

In this long battle, a battle by no means finished, the unforeseeable effects of which will be felt by many future generations, the white man's motive was the protection of his identity; the black man was motivated by the need to establish an identity. And despite the terrorization which the Negro in America endured and endures sporadically until today, despite the cruel and totally inescapable ambivalence of his status in his country, the battle for his identity has long ago been won. He is not a visitor to the West, but a citizen there, an American; as American as the Americans who despise him, the Americans who fear him, the Americans who love him—the Americans who became less than themselves, or rose to be greater than themselves by virtue of the fact that the challenge he represented was inescapable. He is perhaps the only black man in the world whose relationship to white men is more terrible, more subtle, and more meaningful than the relationship of bitter possessed to uncertain possessor. His survival depended, and his development depends, on his ability to turn his peculiar status in the Western world to his own advantage and, it may be, to the very great advantage of that world. It remains for him to fashion out of his experience that which will give him sustenance, and a voice.

The cathedral at Chartres, I have said, says something to the people of this village which it cannot say to me; but it is important to understand that this cathedral says something to me which it cannot say to them. Perhaps they are struck by the power of the spires, the glory of the windows; but they have known God, after all, longer than I have known him, and in a different way, and I am terrified by the slippery bottomless well to be found in the crypt, down which heretics were hurled to death, and by the obscene, inescapable gargoyles jutting out of the stone and seeming to say that God and the devil can never be divorced. I doubt that the villagers think of the devil when they face a cathedral because they have never been identified with the devil. But I must accept the status which myth, if nothing else, gives me in the West before I can hope to change the myth.

25    Yet, if the American Negro has arrived at his identity by virtue of the absoluteness of his estrangement from his past, American white men still nourish the illusion that there is some means of recovering the European innocence, of returning to a state in which black men do not exist. This is one of the greatest errors Americans can make. The identity they fought so hard to protect has, by virtue of that battle, undergone a change; Americans are as unlike any other white people in the world as it is possible to be. I do not think, for example, that it is too much to suggest that the American vision of the world—which allows so little reality, generally speaking, for any of the darker forces in human life, which tends until today to paint moral issues in glaring black and white—owes a great deal to the battle waged by Americans to maintain between themselves and black men a human separation which could not be bridged. It is only now beginning to be borne in on us—very faintly, it must be admitted, very slowly, and very much against our will—that this vision of the world is dangerously inaccurate, and perfectly useless. For it protects our moral high-mindedness at the terrible expense of weakening our grasp of reality. People who shut their eyes to reality simply invite their own destruction, and anyone who insists on remaining in a state of innocence long after that innocence is dead turns himself into a monster.

The time has come to realize that the interracial drama acted out on the American continent has not only created a new black man, it has created a new white man, too. No road whatever will lead Americans back to the simplicity of this European village where white men still have the luxury of looking on me as a stranger. I am not, really, a stranger any longer for any American alive. One of the things that distinguishes Americans from other people is that no other people has ever been so deeply involved in the lives of black men, and vice versa. This fact faced, with all its implications, it can be seen that the history of the American Negro problem is not merely shameful, it is also something of an achievement. For even when the worst has been said, it must also be added that the perpetual challenge posed by this problem was always, somehow, perpetually met. It is precisely this black-white experience which may prove of indispensable value to us in the world we face today. This world is white no longer, and it will never be white again.

## Questions for Discussion

According to Baldwin, where does identity come from? To what extent do individuals have the power to modify identity?

Why does Baldwin use the Swiss village to make points about American history and cultural politics?

*Richard Rodriguez, born in 1944 into a Spanish-speaking, Mexican-American family, was educated at Stanford, Columbia, and Berkeley. Many of his eloquent essays—like the ones in his* Days of Obligation: An Argument with My Mexican Father *(1992) and* Brown: The Last Discovery of America *(2003)—mix memoir and argument, and many measure the gains and losses that result when English replaces Spanish that is spoken at home. This essay, first published in the magazine* The American Scholar *(1981), was incorporated into his acclaimed (and controversial) book* Hunger of Memory *(1982).*

# Richard Rodriguez

## Aria: A Memoir of a Bilingual Childhood

I remember, to start with, that day in Sacramento in a California now nearly thirty years past, when I first entered a classroom—able to understand about fifty stray English words. The third of four children, I had been preceded by my older brother and sister to a neighborhood Roman Catholic school. But neither of them had revealed very much about their classroom experiences. They left each morning and returned each afternoon, always together, speaking Spanish as they climbed the five steps to the porch. And their mysterious books, wrapped in brown shopping-bag paper, remained on the table next to the door, closed firmly behind them.

An accident of geography sent me to a school where all my classmates were white and many were the children of doctors and lawyers and business executives. On that first day of school, my classmates must certainly have been uneasy to find themselves apart from their families, in the first institution of their lives. But I was astonished. I was fated to be the "problem student" in class.

The nun said, in a friendly but oddly impersonal voice: "Boys and girls, this is Richard Rodriguez." (I heard her sound it out: *Rich-heard Road-ree-guess.*) It was the first time I had heard anyone say my name in English. "Richard," the nun repeated more slowly, writing my name down in her book. Quickly I turned to see my mother's face dissolve in a watery blur behind the pebbled-glass door:

Now, many years later, I hear of something called "bilingual education"—a scheme proposed in the late 1960s by Hispanic-American social activists, later endorsed by a congressional vote. It is a program that seeks to permit non-English-speaking children (many from lower class homes) to use their "family language" as the language of school. Such, at least, is the aim its supporters announce. I hear them, and am forced to say no: It is not possible for a child, any child, ever to use his family's language in school. Not to understand this is to misunderstand the public uses of schooling and to trivialize the nature of intimate life.

5    Memory teaches me what I know of these matters. The boy reminds the adult. I was a bilingual child, but of a certain kind: "socially disadvantaged," the son of working-class parents, both Mexican immigrants.

In the early years of my boyhood, my parents coped very well in America. My father had steady work. My mother managed at home. They were nobody's victims. When we moved to a house many blocks from the Mexican-American section of town, they were not intimidated by those two or three neighbors who initially tried to make us unwelcome. ("Keep your brats away from my sidewalk!") But despite all they achieved, or perhaps because they had so much to achieve, they lacked any deep feeling of ease, of belonging in public. They regarded the people at work or in crowds as being very distant from us. Those were the others, *los gringos*. That term was interchangeable in their speech with another, even more telling: *los americanos*.

I grew up in a house where the only regular guests were my relations. On a certain day, enormous families of relatives would visit us, and there would be so many people that the noise and the bodies would spill out to the backyard and onto the front porch. Then for weeks no one would come. (If the doorbell rang, it was usually a salesman.) Our house stood apart—gaudy yellow in a row of white bungalows. We were the people with the noisy dog, the people who raised chickens. We were the foreigners on the block. A few neighbors would smile and wave at us. We waved back. But until I was seven years old, I did not know the name of the old couple living next door or the names of the kids living across the street.

In public, my father and mother spoke a hesitant, accented, and not always grammatical English. And then they would have to strain, their bodies tense, to catch the sense of what was rapidly said by *los gringos*. At home, they returned to Spanish. The language of their Mexican past sounded in counterpoint to the English spoken in public.

The words would come quickly, with ease. Conveyed through those sounds was the pleasing, soothing, consoling reminder that one was at home.

During those years when I was first learning to speak, my mother and father addressed me only in Spanish; in Spanish I learned to reply. By contrast, English (*inglés*) was the language I came to associate with gringos, rarely heard in the house. I learned my first words of English overhearing my parents speaking to strangers. At six years of age, I knew just enough words for my mother to trust me on errands to stores one block away—but no more.

10      I was then a listening child, careful to hear the very different sounds of Spanish and English. Wide-eyed with hearing, I'd listen to sounds more than to words. First, there were English (gringo) sounds. So many words still were unknown to me that when the butcher or the lady at the drugstore said something, exotic polysyllabic sounds would bloom in the midst of their sentences. Often the speech of people in public seemed to me very loud, booming with confidence. The man behind the counter would literally ask, "What can I do for you?" But by being so firm and clear, the sound of his voice said that he was a gringo; he belonged in public society. There were also the high, nasal notes of middle-class American speech—which I rarely am conscious of hearing today because I hear them so often, but could not stop hearing when I was a boy. Crowds at Safeway or at bus stops were noisy with the birdlike sounds of *los gringos*. I'd move away from them all— all the chirping chatter above me.

My own sounds I was unable to hear, but I knew that I spoke English poorly. My words could not extend to form complete thoughts. And the words I did speak I didn't know well enough to make distinct sounds. (Listeners would usually lower their heads to hear better what I was trying to say.) But it was one thing for *me* to speak English with difficulty; it was more troubling to hear my parents speaking in public: their high-whining vowels and guttural consonants; their sentences that got stuck with "eh" and "ah" sounds; the confused syntax; the hesitant rhythm of sounds so different from the way gringos spoke. I'd notice, moreover, that my parents' voices were softer than those of gringos we would meet.

I am tempted to say now that none of this mattered. (In adulthood I am embarrassed by childhood fears.) And, in a way, it didn't matter very much that my parents could not speak English with ease. Their linguistic difficulties had no serious consequences. My mother and father made themselves understood at the county hospital clinic and at government offices. And yet, in another way, it mattered very much. It was unsettling to hear my parents struggle with English. Hearing them, I'd grow nervous, and my clutching trust in their protection and power would be weakened.

There were many times like the night at a brightly lit gasoline station (a blaring white memory) when I stood uneasily hearing my father talk to a teenage attendant. I do not recall what they were saying, but I cannot forget the sounds my father made as he spoke. At one point his words slid together to form one long word—sounds as confused as the threads of blue and green oil in the puddle next to my shoes. His voice rushed through what he had left to say. Toward the end, he reached falsetto notes, appealing to his listener's understanding. I looked away at the lights of passing automobiles. I tried not to hear any more. But I heard only too well the attendant's reply, his calm, easy tones. Shortly afterward, headed for home, I shivered when my father put his hand on my shoulder. The very first chance that I got, I evaded his grasp and ran on ahead into the dark, skipping with feigned boyish exuberance.

But then there was Spanish: *español*, the language rarely heard away from the house; *español*, the language which seemed to me therefore a private language, my family's language. To hear its sounds was to feel myself specially recognized as one of the family, apart from *los otros*. A simple remark, an inconsequential comment could convey that assurance. My parents would say something to me and I would feel embraced by the sounds of their words. Those sounds said: *I am speaking with ease in Spanish. I am addressing you in words I never use with los gringos. I recognize you as someone special, close, like no one outside. You belong with us. In the family, Ricardo.*

15      At the age of six, well past the time when most middle-class children no longer notice the difference between sounds uttered at home and words spoken in public, I had a different experience. I lived in a world compounded of sounds. I was a child longer than most. I lived in a magical world, surrounded by sounds both pleasing and fearful. I shared with my family a language enchantingly private—different from that used in the city around us.

Just opening or closing the screen door behind me was an important experience. I'd rarely leave home all alone or without feeling reluctance. Walking down the sidewalk, under the canopy of tall trees, I'd warily notice the (suddenly) silent neighborhood kids who stood warily watching me. Nervously, I'd arrive at the grocery store to hear there the sounds of the gringo, reminding me that in this so-big world

I was a foreigner. But if leaving home was never routine, neither was coming back. Walking toward our house, climbing the steps from the sidewalk, in summer when the front door was open, I'd hear voices beyond the screen door talking in Spanish. For a second or two I'd stay, linger there listening. Smiling, I'd hear my mother call out, saying in Spanish, "Is that you, Richard?" Those were her words, but all the while her sounds would assure me: *You are home now. Come closer inside. With us.* "*Sí,*" I'd reply.

Once more inside the house, I would resume my place in the family. The sounds would grow harder to hear. Once more at home, I would grow less conscious of them. It required, however, no more than the blurt of the doorbell to alert me all over again to listen to sounds. The house would turn instantly quiet while my mother went to the door. I'd hear her hard English sounds. I'd wait to hear her voice turn to soft-sounding Spanish, which assured me, as surely as did the clicking tongue of the lock on the door, that the stranger was gone.

Plainly it is not healthy to hear such sounds often. It is not healthy to distinguish public from private sounds so easily. I remained cloistered by sounds, timid and shy in public, too dependent on the voices at home. And yet I was a very happy child when I was at home. I remember many nights when my father would come back from work, and I'd hear him call out to my mother in Spanish, sounding relieved. In Spanish, his voice would sound the light and free notes that he never could manage in English. Some nights I'd jump up just hearing his voice. My brother and I would come running into the room where he was with our mother. Our laughing (so deep was the pleasure!) became screaming. Like others who feel the pain of public alienation, we transformed the knowledge of our public separateness into a consoling reminder of our intimacy. Excited, our voices joined in a celebration of sounds. *We are speaking now the way we never speak out in public— we are together,* the sounds told me. Some nights no one seemed willing to loosen the hold that sounds had on us. At dinner we invented new words that sounded Spanish, but made sense only to us. We pieced together new words by taking, say, an English verb and giving it Spanish endings. My mother's instructions at bedtime would be lacquered with mock-urgent tones. Or a word like *sí,* sounded in several notes, would convey added measures of feeling. Tongues lingered around the edges of words, especially fat vowels, and we happily sounded that military drum roll, the twirling roar of the Spanish *r.* Family language, my family's sounds; the voices of my parents and sisters and brother. Their voices insisting: *You belong here. We are family members. Related. Special to one another. Listen!* Voices singing and sighing, rising and straining, then surging, teeming with pleasure which burst syllables into fragments of laughter. At times it seemed there was steady quiet only when, from another room, the rustling whispers of my parents faded and I edged closer to sleep.

Supporters of bilingual education imply today that students like me miss a great deal by not being taught in their family's language. What they seem not to recognize is that, as a socially disadvantaged child, I regarded Spanish as a private language. It was a ghetto language that deepened and strengthened my feeling of public separateness. What I needed to learn in school was that I had the right, and the obligation, to speak the public language. The odd truth is that my first-grade classmates could have become bilingual, in the conventional sense of the word, more easily than I. Had they been taught early (as upper middle-class children often are taught) a "second language" like Spanish or French, they could have regarded it simply as another public language. In my case, such bilingualism could not have been so quickly achieved. What I did not believe was that I could speak a single public language.

20    Without question, it would have pleased me to have heard my teachers address me in Spanish when I entered the classroom. I would have felt much less afraid. I would have imagined that my instructors were somehow "related" to me; I would indeed have heard their Spanish as my family's language. I would have trusted them and responded with ease. But I would have delayed—postponed for how long?—having to learn the language of public society. I would have evaded—and for how long?—learning the great lesson of school: that I had a public identity.

Fortunately, my teachers were unsentimental about their responsibility. What they understood was that I needed to speak public English. So their voices would search me out, asking me questions. Each time I heard them I'd look up in surprise to see a nun's face frowning at me. I'd mumble, not really meaning to answer. The nun would persist. "Richard, stand up. Don't look at the floor. Speak up. Speak to the entire class, not just to me!" But I couldn't believe English could be my language to use. (In part, I did not want to believe it.) I continued to mumble. I resisted the teacher's demands. (Did I somehow suspect that once I learned this public language my family life would be changed?) Silent, waiting for the bell to sound, I remained dazed, diffident, afraid.

Because I wrongly imagined that English was intrinsically a public language and Spanish was intrinsically private, I easily noted the difference between classroom language and the language at home. At school, words were directed to a general audience of listeners. ("Boys and girls . . .") Words were meaningfully ordered. And the point was not self-expression alone, but to make oneself understood by many others. The teacher quizzed: "Boys and girls, why do we use that word in this sentence? Could we think of a better word to use there? Would the sentence change its meaning if the words were differently arranged? Isn't there a better way of saying much the same thing?" (I couldn't say. I wouldn't try to say.)

Three months passed. Five. A half year. Unsmiling, ever watchful, my teachers noted my silence. They began to connect my behavior with the slow progress my brother and sisters were making. Until, one Saturday morning, three nuns arrived at the house to talk to our parents. Stiffly they sat on the blue living-room sofa. From the doorway of another room, spying on the visitors, I noted the incongruity, the clash of two worlds, the faces and voices of school intruding upon the familiar setting of home. I overheard one voice gently wondering. "Do your children speak only Spanish at home, Mrs. Rodriguez?" While another voice added, "That Richard especially seems so timid and shy."

*That Rich-heard!*

25    With great tact, the visitors continued, "Is it possible for you and your husband to encourage your children to practice their English when they are home?" Of course my parents complied. What would they not do for their children's well-being? And how could they question the Church's authority which those women represented? In an instant they agreed to give up the language (the sounds) which had revealed and accentuated our family's closeness. The moment after the visitors left, the change was observed. "*Ahora*, speak to us only *en inglés*," my father and mother told us.

At first, it seemed a kind of game. After dinner each night, the family gathered together to practice "our" English. It was still then *inglés*, a language foreign to us, so we felt drawn to it as strangers. Laughing, we would try to define words we could not pronounce. We played with strange English sounds, often overanglicizing our pronunciations. And we filled the smiling gaps of our sentences with familiar Spanish sounds. But that was cheating, somebody shouted, and everyone laughed.

In school, meanwhile, like my brother and sisters, I was required to attend a daily tutoring session. I needed a full year of this special work. I also needed my teachers to keep my attention from straying in class by calling out, "*Rich-heard*"—their English voices slowly loosening the ties to my other name, with its three notes, *Ri-car-do*. Most of all, I needed to hear my mother and father speak to me in a moment of seriousness in "broken"—suddenly heartbreaking—English. This scene was inevitable. One Saturday morning I entered the kitchen where my parents were talking, but I did not realize that they were talking in Spanish until, the moment they saw me, their voices changed and they began speaking English. The gringo sounds they uttered startled me. Pushed me away. In that moment of trivial misunderstanding and profound insight, I felt my throat twisted by unsounded grief. I simply turned and left the room. But I had no place to escape to where I could grieve in Spanish. My brother and sisters were speaking English in another part of the house.

Again and again in the days following, as I grew increasingly angry, I was obliged to hear my mother and father encouraging me: "Speak to us *en inglés.*" Only then did I determine to learn classroom English. Thus, sometime afterward it happened: one day in school, I raised my hand to volunteer an answer to a question. I spoke out in a loud voice and I did not think it remarkable when the entire class understood. That day I moved very far from being the disadvantaged child I had been only days earlier. Taken hold at last was the belief, the calming assurance, that I *belonged* in public.

Shortly after, I stopped hearing the high, troubling sounds of *los gringos.* A more and more confident speaker of English, I didn't listen to how strangers sounded when they talked to me. With so many English-speaking people around me, I no longer heard American accents. Conversations quickened. Listening to persons whose voices sounded eccentrically pitched, I might note their sounds for a few seconds, but then I'd concentrate on what they were saying. Now when I heard someone's tone of voice—angry or questioning or sarcastic or happy or sad—I didn't distinguish it from the words it expressed. Sound and word were thus tightly wedded. At the end of each day I was often bemused, and always relieved, to realize how "soundless," though crowded with words, my day in public had been. An eight-year-old boy, I finally came to accept what had been technically true since my birth: I was an American citizen.

30     But diminished by then was the special feeling of closeness at home. Gone was the desperate, urgent, intense feeling of being at home among those with whom I felt intimate. Our family remained a loving family, but one greatly changed. We were no longer so close, no longer bound tightly together by the knowledge of our separateness from *los gringos.* Neither my older brother nor my sisters rushed home after school any more. Nor did I. When I arrived home, often there would be neighborhood kids in the house. Or the house would be empty of sounds.

Following the dramatic Americanization of their children, even my parents grew more publicly confident—especially my mother. First she learned the names of all the people on the block. Then she decided we needed to have a telephone in our house. My father, for his part, continued to use the word gringo, but it was no longer charged with bitterness or distrust. Stripped of any emotional content, the word simply became a name for those Americans not of Hispanic descent. Hearing him, sometimes, I wasn't sure if he was pronouncing the Spanish word *gringo*, or saying gringo in English.

There was a new silence at home. As we children learned more and more English, we shared fewer and fewer words with our parents. Sentences needed to be spoken slowly when one of us addressed our mother or father. Often the parent wouldn't understand. The child would need to repeat himself. Still the parent misunderstood. The young voice, frustrated, would end up saying, "Never mind"—the subject was closed. Dinners would be noisy with the clinking of knives and forks against dishes. My mother would smile softly between her remarks; my father, at the other end of the table, would chew and chew his food while he stared over the heads of his children.

My mother! My father! After English became my primary language, I no longer knew what words to use in addressing my parents. The old Spanish words (those tender accents of sound) I had earlier used—*mamá* and *papá*—I couldn't use any more. They would have been all-too-painful reminders of how much had changed in my life. On the other hand, the words I heard neighborhood kids call their parents seemed equally unsatisfactory. "Mother" and "father," "ma," "papa," "pa," "dad," "pop" (how I hated the all-American sound of that last word)—all these I felt were unsuitable terms of address for *my* parents. As a result, I never used them at home. Whenever I'd speak to my parents, I would try to get their attention by looking at them. In public conversations, I'd refer to them as my "parents" or my "mother" and "father."

My mother and father, for their part, responded differently, as their children spoke to them less. My mother grew restless, seemed troubled and anxious at the scarceness of words exchanged in the house. She would question me about my day when I came home from school. She smiled at my small talk. She pried at the edges of my sentences to get me to say something more. ("What . . . ?") She'd join conversations she overheard, but her intrusions often stopped her children's talking. By contrast, my father seemed to grow reconciled to the new quiet. Though his English somewhat improved, he tended more and more to retire into silence. At dinner he spoke very little. One night his children and even his wife helplessly giggled at his garbled English pronunciation of the Catholic "Grace Before Meals." Thereafter he made his wife recite the prayer at the start of each meal, even on formal occasions when there were guests in the house.

35      Hers became the public voice of the family. On official business it was she, not my father, who would usually talk to strangers on the phone or in stores. We children grew so accustomed to his silence that years later we would routinely refer to his "shyness." (My mother often tried to explain: both of his parents died when he was eight. He was raised by an uncle who treated him as little more than a menial servant. He was never encouraged to speak. He grew up alone—a man of few words.) But I realized my father was not shy whenever I'd watch him speaking Spanish with relatives. Using Spanish, he was quickly effusive. Especially when talking with other men, his voice would spark, flicker, flare alive with varied sounds. In Spanish he expressed ideas and feelings he rarely revealed when speaking English. With firm Spanish sounds he conveyed a confidence and authority that English would never allow him.

The silence at home, however, was not simply the result of fewer words passing between parents and children. More profound for me was the silence created by inattention to sounds. At about the time I no longer bothered to listen with care to the sounds of English in public, I grew careless about listening to the sounds made by the family when they spoke. Most of the time I would hear someone speaking at home and didn't distinguish his sounds from the words people uttered in public. I didn't even pay much attention to my parents' accented and ungrammatical speech—at least not at home. Only when I was with them in public would I become alert to their accents. But even then their sounds caused me less and less concern. For I was growing increasingly confident of my own public identity.

I would have been happier about my public success had I not recalled, sometimes, what it had been like earlier, when my family conveyed its intimacy through a set of conveniently private sounds. Sometimes in public, hearing a stranger, I'd hark back to my lost past. A Mexican farm worker approached me one day downtown. He wanted directions to some place. "*Hijito,* . . ." he said. And his voice stirred old longings. Another time I was standing beside my mother in the visiting room of a Carmelite convent, before the dense screen which rendered the nuns shadowy figures. I heard several of them speaking Spanish in their busy, singsong, overlapping voices, assuring my mother that yes, yes, we were remembered, all our family was remembered, in their prayers. Those voices echoed faraway family sounds. Another day a dark-faced old woman touched my shoulder lightly to steady herself as she boarded a bus. She murmured something to me I couldn't quite comprehend. Her Spanish voice came near, like the face of a never-before-seen relative in the instant before I was kissed. That voice, like so many of the Spanish voices I'd hear in public, recalled the golden age of my childhood.

Bilingual educators say today that children lose a degree of "individuality" by becoming assimilated into public society. (Bilingual schooling is a program popularized in the seventies, that decade when middle-class "ethnics" began to resist the process of assimilation—the "American melting pot.") But the bilingualists oversimplify when they scorn the value and necessity of assimilation. They do not seem to realize that a person is individualized in two ways. So they do not realize that, while one suffers a diminished sense of *private* individuality by being assimilated into public society, such assimilation makes possible the achievement of *public* individuality.

Simplistically again, the bilingualists insist that a student should be reminded of his difference from others in mass society, of his "heritage." But they equate mere separateness with individuality. The fact is that only in private—with intimates—is separateness from the crowd a prerequisite for individuality; an intimate "tells" me that I am unique, unlike all others, apart from the crowd. In public, by contrast, full individuality is achieved, paradoxically, by those who are able to consider themselves members of the crowd. Thus it happened for me. Only when I was able to think of myself as an American, no longer an alien in gringo society, could I seek the rights and opportunities necessary for full public individuality. The social and political advantages I enjoy as a man began on the day I came to believe that my name is indeed *Rich-heard Road-ree-guess*. It is true that my public society today is often impersonal; in fact, my public society is usually mass society. But despite the anonymity of the crowd, and despite the fact that the individuality I achieve in public is often tenuous—because it depends on my being one in a crowd—I celebrate the day I acquired my new name. Those middle-class ethnics who scorn assimilation seem to me filled with decadent self-pity, obsessed by the burden of public life. Dangerously, they romanticize public separateness and trivialize the dilemma of those who are truly socially disadvantaged.

40     If I rehearse here the changes in my private life after my Americanization, it is finally to emphasize a public gain. The loss implies the gain. The house I returned to each afternoon was quiet. Intimate sounds no longer greeted me at the door. Inside there were other

noises. The telephone rang. Neighborhood kids ran past the door of the bedroom where I was reading my schoolbooks—covered with brown shopping-bag paper. Once I learned the public language, it would never again be easy for me to hear intimate family voices. More and more of my day was spent hearing words, not sounds. But that may only be a way of saying that on the day I raised my hand in class and spoke loudly to an entire roomful of faces, my childhood started to end.

## Questions for Discussion

Rodriguez argues that language, while certainly bringing people together, can also foster alienation and miscommunication. Can you cite experiences that support that point?

Who is Rodriguez primarily trying to influence with his argument? How can you tell?

*Amy Tan was born in Oakland, California, in 1952 to parents who had emigrated from China. She is the best-selling author of novels, short fiction, and children's books. In college, she became interested in linguistics, eventually earning a master's degree in the subject in 1973. After working as a language development consultant for projects designed to help disabled children, she turned to fiction in the mid-1980s. In 1989* The Joy Luck Club *was published and became a best-seller; in 1994 it was adapted into a movie. She has since completed* The Kitchen God's Wife, The Hundred Secret Senses, *and* The Bonesetter's Daughter. *Her essay "Mother Tongue," first given as a lecture, was chosen for* Best American Essays *in 1991.*

# *Amy Tan*
# Mother Tongue

I am not a scholar of English or literature. I cannot give you much more than personal opinions on the English language and its variations in this country or others.

I am a writer. And by that definition, I am someone who has always loved language. I am fascinated by language in daily life. I spend a great deal of my time thinking about the power of language—the way it can evoke an emotion, a visual image, a complex idea, or a simple truth. Language is the tool of my trade. And I use them all—all the Englishes I grew up with.

Recently, I was made keenly aware of the different Englishes I do use. I was giving a talk to a large group of people, the same talk I had already given to half a dozen other groups. The nature of the talk was about my writing, my life, and my book, *The Joy Luck Club.* The talk was going along well enough, until I remembered one major difference that made the whole talk sound wrong. My mother was in the room. And it was perhaps the first time she had heard me give a lengthy speech, using the kind of English I have never used with her. I was saying things like, "The intersection of memory upon imagination" and "There is an aspect of my fiction that relates to thus-and-thus"— a speech filled with carefully wrought grammatical phrases, burdened, it suddenly seemed to me, with nominalized forms, past perfect tenses, conditional phrases, all the forms of standard English that I had learned in school and through books, the forms of English I did not use at home with my mother.

Just last week, I was walking down the street with my mother, and I again found myself conscious of the English I was using, the English I do use with her. We were talking about the price of new and used furniture and I heard myself saying this: "Not waste money that way." My husband was with us as well, and he didn't notice any switch in my English. And then I realized why. It's because over the twenty years we've been together I've often used the same kind of English with him, and sometimes he even uses it with me. It has become our language of intimacy, a different sort of English that relates to family talk, the language I grew up with.

5    So you'll have some idea of what this family talk I heard sounds like, I'll quote what my mother said during a recent conversation which I videotaped and then transcribed. During this conversation, my mother was talking about a political gangster in Shanghai who had the same last name as her family's, Du, and how the gangster in his early years wanted to be adopted by her family, which was rich by comparison. Later, the gangster became more powerful, far richer than my mother's family, and one day showed up at my mother's wedding to pay his respects. Here's what she said in part:

"Du Yusong having business like fruit stand. Like off the street kind. He is Du like Du Zong—but not Tsung-ming Island people. The local people call putong, the river east side, he belong to that side local people. That man want to ask Du Zong father take him in like become own family. Du Zong father wasn't look down on him, but didn't take seriously, until that man big like become a mafia. Now important person, very hard to inviting him. Chinese way, came only to show respect, don't stay for dinner. Respect for making big celebration, he shows up. Mean gives lots of respect. Chinese custom. Chinese social life that way. If too important won't have to stay too long. He come to my wedding. I didn't see, I heard it. I gone to boy's side, they have YMCA dinner. Chinese age I was nineteen."

You should know that my mother's expressive command of English belies how much she actually understands. She reads the Forbes report, listens to "Wall Street Week," converses daily with her stockbroker, reads all of Shirley MacLaine's books with ease—all kinds of things I can't begin to understand. Yet some of my friends tell me they understand 50 percent of what my mother says. Some say they understand 80 to 90 percent. Some say they understand none of it, as if she were speaking pure Chinese. But to me, my mother's English is perfectly clear, perfectly natural. It's my mother tongue. Her language, as I hear it, is vivid, direct, full of observation and imagery. That was the language that helped shape the way I saw things, expressed things, made sense of the world.

Lately, I've been giving more thought to the kind of English my mother speaks. Like others, I have described it to people as "broken" or "fractured" English. But I wince when I say that. It has always bothered me that I can think of no way to describe it other than "broken," as if it were damaged and needed to be fixed, as if it lacked a certain wholeness and soundness. I've heard other terms used, "limited English," for example. But they seem just as bad, as if everything is limited, including people's perceptions of the limited English speaker.

I know this for a fact, because when I was growing up, my mother's "limited" English limited my perception of her. I was ashamed of her English. I believed that her English reflected the quality of what she had to say. That is, because she expressed them imperfectly her thoughts were imperfect. And I had plenty of empirical evidence to support me: the fact that people in department stores, at banks, and at restaurants did not take her seriously, did not give her good service, pretended not to understand her, or even acted as if they did not hear her.

10    My mother has long realized the limitations of her English as well. When I was fifteen, she used to have me call people on the phone to pretend I was she. In this guise, I was forced to ask for information or even to complain and yell at people who had been rude to her. One time it was a call to her stockbroker in New York. She had cashed out her small portfolio and it just so happened we were going to go to New York the next week, our very first trip outside California. I had to get on the phone and say in an adolescent voice that was not very convincing, "This is Mrs. Tan."

And my mother was standing in the back whispering loudly, "Why he don't send me check, already two weeks late. So mad he lie to me, losing me money."

And then I said in perfect English, "Yes, I'm getting rather concerned. You had agreed to send the check two weeks ago, but it hasn't arrived."

Then she began to talk more loudly. "What he want, I come to New York tell him front of his boss, you cheating me?" And I was trying to calm her down, make her be quiet, while telling the stockbroker, "I can't tolerate any more excuses. If I don't receive the check immediately, I am going to have to speak to your manager when I'm in New York next week." And sure enough, the following week there we were in front of this astonished stockbroker; and I was sitting there red-faced and quiet, and my mother, the real Mrs. Tan, was shouting at his boss in her impeccable broken English.

We used a similar routine just five days ago, for a situation that was far less humorous. My mother had gone to the hospital for an appointment, to find out about a benign brain tumor a CAT scan had revealed a month ago. She said she had spoken very good English, her best English, no mistakes. Still, she said, the hospital did not apologize when they said they had lost the CAT scan and she had come for nothing. She said they did not seem to have any sympathy when she told them she was anxious to know the exact diagnosis, since her husband and son had both died of brain tumors. She said they would not give her any more information until the next time and she would have to make another appointment for that. So she said she would not leave until the doctor called her daughter. She wouldn't budge. And when the doctor finally called her daughter, me, who spoke in perfect English—lo and behold—we had assurances the CAT scan would be found, promises that a conference call on Monday would be held, and apologies for any suffering my mother had gone through for a most regrettable mistake.

15    I think my mother's English almost had an effect on limiting my possibilities in life as well. Sociologists and linguists probably will tell you that a person's developing language skills are more influenced by peers. But I do think that the language spoken in the family, especially in immigrant families which are more insular, plays a large role in shaping the language of the child. And I believe that it affected my results on achievement tests, IQ tests, and the SAT. While my English skills were never judged as poor, compared to math, English could not be considered my strong suit. In grade school I did moderately well, getting perhaps B's, sometimes B-pluses, in English and scoring perhaps in the sixtieth or seventieth percentile on achievement tests. But those scores were not good enough to override the opinion that my true abilities lay in math and science, because in those areas I achieved A's and scored in the ninetieth percentile or higher.

This was understandable. Math is precise; there is only one correct answer. Whereas, for me at least, the answers on English tests were always a judgment call, a matter of opinion and personal experience. Those tests were constructed around items like fill-in-the-blank sentence completion, such as, "Even though Tom was ___ Mary thought he was ___." And the correct answer always seemed to be the most bland combinations of thoughts, for example, "Even though Tom was shy, Mary thought he was charming," with the grammatical structure "even though" limiting the correct answer to some sort of semantic opposites, so you wouldn't get answers like, "Even though Tom was foolish, Mary thought he was ridiculous." Well, according to my mother, there were very few limitations as to what Tom could have been and what Mary might have thought of him. So I never did well on tests like that.

The same was true with word analogies, pairs of words in which you were supposed to find some sort of logical, semantic relationship—for example, "Sunset is to nightfall as ___ is to ___." And here you would be presented with a list of four possible pairs, one of which showed the same kind of relationship: red is to stoplight, bus is to arrival, chills is to fever, yawn is to boring. Well, I could never think that way. I knew what the tests were asking, but I could not block out of my mind the images already created by the first pair, "sunset is to nightfall"—and I would see a burst of colors against a darkening sky, the moon rising, the lowering of a curtain of stars. And all the other pairs of words—red, bus, stoplight, boring—just threw up a mass of confusing images, making it impossible for me to sort out something as logical as saying: "A sunset precedes nightfall" is the same as "a chill precedes a fever." The only way I would have gotten that answer right would have been to imagine an associative situation, for example, my being disobedient and staying out past sunset, catching a chill at night, which turns into feverish pneumonia as punishment, which indeed did happen to me.

I have been thinking about all this lately, about my mother's English, about achievement tests. Because lately I've been asked, as a writer, why there are not more Asian Americans represented in American literature. Why are there few Asian Americans enrolled in creative writing programs? Why do so many Chinese students go into engineering? Well, these are broad sociological questions I can't begin to answer. But I have noticed in surveys—in fact, just last week—that Asian students, as a whole, always do significantly better on math achievement tests than in English. And this makes me think that there are other Asian-American students whose English spoken in the home might also be described as "broken" or "limited." And perhaps they also have teachers who are steering them away from writing and into math and science, which is what happened to me.

Fortunately, I happen to be rebellious in nature and enjoy the challenge of disproving assumptions made about me. I became an English major my first year in college, after being enrolled as pre-med.

I started writing nonfiction as a freelancer the week after I was told by my former boss that writing was my worst skill and I should hone my talents toward account management.

20      But it wasn't until 1985 that I finally began to write fiction. And at first I wrote using what I thought to be wittily crafted sentences, sentences that would finally prove I had mastery over the English language. Here's an example from the first draft of a story that later made its way into *The Joy Luck Club*, but without this line: "That was my mental quandary in its nascent state." A terrible line, which I can barely pronounce.

Fortunately, for reasons I won't get into today, I later decided I should envision a reader for the stories I would write. And the reader I decided upon was my mother, because these were stories about mothers. So with this reader in mind—and in fact she did read my early drafts—I began to write stories using all the Englishes I grew up with: the English I spoke to my mother, which for lack of a better term might be described as "simple"; the English she used with me, which for lack of a better term might be described as "broken"; my translation of her Chinese, which could certainly be described as "watered down"; and what I imagined to be her translation of her Chinese if she could speak in perfect English, her internal language, and for that I sought to preserve the essence, but neither an English nor a Chinese structure. I wanted to capture what language ability tests can never reveal: her intent, her passion, her imagery, the rhythms of her speech and the nature of her thoughts.

Apart from what any critic had to say about my writing, I knew I had succeeded where it counted when my mother finished reading my book and gave me her verdict: "So easy to read."

## Questions for Discussion

Would you agree that "Mother Tongue" is an argument? What is its thesis?

Do you have an intimate "family language" that amounts to a special "dialect" that is distinct from the dialect you use at school?

*Leslie Marmon Silko (born 1948) was raised on the Laguna Pueblo
reservation in New Mexico in a family of Native American (Pueblo and
Laguna), Mexican, and white descent. She first attended the Indian
schools on the reservation, but ultimately she attended Catholic school in
Albuquerque before going on to the University of New Mexico, where she
earned a B.A. in English in 1969. A poet, novelist, short story writer, essayist, literary and social critic, and activist for immigration and women's
issues, Silko writes primarily about Native American culture and the traditions and practices that collide with the dominant white society. Her
best-known novel,* Ceremony *(1977), explores many Native American
themes and narrative techniques, including the importance of the oral
tradition and storytelling. She recently retired as Professor of English and
Creative Writing at the University of Arizona. The following essay was
first published in the* Nation *in 1994.*

# Leslie Marmon Silko
# The Border Patrol State

I used to travel the highways of New Mexico and Arizona with a wonderful sensation of absolute freedom as I cruised down the open road
and across the vast desert plateaus. On the Laguna Pueblo reservation,
where I was raised, the people were patriotic despite the way the U.S.
government had treated Native Americans. As proud citizens, we grew
up believing the freedom to travel was our inalienable right, a right
that some Native Americans had been denied in the early twentieth
century. Our cousin, old Bill Pratt, used to ride his horse 300 miles
overland from Laguna, New Mexico, to Prescott, Arizona, every summer to work as a fire lookout.

In school in the 1950s, we were taught that our right to travel
from state to state without special papers or threat of detainment was
a right that citizens under communist and totalitarian governments
did not possess. That wide open highway told us we were U.S. citizens;
we were free. . . .

Not so long ago, my companion Gus and I were driving south from
Albuquerque, returning to Tucson after a book promotion for the pa-
perback edition of my novel *Almanac of the Dead*. I had settled back
and gone to sleep while Gus drove, but I was awakened when I felt the

car slowing to a stop. It was nearly midnight on New Mexico State Road 26, a dark, lonely stretch of two-lane highway between Hatch and Deming. When I sat up, I saw the headlights and emergency flashers of six vehicles—Border Patrol cars and a van were blocking both lanes of the highway. Gus stopped the car and rolled down the window to ask what was wrong. But the closest Border Patrolman and his companion did not reply; instead, the first agent ordered us to "step out of the car." Gus asked why, but his question seemed to set them off. Two more Border Patrol agents immediately approached our car, and one of them snapped, "Are you looking for trouble?" as if he would relish it.

I will never forget that night beside the highway. There was an awful feeling of menace and violence straining to break loose. It was clear that the uniformed men would be only too happy to drag us out of the car if we did not speedily comply with their request (asking a question is tantamount to resistance, it seems). So we stepped out of the car and they motioned for us to stand on the shoulder of the road. The night was very dark, and no other traffic had come down the road since we had been stopped. All I could think about was a book I had read—*Nunca Mas*—the official report of a human rights commission that investigated and certified more than 12,000 "disappearances" during Argentina's "dirty war" in the late 1970s.

5     The weird anger of these Border Patrolmen made me think about descriptions in the report of Argentine police and military officers who became addicted to interrogation, torture and the murder that followed. When the military and police ran out of political suspects to torture and kill, they resorted to the random abduction of citizens off the streets. I thought how easy it would be for the Border Patrol to shoot us and leave our bodies and car beside the highway, like so many bodies found in these parts and ascribed to "drug runners."

Two other Border Patrolmen stood by the white van. The one who had asked if we were looking for trouble ordered his partner to "get the dog," and from the back of the van another patrolman brought a small female German shepherd on a leash. The dog apparently did not heel well enough to suit him, and the handler jerked the leash. They opened the doors of our car and pulled the dog's head into it, but I saw immediately from the expression in her eyes that the dog hated them, and that she would not serve them. When she showed no interest in the inside of the car, they brought her around back to the trunk, near where we were standing. They half-dragged her up into the trunk, but still she did not indicate any stowed-away human beings or illegal drugs.

The mood got uglier; the officers seemed outraged that the dog could not find any contraband, and they dragged her over to us and commanded her to sniff our legs and feet. To my relief, the strange violence the Border Patrol agents had focused on us now seemed shifted to the dog. I no longer felt so strongly that we would be murdered. We exchanged looks—the dog and I. She was afraid of what they might do, just as I was. The dog's handler jerked the leash sharply as she sniffed us, as if to make her perform better, but the dog refused to accuse us: She had an innate dignity that did not permit her to serve the murderous impulses of those men. I can't forget the expression in the dog's eyes; it was as if she were embarrassed to be associated with them. I had a small amount of medicinal marijuana in my purse that night, but she refused to expose me. I am not partial to dogs, but I will always remember the small German shepherd that night.

Unfortunately, what happened to me is an everyday occurrence here now. Since the 1980s, on top of greatly expanding border checkpoints, the Immigration and Naturalization Service and the Border Patrol have implemented policies that interfere with the rights of U.S. citizens to travel freely within our borders. I.N.S. agents now patrol all interstate highways and roads that lead to or from the U.S.-Mexico border in Texas, New Mexico, Arizona and California. Now, when you drive east from Tucson on Interstate 10 toward El Paso, you encounter an I.N.S. check station outside Las Cruces, New Mexico. When you drive north from Las Cruces up Interstate 25, two miles north of the town of Truth or Consequences, the highway is blocked with orange emergency barriers, and all traffic is diverted into a two-lane Border Patrol checkpoint—ninety-five miles north of the U.S.-Mexico border.

I was detained once at Truth or Consequences, despite my and my companion's Arizona driver's licenses. Two men, both Chicanos, were detained at the same time, despite the fact that they too presented ID and spoke English without the thick Texas accents of the Border Patrol agents. While we were stopped, we watched as other vehicles—whose occupants were white—were waved through the checkpoint. White people traveling with brown people, however, can expect to be stopped on suspicion they work with the sanctuary movement, which shelters refugees. White people who appear to be clergy, those who wear ethnic clothing or jewelry and women with very long hair or very short hair (they could be nuns) are also frequently detained; white men with beards or men with long hair are likely to be detained, too, because Border Patrol agents have "profiles" of "those sorts" of white people who may help political refugees. (Most of the political refugees from

Guatemala and El Salvador are Native American or mestizo because the indigenous people of the Americas have continued to resist efforts by invaders to displace them from their ancestral lands.) Alleged increases in illegal immigration by people of Asian ancestry mean that the Border Patrol now routinely detains anyone who appears to be Asian or part Asian, as well.

10    Once your car is diverted from the Interstate Highway into the checkpoint area, you are under the control of the Border Patrol, which in practical terms exercises a power that no highway patrol or city patrolman possesses: They are willing to detain anyone, for no apparent reason. Other law-enforcement officers need a shred of probable cause in order to detain someone. On the books, so does the Border Patrol; but on the road, it's another matter. They'll order you to stop your car and step out; then they'll ask you to open the trunk. If you ask why or request a search warrant, you'll be told that they'll have to have a dog sniff the car before they can request a search warrant, and the dog might not get there for two or three hours. The search warrant might require an hour or two past that. They make it clear that if you force them to obtain a search warrant for the car, they will make you submit to a strip search as well.

Traveling in the open, though, the sense of violation can be even worse. Never mind high-profile cases like that of former Border Patrol agent Michael Elmer, acquitted of murder by claiming self-defense, despite admitting that as an officer he shot an "illegal" immigrant in the back and then hid the body, which remained undiscovered until another Border Patrolman reported the event. (Last month, Elmer was convicted of reckless endangerment in a separate incident, for shooting at least ten rounds from his M-16 too close to a group of immigrants as they were crossing illegally into Nogales in March 1992.) Or that in El Paso a high school football coach driving a vanload of players in full uniform was pulled over on the freeway and a Border Patrol agent put a cocked revolver to his head. (The football coach was Mexican-American, as were most of the players in his van; the incident eventually caused a federal judge to issue a restraining order against the Border Patrol.) We've a mountain of personal experiences like that which never make the newspapers. A history professor at U.C.L.A. told me she had been traveling by train from Los Angeles to Albuquerque twice a month doing research. On each of her trips, she had noticed that the Border Patrol agents were at the station in Albuquerque scrutinizing the passengers. Since she is six feet tall and of Irish and German ancestry, she was not particularly concerned.

Then one day when she stepped off the train in Albuquerque, two Border Patrolmen accosted her, wanting to know what she was doing, and why she was traveling between Los Angeles and Albuquerque twice a month. She presented identification and an explanation deemed "suitable" by the agents, and was allowed to go about her business.

Just the other day, I mentioned to a friend that I was writing this article and he told me about his 73-year-old father, who is half Chinese and who had set out alone by car from Tucson to Albuquerque the week before. His father had become confused by road construction and missed a turnoff from Interstate 10 to Interstate 25; when he turned around and circled back, he missed the turnoff a second time. But when he looped back for yet another try, Border Patrol agents stopped him and forced him to open his trunk. After they satisfied themselves that he was not smuggling Chinese immigrants, they sent him on his way. He was so rattled by the event that he had to be driven home by his daughter.

This is the police state that has developed in the southwestern United States since the 1980s. No person, no citizen, is free to travel without the scrutiny of the Border Patrol. In the city of South Tucson, where 80 percent of the respondents were Chicano or Mexicano, a joint research project by the University of Wisconsin and the University of Arizona recently concluded that one out of every five people there had been detained, mistreated verbally or nonverbally, or questioned by I.N.S. agents in the past two years.

Manifest Destiny may lack its old grandeur of theft and blood— "lock the door" is what it means now, with racism a trump card to be played again and again, shamelessly, by both major political parties. "Immigration," like "street crime" and "welfare fraud," is a political euphemism that refers to people of color. Politicians and media people talk about "illegal aliens" to dehumanize and demonize undocumented immigrants, who are for the most part people of color. Even in the days of Spanish and Mexican rule, no attempts were made to interfere with the flow of people and goods from south to north and north to south. It is the U.S. government that has continually attempted to sever contact between the tribal people north of the border and those to the south.

15        Now that the "Iron Curtain" is gone, it is ironic that the U.S. government and its Border Patrol are constructing a steel wall ten feet high to span sections of the border with Mexico. While politicians and multinational corporations extol the virtues of NAFTA and "free

trade" (in goods, not flesh), the ominous curtain is already up in a six-mile section at the border crossing at Mexicali; two miles are being erected but are not yet finished at Naco; and at Nogales, sixty miles south of Tucson, the steel wall has been all rubber-stamped and awaits construction likely to begin in March. Like the pathetic multimillion-dollar "antidrug" border surveillance balloons that were continually deflated by high winds and made only a couple of meager interceptions before they blew away, the fence along the border is a theatrical prop, a bit of pork for contractors. Border entrepreneurs have already used blowtorches to cut passageways through the fence to collect "tolls," and are doing a brisk business. Back in Washington, the I.N.S. announces a $300 million computer contract to modernize its record-keeping and Congress passes a crime bill that shunts $255 million to the I.N.S. for 1995, $181 million earmarked for border control, which is to include 700 new partners for the men who stopped Gus and me in our travels, and the history professor, and my friend's father, and as many as they could from South Tucson.

It is no use; borders haven't worked, and they won't work, not now, as the indigenous people of the Americas reassert their kinship and solidarity with one another. A mass migration is already under way; its roots are not simply economic. The Uto-Aztecan languages are spoken as far north as Taos Pueblo near the Colorado border, all the way south to Mexico City. Before the arrival of the Europeans, the indigenous communities throughout this region not only conducted commerce, the people shared cosmologies, and oral narratives about the Maize Mothers, the Twin Brothers and their Grandmother, Spider Woman, as well as Quetzalcoatl the benevolent snake. The great human migration within the Americas cannot be stopped; human beings are natural forces of the Earth, just as rivers and winds are natural forces.

Deep down the issue is simple: The so-called "Indian Wars" from the days of Sitting Bull and Red Cloud have never really ended in the Americas. The Indian people of southern Mexico, of Guatemala and those left in El Salvador, too, are still fighting for their lives and for their land against the "cavalry" patrols sent out by the governments of those lands. The Americas are Indian country, and the "Indian problem" is not about to go away.

One evening at sundown, we were stopped in traffic at a railroad crossing in downtown Tucson while a freight train passed us, slowly gaining speed as it headed north to Phoenix. In the twilight I saw the most amazing sight: Dozens of human beings, mostly young men, were riding the train; everywhere, on flat cars, inside open boxcars, perched on top of boxcars, hanging off ladders on tank cars and between boxcars. I couldn't count fast enough, but I saw fifty or sixty people headed north. They were dark young men, Indian and mestizo; they were smiling and a few of them waved at us in our cars. I was reminded of the ancient story of Aztlan, told by the Aztecs but known in other Uto-Aztecan communities as well. Aztlán is the beautiful land to the north, the origin place of the Aztec people. I don't remember how or why the people left Aztlán to journey farther south, but the old story says that one day, they will return.

## Questions for Discussion

How do myth and history function in Silko's argument?

Why does Silko wait until the end of the essay to introduce her discussion of the cultural ties of the native peoples north and south of the U.S. border?

# APPENDIX

# SOME ARGUMENTS ABOUT ARGUMENT

*Kenneth Burke (1897–1993) was a brilliant and prolific writer, literary critic, and educator who was especially interested in language issues. During the middle years of the last century he wrote a series of books and articles—A* Grammar of Motives *(1945) and* A Rhetoric of Motives *(1950) among many others—that have collectively shaped the ways that many people today think about language use in general and ways of persuading people in particular. In 1951 he wrote "Rhetoric—Old and New" for* The Journal of General Education. *In the following excerpt, he summarizes some of his key concepts and theories in a way that is directly applicable to the topic of argumentation.*

# Kenneth Burke

# Rhetoric—Old and New

On the assumption that writing and the criticism of writing have an area in common, this statement is offered in the hopes that, though presented from the standpoint of literary criticism, it may be found relevant to the teaching of communication.

Let us, as a conceit, imagine a dialogue between two characters: "Studiosus" and "Neurosis." Studiosus would be somewhat of a misnomer for the first figure, who represents a not very interested member of a freshman class taking a required course in composition; and Neurosis would be his teacher. Studiosus has complained bitterly of the work which the course requires of him, whereupon Neurosis delivers a passionate oration in defense of his subject (naturally without mention of a flitting fantasy he sometimes entertains, according to which he has been granted some *other* cross to bear).

Imagining his apology, we found it falling into three stages, that corresponded roughly to an Inferno, a Purgatorio, and a Paradiso. First would be an account of the abysmal problems that beset the use of language. Next would come a movement of transition, whereby the very sources of lamentation could, if beheld from a different angle, be transformed into the promissory. This would be the purgatorial stage. And, despite the mournfulness of our times, a glorious paradisiac ending seemed feasible, if we did a certain amount of contriving—but let us put off for a bit the description of this third stage, while we prepare for it by first giving the broad outlines of the other two.

The first stage would stress the great deceptions of speech. As with Baudelaire's sonnet on "Correspondences," it would note how men wander through "forests of symbols." Man a symbol-using animal. Expatiate on the fog of words through which we stumble, perhaps adding an image (the dog and the waterfall heard enigmatically beyond the mist). Here we would consider the problems of news: the *necessary* inadequacy of the report, even in the case of the *best* reporting; the bungling nature of the medium; the great bureaucratic dinosaurs of news-collecting; the added risks that arise from the *dramatic* aspects of news. (And to get a glimpse of what sinister practices we do accept as the norm, where international relations are concerned, imagine a prize fight reported in the style regularly used for news of international disputes; one fighter's blows would be reported as threats and provocations, while the other's were mentioned in the tonalities proper to long-suffering and calm retaliation regrettably made necessary by the outlandish aggressiveness of the opponent.)

5    If I had to sum up in one word the difference between the "old" rhetoric and a "new" (a rhetoric reinvigorated by fresh insights which the "new sciences" contributed to the subject), I would reduce it to this: The key term for the old rhetoric was "persuasion" and its stress was upon deliberate design. The key term for the "new" rhetoric would be "identification," which can include a partially "unconscious" factor in appeal. "Identification" at its simplest is also a deliberate device, as when the politician seeks to identify himself with his audience. In this respect, its equivalents are plentiful in Aristotle's *Rhetoric*. But identification can also be an end, as when people earnestly yearn to identify themselves with some group or other. Here they are not necessarily being acted upon by a conscious external agent, but may be acting upon themselves to this end. In such identification there is a partially dreamlike, idealistic motive, somewhat compensatory to real differences or divisions, which the rhetoric of identification would transcend.

But we are now ready for our second stage. For, if identification includes the realm of transcendence, it has, by the same token, brought us into the realm of transformation, or dialectic. A rhetorician, I take it, is like one voice in a dialogue. Put several such voices together, with each voicing its own special assertion, let them act upon one another in co-operative competition, and you get a dialectic that, properly developed, can lead to views transcending the limitations of each. At which point, to signalize his change of heart, poor Neurosis might now be renamed "Socraticus."

Socraticus could point out how the very lostness of men in their symbolic quandaries has led to the invention of miraculously ingenious symbolic structures—whereat the very aspects of language we might otherwise fear can become engrossing objects of study and appreciation; and works once designed to play upon an audience's passions, to "move" them rhetorically toward practical decisions beyond the work, can now be enjoyed for their ability to move us in the purely poetic sense, as when, hearing a lyric or seeing a sunrise, we might say, "How moving!" (We here touch upon the kind of heightened or elevated diction discussed in Longinus' *On the Sublime.*)

Considering the relation between rhetoric and dialectic, we come with Socraticus upon the Platonic concern with the Upward Way (linguistic devices whereby we may move from a world of disparate particulars to a principle of one-ness, an "ascent" got, as the semanticists might say, by a movement toward progressively "higher levels of generalization"). Whereat there could be a descent, a Downward Way, back into the world of particulars, all of which would now be "identified" with the genius of the unitary principle discovered en route. (All would be thus made consubstantial by participation in a common essence, as with objects bathed in the light of the one sun, that shines down upon them as from the apex of a pyramid. And the absence of such dialectic journeys on the grand scale should not be allowed to conceal from us the fact that we are continually encountering fragmentary variants of them. For instance, you may look upon a world of disparate human beings; you can next "rise to a higher level of generalization" by arriving at some such abstraction as "economic man"; and, finally, you can look upon these unique human beings simply in terms of this one attribute, thus "identifying" them with a unitary term got by a tiny rise toward generalization and a descent again from it.)

But the mention of the pyramid can lead us nicely into the third state, our Paradiso. Socraticus might now even change his name to "Hierarchicus"—and we might dwell upon the double nature of hierarchy. Thus there is the purely verbal ascent, with corresponding resources of identification (our notion being that a rhetorical structure is most persuasive when it possesses full dialectical symmetry—or, otherwise put, dialectical symmetry is at once the perfecting and transcending of rhetoric). But there is also another line of ascent; and this involves the relation between the dialectics of identification and hierarchic structure in the social, or sociological, sense (society conceived as, roughly, a ladder, or pyramid, of interrelated roles).

10    Here we would consider how matters of prestige (in the old style, "wonder," or in the terminology of Corneille, "admiration") figure in the ultimate resources of "identification." Here we would note how our

ideas of "beauty," and even "nature," are "fabulous," concealing within themselves a social pageantry. Here would be the ultimate step in the discussion of the ways in which man walks among "forests of symbols."

Are things disunited in "body"? Then unite them in "spirit." Would a nation extend its physical dominion? Let it talk of spreading its "ideals." Do you encounter contradictions? Call them "balances." Is an organization in disarray? Talk of its common *purpose.* Are there struggles over means? Celebrate agreement on ends. Sanction the troublously manifest, the incarnate, in terms of the ideally, perfectly invisible and intangible, the divine.

**Deborah Tannen**, *a professor of linguistics at Georgetown University in Washington, D.C., published* You Just Don't Understand: Women and Men in Conversation *in 1990. An exploration of the complexities of communication between men and women, it became a national best-seller. Her subsequent work has continued to explore the interrelations of gender and communication, and she has become a frequent guest on radio and television news and talk shows. In 1998 she published* The Argument Culture, *which won the Common Ground Book Award and from which the following piece has been excerpted.*

# Deborah Tannen

# The Argument Culture: Moving from Debate to Dialogue

In the spring of 1995, Horizons Theatre in Arlington, Virginia, produced two one-act plays I had written about family relationships. The director, wanting to contribute to the reconciliation between Blacks and Jews, mounted my plays in repertory with two one-act plays by an African-American playwright, Caleen Sinnette Jennings. We had both written plays about three sisters that explored the ethnic identities of our families (Jewish for me, African-American for her) and the relationship between those identities and the American context in which we grew up. To stir interest in the plays and to explore the parallels between her work and mine, the theater planned a public dialogue between Jennings and me, to be held before the plays opened.

As production got under way, I attended the audition of actors for my plays. After the auditions ended, just before everyone headed home, the theater's public relations volunteer distributed copies of the flyer announcing the public dialogue that she had readied for distribution. I was horrified. The flyer announced that Caleen and I would discuss "how past traumas create understanding and conflict between Blacks and Jews today." The flyer was trying to grab by the throat the issue that we wished to address indirectly. Yes, we were concerned with conflicts between Blacks and Jews, but neither of us is an authority on that conflict, and we had no intention of expounding on it. We hoped to do our part to ameliorate the conflict by focusing on commonalities. Our plays had many resonances between them. We wanted to talk about our work and let the resonances speak for themselves.

Fortunately, we were able to stop the flyers before they were distributed and devise new ones that promised something we could deliver: "a discussion of heritage, identity, and complex family relationships in African-American and Jewish-American culture as represented in their plays." Jennings noticed that the original flyer said the evening would be "provocative" and changed it to "thought-provoking." What a world of difference is implied in that small change: how much better to make people think, rather than simply to "provoke" them—as often as not, to anger.

It is easy to understand why conflict is so often highlighted. Writers of headlines or promotional copy want to catch attention and attract an audience. They are usually under time pressure, which lures them to established, conventionalized ways of expressing ideas in the absence of leisure to think up entirely new ones. The promise of controversy seems an easy and natural way to rouse interest. But serious consequences are often unintended: Stirring up animosities to get a rise out of people, though easy and "provocative," can open old wounds or create new ones that are hard to heal. This is one of many dangers inherent in the argument culture.

5      In the argument culture, criticism, attack, or opposition are the predominant if not the only ways of responding to people or ideas. I use the phrase "culture of critique" to capture this aspect. "Critique" in this sense is not a general term for analysis or interpretation but rather a synonym for criticism.

It is the *automatic* nature of this response that I am calling attention to—and calling into question. Sometimes passionate opposition, strong verbal attack, are appropriate and called for. No one knows this better than those who have lived under repressive regimes that forbid public opposition. The Yugoslavian-born poet Charles Simic is one. "There are moments in life," he writes, "when true invective is called for, when it becomes an absolute necessity, out of a deep sense of justice, to denounce, mock, vituperate, lash out, in the strongest possible language." I applaud and endorse this view. There are times when it is necessary and right to fight—to defend your country or yourself, to argue for right against wrong or against offensive or dangerous ideas or actions.

What I question is the ubiquity, the knee-jerk nature, of approaching almost any issue, problem, or public person in an adversarial way. One of the dangers of the habitual use of adversarial rhetoric is a kind of verbal inflation—a rhetorical boy who cried wolf: The legitimate, necessary denunciation is muted, even lost, in the general cacophony of oppositional shouting. What I question is using opposition to accomplish *every* goal, even those that do not require fighting but might also (or better) be accomplished by other means, such as exploring, expanding, discussing, investigating, and the exchanging of ideas suggested by the word "dialogue." I am questioning the assumption that *everything* is a matter of polarized opposites, the proverbial "two sides to every question" that we think embodies open-mindedness and expansive thinking.

In a word, the type of opposition I am questioning is what I call "agonism." I use this term, which derives from the Greek word for "contest," *agonia*, to mean an automatic warlike stance—not the literal opposition of fighting against an attacker or the unavoidable opposition that arises organically in response to conflicting ideas or actions. An agonistic response, to me, is a kind of programmed contentiousness—a prepatterned, unthinking use of fighting to accomplish goals that do not necessarily require it.

## How Useful Are Fights?

Noticing that public discourse so often takes the form of heated arguments—of having a fight—made me ask how useful it is in our personal lives to settle differences by arguing. Given what I know about having arguments in private life, I had to conclude that it is, in many cases, not very useful.

10      In close relationships it is possible to find ways of arguing that result in better understanding and solving problems. But with most arguments, little is resolved, worked out, or achieved when two people get angrier and less rational by the minute. When you're having an argument with someone, you're usually not trying to understand what the other person is saying, or what in their experience leads them to say it. Instead, you're readying your response: listening for weaknesses in logic to leap on, points you can distort to make the other person look bad and yourself look good. Sometimes you know, on some back burner of your mind, that you're doing this—that there's a kernel of truth in what your adversary is saying and a bit of unfair twisting in what you're saying. Sometimes you do this because you're angry, but sometimes it's just the temptation to take aim at a point made along the way because it's an easy target.

Here's an example of how this happened in an argument between a couple who had been married for over fifty years. The husband wanted to join an HMO by signing over their Medicare benefits to save money. The wife objected because it would mean she could no longer see the doctor she knew and trusted. In arguing her point of view, she said, "I like Dr. B. He knows me, he's interested in me. He calls me by my first name." The husband parried the last point: "I don't like that. He's much younger than we are. He shouldn't be calling us by first name." But the form of address Dr. B. uses was irrelevant. The wife was trying to communicate that she felt comfortable with the doctor she knew, that she had a relationship with him. His calling her by first name was just one of a list of details she was marshaling to explain her comfort with him. Picking on this one detail did not change her view—and did not address her concern. It was just a way to win the argument.

We are all guilty, at times, of seizing on irrelevant details, distorting someone else's position the better to oppose it, when we're arguing with those we're closest to. But we are rarely dependent on these fights as sources of information. The same tactics are common when public discourse is carried out on the model of personal fights. And the results are dangerous when listeners are looking to these interchanges to get needed information or practical results.

Fights have winners and losers. If you're fighting to win, the temptation is great to deny facts that support your opponent's views and to filter what you know, saying only what supports your side. In the extreme form, it encourages people to misrepresent or even to lie. We accept this risk because we believe we can tell when someone is lying. The problem is, we can't.

Paul Ekman, a psychologist at the University of California, San Francisco, studies lying. He set up experiments in which individuals were videotaped talking about their emotions, actions, or beliefs— some truthfully, some not. He has shown these videotapes to thousands of people, asking them to identify the liars and also to say how sure they were about their judgments. His findings are chilling: Most people performed not much better than chance, and those who did the worst had just as much confidence in their judgments as the few who were really able to detect lies. Intrigued by the implications of this research in various walks of life, Dr. Ekman repeated this experiment with groups of people whose jobs require them to sniff out lies: judges, lawyers, police, psychotherapists, and employees of the CIA, FBI, and ATF (Bureau of Alcohol, Tobacco, and Firearms). They were no better at detecting who was telling the truth than the rest of us. The only group that did significantly better were members of the U.S. Secret

Service. This finding gives some comfort when it comes to the Secret Service but not much when it comes to every other facet of public life.

## Two Sides to Every Question

15  Our determination to pursue truth by setting up a fight between two sides leads us to believe that every issue has two sides—no more, no less: If both sides are given a forum to confront each other, all the relevant information will emerge, and the best case will be made for each side. But opposition does not lead to truth when an issue is not composed of two opposing sides but is a crystal of many sides. Often the truth is in the complex middle, not the oversimplified extremes.

We love using the word "debate" as a way of representing issues: the abortion debate, the health care debate, the affirmative action debate—even "the great backpacking vs. car camping debate." The ubiquity of this word in itself shows our tendency to conceptualize issues in a way that predisposes public discussion to be polarized, framed as two opposing sides that give each other no ground. There are many problems with this approach. If you begin with the assumption that there *must* be an "other side," you may end up scouring the margins of science or the fringes of lunacy to find it. As a result, proven facts, such as what we know about how the earth and its inhabitants evolved, are set on a par with claims that are known to have no basis in fact, such as creationism.

The conviction that there are two sides to every story can prompt writers or producers to dig up an "other side," so kooks who state outright falsehoods are given a platform in public discourse. This accounts, in part, for the bizarre phenomenon of Holocaust denial. Deniers, as Emory University professor Deborah Lipstadt shows, have been successful in gaining television airtime and campus newspaper coverage by masquerading as "the other side" in a "debate."

Appearance in print or on television has a way of lending legitimacy, so baseless claims take on a mantle of possibility. Lipstadt shows how Holocaust deniers dispute established facts of history, and then reasonable spokespersons use their having been disputed as a basis for questioning known facts. The actor Robert Mitchum, for example, interviewed in *Esquire*, expressed doubt about the Holocaust. When the interviewer asked about the slaughter of six million Jews, Mitchum replied, "I don't know. People dispute that." Continual reference to "the other side" results in a pervasive conviction that everything has another side—with the result that people begin to doubt the existence of any facts at all.

## The Expense of Time and Spirit

Lipstadt's book meticulously exposes the methods used by deniers to falsify the overwhelming historic evidence that the Holocaust occurred. That a scholar had to invest years of her professional life writing a book unraveling efforts to deny something that was about as well known and well documented as any historical fact has ever been—while those who personally experienced and witnessed it are still alive—is testament to another way that the argument culture limits our knowledge rather than expanding it. Talent and effort are wasted refuting outlandish claims that should never have been given a platform in the first place. Talent and effort are also wasted when individuals who have been unfairly attacked must spend years of their creative lives defending themselves rather than advancing their work. The entire society loses their creative efforts. This is what happened with scientist Robert Gallo.

20     Dr. Gallo is the American virologist who codiscovered the AIDS virus. He is also the one who developed the technique for studying T-cells, which made that discovery possible. And Gallo's work was seminal in developing the test to detect the AIDS virus in blood, the first and for a long time the only means known of stemming the tide of death from AIDS. But in 1989, Gallo became the object of a four-year investigation into allegations that he had stolen the AIDS virus from Luc Montagnier of the Pasteur Institute in Paris, who had independently identified the AIDS virus. Simultaneous investigations by the National Institutes of Health, the office of Michigan Congressman John Dingell, and the National Academy of Sciences barreled ahead long after Gallo and Montagnier settled the dispute to their mutual satisfaction. In 1993 the investigations concluded that Gallo had done nothing wrong. Nothing. But this exoneration cannot be considered a happy ending. Never mind the personal suffering of Gallo, who was reviled when he should have been heralded as a hero. Never mind that, in his words, "These were the most painful years and horrible years of my life." The dreadful, unconscionable result of the fruitless investigations is that Gallo had to spend four years fighting the accusations instead of fighting AIDS.

The investigations, according to journalist Nicholas Wade, were sparked by an article about Gallo written in the currently popular spirit of demonography: not to praise the person it features but to bury him—to show his weaknesses, his villainous side. The implication that Gallo had stolen the AIDS virus was created to fill a requirement of the discourse: In demonography, writers must find negative sides of their subjects to display for readers who enjoy seeing heroes transformed into villains. The suspicion led to investigations, and the investigations became a juggernaut that acquired a life of its own, fed by the enthusiasm for attack on public figures that is the culture of critique.

## Metaphors: We Are What We Speak

Perhaps one reason suspicions of Robert Gallo were so zealously investigated is that the scenario of an ambitious scientist ready to do anything to defeat a rival appeals to our sense of story; it is the kind of narrative we are ready to believe. Culture, in a sense, is an environment of narratives that we hear repeatedly until they seem to make self-evident sense in explaining human behavior. Thinking of human interactions as battles is a metaphorical frame through which we learn to regard the world and the people in it.

All language uses metaphors to express ideas; some metaphoric words and expressions are novel, made up for the occasion, but more are calcified in the language. They are simply the way we think it is natural to express ideas. We don't think of them as metaphors. Someone who says, "Be careful: You aren't a cat; you don't have nine lives," is explicitly comparing you to a cat, because the cat is named in words. But what if someone says, "Don't pussyfoot around; get to the point"? There is no explicit comparison to a cat, but the comparison is there nonetheless, implied in the word "pussyfoot." This expression probably developed as a reference to the movements of a cat cautiously circling a suspicious object. I doubt that individuals using the word "pussyfoot" think consciously of cats. More often than not, we use expressions without thinking about their metaphoric implications. But that doesn't mean those implications are not influencing us.

At a meeting, a general discussion became so animated that a participant who wanted to comment prefaced his remark by saying, "I'd like to leap into the fray." Another participant called out, "Or share your thoughts." Everyone laughed. By suggesting a different phrasing, she called attention to what would probably have otherwise gone unnoticed: "Leap into the fray" characterized the lively discussion as a metaphorical battle.

25      Americans talk about almost everything as if it were a war. A book about the history of linguistics is called *The Linguistics Wars*. A

magazine article about claims that science is not completely objective is titled "The Science Wars." One about breast cancer detection is "The Mammogram War"; about competition among caterers, "Party Wars"—and on and on in a potentially endless list. Politics, of course, is a prime candidate. One of innumerable possible examples, the headline of a story reporting that the Democratic National Convention nominated Bill Clinton to run for a second term declares, "DEMOCRATS SEND CLINTON INTO BATTLE FOR A 2D TERM." But medicine is as frequent a candidate, as we talk about battling and conquering disease.

Headlines are intentionally devised to attract attention, but we all use military or attack imagery in everyday expressions without thinking about it: "Take a shot at it," "I don't want to be shot down," "He went off half cocked," "That's half the battle." Why does it matter that our public discourse is filled with military metaphors? Aren't they just words? Why not talk about something that matters—like actions?

Because words matter. When we think we are using language, language is using us. As linguist Dwight Bolinger put it (employing a military metaphor), language is like a loaded gun: It can be fired intentionally, but it can wound or kill just as surely when fired accidentally. The terms in which we talk about something shape the way we think about it—and even what we see.

The power of words to shape perception has been proven by researchers in controlled experiments. Psychologists Elizabeth Lofrus and John Palmer, for example, found that the terms in which people are asked to recall something affect what they recall. The researchers showed subjects a film of two cars colliding, then asked how fast the cars were going; one week later, they asked whether there had been any broken glass. Some subjects were asked, "About how fast were the cars going when they bumped into each other?" Others were asked, "About how fast were the cars going when they smashed into each other?" Those who read the question with the verb "smashed" estimated that the cars were going faster. They were also more likely to "remember" having seen broken glass. (There wasn't any.)

This is how language works. It invisibly molds our way of thinking about people, actions, and the world around us. Military metaphors train us to think about—and see—everything in terms of fighting, conflict, and war. This perspective then limits our imaginations when we consider what we can do about situations we would like to understand or change.

## Mud Splatters

30  Our fondness for the fight scenario leads us to frame many complex human interactions as a battle between two sides. This then shapes the way we understand what happened and how we regard the participants. One unfortunate result is that fights make a mess in which everyone is muddied. The person attacked is often deemed just as guilty as the attacker.

The injustice of this is clear if you think back to childhood. Many of us still harbor anger as we recall a time (or many times) a sibling or playmate started a fight—but both of us got blamed. Actions occur in a stream, each a response to what came before. Where you punctuate them can change their meaning just as you can change the meaning of a sentence by punctuating it in one place or another.

Like a parent despairing of trying to sort out which child started a fight, people often respond to those involved in a public dispute as if both were equally guilty. When champion figure skater Nancy Kerrigan was struck on the knee shortly before the 1994 Olympics in Norway and the then-husband of another champion skater, Tonya Harding, implicated his wife in planning the attack, the event was characterized as a fight between two skaters that obscured their differing roles. As both skaters headed for the Olympic competition, their potential meeting was described as a "long-anticipated figure-skating shootout." Two years later, the event was referred to not as "the attack on Nancy Kerrigan" but as "the rivalry surrounding Tonya Harding and Nancy Kerrigan."

By a similar process, the Senate Judiciary Committee hearings to consider the nomination of Clarence Thomas for Supreme Court justice at which Anita Hill was called to testify are regularly referred to as the "Hill-Thomas hearings," obscuring the very different roles played by Hill and Thomas. Although testimony by Anita Hill was the occasion for reopening the hearings, they were still the Clarence Thomas confirmation hearings. Their purpose was to evaluate Thomas's candidacy. Framing these hearings as a two-sides dispute between Hill and Thomas allowed the senators to focus their investigation on cross-examining Hill rather than seeking other sorts of evidence, for example by consulting experts on sexual harassment to ascertain whether Hill's account seemed plausible.

## Slash-and-Burn Thinking

Approaching situations like warriors in battle leads to the assumption that intellectual inquiry, too, is a game of attack, counterattack, and self-defense. In this spirit, critical thinking is synonymous with criticizing. In many classrooms, students are encouraged to read someone's life work, then rip it to shreds. Though criticism is one form of critical thinking—and an essential one—so are integrating ideas from disparate fields and examining the context out of which ideas grew. Opposition does not lead to the whole truth when we ask only, "What's wrong with this?" and never "What can we use from this in building a new theory, a new understanding?"

35     There are many ways that unrelenting criticism is destructive in itself. In innumerable small dramas mirroring what happened to Robert Gallo (but on a much more modest scale), our most creative thinkers can waste time and effort responding to critics motivated less by a genuine concern about weaknesses in their work than by a desire to find something to attack. All of society loses when creative people are discouraged from their pursuits by unfair criticism. (This is particularly likely to happen since, as Kay Redfield Jamison shows in her book *Touched with Fire*, many of those who are unusually creative are also unusually sensitive; their sensitivity often drives their creativity.)

If the criticism is unwarranted, many will say, you are free to argue against it, to defend yourself. But there are problems with this, too. Not only does self-defense take time and draw off energy that would better be spent on new creative work, but any move to defend yourself makes you appear, well, defensive. For example, when an author wrote a letter to the editor protesting a review he considered unfair, the reviewer (who is typically given the last word) turned the very fact that the author defended himself into a weapon with which to attack again. The reviewer's response began, "I haven't much time to waste on the kind of writer who squanders his talent drafting angry letters to reviewers."

The argument culture limits the information we get rather than broadening it in another way. When a certain kind of interaction is the norm, those who feel comfortable with that type of interaction are drawn to participate, and those who do not feel comfortable with it recoil and go elsewhere. If public discourse included a broad range of types, we would be making room for individuals with different temperaments to take part and contribute their perspectives and insights. But when debate, opposition, and fights overwhelmingly predominate, those who enjoy verbal sparring are likely to take part—by calling in to talk shows, writing letters to the editor or articles, becoming journalists—and those who cannot comfortably take part in oppositional discourse, or do not wish to, are likely to opt out.

This winnowing process is easy to see in apprenticeship programs such as acting school, law school, and graduate school. A woman who was identified in her university drama program as showing exceptional promise was encouraged to go to New York to study acting. Full of enthusiasm, she was accepted by a famous acting school where the teaching method entailed the teacher screaming at students, goading and insulting them as a way to bring out the best in them. This worked well with many of the students but not with her. Rather than rising to the occasion when attacked, she cringed, becoming less able to draw on her talent, not more. After a year, she dropped out. It could be that she simply didn't have what it took—but this will never be known, because the adversarial style of teaching did not allow her to show what talent she had.

## Polarizing Complexity: Nature or Nurture?

Few issues come with two neat, and neatly opposed, sides. Again, I have seen this in the domain of gender. One common polarization is an opposition between two sources of differences between women and men: "culture," or "nurture," on one hand and "biology," or "nature," on the other.

40     Shortly after the publication of *You Just Don't Understand*, I was asked by a journalist what question I most often encountered about women's and men's conversational styles. I told her, "Whether the differences I describe are biological or cultural." The journalist laughed. Puzzled, I asked why this made her laugh. She explained that she had always been so certain that any significant differences are cultural rather than biological in origin that the question struck her as absurd. So I should not have been surprised when I read, in the article she wrote, that the two questions I am most frequently asked are "Why do women nag?" and "Why won't men ask for directions?" Her ideological certainty that the question I am most frequently asked was absurd led her to ignore my answer and get a fact wrong in her report of my experience.

Some people are convinced that any significant differences between men and women are entirely or overwhelmingly due to cultural influences—the way we treat girls and boys, and men's dominance of women in society. Others are convinced that any significant differences are entirely or overwhelmingly due to biology: the physical facts of female and male bodies, hormones, and reproductive functions. Many problems are caused by framing the question as a dichotomy: Are behaviors that pattern by sex biological or cultural? This polarization encourages those on one side to demonize those who take the other view, which leads in turn to misrepresenting the work of those who are assigned to the opposing camp. Finally, and most devastatingly, it prevents us from exploring the interaction of biological and cultural factors—factors that must, and can only, be understood together. By posing the question as either/or, we reinforce a false assumption that biological and cultural factors are separable and preclude the investigations that would help us understand their interrelationship. When a problem is posed in a way that polarizes, the solution is often obscured before the search is under way.

## An Ethic of Aggression

In an argument culture aggressive tactics are valued for their own sake. For example, a woman called in to a talk show on which I was a guest to say, "When I'm in a place where a man is smoking, and there's a no-smoking sign, instead of saying to him 'You aren't allowed to smoke in here. Put that out.' I say, 'I'm awfully sorry, but I have asthma, so your smoking makes it hard for me to breathe. Would you mind terribly not smoking?' Whenever I say this, the man is extremely polite and solicitous, and he puts his cigarette out, and I say, 'Oh, thank you, thank you!' as if he's done a wonderful thing for me. Why do I do that?"

I think this woman expected me to say that she needs assertiveness training to learn to confront smokers in a more aggressive manner. Instead, I told her that there was nothing wrong with her style of getting the man to stop smoking. She gave him a face-saving way of doing what she asked, one that allowed him to feel chivalrous rather than chastised. This is kind to him, but it is also kind to herself, since it is more likely to lead to the result she desires. If she tried to alter his behavior by reminding him of the rules, he might well rebel: "Who made you the enforcer? Mind your own business!" Indeed, who gives any of us the authority to set others straight when we think they're breaking rules?

Another caller disagreed with me, saying the first caller's style was "self-abasing" and there was no reason for her to use it. But I persisted: There is nothing necessarily destructive about conventional self-effacement. Human relations depend on the agreement to use such verbal conventions. I believe the mistake this caller was making—a mistake many of us make—was to confuse *ritual* self-effacement with the literal kind. All human relations require us to find ways to get what we want from others without seeming to dominate them. Allowing others to feel they are doing what you want for a reason less humiliating to them fulfills this need.

45      Thinking of yourself as the wronged party who is victimized by a lawbreaking boor makes it harder to see the value of this method. But suppose you are the person addicted to smoking who lights up (knowingly or not) in a no-smoking zone. Would you like strangers to yell at you to stop smoking, or would you rather be allowed to save face by being asked politely to stop in order to help them out? Or imagine yourself having broken a rule inadvertently (which is not to imply rules are broken only by mistake; it is only to say that sometimes they are). Would you like some stranger to swoop down on you and begin berating you, or would you rather be asked politely to comply?

As this example shows, conflicts can sometimes be resolved without confrontational tactics, but current conventional wisdom often devalues less confrontational tactics even if they work well, favoring more aggressive strategies even if they get less favorable results. It's as if we value a fight for its own sake, not for its effectiveness in resolving disputes.

This ethic shows up in many contexts. In a review of a contentious book, for example, a reviewer wrote, "Always provocative, sometimes infuriating, this collection reminds us that the purpose of art is not to confirm and coddle but to provoke and confront." This false dichotomy encapsulates the belief that if you are not provoking and confronting, then you are confirming and coddling—as if there weren't myriad other ways to question and learn. What about exploring, exposing, delving, analyzing, understanding, moving, connecting, integrating, illuminating . . . or any of innumerable verbs that capture other aspects of what art can do?

## The Broader Picture

The increasingly adversarial spirit of our contemporary lives is fundamentally related to a phenomenon that has been much remarked upon in recent years: the breakdown of a sense of community. In this spirit, distinguished journalist and author Orville Schell points out that in his day journalists routinely based their writing on a sense of connection to their subjects—and that this sense of connection is missing from much that is written by journalists today. Quite the contrary, a spirit of demonography often prevails that has just the opposite effect: Far from encouraging us to feel connected to the subjects, it encourages us to feel critical, superior—and, as a result, distanced. The cumulative effect is that citizens feel more and more cut off from the people in public life they read about.

The argument culture dovetails with a general disconnection and breakdown of community in another way as well. Community norms and pressures exercise a restraint on the expression of hostility and destruction. Many cultures have rituals to channel and contain aggressive impulses, especially those of adolescent males. In just this spirit, at the 1996 Republican National Convention, both Colin Powell and Bob Dole talked about growing up in small communities where everyone knew who they were. This meant that many people would look out for them, but also that if they did something wrong, it would get back to their parents. Many Americans grew up in ethnic neighborhoods that worked the same way. If a young man stole something, committed vandalism, or broke a rule or law, it would be reported to his relatives, who would punish him or tell him how his actions were shaming the family. American culture today often lacks these brakes.

50    Community is a blend of connections and authority, and we are losing both. As Robert Bly shows in his book by that title, we now have a *Sibling Society:* Citizens are like squabbling siblings with no authority figures who can command enough respect to contain and channel their aggressive impulses. It is as if every day is a day with a substitute teacher who cannot control the class and maintain order.

The argument culture is both a product of and a contributor to this alienation, separating people, disconnecting them from each other and from those who are or might have been their leaders.

## What Other Way Is There?

Philosopher John Dewey said, on his ninetieth birthday, "Democracy begins in conversation." I fear that it gets derailed in polarized debate.

In conversation we form the interpersonal ties that bind individuals together in personal relationships; in public discourse, we form similar ties on a larger scale, binding individuals into a community. In conversation, we exchange the many types of information we need to live our lives as members of a community. In public discourse, we exchange the information that citizens in a democracy need in order to decide how to vote. If public discourse provides entertainment first and foremost—and if entertainment is first and foremost watching fights—then citizens do not get the information they need to make meaningful use of their right to vote.

Of course it is the responsibility of intellectuals to explore potential weaknesses in others' arguments, and of journalists to represent serious opposition when it exists. But when opposition becomes the overwhelming avenue of inquiry—a formula that *requires* another side to be found or a criticism to be voiced; when the lust for opposition privileges extreme views and obscures complexity; when our eagerness to find weaknesses blinds us to strengths; when the atmosphere of animosity precludes respect and poisons our relations with one another; then the argument culture is doing more damage than good.

55       I do not believe we should put aside the argument model of public discourse entirely, but we need to rethink whether this is the *only* way, or *always* the best way, to carry out our affairs. A step toward broadening our repertoires would be to pioneer reform by experimenting with metaphors other than sports and war, and with formats other than debate for framing the exchange of ideas. The change might be as simple as introducing a plural form. Instead of asking "What's the other side?" we might ask instead, "What are the other sides?" Instead of insisting on hearing "both sides," we might insist on hearing "all sides."

Another option is to expand our notion of "debate" to include more dialogue. This does not mean there can be no negativity, criticism, or disagreement. It simply means we can be more creative in our ways of managing all of these, which are inevitable and useful. In dialogue, each statement that one person makes is qualified by a statement made by someone else, until the series of statements and qualifications moves everyone closer to a fuller truth. Dialogue does not preclude negativity. Even saying "I agree" makes sense only against the background assumption that you might disagree. In dialogue, there is opposition, yes, but no head-on collision. Smashing heads does not open minds.

*Anne Frances Wysocki, a graphic artist and university professor, teaches courses in writing, visual communication, and new media at Michigan Technological University. Before completing her doctoral dissertation on the subject of visual rhetoric, she studied animation and film at the San Francisco Art Institute. In 2003 she published a longer version of the following essay in* What Writing Does and How It Does It, *a collection of essays by a number of people describing how to understand written discourse.*

## *Anne Frances Wysocki*

# Understanding the Visual in Textual Arguments

Every day we are surrounded by visual arguments. Because of the technological developments of the previous century we are regularly presented with photographs, films, television shows, and now Web sites that make appeals about our values, attitudes, and actions in a visual way. Famous photos by Jacob Riis persuaded Americans to pass child labor laws. The documentary film "The Spanish Earth" convinced people to support the loyalist cause in the Spanish Civil War, and CBS News coverage of Martin Luther King, Jr.'s Birmingham Campaign in 1963 aroused the nation in support of the legislation now known as the Civil Rights Act of 1964. The hit movie and subsequent TV series "M.A.S.H" shaped American attitudes toward the Vietnam war, just as "West Wing" now makes arguments about the practices and choices of today's politicians. And now Web sites sell everything from hotels and music supplies to environmentalism and religious groups. At the same time, of course, arguments in text have not lost much ground: indeed, we still depend vitally on newspapers and magazines for the circulation of civic capital, and in those media visual elements work closely with text to make unified appeals that are both literate and visual. This essay is designed to explain how visual arguments work, especially when they are used in conjunction with texts, in a mixed media, that is, in order to persuade. The chapter raises questions about relations among the visual presentations of our texts and about particular values of our culture, such as efficiency, clarity, consumption, standardization, and the "seriousness" of words (against the non-seriousness of images). My fundamental argument is that the visual elements and arrangements of a text all do persuasive work. Someone composing a text that has a visual component—and all of them do—has to learn about and choose among available strategies to build a text that attracts a desired audience, is understandable to that audience, and moves it toward the ends desired by the composer.

## AN OVERVIEW of the visual aspects of texts

Here is one possible way to categorize what we see when we look at a text.

- THE PAGE OR SCREEN ITSELF

- WHAT IS ON A PAGE OR SCREEN

- WHAT HELPS READERS MAKE CONNECTIONS AMONG THE PARTS OF A MULTI-PAGED OR MULTI-SCREENED TEXT

- WHAT "CONTAINS" THE PAGE/SCREEN
  Three of these categories are explicated in the Approach section below. The second category—WHAT IS ON A PAGE OR SCREEN—requires terminology with which you might not be familiar, so let me unpack that terminology next.

■ WHAT IS ON A PAGE OR SCREEN: TYPE
  When a letter or word or sentence or paragraph is placed on a page or screen, it is given visual materiality and hence must be given a particular *lettershape*, *style*, *size*, and *overall shape*.

*Lettershapes: typefaces*
Letters have shape because of their typefaces. Because typefaces are a major visual strategy for a text's composers to signal the genre into which the text is to fit, and because the choice of different typefaces can signal argumentative moves in a text, it is worth giving typefaces—their categories and histories—some attention.
  One possible first step in categorizing a typeface is to ask whether it is most often used in short, quickly read phrases (such as in headers or in advertising catchlines) or in longer blocks or paragraphs for more engaged reading. In the practices we have inherited, designers use the first category when they want a typeface to call attention to itself on the page; designers use the second cat-

egory when the typeface is supposed to attract no attention to it-self. The first category is often named DECORATIVE (although such typefaces function in ways other than decorative); the second, FOR EXTENDED READING. DECORATIVE TYPEFACES can be categorized in several different ways, such as script, novelty, gothic, grunge, and so on. TYPEFACES FOR EXTENDED READING are the kinds you will most likely use in an academic work, and they fall generally into four kinds:

### Roman typefaces

These faces have their origins in the desire of the Renaissance Humanists to give their writing classical weight; therefore they look as though they were drawn with quill and ink, and have lines—called *serifs*—at the end of the main strokes; serifs are supposed to look like the finishing touches a stone carver would give to a letter to clean up its edges. Examples: Garamond, Minion, Baskerville, Times New Roman.

### Modern typefaces

These are typefaces that were modern when they were first de-signed, in the 18th century. Type designers wanted new type-faces to reflect the rationality of the Enlightenment, and new printing technologies allowed them to design faces using very thin strokes. Examples: **Bodoni**, Fairfield, Fenice.

### Slab serif or Egyptian typefaces

When Napoleon set out to conquer Egypt as the 18th century turned into the 19th, he sent artists and historians as well as the army; although the army ended up surrendering to Britain, the artists and historians brought samples of Egyptian art to France, starting a craze for all things Egyptian, including type-faces that looked Egyptian. In the typefaces that have grown out of the original designs, there are no curving transitions into the serifs. Examples: Memphis, Courier.

### Sans serif typefaces

Type designers, in tune with the industrialization of Europe and the United States in the previous two centuries, wanted typefaces that functioned rationally, like machines. They streamlined the typefaces with which they had grown up, re-moving everything they saw as extraneous, such as serifs. ("Sans" is French for "without.") Examples: Avant Garde, Futura, Helvetica.

NOTE how most academic and literary texts use only one or two typefaces throughout, although there are writers experimenting with the argumentative possibilities of mixing multiple typefaces, as one of the examples for analysis shows.

*Styles of type*
The typefaces I have categorized "for reading" can have different styles attached to them. Designers use these styles for different purposes: when applied to only a few words or lines, they call visual and conceptual attention to words or phrases; they can mark text that is supposed to represent spoken words. This **Bodoni** typeface, for example, has regular, *italic*, **semibold**, ***semibold italic***, **bold**, and ***bold italic*** styles. When working with texts that are to have a harmonious appearance, designers often choose a typeface family with multiple styles, such as the Bauer Bodoni, because the lettershapes of the different styles derive from each other, giving the styles a unified and hence harmonious appearance.

*The size of type*

# What do you think when you see type this size?

The different pages we see have different sizes—and mixes of sizes—associated with them. This page is (mostly) set in a size you expect to see in an academic text. Children's books often have very large faces, which are then scaled down somewhat for young adult books, which are then scaled down again for adult texts. (How do you think these size conventions developed?) NOTE how most academic or literary texts, on paper or screen, use the same size of type throughout, although (as with mixing typefaces on a page) some writers are experimenting with the argumentative possibilities of widely varying sizes, on paper and on the Web.

*The overall shape of type*
The shape of type on a page or screen can suggest many things to us; compare, for example, these samples:

Do these layouts suggest different kinds of texts? How difficult do you judge the texts to be, based on the overall shape of the type? (The first and third pages have what is called "left alignment"; the middle page has "fully justified alignment.") Because we have come to associate different kinds of texts with different shapes of type on a page (and hence on a screen), page composers can arrange the shape of text to achieve different ends.

## ■ WHAT IS ON A PAGE OR SCREEN: OTHER VISUAL ELEMENTS

In addition to type, page and screen composers can make their arguments with *shapes, color, photographs, drawings and paintings, charts and graphs, animations, visual transitions, video*, and *sound*.

### Shapes

Look how the authors of the web page on page 506 have used solid-colored shapes not only to differentiate what is clickable or background information from what is 'content,' but also how the shapes—rectangles with curved edges, like a 1950's car fin—signal that this site is supposed to appeal to those who think such techno-nostalgia is hip.

Think also of what the shape of a bullet in text can signal:

- It can be as visually unobtrusive as possible but still perform its function of indicating a point.

■ It can echo the overall shape of text on a page or screen, emphasizing the geometric organization and order of a text.

☛ It can suggest another time period or the physical presence of an author.

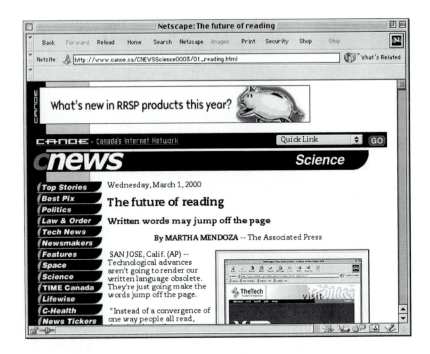

## Color

You've grown up with and into uses of color, and can probably easily describe the colors that would most likely be used in children's books or a Web site promoting health through relaxation, as long as the book or Web site was designed and intended to be read in your country.

**NOTE,** however, that color uses you take for granted do not carry across cultural lines: in China, for example, the traditional color of a bride's clothing was scarlet and the color of mourning was white.

**NOTE** also that, when you are analyzing a text, the amount of color is something to note alongside what colors are used. You do not generally expect to see anything but black and white in academic or literary paper-based texts, except on the covers of books. Web sites that want to give the appearance of being serious tend to use muted colors and a limited number.

In addition, consider the range of black through grey to white as a range of colors. Some typefaces form blocks that are very dark, and some light, in overall tone. Some pages or screens are designed to present a very evenly toned surface (like the pages in this book, for the most part) while others use different typefaces and other graphic elements to create a variable surface that can look playful or create a sense of geometric order.

## Photographs

You are probably well able to look at advertisements in magazines to analyze why a model in a photograph is (for example) white, female, slender, tall, healthy-looking, and gazing at a product she holds at chest-level.

You can probably also say why in this advertisement for netaid.org, a "partnership" between software companies and the United Nations Development Program for addressing world poverty, the designers chose to show a child, and why the child is centered and large and sleeping on piles of clothing and blankets while other people mill in the background, and why the child's arm reaches out as it does, down toward and off the bottom of the page. You can probably also say why the button, as on a

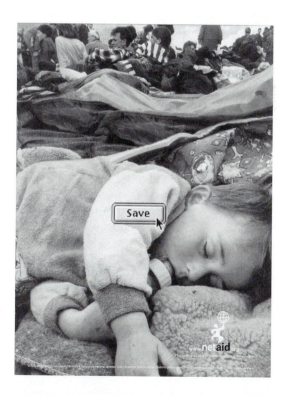

computer screen, is labeled "Save" and placed where it is. Finally, you might also be confident in discussing not only economic reasons why this composition's photograph is black and white (because black and white is cheaper to reproduce than color), but also how this photograph calls to contexts of traditional black and white documentary photography. Each of these aspects of photographs involves choices made by composers for achieving persuasive ends.

NOTE that photographs are often used to bring a sense of immediacy and "reality" to a layout. But photographs can also be fading black-and-white presentations from other times, or be manipulated to look old or dreamy or super-saturated. Photographs can also be manipulated in other ways: a model's face can be made completely and unhumanly blemish free, or people who would or could never be in the same room can be seamlessly aligned. Photographs have never been "caught moments of reality"; they have always been the result of a photographer's attentions, choice of framing, and technological knowledge. Now, however, because of changes in technology, photographers now have many more choices available to them for constructing their work.

NOTE how easy it is to focus almost exclusively on the photograph(s) when you analyze a text composed mostly of photograph and type. Be sure to attend to how the photograph(s) and the type have been designed to interact, and how the typeface, its size, and alignment also work in the whole layout.

### Drawings and Paintings

A drawing or painting (an illustration that is not supposed to look as though it were made with a camera) can look quickly sketched or minutely observed; it can be a technical illustration that seems never to have been touched by a hand; it can be the central focus of a page or a background pattern. The appearance of an illustration is a composer's choice, as is whether to use an illustration or a textual description in a text.

In the screen at the top of the opposite page, from a multimedia CD-ROM about the Beat Generation, the central illustration (the parts of which can be clicked to learn about movies or music or writing of the time) suggests what a living space from that time

could have looked like; but it is also a hard-edged though loose sketch in a limited range of dark colors. The illustration provides a darkly playful frame for looking at the work of the Beats. In the screen illustrated above, if you were, for example, to click on the Super-8 projector, you would see excerpts from films made by the Beats. Imagine how different your experience of this piece would be if this screen were instead simply a list of words to click—Movies, Texts, Recordings, Art, Pornography.

### Charts and graphs

Charts and graphs are sometimes referred to as "data visualizations," which indicates how they are intended to bring a scientific or technical tone to a text. No one chart or graph perfectly represents or encapsulates a dataset: any chart or graph is the result of its maker's decisions about what data to foreground and what not. Someone designing a chart or graph also has to decide what kind of chart or graph (scatterplot vs. pie chart, for example), what typefaces and colors to use, the weights of lines, and whether to include illustrations (as in the charts and graphs of *USA Today*).

Charts and graphs thus function rhetorically as part of a page or screen but also in and of themselves.

## ■ WHAT IS ON A SCREEN: **VIDEO, ANIMATION, VISUAL TRANSITIONS, & SOUND**

### Video

Video can be edgily hand-held or steadily formal. The current but always-being-stretched technical limitations of the Web and desktop computers have restricted video on our screens to small windows and jumpy frames; with the proliferation of digital video cameras and the expansion of computer power we will probably have more, larger, and smoother video to watch and analyze on screen. In CD-ROM-based multimedia applications, video can be shown through masks of any shape and not just in rectangular windows. A video sequence can thus be smoothly integrated into a scene, making it look as though parts of the screen "come alive." When you analyze video, keep in mind the range of choices a videographer has: framing, lighting, color or black and white, visual transition between sequences, use of type or titles, if there are actors and whether those actors address the camera or not, and so on. Each frame and sequence contributes to the overall effect of a video, and so require choice.

### Animation

Like drawings and paintings and video, animations can be presented in many ways: there are the bright colors and broad shapes we associate with children's TV cartoons or many Disney films, and there are finely rendered 3D animations of dinosaurs woven into "live" footage to seem as though we are transported in time. Animations are often used in explanations of technical processes because the processes can be shown abstractly, with direct focus on the important details. The technological capabilities of the Web and various software packages are also encouraging many people to experiment with animations inspired by poetic structures (and sometimes by the practices of experimental film), mixing type, color, drawings, photographs, and movement. As with all these graphic elements, a composer not only decides that an animation is appropriate to her ends but also decides what kind of animation, its colors, and so on.

## Visual Transition

At present, when you click a regular link on most Web pages, the current page disappears from screen to be replaced, bit-by-bit, by a new page; this is close to a jump cut in video or film. Certain software allows developers to incorporate visual transitions in on-screen files; most software for developing CD-ROM-based multimedia applications gives developers choices for how one screen will change into the next. A dissolve between two screens, for example, can make it look as though what is on one screen morphs slowly into what is on the other, implying a relation of similarity between the screens. A push transition can make it look as though you are seeing one long page moving behind the onscreen window, as though what is on the two pages is in one, united, place. Because transitions establish visual relationships between different screens, they are important choices for composers (and analyzers) to consider in arguments.

## Sound

There is no small speaker embedded in this page to suggest how hip-hop or Bach playing while you read affects your sense of my arguments. But you ought to be able to imagine the differences. Sound on screen can be a voiceover, repeating or expanding upon what is onscreen. (Designers choose this strategy sometimes for educational reasons—helping children with difficult words or supplying additional modes of presentation for those who learn in different ways—and sometimes for commercial ends, enthusiastically pitching a product.) Sound can also be ambient, suggesting a mood or place. This strategy can make a text seem more present and real because it encourages us to experience the text similarly to how we experience our day-to-day actions in spaces where sound and movement (and smell) are mixed. Try watching MTV without the music to hone your sense of what sound and visual strategies bring to texts together and separately.

# AN APPROACH for analyzing the visual aspects of texts

In this section I list and discuss questions for considering how the visual elements and contexts of a text contribute to our overall experience of the text. The questions are not exhaustive of what we can ask of the

visual elements of a text, certainly, but they provide an initial framework that can be modified and expanded; these questions ask us to:

1 Name the visual elements in a text.

2 Name the designed relationships among those elements.

3 Consider how the elements and relations connect with different
   audiences, contexts, and arguments.

QUESTIONS FOR LOOKING AT A SCREEN OR PAGE ITSELF

• *Naming the elements:* What is the size of this page/screen? What is
  its shape? Its texture? How is it colored?

• *Naming relationships among elements:* Do the visual elements on
  the page look small and centered and swallowed up by the page, or
  do they take over the whole page? Does the shape of words on the
  page fit and echo the shape of the page, or suggest geometric order,
  or is there incongruence? Is the page/screen designed so that you are
  not supposed to notice it but only the elements on it?

• *Contextualizing the elements:* How would your experience of this
  page/screen be different if it were a different size or shape or color or
  texture? What does this tell you about the expectations about the
  visual you bring to this text, expectations of which the author/
  designer is taking advantage?

QUESTIONS FOR LOOKING AT WHAT IS ON A SINGLE PAGE/SCREEN

• *Naming the elements:* What are the visual elements of this page/
  screen? What kinds of typefaces have been used, or are there any
  visual words at all? Are there photographs, illustrations, charts or
  graphs? What are the sizes of the different elements? Is there color?
  What colors, and how much?

• *Naming relationships among elements:* How does your attention
  move over this page/screen, that is, what catches your eye first, what
  second, what third—and why? (The size and color of something,
  and its placement at top or left or bottom or right, or what it presents—photographs, drawings—help answer this question, although
  it is also important to notice when your attention is directed evenly
  across and down a page). This tells you the order the author/
  designer wants you to see and hence think about what is on the

page/screen, the hierarchical relation between elements. (For example, a block of text that has been made the exact same size and shape as a photograph perhaps tells you that the photograph is just as important in this text as the block of text.)

• *Contextualizing the elements:* With what sorts of audiences do you associate the elements you have named? How would this page/screen be different if one of its elements were different, or if elements were added/removed? (How would this page be different if the type were purple or larger or the page were twice as tall? How would this screen be different if the photograph of Barbie were replaced by GI Joe or Toni Morrison or Rosie O'Donnell? How would this screen be different if its video clip were replaced by a drawing?) Sometimes imagining a page with a replacement or change helps us see much more clearly what the page is intended to achieve, because it helps us denaturalize the page and see its elements as choices that could have been otherwise. What do the author/designer's choices of visual strategies tell you about her/his conception of the audience for this page/screen?

## QUESTIONS FOR LOOKING AT WHAT HELPS READERS MAKE CONNECTIONS AMONG THE PARTS OF A MULTI-PAGED OR MULTI-SCREENED TEXT

• *Naming the elements:* What visual strategies did the designer use to tell you that these various pages or screen are to be understood as one text?

• *Naming relationships among elements:* How are you introduced to this text? What does the opening page or screen lead you to expect about the rest of the text?

• *Naming relationships among elements:* What tells you that this text continues on other pages or screens? How have you come to recognize this visual strategy? (That is, you have been explicitly taught that the lines of text on a book page continue on the next page or have some explanation of how they continue on a later page. But how have you learned about the workings of links on Web pages? How have you learned to recognize what is clickable in texts like video games or exploratory multimedia like *Myst?*) How do the contexts of your learning affect your attitude towards these texts and their pages/screens?

- *Naming relationships among elements:* How do the acts you must take to move through this text affect your sense of the relationships among the different parts of the text? How do the visual relationships between the different pages/screens of this text contribute to your sense of the text? (When you go to the next screen of a Web page by clicking a text link, what sort of relationship do you think exists between the two pages? How is this different from the relationship you imagine between successive pages of a book? How is a graphic link different from a text link? How is a vertical 'listing' of onscreen buttons/icons different from listing of words that are clickable? How is a Web page that ends with multiple links different from a Web or book page that offers no such set of choices?)

- *Contextualizing the elements:* What do your observations tell you about how the designer hoped the audience would approach and move through this text? Does the way this text has been composed for you to move through it suggest other kinds of practices? (For example, do you move through this Web site as though through a deck of cards, or are you supposed to feel as though you are having a conversation with someone? Do these paper pages look mass-produced or have they been designed to make you think of hand-work?) What sort of relationship with the text does the structure of this text ask its audience to have? What sort of relationship with other people?

### QUESTIONS FOR LOOKING AT WHAT "CONTAINS" THE PAGE/SCREEN

- *Naming the elements:* If you close your eyes and "picture" this text as a whole, what do you see? Is it a rectangular shape with cloth covers, or . . . ? Is it a round shiny plastic thing in a clear plastic box with a paper wrapper? How is the cover/wrapper labeled?

- *Naming relationships among elements:* What expectations do you develop in response to the specific visual presentation of this text as a whole object? (With what is shown on its cover, or its size? With the packaging of the CD on which this piece of interactive multimedia arrived? With the window through which I am viewing this Web page? With this computer?)

- *Contextualizing the elements:* With what sort of context do you associate this object and its visual appearance? What kind of people do you think will carry and use this object?

*Finally . . .*

• The questions above ask you to approach a text as a discrete object with distinct visual organization (what is on a page/screen, the page/screen itself, relations between the pages/screens, the 'container' for the pages/screens). Does this organization work for the text you are analyzing? What is left out of this organization, or excluded?

## TWO SAMPLE ANALYSES

Let me now provide two examples of how these questions can guide an analysis of particular arguments—one contained on a single page from a magazine, one in a book. For the sake of space, I do not apply all the questions from the Approach section to each text I analyze below (nor do I apply them always in order); but the following analyses should still give you ideas about how the questions can help you identify the visual elements of a text and relate them to its persuasive aim.

### ANALYSIS OF a page from a magazine

The page I analyze (reproduced on page 517) comes from the March 2000 issue of *WIRED* magazine. An issue from a previous year carried the subtitle "The Business of Change" on its cover, and the magazine's articles cover technological developments (primarily dealing with computers and all things digital) and their economic and social connections. Because this is a magazine devoted to high tech and money, areas where being up-to-date and attentive to future possibilities are important, the pages of this magazine—advertisements and articles—are designed to persuade readers that any information they take from these pages is as close to the moment (or the coming moments) as possible. Given, however, that the business of technology is so much caught up with technological objects like computers and music appliances, the border between knowledge about technological objects and wanting those objects can be thin; the "business of change" can only continue if business, which means consumption, holds a steady course. This analysis examines one page that I think works to create such a steady course by not only informing readers about new technologies but also by shaping desire for those technologies.

The "Fetish" page is a regular feature in recent years of *WIRED*. It shows new technological tools (and toys) that might interest the magazine's readers. While the word-title "FETISH" is certainly an indication of the relationship the authors/designers hope readers will establish with what is on this page, the word is not the only strategy employed to encourage that relationship: the layout of the page is also very much strategized.

This page is on the right side of a two-page spread, and, like all pages in the magazine, is made of a thick, white, semigloss, smooth paper; the paper feels slick to my touch but substantial. The page is in a usual size for magazines. There are no consistent margins anywhere on the page, and the objects shown on the page fill the page and even overflow its edges.

At the top of the page is the word "FETISH," in a blue and light green sans serif typeface; the individual letters look three-dimensional, as though constructed out of sheets of aluminum. There are photographs of three objects on the page: a pocket-size scanner (for scanning business cards or receipts), a mortar (for playing paintball), and see-through loudspeakers; the objects range in price (I learn if I read about them) from $250 to $3100. The three objects are shown in muted colors against the white of the page; they have been cut out from any thing that was around them so that there is nothing to distract my eyes from them. There are also three small columns of text: these columns describe the objects, give pricing and contact information, and are in a sans serif typeface—like "FETISH"—and in a uniform small size in light blue and black ink; they do not overlap or in anyway visually interfere with my view of the objects. At the bottom of the page is the name of the magazine, the issue information, and a page number, as on most other pages of the magazine.

There is an overall balance and harmony to this page: all the elements are muted in color, and the text blocks are close in size to the photographs; there is only one kind of typeface used on this page, and most of the type is in the same size; there is a lot of white space left around all the elements, giving the page an open feeling. The photographs and columns of descriptive text are given an informal but nonetheless careful arrangement: on the left of the page are two objects, each with a column of text aligned evenly to it, creating a solid and balanced shape; to the right, centered to the left side of the page, is the third object, with its corresponding text (in turn) centrally aligned to it. The photograph of the third object, the speakers, is also sized to extend exactly to the top of the scanner and to the bottom of the mortar, so that the objects have an orderly and aligned visual relationship to each other.

Because there is a harmonious arrangement to the page's elements, however, does not mean that some elements aren't emphasized.

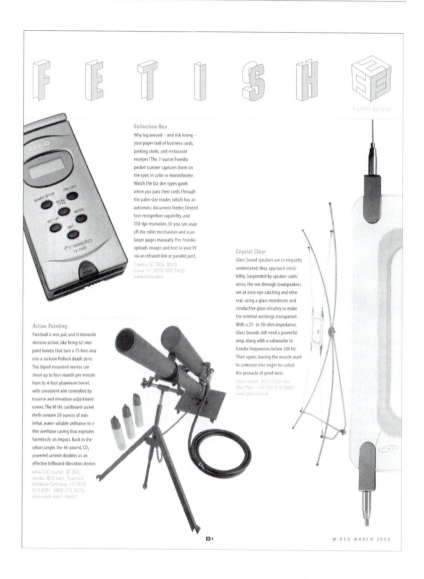

**FETISH**

By Paul Spinrad

**Collection Box**
Why lug around – and risk losing – your paper trail of business cards, parking stubs, and restaurant receipts? The 7-ounce Freedio pocket scanner captures them on the spot, in color or monochrome. Watch the biz-dev types gawk when you pass their cards through the palm-size reader, which has an automatic document feeder, limited text-recognition capability, and 150-dpi resolution. Or you can snap off the roller mechanism and scan larger pages manually. The Freedio uploads images and text to your PC via an infrared link or parallel port.
Freedio FZ-7000: $245. Casio: +1 (970) 361 5400. www.casio.com.

**Crystal Clear**
Glass Sound speakers are so elegantly understated, they approach invisibility. Suspended by speaker-cable wires, the see-through loudspeakers are at once eye-catching and ethereal, using a glass membrane and conductive glass circuitry to make the internal workings transparent. With a 25- to 30-ohm impedance, Glass Sounds still need a powerful amp, along with a subwoofer to handle frequencies below 200 Hz. Then again, leaving the muscle work to someone else might be called the pinnacle of good taste.
Glass Sound: $2,170 per pair. Glass Panel: +49 (20) 615 0557. www.glasspanel.de

**Action Painting**
Paintball is war, pal, and it demands decisive action, like firing 62-mm paint bombs that turn a 75-foot area into a Jackson Pollock death zone. This bipod-mounted mortar can shoot up to four rounds per minute from its 4-foot aluminum barrel, with consistent aim controlled by traverse and elevation-adjustment screws. The M1A's cardboard-jacket shells contain 20 ounces of non-lethal, water-soluble ordnance in a thin urethane casing that explodes harmlessly on impact. Back in the urban jungle, the 46-pound, $CO_2$-powered cannon doubles as an effective billboard-liberation device.
M1A-TOC mortar: $1,300, rounds: $10 each. Toontown Ordnance Company: +1 (970) 613 2051 (980) 315 5270. www.tzlink.com/~martyr

Although the columns of text and the objects are roughly the same size, the text has been shaped into columns that make even, uneventful patterns, with no particular visual emphasis of style or size given them. It is the objects that have been given emphasis: they are differently shaped than the repeated even columns of type, they have been cut off from whatever "reality" surrounded them in their original photographs, and they have been made to extend off the page, so that we have to use our imaginations to complete them. They are not shown in use, but rather stilled, objects to observe and consider and desire.

And because there are only the objects and a few pieces of unemphasized text on this page, arranged as they are, my eyes move around the objects circularly. I see first what is at the top of the page (I have, after all, been taught to read starting at the top), and then move down the left column of objects, up and over to the right object, back to the top, and around again; notice how the objects have been arranged so that their edges and legs point into each other, keeping my eyes moving over them.

I think, then, that the visual strategies used to arrange this page are aimed at catching me up in a circle of desire: I may not have known that these objects existed before I came to this page, but now I am presented with them in an arrangement that keeps my eyes on them, moving over them, seeing little else but them. The harmonious overall arrangement of the page keeps the desire from seeming irrational or out of control; instead, in the world of this magazine, to desire these objects is in order.

## ANALYSIS OF pages from books

The page depicted on page 519 could be in almost any academic journal or book. The page uses one typeface (an oldstyle) in a single size, in even black lines that, interspersed with the spaces between the lines, build a grey rectangle on the page. All this book's pages look the same, and were you to hold this page up to a light, you would see how the text rectangle on the back aligns perfectly with the text rectangle on the side facing you. If I consider the relationship between the pages of this text, the effect is of visual sameness and evenness. Just as spelling and punctuation are consistent, so is there no change of typeface or size or page texture to encourage my eyes to note anything particular as I move over these pages. There is nothing on these pages to encourage me to be attentive to the materiality of the pages, to their context of particular time and place. Instead, what is emphasized by this visual presentation is what is not on the page but rather what is beyond the page: the thinking, the "content."

This sort of visual presentation creates, then, an unremarkable even pattern so that my reading attentions are on—or in?—immaterial thoughts which exist independently of any particular visualization. This presentation works so that I can ignore the materiality and temporality of a text in order that I might range freely and deeply in

260                                                                                          JAY DAVID BOLTER

"imagetext" (Mitchell *Picture Theory*, 83 ff) – can be commonplace or sophisticated. But in each case the image both reaffirms and dominates the verbal text. Words no longer seem to carry conviction without the reappearance as pictures of imagery that was latent in the words.

Throughout the history of writing, there have been genres that combine words, icons, and pictures. Rebus and emblem poetry were popular in the Renaissance. Children today still enjoy rebus books, in which some of the nouns are replaced by stylized drawings. A young child can follow the story and become accustomed to the linearity of reading before he can actually decipher the letters that constitute alphabetic writing. The *USA Today* graphs are also connected to the long tradition of *technopaignia*, poems written in a shape that reflects their content. Panpipes and other shaped poems are as old as the *Greek Anthology*. However, the contemporary examples of visual play are more widespread and have greater significance, coming as they do after five hundred years of printing. They can be seen as part of a general trend to renegotiate the relationship between arbitrary signs and perceptual elements in communication.

The renegotiation is also apparent in the layout and content of the newspaper. In many American papers, for example, pictures are coming to dominate and organize the articles. In some cases a picture and its caption replace a verbal story altogether. The picture catches the reader's eye: he reads the caption and then searches the page in vain for the text that will add detail. The picture has broken free of the prose that would traditionally have explained and justified its presence. The newspaper is becoming a picture book. The situation is still different in Europe, where "serious" newspapers often contain fewer pictures and more prose and where the pictures are more often under the overt control of the text.

If, during the heyday of print in the eighteenth and nineteenth centuries, writers controlled the visual by subsuming it into their prose, writers today seem to be trying to become more visual and sensuous. Eventually, the visual element not only rises to the surface of the text, but escapes altogether and takes its place as a picture on the printed page. It is not only newspapers and magazines that are renegotiating the verbal and the visual. Other forms, including "serious" and popular fiction and academic prose, are also changing, and in all cases verbal text seems to be losing its power to contain and constrain the sensory. Each genre of writing is either experiencing a "breakout of the

thought, as though thinking itself is unbound by time and place. What might then be the effect of the time we spend with books like this, the books that fill our libraries, the books whose pages all look, unremarkably, the same?

The visual presentation of these pages suggests that visual sameness rather than visual difference is valued. Such standardization is not limited to book pages, obviously: I think here of the aisles of evenly stacked goods in supermarkets, of cars coming off assembly lines, of the rows of desks in my elementary school classrooms. Might it be possible to argue that pages like the one I have shown here—when we connect them to the larger contexts in which we see and experience them, when we connect them to the times in which they are produced—align with industrial and educational processes that encourage standardization and evenness?

If that is possible, then if authors/designers wanted to question those other processes, and to question their connections to academic work,

*would it be sensible of them*
*to make a composition*
*that followed the visual conventions of the standard academic page?*

The photograph on page 523 shows the final pages (before the notes) of *Hiding* by Mark C. Taylor (who teaches philosophy and religion at Williams College) in collaboration with the designers Michael Rock, Susan Sellers, and Chin-Lien Chen. These pages call attention to themselves as different from the usual academic page. There is a single sentence, in a bolded slab serif typeface much larger than what we

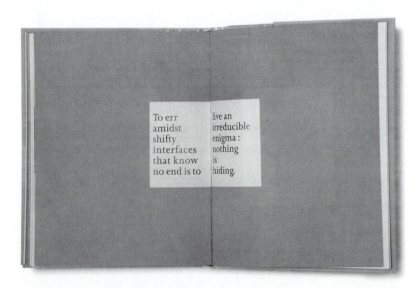

usually find in an academic text, in a small white space, that has the rough proportions of two side-by-side 8½ by 11" pages, surrounded by bright red on a semigloss paper. Only the physical size of this book fits into usual academic possibilities.

The book's closing pages are not the only pages that have been designed differently from academic expectation. The book has five chapters, each of which has its own overall patterning and color scheme, and one of which is printed on different paper from the rest.

The first chapter, "Skinsc(r)apes," has black and white type on red paper printed with blurry images of diseased skin, as though the bumps and blotches of the disease were on the paper itself. In the chapter, Taylor discusses Dennis Potter's *Singing Detective* television drama, which is about, sort of, a man who is in the hospital being treated for psoriatic arthritis who is also writing a detective novel—except that the man's hands are so affected by his disease that he cannot write; it is unclear then where the detective novel is taking shape. Taylor writes that

> *Potter's programs fold back on themselves not once but at least twice to examine questions that televisual and telephonic media raise about the relation between fact and fiction, reality and illusion, truth and appearance, history and story, and surface and depth. When read in the context of contemporary technology and media culture,* The Singing Detective *becomes a story about the possibility or impossibility of detection in a world where all "reality" is rapidly becoming virtual reality.* (24–25)

These then are also Taylor's concerns in the book, the relation (or even existence) of surface and depth, the possibility of anything hiding and needing us to perform detective work to find and understand it. And so the first chapter, both in its writing and in the look of its pages, makes us look at skin, at what it covers, or doesn't, and about what happens when we try to peel away at skins, as with detective or psychoanalytic work: there is only more skin—more layers, more clues—"but no solutions" (71).

Chapter 2, "Dermagraphics," is printed on vellum, a thin translucent paper that allows me to see, somewhat, through to what is on the pages underneath. Taylor and the designers with whom he worked lay out a history of tattoo and body decoration in this chapter, with printed-in-green illustrations and photographs of tattoos and piercings taking up the full left hand page of each spread and even columns of fully justified oldstyle type (printed in black) on the right. This chapter then moves our attentions out from the skin and diseases that seem to erupt from within to the things humans have done and now do to their skins in the hopes of making meaning; but, as all the elements of this text argue, the meaning can only come from referring to other things we have made, to other signs, not to anything hiding behind or underneath a representation.

In chapter 3, "De-Signing," Taylor moves us out again, from skin to what we put over our skin (but which acts like another layer of skin): fashion. The chapter opens with a series of full color page spreads. These full color spreads show photographs from fashion magazines, which are overprinted with phrases like "Falling Apart at the Seems" or "Transparency." The full color spreads are followed by pages in which columns of black type (in a modern typeface) make a continual fully-justified column at the top and bottom of the pages as various texts in a pale blue sans serif face run through the middle of the pages, sometimes in the expected vertical format and sometimes in a horizontal format. The blue texts take their titles from the phrases printed over the color photographs at the chapter opening, and are made to look like fashion magazine layouts. In these blue texts Taylor spreads out his considerations of fashion, using excerpts from fashion magazines that speak about specific fashion trends to show how those trends echo and repeat ideas in other areas—philosophy, literature, architecture; for example, Taylor connects fashion that reveals the seams and linings of clothing to the intellectual habits of deconstruction. In the black text, Taylor links fashion to the overall practices of modernism, the desire to be up to date and current, as well as to intellectual habits of dichotomizing, as with the concepts of *being/becoming*, *masculine/feminine*, *profound/superficial*, and so on.

Chapter 4, "Ground Zero," then takes on what might seem to be the next layer we build around ourselves, architecture. As in chapter 3, the pages in chapter 4 have two texts on them, but these two texts both continue throughout all the pages, one at the top in an oldstyle typeface printed on light green, the other at the bottom of the page, printed in a sans serif face. In both texts Taylor considers what we might consider to be the central problem for architecture, that of space; the top text considers space as something with (economic) value; the bottom text considers space in its relations to time. Occasional sentences in either text are outlined and printed in green and then linked to the other text by a line. On the penultimate page of the chapter, the two texts break in mid-sentence, and when a reader turns the page, there is present only one text, which can be read as the ending to either of the two preceding texts, where "proliferating signs immerse us in a superficial flux that never ends. . . . the substance of our dreams is stripped away to expose the inescapability of time and the unavoidability of death" (266–267).

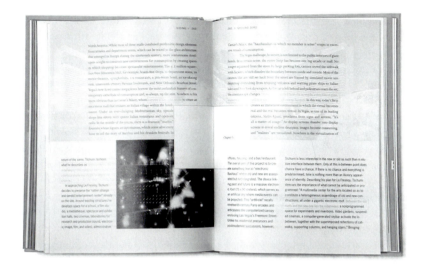

In the last pages of chapter 4, chapter 5, "Interfacing," has been erupting from the middle of the page, which the photograph above shows: the new chapter starts on a small white page-shape in the middle of the pages of chapter 4, and grows progressively larger as the book proceeds, until chapter 5 finally fills the whole page of the book and takes over. In this final chapter, which is printed in a black old-style of varying sizes with various red lines and boxes and photographs and illustrations interspersed, Taylor gives a history of the notion of virtual reality, whose origins he argues develop out of questions about society and culture that are similar to those that shaped Kant's thinking at the end of the eighteenth and beginning of the nineteenth centuries. Taylor steps us through Kant and Hegel and Nietzsche, and through the development of cinema and robotics and molecular biology and neurology to lead us back to the concerns of virtual reality and postmodernity. To the matters of surface and depth, of inner and outer and proper division and boundary, Taylor now adds questions about the divisions between human and machine, biology and machine, information and biology.

As the title of the final chapter together with all the strategies of the preceding pages suggest, Taylor has been building an argument that we need to reconceive the relationships between terms like surface and depth or real and unreal. Rather than relations of opposition, Taylor would rather we work with the notion he develops of interfaces, where boundaries are not fences or walls or barriers but are instead chancy and permeable membranes. Such a conception, he argues, not only addresses the shortcomings of much thinking of our time but also is appropriate for the situations of our time.

The book has thus followed only a baseline of expected visual and structural academic conventions: it is a size that fits on bookstore and office shelves, its text is primarily in fully justified columns of black oldstyle type, it contains chapters (which build out from an introductory idea), its quotations are made visually clear. But the book breaks most other academic conventions in its incorporation of multiple typefaces, chapters that do not look alike, multiple texts on a page, photographs that go underneath columns of text, different texts that end with the exact same words on a page, different kinds of paper, bright colors, and so on. In other words, the pages of this book call attention to themselves. The pages of the book call attention to each page as a surface to be looked at and used and not as a surface that exists merely to indicate some depth of thought hidden somewhere else. The pages call attention to their construction and temporal fashionability (in their use of tattoos and virtual reality, for example). The pages call us to be attentive to surfaces and their temporality as what we have to work with, as what there is.

No matter your tendency to lean toward or away from the arguments of this book, you ought to be able to see that such arguments would be undermined had Taylor and his collaborator-designers produced a book that followed strict academic conventions. You ought to be able to see how, by breaking visual conventions, they have been able to call into question other "less visible" conventions. Notice, that is, how the composers of *Hiding* have made careful choices among visual strategies that we might not previously have considered to be strategies: they've used type color and size to argumentative end, as well as how photographs and type interact, and how the blocks of type are arranged on a page. As you compose your own arguments on paper or screen, you might use the example of *Hiding* to help you discover and use visual strategies that might not previously have seemed like strategies.

# Text Credits

John Adams and Abigail Adams, excerpts from select letters reprinted by permission of the publisher from *The Adams Papers: Adams Family Correspondence, Volume I: December 1761–May 1776*, edited by L. H. Butterfield, Cambridge, Mass.: The Belknap Press of Harvard University Press, Copyright © 1963 by the Massachusetts Historical Society.

Paula Gunn Allen, "Where I Come From Is Like This" from *The Sacred Hoop* by Paula Gunn Allen. Copyright © 1986, 1992 by Paula Gunn Allen. Reprinted by permission of Beacon Press Boston.

James Baldwin, "Stranger in the Village" from *Notes of a Native Son* by James Baldwin. Copyright © 1955, renewed 1983, by James Baldwin. Reprinted by permission of Beacon Press, Boston.

Benjamin Barber, "America Skips School." Copyright © 1993 by *Harper's Magazine*. All rights reserved. Reproduced from the November issue by special permission.

Gwendolyn Brooks, "We Real Cool" from *Blacks*, 1991. Reprinted By Consent of Brooks Permissions.

Susan Brownmiller, "Let's Put Pornography Back in the Closet" from *Take Back the Night*, ed. Laura Lederer. Copyright © Susan Brownmiller, 2003.

Kenneth Burke, "Rhetoric Old and New" from *Journal of General Education*, vol. 5, 1951, Penn State Press, pp. 202–209. Copyright 1951 by The Pennsylvania State University. Reproduced by permission of the publisher.

Rachel Carson, "A Fable for Tomorrow" and "An Obligation to Endure" from Silent Spring by Rachel Carson. Copyright © 1962 by Rachel L. Carson, renewed 1990 by Roger Christie.

# Image Credits

# Index